ROBERT A. LEITCH
University of Georgia

K. ROSCOE DAVIS
University of Georgia

ACCOUNTING INFORMATION SYSTEMS

PRENTICE-HALL, INC., *Englewood Cliffs, New Jersey 07632*

Library of Congress Cataloging in Publication Data

LEITCH, ROBERT A., (date)
   Accounting information systems.

   Bibliography: p.
   Includes index.
   1. Information storage and retrieval systems—
Accounting. 2. Accounting—Data processing.
3. Management information systems. I. Davis,
K. Roscoe, (date). II. Title.
HF5679.L38 1983   657'.028'54   82-21580
ISBN 0-13-002949-1

*Dedicated to **Paula, Bob,** and **Adam** (R.A.L.) and to **Minnie J. Handy** (K.R.D.)*

Editorial/production supervision and interior design: **Joan Foley**
Cover design: **Wanda Lubelska**
Manufacturing buyer: **Ray Keating**

Material from Uniform CPA Examination Questions and Unofficial Answers, copyright © November 1956, May 1963, May 1965, November 1965, November 1967, May 1968, November 1969, November 1971, May 1972, November 1972, November 1973, November 1974, May 1975, November 1975, May 1976, November 1976, May 1977, May 1978, May 1979, and May 1980 by the American Institute of Certified Public Accountants, Inc., is reprinted (or adapted) with permission.

Material from the Certificate in Management Accounting Examinations, copyright © December 1972, December 1973, December 1974, June 1975, June 1976, June 1977, December 1977, June 1978, December 1978, June 1979, December 1979, June 1980, and December 1980 by the National Association of Accountants, is reprinted (or adapted) with permission.

Printed in the United States of America

10 9 8 7 6 5 4 3 2 1

ISBN 0-13-002949-1

Prentice-Hall International, Inc., *London*
Prentice-Hall of Australia Pty. Limited, *Sydney*
Editora Prentice-Hall do Brasil, Ltda., *Rio de Janeiro*
Prentice-Hall Canada Inc., *Toronto*
Prentice-Hall of India Private Limited, *New Delhi*
Prentice-Hall of Japan, Inc., *Tokyo*
Prentice-Hall of Southeast Asia Pte. Ltd., *Singapore*
Whitehall Books Limited, *Wellington, New Zealand*

CONTENTS

CHAPTER 5: ELECTRONIC DATA PROCESSING TECHNOLOGY 108

CHAPTER 6: SYSTEM STRUCTURES AND ASSOCIATED HARDWARE 147

CHAPTER 7: SYSTEMS FLOWCHARTING AND DOCUMENTATION 189

CHAPTER 8: DATA BASE SYSTEMS 217

CHAPTER 9: SYSTEM CONTROLS 259

CHAPTER 13: MARKETING SYSTEMS 414

CHAPTER 14: FINANCIAL ACCOUNTING SYSTEMS 455

CHAPTER 15: CORPORATE PLANNING AND MODELING SYSTEMS 532

CHAPTER 16: LARGE-SCALE SYSTEMS 579

PREFACE

Accounting information systems support the transaction processing, reporting, and decision-making systems of most organizations. To support these systems and their requirements effectively, an accountant must be able to integrate the data processing elements with the managerial activities within the decision-making and organizational framework of the organization.

This text provides a conceptual framework for integrating all the elements required to support accounting information systems. These are: hardware, software, data base, procedures, and personnel. The framework builds on the premise that the elements should be organized to support the transaction processing, reporting, and decision-making requirements of the organization. This framework is well founded in management information systems design theory, and it is the focal point of all the discussion in the text.

The objective of this text is to expose students to the elements that constitute an accounting system and the theory upon which a system should be designed and organized. The material is also written for the education of current or future practitioners who will deal with challenging systems design, operation, and problems of clients or their own organizations.

The text encompasses four major areas: (1) a theoretical framework for accounting systems, (2) procedures for systems analysis and design, (3) decision-making, organizational, behavioral, internal control, electronic data processing technology, and data base concepts, and (4) a broad spectrum of applications of accounting systems to common sets of information requirements. The text covers the entire range of systems now in use or which will be increasingly used in practice. This range comprises the small ledgerless bookkeeping systems as well as the complex decision support systems used by large international corporations.

The sequence followed in the text begins with an outline of a general framework and the theoretical underpinnings of the framework. This is necessary in order to integrate the concepts of all subsequent chapters. The general framework is followed by several chapters on systems elements and technology (Chapters 3–9). It is important that accountants have an understanding of the organizational concepts, behavioral factors, and decision-making processes prior to initiating any systems analysis, design, and implementation activities. These concepts are reviewed in Chapters 3 and 4. A basic understanding of electronic data processing hardware and software concepts is also important. These are reviewed in Chapters 5 and 6. Accountants must also have a working knowledge of flowcharting and documentation concepts as well as an understanding of data base design and systems controls. These topics are covered in detail in Chapters 7, 8, and 9.

Since one of the major roles of accountants is the evaluation of systems, considerable emphasis is given to internal control in this text. In addition to the detailed discussion of controls in Chapter 9, internal control applications are emphasized throughout the text. Appendixes are given later in the text, in application chapters, detailing specific control procedures for the operating and financial cycles of the organization.

The AICPA structure for systems development and implementation is used to integrate the theoretical and technical material in the text. Chapters 10 and 11 set forth a systematic set of procedures for the analysis, design, and implementation of accounting systems. The philosophy upon which these chapters are built is that a well conceived, designed, and implemented system will go a long way toward achieving the control of an organization that both management and accountants desire.

An application section is presented in the final section of the book. The objective is to integrate the theoretical, organizational, decision-making, technical, and design concepts of previous chapters. The emphasis here is on the characteristics of systems that are required to meet the various transaction processing, reporting, and decision-making needs of management. Examples are used to demonstrate the achievement of these objectives. Manual processing, batch processing, real-time systems, and integrated systems, as well as distributed processing, are illustrated.

Many of the illustrations and cases used in this section have been abstracted from actual cases. Chapters 12 and 13 concentrate on logistical and marketing systems, respectively. A complete financial accounting system for a microcomputer is provided in Chapter 14, to illustrate financial information requirements and the technology available to satisfy these requirements. Accounts receivable, accounts payable, payroll, inventory, general ledger, and fixed asset transaction processing systems are discussed. Financial planning/modeling systems used for managerial and strategic decision making are described in Chapter 15. Large complex systems that integrate a number of functional areas are illustrated in Chapter 16. Chapter 17 focuses on systems that are required to satisfy the special needs of small businesses. All of these application chapters emphasize the effective use of an accounting system to meet the information needs of management with respect to transaction processing, reporting, and decision making.

In summary, some of the special features of this text are

1. A theoretical framework for systems design.
2. The AICPA guidelines for systems development and implementation.
3. An emphasis on administrative and accounting controls.
4. A chapter on flowcharting.
5. Chapters on organizational and behavioral theory related to systems design.
6. A chapter on decision-making concepts that support the decision-making needs of management.
7. A substantive review of systems hardware and software.
8. A chapter on data base design.
9. A complete discussion of a small financial accounting system for a microcomputer.
10. A review of financial planning models and systems.
11. A detailed discussion of large complex processing systems.
12. A special chapter on the problems of small-business systems.
13. Many cases and examples based on actual experience.
14. Many cases that require the student to integrate knowledge from several chapters, such as flowcharting, system design, internal control, and software concepts.
15. Many CPA and CMA questions.
16. Several cases designed to help the student integrate and build on previously studied concepts in other courses.

This text is designed for either a one-semester or a one-quarter junior, senior, or introductory graduate-level course. With the addition of outside readings and EDP or system design projects, the text can easily be used for a two-semester or two-quarter course sequence in accounting systems.

This text assumes that students have had a basic course in computers or computer programming. In other words, an elementary understanding of EDP is assumed. If a student has no prior background, a supplement paperback may be used to develop the EDP basics. The text also assumes that students have had some accounting course work, to the extent that they have a basic understanding of the various transaction processing accounting cycles.

The text is flexible enough that the instructor may select subsets of chapters, depending on the background of the students, the material to be introduced, the level at which the course is to be taught, and the credit hours to be assigned. For example, if the course follows an in-depth course in EDP, Chapters 5, 6, and 8 may be used only for review. If it follows an auditing course in which internal control is stressed, Chapter 9 may be reviewed lightly. On the other hand, if the instructor is pressed for time, Chapter 4 and a few of the application chapters may be either skipped or treated lightly.

Moreover, the sequence may be altered. For example, the flowcharting chapter may be taught at an earlier point in time, and the small-business chapter may follow either 11 or 14 if the students need the background earlier in the quarter or semester.

In summary, the core of the text is contained in Chapters 1, 2, 3, 7, 9, 10, 11, 12, 13, 14, and 15. The other chapters build upon and support this basic framework.

The overall objective of the text is to develop a framework for the analysis and design of accounting information systems. Based on this framework, the objective is then to show the student how to analyze, design, and implement accounting information systems that satisfy the transaction processing, reporting, and decision-making requirements of management.

We wish to thank the American Institute of Certified Public Accountants and the Institute of Management Accounting of the National Association of Accountants for permission to use problem materials from past examinations. We also wish to thank Management Sciences of America (Atlanta, Georgia) for the extensive use of its system descriptions.

We are grateful to Sue McKinley, Lydia Schliefer, Steven Connor, Jan Leichti, Greg Prince, Roxanne Lyda, Cynthia Washington, and Virginia Yegal for their willing assistance. We appreciate the hard work and kind suggestions of many of the reviewers of early drafts of this manuscript: Chuck R. Litecky, University of Missouri-Columbia; Richard S. Savich, University of Southern California; Miklos Vasarhelyi, Columbia University; John Wragge, University of Delaware; Harold Wyman, University of Connecticut. We are also grateful to Barbara Cofer, Linda Keith, Betty Brewer and Ann Saye for typing and proofreading the drafts of the manuscript.

We especially thank our wives, Paula and Halaine, and our children, Rob, Adam, Kevin, and Kimberly, for their patience during the long hours involved in the preparation of this text.

1

INFORMATION PROCESSING:
An Overview

INTRODUCTION

Accounting has undergone significant changes during the past decade due to the environment in which it operates. As a result, the roles of the controller and the public accountant have greatly expanded in terms of information processing, information utilization, information system design, and information system review. Two major developments have led to these changing roles: (1) the growth in computer technology and (2) the formalization of information processing.

Since the advent of the first commercial computer in the late 1940s and early 1950s, there has been a tremendous growth in computer technology. The first bulky slow-speed electromechanical computers have been replaced with high-speed electronic computers that provide millions of bits of storage with rapid access and execution times and with desk-top microcomputers. This growth in computer technology has resulted in expanded capabilities in information processing. Payroll, accounts receivable, and accounts payable processing applications were novel ideas in the mid-1950s; today they are routine. Today large complex integrated and/or distributed systems support a whole array of managerial decision-making activities including those related to the controller and the accounting activities of the firm.

Formalization of information processing as it relates to the accounting system is shown in Figure 1–1. Under the classical system, the accounting system constituted the only formal aspect of a firm's information system. Only financial data were processed. The system was transaction oriented and consisted mostly of historical records and financial reports. Little information was generated for planning and control activities. Budgets were developed for internal use but did not focus on decision processes. Nonfinancial data consisted primarily of statistical reports.

Due primarily to the development of sophisticated computer hardware and to developments in information processing technology, this simple system evolved into large complex systems (see part B in Figure 1–1). Under the classical system, the accountant was primarily a provider of information; under the complex integrated and distributed systems, the accountant is both a user and a provider of information. Moreover, today the accounting system interfaces with most other formal information systems.

In general, the integrated and the distributed frameworks have increased the complexity of the accountant's role from that of data processing to

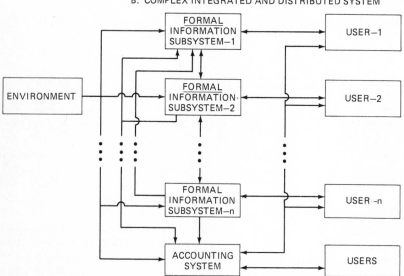

Figure 1-1   Classical vs. Complex Integrated and Distributed Systems

Source: Adapted from "Report of the Committee on Accounting and Information Systems," *The Accounting Review Supplement*, 1971, p. 292.

that of information processing. The accountant's role has changed because information processing and data processing differ. Information processing is not necessarily computer based. Although we have become accustomed to the idea that information processing exists in large corporate firms, its existence is not a function of the size of the firm. Small as well as large firms can benefit from information processing (as will be emphasized in Chapter 17, "Small-Business Systems"). The accountant should recognize, however, that as the size of a firm increases, the need for a properly designed information system increases.

To understand contemporary accounting information systems, an introduction to basic systems concepts is important. Therefore, it is necessary to define *accounting information* and specify the roles now played by the accountant. A broad, general definition of information processing and a look at some historic developments that have supported the development of information processing are also necessary. The accounting implications of different system developments must be identified, and the different dimensions of information processing must be defined. This chapter considers these, as well as other, basic foundation concepts.

ACCOUNTING AND INFORMATION SYSTEMS

Accounting Information

We can begin our analysis by defining what is meant by an accounting system. One definition of *accounting system* follows:

> That portion of the formal information system concerned with the measurement and prediction of income, wealth, and other economic events of the organization and its subparts and entities.[1]

A more narrow definition would include only financial and transaction information, as shown in Figure 1–2. Regardless of the definition we adopt, it should be clear that the boundaries of the traditional accounting system have been expanded to include not only monetary items but all significant economic events that may be quantified and used for both internal and external decisions. For most firms, the accounting system is the most pervasive information subsystem because it interfaces with most of the other subsystems, such as marketing, production, personnel, and finance.

The Role of Accounting

The expanded role of the accountant that has evolved with the developments in information systems is well expressed by the 1971 American Accounting Association's Committee on Accounting and Information Systems:

> The role of accounting, in its conventional sense, has assumed a new

---

[1] "Report of the Committee on Accounting and Information Systems," *The Accounting Review Supplement*, 1971, pp. 289 and 290.

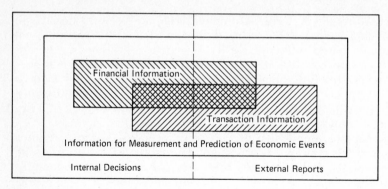

Figure 1-2 Accounting System for Internal and External Decisions and Reports

position in the information environment. The accountant has, to a significant degree, become primarily a *user* of information with only limited attention given to his former data accumulation activities.

As a user of information, the accountant is concerned with the overall classification and coding structure for the series of information systems [Figure 1–1]. He is also concerned with internal controls, management controls, and security measures employed in these data processing and transaction activities. In addition the accountant must clearly examine his own set of activities and responsibilities, and he must specify the set of information requirements that must be satisfied by the series of information systems [Figure 1–1]. Thus, system analysis, systems control, and information systems design are key elements in the accountant's role as an information system user.

The traditional concept of accountants' activities and responsibilities include the following basic activities:

1. Perform and facilitate the attest functions.
2. Keep records on economic performance and related third party needs.
3. Provide an overall management control function.
4. Perform a number of operating duties involving financial management.
5. Design and manage information systems.
6. Provide information for a variety of decision-making purposes.

The effect of the present information environment on the first three of these is relatively limited, but on the last three it is dramatic.[2]

The excerpt from the above report concentrates on the role of the accountant within a firm; and it is important that we recognize this management role, but we must also recognize the increasing role of the public accountant. Accountants play an important role in two areas in information processing in public accounting: (1) in management advisory services where the CPA firm provides technical assistance to the firm on information system design and implementation, and (2) in the auditing of electronic data processing systems where the auditor or audit team must perform tests of compliance and other

[2] Ibid., pp. 279–90.

necessary audit procedures. In the latter case, the accountant often becomes involved with the design of the information system in order to resolve future audit problems.

In summary, the role of the accountant in the changing environment of information systems has become one of a

1. User of information
2. Provider of information
3. Designer of information systems
4. Reviewer of information systems

Thus knowledge and understanding of the basics of information system design, implementation, and control have become essential to the professional accountant.

DEFINITION OF INFORMATION PROCESSING

General Definition

In this text, *information processing* and *information systems* will be used interchangeably. These terms have a much broader connotation than *management information systems* (MIS) in that the provision of information relates not only to providing management with required information but to providing external constituents with required information as well. As we progress through the text, it will also become quite obvious that information systems are not restricted to any particular function (i.e., marketing, production, finance, personnel, etc.) or managerial level within a firm. Nor is the term *information processing* restricted to any particular type of organization (nonprofit, governmental, or profit making). A final reason that would justify use of the term *information processing* or *information system* is that neither term implies a computer-based system. Since it is quite possible for some organizations with low volume, minimal complexity, and less than rigid time requirements to develop viable manual or electromechanical information systems, a term is needed that also encompasses these systems.

All organizations have some form of information system regardless of whether it is merely a manual accounting system consisting of a set of filing cabinets and a chart of accounts in a ledger or a sophisticated on-line interactive system that provides accounting information as well as information for decision making. The latter system, however, is a more viable information system; not because it is a computer-based system, but simply because it has the means by which data pertaining to organizational needs can be recorded, stored, processed, retrieved, and communicated in a form required by individuals within and by constituents outside the firm.

An information system is analogous to a manufacturing process that takes raw material and converts it into a product that either is utilized by a consumer or becomes the input to another manufacturing process. An information system converts raw data, via data processing, into management reports or reports for external users. It can also provide selected data as input to decision models or other systems which further process the data to provide viable decision aids for management.

Within the framework of this text, the term *information systems* is defined as follows:

> Those systems in an organization that (1) meet daily transactional processing requirements, (2) support operational, managerial, and strategic activities of the organization, and (3) provide external constituents with necessary reports.

In a broad sense, this definition is similar to the definition of an accounting system, since it embodies information about economic events.

Historical Perspective

Information systems existed prior to the development of the computer. Computer technology, however, made possible sophisticated integrated as well as distributed information systems. Several other factors and developments in addition to computer technology have influenced and contributed to the growth of the field. Specifically, four concepts that have emerged over the past two decades have had a bearing on the evolution of information systems: (1) the development of the scientific approach to management, which involves the development of decision science (mathematical) models to support decision making, (2) technological developments in both software and hardware in data processing, (3) the idea that activities and operations within a firm can be viewed as a system (i.e., the "systems approach"), and (4) internal and external information requirements. Let us examine each of these in some detail and comment on their accounting implications.

DEVELOPMENT OF MANAGEMENT SCIENCES   The size and the complexity of organizations have changed significantly over the past two decades. To remain competitive it has become increasingly important for organizations to "optimally manage their resources," and this has led to the development of the field of management sciences. *Management science* (often referred to as *operations research* or *decision sciences*) is the application of the scientific method to management problems. Management science is rooted in the use of mathematical models to identify and study solution alternatives.

The field of management sciences grew out of military efforts during World War II. During the war there was a great need to optimize the utilization of resources and to determine the most effective warfare operations. Management science models—such as "linear programming," "queuing theory," "game theory," and "simulation"—were developed to aid military strategists in their decision making. Since a number of military endeavors were successful, many of the models and analyses were transferred to industrial operations after the war.

Like military strategists, managers of organizations are often faced with decisions that deal with the future course or direction of their organization. Managers are often confronted with decisions ranging from basic routine operating decisions to highly complex decisions that involve millions of dollars. The success of management science in organizations has been most apparent in operational problems and tactical decisions. Mathematical models and techniques have been used extensively in inventory management, production scheduling, plant location, cost analysis, and cost allocations, as well as in financial planning and investment analysis.

Obviously the application of mathematical models can never provide the basis for all decisions, and many information needs of an organization can be met by establishing a well-designed data base that will provide timely reports or on-line response to management inquiries. But management science is an important development relative to information processing in that it can provide procedures for analyzing and studying problems. When we move beyond the transaction processing step in information processing, the models and algorithms of management science play an important role in the design of information systems.

COMPUTER TECHNOLOGY   As we indicated earlier, information processing does not necessarily imply the use of computer-based systems. But we can hardly argue that current information systems could exist without the support of computer technology. More than thirty years have elapsed since the emergence of the first commercial computer in 1947; however, the development of sophisticated computer-based information systems has occurred within the past ten years. Early information systems were primarily transaction-based systems which were developed principally to handle day-to-day operations and to provide record-keeping functions. The development of cost-effective systems to support top-level decision-making activities did not occur until the early 1970s, even though cost-effective systems were used to support middle- and lower-level management in the 1960s.

The reason for the time gap in the development of sophisticated information systems was the delayed development of computer software. A basic computer system consists of *hardware* (physical elements such as input/output units, peripheral storage devices, and the central processing unit) and *software* (languages and stored programs that control and/or provide operating flexibility). Hardware and software developments did not occur simultaneously. Computer technology has concentrated primarily on providing computer hardware. Software developments have usually lagged hardware developments.

On-line terminals, telecommunication (telephone and microwave) networks, and high-speed storage devices were developed in the mid-1960s. More recent technology developments have been directed toward minicomputers and microprocessors. Traditionally software development has been left to each respective organization. Sizable software vendors are beginning to emerge, however, and hardware vendors are developing more and more software.

In the late 1960s, computer manufacturers found that hardware usage was less than expected because user organizations could not cost-justify the development of software and because various software developments caused numerous hardware changes. Software is still a greater problem than hardware, but currently a variety of information processing software packages are available from "software houses."

In the early 1970s, telecommunication networks with high-speed video systems were combined with related software. Most of these large systems could provide fast response to system inquiries and could provide access to large data files that were remotely situated. Such systems generally are economically feasible for only larger corporate firms, but with the development of minicomputers and microprocessors, information systems have become more cost effective, even for small (single proprietor) organizations. Most recently communication networks combined with minicomputers and microprocessors have led to the rapid development of distributed processing systems. In the near future this latest development will have a significant impact on the development of information processing.

Because of the impact of minicomputer and microprocessor technology, the accountant must have a broad understanding of information processing. In the 1950s and 1960s large firms and clients utilized electronic data processing technology. But since there were relatively few of these, specialists could be employed. Now many small and medium-sized firms and clients are using small processors. The controllers of these firms and the accountants who audit these firms must be able to understand and deal with this new technology.

THE SYSTEMS APPROACH   Another factor that has affected the evolution of information processing is the emergence of the "systems approach." The systems approach is a way of perceiving the structure that is needed to coordinate the activities and operations within an organization. A fundamental precept of the systems approach is the interrelationship of the parts, or subsystems, of the organization. The systems approach begins with a set of organizational objectives and focuses on the design of the information system as a whole. If the system is designed properly, the effectiveness of its components considered collectively will be greater than the sum of the effectiveness of each component considered separately. The result of proper design is a more efficient system. On the other hand, an evolutionary or piecemeal approach to development often leads to inefficient systems.

In the past, organizations have fallen short of optimal effectiveness because they have failed to interrelate the different functions within the organization. The sales function, for example, was sometimes performed without adequate regard to the production function; production quite often was not coordinated with financial or personnel planning. Manual accounting systems have traditionally been concerned largely with the production of ex post facto information for financial statements, not with providing forward-looking information for management decision making.

In this text we will take a systems approach to information processing, from the standpoint of both design and development. The information needs of the entire organization will be examined. (A more-detailed presentation of the systems approach is included in Chapters 2, 10, and 11.)

EXTERNAL/INTERNAL INFORMATION REQUIREMENTS   Managing and controlling a firm, regardless of whether it is a small single proprietorship or a large corporation, can be enhanced by use of the systems approach. Information systems that support the management and controlling activities of the firm can be developed. However, before we can develop a system to support the firm's activities, we must first define and identify the firm's information needs.

Two global factors determine the firm's information needs: (1) internal information requirements (accounting for managerial decision making and control) and (2) external reporting requirements (accounting for financial reporting). Both factors have an impact on the structure and development of information systems.

The rise of large corporations in the early 1900s created the need for larger and more complex systems than those used to provide internal information. Information systems in the early 1900s concentrated on simple cost accounting and budget reporting, which often proved inadequate in decision making. As firms continued to expand in the 1930s and 1940s, more-detailed cost reporting resulted. Full cost, direct cost, marginal cost, replacement cost, and opportunity cost information began to appear. This detailed cost reporting increased the volume of data handled.

Internal reporting systems then emerged. These systems were built on the idea of responsibility and profitability accounting in which each manager receives reports covering his or her area of responsibility. The reports display *planned* performance and identify variations from the plan. Lower-level reports are summarized for upper-level management. Top-level management receives summary reports that identify problem areas and causes. Obviously the larger the corporation, the larger the volume of data handled, and the greater the need to employ decision support techniques such as capital budgeting, cost-volume-profit analysis, resource allocation procedures, inventory control procedures, cash flow analysis, and sales analysis.

In the large corporations, managerial control problems became more complex, programming and budgeting and planning became necessary, and decision models or management science models became more applicable. To deal with this trend, decision support systems and corporate planning models evolved. Also the advent of minicomputers and microcomputers has helped even small companies to better satisfy these information requirements.

Like internal reporting, external reporting has had an impact on information systems and accounting systems. The most obvious external reporting requirement is that of periodic financial statements, which report the status of the firm and are made available, often on a quarterly basis, to every stockholder. Interest groups other than stockholders also affected external reporting requirements. In the preindustrial 1800s, only a limited amount of external reporting was needed. Corporate enterprises have now grown to the point that suppliers, customers, labor unions, financial institutions, and a variety of governmental agencies require information on the status of different pects of the business. All of these information users have a bearing on the structure of an information system, particularly if the system is to be responsive to all external constituents.

Information Systems in Summary

Figure 1–3 depicts the above-noted concepts and their relationships to information processing. Data are transformed into information via data processing procedures, which are mediated by systems analysis and are designed

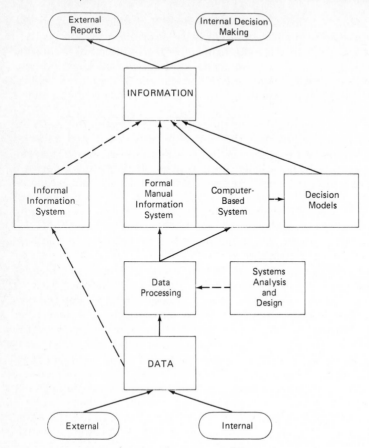

Figure 1-3 Information Systems Perspective

and used by the information system. Information systems supply information to external constituents, to managers (decision makers), or to the decision models employed as an aid in the decision-making process. A distinction between the "formal" and the "informal" systems shown in the diagram should be made. A *formal system* has a prescribed set of rules and procedures for gathering and analyzing data and for disseminating information. An *informal system* involves highly variable information that is not generated routinely; such systems tend to develop noticeably within the organization. In the diagram we also differentiate between computer-based systems and formal information systems. This was done to reemphasize that all information systems are not necessarily computer based.

Data and Information

In previous discussions, the terms *data* and *information* were used in describing information processing. These terms relate to two distinct concepts. Authors often erroneously use the terms interchangeably, despite the two unique but related concepts involved. Thus, before examining additional aspects of information processing, it is necessary that we have a clear idea of this basic terminology.

To understand the difference between data and information, let us examine the general concept of data processing. Data processing can be described as a three-phase process: (1) input, (2) processing, and (3) output (see Figure 1–4).

Data are raw facts, such as transaction details from sales invoices. When data are placed in a significant context by data processing operations, communicated knowledge results. *Information* is communicated knowledge developed by matching and transforming data so that the output is in a form that is useful to the recipient.

The definition of *data* is quite straightforward; data are simply raw facts. However, we must carefully examine the definition of *information*. Information does not result simply because a data processing operation is performed on the data. Consider what will result if we take raw data, store these data, and simply output these data. Information has not been generated. Additional knowledge does not result from reproduction of the original data.

To understand the difference between information and data, each part of our definition of information must be examined. First, *communicated knowledge* means that something previously unknown has been *sent, received, recognized*, and *accepted* by the individual to whom it was directed. Second, the knowledge generated results from performing a series or group of operations, such as classifying, sorting, summarizing, analyzing, or modeling, on input data. Finally, the knowledge must be presented (reported) in such a form that it can be used by the recipient.

One point that should be made regarding the definition of information is that there are varying degrees to which the different criteria of the definition are met. Knowledge is *sent, received, recognized*, and *accepted* to varying degrees. The amount of information generated and then communicated can be placed on a continuum. It is not an either-or question. Some examples will demonstrate the point. Consider the manager who receives a report that is outdated by two months, recognizes that the report is outdated, and discards it. Information, to a certain degree, was created, but since the knowledge contained in the report was outdated the recipient was not willing to accept the information. The information was not useful. Consider as another example the sales manager who receives quarterly territorial reports of product sales by product, by salesperson, and by district. Upon receipt of the reports, the manager summarizes the data into total sales and compares this with the same quarter's total

Phase 1: Input	Phase 2: Processing	Phase 3: Output
1. Capturing of detailed *data* on all transactions 2. Recording of *data* gathered outside the firm	1. Storage and retrieval 2. Classification and sorting 3. Summarization 4. Calculating, analysis, and modeling 5. Report generation	1. Management *information* 2. Historical transaction updates and recordings 3. External reporting

Figure 1-4   The Data Processing Function

Source: George J. Brabb, *Computers and Information Systems in Business*, 2nd ed., p. 6. Copyright © 1980 by Houghton Mifflin Company. Adapted by permission.

sales in the preceding year in order to determine sales performance. If we were to use a strict interpretation of the definition of information, then information was *not* generated because the output information was not in a form that was immediately usable. Such a strict interpretation should not be used. In actuality, information was created to a certain degree. To make the information fully useful to support a management decision, however, further processing was required. Consider, as a third example, the manager who regularly receives a report that provides suggested weekly production schedules. The schedules are developed via a mathematical-programming model. Unfortunately, the manager in this case was never trained in mathematical programming; the output report, therefore, has little meaning to the manager. The manager continued to use a rule-of-thumb technique to schedule operations. Information as we have defined it was not created because the output report was not recognized and used by the recipient and no benefit resulted.

One last comment should be made regarding the definition of information and information processing. Information cannot be created without considering the desires and needs of the recipient. One of the accountant's roles consists of identifying the information needs of the recipient and creating such information. The mere transmittal of relevant and timely facts is not the creation of information or of information processing. Unless the generated facts are accepted as a basis for action, they are mere data.

DIMENSIONS OF INFORMATION PROCESSING

To this point in the chapter we have defined *accounting information*, commented on the changing role of accounting in information processing, defined *information processing*, identified some historical developments that have influenced the area, and differentiated between *data* and *information* and the role that each plays in an information system. We have not developed a framework that integrates these concepts. Before we can do this, we need to examine the different *dimensions* of information processing. Three dimensions exist in any information system: (1) data processing (elements), (2) managerial activities, and (3) organizational functions.

Data Processing (Elements)

The first dimension of information processing is the physical aspects, or elements, of a system. If we were to ask to view an information system, we would probably be shown the physical components, or the *data processing elements*, of the system. These components would include (1) hardware, (2) data storage equipment, (3) software, and (4) operating procedures. A fifth element that would be necessary to make the system operational would be personnel.

The *hardware* for a system consists principally of what in global terms is referred to as "the computer" and includes the central processing unit, input/output devices, storage devices, communication equipment, and data preparation equipment. *Data storage equipment* includes such storage devices as magnetic tapes, disk packs, and drums.

Software is divided into three major areas: (1) general operating software, (2) general application software, and (3) specialized application management systems. General operating software consists of software programs provided by the computer manufacturer that guide the general operations of the computer. Generalized application software includes general analysis programs, such as budget planning, PERT analysis, and basic decision models, many of which are available from the computer manufacturer. Specialized application software consists of programs written specifically for individual applications. (Hardware and software concepts will be examined in Chapters 5, 6, and 8.)

A *data base* consists of data stored on storage devices. (Data base structure and accounting implications of the structure will be examined in Chapter 8.)

Procedures are viewed as physical elements of an information system because they appear in physical form, such as instruction booklets and manuals. In general, two types of procedures are necessary: (1) instructions for system users (these include not only general operating and use instructions but also data preparation instructions), and (2) instructions for computer center personnel who will be involved in running the system. Accountants are generally interested in the internal control and security procedures in items 1 and 2.

Personnel necessary to operationalize an information system include computer operators, who handle the physical aspects of running the system; systems analysts and programmers, who are involved in systems development; data preparation personnel, who are involved in preparing data to be input; and, finally, system users, who are the ultimate recipients of information.

Figure 1–5 summarizes the data processing dimension of an information system.

Managerial Activities

The second dimension of information processing is found when we examine the various managerial activities associated with different levels in an organization. These activities influence information processing because the information required for their support differs for each managerial level in the organization. We can gain an understanding of the different requirements by examining each of these activities. It should be recognized, however, that these activities have subdimensions such as (1) the degree to which decision-making activities are programmable or nonprogrammable, (2) the degree to which decision activities require internal or external information, and (3) the frequency with which the information should be updated. We will examine each of these subdivisions, as well as other points, separately. First we must define *managerial activity levels*.

ACTIVITY LEVELS[3]   The different decision-making activities can best be amplified by using the classical framework developed by Robert Anthony[4] and

[3] This concept or view has often been referred to as the "hierarchical view of information systems design." See John G. Burch, Felix R. Strater, Jr., and Gary Grudnitski, *Information Systems: Theory and Practice* (New York: John Wiley, 1979), pp. 74–75.

[4] Robert N. Anthony, *Planning and Control Systems: A Framework for Analysis* (Boston: Division of Research, Harvard University Graduate School of Business Administration, 1965).

HARDWARE

Central processing unit (CPU)
Input/output devices
Storage devices
Communication equipment
Data preparation equipment

SOFTWARE

Operating system and data management system
General application software
Specialized application software

DATA BASE

Data files of daily transactions, historical records, and information files

PROCEDURES

User instructions: general operations and data preparation
Operating instructions for computer center personnel involved in
   "running the system"

PERSONNEL

System users (management)
System analysts and programmers
Data preparation specialist
Computer operator

Figure 1-5   Data Processing Dimension of Information Processing
Source: George J. Brabb, *Computers and Information Systems in Business*, 2nd ed., p. 6.
Copyright © 1980 by Houghton Mifflin Company. Adapted by permission.

shown in Figure 1–6. Anthony identifies three categories of activities and argues that the decision-making activities differ significantly enough among these categories to warrant the development of different information systems.

The first category or activity level is *strategic planning*, which Anthony defines as follows:

> *Strategic planning* is the process of deciding on objectives of the organization, on changes in the objectives, on the resources used to obtain these objectives, and on the policies that are to govern the acquisition, use, and disposition of these resources.[5]

[5] Ibid., p. 24.

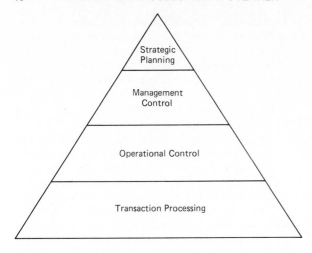

Figure 1-6 The Managerial Activity Dimension of Information Processing

In strategic planning the decision maker is involved with two key issues: (1) the development of organization objectives and (2) the allocation of resources required to attain the objectives. Decisions at this level tend to be made over a long period of time and involve the commitment of substantial resources.

The second category is *managment control,* which Anthony defines as follows:

> *Management control.* . . is the process by which managers assure that resources are obtained and used effectively and efficiently in the accomplishment of the organization's objective.[6]

In this category the decision maker is involved with monitoring the use of both financial and human resources within the organization. Both the efficient use of resources on hand and the provision of tools to aid in future resource usage are important. Most of the decision-making activity at this level is either financial or related to employee problems. A typical problem at the managerial control level is determining the reason for a variance between budgeted and actual costs.

Anthony's third category of managerial activity is *operational control,* which he defines as follows:

> *Operational control.* . . is the process of assuring that specific tasks are carried out effectively and efficiently.[7]

Operational activities are those activities involved in the day-to-day operations of the organization. An example of an operational decision is recognizing the need to reorder an inventory item, preparing appropriate documents, and fol-

[6] Ibid., p. 27.

[7] Ibid., p. 67.

lowing up to see that the item is purchased. The key distinction between operational control activities and management control activities is that operational control is *task-centered*, whereas management control is more *decision-centered*. Less adjustment is required in the operational control area because tasks, goals, and resources have been delineated in management control activity.

To complete the activity level analysis we should include a fourth activity, *transaction processing*. This activity is generally not included in the traditional decision-making activity dimension (Anthony, for example, excludes this in his review) because it does not involve management decision-making tasks or events. Transaction processing involves the handling of the organization's daily business transactions, such as payroll, accounts receivable, accounts payable, sales, updating of expense ledgers, and changes in inventories. It supports a wide variety of clerical decisions. Transaction processing is an important building block in information systems because it furnishes the system data base with many of the data required for decision making, planning, and control. The accountant as a provider of information must interface with other systems most often at this level.

INFORMATION REQUIREMENTS TO SUPPORT ACTIVITY LEVELS Transaction processing does not involve decision making but simply includes the collecting, sorting, editing, and structuring of daily transaction data. Because the other managerial activities do involve decision making and because the activities differ by level, the information required to support them differs. Likewise, data requirements for each activity differ. The accountant, as a user, provider, designer, and reviewer of information, needs to be cognizant of these differences because they affect the transaction processing activities required. Operational control, for example, implies a high frequency of data collection. Decision making at the operational level is based on highly detailed information generated within the organization. Data, as well as information that supports operational control, must be up-to-date, accurate, and precise.

In strategic planning, the frequency of data collection is low, and quite often the data are obtained from external sources. In general, the data, and thus the information employed, cover a wide time span and in many instances do not have to be current. Managers at the strategic level have a greater need for summary or aggregate information than for the detailed information employed at the managerial and operational levels. The triangular shape of Figure 1–6 indicates the greater need. This does not imply that simple aggregation of managerial or operational data will satisfy strategic planning needs, however, because of the essential differences in strategic planning and the other managerial levels.

Information requirements for managerial control decisions fall between strategic planning and operational control requirements. The level of detail included in managerial control information is greater than that required for strategic planning but less than that required in operational control, where weekly or daily updates are often required. Figure 1–7 lists the data/information requirements involved in supporting the three decision activity levels as well as transaction processing.

PROGRAMMED AND NONPROGRAMMED DECISIONS An additional issue that should be noted regarding the managerial activities dimension of information

Figure 1-7 Information/Data Requirements to Support Organizational (Management) Activities

Characteristics of Data/Information	Transaction Processing	Operational Control	Management Control	Strategic Planning
Source	Internal	Largely internal	→	Largely external
Scope	Well defined	Well defined, narrow	→	Very broad
Level of aggregation	Extremely detailed	Detailed	→	Aggregate
Time horizon	Historical	Historical	→	Future
Updating	Daily	Weekly and daily	→	Infrequent
Required accuracy	High	High	→	Low
Frequency of use	Daily	Very frequent	→	Infrequent

Source: Adapted from Lucas, Henry C., Jr., *Computer Based Information Systems in Organizations* (Palo Alto: Science Research Associates, 1973), p. 11. Adapted and reprinted by permission of the publisher.

processing is the distinction between *programmed* and *nonprogrammed* decisions. We include this concept at this point in our discussion, not because it directly influences information requirements, but because it influences the *decision models* that can be used to support decision making (refer to Figure 1–3). Systems built to support programmed, or structured, decision making will differ significantly from those for nonprogrammed, or unstructured, decision making.

The relationship between structured and unstructured decision making and the managerial activities is one in which structured decison making is linked more with operational control and managerial control activities, whereas unstructured decision making is linked more with strategic planning. This seems logical because the information requirements for strategic planning are broad and encompassing, but the requirements for operational and managerial control are more detailed, well defined, and narrow. Herbert Simon, in *The New Science of Management Decision*, argues to the contrary, however. Simon contends that individuals employ the same problem-solving or decison-making process regardless of their position in the organization.[8] We can gain a better understanding of this point if we examine what Simon labels the three phases of decision making:[9]

1. Intelligence—searching the environment for conditions calling for decision
2. Design—inventing, developing, and analyzing possible courses of action
3. Choice—selecting a course of action from those available

A structured problem is one in which all three phases of decison making are structured. An unstructured problem is one in which none of the phases are structured. For handling structured problems, decision models or algorithms are most applicable. Such models are particularly applicable for *identifying solution alternatives* and selecting the best solution. The fact that a problem is structured, however, does not imply that it is associated with any particular managerial level. An EOQ, or economic order quantity, model is an example of a decision model that is applicable to the operational control problem of inventory control. The strategic planning problem of warehouse or facility location can easily be handled with a decision model.

Other examples of the structured and nonstructured relationship to the managerial activities (strategic planning, management control, and operation control) are shown in Figure 1–8.

Note that transaction processing is not mentioned in the above discussion; it is a data/information-handling activity. Its interface with the decision models, however, is critical to any information processing system.

Organizational Functions

The third dimension of information processing is that which results when we view an information system from the organization's perspective. Since

---

[8] Herbert A. Simon, *The New Science of Management Decision*, rev. ed. (Englewood Cliffs, N.J.: Prentice-Hall, Inc., 1977), pp. 45–48.

[9] Ibid., p. 40.

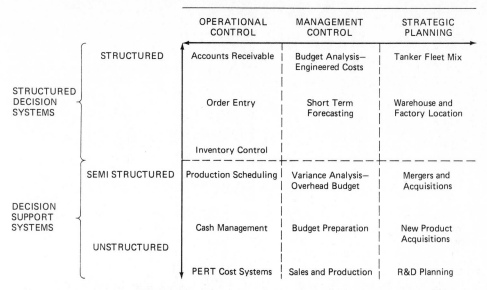

	OPERATIONAL CONTROL	MANAGEMENT CONTROL	STRATEGIC PLANNING
STRUCTURED	Accounts Receivable	Budget Analysis— Engineered Costs	Tanker Fleet Mix
	Order Entry	Short Term Forecasting	Warehouse and Factory Location
	Inventory Control		
SEMI STRUCTURED	Production Scheduling	Variance Analysis— Overhead Budget	Mergers and Acquisitions
	Cash Management	Budget Preparation	New Product Acquisitions
UNSTRUCTURED	PERT Cost Systems	Sales and Production	R&D Planning

STRUCTURED DECISION SYSTEMS

DECISION SUPPORT SYSTEMS

Figure 1-8 Structured/Unstructured Problems Associated with Different Managerial Activities

Source: G. Anthony Gorry and Michael S. Scott Morton, "A Framework for Management Information Systems," *Sloan Management Review*, (Fall 1971), p. 59.

many organizations, particularly larger corporations, are structured and organized managerially in terms of functional activities, such as marketing, production, personnel, accounting, and finance, this is a logical basis for organizing and developing an information system.[10] In designing or viewing an information system from the organizational perspective, we are not restricted from developing functional groupings other than those that exist organizationally. In general, however, the organizational arrangement will dictate system groupings.

Each function, however defined, is viewed as a subsystem having all the elements needed to perform all processing related to that function. Each functional subsystem is assumed to have the personnel, hardware, software, data base, and procedures to support its operation. These facilities could be provided by a centralized (integrated) organizational unit within the firm or by a decentralized unit. Obviously there will be some programs (software), as well as data base and decision models, common to several or all functions. Financial and managerial accounting systems can use common data bases, for example. Thus a combination of centralized and decentralized organizational units may be appropriate. (Additional comments regarding this point are made in Chapter 2.)

In addition to the link between the functional units and the facilities, there is a link with managerial activities. Each function can be viewed in terms of the information required to support operational control, management control, strategic planning, and transaction processing.

[10] Gordon B. Davis, *Management Information Systems: Conceptual Foundations, Structure, and Development* (New York: McGraw-Hill, 1976), p. 214.

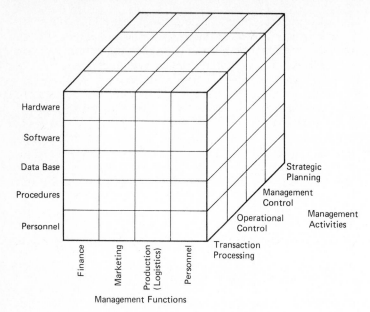

Hardware

Software

Data Base

Procedures

Personnel

Finance

Marketing

Production
(Logistics)

Personnel

Management Functions

Transaction
Processing

Operational
Control

Management
Control

Strategic
Planning

Management
Activities

Figure 1-9 Dimensions of Information Processing

Source: Adapted from Lucas, Henry C., Jr., *Computer Based Information Systems in Organizations* (Palo Alto: Science Research Associates, 1973), p. 11. Adapted and reprinted by permission of the publisher.

Figure 1–9 illustrates the functional dimension of information processing. We identify four basic subunits within the functional dimension: (1) finance, (2) marketing, (3) production (logistics), and (4) personnel. Other subunits are possible and are detailed in Chapter 3. (Chapters 12–15 include detailed descriptions of each of the basic functional subunits and its information requirements. These chapters examine the relationships between each function and the other dimensions of information processing.)

SUMMARY

Before addressing the question of how an information system is designed and developed, we must have a firm understanding of the components and concepts on which a system is built. Some of these basic concepts have been presented in this chapter. First, we emphasized the ever-expanding definition of what constitutes an accounting system and the impact that the information processing and decision-making environment has on accounting systems. We noted that the roles of the controller and public accountant have been greatly expanded from providers of financial information to providers, users, and designers of major portions of the information processed by the firm. We also noted that these emerging roles for an accountant have occurred because of the interfaces between what has traditionally been regarded as accounting information and the information needs of new formalized information systems of the organization.

In this chapter we also differentiated between *data* and *information*, noting specifically that the presence of information can be viewed as a continuum.

At the conclusion of the historical overview of information systems, a summary diagram (Figure 1–3) identified the relationship between data and information. The summary diagram also identified the links between formal information systems, computer-based systems, computer technology, systems analysis and design, and decision models. This "global information systems perspective" is a systematic means for linking the components of an information system. Throughout the text the reader may want to refer to this diagram in order to keep different concepts in perspective.

The final concept presented in this chapter was that of dimensions of information processing. Note that the dimensions described—the system elements, managerial activities, and organizational functions—are not the only available views of the information processing dimensions. Several of the *subdimensions* described are often labeled *dimensions* by other authors. However, the dimensions we have presented appear to be common to most organizations. They are therefore the most suitable for developing a general view of an information system. In Chapter 2 we will examine these dimensions in order to develop an information systems framework.

SELECTED REFERENCES

ACKOFF, RUSSELL, "Management Misinformation Systems," *Management Science*, 14, No. 4 (December 1967).

AMERICAN ACCOUNTING ASSOCIATION COMMITTEE ON INFORMATION SYSTEMS, "Accounting and Information Systems," *Accounting Review, Supplement*, Vol. 46, 1971.

ANTHONY, ROBERT N., *Planning and Control Systems: A Framework for Analysis*. Boston: Harvard University Press, 1965.

ANTHONY, ROBERT N., *Planning and Control Systems: A Framework for Analysis*. Boston: Harvard University Press, 1965.

BRABB, GEORGE J., *Computers and Information Systems in Business*. New York: Houghton Mifflin, 1976.

BURCH, JOHN G., FELIX R. STRATER, JR., AND GARY GRUDNITSKI, *Information Systems: Theory and Practice*. New York: John Wiley, 1979.

CHURCHMAN, C. WEST, *The Systems Approach*. New York: Dell Publishing, 1968.

CUSHING, BARRY F., *Accounting Information Systems and Business Organization*. Reading, Mass.: Addison-Wesley, 1978.

DAVIS, GORDON B., *Management Information System Conceptual Foundation, Structure and Development*. New York: McGraw-Hill, 1974.

DAVIS, KEAGLE W., "The Information Systems Auditor of the 1980s," *Management Accounting*, 43 (March 1980), 40–47.

DORRICOT, KEITH O., "Impact of Small Computers on Auditing," *CA Magazine*, 112, No. 1 (January 1979), 62–64.

GORRY, G. ANTHONY, AND MICHAEL S. SCOTT MORTON, "A Framework for Management Information Systems," *Sloan Management Review*, Fall 1971, pp. 55–70.

LUCAS, HENRY C., JR., *Computer Based Information Systems in Organizations*. Chicago: Science Research Associates, 1973.

Management Advisory Services Education Task Force, *Exposure Draft University Education for Management Consulting*. AICPA, 1977.

Mason, Richard O., "Concepts for Designing Management Information Systems," AIS Research Paper No. 8, October 1969.

Murdick, Robert G., and Joel E. Ross, *Information Systems for Modern Management*. Englewood Cliffs, N.J.: Prentice-Hall, 1971.

Prince, Thomas R., *Information Systems for Management Planning and Control*. Homewood, Ill.: Richard D. Irwin, 1975.

Simon, Herbert A, *The New Science of Management Decision*, rev. ed. Englewood Cliffs, N.J.: Prentice-Hall, Inc., 1977.

REVIEW QUESTIONS

1. Explain how two major factors in the business environment have changed the role of the controller or the accountant.

2. Define the term *accounting system*.

3. How do current accounting subsystems relate to other subsystems, such as marketing and production?

4. What has been the traditional role of the accountant? What aspects of this role have been influenced the most by the changing information environment?

5. How has the current information environment changed public accounting practice?

6. What is the accountant's role in the current information processing environment?

7. Explain the basic differences between *information processing systems* and *management information systems* (MIS).

8. Define the term *information systems*. Give an example.

9. What four factors have had an impact on the evolution of information systems? Elaborate on each.

10. Have *software* and *hardware* traditionally developed at the same rate? What impact has this had on the development of information systems? What are some of the accounting implications?

11. Differentiate between *external* and *internal* information requirements. Give some accounting examples.

12. Sketch a pictorial representation of an accounting system. Include in your diagram *external* and *internal* constituents, decision models, computer technology, and systems analysis and design, as well as the different types of information systems.

13. Differentiate between *data* and *information*. Give a few accounting examples.

14. What are three dimensions of information processing?

15. What elements are associated with the data processing dimension of information processing?

16. Explain Anthony's framework of decision-making activities. How does this framework relate to information processing? What are its accounting implications?

17. Describe the functional dimension of information processing.

18. Differentiate between *programmed* and *nonprogrammed* decisions. How does this distinction relate to information processing?

19. Will aggregation of transaction data be sufficient for strategic decision-making information needs? Why or why not? How does your answer influence accounting systems, such as budgeting?

20. Give an example of a decision-making algorithm for production and marketing for both structured and unstructured decisions and for each management activity level.

EXERCISES AND CASES

1–1

Stewart and Miller, CPAs, have been serving clients in a small town south of Pittsburgh for twenty years. Their clients have begun to ask their advice about the acquisition of microsystems to assist them in managing their firms and keeping their records. Stewart and Miller have not been able to render this service because of their lack of EDP expertise, and they have lost several clients to a new CPA firm in town. Moreover, for those clients who have converted their accounting systems to EDP, Stewart and Miller have felt very uneasy in trying to audit the new system. The partners of this new firm have a strong background in accounting systems and are quite knowledgeable about microsystems. They even use their own Radio Shack TRS–80 for write-up work and tax planning. As Ron Miller's close friend and controller for one of Ron's clients, what action would you suggest that he and Bob Stewart take with regard to this ominous trend in adverse client relations?

1–2

As controller of a quality glass company you have been under a lot of pressure to improve your budget process because of several serious inventory problems. Production never seems to produce the correct style demanded by marketing. Stockouts of one line of glass and an oversupply of another line of glass are common. You use a straightforward budget process. Sales forecasts are made monthly, and production is instructed to produce to meet these forecasts. Production, in turn, is scheduled, and sufficient materials are ordered to comply with the needs of marketing. A manual system of reports is used to implement this system, but it is apparent that a quicker, more flexible system is now needed to accommodate changes in a very competitive retail market. The problem is that you are comfortable with your current batch processing accounting system, which uses card tabulating equipment and magnetic tapes and the manual budget reporting system. Moreover, you do not understand the new on-line system your boss is urging you to consider. Your friend and CPA has suggested that you take a few professional development courses in EDP systems, the systems approach to management general ledger systems, and decision support and planning systems. Should you follow his advice? Why?

1–3

Wilks Ski Company manufactures a wide variety of winter sports equipment. Manufacturing, sales, and distribution decisions are very much a function of projected regional weather and economic conditions. In other words, if discretionary income is high and more than average snowfall is expected for the eastern region, Wilks's management makes every effort to ensure that all retail outlets have a sufficient supply of ski equipment. However, if sales in another region are expected to be slow, every effort must be made to avoid overstocking due to the seasonal nature of its product.

A computer service provides Wilks with the following set of reports (not all are noted here):

a. Current weather conditions by region, average snowfall to date, and temperature in degree days to date
b. Sales of winter sports equipment by region
c. Forecast of economic conditions by region for the next season
d. Meteorological forecast for the next winter season by region
e. U.S. meteorological forecast
f. Inventory of Wilks Ski equipment by retail outlet
g. Forecast of expected seasonal sales by month by region based on a regression model that incorporates items *a* through *f*
h. Correlation statistics between past retail sales and meteorological forecasts

   Which reports constitute *information* and which are just *data*? (Identify them by *I* and *D*.) Are there some that will provide useful information in a limited sense? (Identify these by *P*.)

1–4

Consider again the Wilks Ski Company (Case 1–3). List the operational, managerial, and strategic information requirements that you would expect this type of firm to have.

1–5

The top- and middle-management levels of Wilks Ski Company (Case 1–3) have over the last five years (since they employed the computer service organization to assist them in processing information) received summary reports of the type given to operational management for sales, distribution, and manufacturing. These reports summarize inventory, sales statistics and forecasts, economic statistics and forecasts, and meteorological statistics and forecasts. Top-management personnel have been dissatisfied with these reports. Based on the characteristics of information listed in Figure 1–9, briefly describe why.

1–6

Overweight Trucking Company, located in central Ohio, has just purchased a small computer system to schedule its trucks more efficiently. Included in the package it purchased were the necessary "canned" programs to schedule its trucks. These programs, which were designed for a trucking company with one freight terminal, were thoroughly tested and have been used extensively in the trucking industry. Overweight, however, has had difficulty in operating the system. Why do you think such a problem has arisen, given that the new system is a proven one?

1–7

The Scarf Toy Manufacturing Company has a responsibility accounting system. Managers receive reports on operations which aggregate details of shop operations for each plant. Plant operations are further aggregated in the report received by the vice-president of manufacturing. These reports show the budgeted and actual operating results for the current month and the year to date. They, along with inventory status reports, provide the major source of production information for planning. Management can look at the variances and determine whether manufacturing operations are under control. If the variances are large, management takes appropriate action: changing the manufacturing plans.

The company's profits have been decreasing, and management has requested similar aggregate sales data from marketing. It feels that this added information will suffice for its decision-making needs. It has asked your advice as the company's CPA. Do you agree? Why? Do you foresee any needs that will not be met by this information? If so, what additional information do you suggest that management provide with its accounting system?

1–8

Arment Company has sales that range from $25 million to $30 million, has one manufacturing plant, and employs seven hundred people, including fifteen national account salespeople and eighty traveling sales representatives. The home office and plant are in Philadelphia, and the product is distributed east of the Mississippi River. The product is a line of pumps and related fittings used at construction sites, in homes, and in processing plants. The company has total assets equal to 80 percent of sales. Its capitalization consists of the following: current liabilities, 30 percent; long-term debt, 15 percent; and shareholders' equity, 55 percent. In the past two years sales have increased 7 percent annually, and income after tax has amounted to 5 percent of sales.

REQUIRED: List the strategic-planning decisions that must be made or confirmed during the preparation of the annual profit plan or budget. (Adapted from the CMA Examination)

1–9

Your firm has been asked to design a system for strategic planning for May's, a regional department store. Specifically, May's needs help with planning store locations and the type of merchandise to carry in each store. May's management tried to summarize credit sales by location in the metropolitan area and sales at each of its locations. It felt that the aggregated information was not sufficient to make the decision and called upon your firm for assistance. Why wasn't management satisfied? Characterize the nature of the two decisions involved here.

1–10

The Block Baking Company produces a variety of bread and other baked goods. Block Baking has a perpetual inventory system, which gives inventory on hand at the end of each day. This information is used to schedule the next day's production. Management tries to produce what is in short supply so that it will not incur any stockouts that will send customers elsewhere. This goal has not been achieved, however. Sales are lost, and management is considering increasing its overall inventory so that there will be enough stock. The president, however, has rejected this because of the company's policy of shipping only fresh bread. Large stocks will increase the probability of stale bread being delivered to customers, and fresh products are important in the company's market area. You have been called in to help management resolve this problem. Write a brief assessment of the problem and outline your suggestions for expanding the system to resolve the company's dilemma.

1-11

Classify the following decisions as operational, managerial, or strategic. Also classify them as structured or unstructured.

a. Ordering inventory by using the EOQ model
b. Locating a retail outlet for a large fast-food company
c. Terminating an R & D project that does not seem fruitful
d. Planning the construction of a large office building
e. Adding a second shift
f. Promoting a plant manager to vice-president
g. Adding a new product
h. Merging with a raw material supplier
i. Repairing a lathe
j. Inspecting finished goods by using an electronic tester
k. Selecting a vendor from a catalog

1-12

Johnson Typewriter, Inc., an old line manufacturer of electric and manual typewriters was one of the leaders in the typewriter industry. Commercial and retail sales topped 475 million in 1982. This was up 55 million from 1981 and exceeded 1980 sales by 75 million. Profits, on the other hand, slid from a record high of 45 million in 1980 to a loss of 95 million in 1982. This disastrous profit picture was even more perplexing because a new management team took over the reigns of Johnson

Typewriter in 1979 and they quickly merged with AWP (Automatic Word Processing) to apply state of the art microprocessing to its line of commercial typewriters so as to compete effectively in the market place. Their sales figures reflect the success of this strategy. To compound Johnson Typewriter's troubles, their auditors are the subject of litigation for rendering a clean opinion on what has been described as materially false and misleading financial statements for 1981 and 1982. As a result, the management team which led Johnson Typewriter into their problems has been replaced by long time Johnson employees headed by Mr. Reed, who was V.P. of Research and Development. Mr. Reed promptly engaged the services of another public accounting firm to assist him in his analysis of the current situation.

Upon their joint examination of the operating and financial activities of business, they found that the condition was far worse than their wildest beliefs.

1. Johnson's debt, most of which was short-term had risen drastically. It was nearly equal to the company's equity. Cash reserves were nearly depleted. All of this was necessary according to the previous management team in order to enter the age of microprocessing technology. They said, "It was an investment in the future."

2. Some of the commercial sales contracts were misclassified and as a result of reclassification to the typewriter division, Automatic Word Processing division showed an adjusted loss of nearly 90 million. This misclassification, it was revealed, was due to the absence of simple controls over sales contract classification.

3. A further examination of the financial statements revealed that several of the adjustments made to the financial statements in 1982, which precipitated the heavy loss, should have been recognized in 1981 and 1980. The accounting system again failed to classify these according to generally accepted accounting principles.

4. Assets were misstated in almost every division. Receivables and inventories were consistently overstated in value. Far too much reliance was placed on a perpetual inventory system which lacked adequate controls.

5. Inefficiencies were present throughout the organization.

   a. In accounting, billing was accomplished using an old overloaded system. The result was that customers received multiple statements, received statements prior to delivery of the typewriter or word processor and sometimes never received invoices for delivered equipment.

   b. In the inventory management system, parts were often not on hand for production or service. This resulted in poor service and the return of many pieces of equipment and the loss of many man hours in manufacturing due to unexpected part shortages.

   c. In the distribution of units to commercial distributors and retailers, orders or requisitions for certain popular models would go unheaded and alternative models were frequently shipped as they were produced. The result was the loss of several unhappy distributors and retailers.

   d. In production, insufficient arrangements were made with suppliers of microchips. Orders were often placed two months in advance and not delivered to the appropriate plant until three months had lapsed. The result was that manufacturing often had to "make do."

   e. A careful investigation yielded the striking revelation that Word Processing was selected for merger not because of its R&D technology but because of beneficial tax implications. It was discovered after review that other potential word processing companies with much more advanced and developed micro-processing technology were not even considered for merger.

From the results of the joint investigation above, what information system failures do you recognize? What management decisions were not supported by an effective accounting information system? Classify these decisions as operating, managerial, and strategic.

2

INFORMATION PROCESSING CONCEPTS

INTRODUCTION

In the preceding chapter, different dimensions of information systems were presented and discussed in detail. In our discussion we did not link the different dimensions in order to form a complete system, although this integration was implied. Obviously the dimensions, or components, of a system are interrelated and thus should be linked in order to complete our analysis.

Before addressing the task of linking the dimensions, it is appropriate to examine the systems approach in more detail. This concept relates to the manner in which and the degree to which the dimensions of a system are coordinated. An additional fact that justifies examination of the systems approach is that it can be related to the systems development and implementation process. In this text we will use the AICPA management advisory services guidelines as a basis for defining the systems development and implementation process, although other frameworks are available.

SYSTEM CONCEPTS

Information Systems versus
Management Systems

As we indicated briefly in Chapter 1, the systems approach is a philosophy or perception of a structure that seeks to coordinate, in an efficient manner, the activities or operations of an organization. To employ or develop such a philosophy, systems personnel, accountants, and managers must "think systems." But before one can think systems, it is necessary to define exactly what the term *system* means. In an elementary sense, a system can be described as a set of elements (people, hardware, information, etc.) organized for the purpose of achieving a particular goal. A system, however, is more than a collection of such organizational functions as marketing, manufacturing, and finance or other organizational divisions. The various functions, divisions, and products, and the internal and external factors of the environment, are synthesized to form the firm—or, in other words, "the system." A firm, when viewed as a system, is more than the mere components tied together in a static fashion by the structure of the organization. It is a combination of closely related parts operating in a dynamic fashion. Within the overall system, the accounting subsystem is often the focal point of this relationship.

The obvious question at this point is, How does the concept of a system relate to information systems and how is this related to viewing the organization as a system? Recall our definition of *information systems*:

> Those systems in an organization that (1) meet daily transactional processing requirements, (2) support operational, managerial, and strategic activities of the organization, and (3) provide external constituents with necessary reports.

A key objective of an information system is to make available, on a timely basis, comprehensive information to managers throughout the organization so as to aid management in effective decision making. *Information systems*, however, differ from *management systems*. The dimensions of an information system that we noted in Chapter 1, particularly the organizational functions and managerial activities dimensions, could also be viewed as dimensions of a management system. If we view these dimensions as they relate to planning, organizing, controlling, and managing the objectives of the firm, then the interrelated network could be labeled a *management system*. An information system is tied to a management system in that its objective is to provide information of sufficient quality and quantity to allow the management system to function effectively.

Obviously, management systems and information systems have some characteristics in common, such as the following:

1. Both management systems and information systems can be analyzed, designed, and managed by the general principles of systems design.
2. Both are ongoing processes. They are dynamic rather than static, and their dynamic nature must be planned for in the design and develop-

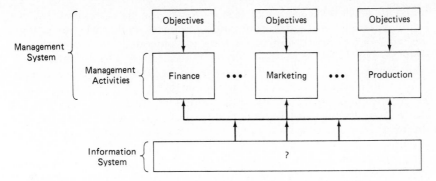

Figure 2-1 Management System-Information System Relationship

ment process. (This concept is reviewed briefly in this chapter and discussed at length in Chapters 10 and 11.)

3. The elements of each are operationally linked, but the information system must be designed to complement the management system, not the reverse. The management system should be designed to achieve the objectives of the organization most effectively; the information system should be designed to complement the management system.

4. Both the management system and the information system have outputs. Output of the information system, however, is an input to the management system. It aids in the operational and decision-making activities of the organization.

5. Finally, an accounting subsystem is at the center of both systems, and, as a result, controllers and CPAs need to understand the structure of the management system and the supporting information system.

Figure 2–1 illustrates schematically the general relationship between a management system and an information system. Note that the information system is undefined in the diagram. The diagram only depicts the fact that the information system supports the management system. Nothing has been said at this point as to how the information system should be designed to accomplish this objective.

The Systems Approach: General

To develop an effective system within any organization, we must consider both the management system and the information system and we must apply the systems approach. As we indicated earlier, the fundamental precept of the systems approach is the interrelationship of the parts or subsystems of the *area, problem,* or *organization* being addressed. When the subsystems are considered collectively as a system, the system's effectiveness is greater than the sum of the effectiveness of each subsystem considered separately. In the past many organizations have fallen short in the development of an effective information system because they failed to relate all components. Such failures can be attributed to several factors. The first factor is the narrow view that has been taken by specialists such as accountants, engineers, and marketing people. There is a tendency in any organization for each individual to concentrate on the different aspects of his or her specialty without relating it to the other activities in the organization. A second factor is "suboptimizing." Traditionally, there has been an emphasis on optimizing the performance of a functional area within the organization (such as marketing, production, or finance). A third factor in information system shortcomings is the failure to realize the potential of an accounting subsystem as a focal point for linking the various subsystems of an organization.

The *systems approach* can best be illustrated by comparing it with a *component approach* (focusing on separate functions). Consider the development of an information system to support the different managerial activities or levels in the organization. If we assume that the different activities or levels can be depicted by the hierarchical structure, one approach would be to develop the information by summing the information upward along the traditional authority lines. This approach, however, will not result in maximum effectiveness. The management system, in this case the hierarchical structure, allows suboptimization of each component within each level. The systems approach would call for linking the components and levels of the organization so that total organization effectiveness is achieved. The accounting system can be utilized effectively to provide this linkage through the transaction, recording, budgeting, planning, and reporting processes.

Two comments should be made about an information system that supports the organization structure. First, it should not be assumed that in a traditional organizational structure information is limited to the chain of command. For example, copies of sales orders have traditionally been forwarded to the credit, production scheduling, shipping, and accounts receivable departments. Although these information flows do provide some degree of integration, maximum effectiveness does not result without crossing organizational boundaries and examining the organization as a whole. Second, the management system and the information system must be considered collectively. Earlier it was implied that the management system should be designed to maximize the firm's objectives, and the information system simply supports this by supplying appropriate and timely information. The two systems—the management system and the information system—are strongly related and should be considered together to maximize their effectiveness for the firm as a whole.

The differences between the *systems approach* and the *component approach* can be illustrated by comparing Figures 2–2 and 2–3. In the *component approach* (Figure 2–2), the focus is on the summation of the parts rather than on an interrelated whole. Component objectives are defined by synthesis of common data. The complete system is defined as the collection of the components. The *systems approach* (Figure 2–3) begins with the objectives of the system as a whole. Requirements of the entire system are defined by evaluating the system objectives. Various configurations of subsystems or components are studied. Based upon selected criteria formulated from the system objectives, the components are evaluated and analyzed, using cost-benefit analysis, to select the configuration of components that best meets the overall firm objectives. The final step is the synthesis of the selected components into the final system.

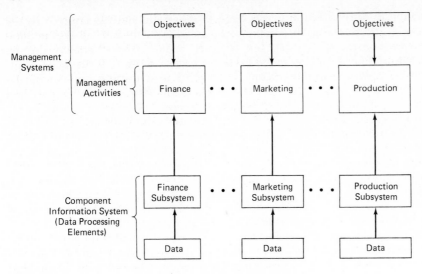

Figure 2-2   The Component Approach to System Formulation

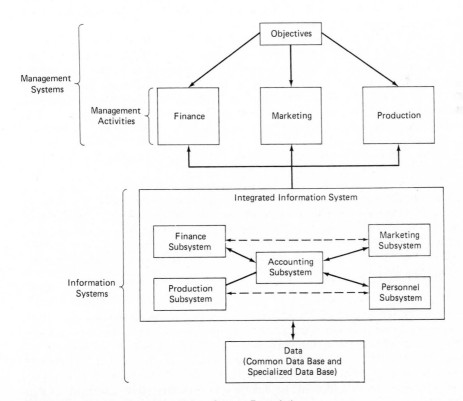

Figure 2-3   The Systems Approach to System Formulation

Often the organization is too large to apply the systems concept to the entire firm. In these situations, boundaries are drawn around subsystems and interfaces are considered so that the analysis, design, and ultimately the accounting system may be more manageable. In each case there is a cost associated with the resulting suboptimization associated with this decoupling of the various components or subsystems. There is a trade-off between this cost and the cost of a completely integrated system. For such subsystems, all the previous decisions apply to that subsystem and its related components.

In the formulation and development of a system, the following factors must be kept in mind: (1) level of integration, (2) information flow, (3) technology utilization, (4) effectiveness, (5) level of decision orientation, and (6) utilization of decision support models. We will examine two different schemes for linking the different dimensions of systems. But regardless of the scheme employed, the system will be influenced by the above factors. It is thus appropriate to examine the factors further.

One objective of employing the systems approach for system formulation and development is to *integrate* the components in a way that takes advantage of the interrelatedness and interdependence between the dimensions and subdimensions of the organization. This integration process must also ensure that communication channels (*information flows*) are open between subsystems and between the firm and the environment. The degree to which this should be accomplished will be a function of the desired independence and subsequent decoupling of the various subsystems or components. Various design trade-offs have a bearing on this information flow.

For a system to be *effective*, it must not only be cost effective but also meet the overall objectives of the organization. Utilization of the systems approach in both system formulation and development can strongly affect both of these goals. One factor that can significantly affect the degree to which these goals are met is the utilization of current *technology* in the development of the system. Where appropriate, integration of up-to-date computer technology into the systems framework should be considered. For example, for small accounting systems, minicomputers with standard accounting packages should be considered.

Finally, to make the management functions of planning, control, and decision making more effective, programmed *decision support models* should be integrated into the system where appropriate. The level at which various decisions are to be made must also be considered in formulating and developing the firm's overall system.

AN INFORMATION SYSTEM FRAMEWORK

In Chapter 1 we identified three dimensions of information systems: (1) the management activity dimension, (2) the organizational function dimension, and (3) the data processing, or elements, dimension. Rather than being viewed separately, these dimensions should be synthesized into a framework, particularly if we take a systems view of an information system. What is needed is a conceptual framework that will allow us to examine and evaluate the interaction of the dimensions and subdimensions.

A conceptual framework can be developed by synthesizing concepts from each of the dimensions previously described. Recall that the managerial activities dimension was defined by examining the different activities associated with the different levels in the organization. The activities identified were transaction processing, operational control, managerial control, and strategic planning. The functional dimension was defined by examining the different functional units in an organization, including marketing, production, personnel, finance, and accounting. (Functional units can also be determined along divisional or product lines or other dimensions, although we did not note these.) The data processing, or elements, dimension was defined by analyzing the physical and procedural activities associated with information processing. The elements associated with the data processing dimension were defined as software, hardware, data base and data management procedures, operating procedures, and personnel. Obviously such factors as personnel, procedures, and applications software are common to several of these dimensions. Likewise, certain factors are unique to a managerial level, organizational function, or processing activity. Figure 2–4 puts this in perspective. Note that the diagram includes each of the dimensions. Note also that the diagram is an extension of Figure 1–9.

An understanding of this conceptual framework of an information system can be developed by examining the different dimensions as they relate to the framework. We will begin by examining the functional dimension. Each

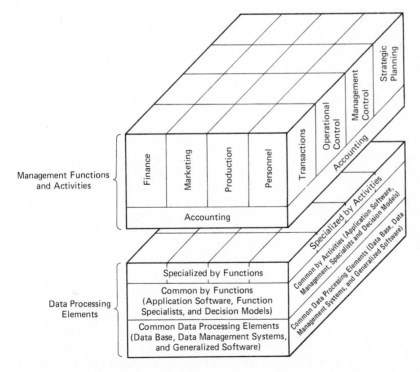

Figure 2-4   Conceptual Framework of an Information System

functional unit (finance, marketing, production, personnel) can be subdivided into activities ranging from transaction processing to strategic planning. The degree of activity in each component (subdivision or subsystem) will vary with the function. Marketing and finance, for example, would obviously have more activity at the strategic level, accounting would have a high degree of activity at the transaction processing level, while production and logistics management would have the highest degree of activity at the operational and managerial control levels. If an organization were organized along product lines, each product would likewise require different degrees of management activity.

The impact of functional-managerial activity subsystems on the information system is through the demand for (1) timely and accurate information, (2) common information (accessible as a data base), (3) common software and hardware, (4) specialized software and hardware, (5) common decision support systems, and (6) unique decision support systems. This impact is represented by the matrix in Figure 2–4. All of these demands may not occur within a firm, depending upon the size and nature of the business.

To gain an understanding of how such demands occur, we can examine the framework further. Each functional unit will probably have unique data files that are used only by that functional area or product division. In fact, some individual applications within some functional units will have unique data files not required by other applications in functional areas. Pricing analysis within the managerial control and strategic planning areas of marketing is an example of an application requiring a unique data file. There will also be files that need to be accessed by more than one functional or divisional unit or application. Files of this nature are generally labeled *common files* and are organized into a general data base. The management of the data base generally requires special software that falls into the category of *data base management systems.*

In addition to common and specialized files, common and specialized software may be required to support the functional and divisional units within the firm. If one of the subunits of a functional area is involved with a special problem, then special applications software must be written for that subunit. A plant layout decision, to be made by a division manager, is an example of a problem that may require special applications software. Many common software packages and decision support models (such as linear programming, regression analysis, and forecasting models) can also be used by all subunits within the functional areas as well as across the areas. Software that spans the functional and divisional areas forms the *decision model base* for the information system.

If we examine information demands from the viewpoint of activity levels rather than functional units, we find demands comparable to those by function. Both unique and common files as well as specialized software, common software, and decision support models will probably be required. Each of these needs is depicted in Figure 2–4.

INFORMATION SYSTEM STRUCTURES

In studying the systems concept and in analyzing the proposed conceptual view of an information system, we could easily conclude that a totally integrated system had been proposed. This is an invalid conclusion. The systems approach shown in Figure 2–3 is a process by which we can *examine and study* the firm's functional and decision activity information needs as a whole. The conceptual framework (Figure 2–4) provides a means for *viewing the relationship* of the different dimensions and subdimensions of an information system. Nothing has been said as to how we go about linking the functional and decision-making activities and the data processing elements in order to form the information system.

The information systems literature indicates that numerous types of linkage exist. Most of these can be classified into two types of system linkages (or a combination of the two types): (1) an integrated system or (2) a distributed system. Since these are two distinct approaches to structuring an information system and since each has certain advantages as well as disadvantages, we will briefly discuss each. (In Chapter 6 we will evaluate system structures and review their associated hardware.) We will also comment briefly on the combination of the two approaches.

Integrated Systems[1]

As we have just noted in our conceptual examination of an information system, both specialized and common data files as well as specialized and common software needs can exist in an information system. The fact that specialized data, software, and other needs exist, however, does not prevent the structuring of a totally integrated information system. Those specialized parts of the total system will simply have limited usage. An integrated information system is designed so that all the data of an organization are channeled into a common data base. The data base, along with all necessary support software and decision models, services all the data processing and information functions of the organization. The key aspect of the integrated approach is the common data base. Figure 2–5 illustrates an integrated system.

Developing and installing an integrated information system requires a total commitment from management at all levels. Since the system spans all or a large part of the organization's functions and divisions, it must have the organization's full support. Commitment is needed for the development of a long-range master plan, the employment of highly skilled personnel, the acquisition of the necessary hardware and software, and the expenditure of sufficient funds. It must also be recognized that the development of this type of system will probably require a change in traditional methods of handling data and information. Changes in organizational structure, particularly at the staff support level, will also be needed. Staff groups that traditionally exist in marketing, production, finance, and other operating areas can be centralized because the data handling and processing are centralized.

Having an integrated system with a common data, software, and decision model base does not necessarily imply that one set of files or programs exists. It means that duplicate files and redundance of files and programs are reduced by having a consolidated set of interrelated files and programs.

One of the things that an integrated system does provide is a reduction in the number of communication channels required to support and interact

[1] See John G. Burch, Felix R. Strater, Jr., and Gary Gruditski, *Information Systems: Theory and Practice* (New York: John Wiley, 1979) for the source of much of this discussion.

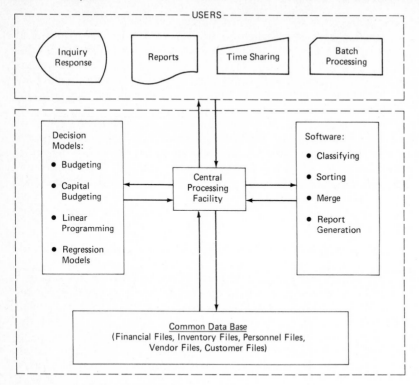

Figure 2-5   An Integrated Information System

with all the organizational activities and functions within the firm. For example, in an organization in which thirty activities or functions exist, only thirty channels are needed to support complete interaction among the different activities or functions. Each activity-function is tied directly to the common data and support bases. Figure 2–6 illustrates the channel arrangement necessary to support an eight-activity or -function firm.

Other advantages and disadvantages of integrated systems are summarized in Figure 2–7. Although there are disadvantages to an integrated system, there are certain advantages that would warrant employing such a structure.

In the late 1960s there was a movement toward integrated systems, which was triggered by at least two factors: (1) fragmentation of computer operations and (2) computer technology. As computer systems emerged in the 1950s, data processing activities tended to be localized within the different functions and operations of the firm because computer hardware and software that could support large centralized operations did not exist. This resulted in fragmentation and noncoordination of data processing activities. With the development of improved computer technology and telecommunications in the early 1960s, technical capabilities that could support large centralized processing facilities emerged.

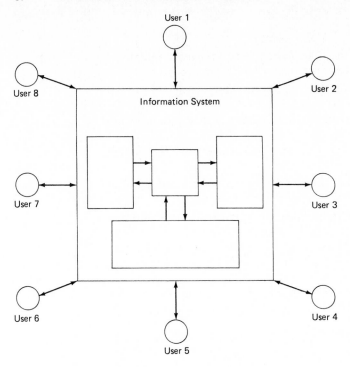

Figure 2-6 Information Channel Network for Integrated Information System

Distributed Systems[2]

To employ an integrated systems approach requires full commitment of the organization, both financially and administratively; lack of this commitment will result in failure. Factors other than financial and administrative can result in poor systems results, however. Some authors argue that the concept of a totally integrated system is logically unsound. Gorry and Morton state:

> Some of the proponents of the *total system* approach advocate that systems through the organization be tightly linked with the output of one becoming the direct input to another, and that the whole structure be built on the detailed data used for controlling operations. In doing so they are suggesting an approach to systems design that is at best uneconomical and at worst based on a serious misconception. The first major problem with this view is that it does not recognize the on going nature of systems development. . . . The second and perhaps most severe problem with this total system view is that it fails to represent properly the information needs of the management control and strategic planning activities. Neither of these areas necessarily needs informa-

[2] Ibid.

ADVANTAGES

-A simple communication network is required.

-The system allows multiple users to concurrently retrieve, update, or delete data from the data base.

-The possibility of errors is minimized because increased attention is generally given to controls.

-More security through control of the system against unauthorized users is possible.

-Economies of scale exist in the development and use of the system, since the system serves the entire organization.

-Since staff support operations are centralized, better opportunities should exist for recruiting skilled professional employees.

-Consistency in accounting and information processing procedures is promoted.

-Better utilization of total processing capabilities is possible. The system avoids having excess capacity in one division and a processing overload in another division.

-Maximum computer capabilities are provided to all divisions or units of the firm.

-The management system is not tied to the traditional hierarchical structure. The information system provides top management with information on any level and regarding any function.

DISADVANTAGES

-The cost of development is extremely high.

-Modification of the system can be lengthy and costly because of interdependencies.

-Unless a complete backup system is available, certain system problems can be catastrophic. Loss of the central processing unit (CPU) will cause the entire system to go down; this could be disastrous for an on-line airline, stock brokerage, or banking system.

-Costs associated with errors are generally higher.

-Development and maintenance of the system requires highly skilled employees.

-Management must be willing to make a long-term commitment that even in the largest organization can be technically and financially risky.

Figure 2-7   Advantages and Disadvantages of Integrated Systems

tion that is a mere aggregation of data from the data base. . . . if such a link is needed, it is most cost effective to use sampling from the data base and other statistical techniques to develop the required information.[3]

[3] G. Anthony Gorry and Michael S. Scott Morton, "A Framework for Management Information Systems," *Sloan Management Review*, 13, no. 1 (Fall 1971), pp. 55–70.

Dearden argues further against the use of a totally integrated system by stating that an integrated system encompasses such a large assortment of different activities that no one person could possess the set of skills required to effectively integrate a firm's total system needs.[4]

To underscore the complexity problem, Vanecek, Zant, and Guynes argue that

> Although DDP could not occur without the necessary advances in technology, a major impetus for change has been the complexities of the centralized system. There is a greater but rapidly growing effort by end users to take charge of their own information processing functions. This desire for more direct management control of computer resources is consistent with current management styles, which tend to be more decentralized. User departments, frustrated by the lack of responsiveness of data processing staff at central locations have found that it is possible to install small, powerful mini-micro computers within authorized departmental spending levels.[5]

One alternative is to decouple the systems and bear the costs of reduced coordination among the more independent subsystems. Another approach is to distribute subsystems throughout the organization and link the subsystems via a communication network. This latter process is the distributed systems approach. While the integrated system utilizes the central data processing facility with a common data base, the distributed system is built by aggregating a group of small separate information systems. The basic philosophy upon which the distributed approach builds is that if an organization develops different information systems throughout, and links these systems via appropriate communication channels, the resulting information system will be as coordinated and as efficient as an integrated approach. An argument often used to support adopting the distributed systems approach is that localized information systems can better serve the subunits of the organization because they are customized to meet the particular needs of each subunit.

A key difference between the integrated approach and the distributed approach is the data base structure. An integrated system has a common data base, as well as a common set of software. To develop a common data base is very costly, and different functional units or areas of the organization may differ significantly enough that only a portion of the data is amenable to consolidation in a common data base. The distributed systems approach takes these factors into consideration. A more rational approach to structuring a data base is to have a small central data base and a network of separate unique data bases. The centralized data base can house common data elements and can act as a central clearinghouse much in the manner of the common data base in the integrated system. The centralized data base, however, is much smaller than

---

[4] John, Dearden, "MIS Is a Mirage," *Harvard Business Review,* January—February, 1972, p. 93. Copyright © 1972 by the President and Fellows of Harvard College; all rights reserved.

[5] Michael T. Vanecek, Robert F. Zant, and Carl S. Guynes, "Distributed Data Processing: A New 'Tool' for Accountants," *Journal of Accountancy,* October 1980, pp. 75–83.

the common data base and contains only elements common to *all* functional units, areas, and levels throughout the organization. Figure 2–8 illustrates the data base structure for a distributed system.

Note that in Figure 2–8 the distributed subsystems are arranged by function. Note also that the accounting subsystem can be used as an integrating force and communication device. It is not mandatory that the subsystems be organized in this manner, but it is a fairly workable arrangement because these functional units are common to most organizations. The important point here is that the subsystem data bases are linked to each other and to the centralized data base. This does not mean that all subsystems will have the same degree of interaction with all other subsystems. Some subsystems will need to interact very heavily with other subsystems. Some may be fairly isolated and self-sufficient.

Another key difference in the distributed systems approach is that users often interact among themselves as opposed to working through a centralized operation. A distributed system in most instances will require a much more elaborate communication network. This is one of the disadvantages of a distributed system. If it is assumed that every subsystem is tied to every other subsystem and to the centralized operation, then $N(N-1)/2$ channels are required. For example, if we have an organization with five subsystems (users) plus the central operations, then fifteen communications channels are required (see Figure 2–9). This is the most complex system.

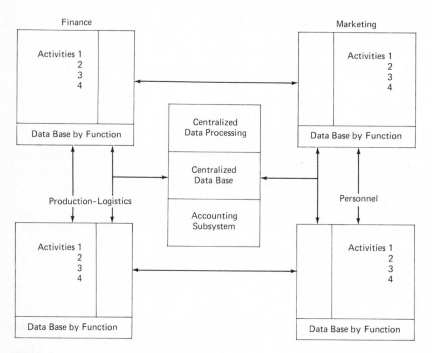

Figure 2-8   A Distributed Information System

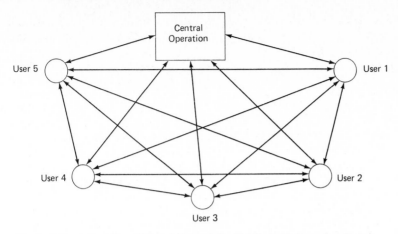

Figure 2-9 Information Channel Network for Distributed Information System

Since a sophisticated communications network can be costly, we might quickly conclude that a distributed system is more costly to develop than an integrated system. This would be an incorrect assumption. In recent years, highly efficient and economical telecommunications equipment has been developed. In addition, the development of economical microcomputers has enhanced the cost effectiveness of the distributed systems approach. By using a distributed system, costs are also reduced because some of the processing burden is removed from the centralized facility, which means that smaller, more economical, computers can be employed.

Other advantages and disadvantages of the distributed systems approach are summarized in Figure 2–10.

Integrated versus Distributed

The integrated and distributed approaches are two extremes to structuring an information system. An *integrated system* is a centralized operation with a limited degree of distribution; a *distributed system* is a decentralized operation with a limited degree of centralization. Some combination of the two approaches may be the most appropriate for a given firm. The problem is to decide whether to lean toward a more distributed system with a limited degree of integration or toward a highly integrated system. The advantages and disadvantages of each approach will influence the decision, but factors other than these must be considered. Several factors that must be evaluated are (1) the overall objectives of the firm and the style of top management, (2) the organization structure, (3) the degree of independence desired for each function or division, and (4) the level of diversity within the firm.

If top management wants a strong centralized organization with limited flexibility at lower levels in the organization, then the information system should be integrated to every degree possible. On the other hand, if the organization is relatively diverse with significantly different operations, then a cen-

ADVANTAGES

-The total system can more easily be designed to meet users' needs, since individualized subsystems are utilized.

-The system, or portions of the system, can more easily be modified to meet changing user requirements.

-New subsystems can be added without greatly affecting other subsystems.

-A breakdown or change in one subsystem will not cause a significant degradation in the total system.

-Software and hardware requirements are not stringent. Most distributed systems will require relatively simple hardware (with the exception of the telecommunication network) and software. A very sophisticated data base management system and costly, large-capacity processing equipment are required for most integrated systems.

DISADVANTAGES

-A distributed system requires more communication channels in order to link the separate data bases and subsystems.

-The probability of a duplication of data is increased because different data bases are employed.

-Additional personnel may be required because processing activities are not centralized.

-If subsystems are fairly independent, then the coordination of activities may be difficult.

-It may be difficult to extract corresponding data from different files.

-The probability of report discrepancies will increase because of the likelihood of mismatches in data handling at subsystem levels.

-Individual accounting systems may not be consistent.

Figure 2-10   Advantages and Disadvantages of Distributed Systems

tralized management structure and an integrated system are probably inappropriate. For example, a commercial airlines organization is likely to need an integrated system because most operations, such as scheduling and maintenance, revolve around passenger activity and the organization is very centralized. On the other hand, a large aerospace organization is more amenable to a distributed systems approach because the organization probably has diverse functions and operations that are relatively independent. In some situations top management should probably not even try to integrate via either type of system. It may be better to have independent systems for each component.

In summary, two types of system linkages form the basis for linking the organizational functions, decision-making activities, and data processing elements in order to form an information system. These are the integrated and distributed approaches. The selection of the approach to be used depends on the firm's environment as well as applicable technology.

A SYSTEMATIC PROCEDURE
FOR SYSTEM DESIGN
AND DEVELOPMENT

It must be recognized that a well-designed information system requires careful planning, organizing, staffing, coordinating, directing, and controlling of all the elements that will be linked to form the complete system. We can accomplish this by employing the systems approach described earlier. Both the integrated approach and the distributed approach provide useful frameworks for system design and development, since they lead to well-organized systems.

In this section we introduce a concept that enhances the design and development of systems. This is the systems development and implementation life cycle concept portrayed in Figure 2–11.[6] This life cycle illustrates the *procedures* for accomplishing the objectives of a well-organized system. These procedures consist of (1) *systems analysis and definition*, (2) *systems design and implementation (synthesis)*, and (3) *evaluation*. Briefly, systems analysis consists of the definition of a new system or the analysis of the existing system. Systems analysis is characterized as follows:

1. Planning—development of a master design plan that is a function of the business environment
2. Decision and Process Network Analysis—identification of major decision-making activities and their respective information and reporting requirements
3. Conceptual Design—information flow and decision model specifications

The AICPA EDP Applications Systems Task Force,[7] in its Management Advisory Services guidelines, denotes (1) Planning and (2) Decision and Process Network Analysis as Phase I (Requirements Definition and Alternative Approaches) (see Figure 2–11). According to the task force study, the basic objectives of this phase are to

1. Provide a clear statement of the application system's overall objectives and requirements
2. Conduct and document a broad study of the existing business systems for attaining these objectives
3. Establish a work program for identifying and developing the new system, and to estimate the required resources
4. Identify, and tentatively evaluate, broad alternative approaches, their preliminary conceptual design, and the feasibility of each

[6] There are other conceptual approaches to systems design and development. See Ron Weber, *EDP Auditing* (New York: McGraw-Hill, 1982) for a discussion of a social technical design approach.

[7] See AICPA, *Guidelines for Development and Implementation of Computer-Based Application Systems*, AICPA Management Advisory Services Guideline Series Number 4 (New York: American Institute of Certified Public Accountants, © 1976) for the objectives quoted for this phase and other phases of systems development and implementation which follow.

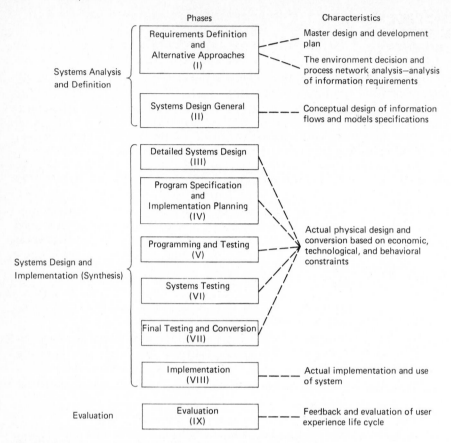

Figure 2-11 Information System Development and Implementation

Guidelines for Development and Implementation of Computer-Based Application Systems, Management Advisory Services Guideline Series Number 4 (New York: American Institute of Certified Public Accountants, © 1976).

In Phase I it is strongly suggested that care be taken to define the environment in which the firm operates and to obtain maximum participation on the part of management.

Following the specification of feasible alternatives, a conceptual or general design phase is initiated (Phase II). The objectives of this general design phase are to

1. Develop functional specifications of the application system requirements
2. Consider alternatives and estimate development and operating resources required for each
3. Establish the general work flow, information requirements, costs, benefits, and limitations of each probable alternative
4. Evaluate the alternatives and develop a specific proposal for implementing the recommended alternatives

During this phase consideration must be given to the firm's capability to implement the selected system. This phase must end in a conceptual network of information flows and decision processes. This completes the System Analysis and Definition process.

Next follows the Systems Design and Implementation procedures, which consist of Phases III through VIII. The conceptual proposal already formulated is subjected to various economic, technological, and behavioral constraints. A workable system is designed in Phase III. Particular attention should be given to such items as system controls, auditability, program change procedures, forms design, files organization, operational procedures, equipment and software selection, maintenance procedures, and flexibility of the system for growth. The principal objectives are to

1. Design the application system/subsystem structure, interfaces, and EDP equipment
2. Establish the file, input, output, processing, control, and resource requirements
3. Develop plans, schedules, and time and cost estimates for programming, conversion, and training

Phase IV, Program Specification and Implementation Planning, has as its objectives:

1. Detailed, programming specifications consistent with client standards
2. Preparation of test plan
3. Implementation plan

Programs are developed and tested in Phase V. Phase VI, System Testing, is initiated next. Phase VI's objectives are to

1. Finalize a set of programs that when processed together interface properly to constitute a single integrated system
2. Test the system thoroughly, evaluating the test results with users to assure compliance with both specifications and current requirements
3. Obtain user acceptances

Comprehensive data testing is a must at this stage of the life cycle and should be accomplished before conversion and implementation.

Phase VII, Final Testing and Conversion, follows, where the principal objectives are to

1. Complete and validate the appropriateness of systems documentation and training materials
2. Correct and verify files and data
3. Perform final testing to obtain user approval

Care should be taken to review the system operating characteristics; the timing of input, processing, and output; and the transaction and data flows.

During this phase and the preceding phase of system testing, it is necessary to run the new and the old systems in parallel and reconcile any differences. Test results are compared with the expectations of the system user. Expectations can be generated via sample test data or actual sets of transactions.

The next aspect of the life cycle is the actual implementation of the preferred system (Phase VIII). The basic objectives of this phase are to

1. Ensure adequacy of user training
2. Start system operation and to review results
3. Effect any required changes in the system, programs, and documentation
4. Turn over system to user

Formal written acceptance must accompany this last objective.

Finally, after the system is operating, Phase IX should be undertaken. This should actually be an ongoing phase. The objective is to review the system, relating it to the original overall objectives and the objectives of each phase with emphasis on costs, benefits, and controls.

In Chapter 10 we will examine Phases I and II, characterized by planning, network analysis, and conceptual design. In Chapter 11 we will examine physical design and implementation. Each step and phase of the life cycle *must* proceed in the order noted or an effective and efficient system will probably not result. Moreover, this analysis is a continuous process throughout the life of a system and serves as a basis for a Master Design Development and Review Plan with many compliance checkpoints and feedback loops. In Chapters 3 through 9 we will review many technological, economic, and behavioral considerations that have a strong bearing on the link between conceptual and actual detailed design and implementation. In essence, these constitute the various elements of an information system.

SUMMARY

The systems approach is the process by which we can examine and study a firm's information needs. We have shown that the process is useful for integrating the management and information systems of an organization. Of equal importance, we have shown that if an organization is to develop a fully effective and efficient system, a systems approach should be encouraged. It provides a viable alternative to the fractionalized component approach which often leads to suboptimization. Sometimes it may be useful to decouple the system, however, and apply the systems approach to smaller units within the firm.

An information systems structure for conceptually integrating the different dimensions of information processing (organizational functions, managerial activities, and processing elements) was defined. This conceptual structure will be used throughout the text in discussing the factors within an information system.

To *structure* an information system, we have three alternatives: a fully integrated system, a distributed system, or a combination of the two. Advantages as well as disadvantages exist with each. The integrated approach provides a centralized data base, avoids duplicate files, and provides centralized data processing activities. The approach is difficult to implement because it encompasses the entire organization and requires the full support of management. With the development of cost-efficient minicomputers and telecommunications equipment, the distributed approach has become a viable information system structure alternative. In this chapter we have noted that rather than selecting a specific alternative, management should structure the information system for the firm in question, taking into consideration the degree of diversification in the organization, the organizational structure, and management's objectives. This may well result in a combination integrated-distributed system.

The final point noted in the chapter was that a planned approach must be employed in the development of an information system. A systematic set of guidelines for development and implementation of systems was presented. The set of procedures is often referred to as a systems life cycle. If we fail to employ this life cycle structure, the developed system is likely to be ineffective and inefficient regardless of how well the system is conceptualized or structured.

SELECTED REFERENCES

ACKOFF, RUSSELL L., "Management Misinformation Systems," *Management Science*, 14 (December 1967), B147–56.

AMERICAN INSTITUTE OF CERTIFIED PUBLIC ACCOUNTANTS, *Guidelines for Development and Implementation of Computer-Based Application Systems.* Management Advisory Services Guideline Series Number 4 (1976).

BOER, GERMAIN, "A Decision Oriented Information System," *Journal of Systems Management*, 23 (October 1972), 36–39.

BURCH, JOHN G., FELIX R. STRATER, JR., AND GARY GRUDNITSKI, *Information Systems: Theory and Practice.* New York: John Wiley, 1979.

CUSHING, BARRY F., *Accounting Information Systems and Business Organization.* Reading, Mass.: Addison-Wesley, 1978.

DANIEL, RONALD D., "Management Information Crisis," *Harvard Business Review,* September–October 1961.

DAVIS, GORDON B., *Management Information System Conceptual Foundation, Structure, and Development.* New York: McGraw-Hill, 1974.

DEARDEN, JOHN, "MIS Is a Mirage," *Harvard Business Review,* January–February 1972, p. 93.

DIETZ, DEVON D., AND JOHN D. KEANE, "Integrating Distributed Processing within a Control Environment," *Management Accounting,* 62 (November 1980), 43–47.

GODFREY, JAMES J., AND THOMAS R. PRINCE, "The Accounting Model from an Information System," *Accounting Review,* January 1971, pp. 75–89.

GORRY, G. ANTHONY, AND MICHAEL S. SCOTT MORTON, "A Framework for Management Information Systems," *Sloan Management Review,* Fall 1974, pp. 55–70.

MARTINO, R. L., "The Development and Installation of a Total Management System," *Data Processing for Management,* April 1963, pp. 31–37.

MASON, RICHARD O., "Concepts for Designing Management Information Systems," AIS Research Paper No. 8, October 1969.

MURDICK, ROBERT D., AND JOEL E. ROSS, *Information Systems for Modern Management.* Englewood Cliffs, N.J.: Prentice-Hall, 1971.

PARETTA, ROBERT L., "Designing Management Information Systems: An Overview," *Journal of Accountancy,* 129 (April 1975), 42–47.

PRINCE, THOMAS R., *Information Systems for Management Planning and Control.* Homewood, Ill.: Richard D. Irwin, 1975.

SCHODERBEK, PETER P., ASTERIOS G. KEFALAS, AND CHARLES G. SCHODERBEK, *Management Systems Conceptual Considerations* (rev. ed.). Dallas, Tex.: Business Publications, 1980.

STATLAND, NORMAN, "Organizing Your Company's EDP: Centralization vs. Decentralization," *Price Waterhouse Review*, No. 2 (1975), pp. 12–17.

STATLAND, NORMAN, AND DONALD T. WINSKI, "Distributed Information Systems: Their Effect on Your Company," *Price Waterhouse Review*, No. 1 (1978), pp. 54–63.

THIERAUF, ROBERT J., *Distributed Processing Systems.* Englewood Cliffs, N.J.: Prentice-Hall, 1978.

VANECEK, MICHAEL T., ROBERT F. ZANT, AND CARL S. GUYNES, "Distributed Data Processing: A New 'Tool' for Accountants," *Journal of Accountancy*, October 1980, pp. 75–83.

WEBER, RON, *EDP Auditing.* New York: McGraw-Hill, 1982.

WINSKI, DONALD T., "Distributed Systems: Is Your Organization Ready?" *Infosystems*, 25 (September 1978), 38–42.

REVIEW QUESTIONS

1. Define the term *system* as it relates to a firm.

2. Differentiate between an *information system* and a *management system.* Identify factors that are common to both.

3. Differentiate between a *systems approach* and a *component approach* in formulating an information system. What factors should be considered in employing a systems approach?

4. Identify data processing elements that might be common between production and marketing.

5. Define what is meant by an integrated systems approach to structuring an information system. What are the advantages and disadvantages of this type of approach?

6. Identify the characteristics of a distributed systems approach for structuring an information system. What are the advantages and disadvantages of this type of approach?

7. Why is the classification of management activities useful in structuring an information system?

8. Does the number of required communication channels differ in the integrated and distributed systems approaches? Explain.

9. What factors should be considered in deciding whether to employ an integrated or a distributed system? Should a totally integrated system, a totally distributed system, or a combination of the two approaches be used?

10. What role does the "systems life cycle" play in information processing? How is it related to systems analysis and systems design?

EXERCISES AND CASES

2–1

Curtis Company operates in a five-county industrial area near Cleveland, Ohio. The company employs a manual system for all its record keeping except payroll; the payroll is processed by a local service bureau. Other applications have not been computerized because they could not be cost justified previously.

The company's sales have grown at an increasing rate over the past five years. With this substantial growth rate, a computer-based system seemed more practical. Consequently, Curtis engaged the management consulting department of its public accounting firm to conduct a feasibility study for converting its record-keeping systems to a computer-based system. The accounting firm reported that a computer-based system would improve the company's record-keeping system and still provide material cost savings.

Therefore Curtis decided to develop a computer-based system for its records. Curtis hired a person with experience in systems development as manager of systems and data processing. His responsibilities are to oversee the entire systems operation, with special emphasis on the development of the new system.

REQUIRED: Describe the major steps that will be undertaken to develop and implement Curtis Company's new computer-based system. (CMA adapted)

2-2

Inner City Bus Company had difficulty in scheduling its drivers, buses, and maintenance operations, particularly when it snowed. To help resolve this problem, Inner City leased a minicomputer that had scheduling capability. Furthermore, radio receivers were installed in each bus so that routes could be altered when the weather created delays. Drivers could immediately be informed of route alterations.

a. Considering the life cycle concept, can you foresee any difficulties Inner City may face due to their purchase and implementation procedures?

b. Can this scheduling system be altered to effect better matching of data and information requirements?

c. Are the communication channels sufficient to alter bus schedules?

2-3

Lakeland Chemical is a middle-sized chemical processing firm with several major products and distribution and sales organizations throughout the upper Midwest. Lakeland had been experiencing coordination problems in marketing, distribution, and production. Each product had its own manager, who was responsible for production, distribution, and sales. Each region also had its own sales and distribution manager. Each manager was paid a substantial bonus on meeting budgeted production or sales. The firm had only one processing facility for all products. In the late 1960s it centralized all EDP for efficiency and control reasons. The system has been upgraded several times in the past ten to fifteen years. The manager of the processing facility was attempting to comply with the requests of the sales personnel by rescheduling production, working overtime, expediting materials, and even contracting some processing.

Top management is worried. Company profits have been falling even though sales have been excellent. Is there a system problem that, if resolved, can alleviate some coordination and decision-making difficulties and improve profits? If so, what is it and what is your suggestion, as the company's CPA, on an alternative system and why?

2-4

Ohio Steel, a medium-sized steel firm that specializes in high-strength steel alloy manufacturing and sales to the automotive industry, has two mills on Lake Erie. Ohio Steel has an older medium-sized computer and an information system that is quite effective for scheduling production, financial planning, sales analysis, inventory control, and general accounting applications. It is a simple batch processing system. A complex system has not been necessary because daily updating of schedules and reports has been more than adequate, given that Ohio Steel has a few large customers in a reasonably stable market.

Ohio Steel's management has decided to diversify and is considering the purchase of a chain of fifty motels in the Midwest. You, the controller of the steel firm, are charged with the responsibility for providing management with the necessary information for decision making. You have been asked to report briefly on the changes in information requirements you would envision if the purchase takes place.

You are also to discuss the cost implications of various alternative systems needed to cope with these possible changes. In your brief report, you should weigh the merits of an integrated versus distributed system and the impact of recent technology.

2-5

Foodway is a regional supermarket chain with two hundred stores in five states, and warehouse and distribution operations in each of these states. Each state has a manager for retail warehouse and distribution operations. Although each state manager purchases from a different set of wholesalers, the operations are virtually identical from state to state. Currently each state has its own computer system for scheduling distribution, inventory reorder, purchasing, sales analysis, and transaction processing. Foodway is considering centralizing its operations.

a. Comment briefly on the pros and cons of such centralization.
b. One of the managers has just attended a conference where the attributes of microcomputers were discussed. Especially interesting was their ability to link up with larger central processing units. Comment briefly on the impact of recent technological developments and Foodway's centralization.

2-6

Minnesota Pump, a manufacturer of industrial pumps for a wide variety of uses ranging from waste treatment to natural gas, has three manufacturing plants. These plants specialize in different types of pumps. Minnesota's sales and distribution function is organized by metropolitan area and is concentrated in the upper Midwest. Its finance function is centralized and located in St. Paul. Each plant and sales district has its own data processing system to support functional decision-making, reporting, and transaction processing needs.

The manufacturing plants are operated as cost centers. Managers are evaluated on how well they meet their production schedule and control their costs. The production schedule is set by the home office.

Sales and distribution districts are contribution centers. Managers are evaluated on their budgeted contribution to the overall profit of the firm. Moreover, they forecast sales that are aggregated by the home office and used as the basis for production planning. Each sales district has its own warehouse to serve customer needs because service is the key to success in the industrial pump business.

The finance function's role is to make sure that all capital requests yield a reasonable return on investment. The company has the final word on all capital requests that originate from the plants or sales offices.

Minnesota Pump has had considerable difficulty in getting its management to work together. Coordination is often difficult and none of the managers seem to take action to maximize long-run returns on equity, which is the company's overall goal.

What kind of management and information system does Minnesota Pump have? Will this management system, along with its supporting system, lead to dysfunctional consequences with regard to achievement of the company's overall goal? Why? Briefly, as Minnesota Pump's CPA, could you render any advice and, if so, what would it be?

3

ORGANIZATIONAL AND BEHAVIORAL PRINCIPLES

OVERVIEW

The systems approach to any management or accounting system is based on the interrelationships of the activities, the functions, and the information processing elements of an organization. These interrelationships involve the firm's objectives, decisions, organization structure, and technology and the behavior of individuals in the organization. Many organizations and their associated supporting information systems have fallen short of their potential because they have failed to coordinate these activities, functions, and data processing elements with the major variables of a firm's management system. Moreover, they have failed to motivate the individuals who are to implement the system.

In Chapters 1 and 2 we noted that it is imperative that the information system be designed to support the management system, not the reverse; in addition, the management system should be designed to achieve the objectives of the organization most effectively. The systems approach should be applied to both the management system and the information system (as was shown in Figure 2–3).

The management system consists of various managerial activities and functions and their interrelationships (as was shown in the upper portion of

Figure 2–4); ideally, the management system should be structured to achieve, through individual behavior, the objectives of the organization as a whole. These activities can be characterized as strategic planning, management control, operational control, and transaction processing (as was shown in Figure 1–6). To accomplish the firm's objectives, management must plan, organize, staff, coordinate, direct, and control these activities. This management process must be implemented through human interaction. These activities, once organized, must be implemented further. Thus both the design and implementation of a system and its subsequent operation are functions of the decision-making activities of the firm, the organization structure of the firm, and the behavior patterns of the individuals involved in the design, implementation, reporting, transaction processing, and decision-making activities of the firm. All of these components make up the *social environment* of the management system and the supporting information system.

The objective of this chapter will be to give the accountant, as information system user and designer, a better appreciation of the impact of organizational and behavioral factors on an information system and vice versa. In Chapter 4 the objective will be to review the impact of decision-making activities on an information system and vice versa.

In this chapter we will consider the key variables with respect to the organization structure of the firm, organization of the accounting and information systems department or departments, and behavioral issues, including the problem of employee resistance to change. We will also consider the impact of the recent changes in data processing technology on the social environment of the firm. We will see that various organization systems follow the needs of management to process information and to make decisions. Technology will clearly influence this causal relationship. We will also see that an information system and its accounting subsystem must fit the organization and its social environment.

ORGANIZATIONAL STRUCTURE

Structure and Process

It is important that accountants understand the structure and processes of the organization so that they can effectively design a system to provide management with its information needs. Patterns of authority, responsibility, and decision processes will dictate the flow of information. Moreover, these activities, along with reward criteria and management policy, will lead to certain types of organization structure. *Structure* is generally defined as how the organization gets work done via lines of authority, assignment of decision-making responsibility, and communication channels through which inquiries, reports, and transaction documents flow. With larger, more mature (in terms of more formalized) systems, and firms with larger time frames (rate of technological change and strategic decision making), this understanding is much easier to achieve because the organization tends to be fairly stable. It is not enough to know the structure of the organization; the transaction and decision-making processes must also be understood. *Process* refers to the actual or needed processing of transactions and reports and the methods of decision making used at all levels of activity and in each functional area. This may not be readily apparent from formal organization charts and descriptions. This information must be obtained to understand the social environment of a firm so that needed information can be provided to the decision maker on a timely basis. Input such as organization charts, descriptions of duties, the flow of documents, charts of accounts, and personal conversations with employees should help the systems designer or accountant gain insight into the organization structure and processes.

Criteria for Assessing Structure and Process

Organizations may take many forms or structures to comply with the nature of the business or organization. Not all structures are equally effective. An organization must continually evaluate its tasks, the uncertainty related to these tasks, and the information requirements of management needed to deal with these tasks.[1] These structures can be assessed in terms of their ability to process transactions and make decisions to meet the objectives of the organization, as outlined in Figure 3–1. *Steady-state efficiency* refers to the organization's economies of scale, optimization procedures, and synergistic aspects. In other words, it is a smooth operation that operates at maximum efficiency. *Operating responsiveness* refers to the organization's responsiveness to operating challenges and opportunities. *Management responsiveness* refers to the organization's responsiveness to the reallocation of its resources to accomplish its objectives. *Strategic responsiveness* refers to the organization's ability to change its objectives and policies when environmental changes occur in products, technology, markets, and society. In other words, the organization is responsive at the strategic level. *Structural responsiveness* refers to the organization's ability to design new organizational structures to meet new challenges and problems as they arise. In general, the more uncertain the environment and the tasks of the organization, the greater the responsiveness needed at all levels of management activity.

These five criteria, which follow from Anthony's decision-making activities, can be used to assess the organization's transaction and decision-making

PROCESS CRITERIA	OBJECTIVES	OUTCOME
1. Steady-state efficiency 2. Operating responsiveness 3. Management responsiveness 4. Strategic responsiveness 5. Structural responsiveness	1. Maximize near-term performance 2. Long-term growth 3. Protection from catastrophic risk	Maximization of return on resources employed by organization

Figure 3–1   Process Criteria, Objectives and Outcome

Adapted from Robert A. Ullrich and George F. Wieland, *Organization Theory and Design.* (Homewood, Illinois: Richard D. Irwin, Inc., 1980.)

[1] For a complete discussion, see Jay R. Galbraith, *Organizational Design: An Information Processing Point of View* (Reading, Mass.: Addison-Wesley, 1974); and Paul R. Lawrence and Jay W. Lorsch, *Developing Organizations: Diagnosis and Action* (Reading, Mass.: Addison-Wesley, 1969).

processes and the organization's related structure that is used to carry out its objectives.

Basic Framework

VERTICAL AND HORIZONTAL DIFFERENTIATION   An organization can be structured *vertically* along hierarchical lines of authority and responsibility with the president at the top, vice-presidents in charge of various functions, and managers reporting to the vice-presidents. Supervisory personnel then report to these managers. This is the most common form of an organization. On the other hand, an organization can be structured around *horizontal* departmentalization. This departmentalization may be by function, location, process, or product. For example, a team of engineers is assigned to a certain research project or a company, such as General Motors, is organized around its product lines.

CENTRALIZED FUNCTIONAL FORM   One of the more common ways for an organization to structure itself to process information and make decisions to meet its objectives is through centralization and vertical differentiation following traditional functional lines. This type of structure lends itself well to an organization that wants its decision making to be highly centralized. Recent advances in computer technology and telecommunications have made this centralization easier to achieve.

Each vice-president or each manager is responsible for a specific part of the organization. This has the advantages of steady-state efficiency in terms of economy of scale and specialization. Moreover, communication and decision-making networks are relatively simple. For example, in Figure 3–2 all sales activities are the province of the vice-president of marketing, who can employ specialists for assistance. Each regional manager, who reports to the vice-president, can do the same. Throughout the organization each manager is concerned with only one function and can therefore do a better job of supervision, especially in such technical areas as engineering and manufacturing. Interfaces with other parts of the organization can be achieved using a centralized information system.

The problem with the centralized functional form is the absence of profit or return-on-investment responsibility other than at the executive level. Management cannot easily use profit or investment center concepts to control the organization.[2] These modes of control are often quite desirable in companies that have diverse products or divisions or are project oriented, such as the construction industry. Functional organizations can effectively be used to control an organization if its product is fairly homogeneous. Cost centers can effectively be used for planning and control, and needed coordination of activities can be achieved at the executive level, which is the only level with a company-wide perspective. A centralized functional form, moreover, suffers

---

[2] See Robert N. Anthony and John Dearden, *Management Control Systems* (Homewood, Ill.: Richard D. Irwin, 1976) for a description of these concepts.

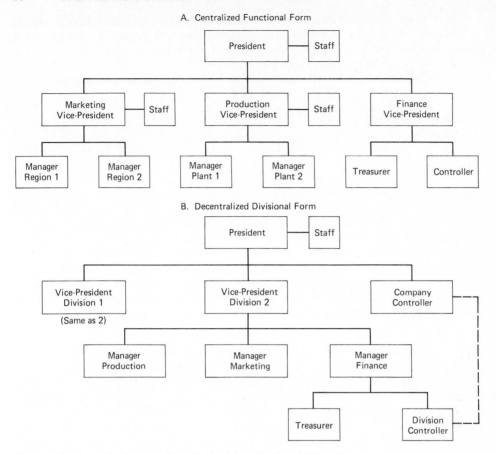

Figure 3-2   Centralized versus Decentralized Organizational Structure

from low strategic and structural responsiveness because top management is often overloaded with operating problems and has little time for managerial and strategic decision making. In terms of the flow of information, top management often suffers from information overload because of this focus on operating problems and cannot make effective decisions because it may be swamped with too much operating detail. There is also an absence of coordination except via a large, complex, centralized computer processing system between various functions, such as marketing and production, to ensure a smooth flow of a product at a profit. As a result, there is little product or project orientation in the management information system.

DECENTRALIZED DIVISIONAL FORM   If a firm wants its organization to be more responsive to opportunities for profit and return on investment for each division or product line, it may structure its organization along divisions or product lines, as shown in part B of Figure 3–2.[3] Note that this figure is only schematic; the divisional forms may be used through several levels before a functional form is used. Also, this structural form has good steady-state efficiency and operating responsiveness.

Due to the shift at the highest level, and possibly at several other levels, to a functional, location, process, or product departmentalization, strategic and structural responsiveness is better than for the centralized structure.[4] This structural form can be effective in controlling an organization through profit and investment planning responsibility and control. It can also be effective in training managers to deal with problems from the perspective of the organization as a whole.

The decentralized divisional organization form also has disadvantages. The degree of specialization existing in the centralized form will generally not exist in this structural form. Divisions and product lines will necessarily vie for scarce company resources that will have to be allocated, resulting in competition instead of cooperation. Therefore this type of organization is generally characterized by decentralized decision-making activities. Minicomputers have, moreover, given even small divisions the ability to have their own EDP operations. From an information processing perspective, one of the problems often found in a divisional structure is a lack of consistency among divisions in managerial, data processing, and accounting procedures.

RESPONSIBILITY AND PROFITABILITY ACCOUNTING SYSTEMS   To aid in the planning and controlling of management activities in both of these hierarchical organization forms, a responsibility accounting system may be used by management as a focal point for its information system.[5] Such a system followed from the evolution of accounting system structures and computer hardware. In a responsibility, or profitability, accounting system each manager or vice-president is responsible for all of those costs, revenue, and investments that are under that person's control. *Control* is defined as significant influence (delegated authority) over the expenditure or sale. All plans, programs, budgets, and reports follow these lines of responsibility. For example, consider the centralized functional form for a small company. Plant supervisors are responsible for direct labor, overtime premiums, direct materials, tools and supplies, setup and rework costs, and repairs. They each report to the plant manager, who is responsible for all the operations of the plant, including machining, assembly, and finishing, as well as plant overhead operations, such as engineering, and the manager's own office. The plant manager along with the sales manager reports to the president, who is responsible for all the operations of the firm and the

---

[3] For a discussion of General Motors' and Du Pont's organization structure, see Alfred P. Sloan, Jr., *My Years with General Motors* (Garden City, N.Y.: Doubleday, 1964); and Alfred D. Chandler, Jr., *Strategy and Structure: Chapters in the History of American Industrial Enterprise* (Belmont, Calif.: Brooks/Cole, 1965).

[4] See almost any text on strategic management such as La Rue T. Hosmer, *Strategic Management* (Englewood Cliffs, N.J.: Prentice-Hall, 1982) for a discussion of strategic planning issues.

[5] See Charles T. Horngren, *Cost Accounting: A Managerial Emphasis*, 5th ed. (Englewood Cliffs, N.J.: Prentice-Hall, 1982), for a more complete description.

resulting profitability and return on investment. Table 3–1 illustrates a typical performance report for such a system. Note that each supervisor and manager is only held responsible for controllable costs. In this case, performance evaluations at the managerial level are based on the difference between the actual and budgeted costs or the variance. Often a flexible budget is used to set standards based on actual levels of activity, such as units produced.[6] For a divisional hierarchy, this type of performance report may also include revenues, since a division or product manager is often responsible for profit. Investment in the division is sometimes included in the performance report to assess a manager's profit performance relative to the investment if revenues and expenses are under the manager's control.[7]

Table 3-1   Responsibility Accounting System

PERFORMANCE REPORTS

	Amount		Variance F(u)	
	Current Month	Year to Date	Current Month	Year to Date
President's Report				
President's office	8,600	17,200	(600)	(1,200)
Controller	2,700	5,400	0	0
Sales—manager	42,500	90,300	500	(4,000)
Plant—manager	34,700	71,640	150	210
Total controllable costs	88,500	184,540	50	4,990
Plant Manager				
Manager's office	3,500	7,000	0	0
Machining dept.	9,650	20,100	300	400
Finishing dept.	13,900	28,200	400	500
Assembly dept.	7,650	16,340	(550)	(690)
Total controllable costs	34,700	71,640	150	210
Assembly Dept. Supervisor				
Direct labor	2,550	5,400	(150)	50
Direct materials	3,750	8,500	50	(100)
Supplies and tools	150	250	(50)	(50)
Setup and rework	700	1,500	0	(100)
Repairs	500	600	(400)	(400)
Overtime premium	0	90	0	(90)
Total controllable costs	7,650	16,340	(550)	(690)

Charles T. Horngren, *Cost Accounting: A Managerial Emphasis*, 5th ed.,© 1982, p. 146. Adapted by permission of Prentice-Hall, Inc., Englewood Cliffs, N.J.

[6] See Horngren, *Cost Accounting*, for more detail.

[7] See Anthony and Dearden, *Management Control Systems*, for a full discussion of cost, profit, and investment centers.

GENERAL STRUCTURE PRINCIPLES   For either of the two basic organization structures, several basic principles must be followed if an effective management system is to operate.[8] These principles include the following:

1. Authority and responsibility must be specified.
2. Structure should follow from the objectives of the organization. This must be the case or no system will function well in the organization.
3. A person should report to only one supervisor.
4. Levels of supervision should be minimized to the extent feasible.
5. The span of control (number of employees supervised) should not be too large; it will be a function of the organization's task complexity, responsibilities, and the character of the employees supervised.
6. The organization should permit expansion and contraction for new product lines and growth.
7. Activities with conflicting objectives should be separated. Examples of conflicting activities are the credit and sales functions.
8. Similar activities, such as data processing and accounting, should be grouped together.
9. Line and staff responsibilities must be clearly stated. Basically, the staff is to assist the line manager in exercising line authority. The staff, however, may act as an agent for the line manager. This must be specified. For example, the controller may be delegated to act in the manager's behalf in accounting policy matters.

Adaptive Framework

PROJECT MANAGEMENT   If a firm's operations require a project orientation with a specific beginning and end, such as the construction of a building or the manufacture of a specific number of aircraft of a certain type, it may be useful to combine both the divisional and the centralized structures. Functional resources can then be assigned to specific projects for their duration. Upon completion of the project, these resources (personnel, financial, manufacturing facilities, construction equipment, etc.) are returned to a pool for utilization on another project. Such a structure is generally called a project management structure. As can be seen in part A of Figure 3–3, the organization structure has permanent functions such as marketing, production, and finance, and flexible project groups that are drawn from the permanent functional areas and assigned to specific projects for their duration. Project managers can then integrate all the functions in order to accomplish their mission or objectives. As a result, such an organization has much greater managerial, strategic, and structural responsiveness than the previously discussed structures. This type of organization is also quite useful in companies where technology, markets, and products are rapidly changing and responsive strategic decision making is essential to the company's success.

Project management organizations will have more complex transaction processing and decision-making networks. Examples of the use of this type of

---

[8] Adapted from James B. Bower, Robert E. Schlosser, and Charles T. Zlatkovich, *Financial Information Systems: Theory and Practice* (Boston: Allyn & Bacon, 1969), pp. 60–65.

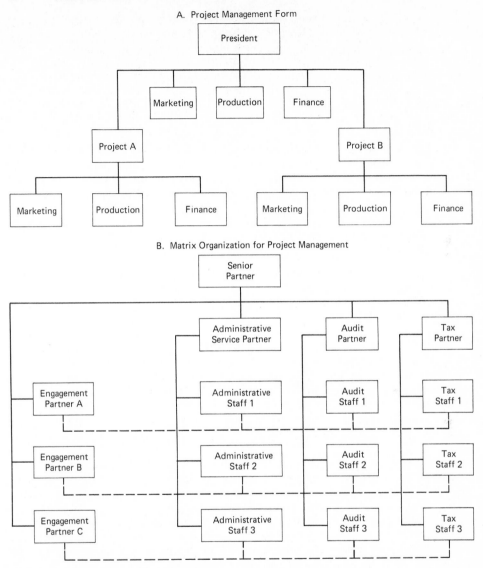

Figure 3-3 Project Management Structures

structure can be found in construction companies, consulting firms, and, perhaps, aerospace.

MATRIX STRUCTURE In a matrix structure each member is responsible both to the project manager (or, as illustrated in Figure 3–3, the partner in charge of a specific engagement) and to a functional manager. This state of dual responsibility and authority is much more permanent in a matrix organization than in a project management form, even though projects begin and end. In fact, a particular individual may even be working on more than one project team (engagement) at one time.

Such an organization has good strategic and structural responsiveness but very poor steady-state efficiency. Economies of scale and technical efficiency are hampered by dual responsibilities and competition for resources. With a matrix structure a very high degree of integration is required. This integration will be reflected in a very complex decision and transaction flow network. The network not only will have formal lines of responsibility, as in the division structure, but also will have technical lines of responsibility for the functional areas as in the functional form.

INNOVATION STRUCTURE Hybrids of these structures can be used effectively. For example, the centralized or divisional form, which maximizes steady-state efficiency, can be used for current business, and the matrix structure can be used for innovative products and projects, for example, the R & D department.

Decision and Transaction Flow Network

Management must operate, control, and report the activities of the firm. Transaction processing and operational, managerial, and strategic activities are required to accomplish these managerial and reporting tasks. Moreover, management must somehow organize and integrate the functional activities to achieve the organization's objectives and report these activities. Several structural and processing methodologies have been proposed to help achieve this integration. A reponsibility accounting system is one such structural and processing methodology for structuring the organization, controlling its operations, and providing information for decision making. As we noted in our discussion of division organization structures, revenue and investment responsibilities may be added to give the organization a profit and return-on-investment objective. This added emphasis or profit is often called *profitability accounting*.

Other methods have been proposed. One frequently used method where there are multiple and often nonquantifiable organizational goals is *management by objectives*.[9] The manager sets personal objectives with the guidance and counsel of superiors and is evaluated on the accomplishment of these objectives. Another method combines planning, programming, and budgeting systems into an integrated control system known as PPBS.[10] This system is primarily used in large organizations, especially those that are program- or project-oriented, such as construction or aerospace.

Regardless of the organization structure and method of planning, control, and reporting used, the information system, and specifically the accounting system, must be designed to support the organization's transaction processing and decision-making networks and the people who operate these networks. (More will be said about design, development, and implementation of information systems in Chapters 10 and 11.)

---

[9] See George S. Odiorne, *Management by Objectives* (Englewood Cliffs, N.J.: Prentice-Hall, 1970).

[10] See Anthony and Dearden, *Management and Control Systems.*

Data Structure

To provide effective information for the organization, the information system's data base must be structured around the organization framework. For example, if a matrix structure is used, the data base must permit efficient updating, summary, and retrieval of information for projects as well as for functional areas, in order to help project and functional managers make decisions and control their operations to achieve the firm's objectives.

ORGANIZATION OF ACCOUNTING AND MIS DEPARTMENT

MIS Location Issues

The location of the information systems department within the organization is the subject of a great deal of controversy. The fact that the information emanating from this department is the lifeblood of the organization's decision network gives the manager or the vice-president of this department considerable influence over the decision-making activities at all levels within the organization. Specifically, the advent of the computer has definitely shifted the power locus within the organization more toward the manager of the information system or more toward the home office in centralized processing systems.[11]

The general consensus is that the information systems department should be located under either a vice-president of information at the corporate level or a vice-president or manager of information at the divisional level, where the vice-president or manager reports directly to the president or division vice-president, respectively. This location tends to ensure a more company-wide or division-wide perspective for information processing and communication. This is in contrast to another common location in the controller's department or under the vice-president of finance. The problem with this latter location is that financial information tends to dominate the system. Most computerized information systems probably started in this location because transaction information was the first to be incorporated into the computer system. The problem of dominance of transaction information has been aggravated by a narrow view of the controller's role. In fact, if the controller is concerned only with financial matters, other parts of the organizations will, as indicated, not have many of their information needs satisfied.

On the other hand, if the controller's role is expanded as it should be to include all information (not only financial), many of these problems will be mitigated and both locations, in effect, will be similar in organizational behavior. In this text we assume that this expanded role of the controller includes all information, recognizing that this is not always the case. The trend in the locus of information systems is actually out of the controller's organization and into a separate department because of the narrow financial view adopted by many financial vice-presidents and controllers in practice.

---

[11] See Martin L. Bariff and Jay R. Galbraith, "Intraorganizational Power Considerations for Designing Information Systems," *Accounting, Organizations and Society*, 3, No. 1 (1978), 15–27. Copyright © 1978, Pergamon Press, Ltd. Reprinted with permission.

Controllership and Treasurership Functions

One of the cardinal principles of any organization is the separation of the duties of the custody of assets and the recording of transactions pertaining to these assets. Based on this premise, the Financial Executives Institute (FEI) has proposed that controllership and treasurership functions be separated, as shown in Figure 3–4. The treasurership is basically a custodial function, and the controllership is basically an information and reporting function. Note that according to the FEI, systems procedures and electronic data processing, if located in the financial area, are controllership functions.

The controller is thus charged with two types of activities. One can be categorized as day-to-day accounting activities and the other as planning and control activities. These must be separated, or the latter will never be accomplished because day-to-day problems will dominate the schedule. Thus it is further suggested that the controller's department be organized so that the day-to-day activities are grouped together under a chief accountant or assistant controller (see Figure 3–5). Using this type of organization, there is an assistant controller for planning and control and for information systems. Moreover, there are managers for economic analysis, tax planning, internal auditing, and special projects. In many firms, internal audit and information systems may not be located here. As with information systems, it is often recommended that the internal audit department report to the highest level within the firm.

Organization of EDP Department

Regardless of the location of the information systems department within the firm, certain functions must be kept separate, as shown in Figure 3–6. The actual operation of the computer system (running of the computer programs) must be separate from the designing of the system and the programming of the various jobs to be run. To guarantee the security of the firm's assets and reliability of information, these two functions must never be com-

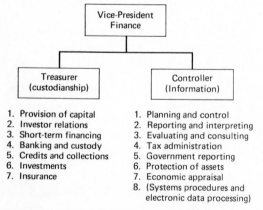

Figure 3-4 Controllership and Treasurership Functions Defined by Financial Executives Institute
Adapted from Financial Executives Institute with permission, New York, N.Y.

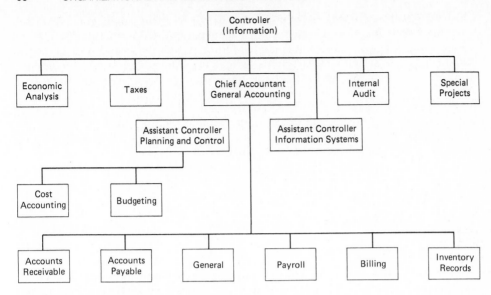

Figure 3-5 Organization of Controller's Department

bined. The manager of systems design and analysis is responsible for the development and design of all the system projects within the firm. These projects should be coordinated by the executive responsible for the management information system and the manager in charge of the EDP system, in conjunction with the directives given by the steering committee. Moreover, the development and implementation of these projects should follow a well-conceived plan such as the one outlined by the AICPA (see Chapters 10 and 11). For larger organizations, each systems project will have a manager. The manager of systems design and development is also responsible for the programming, testing, and maintenance of the system. Personnel in the systems design and analysis section, because of their knowledge of the system and their technical expertise, must not have access to the system other than in a very controlled situation that involves systems development and implementation.

Custody of information in the form of cards, tapes, and disks must be separate from both of these functions for the same reason that the treasurership and controllership functions must be separate. Generally there is a tape or disk library with a librarian. Finally, input, output, and processing flows, as well as programming and systems design, must all be controlled by a third party,

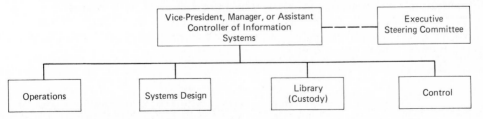

Figure 3-6 Organization of Information Systems Department

which in small organizations may be the data processing manager. Nevertheless, this fourth function of control must be separated from operations, systems design, and custody of the information. Other functions should also be segregated for larger systems departments. These are data preparation, documentation library, security, and, for data base management systems, data base administration.[12] A data base administrator is responsible for defining the data base schema, organizing data base controls and logical relationships, securing the data, and monitoring data base operations as well as servicing user needs with respect to the data base. Separation of these functions forms the cornerstone of good internal control (see in Chapter 9).

In addition, the EDP operation may be centralized in an integrated system or decentralized in a distributed framework. The EDP organization should follow the management systems organization, otherwise conflict will often develop because the system will in general not effectively support management, decision making, reporting, and transaction needs.

Management of EDP Systems

Regardless of the specific location of the information systems processing function, long-range planning of the utilization of systems resources is necessary. All projects and changes in hardware, software, and applications must conform to a master long-range plan. For example, each project must conform to this plan during the early phases of systems development and implementation. To assist in this planning process, an accounting information system should have an executive systems steering committee to help set broad policies and plans for the firm's information system. The chairman of this committee must be the senior executive who is responsible for the firm's information system. For example, this could be the vice-president for management information or the controller. Members should include the manager of EDP systems, the controller, and the senior managers from major users within the organization. This committee can also review major projects, changes, purchases, application systems, exceptions to internal control procedures, and hiring of key personnel. A further benefit of such a committee is that it involves top management in the firm's information and accounting activities. Without top-management support and a steering committee directing EDP management and planning, no system can be successful.

In addition to these organization and planning activities, it is also necessary to price information and data processing services. There should be an equitable allocation of resources, costs for these services, and motivation to provide service to users so that users can fully utilize the resources of the information or accounting department. The information systems center can be either an information center or an accounting center. The center can also be either a profit or a cost center, but its information pricing structure will have a great impact on its utilization.[13]

---

[12] For a complete discussion of the data base administration, see Ron Weber, *EDP Auditing: Conceptual Foundation and Practice* (New York: McGraw-Hill, 1982) pp. 164–82.

[13] See Richard L. Nolan, *Managing the Data Resource Function* (St. Paul, Minn.: West Publishing, 1974).

BEHAVIORAL CONCEPTS

Basic Motivation Concepts

Any organization is basically the coalition of individuals working toward their own set of goals. The job of management, and, in turn, of the information system that supports management, is to obtain some sort of congruence of these individual goals and the objectives of the entire organization. This is not easy. It may never be achieved completely in practice, but management must at least attempt to obtain a reasonably high degree of congruence. To accomplish this, a reasonable understanding of human behavior and motivation in an organizational setting is necessary for the systems designer and the accountant, who assists management in the development and implementation of information systems.

Motivation can be described as a function of many factors, and it is the task of the systems designer or accountant to work with these various factors to motivate individuals or groups of individuals to achieve the overall goals of the organization. Based on a composite of the prevailing literature,[14] the performance of individuals and groups is a product of (1) aptitude, (2) skill level, (3) understanding of the task, (4) choice to expend effort, (5) choice of degree of effort to expend, (6) choice to persist, and (7) facilitating and inhibiting conditions not under the individual's control. Most of these are directly related to a person's motivation.

To further compound the motivation problem, organizations are dynamic and every management decision or absence of a decision, change in the social environment, or impact of the external factors (including system changes) will have an effect on one or more of the factors summarized above. The effect will be different for each individual and will lead to both functional and dysfunctional motivational consequences with respect to overall goal congruence. Functional consequences enhance the degree of goal congruence, and dysfunctional consequences distract from overall goal congruence.

Motivational theories can be classified as *process* theories, which attempt to define the major processes and variables leading to choice, effort, and persistence; or they can be classified as *content* theories, which attempt to identify the variables that influence behavior, such as needs, rewards, and punishment.

The dominant cognitive process theory of motivation is Vroom's *expectancy-valence* model,[15] which states that motivation is a function of the product of (1) expectancy that an effort results in attaining outcomes and (2) the valence of the outcomes. *Valence* is defined as the perceived value of outcomes stemming from the action. From the accountant's or the systems designer's perspective, this means that individual motivation to comply with an organization's policies is a function of individuals' expectations and perceptions of the future consequences of their actions and the probability that their individual actions

---

[14] This discussion is based in part on John P. Campbell and Robert D. Pritchard, "Motivation Theory in Industrial and Organizational Psychology," in *Handbook of Industrial and Organizational Psychology*, ed. Marvin D. Dunnette (Rand McNally: Chicago, 1976), pp. 63–130.

[15] Ibid., pp. 74–75.

will succeed. Others have extended this theory to emphasize the feedback loops of past experiences, and how they alter perceptions of probability of success, and perceptions of values. In other words, if all previous system changes were successful in terms of the individual's ability to adapt, that individual would perceive the probability of success of the next system change to be high. This would probably lead to a greater degree of functional behavior on the part of the individual within the organization.

Content theories are, to a large extent, founded on several theories of individual need and performance outcomes and the way in which they influence behavior. Maslow ranks these needs starting with basic physiological needs and ending with self-actualization or fulfillment. The hierarchical rank is as follows: (1) Physiological needs (hunger, thirst, etc.); (2) Safety needs (protection from injury); (3) Social needs (love, friendship, affection, etc.); (4) Esteem needs (self-respect); and (5) Self-actualization needs (achieve fulfillment).[16] Basic, lower-level needs must be satisfied to some degree before higher-level needs will motivate the individual. On the other hand, Herzberg concentrates on extrinsic and intrinsic performance factors related to the workplace environment. His job satisfaction and work motivators are classified as follows: Extrinsic factors that stem from organizational context—(1) Pay (salary increase); (2) Technical supervision (competent supervisor); (3) Human relations (quality of supervision); (4) Company policy and administration; (5) Working conditions (safety/physical surroundings); and (6) Job security and Intrinsic factors or motivators that are related to a person's job—(1) Achievement (success and personal worth); (2) Recognition (praise); (3) Responsibility (status); and (4) Advancement (status).[17] The first group, the extrinsic factors, are the rewards and needs related to the job environment and are sometimes called "hygiene" factors. The second group, the intrinsic factors, describe the individual's relation to the job. These are the "motivators." Absence of the first will cause dissatisfaction and probably a greater degree of dysfunctional activities, and presence of the latter will motivate people toward their individual goals. Job-satisfaction rankings assume that the basic physical needs have been fulfilled and that they start with Maslow's concept of safety—i.e., working conditions. In other words, in the development, implementation, and operation of an information system the accountant must be cognizant of the need to satisfy the variables that influence an individual's behavior and the fact that the variables involved are ordered. Without satisfactory interpersonal relationships, there is little reason to worry about the higher-order needs. In terms of information systems design success, an overview of the higher-order factors that most influence human behavior is presented in Figure 3–7. Of these, job social structure is perhaps the most important single factor—according to Herzberg, disruption of the social structure via system change affects a key environmental factor (interpersonal relations). These higher-order needs are reinforced either positively or negatively by top-management support, clear communication of objectives, past experience, job complexity, an individual's aptitude, and the extrinsic factors noted by Herzberg. Although this summary is not all-inclusive, it does present the key

[16] See Abraham H. Maslow, *Motivation and Personality* (New York: Harper & Row, 1970).

[17] See Frederick Herzberg, *Work and the Nature of Man* (Cleveland: World Publishing Co., 1966).

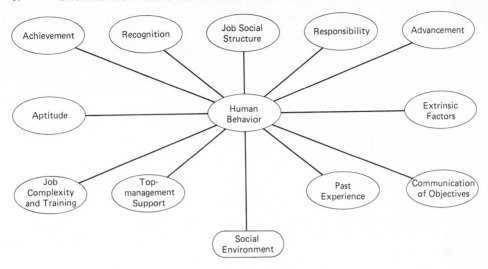

Figure 3-7   Major Factors That Influence Human Behavior and Its Impact on an Information Systems Social Environment

variables of which an accountant or a systems analyst must be aware in the development and implementation of a system.

In addition to these factors that influence human behavior and, in turn, the social environment of the information system, leadership styles must be considered. At the extreme they can be characterized as authoritarian and participative. They will have an impact on the design procedures as well as the operation of any information system. The latter is more likely to set a better psychological climate for systems change than the former because employees will be more a part of the change. "Theory Z," which projects a broader base for decision-making authority with more supervisors and employees participating in the decision process, has recently been promoted as an effective way to utilize the insight of the key participants in the decision process.[18] A better "psychological climate" through participation, however, may or may not result in a more efficient system because some employees are better motivated by authoritarian leadership.

Levels of Management

The impact of these behavioral factors varies at different levels of management within an organization.[19] Moreover, the actions of different levels of management will directly influence the psychological climate for the organization and thus the success of the information system.

[18] William G. Ouchi, *Theory Z: How American Business Can Meet the Japanese Challenge* (Reading, Mass.: Addison-Wesley, 1981).

[19] The framework for some of the discussion of top management, middle management, and non-supervisory personnel characteristics which follows is summarized in James B. Bower, Robert E. Schlosser, and Charles T. Zlatksovich, *Financial Information Systems: Theory and Practice* (Boston: Allyn & Bacon, 1972), p. 164.

One of the major contributing factors having a bearing on successful information system implementation is the way each of the levels deals functionally or dysfunctionally with an inherent *resistance to change*:

> Such resistance may take many forms—persistent reduction in output, increase in the number of "quits" and requests for transfer, chronic quarrels, sullen hostility, wildcat or slowdown strikes, and of course, the expression of a lot of pseudological reasons why the change will not work.[20]

It is necessary for each of these levels to deal with these problems, and it is suggested that

> the key to the problem is to understand the true nature of resistance. Actually, what employees resist is usually not technical change but social change—the change in their human relationships that generally accompanies technical change.[21]

The need for a stable social structure is very important, as was suggested earlier in this chapter in the discussion of content theory. Employees will resist any change that threatens to disrupt this structure, which support many of their needs, such as love, friendship, affection, self-respect, self-fulfillment, achievement, recognition, responsibility, and advancement.

TOP MANAGEMENT   A summary of major research on the impact of organization structure and human behavior suggests that some variables that play a key role in the success of any information system and its accounting subsystem are controllable; others are either partially controllable or uncontrollable. Top management controls many of these variables. The effective participation of the senior executives, decision makers, controller, and systems personnel on a steering committee for systems development, implementation, and ongoing operations is controllable by management and necessary for a system's success.[22] The assignment of responsible executive personnel to the steering committee is essential. Success can be enhanced by devoting organizational resources such as time and money to the project. Furthermore, success can be facilitated by top management's providing a positive behavioral climate for implementation of a project. To reduce uncertainty, the objective of the present system, change in the system, or new system must be clearly communicated to all personnel involved. Support and communication of objectives are necessary prerequisites for a good psychological climate. Other factors that top management can influence to help achieve a more positive climate include a concern for employees, use of employee input and participation in systems planning, training and placement programs to retrain displaced employees, encouragement of team-

---

[20] Reprinted by permission of the *Harvard Business Review*. Excerpt from "How to Deal with Resistance to Change" by Paul R. Lawrence (January–February 1969). © 1969 by the President and Fellows of Harvard College; all rights reserved.

[21] Ibid.

[22] Phillip Ein-Dor and Eli Segev, "Organizational Context and the Success of Management Information Systems," *Management Science*, June 1978, pp. 1064–77.

work with regard to systems design, and assignment of reliable people to the development and implementation of the project. It is also important that management set a good pattern over the years for change, for past experience will greatly affect employee attitudes and cooperation (as outlined in the earlier review of process motivational theory). All changes should be well organized, well supported, and effectively communicated to the entire organization. All of this is easier to accomplish with more mature and larger organizations, which have a reasonably long time frame for change. If these variables are positive, the system will be more successful.

Other variables such as the size, structure (in many cases), and time frame (rate of change in the decision-making activities and information processing technology) of the organization and external pressures are generally uncontrollable. These variables must be considered, however, for they do influence the success of any accounting or information system. *Success* is defined as the final implementation of an information system that supports the strategic, managerial, operational, and transaction processing needs of the management system.

MIDDLE MANAGEMENT   Middle-management cooperation is necessary for the successful design and implementation of a system. These managers are the ultimate users of most of the information generated by the system in making managerial and operating decisions and in preparing reports. As such, they must be involved and consulted during all nine of the information systems development and implementation phases noted in Figure 2–11. A tremendous amount of work involving long hours is required of these middle managers in the testing, conversion, and implementation phases; they are the people who ultimately make the system work. Their acceptance is a must if the system is to function as designed.

The problem with middle-level managers often is their great resistance to change, because system changes can alter their job social structure, including the status quo in terms of responsibility, reporting, decision making, and, most important, interpersonal relationships. Often middle-level managers fail to recognize the need for any change because they have a narrow or technical perspective of the organization. Communication of objectives from top management is crucial in overcoming this perception. Middle-level managers need to understand the reason for any change and the forthcoming benefits, and they must be assured that they will be capable of performing any new responsibilities and making any new decisions under the new system. Above all, their sense of status and personal worth must be maintained. Their reluctance to accept a new system is often magnified, as suggested in the expectation-valence motivation theory, by any bad prior experience with systems that did not deliver and lack of top-management consideration for their situation. On the positive side, these managers are capable of working toward long-term objectives and capable of allowing a reasonable time period for a system to demonstrate its worth.

NONSUPERVISORY PERSONNEL   For nonsupervisory personnel, the positive trait of patience exhibited by middle management does not exist. These individuals can best be characterized as employees with short-range goals and a group orientation. They also must be kept well informed and, to the extent possible, reassured that they will be treated with equity, will be trained if necessary, and, above all, will not be out of work. Changes to their job social structure must be made carefully because of their strong group orientation. This can be a problem because increased automation (information systems as well as production) usually leads to a more rigid job structure due to increased coordination with other aspects of the organization and deadlines. These employees may feel "driven" in their job by the computer time schedule.

Impact of EDP on Business Organizations

The impact of the advent of electronic data processing on business organizations, their mode of decision making, their flow of transactions, and their employees' behavior has been profound for all functions at all levels of activity. The exact nature of this impact is debatable; a good synthesis of several opinions and studies is offered by Hofer.[23] Some more recent technological breakthroughs in communication in minicomputers will further add to the debate over the impact because they may reverse some of the earlier trends. If we were to analyze the essential characteristics of the decision-making and transaction process, which can be classified as (1) reliability, (2) speed, (3) accuracy, and (4) intelligence, we would expect the greatest impact on reliability, speed, and accuracy, areas in which the computer clearly has superiority.

Some authors, including Leavitt and Whisler,[24] have suggested a downgrading of middle management in the sense that decision making and creative activities would become more concentrated at higher levels. Others, including Burlingame,[25] predicted that middle managers would be given the tools to do a better job. Blumenthal[26] predicted that the number of middle managers would decline with increased centralization. Schaul,[27] in a study of fifty middle managers, found no reduction, but a small increase with expanded and more complex assignments, particularly in planning.

Hofer,[28] in a comparative study of two companies, found the following:

[23] Charles W. Hofer, "Emerging EDP Pattern," *Harvard Business Review*, March–April 1970, pp. 16–18, 20–22, 26, 28–31, 169–71. Copyright © 1970 by the President and Fellows of Harvard College; all rights reserved.

[24] Harold Leavitt, *Managerial Psychology* (Chicago: University of Chicago Press, 1964) and Harold Leavitt and Thomas L. Whisler, "Management in the 1980's," *Harvard Business Review*, November–December 1958, p. 4. Copyright © 1958 by the President and Fellows of Harvard College; all rights reserved.

[25] John F. Burlingame, "Information Technology and Decentralization," *Harvard Business Review*, November–December 1961, p. 121. Copyright © 1961 by the President and Fellows of Harvard College; all rights reserved.

[26] S. C. Blumenthal, "Breaking the Chain of Command," *Business Automation*, November 1963, pp. 20–27.

[27] Adapted from Donald R. Schaul, "What's Really Ahead for Middle Management," *Personnel*, November–December 1964 (New York: American Management Association, Inc., 1964).

[28] Charles W. Hofer, "Emerging EDP Pattern," *Harvard Business Review*, March–April 1970, pp. 16–18, 20–22, 28–31, and 169–71. Copyright © 1970 by the President and Fellows of Harvard College; all rights reserved.

1. Not much effect on decision making at the very top level (strategic activities), but at the top functional levels (managerial activities) considerable delegation of analysis and evaluation activities took place.

2. At the operational level, better decisions were made because the data were more accurate.

3. Operational planning was improved at the lowest level (operations) due to increased accuracy, and planning at the top level was increased due to more time.

4. Top functional (managerial) managers were able to alter budgets frequently due to speed, and the budget process was more accurate at the operational level.

5. Measurement was improved at all levels, and top management was more easily able to request backup information.

6. The organization structure at the top was not affected; but at the operational level for large-volume activities, major changes took place. For example, a 30 percent reduction in the general and cost accounting sections.

In summary, the empirical evidence suggests that the greatest impact is in the area where the computer has the edge in reliability, speed, and accuracy—i.e., in the routine tasks that can be programmed, and in which measurement is relatively straightforward and volumes are large. With the new developments in minicomputers, these criteria will apply to smaller units in an organization. With improved communication technology, this will have a bearing on what the computer can do better than man and, in turn, on the organization.

SUMMARY

The accountant and the systems designer must consider several variables in the analysis, design, and implementation of information systems. These variables consist of the objectives of the organization, the decisions related to the accomplishment of these objectives, the organization structure, the people who operate within this structure and who process transactions and make decisions, and the technology used for information processing and decision making. Organizations can be structured in many ways, and the information and accounting systems must adapt to and support the management system structure. Special care must be given to the structure of the EDP system and the accounting organization.

An understanding of the behavioral and motivational factors is key to the successful analysis, design, and ultimate implementation of an information system. Of these, the key factors seem to be the employee's job social structure, higher-order needs, and perception of the probability of system success and its resulting value to the individual. Top management's control of the key behavioral variables will greatly influence the system's success or failure.

Finally, the greatest impact of systems changes resulting from improvements in technology has been wherever data processing has been superior in terms of reliability, speed, and accuracy. In varying degrees, these changes have influenced the social structure of the firm at all levels.

SELECTED REFERENCES

ANTHONY, ROBERT N., *Planning and Control Systems: A Framework for Analysis.* Boston: Harvard Business School, 1965.

ANTHONY, ROBERT N., AND JOHN DEARDEN, *Management Control Systems.* Homewood, Ill.: Richard D. Irwin, 1976.

BARIFF, MARTIN L., AND JAY R. GALBRAITH, "Intraorganizational Power Considerations for Designing Information Systems," *Accounting, Organizations and Society*, 3, No. 1 (1978), 15–27.

BLUMENTHAL, S. C., "Breaking the Chain of Command," *Business Automation*, November 1963, pp. 20–27.

BOWER, JAMES B., ROBERT E. SCHLOSSER, AND CHARLES T. ZLATKOVICH, *Financial Information Systems: Theory and Practice.* Boston: Allyn & Bacon, 1969.

BOWER, JAMES B., AND J. BRUCE SEFERT, "Human Factors in Systems Design," *Management Services*, November–December 1965, pp. 39–50.

BURLINGAME, JOHN F., "Information Technology and Decentralization," *Harvard Business Review*, November–December 1961, p. 121.

CAMPBELL, JOHN P., AND ROBERT D. PRITCHARD, "Motivation Theory in Industrial and Organizational Psychology," in *Handbook of Industrial and Organizational Psychology*, ed. M. V. Dunnette, Chicago: Rand McNally, 1976, pp. 63–130.

CHANDLER, ALFRED D., JR., *Strategy and Structure: Chapters in the History of American Industrial Enterprise.* Belmont, Calif.: Brooks/Cole, 1965.

CYERT, RICHARD M., AND JAMES G. MARCH, *A Behavioral Theory of the Firm.* Englewood Cliffs, N.J.: Prentice-Hall, 1963.

DAVIS, GORDON B., *Management Information Systems: Conceptual Foundations, Structure and Development.* New York: McGraw-Hill, 1974.

EIN-DOR, PHILLIP, AND ELI SEGEV, "Organizational Context and the Success of Management Information Systems," *Management Science*, June 1978, pp. 1064–77.

ETZIONI, AMITAI, *Modern Organizations.* Englewood Cliffs, N.J.: Prentice-Hall, 1974.

FEIN, MITCHELL, "Motivation for Work," in *Handbook of Work, Organization and Society*, ed. Robert Dubin. Chicago: Rand McNally, 1976.

GALBRAITH, JAY R., *Organizational Design: An Information Processing Point of View.* Reading, Mass.: Addison-Wesley, 1974.

HERZBERG, FREDERICK, *Work and the Nature of Man.* New York: World, 1966.

HOFER, CHARLES W., "Emerging EDP Pattern," *Harvard Business Review*, March–April 1970, pp. 16–18, 20–22, 26, 28–31, 169–71.

HOPWOOD, ANTHONY G., "Towards an Organizational Perspective for the Study of Accounting and Information Systems," *Accounting, Organizations and Society*, 3, No. 1 (1978), 3–13.

HORNGREN, CHARLES T., *Cost Accounting: A Managerial Emphasis* (5th ed.). Englewood Cliffs, N.J.: Prentice-Hall, 1982.

HOSMER, LaRUE T., *Strategic Management*, Englewood Cliffs, N.J.: Prentice-Hall, 1982.

LAWLER, E. E., AND J. L. SUTTLE, "Expectancy Theory and Job Behavior," *Organizational Behavior and Human Performance*, 9 (1973), 482–503.

LAWRENCE, PAUL R., "How to Deal with Resistance to Change," *Harvard Business Review*, January–February 1969, pp. 4–176.

LAWRENCE, PAUL R., AND JAY W. LORSCH, *Developing Organizations: Diagnosis and Action*, Reading, Mass.: Addison-Wesley, 1969.

LEAVITT, HAROLD J., *Managerial Psychology*. Chicago: University of Chicago Press, 1964.

LEAVITT, HAROLD J., AND THOMAS L. WHISLER, "Management in the 1980's," *Harvard Business Review*, November–December, 1958.

MARCH, JAMES G., AND HERBERT A. SIMON, *Organizations*. New York: John Wiley, 1958.

MASLOW, ABRAHAM H., *Motivation and Personality*. New York: Harper & Row, Pub., 1970.

NOLAN, RICHARD L., *Management Accounting and Control of Data Processing*. New York: National Association of Accountants, 1977.

———, *Managing the Data Resource Function*. St. Paul, Minn: West Publishing, 1974.

ODIORNE, GEORGE S., *Management Decisions by Objectives*, Englewood Cliffs, N.J.: Prentice-Hall, Inc., 1970.

OUCHI, WILLIAM G., *Theory Z: How American Business Can Meet the Japanese Challenge*, Reading, Mass.: Addison-Wesley, 1981.

SCHAUL, DONALD R., "What's Really Ahead for Middle Management," *Personnel*, November–December 1964. New York: American Management Association, Inc.

SCHODERBETCK, PETER P., *Management Systems*. New York: John Wiley, 1967.

SIMON, HERBERT A., *Administrative Behavior*. New York: Macmillan, 1957.

SLOAN, ALFRED P., JR., *My Years with General Motors*. Garden City, N.Y.: Doubleday, 1964.

ULLRICH, ROBERT A., AND GEORGE F. WIELAND, *Organization Theory and Design*. Homewood, Ill.: Richard D. Irwin, 1980.

VROOM, V. H., "Organizational Choice: A Study of Pre- and Post-decision Processes," in *Organizational Behavior and Human Performace*, 1966 Vol. 1, pp. 212–25.

———, *Work and Motivation*. New York: John Wiley, 1964.

WEBER, RON, *EDP Auditing*, New York: McGraw-Hill, 1982.

WHISLER, THOMAS, "The Manager and the Computer," *Journal of Accountancy*, January 1965, pp. 27–32.

WILLIAMS, EDGAR G., "Changing Systems and Behavior," *Business Horizons*, August 1969, pp. 53–58.

REVIEW QUESTIONS

1. What major variables are involved in the social environment of the management and information system?

2. Contrast the advantages and disadvantages of the centralized functional form and the decentralized divisional form of organizational structure.

3. Contrast the matrix form and the cen-

tralized functional form of organizational structure with respect to the five process criteria outlined in Figure 3–1.

4. Define *profitability accounting system* and explain why it would work better in a decentralized divisional form than in a centralized functional form of organizational structure.

5. What are the pros and cons of locating the MIS department in the controller's office?

6. Describe the controllership and treasurership functions.

7. How should an EDP department be organized and why?

8. What variables have a bearing on job performance?

9. Contrast Vroom's expectancy-valence process theory and Maslow's need content theory of motivation.

10. Contrast the impact that various levels of management have on systems change.

11. What is the key issue in a nonsupervisory employee's resistance to change?

12. Where have the greatest changes occurred when any businesses have switched from manual systems to EDP systems?

EXERCISES AND CASES

3–1

The Hooper Company is considering a reorganization. The company's current organizational structure is represented by the chart shown in Figure C3–1(A).

The company recently hired a new vice-president for metal products. This vice-president has an extensive background in sales, which complements the production background of the vice-president for plastic products. The new vice-president for metal products believes that Hooper Company would be more effective if it were reorganized according

to the organizational structure shown in Figure C3–1(B).

REQUIRED:

a. Identify the two types of organizational structure depicted by the two charts.

b. Compare the two organizational structures by discussing the advantages and disadvantages of each using the criteria suggested in the chapter.

c. Which structure would be more conducive to profitability objectives and responsibility? Why?

d. Which structure would be more likely to overload the president's office with data for decision making? Why? (CMA adapted)

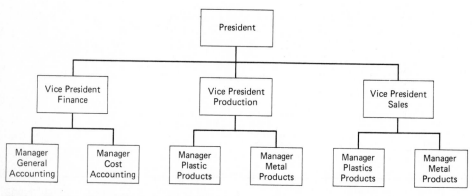

Figure C3–1(A)   Current Organizational Structure

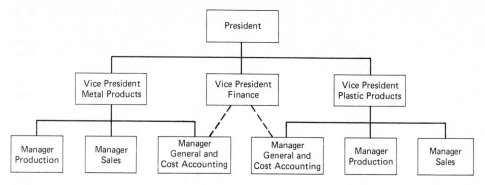

Figure C3–1(B)   Proposed Organizational Structure

3–2

Contronics Inc. is a large electronics-component manufacturer in Fort Wayne, Ind. It has grown substantially during the past four years. As the company has expanded its operations, the duties and responsibilities of the accounting department have increased. Both the size of the controller's staff and the number of the department's responsibility centers have also increased.

Each responsibility center manager reports directly to William Smart, the company controller. An organization structure in which all subordinates report directly to a single supervisor is referred to as a flat organization. The organization chart in Figure C3–2 represents the controllership function of Contronics Inc.

Each manager of a responsibility center supervises a moderate-sized staff and is responsible for undertaking the tasks assigned to the position to accomplish the designated objectives of the individual responsibility center. The managers depend on William Smart for direction in coordinating their separate activities.

Redraw the organization chart of the controllership function to reflect sound organizational standards; add one or more staff units that should facilitate the communication process of Contronics Inc.'s controllership function. (CMA adapted)

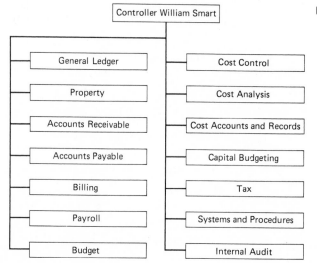

Figure C3–2   Controller's Department

3–3

Bluestone Foundry and Metal Products Company of Youghiogheny City, Pennsylvania, produces small tools for craftsmen for various industries and for wide distribution throughout the nation under various house brands used by discount department stores. Bluestone, at another plant, produces high-quality roller and ball bearings for industrial use. Recently it has added a metal products division that markets metal castings to a wide variety of industries ranging from toys to aerospace. Many of its products require state-of-the-art chemical and metallurgical technology and the best in industrial engineering know-how so that they can be manufactured to rigid specifications. Bluestone has therefore employed a large staff of engineers in research and development. Currently they are organized as shown in the organization chart in Figure C3–3(A). Four vice-presidents report to the president. Since the company places considerable emphasis on marketing its products and on customer service, three marketing managers report to the vice-president of marketing. Plant managers report to these marketing managers to achieve effective coordination of production and marketing for each product. The rest of the organization is shown in Figure C3–3(B).

Bluestone has used a local CPA in Youghiogheny City for twenty years, but due to its growth and the acquisition of the metal products division, it has asked your firm to conduct the annual audit and give advice on modernizing its information system, which is strictly a transaction-based financial and cost accounting system. Bluestone does use a standard cost system and a flexible budget, and the standards are set by the industrial engineering staff. As part of your report, the company would like you to prepare a brief outline giving your suggestions on the following issues:

a. Any organization structural changes you consider necessary and why. Draw the new organization charts involved.

b. The inability of Bluestone's R & D department to deal with its various assignments.

c. The coordination of manufacturing, purchasing, and inventory with respect to the contribution of each product to profit.

d. The location of EDP.

e. Behavioral implications of any structural and information changes you propose at

(1) The vice-president's level

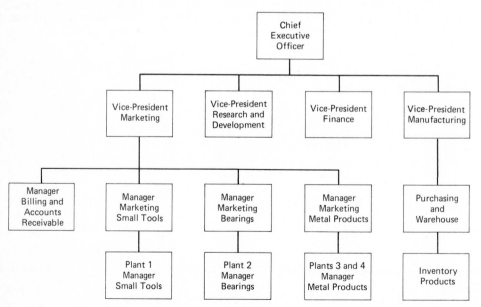

Figure C3–3(A)   Bluestone Foundry and Metal Products

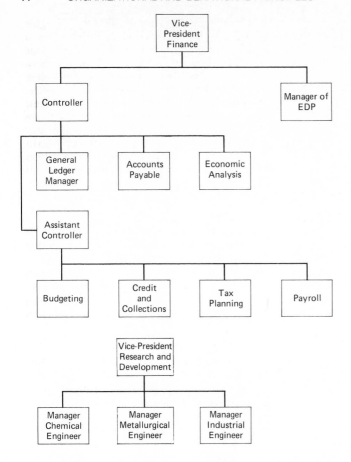

Figure C3–3(B)   Bluestone Foundry and Metal Products

(2) The manager's and supervisor's level

(3) The lower levels

f. How Bluestone should deal with these potential changes.

3–4

CSI&F Inc. is a successful Midwest corporation that had more than $200 million in sales in 1982. Carl Sedlitsky, president and majority stockholder of CSI&F Inc., started Carl's Scrap Iron Company shortly after World War II to take advantage of the surplus scrap iron that he knew would be available. The company thrived during the late 1940s. In 1950 Sedlitsky bought a cast iron foundry from a customer because he needed an outlet for the surplus scrap iron his company was accumulating.

Sedlitsky incorporated his business after purchasing the cast iron foundry. As part of the transaction, the name of the company was changed to Carl's Scrap Iron and Foundry Incorporated; this was later shortened to the present name—CSI&F Inc.

CSI&F Inc. continued its acquisition activities during the next thirty years, so that the corporation now has twenty-two separate divisions consisting of three malleable iron foundries, four ductile iron foundries, five cast iron foundries, four specialty heat-treating plants, five finishing and fabricating plants, and the scrap iron yard.

Carl Sedlitsky has been known as a fair employer. The company's compensation and fringe benefit plans have been excellent and include a profit-sharing plan instituted in 1967.

Mutual respect and personal contact with each management employee were standard when the company was small. Unfortunately, Sedlitsky had to cut back on personal contacts in the 1960s as CSI&F continued to expand.

Sedlitsky still maintains personal contact with all division managers and their immediate assistants through quarterly meetings. The meetings are used to review the divisions' results and are held on three days during each quarter. This rarely allows sufficient time for all division managers to make their oral presentations and to discuss various problems with corporate management. Sedlitsky has the five to seven division managers who are unable to complete their reviews stay over for an additional meeting the following day, or he follows up by telephone in the next few days.

The quarterly meetings not only provide personal contact with the division managers but also provide an opportunity for clarification of monthly written reports. Because CSI&F Inc. has grown in a somewhat haphazard fashion, the accounting system for each of the divisions is different. Consequently the division managers' written reports lack comparability, thus making it difficult for Sedlitsky to digest and integrate the information in a reasonable period of time. In addition, Sedlitsky has been unable to devote the time necessary to analyze the written reports.

In an attempt to alleviate the reporting problems and the lack of comparability in reports, Sedlitsky's executive financial vice-president has drafted a plan that would establish a common accounting and reporting system for those divisions with similar activities. This plan also proposes that the number of divisions be reduced to six—malleable iron, ductile iron, cast iron, finishing and fabricating, specialty heat treating, and scrap iron. Six of the current division managers will head the six new divisions. The remaining sixteen managers will be reassigned and will be responsible for the operations that were formerly administered by the twenty-two division managers. However, the sixteen managers will now report to their respective new division managers rather than to the president. Thus the plan would change Sedlitsky's span of control.

REQUIRED:

a. Discuss the effect the new accounting and reporting system and reduced number of division managers as proposed by the executive financial vice-president should have on Carl Sedlitsky's ability to manage CSI&F Inc. effectively.

b. Discuss how the executive financial vice-president's proposal to reduce the number of divisions is likely to affect the behavior of the two groups of CSI&F's division managers—the six who will head the six new divisions and the remaining sixteen who now will report to the six new division managers. (Adapted from the CMA Examination.)

3-5

Your accounting firm has been asked to design and install new microprocessing cash registers in thirty store locations of Shells, Inc., a regional department store specializing in sportswear, beach supplies, and souvenirs on the Florida east coast. Management wants these to control its vast inventory of numerous small items, which are spread over thirty locations. These new registers will gather data on a cassette tape, which can be transferred at the end of each day to the home store in Sea Oats Beach.

The last time Shells tried to implement a new system, it turned out to be a nightmare for the store managers who were trying to operate this system, and the reports generated were useless in managing their respective stores. Moreover, the clerks found that it was a real hassle to use the system that had been tried before, and they couldn't care less about the corporation's inventory problems.

Do you expect any motivation problems with the new system even though *no* employees will be laid off, the system is in fact easy to operate, reports are purported to be useful to store managers, and very little training is needed by clerks and management who use the system? If so, why, in terms of motivation theory?

3-6

Greengrass Company is an established manufacturer and wholesaler of a broad line of lawn fertilizer and yard maintenance products. The company has annual sales of approximately $100 million and has been a wholly owned subsidiary of a large conglomerate, KSU Corporation, for the past five years. Prior to that, it was an independent corporation whose stock was controlled by the founding and managing family.

A. B. Cardwell, son of the founder, is currently the president of the company, but he is scheduled to retire in May 1984. His nephew, B. C. Cardwell, is currently executive vice-president and has been heir apparent to the presidency ever since A. B. Cardwell became president.

Greengrass had maintained a pattern of increasing profits for many years. During the past three years, however, profits have decreased significantly. Management has attributed this to reduced demand caused by cool, wet summers in the company's primary marketing area coupled with intense competitive activity.

Following his return from a week-long corporate management planning meeting, A. B. Cardwell called a staff meeting to discuss plans for the 1984 marketing season. At the close of the meeting, he announced that the KSU board had named William Thoma president of Greengrass Company in May 1984. Cardwell explained that KSU's management was concerned about the subsidiary's slumping profits and had decided to assume a greater degree of control over Greengrass operations. Thoma's appointment was the first step in this direction. In addition, a new system of financial reporting to KSU management is to be installed.

Mr. Thoma's reputation was well known by the entire staff. He had been executive vice-president of two other KSU-owned companies during the previous three years. In both cases, the companies had records of declining profits prior to his appointment. A significant management reorganization occurred in each of those companies within twelve months after his appointment. In each case, some members of senior management were given early retirement or released, depending on their age. Their replacements usually came from other KSU companies with which Thoma had been associated. Although earnings did increase following the reorganizations, the entire "personality" of the companies was changed.

REQUIRED: As Greengrass's auditor, write a memo explaining the potential need for additional audit work on the new financial reporting system due to your expectations regarding the quality of the financial data generated by the new system. This report should focus on the enthusiasm given the development and implementation of the new system. Specifically, do you expect the current management to be motivated to support the new system? (Adapted from the CMA Examination.)

3–7

Gulf and Northern, a wood product corporation with forests, lumbering operations, and paper mills throughout the Northwest and Southeast, has been experiencing astronomical travel costs between its widely scattered field and plant offices, divisional offices, and corporate offices. It has decided to install a system of video communications equipment at each location so that managers, engineers, accountants, and many of the others who regularly travel can substitute conference calls using video equipment for these person-to-person meetings. It also intends to have the capability to transmit documents so that all parties to the video conference can talk about the same set of figures and documents. Top-management personnel expected praise from their subordinates when they first mentioned this system, but a lot of skepticism and "but it won't work" from the potential users resulted. Why?

3–8

A nationwide survey was conducted recently by an independent research center among professional engineers employed in industrial, academic, and governmental and other not-for-profit organizations. The survey concerned the "wants" of the engineers. The results of the survey are listed below. The order of the items does not indicate the degree of importance; the importance varied with the type of activities and type of organization in which the engineer was associated.

1. Freedom to publish and discuss work with other professional engineers
2. Association with, and intellectual stimulation from, high-caliber colleagues
3. A technically trained management
4. Freedom in solving problems and managing own work (within specified limits)
5. An organization with a reputation for engineering advancement
6. Adequate facilities, resources, and assistance from technicians

7. Opportunity for advancement in salary and status along either the management route or the technical route
8. Competitive salaries and benefits
9. Job security based on achievements
10. A community providing schools, colleges, libraries, other cultural opportunities, and good transportation
11. Treatment as professionals
12. Opportunity to continue formal education while employed
13. Variety and challenge in work
14. Opportunity to see ideas put to use

REQUIRED:

a. Identify and discuss the specific needs of people that are described in motivational theories.
b. Relate each of the specific wants identified in the survey to the specific needs described in motivational theories. (Adapted from the CMA Examination.)

3–9

Although some physiological functions take place without motivation, nearly all conscious behavior is motivated by some need or desire. In recent years psychologists, sociologists, and others have been placing increased emphasis on the importance of human motivation both in general and in business organizations in particular.

Some observers of employee motivation have developed theories that have identified specific types or classes of needs, and they have categorized these needs into levels or priorities. By identifying and classifying its employees' needs, the company hopes to take actions that will improve its employees' motivation and job performance.

REQUIRED:

a. Identify and explain the various types of needs that motivate employees.
b. Place each of the needs identified in your answer to requirement *a* in a hierarchy ranging from lower-level needs to higher-level needs.

c. Explain how an employee's job can satisfy the needs in each major level of the hierarchy. (Adapted from the CMA Examination.)

3–10

Huron Lighting manufactures a line of lighting products and markets them via a series of dealers in thirty-five states. All decisions are made centrally in Bay City. Manufacturing plants and dealers send their cost and sales statistics to Bay City for consolidation and comparison with various budgets. All manufacturing plants report to a vice-president of manufacturing, and all dealers report to a vice-president of marketing and distribution.

Top management has been complaining for a long time that dealers are not selling the higher-margin items. Manufacturing plants have production runs that are too long. These reduce costs but result in many shortages and lost orders at the dealer level.

Management of Huron Lighting has asked you, the company's accountant, to suggest a budget system to motivate the managers to make decisions more consistent with the firm's objective of profit maximization. In general terms, write a brief memo outlining your suggestions and rationale.

3–11

Super Play Toy Company manufactures, distributes, and markets several lines of children's toys. The lines are best described by the age brackets of the children for which they are produced: baby, preschool, and youth. The toys are marketed separately through different outlets and jointly through large discount stores. Super Play is currently organized with a vice-president for each of the functional areas: production, marketing, distribution, finance, and information systems.

Sales have been booming for Super Play because parents like the fact that its toys are almost indestructible, and they are willing to pay a little more for Super Play's products. In spite of this, however, certain items are often sold out at both large discount stores and specialty stores. Moreover, some toys are gathering dust in the factory, warehouse, and retail outlets.

Management thinks that "better" information may help reduce these problems, and you have been called in to assist in a review of its information system. Is the lack of effective information the problem? Why or why not? Comment on these questions in a brief memo.

3-12

Roadway Engineering specializes in the analysis, design, and supervision of interstate highways in and around large metropolitan areas. It has engineers, accountants, financial advisers, draftsmen, and urban planning specialists located in major cities throughout the United States. The company is currently organized in such a way that each of these cities is a profit center and the manager is responsible for all activities at the locations. Because of the nature of government contracts, however, the company has experienced wide fluctuations in the performance of these managers. Due to several large contracts, business is sometimes so good that employees must work overtime to complete these contracts. The company must even subcontract much of the work locally to get it done on time. On the other hand, other locations are hurting; engineers are just sitting around waiting for a new contract. Roadway is reluctant to let these experienced personnel go because next month they may be needed again.

REQUIRED: As an information systems expert, where might you begin to advise Roadway on possible solutions to these problems? Write a brief memo explaining any organizational changes Roadway should consider and the possible functional and dysfunctional consequences of these changes.

3-13

At Efficient Manufacturing, employees take great pride in personal responsibility for manufacturing, sales, and managerial activities.

The whole company is organized around profit centers, including the EDP department. With this prevailing organizational philosophy, the manager of the EDP department has taken each set of application computer programs and assigned it to an individual analyst in the computer center. An individual is responsible for writing the program, testing it, running it on a daily basis, reviewing the output, and resolving any errors that may occur. The manager takes great pride in this efficient system and its smooth operation.

REQUIRED: As an auditor, would you concur with this manager? Write a brief memo describing (1) what dangers are associated with the current organization and (2) how the company should reorganize.

3-14

Williams and Kiger, partners of an Ohio CPA firm, recently read some literature on the use of matrix organization structures in professional organizations. They have decided to change their information system and data base from one that is oriented toward each office in the state to one that will also collect, store, and report information by various technical skills (tax, MIS, auditing, operations research, and SEC practice) within their firm. They also plan to add five new managers to be located in the home office in Columbus to coordinate these activities.

What motivational and behavioral consequences do you expect, if any, from the impact of this new system?

3-15

Case 10-4 (Audio Visual Corporation) may be used here.

4

DECISION MAKING, INFORMATION, AND COMMUNICATION CONCEPTS

OVERVIEW

Management must select courses of action consistent with its objectives in an uncertain, complex, and dynamic environment. As noted in Chapter 2, the management system designed to implement these operational, managerial, and strategic decisions must be supported by an effective and efficient information system. This system is often called a decision support system (DSS). (Decision support systems will be illustrated in Chapter 15.) The accounting system is a major subsystem of such a decision support or information system. In many cases the accounting system is the dominant subsystem; in some cases it is the only component of the system. As noted in Figure 4–1, it is generally the focal point of the information system.

The combined management and information systems are used to plan and control the firm's operations. This planning and control process relies on effective communication; the accountant is a major participant in the design and use of the control and communication network of the firm.

The information system must support the management system. Specifically, it must support decision-making activities. As noted in Chapter 3, these decision-making activities are the third major component of the social and decision-making environment in which the information or accounting system must operate. The other two major components are the organization structure and human behavior. Thus it is vital that accountants and system designers understand the decision-making process, for the decision network will ultimately be the basis for system design.

In this chapter a conceptual framework for decision making will be developed for use in understanding and specifying various decision activities. Decision-making systems will be classified based on this framework, to assist the designer in assessing the key parameters of new and old systems. Measurement and communication concepts will be related to this framework. The key mathematical and behavioral features of decision theory, decision models, and information value will be reviewed relative to this framework. Finally, the important concept of feedback in control and communication systems (cybernetics) will be discussed relative to this basic framework.

Particular attention will be given to the management and accounting system implications of the point of articulation or interface between the information system and the management system.

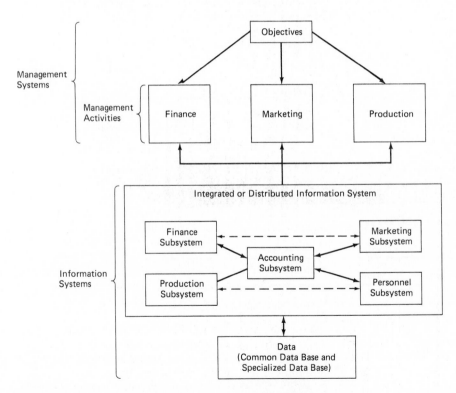

Figure 4-1 Information and Management Systems Formulation

CONCEPTUAL FRAMEWORK
FOR DECISION MAKING

Decision-Making Systems

Management decision making is carried on in an uncertain, complex, and dynamic environment. According to Simon, the process can be characterized as follows.[1] First, intelligence must be gathered in such a way that management is able to identify all the alternative strategies or solutions to a problem. Second, the consequences that would follow upon the adoption of each strategy must be determined. Third, a course of action must be chosen after comparative evaluation of all of these sets of consequences. In addition, this process incorporates review, or feedback, that corrects the decision-making process when needed and communicates the results of the action, which influence subsequent decisions. Many other authors have proposed similar sequences of events for the decision-making process. In this text we will use Mason's framework,[2] which is outlined in Figure 4–2 and parallels Simon's fundamental precepts. This framework is especially useful in classifying the level of support the information system gives to the management system in the decision-making process.

The decision-making process starts with relevant objects, activities, and results of prior actions. These are denoted as data *sources.* For example, in the budget process the sources may represent such objects and activities as histori-

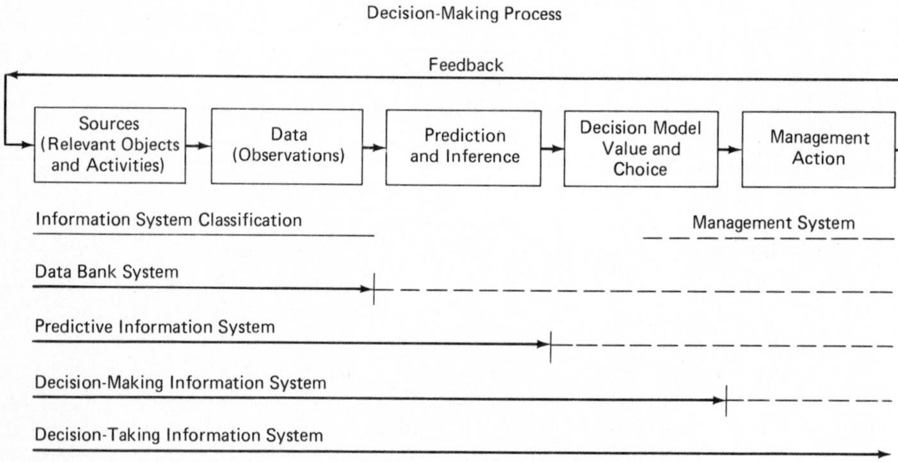

Decision-Making Process

Figure 4-2   Information and Management System Framework for Decision Making

Adapted with permission from Richard O. Mason, "Basic Concepts for Designing Management Information Systems."

[1] Herbert A. Simon, *Administrative Behavior,* 3rd ed., (New York: Free Press, 1976), pp. 67, 97, 232–34. Copyright © 1947, 1957, 1976 by Herbert A. Simon.

[2] Richard O. Mason, Jr., "Basic Concepts for Designing Management Information Systems," (AIS Research Paper No. 8 Los Angeles: UCLA Graduate School of Administration, October 1969). Printed with the permission of the author. This framework forms the basis for the decision making framework presented in this chapter.

cal costs, sales, inventory, and assets. These sources must ultimately be relevant to the decision. These sources are observed, selected, filtered, classified, and measured using a code or scale that will be helpful for decision-making purposes. At this juncture we have *data* that may be called information in an elementary sense. The measurement process will be discussed at greater length later in the chapter. In the budget process, cost behavior patterns—sales statistics such as market shares, accounts receivable, aging reports, and inventory status reports—may represent such data. Next, functional relationships and behavioral patterns are sought for the data and the relevant variables upon which management will make a decision. Regression analysis and cost-volume-profit analysis are useful techniques for such an analysis. The end result will be a set of *predictions* and *inferences* from the data which will be useful to the decision maker. In the budget process this may be represented by forecasts, flexible budgets, and other plans regarding future courses of action. In capital budgeting, revenue and cost forecasts for several alternative courses of action may constitute the predictions and inferences. Inferences regarding competitors' actions may also be useful in such decisions.

These three steps in the decision-making process constitute the ongoing planning process in which data are gathered and forecasts are made for a variety of relative alternative courses of action. This part of the process is followed by a choice among these alternatives. Some *decision model* (formal or informal) is used to *value* these alternatives and choose the most appropriate, best, or in some cases optimal, based on the goals of the organization. To accomplish this, clear objectives must be set for the organization. These objectives must be translated into criteria for selection of a course of action. For example, in the budget process management may select the set of plans that maximizes profit, maximizes market share, minimizes costs, yields a satisfactory profit with little risk, yields the maximum return on investments, yields the largest net present value, and so on. Finally, *action* is taken by management to implement the choice.

After the sequence has been completed, the results of the action are fed back and become one of the sources for the next set of decisions in this dynamic environment. In Simon's conceptualization all of these steps are required just to determine whether a problem or opportunity exists for which some action should be taken. A decision is required in the determination of the existence of a problem.

Sometimes this decision process is insulated from the unknown influences of the environment. The decision maker has complete knowledge of the relevant alternatives and the outcomes resulting from management action for each alternative. Moreover, the decision maker has a model that will permit an ordering of alternatives in accordance with the firm's objectives. In such cases we have a *closed system*. Closed systems are more likely to be found in cases in which an information system encompasses most or all of the decision-making steps in Figure 4–2. More-automated systems will fit this pattern, in which there is a lack of unknown environmental influences.

On the other hand, if the decision process in Figure 4–2 is heavily influenced by an unpredictable environment, the decision maker has knowledge of neither all the alternatives nor the consequences of management action for each alternative. As a result, the model used must be applied to an incomplete set of alternatives for which the outcomes are not certain. Moreover, the model may not be capable of dealing with uncertainty and the complexity of the many environmental variables bearing on the decision. Such a system is an *open decision system*. In cases such as this the decision is clearly influenced by the environment and, to further complicate the situation, the environment may even be influenced by the decision.[3] In open systems the decision-making process will be left up to the individual decision maker to a greater degree. Fewer steps will be formally incorporated into the information system, and more of the steps will be part of the management system.

Type of Decision-Making System

Within the social and decision-making environment (organization, human behavior, and decision making) described in Chapter 3, the accountant or system designer must implement an information system that will ultimately reduce the uncertainty of the consequences of various actions for all levels of management in their decision-making roles. Moreover, this must be done so that the incremental value of the information exceeds the incremental cost. Given the social and decision-making environment of the firm, the accountant must decide where the formal information system stops and the management system (human information processing) begins in the decision-making process. This is called the point of articulation between the information and the management decision-making system.[4] In this text decision-making processes are classified based on this interface between the management (decision) system and the information system. This interface classification can be used to define the level of support that the information (or decision support) system gives to management in the decision-making process.

DATA BANK SYSTEMS A data bank information system is structured to collect, classify, and store data by applying the lowest common denominator that will suffice for a variety of uses. The interface between the information system and the management system is between data and predictions. It becomes the function of management to request the data needed, make predictions and inferences from these data for various alternatives, and select and follow what seems to be the best course of action. Many of these requests will be routine and will constitute a set of management reports. Most traditional accounting systems found in practice will probably fall into this class. The objective of the information system is simply to support management decision making with a timely supply of reliable data. This is all that can be done in many open systems. The data bank system has two main deficiencies: (1) irrelevant data that do not relate to any decision are often collected, and (2) data manipulation and calculations are left to the manager (decision maker). As a result, the manager is often offered more detailed data than can possibly be organized for an effective and efficient evaluation of alternative courses of action. Information overload often exists with these systems.

[3] For an excellent review of this last issue, see J. Forrester, *Industrial Dynamics* (Boston: MIT Press, 1961).

[4] R. O. Mason, "Basic Concepts for Designing Management Information Systems" (AIS Research Paper No. 8, October 1969).

PREDICTIVE INFORMATION SYSTEMS   In a predictive information system the manager asks "what if" questions. The information system is based on a set of assumptions about the behavior of the relevant objects and activities of the firm and the environment. The system predicts a set of expected results (perhaps even probability distributions) for various alternative courses of action deemed relevant by the decision maker. This type of system supports managers by focusing on the relevant information for particular decisions, thus reducing the information overload. Financial planning and budget simulation models are excellent examples of this type of system. Most of these financial planning models are founded on simple financial and cost accounting relationships and transactions, which can be expressed as systems of equations as will be demonstrated in Chapter 15.[5] The manager may give the information system the current financial position of the firm, a sales forecast, a set of revenue and cost transaction assumptions, and a set of collection and inventory policies or assumptions. A pro forma income statement, balance sheet, and statement of changes in financial position, as well as information such as return on investment and earnings per share, can be generated by the system given these assumptions.

The impact of these alternative assumptions and actions on the financial statement is thus inferred by the system. No attempt is made by the system to evaluate the predicted results or, in the example cited, the pro forma set of financial statements. The manager must do the evaluation and ultimate selection of a course of action. Thus the interface (level of support) between the information system and the management system is schematically located between the prediction and the decision model steps in Figure 4–2.

This type of system works well when the volume of data is large, interrelationships among the data items are complicated, and the interrelationships are predictable or, in the case of financial statements, follow a general set of rules, such as generally accepted accounting principles. As in budgeting, many alternatives can be assessed by the decision maker. Many "what if" questions, such as, What is the impact on the financial statements of a price decrease of 10 percent, which according to market research will yield a 5 percent increase in sales?, can also be asked. When using such a system, management must be cognizant of all underlying assumptions to ensure that they coincide with the manager's best assessment of reality and with corporate policies. Because of the advantages offered by such systems in terms of reducing masses of data to commonly used accounting reports familiar to managers, it is strongly suggested that more traditional accounting systems move in this direction. Managers will be able to make better, more-informed decisions. Software ("VisiCalc") is even available for the more popular microcomputer systems to assist managers in establishing this type of decision-making system.[6] (Examples

---

[5] See Steven C. Wheelwright and Spyros G. Makridakis, *Computer Aided Modeling for Managers* (Reading, Mass.: Addison-Wesley, 1972); Execucom, *IFPS User's Manual* (Austin, Tex.: Execucom System Corporation, 1979); and Y. Ijiri, F. K. Levy, and R. C. Lyon, "A Linear Programming Model for Budgeting and Financial Planning," *Journal of Accounting Research*, Autumn 1963, pp. 198–212.

[6] *VisiCalc* is a commonly used spread sheet analysis package offered by software vendors for microcomputers.

of this and the more popular corporate planning models will be given in later chapters of this text.)

DECISION-MAKING INFORMATION SYSTEMS   When relevant data can be collected, and sufficient structural and behavioral relationships exist among data elements and the environment so that the outcomes can be predicted for a set of alternatives, it is sometimes feasible to incorporate the organization's set of values and choice criteria into the information system. Such a system is called a decision-making information system. Management merely asks which action is best, and the information system responds using a programmed decision model that selects the best alternative based on the organization's goals. A good example would be a linear-programming model used to allocate scarce resources, such as labor, to competing jobs to maximize contribution to profit. Generally such systems use operations research, management science, and mathematical or statistical models to sort through the various alternatives to select the "best" course of action for management. In such a system, therefore, the locus of the interface between the information system and management system is between the decision model and management action. Widely used corporate planning model software is also available for this type of system for larger computer configurations. (These systems will be discussed in Chapter 15.)

DECISION-TAKING INFORMATION SYSTEMS   Sometimes, usually in a closed system, the information system can be designed not only to collect data, draw inferences from the data, and select the best course of action but also to implement the selected action. A good example of this type of decision-taking information system is a purchase order and inventory system. In these systems the objective is inventory control. Data consist of the status of inventory items, stockout levels, lead times, carrying costs, and reorder and setup costs. Inferences are drawn from usage rates and the cost structure to set reorder points. The decision model is generally some variation of the EOQ (economic order quantity) model, which minimizes costs. When the reorder point is reached, action is taken in the form of automatic issuance of purchase orders by the information system. Most information systems of this type operate in limited environments, such as the inventory control system in the example just given. Clearly, for such a system to operate without management's interaction, management must have complete confidence in the model and the assumptions upon which it is founded. Again, widely used software is even available for microcomputers for operational decision-making activities of this type.

In summary, the interface between the information and the management system (decision maker) can take place at any juncture in the decision process. This point of articulation or level of decision-making support is a function of the firm's social and decision-making environment. The accountant and the system designer must be aware of the factors influencing this interface in the decision process so that he or she will be able to assess the decision network of the organization to design an effective system. This awareness is critical, for the decision network and the level of support to be rendered by the information system are the basis for system design and implementation.

INFORMATION AND COMMUNICATION CONCEPTS— OVERVIEW

This part of the chapter gives an overview of measurement and communication concepts. Some appreciation of these is helpful for the accountant in using and designing the system. These concepts add some depth to the understanding of the firm's decision-making and communication environment.

Measurement

The collecting, sorting, and storing of data (noted in Figure 4–2 between the sources and the data in the decision-making process) requires the classifying, coding, and assigning of numbers to events, objects, and even other measurements by using a set of rules. Surrogates must often be used for measurement of economic events and activities in decision-making models. The effective assignment of appropriate surrogates presents a difficult problem for the accountant. Timeliness, reliability, objectivity, and relevance must all be weighed and balanced. There is probably no such thing, in practice, as a perfect representation of the various events and activities observed.

Nominal, ordinal, interval, and ratio scales can be used as units of measurement. On a nominal scale, events are only classified. An example of a nominal classification is that of an inventory item as an asset. An ordinal scale, which expresses position in a series, or an interval scale, which expresses magnitudes of differences, can also be used. A ratio scale enables the manager to use numerical manipulation, such as addition or multiplication.

Regardless of the measurement or scale used to encode the relevant economic events and activities for decision making, the generation of useful data must follow the process outlined in Figure 4–3. Events, objects, and possibly other measurements, such as competitors' financial statements, are selected, observed, and filtered. Next they are classified using the assignment of classification codes, such as chart-of-account numbers. An appropriate scale, generally a ratio scale such as dollars or units, is used to assign a number to the observation. Once this measurement process has been completed, the measurements are recorded and transmitted to the data file or data base for future reference by the information system or management. More will be said about data file and data base organization later in the text.

Communication

An accountant, in the role of user and designer of information systems, should be aware of the basic communication concepts related to the decision-making process (outlined in Figure 4–2). Shannon and Weaver state that there are three types of problems associated with communication:[7]

1. The technical problem—"How accurately can the symbols of communication be transmitted?"

[7] C. E. Shannon and W. Weaver, *The Mathematical Theory of Communication* (Urbana: University of Illinois Press, 1949), with permission.

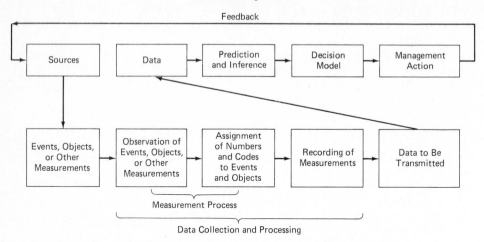

Decision-Making Process

Feedback

Sources → Data → Prediction and Inference → Decision Model → Management Action

Events, Objects, or Other Measurements → Observation of Events, Objects, or Other Measurements → Assignment of Numbers and Codes to Events and Objects → Recording of Measurements → Data to Be Transmitted

Measurement Process

Data Collection and Processing

Figure 4-3 Basic Measurement Concepts for Designing Management Information Systems

Adapted with permission from American Accounting Association Committee on Information Systems, "Accounting and Information Systems." *The Accounting Review Supplement*, vol. XLVI (1971), and R. O. Mason, "Basic Concepts for Designing Management Information Systems."

2. The semantic problem—"How precisely do the transmitted symbols carry the desired meaning?"

3. The effectiveness problem—"How effectively does the received meaning affect conduct in the desired way?"

The first problem is primarily a *transmission problem*, and it exists at each juncture in the decision-making process. Data, including results of predictions, decision models, or management actions, must be encoded, transmitted, and then decoded to provide a signal for the next step in the decision process. This transmission may be part of either the information system or the management system. Statistical communication theory has shed some light on procedures for converting data into messages that may be transmitted, characteristics of transmission channels, and eventual conversion into usable signals. Measures of entropy, or disorder, have been useful to a limited degree in assessing the amount of information transmitted through the system and the loss of information due to aggregation in the coding process. A full discussion of entropy is beyond the scope of this text.[8] Other statistical measures can be used for noise in the transmission process.

It is important that the accountant be aware of the encoding, transmission, and decoding problems associated with the amount of information actually conveyed. Only the information conveyed can be used in decision making. Aggregation of data for more efficient communication, losses associated with this aggregation, and the presence of noise in the system are also important to

---

[8] For a full discussion in the accounting literature, see Baruch Lev, *Financial Statement Analysis: A New Approach* (Englewood Cliffs, NJ.: Prentice-Hall, 1974); and H. Theil, "On the Use of Information Theory Concepts in the Analysis of Financial Statements," *Management Science*, May 1969.

the accountant. Noise results from (1) conflicting signals from like data or (2) different data causing a similar signal due to coding, transmission, and decoding processes. This is an especially critical problem for on-line information systems where the user must communicate in English with a very structured data base. Special care must be taken in designing the interactive language to reduce the noise in the system at the juncture between the system and the decision maker. Outside interference probably falls into the second type of noise.

The *semantic problems* as well as the *effectiveness problem* are, to a large extent, behavioral problems. As a result, the accountant should continually be aware of the individual's role in collecting, processing, and transmitting data, and decision making in the communication process. The individual receives signals, makes observations from these signals based on individual perceptions, and processes and filters these observations according to a personal set of biases. The individual then takes action or sends signals based on these filtered signals. Because of this role, it is important that the system designer understand the impact of signal differences on perceptions, filtering methods, and the ultimate actions of the individuals who make the decisions in a firm. Expertise in communication, semantics, social psychology, sociometrics, learning theory, and psychology may be needed to resolve some of the problems associated with this process. The strategy by which individuals reach a decision is also important in understanding the behavioral process. The accountant and the system designer are challenged to design a system that is usable by a wide range of employees who have different ways of solving problems. Some of the corporate planning models have attempted to deal with this challenge by developing a flexible interactive language that corporate executives can understand.[9]

DECISION THEORY—OVERVIEW

Decision theory issues are important for two reasons. First, the decision model is dependent on the accounting and information system, which provides signals to the model. Second, the selection of the type of information system required is influenced by decision theory issues. In this section we will outline a descriptive set of issues for decision making and the role of individuals in this process. Mathematical and statistical decision models for the more-structured information systems, such as decision-making and decision-taking information systems, will be reviewed briefly. The value of information and information economics issues will also be discussed.

Descriptive Theory

Cyert and March,[10] in an effort to describe organizational decision making while developing a behavioral theory of the firm, outline four major decision-making concepts: (1) *quasi-resolution of conflict*, (2) *uncertainty avoidance*, (3) *problemistic search*, and (4) *organizational learning*. First, they recognize that any or-

---

[9] See Execucom, *IFPS User's Manual* (Austin, Tex.: Execucom System Corporation, 1979).

[10] The descriptive theory of decision making presented here is based largely on Richard M. Cyert and James G. March, *A Behavioral Theory of the Firm* (Englewood Cliffs, N.J.: Prentice-Hall, Inc.,© 1963). Used with permission.

ganization is a coalition of individuals (or segments of the organization), each with different goals and each with some influence to alter the organizational objectives (see Chapter 3). These different objectives must be resolved in the decision-making process. According to Cyert and March, they are resolved by (1) allowing subsystems (or individuals) to pursue their own goals (local rationality), (2) permitting subsystems (or individuals) to make their own decisions within specified limits (acceptable-level decision rules), and (3) resolving conflicts sequentially so that they are not handled at the same time and each decision is based on the prior decisions (sequential attention to goals). These strategies constitute quasi-resolution of conflict.

Uncertainty is generally avoided in practice by using a system that facilitates fast feedback and by encouraging short-run decisions, thus reducing the uncertainty associated with long-range decisions based on old information. Fast feedback must therefore be incorporated into many decision-processing systems and the information systems that support them. The desirability of these shorter planning horizons is an issue that will not be discussed here.[11] Other measures are used to avoid uncertainty, such as long-term contracts which help control the environment through negotiation.

Problemistic search is widely used in practice. The search for a solution to a problem is started with the statement of the problem itself and its obvious symptoms. If a solution to the problem is not found in the location of its origin, the problem is moved to other parts of the organization structure for attempts at finding a solution. This implies that in many systems there may be a sequence imbedded in the process outlined in Figure 4–2. The first set of solution alternatives considered are the obvious. If these are not satisfactory, others are sought. There may be a feedback loop between prediction and decision model steps in the process.

Finally, organizations adapt their behavior over time. Goals and procedures are modified as environmental conditions change. Cyert and March refer to this process as *organizational learning.* The decison maker's style can be *heuristic* and follow a logical process founded on experience with similar problems, common sense, and emotion. The style can be *systematic* and *analytic* and follow a sequential (often mathematical) set of problem-solving steps generally based on a search procedure for underlying cause-and-effect relationships. These styles will influence the decision maker's approach to decision-making processes outlined earlier. The system designer or the accountant must be aware of the various cognitive styles involved in designing an information system that will support a management system consisting of individual decision makers, each with a different level of expertise, educational background, and behavioral history, all of which influence that individual's cognitive style.

Decision Models[12]

Many methods can be used for deciding among alternatives. Some are heuristic and result from experience, emotion, common sense, business intu-

---

[11] See "The Reindustrialization of America," *Business Week,* June 30, 1980 (Special Issue), pp. 74–82 and 92–94.

[12] See W. M. Wagner, *Principles of Operations Research* (Englewood Cliffs, N.J.: Prentice-Hall, 1969), or any other operations research text.

ition, and past trial and error. Management can develop a logical process for resolving problems based on a heuristic approach.

As an alternative, more analytic and systematic logical processes can be utilized. These can be mathematical optimization procedures, such as linear programming and queuing theory, which mathematically choose the best solution given a certain set of input data and assumptions. In some mathematical procedures the input may be in the form of probability distributions. To use these techniques, we must be able to formulate the problem in terms of the assumptions and variables of the model. As a result, the use of mathematical procedures in practice is limited to the more closed operational system. Only a small fraction of management decisions are made using mathematical procedures. They should be used when possible because they can yield an optimal solution and can handle many more input variables than the human mind can comprehend.

Payoff matrices are useful in limited cases where the outcomes bear a direct and clear relationship to alternative actions. Game theory is another useful mathematical model for resolving and understanding the essential character of bargaining situations. Decision trees can be used for a sequence of decisions and evaluation of the impact of various sequences on the expected present value of a course of action. Again, we must be able to make certain assumptions and specify input for these models.

The output criteria for selecting among alternatives cannot always be expressed as an expected value or the maximum contribution to profit, as we noted above, because there are various degrees of risk associated with each outcome. In this case utility and indifference curves can be used in conjunction with several of these mathematical models. Moreover, statistical inference can be used for sampling, correlation analysis, testing hypotheses, and determining probability distributions for both input into the models and output from some of the models.

In cases where heuristic or mathematical or statistical models are used, the accountant or system designer must understand the essential nature of the model (not necessarily the mathematical manipulation or derivation), the necessary assumptions, and the character of the input and information requirements. Design of an effective and efficient information system to support a management decision-making system is impossible without this knowledge. Often outside advice should be sought to gain the necessary understanding of this aspect of the management decision network.

The Value of Information

Our basic premises are (1) that information is a commodity whose acquisition, like that of other commodities, constitutes a problem of economic choice, and (2) that one can obtain insight into this vague problem by viewing information issues within the formal structure of decision theory. . . .[13]

---

[13] Joel S. Demski, *Information Analysis* (Reading, Mass.: Addison-Wesley,© 1972), p. 1. Reprinted with permission.

Information is a resource to be used like any other resource and should not cost more than the value derived from the system. Moreover, the signal from the system has value only if it is relevant and only if it may result in a course of action other than the one that would be taken if the information were not present. In addition to relevance, information must be as timely and accurate as possible without incurring excessive costs. The sequence of events relating cost to value to relevance to potential courses of action must be considered in the design and implementation of any information system. Decision tables and payoff matrices can help the accountant or system designer gain insight into the economic parameters affecting the value of an information system. These are illustrated in the appendix.

Sensitivity analysis is useful in assessing the possible impact of an information system on a decision. To assess this impact, alter the parameters of the problem to see whether information from the system can alter a decision; it may be that no matter what information is received, the decision will not change. The system may have no value in this case.

Relevance can also be defined in a logical manner to be the set of information that has the greatest predictive ability.[14] This set of relevant data may be quite different from the set actually used in making a decision. An accountant trying to design a system might therefore conclude that considerable attention must be given the latter definition of relevance. The problem with this assumption is that the latter set of "relevant" information is often a function of the current system. This represents a narrower view of the decision environment (for example, a manual processing system) than what would be the situation given a new system (for example, on-line computer system). Neither set of information will comprise relevant information for a new system. Therefore the accountant must, as was suggested in earlier chapters, consider the business environment and decision network and build from that point to obtain a relevant set of information.

Cybernetics

Cybernetics is the science of control and communication. There are natural laws, similar to those found in physics and chemistry, that govern control and communication. Since the accountant and the system designer are intimately involved in this process, cybernetic concepts can be helpful in providing much needed insight into the decision and feedback process illustrated in Figure 4–4. The science of cybernetics has a bearing on pattern recognition, data recording, data analysis, heuristic decision rules, accounting principles, learning models, and human behavior. Almost everything influencing an accounting and information system that operates in the uncertain complex and dynamic environment of today's world of business is subject to the laws of cybernetics. The accountant and the system designer are specifically interested in the feedback loops in the decision process shown in Figure 4–4.

---

[14] See Robert Libby, *Accounting and Human Information Processing: Theory and Applications* (Englewood Cliffs, N.J.: Prentice-Hall, 1981) for a discussion of the use of the Brunswick Lens model to assess this data set.

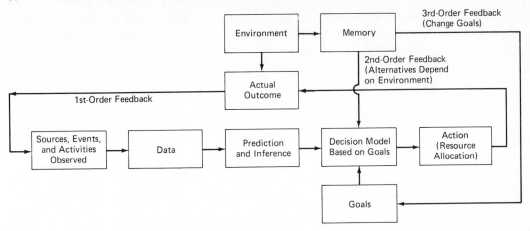

Figure 4-4   Feedback Loops in the Decision-Making Process

Adapted with permission from the American Accounting Association Committee on Information Systems, "Accounting and Information Systems," *The Accounting Review Supplement*, vol. XLVI (1971), pp. 318–320.

First, the state of the system is observed after the actions have taken place. Then results are compared with standards (predictions and inferences) and corrective action (decision model) is often suggested. This process is found in the first-order feedback system.

A memory of past events and actions may be used to help the decision model decide which alternative is best when environmental conditions change. The criteria for choice becomes a function of the environment. This process is found in a second-order feedback system.

Moreover, the memory may suggest new alternatives, goals, or criteria for choice (such as cash flow instead of profit maximization) when environmental conditions change. A third-order feedback loop is present in this case. Learning takes place in the second- and third-order feedback situations. In a sense the system has "artificial intelligence" if second- and third-order feedback loops are present.

Therefore it is important that accountants or systems designers be aware of the complexities in the decision-making process so that they can design the system to support the decision maker.

IMPLICATIONS

The decision-making process, whether it involves a decision regarding the need to resolve a problem or take advantage of an apparent opportunity, or involves the actual selection of a course of action, is comprised of the sequence of steps outlined in Figure 4–2: (1) identification of sources of data, (2) extraction and measurement of data from these sources, (3) predictions and inferences drawn from the data for several alternatives, (4) definition of decision criteria and choice of the best alternative, (5) managerial action, and (6) eventual feedback.

The information system may complete this process or it may only begin it by offering management a set of data from which to make decisions. The management system will complete the process where the decision support system stops. This interface will be a function of many social and decision-making environmental factors, such as the nature of the decision, the behavior of the firm, and the style of its management. The accountant must understand this process and, most important, the interface between the information system and the management system to effectively design a system to support management needs.

The decision-making process outlined in the chapter is not simple. Many complex factors influence the process. Objects and activities must be measured and these must be encoded, transmitted, and decoded into signals that are significant to the decision maker. This is an imprecise and complex task that often involves many sets of behavioral assumptions. Measurement and communication concepts can be quite useful in understanding this part of the process.

Decision theory can give the accountant or system designer important guidelines in system design. An understanding of the decision-making practice in organizations where individual goals must be reconciled with corporate goals, an understanding of decision models, and an appreciation of the basic economic issues regarding the value and potential value of information systems are all important to anyone who must design an effective, efficient, and cost-justified system that managers can use. Finally, recognizing that most of the key variables in business systems can be cast as control and communication variables is important, the science of cybernetics, which deals with such variables, may be helpful in systems design.

In summary, the accountant or systems designer must strive to better understand the social and decision-making environment in which the system must function.

SELECTED REFERENCES

American Accounting Association Committee on Information Systems, "Accounting and Information Systems," *Accounting Review Supplement*, Vol. XLVI (1971).

Bedford, N. M., and M. Onsi, "Measuring the Value of Information—An Information Theory Approach," *Management Science*, January–February 1966.

Bellman, R., and L. A. Zadeh, "Decision-Making in a Fuzzy Environment," *Management Science*, December 1970.

Cyert, Richard M., and James G. March, *A Behavioral Theory of the Firm*, Englewood Cliffs, N.J.: Prentice-Hall, Inc., 1967.

Demski, Joel S., *Information Analysis*. Reading, Mass.: Addison-Wesley, 1972 and 1980.

Execucom, *IFPS User's Manual*. Austin,Tex.: Execucom System Corporation, 1979.

FELTHAM, G. A., "The Value of Information," *Accounting Review*, October 1968.

FELTHAM, G. A., AND J. S. DEMSKI, "The Use of Models in Information Evaluation," *Accounting Review*, October 1970.

FORRESTER, J., *Industrial Dynamics*. Boston: MIT Press, 1961.

HORNGREN, C. G., *Cost Accounting: A Managerial Emphasis*. (5th ed.). Englewood Cliffs, N.J.: Prentice-Hall, 1982.

IJIRI, Y., *The Foundations of Accounting Measurement*. Englewood Cliffs, N.J.: Prentice-Hall, 1967.

IJIRI, Y., AND R. K. JAEDICKE, "Reliability and Objectivity of Accounting Measurements," *Accounting Review*, July 1966.

IJIRI, Y., F. K. LEVY, AND R. C. LYON, "A Linear Programming Model for Budgeting and Financial Planning," *Journal of Accounting Research*, Autumn 1963, pp. 198–212.

LEE, L. C., AND N. M. BEDFORD, "An Information Theory Analysis of the Accounting Process," *Accounting Review*, April 1969.

LEV, BARUCH, *Financial Statement Analysis: A New Approach*. Englewood Cliffs, N.J.: Prentice-Hall, 1974.

LIBBY, ROBERT, *Accounting and Human Information Processing: Theory and Applications*. Englewood Cliffs, N.J.: Prentice-Hall, 1981.

LOBO, GERALD, AND MICHAEL MOHER, eds., *Information Economics and Accounting Research*. Ann Arbor: University of Michigan, 1980.

MCCOSH, ANDREW M., AND M. S. SCOTT MORTON, *Management Decision Support Systems*. New York: Macmillan, 1978.

MASON, R. O., "Basic Concepts for Designing Management Information Systems." AIS Research Paper No. 8, October 1969.

MOCK, THEODORE J., AND HUGH D. GROVE, *Measurement, Accounting, and Organizational Information*. New York: John Wiley, 1979.

RAIFFA, H., AND R. SCHLAIFFER, *Applied Statistical Decision Theory*. Boston: Harvard University Press, 1961.

RAPPAPORT, A., "Sensitivity Analysis in Decision Making," *Accounting Review*, July 1967.

RAPPAPORT, ALFRED, ED., *Information for Decision Making: Quantitative and Behavioral Dimensions* (3rd ed.). Englewood Cliffs, N.J.: Prentice-Hall, 1982.

"Reindustrialization of America," *Business Week*, June 30, 1980.

SHANNON, C. E., AND W. WEAVER, *The Mathematical Theory of Communication*. Urbana: University of Illinois Press, 1964.

SIMON, HERBERT A., *Administrative Behavior* (3rd ed.). New York: Free Press, 1976.

THEIL, H., "On the Use of Information Theory Concepts in the Analysis of Financial Statements," *Management Science*, May 1969.

WAGNER, G. R., "The Future of Corporate Planning and Modeling Software Systems." Paper presented at the Corporate Planning Models Conference at Duke University, 1981.

WAGNER, W. M., *Principles of Operations Research*. Englewood Cliffs, N.J.: Prentice-Hall, 1969.

WHEELWRIGHT, STEVEN C., AND SPYROS G. MAKRIDAKIS, *Computer Aided Modeling for Managers*. Reading, Mass.: Addison-Wesley, 1972.

APPENDIX: THE VALUE OF INFORMATION[1]

To illustrate the use of decision tables, consider two alternative management actions in a simple breakeven context. Both alternatives have a selling price of $5 per unit. Alternative A_1 has a variable cost of $4 per unit and a total fixed cost of $500,000. Alternative A_2 has a variable cost of only $3 per unit and a total fixed cost of $1,200,000. In the former case the unit contribution is $1 per unit, and in the latter case it is $2 per unit; the breakeven points are 500,000 and 600,000 units, respectively. Clearly, higher sales will favor A_2 and lower sales will favor A_1. The problem is that higher sales of 1,000,000 units and lower sales of 600,000 units are equally probable as far as management is concerned. Each alternative contribution to profit is analyzed in Table A4–1. Given this example, there are *two questions* facing management:

Table A4-1   Decision Table: Contribution to Profit Analysis—Cost-Volume-Profit Analysis of Alternatives

	EVENTS	
	High Sales	Low Sales
ACTION	Resulting Contribution to Profit	
A_1	$500,000*	$100,000
A_2	800,000	0

*Sample calculation:
  Unit contribution=$5/unit−$4/unit=$1/unit
  Total contribution=1,000,000 units×$1/unit= $1,000,000
  Less fixed costs   (500,000)
  Expected Total contribution to *profit* $ 500,000

Management Activities Summary

Management Actions:

  Alternative A_1
    Selling price $5/unit, variable costs $4/unit, and fixed costs $500,000
    Unit contribution $1/unit, and breakeven 500,000 units

  Alternative A_2
    Selling price $5/unit, variable cost $3/unit, and fixed cost $1,200,000
    Unit contribution $2/unit, and breakeven 600,000 units

[1] With permission this illustration is based in part on "Report of the Committee on Managerial Decision Models," *The Accounting Review Supplement* vol. XLIV (1969).

1. Should more information be bought? (Should the firm pay for an information system that will give management a better feel for the level of sales?)
2. Which action will maximize contribution to profit? (Other situations could require management to minimize costs, maximize sales, or optimize other objective criteria.)

To decide what action is preferable given *only* the information in Table A4–2, management uses the following procedure:

1. The expected value of each action is calculated by multiplying the contribution to profit for each alternative possible for each event by the probability of the event's occurrence. For example, the expected value of alternative A_1 is the contribution to profit for A_1 for the high sales condition ($500,000) times the probability of high sales (.5), plus the contribution to profit for the low sales condition ($100,000), times the probability of low sales (.5). The expected value of alternative A_1 is therefore $300,000.
2. Because management wishes to maximize contribution, alternative A_2 (higher fixed costs and lower variable costs) is selected. This alternative yields the higher expected contribution to profit.

To answer the first question about the potential value of added information, we must analyze how the added information will affect the decision process, the costs associated with the added information, and the information system needed to provide it to management. The value of the information is related to its ability to reduce the uncertainty surrounding the choice of courses of action. Such an analysis should proceed by first considering the value of *perfect information*. In the case of perfect information, the information sys-

Table A4-2 Decision Table: Expected Values for Contribution to Profit for Alternatives A_1 and A_2 Given No Information

	EVENTS		EXPECTED VALUE OF CONTRIBUTION*
	High Sales 1,000,000 units	Low Sales 600,000 units	
Probability	.5	.5	
ACTION	CONTRIBUTION TO PROFIT		
A_1	$500,000	$100,000	$300,000
A_2	800,000	0	400,000

* Expected value $A_1 = E(A_1) = \$500,000(.5) + \$100,000(.5) = \$300,000$
Expected value $A_2 = E(A_2) = \$800,000(.5) + 0(.5) = \$400,000$

tem will give the decision maker perfect foresight upon receipt of the signal from the system. This perfect foresight eliminates the possibility of making a wrong choice. The signal in the example considered above is whether there will be high or low sales. This signal cannot be known prior to its receipt and the probability of high or low sales, in this case a 50 percent chance of each sales event, will not change. *After* the decision maker receives the information, the course of action yielding the highest contribution will be chosen. The procedure for determining the value of this "perfect" information or "forecast" is as follows:

1. Select the action that will yield the highest contribution to profit for each possible forecast. Specifically, if the new information indicates low sales, alternative A_1 is preferable because it will yield a $100,000 contribution, whereas A_2 will yield 0. Likewise, if high sales are forecast, A_2 is preferable, as indicated in Table A4–2.

2. Calculate the expected value of each action choice, since it is *not* known in advance which perfect forecast will come out of the information system. For each forecast, this is accomplished by multiplying the contribution of the action that would have been chosen given a particular forecast by the information system, as shown in Table A4–3.

3. Add the expected values of each action to get a total expected value for the perfect information. The total expected value for perfect information in this example, shown in Table A4–3, is $450,000.

4. Finally, the value of the perfect information provided by the forecast is calculated by subtracting the expected value of the action taken with no information from Table A4–2 from the expected value of the perfect information calculated in step 3 above. In this example, we calculate the value of the perfect information to be $450,000 − $400,000 = $50,000, where $450,000 is the expected value of perfect information

Table A4-3 Decision Table: Perfect Information—Expected Values for Contribution to Profit for Alternatives A_1 and A_2 Given Perfect Information

	EVENTS		EXPECTED VALUE OF CONTRIBUTION*
	1,000,000 units	600,000 units	
Probability	.5	.5	
ACTION	CONTRIBUTION TO PROFIT		
A_1		$100,000	$50,000
A_2	$800,000		400,000
Total expected value of perfect information			$450,000

* $E(A_1) = .5(0) + .5(\$100,000) = \$50,000$
$E(A_2) = .5(\$800,000) + .5(0) = \$400,000$

from Table A4–3 and $400,000 is the expected value from Table A4–2 for the best choice, A_2, which could be made without any information.

Any system costing more than the value of perfect information, which eliminates the possibility of making a wrong decision, can be rejected immediately as costing more than it can possibly benefit the firm.

Most information is not perfect but is *imperfect information*. Consider an information system that *may* yield a more optimistic forecast for high sales, a forecast of a stable sales level, or a more pessimistic forecast for low sales. The information is relevant in the sense that the probabilities associated with potential outcomes (events) are altered given the information provided by the system. For example, assume that an 80 percent conditional probability is now associated with high sales given an optimistic forecast, and a 20 percent conditional probability is associated with low sales given this forecast. Given a pessimistic forecast, assume a 20 percent conditional probability for high sales and an 80 percent conditional probability for low sales.

Calculation of the value of the imperfect information proceeds as follows:

1. The *revised expected values* of each action are calculated as was done in Table A4–3 for the decision given no information. This is done for each possible outcome from the system and for each action. In this example, one outcome, the stable sales forecast, has the value that was calculated with no information. Only the expected values for the optimistic and pessimistic forecasts are calculated.

2. As before, the action with the greatest expected value is selected for each alternative. For the optimistic, same, and pessimistic forecasts, the actions chosen in this example are A_2, A_2, and A_1, respectively, as shown in Tables A4–2 and A4–4. For example, if an optimistic forecast is obtained from the information system, alternative A_2 should be chosen because it yields the greatest expected contribution to profit ($640,000). The $640,000 is calculated as before: .8($800,000 + .2(0) = $640,000.

3. Management must next estimate the probability of each type of forecast or report. This is necessary to assess the expected value of the imperfect information. For example, assume that in this case management estimated the probabilities of pessimistic, same, and optimistic forecasts as .4, .2, and .4, respectively.

4. Next the expected value of contribution to profit for the alternative that would be chosen for each type of forecast is weighted by its respective probability, as shown in Table A4–5. The calculation is .4($640,000) + .2($400,000) + .4($180,000) = $408,000. In other words, a system that would generate this information has a total value with respect to contribution to profit of $408,000. Finally, the expected value of the imperfect information, as shown in Table A4–5, is compared with the expected value of the action chosen given no information, as shown in Table A4–2. The value of the imperfect information is the amount of the expected value of the imperfect information less the expected value of the action given no information. In this example,

Table A4-4   Decision Table: Imperfect Information—Expected Values of Contribution to Profit for Alternatives A₁ and A₂ Given Optimistic and Pessimistic Imperfect Information

	EVENTS		EXPECTED VALUE OF CONTRIBUTION
	High Sales 1,000,000 Units	*Low Sales 600,000 Units*	
Optimistic probability	.8	.2	
ACTION	CONTRIBUTION TO PROFIT		
A_1	$500,000	$100,000	$420,000
A_2	800,000	0	640,000
Pessimistic probability	.2	.8	
ACTION	CONTRIBUTION TO PROFIT		
A_1	$500,000	$100,000	$180,000
A_2	800,000	0	160,000

that value is $408,000 - $400,000 = $8,000$. In other words, the value of the new system is $8,000 given this set of reports or forecasts with their estimated probabilities of occurrence, sales levels, and alternative actions.

If the system yielding the imperfect information costs less than $8,000, it should be implemented. Otherwise its costs exceed its benefits and it should not be implemented. Note that the value of the system is totally dependent upon the potential alternative actions, the cost behavior patterns of these alternatives, the reports generated by the system, and the probabilities and conditional probabilities associated with these reports. This will always be the case, and the accountant or systems designer must always be cognizant of these factors when considering the economic value of an information system.

Table A4-5   Decision Table: Expected Value of Imperfect Information—Predictions from New Information System

	PESSIMISTIC	SAME	OPTIMISTIC	EXPECTED VALUE OF CONTRIBUTION
PROBABILITY	.4	.2	.4	
ACTION	CONTRIBUTION TO PROFIT FOR OPTIMAL COURSE OF ACTION FOR EACH PREDICTION			
A_1	$180,000			$ 72,000
A_2		$400,000	$640,000	$336,000
Total expected value of imperfect information				$408,000

REVIEW QUESTIONS

1. According to Simon, what is the first step in the decision-making process and what implication does this have for accounting information systems?

2. Explain why Mason's framework or other such frameworks for decision-making activities are useful for systems design.

3. At what point in the decision-making process are models, such as break-even analysis, located? In what type of system would you expect to find breakeven analysis used?

4. What assumptions are necessary for the use of decision models in the decision process?

5. Contrast an *open* and a *closed* system.

6. When are *predictive information systems* useful? What must be true of the environment and what are the assumptions?

7. What must be quantifiable for a *decision-making information system*?

8. What are the essential steps in the measurement process and why is knowledge of these steps important in the design of an accounting system?

9. Contrast transmission, semantic, and effectiveness problems of communication.

10. How do the concepts of quasi-resolution of conflict, uncertainty avoidance, problemistic search, and organizational learning have an influence on an accountant in the design of an accounting system?

11. Contrast *heuristic* and *analytic* cognitive styles and their influence on an accounting system.

12. How do you assess the value of perfect information and how is this important to accountants as they prepare to design accounting systems?

EXERCISES AND CASES

4–1

Wright Manufacturing Company employs a computer-based data processing system for maintaining all company records. The present system was developed in stages over the past five years and has been fully operational for the past two years.

When the system was being designed, all department heads were asked to specify the types of information and reports they would need for planning and controlling operations. Moreover, they were asked to specify the assumptions and decision criteria for some of the information. The systems department attempted to meet the specifications of each department head. Company management specified that certain other reports be prepared for department heads. During the five years of systems development and operation, there have been several changes in the department head positions because of attrition and promotions. The new department heads often made requests for additional reports according to their needs. The systems department complied with

all of these requests. Reports were discontinued only upon request by a department head, and then only if it was not a standard report required by top management. As a result, few reports were actually discontinued and the data processing system was generating a large quantity of reports each reporting period.

Company management became concerned about the quantity of information that was being produced by the system. The internal audit department was asked to evaluate the effectiveness of the reports generated by the system. The audit staff determined early in the study that more information was being generated by the data processing system than could be used effectively. They noted the following reactions to this information overload:

1. Many department heads would not act on certain reports during periods of peak activity. The department head would let these reports accumulate until he or she had sufficient time to analyze the data.

2. Some department heads had so many reports that they could not filter out the rel-

evant information for timely decision making.

3. Frequently reports were ignored because department heads did not agree with the assumptions underlying the analysis of the data.

4. Department heads would often develop the information they needed from alternative, independent sources, rather than utilizing the reports generated by the data processing system. This was often easier than trying to search among the reports for the needed data.

REQUIRED: From the decision process outlined in the text, outline the problems associated with the new system. Briefly note how you would suggest that the company remedy these problems. (Adapted from the CMA Examination)

4-2

Fargo Creek Chemical Company, a vertically integrated chemical processing company, specializes in agricultural chemicals such as pesticides and fertilizer. The company is organized functionally into a manufacturing division, a distribution and warehouse division, and a marketing division. The corporate budget is usually prepared by first working with a sales forecast. Then the distribution of resources is made, based on these forecasts. From this distribution, inventory decisions are made. These budgets are finally forwarded to the manufacturing division, which produces the company's chemical products from natural gas and petroleum products. This system of manually prepared budgets has worked well for years.

The high cost of gas and petroleum products, however, recently caused Fargo Creek's corporate management to question the profitability of some of its products. The marketing manager was asked to work with the manufacturing manager in developing a new budget based on an assessment of each product's contribution to the company. After a week of discussion, these managers both submitted a letter of resignation. Each stated that it was not possible to work with the other and that they needed more support for their decision making.

Why did these problems never occur before? Given your answer to this question, should Fargo Creek try to coordinate its activity? As its accountant, corporate management has asked for your assistance in reconciling this sticky budgeting problem. What brief comments would you have for management from an organizational and behavioral point of view as well as from a decision support perspective? (From your previous visits to Fargo Creek, you would have classified its information system as a data bank system.)

4-3

Smith, Davis, and Davis Brokers, Inc., has recently installed a new security analysis system that calculates how each security price moves relative to a market index and even calculates "optimal" portfolios for clients who have particular risk-and-return preferences. The system also displays coded reports pertaining to a company's earnings, product acquisitions, financial activities, management decisions, asset acquisitions, and so on. It is very efficient and quickly gives feedback to individual brokers while they are advising their clients.

Many of the brokers really like the new system; however, others miss the older, more-detailed reports that formed the basis of their "hunches," which they claim have had a major impact on their success as brokers. Moreover, some of the clients don't like the new system's analytic approach and don't trust the models.

From a behavioral and a decision-making perspective, what have the systems designers and analysts overlooked, if anything?

4-4

The management of Cabin Creek Chemical Company has recently had considerable difficulty in sorting through the large volume of computer output while trying to schedule manufacturing processes. Cabin Creek has had a series of problems such as insufficient raw materials, lost sales due to late deliveries, and idle plant facilities over the past few years. These problems have prompted management to ask for some assistance in allocating manufacturing resources.

Currently, management receives information on

Sales forecasts

Inventory (raw chemical stock, in-process chemicals, and manufactured products)

Machine and plant capabilities

Labor resources

Maintenance schedules

Can you advise management on any changes it should consider in its information and decision support system and why these changes should be made?

4-5

Fresno Valley Frozen Foods management has had considerable difficulty in planning its operations (sales, distribution, and manufacturing) each year due to the large volume of detailed data on supplies of produce and marketing and distribution requirements. The relationships between the supply and marketing data have become too complex for Fresno Valley's management to comprehend.

Fresno Valley currently has what could be classified as a data bank system. What level of decision support would you recommend that it consider? Why? What assumptions are necessary for this level of support?

4-6

The management of ABC Retailers is constantly faced with decisions regarding sales promotions. ABC's management is considering an information system that would generate market information and would cost approximately $30,000 per market survey, and it is trying to assess the value of the information generated by this system. A "typical" sales promotion decision for ABC's business involves the following information, which is now obtainable by the company: With promotion there is a 60 percent chance of a sales increase and a 40 percent chance of no sales increase. The sales increase will result in a $500,000 contribution to profit and fixed costs. The promotion expenditure is $300,000 and is considered a fixed cost. Without promotion there is a 0 percent chance of a sales increase and a 100 percent chance of no sales increase. Adoption of the new information system would add the following information:

1. The expected results of a survey may be positive or negative. If positive, the results are expected to show a 90 percent chance of a sales increase with promotions. If negative, results are expected to show a 30 percent chance of a sales increase with promotions. There will therefore be a 10 percent and a 70 percent respective chance of no increase in sales for the two possible survey results.

2. The probability of a positive survey is 50 percent, and the probability of a negative survey is 50 percent.

ABC's management has asked you, its accountant, to assist in the analysis and comment on the following:

a. Should ABC Retailers use sales promotions, given no information other than what it currently has for a typical case?

b. What is the maximum amount ABC should pay for the additional information generated by the new system in the typical case?

c. Given positive or negative survey results, what action should it take in each case for the typical situation noted here?

d. Should ABC adopt the market survey information system?

4-7

Ohio Valley and Citizens National Bank has twenty branch offices in addition to the home office in River City. Management receives daily transaction summaries from all the branches. Ohio Valley's management is proud of the system that generates this information. These summaries include not only the withdrawals, deposits, transfers, loans, and other typical bank transactions but also many ratios, statistical analyses, and even profit-and-loss statements for each branch.

One day, however, a power outage in River City prevented the EDP department from receiving the ratio, statistical, and financial analysis information at the home office. Much to its surprise, the EDP department never received a phone call asking for the missing information. This was particularly discouraging to the EDP manager. The transaction summary information that was forwarded was exactly the same as the information generated by a previous manual system and consisted of a three-page summary for each branch and totals for the entire bank. The new automated system had been designed to ensure that the home office would receive this information daily.

Should Ohio Valley and Citizens National Bank be proud of this new system? Do you have any suggestions for improving the system, given that many banking decisions are rather routine and assumptions are easily specified?

4–8

Seventy-Six Frozen Seafood Wholesalers needed a system to control its inventory. Carrying costs were extremely high because frozen-food lockers were expensive to build and operate, especially given the high cost of energy. As a result, management asked your firm to help it establish a simple automatic EOQ (economic order quantity) system so that it would know when to order and how much to order. Your firm complied with this request. As manager of the project, you found the average usage rates and average lead times for each item in stock, calculated the cost of processing an order and storing the frozen seafood item, and established an optimal reorder point and quantity for each item. You also added a small buffer stock for each item in case more than an average usage rate was encountered during the period between the reorder point and ultimate delivery of the item. You presented this plan to the management of Seventy-Six Frozen Seafood. In summary, your plan suggested great reductions in the current stock of many items. Management balked at implementing this automatic reorder point system. Management felt that with so little stock the company would constantly stock out because of the great uncertainty in demand and delivery schedules from the docks.

1. How would you convince management to try the system?
2. Could it be that the managers are correct

and you have overlooked some aspects of the problem?
3. What must be true for this type of automatic system to be implemented successfully?

4–9

King's Mountain Quarries, Inc., a large extractor of rock, aggregate, gravel, sand, and other rock products used in the construction industry, has several quarries throughout northern Georgia, western North Carolina, and eastern Tennessee. The firm uses an annual budget to communicate its plans to quarry managers. Monthly budgets detail the amount and type of aggregate quarry managers should extract, process, stockpile, and deliver. Managers are rewarded on how well they meet their budgets. They are, however, expected to react to special orders as they arrive so that the company will not lose any lucrative contracts. Quarry managers are expected to maintain their equipment, train their subordinates, and find new quarry locations within their geographic area. On the other hand, they are expected to keep costs to a minimum.

Corporate management, after a few years of operating under this budget system, has discovered several types of managerial behavior leading to the following typical results:

Manager A—meets budget, but equipment is in disrepair

Manager B—meets budget, but no new rock locations were found

Manager C—costs exceeded budget, but equipment is in good repair

Manager D—costs exceeded budget, but three new quarry locations were found

Manager E—costs are less than budget, but equipment is in disrepair and no new gravel pits were found

Managers C and D—resigned due to low salary and bonus

Corporate management was distraught because C and D were the two finest managers it had. What led to these problems in terms of the desire to communicate objectives via the budget information system?

4-10

Jackson EMC, a corporate utility company, uses two decision models. First, it produces or purchases kilowatts to meet demand fluctuations; if demand goes up, it either places more generators into service or purchases the necessary kilowatts from nearby Alabama Power and Light. However, during peak demand periods Jackson switches to a consumer volunteer load-management system where it can shut down air conditioners for twenty-minute periods by transmitting signals to devices attached to the air-conditioning units. Somehow Jackson must plan for this and decide when to switch from an objective of meeting demand to one of smoothing demand. What types of cybernetic feedback systems are used in this case? Explain. What types of information systems do you think would be necessary to support the demand compliance, demand smoothing, and switch and overload decisions noted above?

5

ELECTRONIC DATA PROCESSING TECHNOLOGY

INTRODUCTION

In Chapter 1 we identified three dimensions of information processing: (1) systems elements, (2) managerial activities, and (3) organizational functions. In Chapter 2 we noted that in designing an information system, these dimensions should be synthesized into a framework, particularly if the "systems view" of information processing is employed. A conceptual framework for synthesizing the dimensions was given (refer to Figure 2–4). In this chapter we will examine one of the dimensions of the framework, the systems elements dimension.

      Recall from Chapter 1 that the *elements* of a system consist of (1) hardware, (2) software, (3) data base, (4) procedures, and (5) personnel. Basic concepts relating to personnel were discussed in Chapter 3. Decision-making and data processing activities (procedures) were discussed in Chapter 4 and will be further discussed in Chapters 12, 13, and 15. Data base concepts are covered in Chapter 8. This chapter, therefore, will focus on hardware and software concepts. Specifically, we will examine the basic physical components that make up a computer system (the central processing unit, input/output devices, and storage devices) and the computer programs that are employed in data processing.

Both this chapter and Chapter 6 deal with hardware and software concepts. In this chapter fundamental hardware and software concepts are presented, with the emphasis on "batch" processing. In Chapter 6 we will focus on "real-time" systems and distributed processing systems and the hardware associated with these systems.

HARDWARE COMPONENTS

Central Processing Unit

The central processing unit (CPU) is the focal point of an EDP system. It controls the entire data processing (hardware) system and performs arithmetic and logical operations on data. The CPU includes a *control section*, an *arithmetic-logic unit*, and a *high-speed storage unit* (primary storage).

To better understand the structure and function of the CPU as well as the overall computer, we can view the "computer" in the block diagram form shown in Figure 5–1. A computer system consists of six basic items: (1) an input medium or device, (2) primary storage, (3) an arithmetic-logic unit, (4) a control unit, (5) secondary storage devices, and (6) an output medium or device.

These items can be described as follows:

1. *Input medium.* Data, as well as the instructions for handling the data, are input to the computer and are made available to the CPU via an input device such as a card reader or a magnetic tape reader.

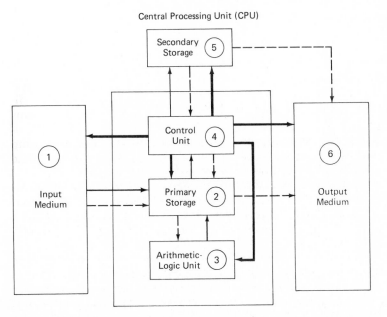

Central Processing Unit (CPU)

Figure 5-1 Block Diagram of a Computer

Note: Data flows are represented by — —▶
Instruction flows are represented by ——▶
Control flow is indicated by ——▶

2. *Primary storage.* Data and instructions received from input devices are transferred to the main (primary) storage section of the CPU. Instructions from the control section and results from the arithmetic-logic section of the CPU also reside in primary storage. When a software program is executed (run), this occurs in primary storage in conjunction with the arithmetic-logic and control units.

3. *Arithmetic-logic unit.* All computational processing in the computer (the manipulation of data in accordance with given instructions) occurs in the arithmetic-logic unit. The computational operations include addition, subtraction, multiplication, division, and logic operations such as comparing the magnitude of numbers.

4. *Control unit.* The focal point of the CPU is the control unit. The input devices, primary storage, secondary storage, arithmetic-logic unit, and output devices all interact to perform a data processing task. The control section's role is to coordinate all the components of the computer. Specifically, the control section (a) indicates to the input medium when data are needed by primary storage and the type and quantity of data needed; (b) indicates where the data entering primary storage (from the input medium) are to be stored; (c) informs the arithmetic-logic section when a computational operation is required, the type operation required, where the associated data are to be found, and where to store the results; (d) "flags" the appropriate secondary storage device indicating where the data are to be found and what data to access; and (e) indicates to the specific output medium which results are to be displayed.

5. *Secondary storage.* Because primary storage is expensive relative to other storage devices and because it is not necessary that all data at all times reside in primary storage, secondary storage devices (such as magnetic tapes, disks, and data cards) were developed. Quite often these can be "added on" to a computer system as needed, whereas primary storage is usually defined when the computer system is designed.

6. *Output medium.* Results from the data processed in the CPU are output (reported or stored) in some form. Several output media such as printers, CRT terminals, and microfilm may be used.

When comparing one computer system with another, factors such as size, speed, and cost are often considered. These terms generally relate to the CPU. When manufacturers state the size of their computer, it is the size of the primary storage section of the CPU to which they refer. The maximum size of a program and the associated data available for processing at any one time is mainly determined by the size of primary storage; therefore the size of primary storage has a large bearing on the computer's capability to process the program.

Primary storage is structured so that each storage location has a unique address. To store or access data or instructions, we must therefore employ a specific storage address. Although all data are stored in a computer in a binary form, or *bit* as it is commonly called, the smallest addressable location in primary storage is not a single binary digit (bit). This is because a series of binary digits are required to store a decimal number or an alphabetic character in binary form. Thus the basic storage unit of most computers is a *byte*. A byte is made up of either six or eight or more bits (plus an additional parity or check bit) depending upon the design of the computer. The byte arrangement is fixed for a given computer but can be strung together in different ways to provide structures of varying length. Within the byte structure, each byte of primary storage is addressable and the number of addressable bytes determines the *size* of primary memory. Therefore a computer with 32K memory (where *K* is the metric notation for thousands) has approximately 32,000 bytes of addressable main storage in the CPU.

As we have noted, size is not the only factor that must be examined when evaluating the CPU. Speed is also important. Speed of the CPU is measured by two factors: (1) access time and (2) execution time. *Access time* refers to the time it takes the control section to locate and retrieve data and instructions for processing. Access time is measured in microseconds[1] for most modern computers, although costly technology exists in which access time is measured in nanoseconds.[2] *Execution time* is the time interval required to execute an instruction in the arithmetic-logic unit. An instruction is obtained from primary storage and transferred to the arithmetic-logic unit (access time). Here it is decoded according to its *operation code*, which specifies the address of the data to be operated upon. The decoded instruction is then executed using the data specified in the instruction. Execution times in modern computers vary from less than one microsecond to several hundred microseconds.

In developing computer systems, access time and execution time are considered jointly because the *total* cycle time (access time plus execution time) is what actually determines the speed of the CPU. In addition, cost trade-offs exist between access time and execution time. Therefore in determining the cost per bit of data (stored and processed), we must consider both factors.

The key cost factor of the CPU is primary storage, or memory. Magnetic cores (very tiny doughnut-shaped ferrite rings that can be magnetized in either a clockwise or a counterclockwise direction) were the predominant form of primary storage throughout the 1960s and early 1970s. Semiconductor memories (which are structured by taking a tiny chip of silicon and inscribing a number of miniature circuits, each of which may be "conducting" or "not conducting") first appeared in 1971. Semiconductor memory is smaller and faster than magnetic core memory but has traditionally been more expensive. Today a number of medium-sized computer systems exist with semiconductor memories. Because of the cost factor, semiconductor memories, though fast and small, have mainly been employed in primary storage. Semiconductor memories are seldom employed in secondary storage devices.

Additional memory storage devices also exist. These include bubble memory, large-scale integration (LSI), thin film, holographics, magnetic disks, and others. All of these devices vary in size, speed, and cost. In general, decreases in primary memory size and increase in performance (speed) correspond to increases in cost. The computer hardware elements that make up the overall computer system and other multiprocessor configurations can often be

---

[1] A *microsecond* is one/one-millionth of a second, or .000001 seconds.

[2] A *nanosecond* is one/thousand-millionth of a second, or .000000001 seconds.

combined to provide the maximum-performance/least-cost system, however. These and other CPU concepts are discussed later in the chapter.

Input/Output Devices

As we indicated in the preceding discussion of the CPU and in Figure 5–1, input and output devices are also integral hardware components. A number of input and output mediums (devices) exist. Figure 5–2 illustrates the vari-

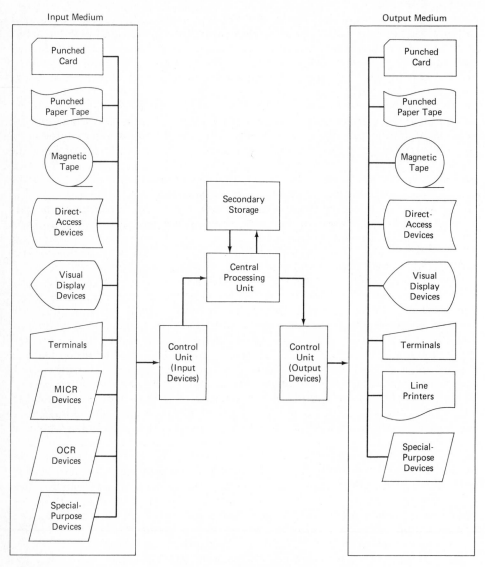

Figure 5-2 Input/Output Devices Employed in a Computer System

ous types of input and output devices found in a computer system. In the figure, magnetic tape, direct-access devices, and special-purpose devices are shown as both input and output devices. These devices can also serve as secondary storage devices, which will be discussed later in this chapter.

Typically, input and output devices are classified as either slow-speed or high-speed. Card readers, direct-input devices, card punches, and printers are slow-speed devices. Magnetic tape units and direct-access devices (disk storage drives, drum storage units, data-cell drives, and others) are high-speed devices. These, as well as other devices, are described below.

Card reader. In the 1960s and 1970s most computer systems were primarily card input systems, or "batch systems." Card-reading devices feed a single card at a time through either a metal brush or a photoelectric cell-reading mechanism that converts the data on the card into electronic form. Card-reading speeds vary from about 12 to 1,000 cards per minute, depending on the type of card reader. A typical card reader operates at a speed of 500 cards per minute.

The processing of data onto and from cards is referred to as a *unit-record concept*, in which all data relating to a transaction are recorded on a single document, the punched card. Figure 5–3 illustrates the standard 80-column punched card utilized in most card input systems.

Although the commercial use of punched cards only dates back to the mid-1950s, the punched-card code shown in the figure and utilized in most card-reading devices was invented in the 1880s by Herman Hollerith, a U.S. Census Bureau statistician. Hollerith later founded the Tabulating Machine Company, which after several mergers changed its name to International Business Machines Corporation in 1924.

Card punches. Output, if stored on cards, is recorded via a card-punching device. Card-punch unit speeds vary from 15 to 500 cards per minute, depending on whether a serial punch operation (column by column) or a parallel punch operation (row by row) is employed. In many cases card-reading and card-punching devices are combined into one unit.

Punched-paper-tape readers–punches. Input and output of data can be accomplished by using punched paper tape in much the same manner as punched cards. A hole combination code is employed, which is different from the Hollerith code shown in Figure 5–3.

Paper tapes use five, six, seven, or eight rows (or channels) in their coding structures. Each tape structure employs a different hole combination code. All code structures include a parity check bit. Figure 5–4 illustrates a five-channel and an eight-channel code. The check bit is actually not part of the code for a character but is simply used in checking the accuracy of each character.

The tape feeds through a read unit in a punched-paper-tape reader. The presence or absence of holes in the tape is sensed and converted to electronic pulses that are then accepted as data inputs. Paper-tape readers are available that have reading speeds varying from 150 to 1,000 characters per second, depending on the tape reader. A rate of 1,000 characters per second is roughly equivalent to a rate of 750 punched cards per minute.

When data from the CPU are to be output onto paper tape, they are decoded to paper-tape code (within the paper-tape punch) and punched onto a

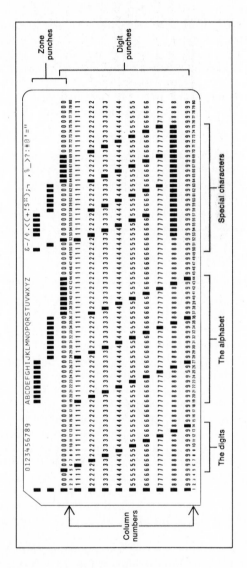

Figure 5-3 Standard Eighty-Column Punched Card

Courtesy of IBM Corporation

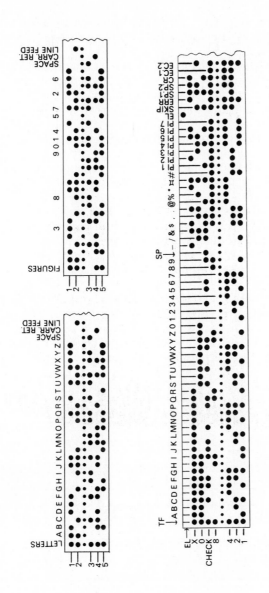

Figure 5-4 Code for Five-Channel and Eight-Channel Paper Tape

From *Information Processing* by Marilyn Bohl, ©1980, 1976, 1971, Science Research Associates, Inc. Reprinted by permission of the publisher.

new tape as it moves through a punch mechanism. The tape is punched with a density of 10 characters to the inch and at a rate of 15 to 150 characters per second, depending on the type of punch.

Paper-tape readers and punches are often combined into a single input/output unit, in much the same fashion as combined card readers and punches.

Magnetic tape. Magnetic tape is a primary input/output medium for data processing systems. It is also used extensively for storing large files of data between processing runs.

Data are recorded on magnetic tape as magnetized dots (called bits) rather than as holes (which is the case for punched cards and punched paper tape). Therefore the data can be retained indefinitely if desired, or they can be erased automatically and the tape reused. A reel of tape is typically one-half inch in width and comes in lengths of up to 2,400 feet. When all capacity has been used, the data that can be stored on a magnetic tape are equivalent to approximately 500,000 punched cards.

Similar to paper tape, magnetic tape is structured in rows or tracks. Recall that in paper tapes these rows are referred to as *channels*. Magnetic tapes are available in 7-track or 9-track structures. Figure 5–5 illustrates the code structure for a 7-track tape. Note that a check (parity) bit is used in the structure, in much the same manner as that used with paper tapes.

Nine-track tapes differ from 7-track tapes in that two numeric characters, each using four bits, can be recorded in a single 9-track column. Therefore more data can be stored in the same physical space on a 9-track tape. The majority of tapes in use today are 9-track.

Data on magnetic tapes are read into or output (written) from the CPU by means of a magnetic tape drive unit (See Figure 5–6). Data are read or written as the tape moves, at a constant speed, past a read/write head. Operating speeds of existing tape drive units range from 60,000 to 1,250,000 characters per second. (Magnetic tape drives are also discussed in the "Secondary Storage Devices" section of this chapter.)

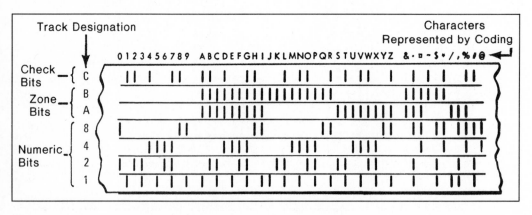

Figure 5-5   Code Structure Employed in a Seven-Track Magnetic Tape

From Feingold, Carl, *Introduction to Data Processing,* 3rd ed., ©1971, 1975, 1980, Wm. C. Brown Company Publishers, Dubuque, Iowa. Reprinted by permission.

Figure 5-6 Magnetic Tape Drive (Read/Write) Unit
Courtesy of IBM Corporation

Original (source) data can be recorded onto magnetic tape off-line from the computer via a keyboard-to-tape encoder. This device operates in a manner similar to that of the keypunch except that the data are recorded on magnetic tape instead of punched cards.

Other means exist for inputting the source data to tape. These include a microcomputer or minicomputer key-to-tape system, a key-to-disk-to-tape system, or a key-to-card-to-tape system. In the key-to-tape and the key-to-disk-to-tape systems, a minicomputer is tied to a number of magnetic drives; the source data are entered via the keyboard (terminal) of the minicomputer and are either written to the tape drive or written to the disk and then to the tape drive. A minicomputer system could also be used to read punched cards and output the source data onto magnetic tape. This latter task could be and often is performed on a large mainframe computer as a data preparation step.

Direct-access devices. Direct-access devices are primarily used as secondary storage devices rather than input/output devices; however, as we noted, direct-access disks can be used in conjunction with other input/output equipment to form "data preparation systems." A key direct-access device, which was first employed in the early 1970s in this manner, is a diskette, or "floppy disk." A *diskette* is a round flexible magnetic disk about eight inches in diameter with a hole in the center. The disk is encased in a permanent plastic envelope for protection, with a small oval-shaped opening to allow access by a read/write mechanism (see Figure 5–7). Data are recorded on one or both sides of a diskette in

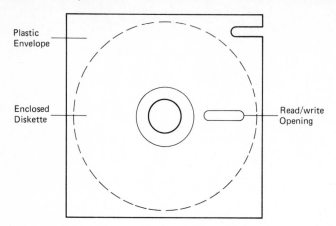

Plastic Envelope

Enclosed Diskette

Read/write Opening

Figure 5-7 A Standard Diskette

concentric circular tracks on its surface. Each diskette contains 77 tracks and when fully utilized can store up to 400,000 characters.

A diskette input/output unit, which is the actual direct-access device for reading and writing data to the diskette, has a high transfer rate. Equipment is currently available that allows reading and writing speeds of up to 4,000 records per minute. Most diskette input/output units are actually miniprocessors or microprocessors with an attached disk drive (read/write) unit. The disk drive portion of the system is relatively inexpensive. By attaching other peripheral equipment such as a telephone modem, tape drive, and printer, the system can serve as a terminal input/output device, can access a larger mainframe computer, or can stand alone as a small computer.

Other direct-access devices, such as drums, data cells, and large magnetic core storage devices, can also be used as input/output devices; however, as we noted earlier, these are primarily viewed as storage devices. (We will examine these devices in the "Secondary Storage Devices" section.)

Visual display/terminal devices. Two major types of devices fall under the heading "visual display/terminal devices": (1) the cathode ray tube, or CRT as it is traditionally called, and (2) the data terminal, or hard copy terminal. Figure 5–8 illustrates a CRT terminal. Figure 5–9 illustrates one type of data terminal.

Visual display, or CRT, terminals are widely used with mainframe, minicomputer, and microcomputer systems. In addition, the unit is used as a remote terminal where data are transferred from a remote location over telephone lines. The line speeds (transfer speed) for these devices occur at 120 or 240 characters per second.

Input to the CRT is entered by means of an alphanumeric keyboard. The input is buffered and immediately displayed on the screen. Before the data are forwarded to the CPU they can be corrected, erased entirely, or reentered. This capability is very useful for internal control. Under control of the CPU, output information can be displayed on the screen. If a hard copy printer is attached to the system, the output on the screen can be directed to the printer.

Figure 5-8 Cathode Ray Tube (CRT) Terminal

From *Information Processing* by Marilyn Bohl, ©1980, 1976, 1971, Science Research Associates, Inc. Reprinted by permission of the publisher.

The advantage of the data terminal over the CRT is that a "hard copy" of input/output is always available for future reference and audit trail. In addition, the data terminal is frequently equipped with magnetic tape read/write capabilities and a telephone modem, and therefore the unit can serve as a multifunction input/output unit. Data terminals are also an integral part of telecommunication and real-time processing systems.

Magnetic-ink character recognition (MICR) device. Data can be represented by magnetic-ink characters and symbols that are readable by both the computer and human beings; the technology is referred to as MICR. The primary application of MICR has been in the banking industry where account numbers, routing numbers, process control numbers, and the amount of the check are recorded with magnetic-ink characters. Figure 5–10 shows a sample check bearing magnetic-ink characters.

Optical character recognition (OCR) device. Data can also be recorded on and read from paper documents by means of optically readable characters. A basic, and probably the most familiar, optical readable character is a pencil mark, used on multiple-choice tests. Optical characters, however, are not limited to simply marks or dots. Most OCR devices can handle the letters of the alphabet, the ten decimal digits, and several other special characters such as standard product codes on retail store merchandise. (Point-of-sale systems that use this equipment are discussed in Chapter 13.)

Some principal applications of OCR devices include the reading of utility company billings, insurance premium notices, product codes, and sales invoices. Figure 5–11 illustrates an OCR utility bill. This particular form can be used to handle both full payment and partial payments, all automatically. If the

Figure 5-9 "Hard Copy" Data Terminal

Courtesy of IBM Corporation

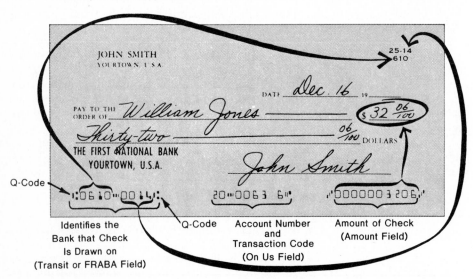

Figure 5-10 Magnetic-Ink Characters Utilized on a Personal Check

From Feingold, Carl, *Introduction to Data Processing,* 3rd ed., ©1971, 1975, 1980, Wm. C. Brown Company Publishers, Dubuque, Iowa. Reprinted by permission.

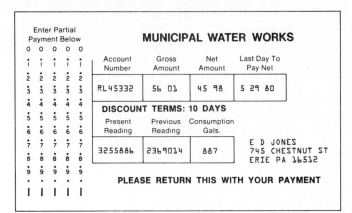

Figure 5-11 Utility Bill Employing OCR Structure

From *Information Processing* by Marilyn Bohl, © 1980, 1976, 1971, Science Research Associates, Inc. Reprinted by permission of the publisher.

bill is returned with full payment, the document is simply processed unmarked. If the bill is returned with partial payment, a clerk marks the amount of payment before the document is processed. The OCR reader reads both the hand-marked portion and the optical characters. Reading speeds of OCR devices range from 500 to 1,600 characters per second.

Printers. Several types of printers exist for outputting data from a computer system. As we noted in our discussion of terminal devices, a "hard copy" data terminal can be used to obtain printed output. Recall that the speeds of these devices vary from 120 to 240 characters per second. Microfilm devices, which use a photographic reduction process to produce output, can also be viewed as output printers, since the output is in printed form and can be stored for future reference. The output speeds of these devices range from 20,000 to 50,000 lines per minute. The true printer, or what is typically referred to as an output printer, is the electromechanical line printer which produces a line with up to 132 positions at speeds of up to 1,100 lines per minute.

At this point the obvious question regarding printers is, since high-speed output capability exists using photosensitive printing, such as that used with microfilm output, why are electromechanical devices used? Two reasons can be given to support the use of electromechanical, or *impact*, printers: (1) electromechanical printers are generally less expensive, and (2) they can produce multiple printed copies of the output document by using traditional carbon duplication methods. Photosensitive as well as other thermal or xerography devices can only produce single versions of the output document.

Secondary Storage Devices

The most common types of secondary storage devices available for use in data processing systems are (1) magnetic disks, (2) magnetic drums, (3) data cells, and (4) other mass-storage devices. Magnetic tape, in addition to being considered an input medium, is a highly utilized secondary storage device.

For operating purposes, secondary storage devices are categorized as either *sequential access* or *direct access* (random access).

A sequential-access storage device is one in which any single record stored on the medium can be accessed only after all other preceding records have been read or processed. If a file is created on a sequential device, all records in the file are maintained in sequential order, utilizing a name or number field common within each record. A magnetic tape is a sequential-access storage medium.

On direct-access storage devices any single record stored on the medium can be accessed directly without reading or processing other records. The file structure on these devices employs *primary* and *secondary* fields (or keys) for locating records, and therefore a file may or may not be ordered sequentially according to its "locator fields." Direct-access files are often maintained and available at all times in an "on-line mode." Magnetic disk, drum, data cells, and mass storage are all direct-access storage devices.

Magnetic tape. The storage capacity of a magnetic tape depends upon the density of the tape and the manner in which records are stored. The density of magnetic tape is represented by the number of characters recorded per inch, or *bytes* per inch if we are referring to the manner in which characters are represented in the CPU. The most common tape densities are 800 and 1,600 characters per inch, although tapes with densities of up to 6,250 characters per inch exist.

Use of a high-density tape does not necessarily mean that a large quantity of data can be stored on a small segment of tape unless an efficient record storage (blocking) procedure is employed. Each *physical* record that is written on or read from a tape is separated by a blank segment of tape (usually 1/2″ or 3/4″), referred to as an *interblock gap* (IBG). The tape drive used in reading or writing information stops and starts at each IBG. That half of the IBG preceding a record allows the tape unit to reach its operating speed before reading or writing. The first half of the IBG following a record allows time for the tape unit to decelerate after a read or write operation. The tape must be moving at its designated operating speed before it can be read from or written on; when the end of a record is reached, the unit must be stopped. The IBG allows for both procedures to occur.

If an 800-character-per-inch density tape is employed with a half-inch IBG, and 80-character records are to be stored on the tape, then 83.33 percent of the tape storage area as well as 83.33 percent of the processing-time will be consumed in processing the IBG. This occurs because each 80-character record requires 0.10 inches of tape (80 ÷ 800), and the IBG requires 0.50 inches of tape. In each 0.60-inch segment of tape, 0.10/0.60 (16.66 percent) of the length is used to store the record, and 0.50/0.60 (83.33 percent) of the length is consumed by the IBG.

To avoid this waste in storage and time, records can be grouped into a block. By grouping or blocking a number of records, most interblock gaps can be eliminated. Each block of record is preceded by an IBG. The number of records contained in a block is referred to as the *blocking factor*. For example, if five records were grouped into a block, the blocking factor would be 5. Using the example above, with a blocking factor of 5, each block of records would contain 400 characters; therefore, in each inch of tape 50 percent of the area (400/800) is utilized for storage and 50 percent (1/2 inch) of the area is consumed by the IBG. Storage space and access time are thus improved with blocking. By employing a large blocking factor, a large amount of data can be stored on a magnetic tape. A single reel of tape can hold up to 40 million characters. Based on 80 characters per card, which would mean that every column on the card was employed, this would be equivalent to 500,000 punched cards. Figure 5–12 illustrates the concepts of *blocked* and *unblocked* records.

When records are blocked, each single record in the block is referred to as a *logical record*; the complete block is referred to as a *physical record*. When the input/output device processes records, it handles physical records or the complete block of logical records. The CPU, however, processes one logical record at a time. Therefore, when a block of records is read from or written to tape, adequate storage space must be available in main memory to store the entire block. Fortunately the operating system software in the CPU controls the reading and writing of blocked records. It accepts single records from CPU processing and holds them until a block has been accumulated; or conversely, it can deblock a block of input records such that single records are made available to the CPU as needed.

In addition to being an efficient storage medium, magnetic tape is also relatively inexpensive. Typical costs for tape reels vary between $20 and $100, depending on the quality and kind of tape. In terms of storage cost, this means that approximately 10,000 characters cost less than $0.01.

Obviously the disadvantage of magnetic tape is that it is a sequential medium. Thus access to a particular record is obtained only after all preceding records have been read. If rapid direct access to specific records is required, magnetic tape is not the appropriate storage medium. However, we should not overlook the fact that tapes play an important role as a "backup storage" medium and are unchallenged for low-cost, high-capacity applications requiring only sequential access.

Magnetic disk. A magnetic disk storage unit is a device that contains magnetic disks and the mechanism for reading and writing data onto the disks. Disk storage, unlike tape storage, allows data to be read or written directly. Access to specific information is immediate; the preceding records in a file do not have to be examined.

A magnetic disk is a thin circular metal disk, similar to a phonograph record, coated on both sides with a magnetic recording material. Data are

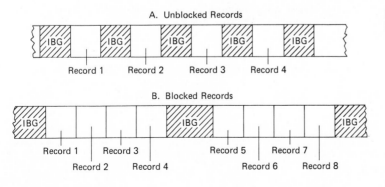

Figure 5-12 Blocked and Unblocked Records

stored on the disk by using the same general principle employed with magnetic tapes: Characters are formed by grouping a series of magnetized or nonmagnetized bits. Characters/bytes are grouped together to form words, and groupings of words form records. Physically, the disk is structured in a series of concentric circles called *tracks*. Records are grouped together and stored in the tracks.

In most disk storage units, several disks are stacked on a vertical shaft. Space is left between each disk to allow for the reading or writing of data on both the upper and lower surfaces of the disk. Data are accessed or written by a read/write head that can move to any location on the surface of the disk. Most disk units have one read/write head for each disk recording surface. The stacked set of disks referred to as a disk pack is removable from most disk drive systems; however, units do exist in which the pack is not removable. Figure 5–13 illustrates a disk access mechanism and a disk pack. Figure 5–14 illustrates a disk storage unit.

Data stored on a magnetic disk are accessible through a surface number, track number, and record number. Any record on any disk surface can be accessed directly, since the surface, track, and record numbers provide a unique address for each record. As with magnetic tape, each physical record on

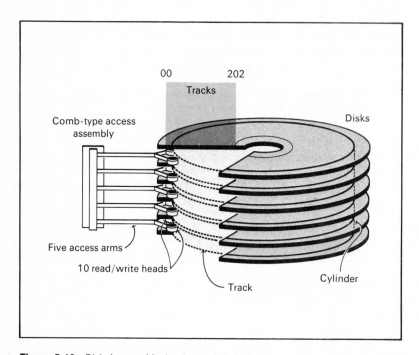

Figure 5-13   Disk Access Mechanism and Disk Pack

From *Information Processing* by Marilyn Bohl, ©1980, 1976, 1971, Science Research Associates, Inc. Reprinted by permission of the publisher.

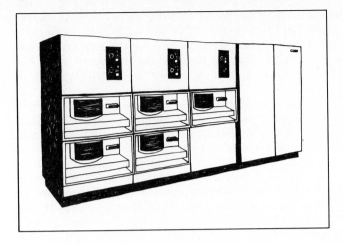

Figure 5-14 Disk Storage Unit

From *Information Processing* by Marilyn Bohl, ©1980, 1976, 1971, Science Research Associates, Inc. Reprinted by permission of the publisher.

disk is separated by interrecord gaps. To conserve storage space it is customary to block records, using the same general procedure employed with tapes.

The capacity of a disk pack depends upon the number of bytes per track, the number of tracks per surface, and the number of surfaces. Utilization of the capacity will obviously depend on how records are blocked. A disk pack with ten recording surfaces, each with 200 accessible tracks with 3,625 bytes per track, will provide storage for up to 7.25 million characters of data. A disk system consisting of eight on-line drives, each utilizing a disk pack with twenty recording surfaces having 200 tracks per surface and 7,294 bytes per track, will provide storage for more than 200 million bytes of data.

Costs, access time, and reading speeds of disk storage units vary widely, in much the same manner that the capacity of these units varies. The average annual cost to lease a single-drive disk unit ranges from $6,000 to well over $12,000. Individual packs with ten recording surfaces can be purchased for less than $200. The expensive portion of the system is the disk drive rather than the pack. The average time required for accessing a record (the time required to position the read/write head) ranges from 20 to 75 milliseconds, depending upon the drive employed. Data can actually be read or written at rates ranging from 156,000 bytes per second to over 1 million bytes per second. The total time for the entire operation (access time plus reading/writing) ranges from 40 to 100 milliseconds.

As we noted in our discussion of input/output devices, magnetic disks are also available in diskette, or "floppy disk," form. A diskette storage unit employs the data storage and access methods of the large magnetic disk system. A diskette unit, however, operates with a single diskette as opposed to a disk pack that contains multiple disks mounted on a spindle. In terms of data storage, the diskette has a much smaller storage capacity than the magnetic disk pack. The access and read/write times are also much slower. The diskette unit is more commonly used as a secondary storage device in small accounting information systems and microcomputer-based systems or as an input/output device.

The advantages of using the magnetic disk or the diskette rather than magnetic tape as a storage device are that (1) data can be organized and stored sequentially and processed like a magnetic tape, but at a faster rate, even though direct access capabilities exist; (2) transactions can be processed as they occur; and (3) files can be structured and stored in a manner that permits transactions to be processed against multiple files simultaneously. The disadvantage of the magnetic disk is the cost of storage; in terms of cost per character stored, magnetic disk storage is ten times as expensive as magnetic tape. An additional disadvantage of using a disk system is that it is often difficult to clearly discern an *audit trail.* If in updating a file on magnetic disk a record is read, updated, and written back to the same location, the original contents are destroyed. And if no provision is made for recording transactions and detecting errors, errors may go undetected and file reconstruction becomes impossible.

Magnetic drum. Magnetic disk storage devices are efficient and suitable for many applications, particularly applications that are high volume and require direct access. However, all applications are not of this nature; some data processing problems require a small volume of data and a rapid processing time. In such situations magnetic drum storage is probably the most suitable.

A magnetic drum is a high-quality metal cylinder coated on its outer surface with magnetically sensitive film. The surface of the drum is divided into tracks around its circumference. Each track has a separate and distinguishable read/write head. Because each track on the drum has a read/write head and because the drum rotates at a constant speed, data can be accessed or written very rapidly. An access-transfer rate of more than one million characters per second is not uncommon. Speeds at this level are important for jobs that require rapid intermediate storage or jobs that repeatedly refer to data throughout processing (such as actuarial tables, logarithmic tables, or other mathematical tables). One disadvantage of the magnetic drum, however, is that it cannot be removed from the drum storage unit and used elsewhere. It cannot be physically structured in "drum packs" like the magnetic disk.

Data-cell/mass-storage devices. In designing and structuring an information processing system, speed is not always the key criterion. A number of systems exist in which the need is to store large data files and backup files, and because the files are seldom used or do not require rapid access, a low-cost, medium-to-slow direct-access device is desirable. Devices that meet this need are generally referred to as mass-storage devices. A data cell is one form of mass-storage device.

A *data-cell drive* is a cylindrical-shaped device that has ten or more removable data cells, with each cell being divided into twenty subcells. Each subcell in the drive contains strips of magnetic-oxide coated tape. This tape is about three times as thick as magnetic tape and is coated on both sides.

When accessing or writing data to a specific location in storage, the cells are rotated until the subcell containing the location is under a fixed-position read/write drum. The strip on the subcell containing the location is withdrawn mechanically and wrapped around the drum. The data are written or read as the strip passes under a read/write head attached to the drum. After processing, the strip is reinserted into its subcell position. Since so much physical movement is required to gain access to a particular location, access time is slow compared with other direct-access storage devices. More than 400 million bytes of data (characters) can be stored on a typical data cell drive, however.

Another example of a large-capacity, medium-to-slow access device is Control Data Corporation's 38500 Mass Storage System. This system is built utilizing magnetic tape cartridges. Each cartridge contains a 150-inch-by-2.7-inch magnetic tape, capable of storing up to 8 million characters of data. The storage unit consists of 2,052 cartridges arranged in a clustered fashion. The storage capacity of the system ranges from 16 million to more than 980 million bytes, with an average access time of 2.5 seconds.

Comparison of storage device characteristics. From the preceding overview of magnetic tapes, magnetic disks, drums, data cells, and other direct-access storage devices, it should be obvious that price, capacity, and speed differences exist for each. In structuring an accounting information system, the type of device chosen will depend on trade-offs among these factors.

Additional Hardware Concepts

In Figure 5–2 we showed a variety of input/output devices that could be employed in a data processing (computer) system. In the figure we did not tie the devices directly to the CPU. *Control units* connected the CPU to the input and output devices. Control units are an integral part of a data processing system. *Channels* and *buffers* are also important components. In this section we will examine these components and describe their relationship to the hardware devices discussed thus far.

Control units. Every input/output device and every secondary storage device will have been or will be tied to a control unit. The control unit governs the activity of the device. In some cases the control unit is built into the devices; in other cases the unit is separate and may control several devices. Figure 5–15 illustrates an IBM 2841 Storage Control Unit tied to four separate storage devices.

Several functions are performed by the control unit: (1) code conversion between the machine language of the CPU and the input/output or secondary storage device, (2) validity checking of data, and (3) data buffering (which we examine shortly). Additionally, if several devices are controlled by a single unit, the unit must (1) determine the priority of servicing of the devices, and (2) generate and transmit the device number when servicing an input device or secondary storage unit or routing data to a particular output device or storage unit.

Channels. It may not have been obvious in the overview of input/output devices and secondary storage devices that the speeds of these units are slow relative to the speed of the CPU. Data can be transferred or processed at a very high rate of speed by the CPU, but some input/output devices are very slow. Recall that card readers and card punchers are very slow input/output devices. To avoid having the CPU sit idle while data are being input or output, channels are included in data processing systems.

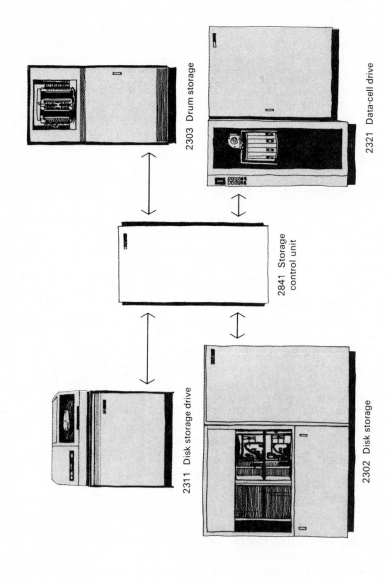

Figure 5-15 Storage Control Unit Tied to Multiple Storage Devices

From *Information Processing* by Marilyn Bohl, ©1980, 1976, 1971, Science Research Associates, Inc. Reprinted by permission of the publisher.

A channel is located between the CPU and the control unit or units. Physically it is usually contained within the housing of the CPU, although it may be a separate piece of equipment. Functionally the channel operates much like a small computer, with its primary responsibility being to direct input/output operations in coordination with the CPU.

There are two types of channels: (1) a selector channel and (2) a multiplexer channel. A *selector channel* transmits information in the form of records. Records are transmitted from an input device to primary storage or are transferred from storage to an output device. Selector channels are generally employed with high-speed input/output devices or storage units, such as magnetic tape, disk, and drum units, and the devices usually employ separate control units.

A *multiplexer channel* operates by transmitting a single *byte* of information. Several operations are thus required to transfer a record to or from primary storage using a multiplexer channel. These channels are generally employed with slow speed devices such as card readers, punchers, and printers, and usually several control units are attached to a single channel.

Regardless of whether a selector channel or a multiplexer channel or both are employed, the CPU operates in conjunction with, but independently of, the channel. When an input/output operation is to be performed, the CPU identifies the proper channel and issues a command (input or output) to the channel. The CPU then is free to perform processing on other programs. The channel operates on its own, working with several input/output control units simultaneously, maintaining communication with each. Just as the CPU is free to continue further processing once it has given an instruction to the channel, a channel is free to execute other commands once a control unit has been instructed as to what to do and which device to employ. Thus a channel is constantly juggling various input/output operations to make the most efficient use of time and to avoid tying up the CPU with input/output operations.

Buffering. The use of channels can improve the efficiency of the CPU. Maximum efficiency, however, will result only when *buffering*, or *overlapped processing*, is employed. In earlier computers, the read-compute-print cycle was performed in a serial fashion. Even though channels were able to reduce the total cycle time by increasing the speed at which data were input and output, the total time was the sum of the input time, processing time, and output time. With overlapped processing, the total time for handling a transaction is the time it takes to handle the longest operation (input, processing, or output).

Figure 5–16 illustrates serial and overlapped processing. With serial processing, three transactions can be read, processed, and output in nine time slices. In contrast, with overlapped processing, seven transactions can be handled in the same total time period. With overlapped processing, buffering of the input (or output) into primary storage is required while the CPU is processing a previous transaction. The term *buffering* is often used to refer to the overlapped processing concept. In Figure 5–16 we have assumed that the same length of time is required for input, processing, and output, although this may be unrealistic because the processing time is generally faster than input or output. The diagram, however, illustrates the obvious benefits of overlapped processing.

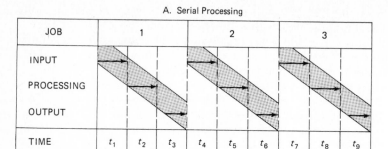

A. Serial Processing

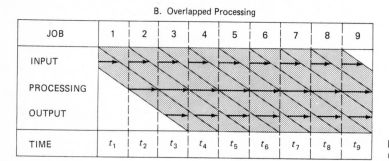

B. Overlapped Processing

Figure 5-16 Serial versus Overlapped Processing

SOFTWARE

Software is as essential a part of a computer system as hardware. The term *software* refers primarily to computer programs, although it encompasses program documentation as well as the standards and techniques used in systems analysis and program development. In this section we will focus on the subset of software related to computer programs.

A variety of software programs exist in most computer systems. These include job-control programs, supervisor routines, file maintenance programs, report generators, information retrieval routines, utility programs, library programs, language translators (such as Assembler, FORTRAN, and COBOL), specific user-written programs, and operating systems. In actuality all the programs and routines are components of the operating system; therefore we will first examine the functions, types, and structure of an operating system and then examine each of the specific component programs. In the latter part of the section we will examine some advanced software concepts such as multiprogramming, virtual storage, and multiprocessing.

Operating Systems: Functions, Types, Structure

In early computer systems, a human operator monitored computer operations, determined the order in which submitted programs were to run, and handled input/output operations. With the significant increases in processing speeds of CPUs and the desire and need to install and use all computer resources efficiently, it was recognized that human operator intervention for control purposes was unrealistic. Therefore, in the early 1960s, software operating systems were developed to help overcome the problem. An operating system is designed to permit a computer system to manage its own operations; in addition, the operating system can operate at the speed of the computer.

The functions of an operating system are directed toward obtaining maximum efficiency in processing operations. Thus the operating system is responsible for scheduling jobs on a priority basis, handling the allocation of resources requested by users, and resolving conflicts that occur when multiple users request the same input/output device, storage device, or storage area. In addition, the operating system performs the accounting function for the computer; it keeps track of all resource usage.

As we indicated earlier, a variety of software programs make up an operating system. Since all the programs are not utilized simultaneously, they are stored on a secondary storage unit called the *system residence device*. The programs are called into primary storage in the CPU (to be executed) at the time they are needed. Figure 5–17 identifies the component programs of an operating system and depicts other areas and functions of the system residence device.

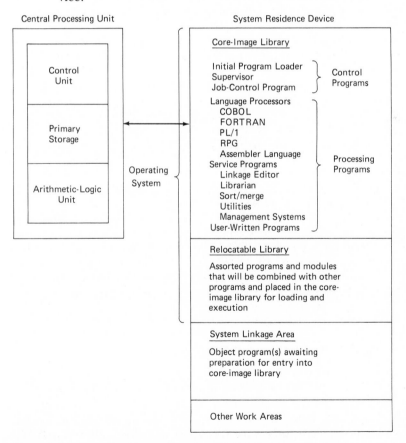

Figure 5-17   Operating System Stored on System Residence Device

A variety of operating systems are available for use with most computer systems, particularly with large computer systems. A computer system, however, will employ only a single operating system. The operating system used will depend upon the computer's purpose, design, and structure. The most basic operating system is a *batch system*, structured principally to handle card input and to process a multiple number of jobs in a predetermined priority sequence. A *real-time operating system* can respond to spontaneous requests for resources, such as inquiries entered from on-line terminals. A *multiprogramming operation system* can operate upon a multiple number of jobs concurrently. Some operating systems, particularly the more sophisticated, can handle *batch, real-time,* and *multiple tasks.* (Types of operating systems are also discussed in the "Advanced Software Concepts" subsection of this chapter.)

Operating System: Components

An *operating system* is an integrated collection of programs, each performing specific duties. In order to better understand the function of each program and how they interrelate and work in unison with the CPU, the programs are generally classified as control programs or processing programs.

Control programs control system operations and perform such tasks as scheduling jobs; handling interrupts caused by error conditions; locating, storing, and retrieving data; and communicating with the computer operator and programmers. In addition, the control programs supervise the execution of processing programs. The *initial program loader routine* (IPL routine), the *supervisor*, and the *job-control program* are control programs.

Processing programs facilitate efficient processing operations and are available to the computer user to simplify program preparation and execution. The major processing programs contained in a typical operating system are *language translators* (Assembler, FORTRAN, COBOL, PL/1, RPG, and others), *service programs* (*linkage editor, librarian, sort/merge,* and *utilities*), and *user-written programs.*

The functions of some of the control programs and processing programs are described in the following paragraphs.

Initial program loader (IPL). The initial program loader is a small program that is loaded into the CPU from the residence device by a manual command from the computer console. Once the IPL program has been loaded, control of the computer is passed to it. The program then performs the single function of locating the supervisor on the residence device and loading it into primary storage. Control is then passed to the supervisor.

Supervisor. The supervisor routine (or monitor or executive) is the major control program and the major component of the operating system. It coordinates all the other activities and parts of the operating system. Figure 5–18 depicts the relationship between the supervisor and the other component programs. After the supervisor has been loaded into the CPU, it calls the other programs as needed and loads them into primary storage. It remains in primary storage throughout all operations. The supervisor also schedules I/O operations and allocates channels to various I/O devices.

Job-control program. Since the supervisor is the control mechanism for the operating system, a means must exist for communicating with it, particularly regarding jobs to be processed and resources required. A job-control lan-

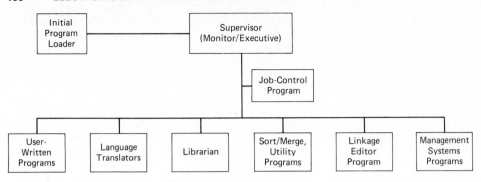

Figure 5-18 Components of an Operating System

guage (JCL) serves as this link. Job-control statements are used to specify (1) the beginning of a user's job (program), (2) the utility, library, or management system routines that are required, and (3) the I/O devices required. A *job-control program* takes the job-control statements written by users and translates them into machine-language instructions that can be executed by the CPU.

A number of job *steps* are often required for a given job. Therefore several job-control statements are required, each specifying the specific step to be performed and the I/O devices needed. All job-control statements are not translated and processed simultaneously; they are handled sequentially. Therefore the supervisor calls the job-control program into primary storage only when a job-control statement needs to be interpreted. A multistep job may require multiple loading of the job-control program into primary storage.

Sort/Merge and Utility programs. Two of the most useful sets of processing programs are the sort/merge and utility programs. Sort/merge programs are employed in organizing records in a file and in merging multiple files of sequence records into a single sequential file. Usually a sort/merge program is written as a set of generalized modules so that the program can be tailored for a variety of applications. As the number of jobs handled by the computer system increases and as the number of data files within the system increases, sort/merge facilities are needed.

A sort/merge program is sometimes labeled a utility program. A number of other utility programs, however, have been designed to perform data processing tasks common to many user jobs. Programs that transfer data from one medium to another, such as from card to tape, tape to disk, tape to printer, and disk to printer, are utility programs. Other examples include debugging aids such as memory dump programs that provide a diagnostic printout of primary storage, or a trace routine, after the execution of each instruction in a user's program.

Librarian. The librarian is a set of service programs that performs the cataloging and management function associated with the libraries. These programs maintain, service, and organize all libraries, including those required by the operating system as well as user libraries. Librarians provide capabilities such as adding, deleting, and removing programs; iisting the contents of different libraries; and repositioning programs in the library after deleting a program.

Linkage editor. The linkage editor is a service program that is actively involved in the execution phase of processing a job. When a job (user program) has been input to the computer and translated to machine language, it is output in object program form on the residence device. The linkage editor will edit the object program and will pull together ("link") all library programs, utility programs, and management system programs that the job requires. Recall that these user program specifications are identified in the job-control language. Once all the programs have been linked together in the system linkage area of the residence device (see Figure 5–17), the linkage editor will specify a "start address" for the entire group of programs. The start address is the location in primary storage in which the programs will be loaded for execution when the supervisor is ready for the job.

Management system programs. Management system programs include file maintenance routines, report generators, and information retrieval routines. In general, a wide range of file activity demands will exist on a computer system, particularly if the computer is employed in an accounting/information system role. Daily, or more frequent, transaction processing must be available. In addition, file capabilities must exist for adding or deleting a record, depending upon the transaction and program requirements. File maintenance programs can provide these file activity capabilities.

User-written programs. As the label implies, user-written programs are the programs actually written by the user. These programs are usually written in a high-level computer language and translated into the machine language of the computer by a language translator. When the term *software* is used by an individual with limited knowledge of the computer, the reference is generally to user-written programs.

Language translators. Language translators are used by the operating system to translate user-written and other software programs to a machine language that the computer can understand and employ. Because the electrical design and structure of most computers differ, translators are tailor-made for specific computers. Generally these software programs are written by a specialized staff within the company that manufactures the computer; therefore most translators are available as a software component when the hardware is purchased. (Additional comments relating to language translators are included in the following section.)

Programming Languages

A computer user employs a sequence of instructions to perform a certain task. These instructions can be written in different programming languages, depending upon the knowledge of the user and the availability of a language translator to convert the input language to the machine language of the computer. Thus a programming language is a basic tool that a user employs in instructing the computer to perform tasks.

Three *levels* of computer languages exist on most computer systems: low-level (machine) languages, assembly languages, and high-level (compiler) languages. Because each of these has advantages as well as disadvantages, and because each is employed in most computers, it is appropriate that we review them in detail.

Machine languages. The first computers that were developed in the late 1940s used only machine instructions. Machine language is therefore as old as the computer. This language is expressed in binary form (combinations of 0's and 1's) and is coded to designate the proper electrical conditions and states in the computer. Machine language is the only language the computer can execute directly. Since it can relate directly to the execution process, it is referred to as a low-level programming language.

The actual writing of machine-language instructions is not expressed in binary form but in hexadecimal, octal, or some other number system, depending on the design of the computer. Regardless of the number system used, the process is complex because the instructions must contain operation codes and primary storage addresses, expressed in an appropriate numbering system.

Since the design and structure of most computer systems differ, each type of computer has a unique machine language. In learning a machine language, a user is therefore tied to a particular computer. For this reason, plus the fact that machine-language programming in general is extremely complex, tedious, and time consuming, limited use is made of this level of language.

Assembly languages. Because of the difficulty involved in using, and in learning, machine-language programming, other languages have been developed. One of these is assembly language, which is similar to machine language with some of the complexities of programming removed through the use of mnemonic symbols within the language.

The language is often referred to as a symbolic language. For example, rather than employing the hexadecimal number that represents the STORE instruction, the assembly language would employ a symbol such as STO. The programmer must still designate the operation to be performed and the storage locations to use, and therefore assembly languages have some of the complexity of machine languages. Assembly languages are also similar to machine languages in that they are machine dependent; each assembly language is related to a specific machine and is not transferable.

High-level programming languages. High-level languages are procedure or problem-oriented languages. They are designed so that the user can focus on the problem or on the procedure for solving the problem, rather than on the computer operations that are the focus in machine and assembly languages. COBOL, FORTRAN, BASIC, PL/1, and RPG are examples of high-level languages.

The label *high level* is used as the language designator because such languages are far removed from the hardware. These languages employ English-like terms and symbols and require much less programming effort than assembly and machine languages. Storage addressing is not required and fewer instructions are needed. While one assembly-language instruction is generally equivalent to one machine-language instruction, one high-level language statement can accomplish the same objective as several machine instructions. This is possible because the language translator for the high-level language carries the burden of generating the equivalent machine instructions.

In contrast to assembly languages and machine languages, high-level languages are machine independent. A program written in a high-level language can therefore be used on many different computers, although some minor changes may be necessary because of differences in machine capabilities.

Compilers and Assemblers. As we noted earlier, before a program can be executed it must exist in machine-language form. Since assembly languages and high-level languages are not in machine language, they must be translated into machine instructions. The translator for an assembly language is called an *assembler* program. A high-level language translator is called a *compiler* program. Both assemblers and compilers are designed for specific computers, since differences exist in the design and structure of computers. Only one assembler is needed for a given computer, since each computer has a unique assembly language. In contrast, a compiler is required for each high-level language used on a given computer. A FORTRAN compiler will translate from FORTRAN to machine language; a COBOL compiler is required to translate from COBOL to machine language.

Advantages and disadvantages of languages. The majority of user-written programs are written in assembly languages or high-level languages rather than machine language. Both levels of language have distinct advantages and disadvantages; for business data processing applications it is important that we be aware of these.

High-level languages are generally much easier to learn than assembly languages. Therefore it takes less time for the user to develop a program. Because the statements are English-like and fairly easy to interpret, they provide better documentation than assembly statements and make it easier to modify existing programs.

Because high-level languages are machine independent, programs do not become obsolete when a new computer is installed. In addition, machine independence allows programs to be shared with other users and general application programs to be purchased at low cost, since they are not written for a specific machine.

One disadvantage of high-level languages, as compared with assembly languages, is that user-written programs are not efficient. Because there is a one-to-one correspondence between assembly-language instructions and machine-language instructions, a program written in assembly language can take full advantage of computer capabilities. A high-level language program will probably take longer to run and will require more core storage, since it must rely on the machine-language instruction generated by the compiler. The difference in computer run time can become significant if the program being run is used on a regular basis.

Another disadvantage of high-level languages is that significant quantities of computer time may be consumed in the compilation process, even though it is a one-time process. In contrast, the conversion of assembly-language programs to machine language will be likely to consume a relatively small amount of time. On some computer systems, particularly minicomputers, the size of the compiler may be a negative factor, since it requires much more storage space than the assembler.

Advanced Software Concepts

In our discussion of hardware we noted that though the CPU is designed to handle a large volume of data processing activities, it is often "I/O bound" because input/output (I/O) devices have limited capabilities (speeds). Hardware components such as channels and buffers are used to improve the interface between the CPU and input/output devices. In this section we will examine three software programs that can improve the operating efficiency of the CPU: *multiprogramming, virtual storage,* and *multiprocessing.*

Multiprogramming. Although the CPU can process instructions very rapidly, it can operate on only one instruction at a time. In addition, the CPU cannot operate on data until the data are in primary storage. Since the speed of I/O operations is slower than the CPU processing speed, a significant amount of CPU time is wasted waiting on I/O operations. To help overcome this problem, multiprogramming allows several programs and their associated data to reside in primary storage at the same time. Under multiprogramming, the CPU executes only one instruction at a time, but it has flexibility in moving from one program to another, then another, and then back to the first program. Instructions from a program are executed until an instruction for an input or output device occurs. The I/O instruction passes control to a channel, thus freeing the CPU to rotate and begin processing instructions from another program. The CPU processes the second program until that program requires input or output, at which time the CPU rotates to another program or back to a previously partially executed program, and so on.

When more than one processing program is loaded into primary storage during multiprogramming, the programs must be held in separate areas. To accomplish this, primary storage is subdivided into areas called partitions. Each partition can handle one program. The size and structure of the partitions are determined by the type of operating system that the computer utilizes.

Virtual Storage. Multiprogramming overcomes the problem of the CPU's having to wait on an I/O operation. A limitation of multiprogramming, however, is that a partition must be large enough to hold an entire program and the entire program remains in the partition until it is fully executed. This results in inefficient use of main memory, particularly if a program contains a large sequence of instructions that is used infrequently and a small group of instructions that is used repeatedly. Since the size of main memory is limited, a procedure was necessary for handling the holding and execution of instructions for a program.

Traditionally, programmers utilized the general multiprogramming framework by trying to trim the sizes of programs so they would fit within smaller partitions of main memory. In some cases, programs have been separated into modules or program segments and executed in separate job steps under a single job run. These activities are tedious and time consuming for the programmer and are seldom beneficial in terms of reduced storage requirements.

To overcome the necessity of having to hold an entire program in memory while it is executing, an extension of multiprogramming, called *virtual storage,* has been developed. The basic concept behind virtual storage is that only the portion of a program and data that is needed immediately must be held in primary storage; the remaining part of the program and any associated data can be held in an auxiliary storage device. The virtual storage technique gives the illusion that main memory is unlimited because only a portion of a program is in main memory at any point in time, and therefore more programs can reside in main memory simultaneously.

A direct-access storage device such as a magnetic disk unit is used to establish a virtual storage system. The term *virtual storage* is given to the access storage, while *real storage* is the term used when referring to primary storage locations given addresses by the operating system. All instructions and data for a given program reside in virtual storage at all times. When data or instructions for a given portion of a program are needed in real storage, they are transferred from virtual storage to real storage.

Two methods exist for storing and transferring data from virtual storage to real storage: (1) segmentation and (2) paging. In *segmentation* each program is broken into variable-size units referred to as segments. The segments could easily be defined as data, the main program, a subroutine of the program, and so on. Based on the size of the segments, the operating system allocates appropriate space in virtual storage. Since any segment in virtual storage must be readily available to be transferred to real storage, the addresses in virtual storage of all segments are kept in real storage in a segment table. Bringing a segment into real storage thus simply involves referencing the table and a transfer.

Paging is similar to segmentation except that all storage areas, both in main memory and in virtual memory, are of a standard fixed size called a page. The size of the page is determined by the characteristics of the given computer. Unlike segmentation, paging does not consider the logical subunits or portions of a program when storing the program. The programs are simply broken into equal-size pages. The transfer of a page of a program from virtual memory to real memory is similar to segmentation. An address is kept in a page table in real storage for each program page in virtual memory. A table reference and transfer are required to move a page of the program to real memory when the page is required during processing.

Fortunately the operating system handles all of the storage, development of tables, transfer of segments or pages, and other tasks associated with virtual storage operations. Virtual storage, however, has some basic limitations. First, an on-line auxiliary storage unit is required. Second, the operating system associated with virtual storage is highly sophisticated, requires a significant amount of storage in main memory, and is often rather expensive. Third, if a virtual storage system is not structured properly, a significant amount of time can be wasted in locating and exchanging program segments or pages.

Multiprocessing. Multiprocessing involves the use of two or more central processing units linked together to form a coordinated data processing operation. Multiprocessing is quite different from multiprogramming. Recall that multiprogramming involves the concurrent execution of instructions from two or more programs, all of which utilize one CPU controlled by a single operating system. In multiprocessing, more than one instruction can be executed simultaneously because two or more CPUs are available. The CPUs can execute different instructions from the same program, or instructions from totally different programs.

One benefit that results from the multiprocessing structure is the "freeing up" of one CPU to primarily handle computational operations. One CPU handles such tasks as scheduling, editing data, and file maintenance while the second CPU is free to handle high-priority or complex processing such as large mathematical calculations. One configuration used to provide this operating arrangement is a medium-size CPU, often a minicomputer, linked to a large CPU. Input/output operations and communications with peripheral devices are chan-

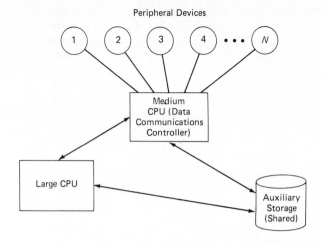

Figure 5-19 Multiprocessing System (Medium-Large, Two-CPU Arrangement)

neled through the medium-size CPU while the large CPU concentrates on computational processing. Figure 5–19 illustrates a medium-large, two-CPU multiprocessing system.

A multiprocessing system can also consist of two or more large CPUs, with each CPU having its own separate memory as well as a single shared memory. Figure 5–20 illustrates this type of configuration. In this figure a small CPU is used as a data communications controller and two large CPUs provide processing services. Under this arrangement, specific CPUs may be dedicated

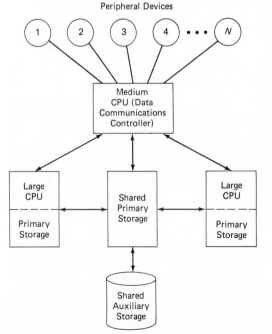

Figure 5-20 Multiprocessing System (Multiple-Large CPU Arrangement)

to specific tasks such as I/O processing, computational processing, or data management; or one CPU can handle on-line processing while another handles only batch processing. Some multiprocessing systems are also designed so that one or more of the CPUs is employed as a backup for the other CPUs. Obviously, multiprocessing systems of this nature are used by organizations with extremely large and complex information processing needs.

A multiprocessing system involves a great deal of hardware and software. A highly sophisticated operating system is needed if the CPUs and other resources are to be used effectively. The implementation of this type of system may also be very time consuming. The payoff from such systems is tremendous, however, particularly if the system is configured so that additional CPUs or storage can be added in the future as needed without reworking the entire system or having to adopt a totally new system.

SUMMARY

This chapter has focused on the hardware and software components of a computer system. In the hardware area we identified the elements that form the central processing unit (CPU), the unit that controls the entire computer. We discussed devices that are used as input/output units, including card readers, terminals, magnetic tapes, and optical character recognition (OCR) devices. We also considered storage devices such as the magnetic disk, magnetic drum, and data cell. An additional topic area included in the examination of hardware was channels and buffers. These devices play an important role in the efficient operation of a computer system, particularly when a large number of peripheral devices are utilized in the system.

Our discussion of software included a coverage of the functions, types, and structure of operating systems. Specific topics examined included supervisors, initial program loader, job-control program, linkage editor, and librarian. A detailed coverage of programming languages was not provided, but we discussed the differences between machine languages, assembly languages, and compiler languages, along with their advantages and disadvantages. Some advanced software concepts were presented, such as multiprogramming, virtual storage, and multiprocessing. We noted that multiprogramming and virtual storage software can improve the efficiency and operation of a single computer system, whereas multiprocessing software is required when two or more CPUs are linked together. Examples were given to highlight the specific aspects of each software package.

SELECTED REFERENCES

BOHL, MARILYN, *Information Processing*, 3rd Edition, Science Research Associates, Palo Alto, Calif., 1980.

FRATES, JEFFREY AND MOLDRUP, WILLIAM, *Introduction to the Computer: An Integrated Approach*, Englewood Cliffs, N.J.: Prentice-Hall, Inc., 1980.

KINDRED, ALTON R., *Introduction to Computers*, 2nd Edition, Englewood Cliffs, N.J.: Prentice-Hall, Inc., 1982.

MANDELL, STEVEN L., *Computers and Data Processing: Concepts and Applications*, St. Paul, Minn.: West Publishing Co., 1979.

SHELLEY, GARY B. AND CASHMAN, THOMAS J., *Introduction to BASIC Programming*, Brea, Cal.: Anaheim Publishing Co., 1982.

REVIEW QUESTIONS

1. Identify in pictorial block diagram form the basic items that constitute a computer.

2. The central processing unit is generally considered to be made up of which of the following two parts?
   a. Control and arithmetic/logical
   b. Input/output and processing
   c. Arithmetical and logical
   d. Storage and processing
   e. None of the above (Adapted from the CMA Examination)

3. What is the function of the following?
   a. Primary storage
   b. Arithmetic-logic unit
   c. Control unit
   d. Secondary storage

4. What factors are used to characterize or describe a central processing unit (CPU)?

5. What is the key cost factor associated with the purchasing of a CPU?

6. Which of the following best describes business and scientific computing needs for input/output and computing speed?
   a. Business needs both and scientific needs neither.
   b. Business needs both and scientific only needs input/output.
   c. Business needs computing speed and scientific needs input/output.
   d. Business needs neither and scientific needs computing.
   e. Business needs input/output and scientific needs computing. (Adapted from the CMA Examination)

7. Which piece of data processing equipment *is not* considered to be an input/output device?
   a. CRT
   b. Magnetic tape
   c. Card reader
   d. JCL
   e. Magnetic disk

8. In which regard do cards have an advantage over magnetic tape?
   a. Speed
   b. Cost per character
   c. Protection against loss
   d. Human readability
   e. Compactness

9. Identify some of the more common input/output devices employed in a computer system.

10. Identify the characteristics of magnetic tape.

11. What are the characteristics of an MICR device? How is it used?

12. Describe how an OCR device is used.

13. Identify some of the more common secondary storage devices.

14. Explain the following concepts used in relationship to a magnetic tape:
    a. Density
    b. Logical record
    c. Physical record
    d. Blocking
    e. Interblock gap (IBG)
    f. Blocking factor

15. Which of the following contains all of the other (with regard to data)?
    a. A record
    b. A field
    c. A file
    d. A character
    e. A block

16. Identify the structure of a magnetic disk. What is a disk pack?

17. Compare the capacity, access time, and average cost of a magnetic tape, magnetic disk, magnetic drum, and data cell.

18. Which of the following is not a direct-access storage device (also called random access storage)?
    a. Disk
    b. Core

c. Drum
d. Data cell
e. None of the above

19. What is the function of the control unit in a computer system?

20. A large bank is considering the implementation of a fast-response teller system. What type of peripheral equipment is normally associated with such fast-response computer systems?
    a. Magnetic tape
    b. Magnetic disk
    c. Magnetic core
    d. Punched cards
    e. Punched paper tape (Adapted from the CMA Examination)

21. Explain the function of a channel.

22. Differentiate between a *selector channel* and a *multiplexer channel*.

23. Explain what is meant by "buffering."

24. What are the functions of an operating system?

25. Explain the term *system residence device*.

26. Differentiate between *control programs* and *processing programs*.

27. What components go together to make up an operating system?

28. Explain the function of each of the following:
    a. Initial program loader (IPL)
    b. Supervisor
    c. Job-control program (JCL)
    d. Sort/merge and utility programs

    e. Librarian
    f. Linkage editor
    g. Management system programs
    h. Language translators

29. What three levels of computer languages exist on most computer systems?

30. Which of these languages was developed to ease the transition from punch-card equipment to computers?
    a. JCL
    b. FORTRAN
    c. RPG
    d. COBOL
    e. Assembly (Adapted from the CMA Examination)

31. Why are assembly languages "machine dependent" while high-level languages such as COBOL are "not machine dependent"? Explain what is meant by "machine dependent."

32. What is the function of a compiler?

33. Differentiate between *multiprogramming* and *multiprocessing*.

34. Explain the structure as well as the use of "virtual storage."

35. Differentiate between *segmentation* and *paging*.

36. Which of the following involves concurrent execution of two or more programs within a single computer?
    a. Multiprogramming
    b. Time sharing
    c. Virtual storage
    d. Multiprocessing
    e. Paging

EXERCISES AND CASES

5–1

For each of the following situations, identify the suitable input/output device or devices. (Refer to Figure 5–2.)

a. An electronics firm has decided to eliminate the use of time cards for recording the work/attendance times of its employees; instead, the company has adopted plastic badges that contain employee identification numbers. The badges can be read by an input device tied to the company's computer system.

b. A building contractor wants to process its weekly payroll on the company's computer system, although the hours that employees work are recorded in pencil on time documents.

c. A metropolitan bank wants to employ a specialized means of inputting to the computer the large volume of checks it must process daily.

d. A television manufacturer wants to receive from its wholesalers orders that have been directly entered into its computer and transmitted to the manufacturer's shipping department.

e. A university wants to employ a specialized procedure to handle the registration forms used by students during the registration process. A semiautomated system is desired.

f. A public water works office wants to employ a procedure for handling the monthly water bills returned by customers with their checks.

g. A large retail clothing outlet wants to capture sales data so that each sales transaction can automatically be read, transmitted, and immediately completed via its central computer facility.

h. A stock broker wants to provide stock prices to prospective customers by entering the appropriate request via a special telephone with a keyboard attachment.

i. A bank that has numerous branches wants to transmit data from its regional offices for rapid processing by the central computer at the central office.

j. A large wholesale organization wants to record the receipt and/or shipment of merchandise on documents that can be handled in batches by its computer system.

5–2

Rank the following secondary storage devices according to the four criteria indicated:

| | CRITERIA | | |
	Access (random/sequential)	Speed (fast/slow)	Cost (expensive/cheap)	Volume (high/low)
Magnetic tape Magnetic disk Magnetic drum Data cell				

5–3

There is no universal I/O device nor storage device that can satisfy all applications; however, under certain circumstances a given I/O as well as a given storage device has advantages over other corresponding types of devices. Shown in columns 1 and 2 of the following table are two sets of devices:

	(1) Device	(2) Device
1	Printer	Card punch
2	Magnetic tape (storage)	Disk (storage)
3	Card reader	CRT terminal

a. Under what circumstances would each item in column 1 have advantages over the corresponding item in column 2?

b. Under what circumstances would each item in column 2 have advantages over the corresponding item in column 1?

5–4

Following is a list of devices. Arrange the devices in descending order of I/O speed.

a. Magnetic tape drive
b. CRT terminal
c. Paper-tape reader
d. Magnetic drum
e. Card punch
f. Data cell
g. Magnetic drum
h. Paper-tape punch
i. Card reader

5–5

The First Bank of Athens has fifty thousand savings accounts. All accounts are maintained on a single master file where each account consists of a record 200 characters in length.

a. If the bank were to use punch cards as an input medium, how many cards would be needed for each account record?
b. What volume of cards would be required if the entire fifty thousand accounts were to be processed?
c. Assume that the bank elected to store the master file of fifty thousand records on a magnetic tape. Determine the number of inches of tape required to store the file using unblocked records and a tape density of 800 characters per inch.
d. Determine the inches of tape required to store the master file using a blocking factor of 5 and a tape density of 800 characters per inch.
e. Assuming that tapes were created under steps *c* and *d* above, which tape would take the least time to read? Why?

5–6

The Ben Davis Supply Company of Swanee, Georgia, employs card equipment in its mail-order processing operation. Each order that is received may be made up of a number of different items. A card is punched for each item on an order. The company receives about eight hundred orders per week; each order, on the average, contains six different items. Each item, on the average, contains 60 characters of information.

Equipment requirements and the associated costs are as follows:

1. Computer cards: $8 per box, 2,000 cards per box
2. Keypunch machines: monthly rental, $100 each
3. Card verifiers: monthly rental, $100 each
4. Salary of equipment operators: $900 per month per person

All orders received are forwarded to the keypunch area for preparation. Upon completion of the keypunch operation, the order, along with the cards, is passed to a verification operation (for checking). The company has found that, on the average, the error rate during keypunching is 15 percent; however, all errors are corrected once they have been sent back to keypunching (no verification is required on the corrected cards).

For this operation:

a. Determine the number of keypunches and verifiers required if it is assumed that exactly four weeks make up a month and an operator (regardless of whether keypunching or verifying is involved) works at a rate of 1,500 characters per hour.
b. Determine the monthly cost for the company.

5–7

Indicate whether a magnetic tape or a magnetic disk system would be more applicable for the following applications. Justify your choice in each case.

a. Airlines reservations
b. A clothing store inventory control system
c. A billing system for a doctor's office
d. State automobile registration of licenses

5–8

Given the following situations, specify a suitable storage medium and a suitable access medium (method). Justify your recommendations in each case.

a. A large hotel has a room reservation system that keeps track of the status of all rooms in a multibuilding complex. The system is maintained on a "room" master file. Each room in the hotel complex appears as a record on the master file. The system is such that each record must be updated and/or changed to reflect new occupants, food and phone charges, and checkout/departure of occupants. The system is linked to the billing process and is used to generate a customer's final bill. On the average, a room in the hotel has an 85 percent occupancy rate and each occupant stays two nights.

b. A large earth-moving equipment company maintains ten thousand parts on an inventory system. Each item in inventory is identified with a unique record. Records are updated and/or deleted daily, depending on the sales activity. On the average, six hundred orders are received daily; each order, on the average, contains six items. New parts or deletion of old parts occurs at a rate of twenty-five per day. The system is designed so that when a customer calls to place an order, an inquiry can be made to determine the status of parts-on-hand. An inventory status report is generated at the end of each day. The report highlights, among other things, when parts-on-hand have declined to their reorder points.

c. The electric utility department in a major city maintains a master file of approximately 250,000 customers. Once a month the customers' electric meters are read to determine consumption. A card is prepared on each customer account to reflect the meter reading. All customer records in the master file are updated to reflect monthly usage. Bills are prepared and a master list, which reflects the customer's name, address, and amount billed, is generated.

5-9

The B & H Drug Company, Inc., owns a chain of stores throughout the Southwest. The store in Houston, Texas, has recently acquired a medium-sized computer and associated peripheral equipment. The configuration includes the following: (1) a CPU having 320,000 bytes of primary storage, (2) a card reader and punch, (3) three magnetic tape drives, (4) two magnetic disk drives with backup, removable disk packs, (5) a high-speed line printer, (6) two keyboard/printer terminals, and (7) five CRT display terminals.

a. Draw the configuration of equipment assuming that no overlapped processing capabilities exist.

b. Draw the configuration of equipment assuming that additional equipment is to be purchased (if necessary) so that overlapped processing exists.

5-10

The L & D Video Company is a manufacturer of video terminals as well as parts for maintaining terminals. The terminals are primarily used in commercial video game equipment. The company produces eighty to ninety different varieties of terminals and markets them throughout the entire United States. The company has a work force of 150 employees and six managers. Sales revenues for Video were $9.2 million last year. The company foresees rapid growth in sales during the next five years.

Bob Lennox, owner of the company, is concerned about the current problems the company is experiencing as a result of rapid growth. For example, the number of sales orders has increased considerably and the company is having problems meeting promised delivery dates. When customers call to check on the status of their orders, it often is several hours before a response can be given. Materials and parts needed in the manufacturing area are frequently out of stock, and long delays occur in replenishing the critical items. Bad debt expense has begun to increase at an alarming rate.

a. Identify a suitable computer hardware configuration that could be used to help improve the operation at Video.

b. Identify the software that would be required to support the hardware in part a. Explain the purpose of each software item.

c. Identify some computer applications that might help Video handle its "growth problems."

5-11

The Bendix Company currently schedules its computer job stream so that one job has the full attention of the central processing unit (CPU) at a time. The company wants to increase the efficiency of its system.

1. One alternative available to the company is to apply the concept of multiprogramming. In doing this, the company would
   a. Obtain two CPUs in order to run two jobs simultaneously
   b. Alter programs to perform more than one job in each program
   c. Utilize an operating system feature that splits the CPU's attention to more than one job
   d. Utilize a minicomputer associated with the main computer to run small jobs
   e. Apply none of the concepts described above
2. A second alternative would be to use multiprocessing. In doing this, the company would
   a. Operate two independent computer systems
   b. Operate two CPUs sharing the same memory
   c. Operate two sets of on-line storage for access by different jobs
   d. Operate a minicomputer for preprocessing data before transmission to the main system
   e. Operate some system other than those described above

5-12

Sobig Company is faced with a situation in which many of its programs are too large for the memory of its current computer. In attempting to solve this problem, Sobig could make use of the modular feature built into its system. In doing this, the company would

a. Break programs into modules, thus permitting one module to be resident in memory at a time
b. Use virtual storage, which allows the programs and data to be moved between primary and secondary storage and thus negates the memory size constraint
c. Be able to add modules of memory, thus expanding the size of the main memory
d. Allocate sections of the system to each program to be processed
e. Be able to switch to a larger computer in the same family, thus preventing the need to reprogram

6

SYSTEM STRUCTURES AND ASSOCIATED HARDWARE

INTRODUCTION

In Chapter 2 we discussed the three dimensions of information systems (management activities, organizational functions, and data processing [elements]) and noted that these can be linked in a variety of ways. We described and discussed in some detail linkages referred to as integrated systems and distributed processing systems. A number of firms still employ very centralized and integrated information systems; but because of the expanding technology of minicomputers and microprocessors, distributed processing has become a widely used structure in information systems. The objective of this chapter is to further examine system structures. To provide a better understanding of these and other systems, we will trace the evolution of information systems from the basic custodial accounting systems that existed prior to computers, up to and including distributed systems. And to better understand the more complex systems (integrated and distributed), we will examine some of the hardware used to support each of these systems.

Because batch processing and real-time processing are types of operations that can be employed in a variety of system structures, including integrated and distributed systems, we will discuss these processing modes prior to examining the evolution of systems.

BATCH PROCESSING
AND REAL-TIME PROCESSING

The two general types of operations that can exist, separately or jointly, in an information system, regardless of whether the system is integrated, distributed, or some other form, are *batch processing* and *real-time processing*. Under batch processing, transactions are accumulated into "batches" and processed periodically. In using real-time processing, records are updated as transactions occur. *Real-time* means that data are processed and handled so that the resulting information is retrieved in sufficient time to control the operating environment.

Quite often the term *on-line* is used in conjunction with batch as well as real-time processing. On-line refers to the fact that input/output devices, data files, and other associated equipment are connected to the computer so that transactions can be transferred to and from the computer with a minimal of manual intervention. Examples of on-line batch processing and on-line real-time processing will be given in order to clarify the concepts.

Batch Processing

As we have just noted, in batch processing the data relating to the same type of transaction are gathered into a particular file in a logical order, sequenced, and processed as a batch. A payroll system is an example of a batch processing system. All data relating to payroll checks (such as hours worked during the time period, vacation days taken, and routine hours worked) must be accumulated before the processing of checks can be accomplished. For a batch processed payroll system, employee number or department number would probably be sequenced to control the batching of the input data.

Batch processing systems have been used for many years in accounting and have been modeled around a number of accounting control techniques, computer operation systems, and data storage structures. In the typical accounting department, each employee performs a particular function or functions. The functions are generally defined to meet the internal control goals of separating the physical handling of assets and the accountability for the asset, and of preventing unintentional mistakes. A batch processing system can be divided into separable subsystems in much the same manner that the accounting functions are divided.

A batch processing system (or subsystem if we were referring to a number of functional operations tied together to form a system) can be designed with *sequential access file storage* or *random access file storage*. Each structure has advantages and disadvantages.

BATCH PROCESSING WITH SEQUENTIAL ACCESS FILES   Figure 6–1 illustrates the structure of a batch processing system with sequential access files. In this type of system the entire master file is read and written each time transactions are processed against it. This update activity requires sorting all input transactions into the same sequence that is found in the master file. In terms of hardware, a card reader, a printer, and two tape drives are required. Obviously the

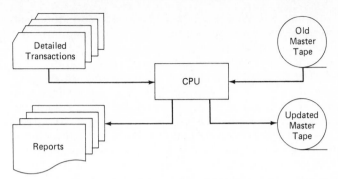

Figure 6-1 Batch Processing with Sequential Access Files

operating system within the CPU and the software required for this processing procedure would be very elementary.

To better understand the structure of a sequential batch processing system, we will examine the detailed operation of a payroll system. A master file contains permanent or semipermanent employee information, such as the (1) name, (2) badge number, (3) address, (4) department, (5) number of exemptions, (6) miscellaneous deductions (such as insurance premiums or retirement contributions), (7) year-to-date pay, and (8) year-to-date withholdings. Transaction data in this case would be on employee time cards, which contain the (1) badge number, (2) hours worked, (3) overtime hours, (4) job classification (if variable), and (5) incentive bonus (if applicable). Using the transaction data and the master file, the payroll processing program performs three functions: (1) it checks the master file employee number and matches it with the employee number on the transaction card (recall that the input data are sorted prior to processing); (2) it generates employee payroll checks, as well as information for cost control and the general ledger; and (3) it updates the master file so that current records will be available for the next processing cycle.

A basic batch processing system of this nature is applicable to many business firms, particularly small firms. This applicability is enhanced further by the fact that microcomputer technology is available to support such systems. However, there are a number of other reasons for the continued use of such basic systems. First, this basic subsystem structure is applicable to such accounting functions as accounts receivable and accounts payable. Second, once a sequential batch processing program has been developed, it can generally be applied to the problems of another business firm with some straightforward variations in the program. These generalized software programs are readily available from the computer manufacturer and are easy to modify or design for any business. Third, since the system is designed and operated around the traditional accounting process, it can easily be controlled and audited. Fourth, management can easily understand the system without a great deal of study of computer hardware or software.

Though a number of advantages exist for batch processing systems with sequential files, there are also limitations and shortcomings. First, because a multiple number of basic subsystems go together to make up a total accounting information system, duplicate items of information exist on many files. Second, a large amount of manual handling of data is involved, and duplicate input data are often required because each processing program essentially operates independently of other programs.

BATCH PROCESSING WITH RANDOM ACCESS FILES   Batch processing is not limited to sequential access files. The basic batch processing system shown in Figure 6–1 can be modified by replacing the magnetic tape units with some type of mass-storage device (magnetic disk, magnetic drum, data cell, etc.). Figure 6–2 illustrates a typical modified batch processing system with random access files. In the random access system, the master files are maintained on the mass-storage device. In addition, an on-line input/output device, which is traditionally used to query the status of any particular record or portion of a file on a "real-time" basis, is used.

There are several key advantages of random access batch processing: (1) it allows quick-response interrogation of the status of information in the system; (2) if the mass-storage device is used in a virtual storage fashion, the memory capabilities of the computer are increased; (3) user-written programs can be stored within the mass-storage device, thus eliminating the need for inputting the programs each time the application is to be used (which is necessary under the basic batch processing system); and (4) it is not necessary to sequence the input data, since any record in the mass-storage device is readily available regardless of the order in which records are input. Therefore extensive editing and sorting of data are eliminated.

Like the sequential batch processing approach, random access batch processing has some disadvantages and limitations. One of the key disadvantages is that an audit trail is difficult to maintain. When transaction data are processed, the master record is read (but not destroyed) from storage. The record is updated in the CPU, and the updated record is written back into mass storage. The writing of the updated record back into mass storage automatically eliminates the old record. Thus the audit trail is destroyed unless the mass storage is periodically dumped to another medium of storage and all transaction data are preserved. Dumps for a particular accounting period would be very expensive compared with storage of the data on tape (on the old master file).

A second problem associated with the random access batch processing approach results from the fact that data need not be sorted sequentially before

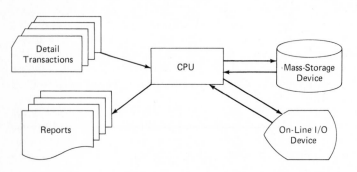

Figure 6–2 Batch Processing with Random Access Files

being input to the computer. Because the data are input chronologically, the audit trail is significantly complicated. Elimination of prior master file data with each new update can be overcome by the procedure discussed above: dumping the mass-storage device at specific periods of time. The dumping of the mass-storage device provides information as to the status of records at specific points in time, but with chronological data it is difficult to trace changes that have occurred. For example, the most recent balance for a given data item can be determined from a current dump, and the balance at the beginning of the period can be determined from the previous dump. To determine the specific transactions that affected the balance, it would be necessary to search through all the transactions during the period between dumps.

BATCH PROCESSING: MODES OF OPERATION Batch processing, regardless of whether it is accomplished with sequential access or random access files, can be structured to operate in two modes: (1) local batch and (2) remote batch.

In *local batch processing*, data are accumulated into batches within the firm and sent directly to the computer for processing. Reports and printed output documents are returned to the user within the firm. No data communication equipment is required, since the input data are processed on the firm's premises. Figures 6–1 and 6–2 are illustrations of local batch processing.

In *remote batch processing*, a data communication system is employed to process data generated at locations that are distant from the main computer installation. Two submodes of operation exist under remote batch processing: (1) *off-line* processing and (2) *on-line* processing.

When there are not enough transactions to warrant a permanent communication link with the computer or when an immediate response from the computer is not necessary, an *off-line* mode of operation can be employed. Under this type of arrangement, data are transferred at predetermined times over the communication channel and transferred to a machine-processible medium, such as magnetic tape, punched cards, or disk. At a specific point in time, the data are processed at the computer facility. The output is transferred back through the communication system to the outlying data-handling facility. Figure 6–3 illustrates an off-line remote batch processing system. One of the key advantages of this mode of operation is low data communication costs. Telephones are used to transfer data/information to and from the computer via the data transmission terminals. The computer is manually linked to the data system.

The second mode of operation of remote batch processing is *on-line*. Under this structure, a permanent communication link is maintained between the remote site and the computer facility. No telephone link is necessary to tie the data communication terminals. Data are still collected onto a machine-processible medium for input and transferred at predetermined times to the computer for processing. The processing occurs on receipt by the computer, and the output is returned upon completion of processing. This type of remote batch system is used when many locations are tied to the central computer and when many transactions are handled on a repetitive basis. Figure 6–4 illustrates an on-line remote batch processing system. The computer is tied directly to the communication device for *on-line* processing.

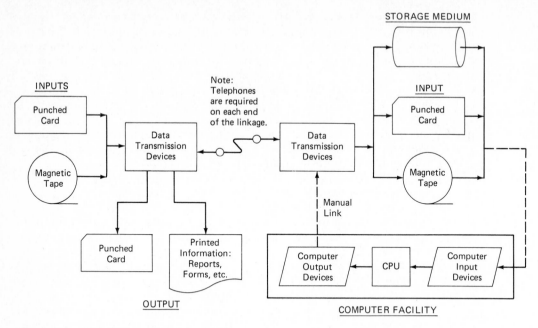

Figure 6-3 Off-Line Remote Batch Processing

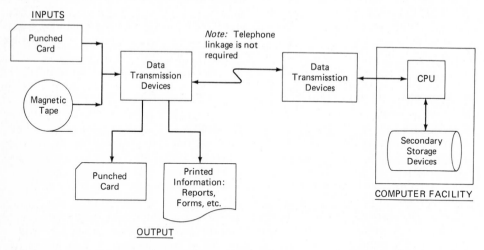

Figure 6-4 On-Line Remote Batch Processing

Real-Time Processing

Typical applications of real-time processing are airlines reservation systems, bank deposit and transfer accounting, hotel accounting and reservation systems, law enforcement systems, patient hospital record systems, savings and loan accounting, and stock market information systems. Transactions and inquiries into these systems are processed as they occur. Data stored in direct-access media are always kept current in order to reflect the status of the firm. All information is available at all times for immediate interrogation.

Recall that a real-time system is one in which data are processed and handled in a small enough time interval so that the resulting information is available in sufficient time to control an activity or process in the operating environment. A key concept in this definition is *response time*. Quite often real-time systems are viewed as being capable of providing an immediate response. In actuality, the nature of the activity being controlled determines the length of the response time. If the activity involved happened to be the flight of an aircraft, then a response time measured in fractions of a second would be necessary for the system to control the activity. If the activity is within the business environment, a response time of several seconds or even several minutes may be immediate enough to control the process or activity. Thus the nature of the activity determines the required response time for a real-time system.

Two additional factors relating to real-time systems should also be highlighted. First, real-time systems, particularly those in the business environment, may be subsystems of larger systems. The real-time subsystem may be applied to one, two, or many particular activities in the firm, while batch processing is employed in all other activities. Second, a real-time system must have an on-line capability; but as we noted in our examination of batch processing, an on-line capability alone does not qualify a system as real-time. The system must contain hardware and software that will enable it to process input data and generate a response that is useful for control purposes.

Unlike batch processing systems where both sequential files and random access files can be used, real-time systems principally employ random access devices. The only uses made of sequential files are to hold master file records before and after updates in case a data base recovery is necessary and to back up the software programs that constitute the system.

In real-time processing, each transaction- or input-originating point has an input/output device that is linked to the computer. These terminals are used to send transactions to, and receive responses from, the computer facility. Thus real-time processing also differs from batch processing in that the input/output devices such as card readers, printers, paper-tape and magnetic-tape readers, and card punches, which are used in batch processing, are not very useful.

REAL-TIME PROCESSING: MODES OF OPERATION   Two modes of operation exist in real-time processing: (1) time sharing and (2) on-line. *Time sharing* is a special-purpose form of real-time processing designed to serve the problem-solving, instead of transaction-handling, needs of users. Many users at different locations can be linked to one computer facility in a time-shared network. *On-line* real-time processing, on the other hand, is designed to fulfill the data processing requirements for only one firm and is capable of processing information within a very short time interval.

Figure 6–5 illustrates a time-sharing system. Under a time-sharing structure, remote terminals are used for developing and testing programs as well as for entering data and retrieving information from files. A large number of users are handled in the time-sharing mode by allocating and controlling the amount of CPU time available to each user. The operating system within the

INPUT/OUTPUT TERMINALS:

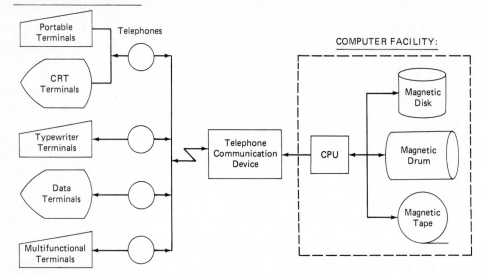

Figure 6–5   Time-Sharing System

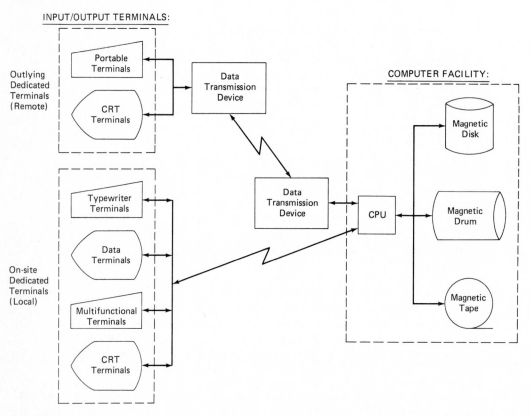

Figure 6–6   On-Line Real-Time System

CPU allocates time so that each user is unaware that access to the CPU is being shared.

A key feature of time sharing is the "conversational" nature that is used when programs are being developed. Data input errors can be detected by the computer and displayed on the terminal, and new data input can be accepted before processing continues.

Figure 6–6 illustrates that, physically, an on-line real-time system is similar to a time-sharing arrangement with one exception: Dedicated terminals are employed and have a continuous connection with the computer facility. Obviously the operating system within the CPU will differ between time-sharing and on-line systems. Real-time processing in the on-line mode requires continuous access to the CPU in most applications.

It is not necessary to have all terminals within a real-time network physically located close to the computer facility; data communication systems can be used to link geographically dispersed terminals. However, as we will note shortly in our overview of integrated systems, a real-time system must be integrated in order to be most effective.

EVOLUTION OF SYSTEMS[1]

From the material in the preceding section, we might conclude that batch processing and real-time processing are system structures, particularly since we used the terms *batch processing system* and *real-time processing system*. In actuality the terms refer to types or modes of operations employed in various information system structures. In this section the term *batch processing* as well as *real-time processing* will be used in conjunction with *integrated systems, real-time integrated systems*, and *distributed processing systems*.

Various approaches to information system designs have evolved over the past twenty-five to thirty years. In each case each new design has sought to correct the deficiencies of the previous design. Currently the thrust in information systems appears to be toward distributed processing systems. This trend has been brought on by the rapidly declining cost of microcomputers, minicomputers, and small general-purpose terminals, and by a number of deficiencies in integrated real-time systems. To better understand this transition, we will examine the evolution of systems, including (1) traditional accounting systems, (2) responsibility reporting systems, (3) integrated data processing systems, (4) integrated management information systems, (5) real-time integrated information systems, and (6) distributed processing systems.

Traditional Accounting Systems

Prior to the introduction of computers, information systems were concerned with providing historical summaries of a company's performance. The focus was on providing the balance sheet and income statement. Little, if any, emphasis was placed on providing information related to controlling day-to-day operations. There was little concern for obtaining feedback of critical informa-

[1] Much of the material in this section summarizes the concepts described in detail by Robert J. Thierauf in *Distributed Processing Systems* (ⓒ1978, pp. 3–52, 102, 105, 136–52. Adapted by permission of Prentice-Hall, Inc., Englewood Cliffs, N.J.)

tion to compare actual performances with preestablished plans. Traditional information systems, therefore, were historically oriented.

The traditional accounting systems consisted of a number of major subsystems such as accounts payable, accounts receivable, and the general ledger. There was no attempt to integrate records that might serve several subsystems. Each subsystem was treated as a separate entity; each was concerned with its own record-keeping task. Because of the individual subsystem focus, a proliferation of excess records occurred within the overall accounting system. In addition, it generally took long periods of time to produce historical reports. Each transaction was handled individually. Manual methods, bookkeeping equipment, and punched-card equipment were employed in traditional accounting systems before computers appeared in the business environment.

Responsibility Reporting Systems

Traditional accounting systems provided an overall historical picture of the firm but did little in terms of providing information to the managers responsible for activities at different levels within the firm. To overcome this deficiency, responsibility reporting systems emerged. A responsibility reporting system was molded around a firm's organizational structure; it was designed to provide historical data at specified time intervals to the various managerial (responsibility) levels within the firm. The system focused on providing information concerned with activities over which specific individuals had accountability and control. (An example was given in chapter 3.)

Responsibility reporting systems, like traditional accounting systems, involved the historical reporting of accounting activities; however, they differed from the traditional system in that they were budget based. A budget was constructed from the top level of management to the lowest responsibility level in the firm. Every manager at every level participated in the preparation of the budget at his or her level of responsibility. Monthly reports resulting from the responsibility reporting system were compared with the preestablished budget. A manager was held responsible for unfavorable deviations of actual costs or other goals from budgeted goals at his or her responsibility level.

The responsibility reporting system overcame some of the deficiencies of the traditional accounting systems. At the time of its initial development, however, it was plagued by the absence of the computer. An extreme amount of time was required to implement the system using manual methods and bookkeeping machines. With punched-card equipment, the procedures involved in manually handling cards, preparing detailed cards, and generating reports were still very lengthy and time consuming. It was not until the introduction of batch processing computer systems that managers readily adopted responsibility reporting systems. Computer batch processing significantly reduced the labor required in manipulating and handling data and provided an easy means for storage of historical data.

Integrated Data Processing Systems

The responsibility reporting systems were an improvement over the traditional accounting systems, but several deficiencies existed in the overall systems available for use in business. First, because computers were first utilized in the accounting function, many of the early developments in the systems area were justified on the basis of the computer's ability to perform accounting activities rather than on providing management with more information and better control over different operations. Second, a piecemeal approach to the development and use of systems occurred even though data processing became more widely used, because applications tend to follow the organizational boundaries of the firm. Duplicate data and, in many cases, duplicate computer programs and subsystems existed.

The next development in systems thus focused on integrating the data processing activities of the firm by integrating the organization's major functions such as finance, marketing, and production. In terms of the conceptual framework of an information system discussed in Chapter 2, integrated data processing was directed at integrating the data processing elements with the management functions dimension.

A distinguishing characteristic of an integrated data processing system is a common set of software by function. This, however, does not mean that all software is common (refer to Figure 2–4). This type of system is flexible; it responds easier to changes in activities, methods, procedures, and responsibilities within the organization because a single software change can be reflected across the organization.

The key factor that differentiated integrated data processing from prior systems was the single record concept. A single data entry is employed in a multiple number of subsystems. Under the single record concept, data are stored in a processible form that can be used by many functional areas across the firm. An example application would be the records associated with the bill of materials created in the manufacturing of a product using several parts. The manufacturing function can use the records in determining material requirements and in placing orders with vendors. Accounting can use the records in conjunction with accounts payable. Marketing can use the information in pricing the final product.

Integrated data processing systems have two deficiencies, however: (1) they employ historical data, and therefore historical output reports are generated; and (2) they fail to include the managerial activities dimension of an information system (refer to Figure 2–4).

Integrated Management Information Systems

The development of integrated information systems occurred in a two-step process. First, integrated management information systems appeared, followed by the development of real-time integrated information systems. In this section we will focus on integrated management information systems.

By incorporating the management activities dimensions of information systems into the integrated data processing system, integrated management information systems emerged. The net result of this system structure was a framework designed to provide decision-oriented information needed by management to plan, control, and evaluate the organization's activities. The focus of all systems prior to integrated MIS was primarily on providing financial information; an integrated management information system focuses on generation of reports and information that will assist management. Financial reports are generated through the system but are a byproduct of the information processed in generating management reports. Such a system also goes beyond merely linking the managerial activities and providing reports; it aids management by taking over routine decision making, thus allowing management to focus on areas that are not routine.

Figure 6–7 illustrates an integrated management information system. To specifically illustrate the integrated framework, consider the receipt of a customer order. The order becomes part of an open order file that is used for preparing invoices and ultimately updating the accounts receivable file. Since the order will result in the production and shipment of a product, it has an impact on the raw material inventory file, production scheduling plans, labor scheduling routines, finished goods inventory file, shipping orders file, sales commission records, and market forecast routines. On the processing of a number of incoming customer orders, the raw material inventory subsystem will probably trigger the issuance of a purchase order for raw materials. The raw material subsystem includes a routine decision-making program that will compute the reorder quantity, reorder point, and economic order quantity using mathematical models. Since the purchase order results in a liability, the accounts payable file is also affected. The integrative features of this system do not occur by chance but are a result of the operational aspects of transactions flowing through the system. Thus the integrated MIS framework simply complements the flow of transactions.

The integrated management information system rectified the problem of the system's being accounting based and directed toward the functional areas of the firm. However, the early versions of such systems were deficient in that they were batch processing oriented (refer to Figure 6–7). This was true even when random access devices were employed. Data thus had to be accumulated over time before processing occurred. This meant that the system was still historical, since the output reports were based on past rather than current data.

This deficiency in integrated systems was primarily due to the lack of equipment and software necessary to support on-line processing. This support was a necessary prerequisite to an emphasis on random access. The emphasis placed on moving away from the functional structure of integrated data processing to a combined functional/managerial activity structure also slowed the movement from integrated information systems to real-time systems.

Real-Time Integrated Information Systems

Many versions of integrated management information systems, responsibility reporting systems, and the other systems we have discussed previously in our overview are still being used by firms within the business environment. The development of hardware and software capabilities, however, brought to fruition real-time integrated information systems. Real-time systems emerged when on-line input/output devices became readily available and when advanced software in the form of operating systems, multiprogramming, and multiprocessing were developed.

Inputs From Major Business Functions

Function	Inputs
Corporate Planning	Short Range Planning (Budgets) Medium Range Planning Long Range Planning
Marketing	Sales Forecasts Customer Orders Advertising Data Shipping Orders Back Orders Commission Data
Research and Development	Current R & D Projects Applied Research Data Pure Research Data
Engineering	Engineering Data Engineering Orders Plant Engineering Data Special Engineering Data
Manufacturing	Manpower Data Production Schedules Quality Control Data
Inventory	Bills of Materials Inventory Data — Raw Materials and Work in Process Cost Cards
Purchasing	Purchase Orders Data on Vendors Economic Ordering Quantity Data Receiving Data Purchase Requisitions
Physical Distribution	Inventory Data — Finished Goods Shipping Data
Accounting	Customer Billing Accounts Receivable Accounts Payable Payroll Data Cost Data Actual Versus Budget Data
Finance	Cash Flow Capital Projects Sources of Funds
Personnel	Personnel Data Personnel Forecasts Contract Negotiation Data Wage Adjustment Factors

Current (Old) Master Files

- Corporate Planning Files
- Sales Data Files
- Customer Master File
- Research and Development Files
- Engineering Files
- Inventory and Price Files
- Production Scheduling and Shipping Files
- Accounts Receivable and Payable Files
- Budgets and Ledger Balances
- Employee and Payroll File
- Other Input Files

Computer Processing

Various Inputs for Computer Processing Runs → Computer Processing Runs (Batch Processing) → Outputs — Daily, Weekly, Monthly, and Special Reports

Updated (New) Master Files

- Corporate Planning Files
- Sales Data Files
- Customer Master File
- Research and Development Files
- Engineering Files
- Inventory and Price Files
- Production Scheduling and Shipping Files
- Accounts Receivable and Payable Files
- Budgets and Ledger Balances
- Employee and Payroll File
- Other Output Files

Output — Management Reports

Daily	Weekly	Monthly	Special Reports
Sales	Inventory Status	Balance Sheet and Income Statement	Profit Planning Reports
Unfilled and Back Orders	Delinquency Notices	Profit Centers Performance Reports	Revised Sales Forecast
Cash Position	Factory Utilization Projections	Overhead Budget Reports	Sales Trend Analyses
Warehouse Shipments and Replacements	Raw Material Status and Shortages	Product Performance Reports	Share of Market
Anticipated Stockouts	Payroll Distribution	Raw Material Forecasts	Results of Special Promotions
Factory Capacity Available	Order Summaries	Variance Analysis	Reports on Capital Projects
Work in Process Summary		Profitability by Product Lines	Outstanding Purchase Commitments
Expediting Information		Aged Trial Balance	Inventory Trends

Key to Reports

- Control Reports
- Information Reports

Integrated management information system for a typical manufacturing firm — data stored on magnetic tapes can be used for more than one report.

Figure 6–7 Integrated Management Information System

Source: Robert J. Thierauf, *Distributed Processing Systems*, © 1978, pp. 18–19. Reprinted by permission of Prentice-Hall, Inc., Englewood Cliffs, N.J.

Real-time processing capabilities provide a control feedback mechanism to complement integrated systems. Figure 6–8 illustrates a real-time integrated information system for a manufacturing firm. To clarify the real-time nature of the system, we will focus on the production area. We will assume that on-line terminals exist throughout the area and all variable manufacturing data are entered as they occur. The on-line data base for this function, as well as those for related managerial activities, are thus always up-to-date. We will also assume that a scheduling subsystem is used to aid management in controlling the manufacturing area. At the beginning of each day the computerized scheduler simulates the activities in the manufacturing area and identifies work assignments and flow rates for all operations. When a breakdown or an unexpected bottleneck occurs in the area during the day, the information is fed back to the scheduler and to management. The scheduler computes multiple alternative work assignments and sends the information to the production manager for a decision. A report is also generated showing the impact on flow rates and shipping schedules, and the critical areas that require immediate attention. The system in essence provides a response that is fed back in sufficient time to control the daily manufacturing activities.

To further illustrate a real-time integrated information system, we can highlight some of its key characteristics. First, there are a number of on-line input/output devices located throughout the organization. These may be teletypewriters, cathode ray tubes, or other devices capable of sending as well as receiving information. These may be physically located in the same building or office or may be miles apart and linked through a data communications network to the computer.

Second, the system is "forward looking" rather than historical. The firm's data base is maintained on-line, is updated as events occur, and can be interrogated from many I/O terminals as the need arises. Feedback of vital information is available when needed, since source data are entered as they occur. Errors and conflicting reports are minimized, since all areas have access to and use the same data and report-generating subsystems. Because the system can provide important information on a timely basis, control of current operations is possible. Decision models are also available to aid in evaluating trends, identifying favorable or unfavorable deviations in preestablished plans, and suggesting corrective action for areas that are out of control.

A third characteristic of a real-time integrated information system is that it focuses on the principle of "management by exception." Only unusually favorable or unfavorable events are brought to the attention of those responsible and accountable for them. Normal events are processed without management's attention, freeing the manager to give attention only to those matters that deviate from the planned levels of operation. Management by exception provides better control over operations and more efficiency. It also serves several other key purposes: (1) it reinforces the need for clearly identifying specific areas of responsibility within the firm, (2) it highlights problems of which upper-level management should be aware, and (3) it necessitates clear procedures for handling problems on a higher level when they cannot be solved on the level on which they occur.

A fourth characteristic that differentiates a real-time integrated system from prior systems is its modular structure. The data base and the software

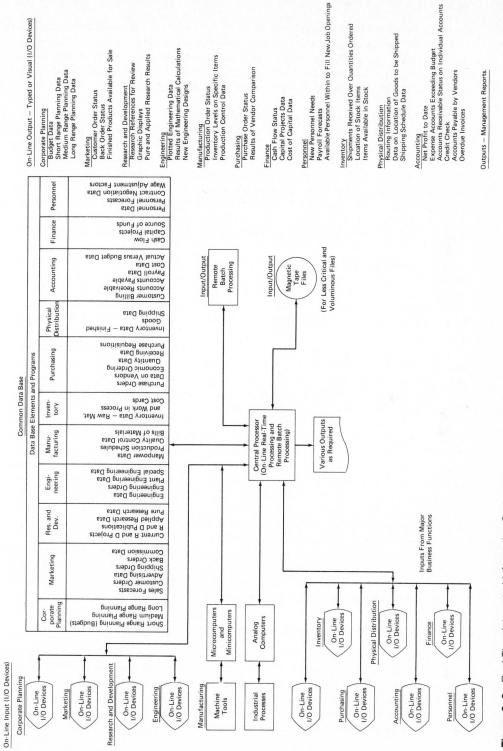

On-Line Input (I/O Devices)

Corporate Planning
- On-Line I/O Devices

Marketing
- On-Line I/O Devices

Research and Development
- On-Line I/O Devices

Engineering
- On-Line I/O Devices

Manufacturing
- Machine Tools
- Microcomputers and Minicomputers

Industrial Processes
- Analog Computers

Inventory
- On-Line I/O Devices

Purchasing
- On-Line I/O Devices

Physical Distribution
- On-Line I/O Devices

Accounting
- On-Line I/O Devices

Finance
- On-Line I/O Devices

Personnel
- On-Line I/O Devices

Inputs From Major Business Functions

Common Data Base
Data Base Elements and Programs

Corporate Planning	Marketing	Res. and Dev.	Engineering	Manufacturing	Inventory	Purchasing	Physical Distribution	Accounting	Finance	Personnel
Short Range Planning (Budgets)	Sales Forecasts	Current R and D Projects	Engineering Data	Manpower Data	Inventory Data – Raw Mat.	Purchase Orders	Inventory Data – Finished	Customer Billing	Cash Flow	Personnel Data
Medium Range Planning	Customer Orders	R and D Publications	Plant Engineering Data	Production Schedules	and Work in Process	Data on Vendors	Goods	Accounts Receivable	Capital Projects	Personnel Forecasts
Long Range Planning	Shipping Orders	Applied Research Data	Special Engineering Data	Quality Control Data	Cost Cards	Economic Ordering	Shipping Data	Accounts Payable	Source of Funds	Contract Negotiation Data
	Advertising Data	Pure Research Data	Engineering Orders	Bills of Materials		Quantity Data		Payroll Data		Wage Adjustment Factors
	Shipping Orders					Receiving Data		Cost Data		
	Back Orders					Purchase Requisitions		Actual Versus Budget Data		
	Commission Data									

Central Processor
(On-Line Real-Time Processing and Remote Batch Processing)

Various Outputs as Required

Input/Output — Remote Batch Processing

Input/Output — Magnetic Tape Files
(For Less Critical and Voluminous Files)

On-Line Output — Typed or Visual (I/O Devices)

Corporate Planning
- Budget Data
- Short Range Planning Data
- Medium Range Planning Data
- Long Range Planning Data

Marketing
- Customer Order Status
- Back Order Status
- Finished Products Available for Sale

Research and Development
- Research References for Review
- Graphic Displays
- Pure and Applied Research Results

Engineering
- Plotted Engineering Data
- Results of Mathematical Calculations
- New Engineering Designs

Manufacturing
- Production Order Status
- Inventory Levels on Specific Items
- Production Control Data

Purchasing
- Purchase Order Status
- Results of Vendor Comparison

Finance
- Cash Flow Status
- Capital Projects Data
- Cost of Capital Data

Personnel
- New Personnel Needs
- Payroll Forecasts
- Available Personnel Within to Fill New Job Openings

Inventory
- Shipments Received Over Quantities Ordered
- Location of Stock Items
- Items Available in Stock

Physical Distribution
- Routing Information
- Data on Location of Goods to be Shipped
- Shipping Schedule Data

Accounting
- Net Profit to Date
- Expense Accounts Exceeding Budget
- Accounts Receivable Status on Individual Accounts
- Credit Check
- Accounts Payable by Vendors
- Overdue Invoices

Outputs — Management Reports.

Figure 6-8 Real-Time Integrated Information System

Source: Robert J. Thierauf, *Distributed Processing Systems*, ©1978, pp. 22-23. Reprinted by permission of Prentice-Hall, Inc., Englewood Cliffs, N.J.

161

that support different subsystems are not permanent, and their relationships to other subsystems are not fixed. The subsystem modules are flexible enough to accommodate new internal and external factors and have the ability to take source transactions and "explode" them into other related transactions for other applications. This latter feature allows one module to "cross-talk" with other modules on-line and in real-time.

The final characteristic common to real-time integrated systems is that they can handle *batch processing* as well as *on-line processing* for applications that are not ideally suited for real-time processing. (Note that Figure 6–8 provides these features.) All processing activities need not be real-time; in many cases it is more economical to employ a batch processing approach. If the areas involved are widely dispersed geographically, then remote batch processing may be applicable, even if hardware may exist to support real-time processing. The cost or processing in real-time, in general, is more than that of batch processing. If real-time is not required, batch processing may be the desired alternative.

On-line updating is a form of on-line processing in which individual transactions are processed in order to update a master file immediately. The on-line updating process is initiated by the keying of transactions into the system. The input transaction initiates the accessing of the record with which the transaction is associated in storage. The record is read into the CPU, updated, and then written back onto the on-line storage device. At the same time, a copy of the transaction may be output onto the input terminal to verify completion of the update. On-line updating is not a form of real-time processing because all that is accomplished is the updating of a record. On-line updating, however, is required in real-time processing because it is the means by which the data base is kept up-to-date.

In Chapter 2 we identified and summarized some major advantages of integrated systems. The major points identified are applicable to a real-time integrated information system, and therefore it is suggested that the reader review the section entitled "Integrated Systems." One of the concluding comments in the chapter was that quite often in discussing integrated systems, some individuals view the structure as a "total system." A real-time integrated information system is not a total system, but of all the systems developed to date it comes closest to the total systems concept.

A number of disadvantages of integrated systems were identified in Chapter 2, such as the extremely high cost of development, the catastrophic nature of certain system problems (loss of the CPU, for example, unless a complete backup system is available), and the system's requirement for development and maintenance of skilled employees.

Distributed Processing Systems

Just as real-time processing was brought about by the development of hardware such as on-line CRT terminals and support software such as multiprogramming, distributed processing became economically feasible when low-cost minicomputers, microprocessors, and "intelligent" terminals became readily available. A number of other factors, however, also had a strong bearing on the development of new types of systems configurations. First, because integrated systems were built around one or more large centralized processing units, bottlenecks often occurred both in the input of data and in the feedback of output information. This weakness could be overcome to some extent by employing on-line real-time capabilities. The costly random access devices and remote terminals employed in a real-time structure require large financial commitments at the initial development of the system; however, many companies were unwilling or unable to commit the enormous amounts of required capital and time. Second, in an integrated system data integrity often becomes a problem. An integrated data base exists, and therefore all data are forwarded to the central facility. In a large integrated system operating in a heavily loaded multiprogramming and/or teleprocessing environment, line failures and teleprocessing problems separate remote users from the data. Security of data is often a concern of users, but the transmission of erroneous data occurs because data are transferred to the central facility before error checks can be made.

Distributed processing overcomes some of the limitations and deficiencies of integrated systems by organizing the data processing resources to support remote applications rather than organizing the system around the needs or constraints of a centralized computer site. In essence, distributed processing takes the computer to the job rather than the job to the computer. Distributed processing does not mean that a front-end processor is used to handle data communications from the central computer facility, nor does it mean using several minicomputers or general-purpose computers located at the central site to replace one large computer. Rather, distributed processing means that individual processors, minicomputers, microprocessors, and small-business computers are located at sites remote from the central facility and that these machines handle the major processing operations that were originally handled at the central site. Management at the local and regional levels is responsible for processing and maintaining many of these applications.

CHARACTERISTICS OF DISTRIBUTED PROCESSING SYSTEMS In our discussion of real-time integrated information systems we noted that integrated systems are characterized by (1) the use of on-line input/output terminals, (2) a "forward looking" rather than a historical approach to report generation, (3) the use of "management by exception" reporting, and (4) the ability to handle *batch processing* as well as *on-line processing*. Distributed processing systems are also built around these characteristics, with major differentiating factors being the type of I/O terminals employed. Distributed systems make heavy use of "intelligent" and "clustered" terminals, whereas most on-line real-time systems employ "dumb" terminals. We will discuss these terminals in detail in the next section, "Hardware of Integrated and Distributed Systems." The key characteristics that differentiate distributed systems from integrated systems, however, are not the use of terminals or the other three characteristics but rather are (1) the *employment of a distributed data base*, and (2) as we noted earlier, *local autonomy of data processing operations*.

Distributed data base. By employing a distributed data base, some of the problems encountered with a large centralized data base can be overcome. In a distributed data base structure, the users' files are placed near the point at which the transactions occur, and therefore the users' data are always available. If data communication failures occur between the distributed site and the central facility, access to the local data is not lost. Likewise, by employing a distributed data base, the volume and accuracy of data transmitted to the central site can be controlled. Distributed processing is based on the premise that remote systems with local data bases can process and store many of the data that under an integrated framework would be sent to the main computer. In an integrated system, error-ridden data are often transmitted from a "dumb" terminal to the CPU where error checks, processing, and storage take place. Under a distributed data base structure, data are processed and stored locally, with summary information or error-free data being transmitted to the centralized data base.

One of the arguments for a centralized integrated data base is that redundant data are avoided. In a distributed data base, a number of separate data bases exist and therefore redundant data may occur. The problem of redundant data in a distributed framework can, however, be controlled by logical integration of related data bases. The task of integrating the data can be minimized by employing a data base management system. Numerous data base management systems are currently available for creating multiple data bases and handling the integration of the data bases efficiently and economically. (Data base management systems are examined in Chapter 8.)

Autonomy of data processing operations. In a distributed processing structure, local and regional management have more control over hardware and operations as well as data processing applications. As we noted earlier, remote distributed systems can continue to operate even when access to the centralized computer systems is impossible. Transaction processing as well as a number of other broad applications are not dependent upon the central site, particularly if a distributed data base exists at the remote site. When easy-to-operate data-entry and processing equipment are employed, source data can be collected and processed and summary management reports can all be generated by non–EDP personnel. In addition, unique or critical processing needs can be handled at the local level because program development on a small independent system is usually less demanding and more economical than developing all programs at a central site. The development of unique applications at the local level not only ensures responsive service to lower-level needs and provides more control to the responsible managers but also minimizes the impact on central site resources. The central facility can therefore concentrate on programs and problems that have an impact on the entire distributed system or improve the efficiency of the overall system. Local autonomy thus benefits both the distributed site and the central site.

In Chapter 2 we identified and discussed some of the advantages and disadvantages of distributed processing systems. Since that material complements our current discussion, it is suggested that the reader review the material.

FORMS OF DISTRIBUTED PROCESSING SYSTEMS   To better understand distributed computing, it is necessary that we examine three concepts: (1) data-entry processing, (2) local processing/management reporting, and (3) network structures.

Data-entry processing. The most basic distributed processing system centers on the local processing of source data. Fundamentally the system consists of single or multiple data-entry units that are distributed throughout the organization at local or regional sites. The system is designed to capture business data at distributed field locations in an organization.

Figure 6–9 illustrates a data-entry processing arrangement. In the figure, data are entered at the local level via key entry units which are under the control of a small processor. Data entered on the keyboard are processed by the local system, using a magnetic disk to temporarily hold data. Once the entries have been verified and errors have been corrected, the data are automatically transferred onto magnetic tape and are then transferred in batch mode via a telecommunication device to the central computer facility.

One mode of operation in the data-entry processing arrangement consists of using the data-entry devices in an interactive processing environment. This approach allows concurrent entry of source data while batch processing operations take place. Under this arrangement, the local processor must have a partitioned supervisor that can handle batch processing communications or other "background processing" activities while simultaneously servicing data-entry devices. In employing this latter approach it is not necessary to restrict input to local data-entry units while batch processing communications are being handled, which is the case for the more basic arrangement. The batch input data are stored on the magnetic tape medium until a predetermined time or until a specified volume of data is reached, at which point the batch data are transmitted to the central site.

It should be noted that in Figure 6–9 a means is provided for on-line processing of source data via a telecommunication device to the central facility. This is an alternative mode of operation. In essence the diagram represents a hybrid form of a distributed-integrated system wherein the distributed aspect of the system is designed to be the more economical and efficient means for handling data-entry processing. In this distributed arrangement a data base does not exist at the local level. The magnetic disk unit associated with the local processor is used for temporary storage of input data. All error-free data are transmitted to the central site.

Local processing/management reporting. The second form or level of distributed processing, which we label *local processing/management reporting*, builds upon the framework of data-entry processing by adding local processing of transactions and local preparation of management reports. This is made possible primarily by providing the appropriate hardware and software at the local level to build and maintain a data base and to handle local processing. A variety of equipment configurations can be employed in order to operate in such an environment. To be most effective, each system will be tailor-made for a given application. Figure 6–10 shows how this type of system might be arranged.

In essence, the framework of Figure 6–10 is an elaboration of Figure 6–9, with the key difference being the inclusion of a local data base, a local computer that is capable of handling transactional processing of source input data, and other peripheral devices for input/output at the local level. A means is also provided for on-line updating directly to the central computer via a communication device. This procedure is used for source data that are not locally related but are pertinent to the central site or the overall organization.

The operation of this form of a distributed system is built upon processing at the local level. The system is capable of handling local operations and producing management information. After source documents are entered

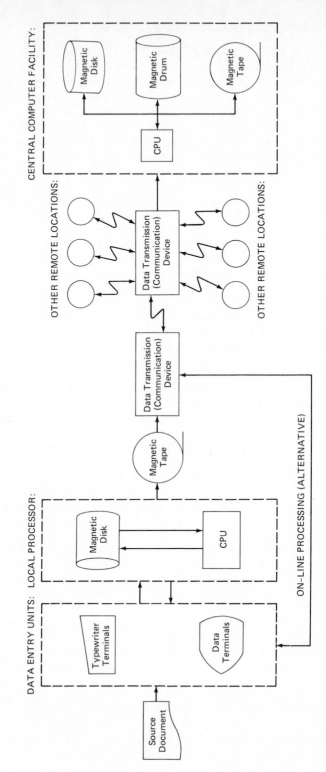

Figure 6-9 Data-Entry Processing Arrangement of Distributed Processing

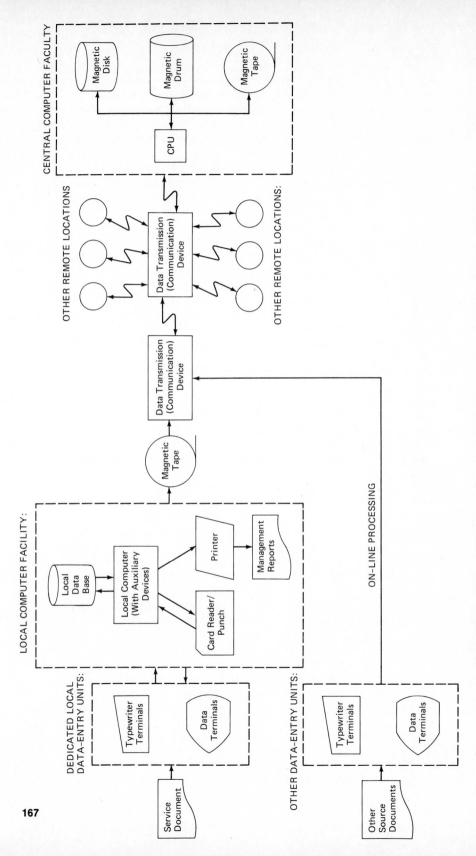

Figure 6–10 Transaction Processing/Management Reporting Arrangement of Distributed Processing

and validated using the local computer, transactions are processed and managerial reports are generated. In effect, the system gives both the local managers and the operating personnel more control over existing operations. Operating personnel handle the entire transaction process rather than just capturing source data that are then forwarded to the center site. Managers receive reports about current operations and have inquiry access to the local data base.

The actual output from the local processing is varied. First, and the most obvious, managerial reports that serve the needs of local managers can be generated. Second, detailed as well as summary information that is to be forwarded via the communication device to the central computer center may result from the daily processing of transactions. Third, if the processing of transactions has an impact on the data base, then a provision must be made to update all data files. Finally, output from the system may simply be historical data that are accumulated for projected needs in the future. Figure 6–10, however, is not the only form in which a local processing structure can exist. As we have noted, the system may have a variety of structures in terms of hardware configurations. The key element is whether local processing/management reporting capabilities exist.

Network structures. Data-entry processing and local processing focus on the needs and operations of local sites; network structures focus on the needs across the firm and at the corporate level or central site. These latter needs arise from two sources: (1) some local operations may need data that are processed and/or stored at other local data bases (rather than having duplicate data in each local data base, a means should exist for accessing data at all or specific local sites); and (2) management at the corporate level is more interested in how the firm is operating as a total unit (corporate needs thus call for the linking of information from local sites). Networks, structured by employing hardware such as multiplexers, line adapters, modems, and other communication equipment, are the means for linking remote processing centers. At least five basic network structures exist: (1) point-to-point network, (2) hierarchical or tree network, (3) star network, (4) loop or ring network, and (5) fully connected ring network. We will examine each briefly.

Point-to-point network. The point-to-point network, which consists of two processors, minicomputers, or general-purpose computers—or a combination of these—linked together by a communication line, is the simplest form of a network (see Figure 6–11). In this arrangement each machine performs a specific function. For example, one can be devoted to data processing, while the other, which may be a special-purpose device, performs I/O control functions, including buffering and message switching. In essence, each machine performs a complementary function for the other.

Hierarchical or tree network. This network configuration complements the hierarchical structure of most firms in that a large or host computer provides the central processing function and dedicated microprocessors, minicomputers, or general-purpose computers perform functional processing that is input to the next higher level in the organization. In each case in a hierarchical configuration, the communications that take place are between microprocessors, minicomputers, or general-purpose computers that exist on different levels. No communication link exists between machines at the same level. Figure 6–12, part A illustrates a hierarchical or tree network.

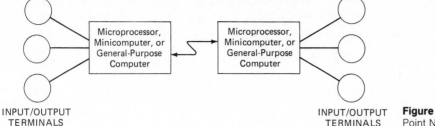

INPUT/OUTPUT
TERMINALS   INPUT/OUTPUT   **Figure 6–11**   Point-to-
                                             TERMINALS   Point Network

Star network. In the star network a multiple number of remote microprocessors and/or minicomputers are tied, each with separate lines, to a central (host) computer (see Figure 6–12, part B). Structurally a star network is similar to a two-level hierarchy network but differs in that a heavier flow of communication exists between each sublevel computer and the central computer. Branch (remote) computers perform all local operations and communicate with the central site; the central computer controls the combined operations of the network and supplies centralized data as required by the branch units. A typical application of a star network is an airlines reservation and ticketing system.

Loop or ring network. A loop or ring network is simply a group of microprocessors, minicomputers, or general-purpose computers—or some combination of these—linked together to form a ring. Each computer is serially linked to the nearest adjacent computer via a communication line. If a unit needs data from a unit not linked directly to it, the request must be routed through all intermediate units. For this reason, a ring configuration is only used when the remote units are physically close together. Otherwise inquiry and data transfers become uneconomical. A loop or ring configuration is shown in Figure 6–13, part A.

Fully connected ring network. The standard form of the ring or loop network is very limited; because of this it is seldom employed in practice. The more commonly used form of a ring is the fully connected ring shown in Figure 6–13, part B. In this configuration each microprocessor, minicomputer, or general-purpose computer is cross-linked to every other unit. There is no central computer, and the cross-linking circumvents any breakdown in the flow of data or communications anywhere in the system. Obviously the cost of communication equipment for this configuration is much greater than that for other network structures. Some banking institutions utilize this form of network.

Other network structures—general comments. As we have already noted, the structure of most distributed processing systems will probably not conform strictly to any of the previously defined networks. Most systems will be an elaboration of one of the structures, tailored for the specific firm or organization. In designing a system we must always remember that the major objective of distributed processing is to organize data processing resources to support remote applications, rather than to organize a central site and support remote sites to the extent that resources permit.

Several additional factors must also be considered in the design of distributed networks. First, hardware as well as software make up a network. Hardware generally includes data transmission equipment, multiplexers, line

A. Hierarchial or Tree Network

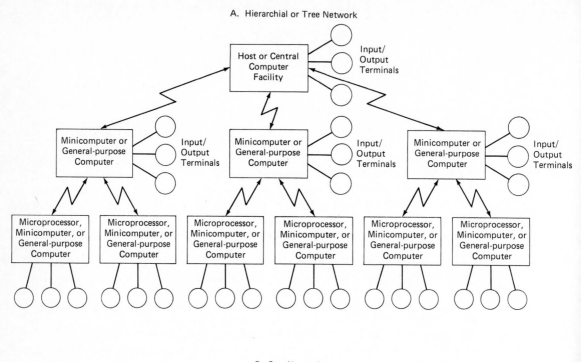

B. Star Network

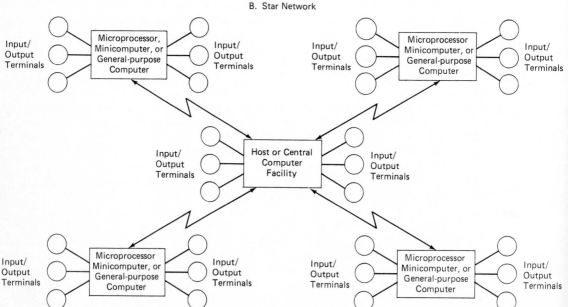

Figure 6–12 Hierarchical and Star Networks

A. Loop or Ring Network

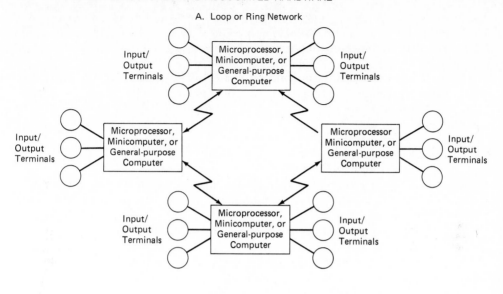

B. Fully Connect Ring Network

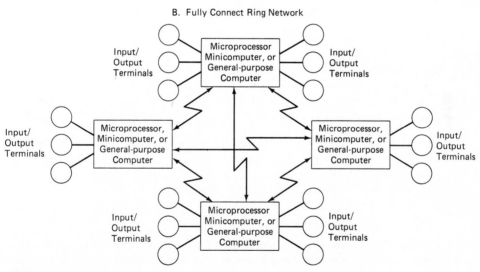

Figure 6–13 Ring Networks

adapters, modems, and other peripheral devices. Software consists of the operating system in the host computer, data base management systems, front-end processors, and remote processors for handling services provided to remote users. The term *network architecture* is used in referring to the combination of hardware and software that constitutes a network.

Second, the architecture of networks differs depending on whether the structure is designed around a general-purpose mainframe computer or minicomputers/microprocessors. General-purpose computer networks evolved from central processing systems; thus many use medium-to-large host processors to execute programs that are batch-stream collected from remote and local terminals in a star network. Minicomputer networks, on the other hand, usually consist of interconnected but independent computers in a ring or loop network.

In general there is no one dominant or best structure for a network; each must be designed for the particular firm or organization involved. However, the following factors must be considered if the distributed network is to be effective:

1. Data must be edited as close as possible to the point of origin in order to detect and correct errors.
2. Processing requirements should be clustered to the degree necessary to make the purchase and operation of processing equipment cost effective.
3. Data should be moved from one place to another only when it is absolutely necessary.
4. The data flows upward within the network should include only data that are significant to the upper levels of the organization.
5. Computing power should be placed at each hierarchical level or remote site to the extent that it can be best used and cost justified.

HARDWARE OF INTEGRATED AND DISTRIBUTED SYSTEMS

Up to this point in the chapter we have focused on the structure of systems (integrated MIS, integrated real-time systems, and distributed processing systems) and have examined different modes of operation (batch versus real-time). Little has been said about the hardware that is necessary to support these systems or operations. In this section we examine hardware elements, particularly those that relate to integrated and distributed processing, including (1) data communication equipment, (2) terminals, and (3) minicomputers/microcomputers.

Data Communications

Data communication is the process of transmitting data from one location to another, over communication channels such as telephone-telegraph lines and microwaves. When a CPU is a great distance from user terminals and I/O devices or from other computers with which it must interact, some form of data communication system is required. For example, when a time-sharing mode of operation is used and remote users access the central computer site, modems (message sending and receiving units), telephones, and telephone lines are required in addition to I/O terminals.

In general, data and communication systems can be subdivided into four major components: (1) *communication channels*, (2) *modems*, (3) *multiplexers and concentrators*, and (4) *communication processors*. All of these components are not required in every data communication system; however, a major data processing structure such as the real-time integrated system we identified earlier in the chapter (see Figure 6–8) would be likely to contain all of them, particularly the first three. The fourth component is used extensively in distributed processing systems.

COMMUNICATION CHANNELS Telephone and telegraph lines, often called carrier media, are examples of communication channels used for data transfer. Other varieties of communication channels are coaxial cables, microwave links, communication satellites, high-speed helical waveguides, and laser beam systems. These channels as a group cover the entire spectrum of data transfer capabilities including low, medium, and high transfer rates.

The transfer rate or capability of a channel is determined by its *grade*, or *bandwidth*. Telegraph lines are narrow bandwidth channels; they can transfer data at a rate of 45 to 90 bits per second. Telephone lines, which are voice grade-level, offer a broader bandwidth and thus a greater transfer rate. The transmission rates of telephone lines vary from 300 to 9,600 bits per second. Coaxial cables and microwaves provide broad-band channel capabilities, as do communication satellites, helical waveguides, and laser beam systems. Leased broad-band services are offered by both Western Union and the Bell System. Currently leased line services exist that provide data transmission rates of up to 120,000 bits per second.

MODEMS Special equipment is used in conjunction with a communication channel to send, code, amplify, and receive data. One of these special devices is a modem. The word *modem* is an acronym for "modular/demodulator." Computers store data in *digital pulse* form. Electrical signals are transmitted in *wave* form. Consequently, when data from a computer are transmitted via a communication channel, they must first be converted from pulse form to wave form. This process of conversion is called *modulation. Demodulation* is the reverse process. The wave form is converted to pulse form when data have been transferred through the channel and are to be received by the I/O device or by the computer if the transmission is in the opposite direction. Both modulation and demodulation functions are performed by the modem. Figure 6–14 illustrates the modulation/demodulation process.

MULTIPLEXERS AND CONCENTRATORS In Chapter 5 we discussed how a multiplexer unit could be used in conjunction with the CPU and associated peripheral devices. Recall that the multiplexer was placed between the CPU and the peripherals and involved the function of polling the low-speed peripherals

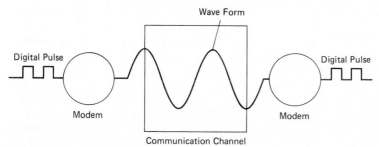

Figure 6–14
Modulation/Demodulation
Process

and combining data inputs and commands from each to provide a concentrated high-speed input to the CPU. This arrangement was necessary in order to avoid having the CPU sit idle while waiting on the low-speed peripherals. Multiplexers and concentrators are used in conjunction with communication channels to perform a similar function: They provide the means by which a number of input and output terminals can utilize a single communication channel.

The most widely used remote terminals operate at speeds ranging from 45 to 300 bits per second, with 100–150 bits per second being the most typical. When a number of these low-speed units are connected on-line to a CPU, each via a voice band (telephone) grade channel, communication can become very expensive, particularly if one or more of the terminals are outside the toll-free zone of the CPU. Since a voice-grade-level channel can transmit up to 9,600 bits per second, it would seem logical that more than one terminal can utilize the same channel, particularly if data transmission from different terminals can be kept separate. This is precisely the multiplexer's function. A multiplexer is able to subdivide a typical voice-grade line into narrower bandwidths so that each seems to become a separate channel. The multiplexer assigns each of the "subchannels" to a specific terminal or remote site, codes data for transmission, and decodes and reroutes communications at the receiving end. Figure 6–15 illustrates this concept.

In employing a multiplexer it is assumed that all terminals will be used 100 percent of the time. The multiplexer, therefore, subdivides the voice-grade channel into narrower bandwidth subchannels and allocates each to a given terminal. A concentrator differs from a multiplexer in that it is assumed that all terminals will not be in use at the same time; therefore a low-grade channel can be employed and terminals can "share" the channel. Data from only one terminal at a time can be transmitted over a channel when it is controlled by a concentrator; however, this does not mean that the communication network is limited to a single channel. The more typical case would be where, for example, six terminals utilized three channels (see Figure 6–16).

The concentrator controls access to the channels in the communication network by polling terminals when a channel becomes idle. The first terminal that is ready to transmit or receive data when polled is given control of the channel. The terminal retains control until its transmission is complete. The concentrator continues to monitor all channels to determine when the next channel will become available. When another channel is free for transmission, the terminal polling process is once again repeated. If several terminals are

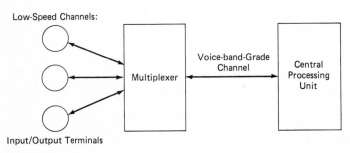

Low-Speed Channels:

Input/Output Terminals

Figure 6–15 Communication System Using Multiplexing

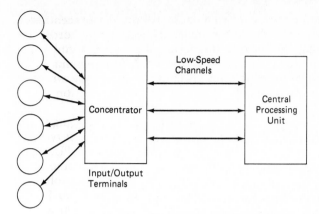

Figure 6–16 Communication System Using a Concentrator

awaiting use of a channel when it becomes available, the terminals are assigned to the channels on a FIFO (first-in, first-out) basis.

COMMUNICATIONS PROCESSOR Typically a data communications system will contain a number of different types of terminals, along with a variety of peripherals (both local and remote), a number of modems, possibly a multiplexer or concentrator unit or both, and other electronic control devices. As long as the total number of electronic devices and the amount of data transmitted are maintained at certain levels, the operating system of the central computer can be programmed to handle message switching, error checking, directing of message queues and priorities, and other duties associated with the throughput of data and information. However, if the number of terminals, peripheral devices, and other components and/or the volume of data transmission surpasses a certain level, a programmable communications processor can handle these tasks more economically than the central processor. A separate processor is thus economically justified.

Terminals

In Chapter 5 we identified and discussed a number of input/output terminal devices including the card reader, card punch, keyboard-to-tape encoder, visual display terminal, magnetic-ink character recognition (MICR) device, optical character recognition (OCR) device, and printer. In this section we will extend this discussion by focusing on three levels of terminal devices: (1) "dumb" terminals, (2) "smart" terminals, and (3) "intelligent" terminals. These classifications of terminals are widely used in the system literature, making it important that the reader have a clear understanding of what differentiates one class of terminal from the next. Examples will be given to illustrate specific points or concepts, but our objective is not to provide a survey of terminal hardware. Our discussion will be oriented toward on-line terminal processing.

"DUMB" TERMINALS A "dumb" terminal is a device connected to some form of computing capabilities and simply provides a direct-access method to and from the computer. No error checking, editing, or other capabilities can be performed by the terminal. The terminal has no storage capabilities other than a single line buffer for inputting strings of characters. All the devices discussed in Chapter 5 would be classified as dumb terminals. The most versatile device (in terms of on-line processing) fitting into this terminal category is the visual display terminal, more commonly referred to as the CRT (cathode ray tube) terminal. Data editing can be performed using a dumb terminal, but the work is performed by the user, not the terminal.

"SMART" TERMINALS "Smart" terminals differ from "dumb" terminals in that they are microprogrammable and thus are designed to perform a data input, data output, editing, and some other function automatically. Such terminals are not user-programmable. The logic for the function to be performed must be preprogrammed through the internal read-only memory of the device, a task usually performed by the manufacturer. The architecture of most smart terminals is such that a limited number of functions are performed by a given terminal.

A point-of-sale (POS) terminal is an example of a smart terminal. This terminal performs the functions of a cash register and also captures sales data. The POS terminals have a keyboard for data entry as well as a character recognition reader, a panel for displaying the price, a cash drawer, and a printer that generates a receipt. The factors that set the terminal apart as a smart terminal are that it can (1) read the Universal Product Code (UPC) stamped on an item as the item is being passed over the character recognition reader, (2) update the sales subtotal, and (3) create the sales receipt. If the terminal is directly connected to a central computer, inventory and sales information can also be updated automatically.

Another widely used smart terminal is the Touch-Tone terminal marketed by the Bell System. This device is used to input data from remote sites to a central computer. Several models of this terminal are available. A popular version of the terminal is that used in processing information relating to the credit status of credit-card customers. A clerk dials an access number (code) to the central computer and inserts the customer's card. The customer's account is checked, and the remaining credit balance for the customer is displayed on the phone's video read-out. A more sophisticated version of the terminal provides audio input/output capabilities allowing the clerk to provide all input information through a voice processor.

"INTELLIGENT" TERMINALS The characteristic that differentiates an "intelligent" terminal from other terminals is that it can be programmed using stored-program instructions. It has storage, control functions, a set of instructions, and other components similar to a standard computer, but these components are limited. Most intelligent terminals employ a CRT and in some cases a reader/printer as input/output devices. In general an intelligent terminal must include, as a minimum, the following:

1. Self-contained storage (random access memory)
2. Stored program capabilities
3. A keyboard or some other form of human-oriented input device

4. A CRT or some other form of human-oriented output device
5. Ability to process, within the terminal, a user-written program
6. Ability to process on-line data communications from other intelligent terminals or from one or more computer sites

Intelligent terminals can serve a variety of functions, particularly if they are connected to other peripheral devices. By connecting a terminal to a communication data control unit, and then to a central computer through a communication channel, a remote job-entry (RJE) system is developed. By using a different set of peripherals and programs, a data-entry system such as a remote key-to-disk system can be created. By connecting the terminal to the proper set of I/O devices, a stand-alone computer for low-volume or special-purpose processing is created. An intelligent terminal can also be used to coordinate data entry from nonprogrammable terminals at remote locations.

Intelligent terminals are extensively used in distributed processing networks, primarily for two reasons. First, the operation of the terminal is not dependent upon a central computer or any other terminal. If nonintelligent terminals are connected to the central processor and the processor breaks down, the terminals are not able to function and the entire system is inoperable. If intelligent terminals are employed in a network and the central computer or part or all of the data communication system breaks down, the terminals can still accept input transactions and can perform certain processing functions. Banks and retail stores have adopted intelligent terminals in many of their customer processing operations because of this key factor; sales transactions in a store or account transactions in a bank can be recorded at the terminal and made ready for later transmission even when the central processor is off line. The second reason for using an intelligent terminal is that it can relieve the central processor workload. If data editing or control of a set of nonintelligent terminals is handled by an intelligent terminal, then the workload at the central site can be reduced. In some cases this may mean that a smaller central processor can be employed. Today a single intelligent terminal has the capability of handling data entry, data retrieval, inquiry, response, monitoring, and control. These increased capabilities have been brought about by cost reductions in microprocessing technology.

Minicomputers and Microcomputers

Transistor circuitry was first used in computer systems in the latter part of 1959, integrated circuits were first used in the late 1960s, and by the middle to late 1970s microtechnology was being widely used. These technological changes resulted in the miniaturization of circuitry, which allowed a reduction in the size of central processors as well as associated peripheral hardware. However, this miniaturization had far more impact than simply reducing the size of the computer. The cost of manufacturing a computer and the selling price of computers dropped significantly. Once the devices had become economically attractive, their use spread rapidly from large corporations to small business firms as well as to private homes. These economic changes also had an impact on the manner in which large corporations structured their computer systems. Once small inexpensive computers had become available, decentralization of the computer resources became possible; distributed networks were a reality. The technological changes and miniaturization of computer systems resulted in two new types of computers: the minicomputer and the microcomputer. We will examine each briefly.

MINICOMPUTERS In the early 1960s there was a need, particularly in the process control and telecommunication areas, for an inexpensive programmable device to perform specific functions. Such a device needed only to provide computer logic; virtually no peripheral devices were needed. A process-oriented minicomputer emerged to fill this demand. Within a few years, however, the technology used within the mini was applied to the development of peripheral devices, and soon after stand-alone machines that could be used in a variety of commercial operations such as airlines reservations, car rentals, banking transactions, and inventory control became available.

A typical minicomputer has a 16-bit word length, weighs less than one hundred pounds, and requires no special air conditioning or other support system. Most have from 5,000 to 10,000 logic circuits, have internal storage capacities ranging from 4,000 to 64,000 bytes, consume less than 500 watts of electrical power, and cost less than $50,000.

The central processing unit for most minicomputers can be contained on a circuit board that measures approximately 8½ inches by 11 inches. Therefore the smallest mini system, which would consist of a CPU, one input/output device, and one small secondary storage device, can be operated on a desk top. Systems of this size cost between $3,000 and $10,000 and are used in some small businesses.

In general, most minicomputer systems are larger than a desk-top model; most include a number of peripheral devices and have medium-to-large expandable internal memories. The actual size, cost, and capabilities of the system increase in proportion to the number of peripheral devices involved and the size of the internal storage.

Most minicomputers can be adapted to utilize the peripheral devices involved in large mainframe systems; however, a complete line of low-cost, lightweight, portable peripheral devices have been developed for use with minicomputers. These devices include card readers, floppy as well as hard disk storage devices, line printers, paper-tape readers, cassette readers, optical scanners, and audio output devices. Like the minicomputer itself, the size of these devices has been reduced, particularly when compared with their counterparts in mainframe systems.

The reduction in the size and cost of minis and their associated hardware has been beneficial to small businesses and private users and has brought about an expansion in distributed processing systems. Minicomputers still have certain limitations and restrictions, however. These include the following:

1. Smaller word sizes are used in the design of minicomputers than are traditionally employed in mainframe computers, and therefore the programming languages used on mini systems are not statement-by-statement compatible with mainframe equipment.

2. The minicomputer itself, as well as the related mini equipment, cannot be used directly in conjunction with larger standard-size peripheral devices. Special adapters are necessary.

3.   The typical minicomputer system has limited internal storage capabilities, and therefore certain levels of programs cannot be run on the system regardless of whether there is language compatibility. A program that will compile and run on a mainframe system may not run on a mini. The reverse, however, may be true; a program that will run on a mini will probably run on a mainframe.

4.   The decreased size of the minicomputer means decreased speed, and therefore the time needed to process data will increase. A program that takes a fraction of a second to execute on a mainframe may take several minutes on a mini system.

5.   Because of the limited internal storage of some minicomputers, some business applications must be written in the assembly language of the mini in order to produce a compact program that will execute in the available memory area. In addition, the assembly languages of most minis are machine dependent, and programs cannot be transferred from mini to mini or to a mainframe.

6.   When minis were developed in the late 1960s, they did not have COBOL, FORTRAN, and some of the other commonly used computer languages. Some systems are still deficient in software; however, a number of companies now provide a variety of languages. This deficiency is becoming less of a problem.

On the positive side, minicomputer systems have experienced a phenomenal growth since the 1960s, and mini systems are now available with more power and capabilities than a typical IBM System 360 (a mainframe system) that was introduced less than twenty years ago. Some of this growth has occurred from data base management systems (DBMS), which can be used to reduce the burden of developing computer programs and creating and manipulating data files. At one point in time only large million-dollar computer systems had data base software to support their operation. Now minicomputer manufacturers are beginning to make available DBMS software packages, either by developing their own or by acquiring packages developed by independent software houses.

MICROCOMPUTERS   The primary physical difference between a minicomputer and a microcomputer is their size, but their internal structure is also quite different. A microcomputer is built upon a microprogramming structure. Microprogramming is a process in which each machine instruction initiates a sequence of more elementary instructions (microinstructions). By using a microprogramming approach, the fixed conventional CPU control *logic* of a minisystem can be replaced with a CPU control *memory*, which contains the basic microinstructions for the microcomputer's fundamental operations.

Using a microprogramming design and microcircuit technology, engineers were able in the mid-1970s to produce the entire central processing unit (CPU) on a single silicon wafer or "chip" about a quarter-inch square. This "micro chip CPU," referred to as a microprocessor, is about the size of a dime and costs less than $30 to manufacture. A microprocessor is not a computer, but when it is coupled with memory chips and attached to an input/output device it becomes a microcomputer.

A microcomputer is actually the integration of five basic components: (1) a processor, (2) random access memory, (3) preprogrammed read-only memory, (4) a clock, and (5) input/output peripheral devices.

As we have just noted, the heart of the microcomputer is the microprocessor. Like the processor of minis and mainframes, the microprocessor performs all data manipulation, program and decision-making logic, and arithmetic functions.

The memory section of the micro is divided into two subsections. The most common type of memory is random access memory, or RAM as it is often called. Random access memory is the direct functional equivalent of the core memory that is used as primary storage in both mainframe and minicomputer systems. Unlike core memory, however, RAM is a semiconductor micromemory, or a "memory on a chip." This type of memory is small, fast, and economical and provides the bulk of the microcomputer's internal storage. The only limitation of RAM is that when the electrical power to the system is turned off, data stored in memory are lost.

The second type of memory employed in the microcomputer is read-only memory (ROM), or programmable read-only memory (PROM) as it is often called. The ROM has a permanent set of instructions that the microprocessor uses each time the system is operated. Since the functions performed by the processor are directly related to the ROM, the machine's characteristics can easily be altered by employing a different ROM.

The ROM read-only memory is a semiconductor micromemory. Unlike RAM memory, however, ROM memory does not lose the data or instructions when power is removed from the system, and ROM memory can only be read. Data or instructions cannot be written into the ROM during operation of the system; data and instructions are preprogrammed by the manufacturer.

The electronic clock within the microcomputer is used to synchronize internal and external operations. The processor, when solving problems or handling data and instructions related to a problem, often subdivides individual problems into several component parts. The clock is the coordinating mechanism that brings together, at the proper time, each of the separate processing functions.

A fully operational microcomputer typically has a keyboard for input and some display device for output. A variety of keyboards exist, ranging from a simple 10-key numeric pad to full typewriterlike alphanumeric keyboard units. Visual output devices that range from simple precoded lights to a full-color CRT screen are available. Other peripheral input/output devices are available, including cassette tape units, paper-tape units, floppy disks, and audio-response units.

Figure 6–17 illustrates a typical microcomputer. A system such as this is capable of computational processing, can handle input/output operations, and has an internal storage of 4K to 64K bytes. A system with this configuration costs between $1,500 and $3,500.

Originally microcomputers were principally used by hobbyists, but they are beginning to be used by small businesses and are becoming an integral part of terminal devices and other equipment. Low-cost data terminals have incorporated microprocessors in order to enhance simple data-handling tasks. By adding a microprocessor to a "dumb" or "smart" terminal, an "intelligent" ter-

Figure 6–17   TRS–80 Microcomputer
Courtesy of Radio Shack, A Division of the Tandy Corp.

minal that can perform editing, compiling, and processing can be produced. A complete discussion of small business and accounting applications is in Chapter 17 and a typical financial accounting software package is illustrated in Chapter 14.

SUMMARY

In this chapter we have attempted to integrate some of the ideas and concepts discussed in previous chapters, particularly in regard to types of systems and the hardware that is required to support these different system structures. We traced the evolution of systems, which included (1) traditional accounting systems, (2) responsibility reporting systems, (3) integrated data processing systems, (4) integrated management information systems, (5) real-time integrated information systems, and (6) distributed processing systems. The focus of the coverage was on the latter two systems: real-time integrated information systems and distributed processing systems.

Real-time integrated systems emerged when on-line input/output devices became readily available and when advanced software in the form of operating systems, multiprogramming, and multiprocessing became available on large mainframe computers. In our discussion, however, we noted that because integrated systems are built around one or more large centralized processing units, bottlenecks often occur, both in the input of data and in the feedback of output information. Some of these weaknesses can be overcome by employing on-line real-time capabilities, but costly random access devices and remote terminals are required. Many companies are unwilling and unable to commit the capital and time required to develop a real-time integrated information system.

Distributed processing can overcome some of the limitations and deficiencies of integrated systems by organizing data processing resources to support remote applications rather than organizing the system around the needs or constraints of a centralized computer site. Distributed processing systems became economically feasible when low-cost minicomputers, microcomputers, and intelligent terminals became readily available. The key characteristics that differentiate distributed systems from integrated systems are the employment of a distributed data base and local autonomy of data processing operations.

The hardware required to support both integrated and distributed systems includes (1) communication channels, (2) modems, (3) multiplexers and concentrators, and (4) communication processors. The first three devices are heavily used in integrated systems, while distributed systems require all four devices. The key hardware developments that actually brought about the evolution of both integrated and distributed systems were in minicomputer and microcomputer technology. The last section of the chapter examined the nature of minicomputers and microcomputers, how and when they emerged, and their impact on the information systems field.

SELECTED REFERENCES

BODNER, GEORGE H., *Accounting Information Systems*. Boston: Allyn & Bacon, 1980.

BOOTH, G. M., "Distributed Information Systems," AFIPS Conference Proceedings, National Computer Conference, Vol. 45, 1976.

BOROVITS, I., AND E. SEGEV, "Real-Time Management—An Analogy," *Academy of Management Review*, April 1977.

BURCH, JOHN G., JR., FELIX R. STRATER AND GARY GRUDNISKI, *Information Systems: Theory and Practice* (2nd ed.). New York: John Wiley, 1979.

DEARDEN, J., "Myth of Real-Time Management Information," *Harvard Business Review*, May–June 1966.

DIETZ, DEVON D., AND JOHN D. KEANE, "Integrating Distributed Processing Within a Central Environment," *Management Accounting*, Vol. 62, November 1980.

ELIASON, ALAN L., AND KENT D. KILTS, *Business Computer Systems and Applications* (2nd ed.). Science Research Associates, 1979.

FOSTER, J. D., "Distributed Processing for Banking," *Datamation*, July 1976.

LLEWELLYN, R., *Information Systems*. Englewood Cliffs, N.J.: Prentice-Hall, 1976.

MOSCOVE, STEPHEN A., AND MARK G. SIMKIN, *Accounting Information Systems*. New York: John Wiley, 1981.

MURDICK, ROBERT G., THOMAS C. FULLER, JOEL E. ROSS AND FRANK J. WINNERMARK, *Accounting Information Systems*. Englewood Cliffs, N.J.: Prentice-Hall, 1978.

REISER, R., "Interactive Modeling of Computer Systems," *IBM Systems Journal*, November 4, 1976.

THIERAUF, ROBERT J., *Distributed Processing Systems.* Englewood Cliffs, N.J.: Prentice-Hall, 1978.

WINSKI, DONALD T., "Distributed Systems: Is Your Organization Ready?" *Infosystems*, Vol. 25, September 1978.

YOURDON, E., *Design of On-Line Computer Systems.* Englewood Cliffs, N.J.: Prentice-Hall, 1972.

REVIEW QUESTIONS

1. Identify the two types of operations that can exist, separately or jointly, in an information system.

2. Differentiate between *batch processing* and *real-time processing*.

3. Differentiate between *batch processing with sequential access files* and *batch processing with random access files*. What are the advantages and disadvantages of each?

4. Explain the meaning of the terms *local batch* and *remote batch* processing.

5. Differentiate between *on-line* and *off-line* processing. Give a pictorial example of each.

6. Identify some typical real-time processing applications.

7. Explain the concept of response time as associated with real-time processing.

8. Is an on-line system a real-time system? Explain.

9. Differentiate between *time sharing* and *on-line processing* as modes of operation in real-time processing. Give examples of each.

10. Identify the system structures that have evolved over the past twenty-five to thirty years.

11. What is meant by the term *traditional accounting system* responsibility reporting system?

12. What are the distinguishing characteristics of an integrated data processing system? What are some of the key deficiencies?

13. How does an integrated management information system differ from other systems? What are some of the deficiencies of such systems?

14. Identify some of the characteristics of a real-time integrated information system.

15. What factors brought about the development of distributed processing systems?

16. Identify some of the key characteristics of a distributed processing system.

17. Explain the meaning of the terms *distributed data base* and *autonomy of data processing operations*.

18. What is the meaning of the term *data-entry processing* in relationship to distributed processing? Give an example.

19. Explain the concept of "local processing/management reporting" as related to distributed processing.

20. Identify five basic network structures used in distributed processing. Give an example of each.

21. Identify the major components of a data communications system.

22. Explain the term *bandwidth (grade)* used in conjunction with a communication channel.

23. What role does a modem play in a data communication system? Give an example.

24. Differentiate between a *multiplexer* and a *concentrator*.

25. What role does a communications processor play in a data communications system?

26. Differentiate between a *"dumb"* terminal, a *"smart"* terminal, and an *"intelligent"* terminal.

27. Identify some of the positive as well as negative characteristics of minicomputers.

28. Identify the basic components that make up a microcomputer. Differentiate between a *random access memory* (RAM) and a *read-only memory* (ROM).

29. What roles have minicomputers and microcomputers played in the development of distributed processing?

EXERCISES AND CASES

6–1

The Beta Corporation is preparing to computerize its payroll records using magnetic tape for its employee master file. In designing this system, the best choice for file organization would be

a. Sequential
b. Batch
c. Random
d. On-line
e. Real-time

Give the justification for your answer. (Adapted from the CMA Examination)

6–2

The Wees Company has designed its order entry system so that salespersons can send orders in from a terminal connected via telephone lines to the central processing unit (CPU). Programmed input control checks are performed at this time. However, files are not updated until a run at 1:00 A.M. the next day. This system is

a. On-line and real-time
b. Real-time but not on-line
c. A sequentially organized system
d. Batch processing with random access files
e. On-line but not real-time

6–3

The Petman Company is planning to acquire several "dumb" terminals to place in offices that are remotely located from the computer. What additional devices will the company need to acquire so that the terminals can operate properly?

a. Keypunch machines for coding data
b. Teletypes for transmitting data
c. Cathode ray tubes (CRTs) for displaying data
d. Modems for translating electronic impulses to audio impulses and vice versa
e. Floppy disk units for storing data

6–4

Which of the following applications would be least likely to be done on a real-time basis?

a. Airlines reservations
b. Preparation of payroll checks
c. A "dial-a-computer" stock market quotation system
d. A computerized traffic light control system
e. Computer monitoring of coronary care patients in a hospital

6–5

The meaning of the term *distributed data processing* is most closely associated with

a. Computer networks
b. Batch processing
c. PERT networks
d. Data base management systems
e. Centralization of corporate data bases

6–6

Direct-access storage devices are

a. Basic to real-time operations
b. Supplementary to real-time operations
c. Harmful to real-time operations
d. Incompatible with real-time operations
e. None of the above

6–7

Indicate whether a batch processing or a real-time processing system would be more appropriate for each of the following situations. Explain your answer.

a. Highly integrated operations that require close monitoring

b. Large volume of transactions that peak on a biweekly basis

c. Widely dispersed units within a corporation that require rapid transmittal of data and information

d. A small company that has a small volume of transactions but requires up-to-date and accurate records

e. A company that has a high volume of transactions but can tolerate a slow response time

f. Weekly inquiries relating to the status of certain items or products (i.e., a weekly status report on outstanding orders)

g. Managerial reports that need to be available on a demand basis

6–8

Given each of the following applications, indicate (1) whether a batch processing or a real-time processing operation is more applicable; (2) if batch processing is applicable, indicate whether sequential or random access files are needed and whether a local batch or a remote batch (off-line or on-line) mode of operation is applicable; (3) if real-time processing is applicable, indicate whether an on-line or a time-sharing mode of operation is applicable. Explain your answer.

a. Monthly preparation of financial statements

b. A patient-care system in a large metropolitan hospital containing six hundred beds

c. A payroll system used weekly or biweekly to produce employee checks and payroll records and statements

d. A system designed to keep track of "special orders" that have critical time schedules

e. Preparation of utility bills that are payable on a monthly basis

f. Access and maintenance of records at a credit bureau that processes 2,500 inquiries a week and maintains 350,000 records

g. A reservation system, used by a major airline, to determine and schedule seat occupancy

h. Preparation and generation of internal monthly responsibility reports

i. A system used to support the processing of orders received by mail for a "mail-order house" that stocks 2,500 different products

6–9

Ed Weeks is the manager of a medium-sized retail store. All of the inventory and billing, as well as accounts receivable, general ledger, and other accounting information, have been handled manually. Mr. Weeks has asked for your advice regarding the purchasing of a computer system. After some discussion with Mr. Weeks you learn that he has contacted a service bureau about local batch processing services; however, he does not believe that this will meet his needs. Upon further discussion you determine that Mr. Weeks does not know how a time-sharing system operates.

Explain to Mr. Weeks the structure and operation of time-sharing. Discuss the advantages of both batch processing via a service bureau and real-time processing via time-sharing. Point out the factors that Mr. Weeks should consider regarding the use of some combination of these services before deciding to purchase his computer. Finally, indicate to Mr. Weeks the advantages and disadvantages of purchasing a microcomputer.

6–10

For each of the following cases, indicate whether the described system is *batch processing,* *real-time processing,* or a *combination of both.* Sketch a pictorial configuration of the system. (*Hint:* You may need to refer to Figures 6–3, 6–4, 6–5, or 6–6.)

a. A medical service bureau performs patient billing for numerous medical groups in a large city. Formerly, clients mailed their information to the bureau's data processing center where it was keyed and processed on the bureau's computer. However, third-party billing, such as Blue Shield, Medicare, and Welfare, created bottlenecks as claims forms became more complex. As part of an expansion effort, the service bureau installed communicating processors as data-entry terminals at the offices of ten high-volume clients. For each of these clients the system allows efficient "fill-in-the-blanks" type of data entry. Formats appear on the CRT screen and prompt the user for all necessary information. As data are entered, the processor checks for mistakes, such as an operation date earlier than date of admission. Delays that used to occur in resolving such troublesome errors have now been completely eliminated.

Data recorded on tape cassettes are the validated source files. All billing data are accumulated on reusable cassettes, and at the end of the day, these files are communicated via high-speed communications to the central computer. The central system spools the files to magnetic tape that is in the proper format for final processing on the service bureau's computer. Billing is merely the first phase of a total medical system. Phase 2 is medical records, while Phase 3 involves diagnostics.

b. A major oil company maintains regional marketing centers which are responsible for order entry, invoicing, distribution, and sales analysis of the company's products. Previously the manual system involved processing four hundred orders per day. Invoices had to be typed and were then sent by manual teletypes to twenty distribution centers within each region. Complex tax codes and pricing and product information compounded the need for some system of local file maintenance, computation, and high-speed transmission.

After instituting a feasibility study, a key-to-diskette data-entry system was installed. It allows rapid data entry, and its diskettes provide unlimited storage, easy handling, and fast access to local files. After the operators key in the orders, the processor automatically verifies customer files and product codes. It also calculates price extensions and taxes, appends any special terms, and then stores the completed invoices on diskettes. In two hours of high-speed data transmission per day, all invoices are printed on remote receive-only teletype-writers. The complete invoice transaction file, in turn, is communicated to the corporate data center and is entered into the accounts receivable system on the host computer. At the regional level, the processors accumulate managerial sales analyses for summary reports that were previously unavailable at this level. In this sample application, regionally installed processors serve as "intelligent" data-entry systems for the central computer and act as transaction processing output systems for distributing a high volume of data to numerous field sites.[1]

6-11

Each of the following cases represents a network structure of distributed processing (i.e., point-to-point, hierarchical, star, loop, or fully connected ring). Identify the type of network represented and sketch a pictorial configuration of the system.

a. In a large midwestern city, a motor freight carrier operates a central data processing center for the carrier's regional terminal centers in five large cities. Before the installation of the current distributed processing network, the payroll data had to be keyed in twice, once at the regional level and once at the headquarters level. Time slips had to be checked manually for accuracy of such data as drive time miles, stops, load weights, and route codes. To eliminate multiple-data entry, a processor was placed in each regional center as well as in the central DP center. Currently, payroll data are keyed daily into the regional processors for storage on diskettes; the daily files become the input for the weekly accumulations. The weekly data are then communicated to the central system and merged into a summary payroll file.

This multisite network system processes truckers' payroll at the regional level before transmitting the summary data to the central system. This system then stores the data on magnetic tape for further exception processing at the central processing center. Nothing is ever keyed more than once. Because the rekeying bottleneck at the central level has been eliminated, attention is given to generating detailed reports for management, such as weekly summary reports, driver performance, equipment optimization, route-loading comparisons, and overall productivity.

b. A medium-sized bank, after an exhaustive study of its entire DP operations, concluded that its current centralized DP operations are very expensive. At the hub of the current system is a large computer used for on-line real-time processing by tellers in all of the bank's branch offices. When the first system fails, pro-

[1] Adapted from Robert J. Thierauf, *Distributed Processing Systems*, pp. 102, 105).

cessing is switched to a second computer of the same size for continuous real-time processing by bank tellers. It should be noted that the second computer system is regularly used for batch processing until the first computer fails.

Recognizing the need for lower processing costs and reliability of processing for real-time operations by bank tellers, the bank decided to restructure its DP operations. To achieve this, a software house, working in conjunction with the bank's systems analysts, decided to install a group of four minicomputers to service all banking operations handled by bank tellers. Each minicomputer services forty bank-teller terminals. Not only can tellers inquire about the status of bank balances, but they can also enter deposit items or deduct items in real-time throughout the day. Thus several offices will be linked to one minicomputer. In turn, all minicomputers are linked together so that they can communicate directly with one another. This linking of all minicomputers is necessary in order to enable a teller to interrogate the data base for a customer's account situated in a location other than that for the one being used. Likewise, all minicomputers are linked to the central banking office. This communication arrangement allows the main computer to post all cleared checks as well as debit and credit items against each account at the end of the banking day, that is, in the evening. During the day, however, the main computer is busy performing routine and special batch processing functions for the entire bank. Similarly, appropriate reports about bank operations are prepared daily and periodically to meet management needs.

c. A consumer products manufacturer found that its current DP system failed to produce timely management information. Based on this shortcoming and others, it decided to undergo a feasibility study which resulted in a decision to install a distributed processing system. The areas included were sales, research and development, and manufacturing. A communications network was designed to provide the mechanism for data communications between programs and devices on different systems and on computers running under different operating systems. All three functional areas were designed to run on a single network using minicomputers, including a general-purpose computer at central headquarters.

Sales offices that perform sales order processing are widely dispersed but need to access current inventory information and shipping data. Because individual telephone lines to a central computer are expensive, a communications network is used to reduce line costs. It contains terminal concentrators at local regional centers to send data over high-speed lines to the central system. These data are terminal input or data preinput on disk or tape. Processed sales information can be communicated back to the offices—to terminals or disk storage for later off-line printing, depending on the needs of the sales offices. However, at the highest level, weekly sales data (budget versus actual) are processed on Saturday and are available on Monday morning for evaluation by sales managers at the headquarters level. The ability of the distributed network, then, to provide timely sales reports gives the company "a handle" on where to focus its current sales efforts.

6-12

Quik-Shop Inc. owns and operates a number of twenty-four-hour convenient stores throughout the northeastern United States. The company is now using a second-generation batch-oriented computer system, at its main offices, to process accounting information and produce monthly reports. Currently the company produces monthly reports relating to (1) inventory status by store and (2) sales statistics by product and store. The centralized data center also processes employee weekly payroll, processes purchases by vendors, prepares an accounts payable summary, and prepares vendor checks.

Management at Quik-Shop believes that the existing computer system should be upgraded, possibly to an on-line real-time system. As a systems consultant, you have been asked to prepare a report that highlights the advantages and disadvantages of different configurations of third- or fourth-generation equipment. Include in your report an examination of point-of-sale terminals as well as any other equipment that could be cost justified, based on the nature of the business.

6-13

Sketch a real-time integrated information system configuration that will support a large commercial bank operation. Assume that the bank uses magnetic-ink character recognition (MICR) equipment to process customer checks and deposit slips. Identify other types of terminals or equipment that would be required. In addition, indicate under what conditions it would be desirable to employ a distributed system rather than an integrated system.

6-14

The following multiple-choice questions are designed to test your basic understanding of hardware concepts related to integrated and distributed systems.

1. When a CPU is a great distance from user terminals, some form of communication system is required. Which of the following is *not* a component of a communication system?

a. Modem
b. Concentrator
c. Multiprogramming
d. Multiplexer
e. Channel

2. Current communication technology exists such that systems are available that have a bandwidth from

a. 800 bits per second to 10,000 bits per second
b. 20 bits per second to 1,000 bits per second
c. 300 bits per second to 9,600 bits per second
d. 45 bits per second to 120,000 bits per second
e. 4,000 bits per second to 200,000 bits per second

3. Eaton University is in the process of linking thirty CRT terminals from the School of Accounting to the central computer center located across campus. To link the terminals to the central facility, the following equipment would probably be required:

a. A multiplexer and a concentrator
b. A multiplexer and a voice-band modem
c. A multiplexer and a compiler
d. A concentrator and an MICR
e. A multiplexer only

4. The B & L Bookstore would like to purchase a terminal that could be used to capture sales data, generate receipts, and interface with a central inventory system. The type of terminal the store should consider is classified as

a. An intelligent terminal
b. A dumb terminal
c. A touch-tone terminal
d. A microcomputer
e. A smart terminal

5. A permanent set of instruction for a microcomputer is located in

a. Secondary storage
b. Diskett
c. ROM memory
d. RAM memory
e. Arithmetic-logic unit

7

SYSTEMS FLOWCHARTING AND DOCUMENTATION

BASIC CONCEPTS

Introduction

An accounting information system and information systems in general should be designed to support the management system of the organization. This is accomplished by processing transactions and providing information for the decision-making and reporting requirements of the business. The focus of these transaction processing, operational, managerial, and strategic activities should be to further the objectives of the organization.

Systems flowcharting is an effective way to describe an information system to trained users, such as accountants and systems analysts. The essential characteristics of accounting and information systems can be described much more effectively through the use of standardized symbols than by using a narrative description. This is true for the following reasons:

1. The description is simpler and concentrates on the essential components that are relevant to the professional user.
2. A picture is always easier to use to communicate a message than an oral or written description.

3. A multitude of interrelationships can be communicated easily via a flowchart; a narrative can only be used to effectively describe a linear relationship, whereas a diagram can more easily convey a variety of interactive relationships.

The more complex the accounting system, the more difficult it will be to describe relationships. For the untrained user often found in management, a narrative description may be an essential supplement by a systems flowchart.

Focus of Flowchart

A systems flowchart is basically a communication document. It should therefore be organized with this purpose as its focus. The auditor, manager, accountant, or systems designer who prepares the flowchart should organize the systems flowchart around the relevant information he or she is trying to convey to the current or future users. As outlined in Chapter 4, relevant information is a function of the decisions or reports of the users. This organization effort must consider the (1) flow of transactions, (2) interaction of these flows, (3) decisions, (4) personnel or departments, (5) processing steps, (6) reports to be generated, (7) files used, (8) input preparation, (9) disposition of input, and (10) controls.

The following are some suggestions for the organization and focus of the systems flowchart:

1. The accounting transaction processing cycle. These cycles are commonly referred to as
   a. Sales and collection cycle
   b. Payroll and personnel cycle
   c. Purchasing, production, inventory, and warehousing cycle
   d. Capital acquisition cycle
   e. Financial cycle
   The appendixes of the logistical, marketing, and financial chapters of this text outline the substance of these cycles. This is probably the most common approach used by auditors, due to the focus on the transaction processing cycle.

2. An organizational entity such as a store, warehouse, plant, department, or individual. All activities of the entity would be grouped together to focus on the activities of the entire entity. Often this is used to describe overall activities, and the cycle approach is used to give more-detailed information about the system.

3. A decision, transaction, or report may be the focal point of the flowchart. An example of this for the inventory update and purchase order decision is given later in this chapter. This procedure is most useful in focusing on the transaction processing, reporting, and decision-making requirements of the information system. Moreover, it is valuable for an analysis of administrative controls.

4. A file may be the focal point of the flowchart that is used to communicate the level of interaction with the file. This will be useful in designing and analyzing a random access system where file organization and retrieval requirements are important.

5. For manual systems, the *flow of documents* using a document flowchart (a version of a systems flowchart) is useful for tracing documents as they flow from department to department in the transaction cycle. This is most useful for an analysis of accounting controls for a manual system.

All systems flowcharts contain some elements of each of these items and can be used to assess accounting and administrative controls, but the organization of the document flows, processes, interaction of processes and information flows, personnel descriptions, report generation, files used, input preparation procedures, disposition of input, and controls is critical to effective communication of the system to the users in the systems flowchart. Therefore care must be taken to arrange the presentation of the information.

Another important decision related to the focus of the flowchart is the level of detail presented. Some users require only a broad overview of the system. (A block diagram consisting of all rectangles is often used here.) Others need considerable detail. Generally, even in the latter case, a broad flowchart is still prepared to give the "big picture" of the information system.

The Art of Flowcharting

The basic flowcharting guidelines, such as those above and those presented later in terms of techniques, can be outlined as follows:

1. Start with the focus of the flowchart.
2. Show input and output related to the focal point.
3. Show how input and output are prepared, filed, and distributed.
4. Show interface with other systems.
5. Show other relevant information using annotations, striping, and various codes. This may include departments, personnel, controls, interfaces, and references to other flowcharts.

Beyond guidelines such as these, an emphasis on communication of relevant information about the system (which is the purpose of flowcharting), and the use of standardized symbols and conventions, flowchart preparation is much more of an art than a standardized procedure. No two auditors, controllers, managers, systems analysts, or systems designers will perceive the system the same way or in the same detail at every point. Thus all flowcharts will be different in terms of their emphasis in much the same way that narrative description of an event or process will be different. Moreover, the style of each person who prepares the flowchart will be evident. Therefore, beyond the main characteristics of the system and the main facts that must be conveyed, flowcharts will always reflect the perceptions and style of the preparer.

SYSTEMS FLOWCHARTING TECHNIQUES

Symbols

In 1966 the United States of America Standards Institute (USASI) adopted a standard set of systems flowchart symbols. These symbols are shown in Figure 7–1. Prior to this there was a maze of conflicting symbols. A few modifications of the USASI symbols have been added in practice, and these are indicated in Figure 7–2, with a note describing their use. In this chapter we use only those symbols adopted by the USASI. Others, however, are used elsewhere in the text.

First, there are four general symbols. The *parallelogram* is used to represent input to and output from the system. Generally, however, specialized symbols are used for documents, cards, tapes, and random access files. The parallelogram is most frequently used to represent manual accounting records such as inventory, accounts receivable, accounts payable, and the general ledger. For every system, the flowchart should begin with an input and end with an output, and each input into the system must be shown as an output, that is, its final disposition must be shown. The second basic symbol is the *rectangle*, which represents a processing operation or group of operations. Specialized symbols should be used for many processing operations, and in practice the rectangle is most frequently used for operations performed by the computer (CPU) in data processing operations. A single rectangle may be used to represent many more-detailed operations. Input/output symbols are always separated by one or more processing steps. The third major symbol is the *flow line*. The flowchart should flow from top to bottom[1] and left to right; if not, the lines should have an arrow indicating the direction of flow. Flow lines are always horizontal and vertical, and crossing lines should be avoided if possible. A

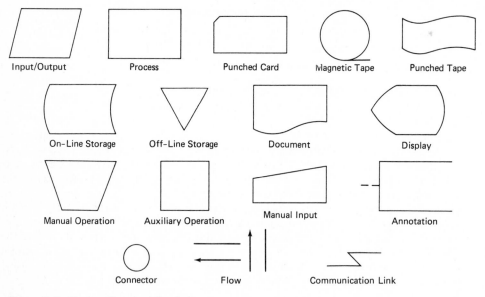

Figure 7–1 System Flowchart Symbols

Adopted by United States of America Standards Institute in 1966.

---

[1] An interesting exception to this is the flowcharting procedure suggested by Peat, Marwick, Mitchell & Co. in its *Systems Evaluation Approach: Documentation of Controls* (*SEADOC*) where the flow is from the bottom to the top.

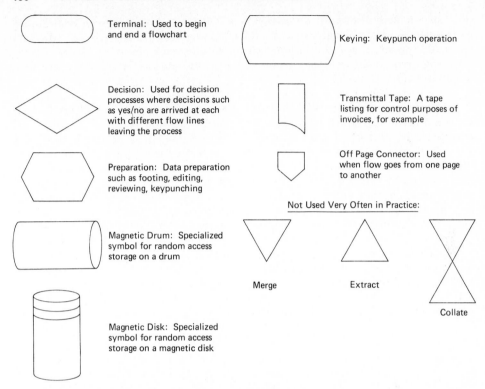

Figure 7–2   Other Frequently Used System Flowchart Symbols

fourth basic symbol is the *annotation*. It is used to provide explanatory comments such as file contents, processing steps, and decisions to be made.

Added information or reference to more-detailed flowcharts also can be added by *striping*. The rectangle, for example, is divided into two sections where in the top section a code such as *C* representing cashier, or *106* representing a detailed flowchart, is noted to show *who* does the processing and *reference* to another more-detailed flowchart, respectively. Sometimes references and identifications are noted at the top left or right outside the symbol.

Whenever feasible, the accountant or system designer should use the more descriptive specialized flowchart symbols shown in Figure 7–1.

There are four specialized symbols for different input and output media. The *document* symbol is used to represent paper documents such as invoices, checks, and reports. As we noted earlier, only the parallelogram, however, is used for basic accounting records, even though these can be defined as documents. In addition to this symbol, there are specialized symbols for *punched* or *mark-sense cards, punched paper tape*, and *magnetic tape*.

There are also three specialized input/output symbols representing input/output devices rather than media. The *manual input* is used in computer systems to permit the operator to communicate with the computer while in operation using an on-line keyboard. Visual *display* devices such as cathode ray tubes (CRTs), console printers, and graph plotters also require the use of a specialized symbol. Finally, a *communication link* is used to represent communication between the computer system (CPU) and remote terminals and displays. As in flow lines, these communication links designate the flow of information by using arrows; these arrows are located in the line rather than at the end of the line.

The latter two specialized input/output symbols represent storage. First, the *triangle* represents off-line storage, regardless of the medium. Such information is not under the control of the CPU. Striping is often used to locate a code at the bottom of the triangle—i.e., the point—to indicate the organization of the file. For example, the codes N and A may represent a numeric and an alphabetic file, respectively. The other storage symbol represents *on-line direct-access storage,* such as magnetic disk, magnetic drum, magnetic strips, magnetic cards, and automatic microfilm systems. Several refinements of the *on-line storage* symbols are shown in Figure 7–2 and are frequently used in practice.

The remaining two specialized symbols are used for specific types of processing. The *square* represents auxiliary operations (off-line mechanical devices) not under the control of the CPU, such as a card sorter, reproducer, optical scanner, punched tape to magnetic tape converter, and mark-sense card punch, which reads cards and punches them according to the marks on the cards. The *trapezoid* is used to represent any manual off-line operation, such as filing, inspecting, keypunching, posting, or reviewing. This symbol is used extensively in practice to describe manual systems.

Often there is no clear indication of which specialized symbol to use. The question might arise, for example, as to the proper representation of a particular file: the magnetic tape, which represents the medium, or the triangle, which describes the off-line state of the file. The accountant or systems designer must use that symbol which best characterizes the message he or she is trying to communicate with the flowchart.

The last symbol shown in Figure 7–1 is the *connector,* and it is used when several charts or pages are used to describe the flowchart (the *off-page-connector* symbol in Figure 7–2 is often used also). A reference number is inserted in the center of the circle, and the circle is inserted at the end of the flow line to connect the various aspects of the flowchart.

ILLUSTRATIONS

Manual

Consider the following illustration.[2]

The Buymore Corporation follows specific procedures in updating its inventory files and in issuing new purchase orders. Following are excerpts taken from the company's "Procedures Manual" as it applies to these procedures.

Entries to stock inventory records are made from four sources:

---

[2] AICPA, *Staff Level 1 Training Program—System Flowcharting* (New York: American Institute of Certified Public Accountants)—adapted.

a. Copies of issued purchase orders
b. New receipts of stock as indicated by copies of approved receiving reports
c. Stores requisition as approved by the storekeeper
d. Miscellaneous transactions such as returns and adjustments

(1) The incoming documents are posted manually each day to the stock inventory records by a special group of clerks in the accounting department. After the posting is completed, the source documents are filed together by date of posting. The ledger cards are analyzed as each posting is made to determine if items on hand plus on order are below the reorder level. (2) If a "below-minimum" condition exists, a purchase requisition is prepared and forwarded to the purchasing department. (3) Vendors are selected from a master vendor file by employees in the purchasing department. A purchase order is prepared and mailed to the vendor. The master vendor file is updated when an order is placed. Four copies of the purchase order are prepared and routed as follows:

a. Original is sent to the vendor.
b. Copy, with purchase requisition attached, is filed in the purchasing department.
c. Copy is filed in the receiving department.
d. Copy is sent to the accounting department to adjust stock inventory records.

The systems flowchart for the manual system is shown in Figure 7–3. The flow of transactions is clearly shown by noting the four input documents across the top of the figure, the processing steps with files accessed at the center, and the output at the bottom—i.e., a top-to-bottom flow paralleling the sequence of processing steps is used. An annotation is used to expand the description of the manual processing step, the descriptions in the symbols are brief, striping is used to show who or what department performs what task and how files are organized, and a feedback loop is used to show that the output of the last processing step becomes input to the first processing step, which is the posting of inventory records. A key on the chart explains the notation used in the symbols. Moreover, bidirectional flow lines are used to represent interaction (reference and updating of perpetual records, i.e., the stock record and vendor file) with records to simplify the flowchart.

Batch Processing

Consider again the same illustration with the same input sources and output information requirements.[3]

The Buymore Corporation has decided to automate. A new computer is to be installed, and the purchase order procedures are among the first to be programmed. The following changes will be required in the system.

[3] Ibid.

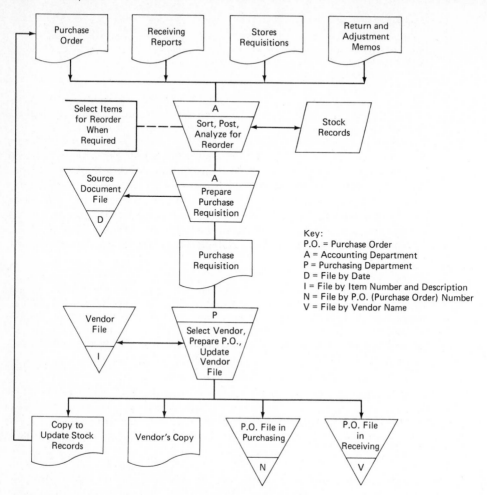

Figure 7–3   Manual System
AICPA Staff Level I Training Program—adapted.

INPUT DOCUMENTS   Receiving reports and return and adjustment memoranda will be transferred from source documents to punched cards before they enter the system. Stores requisitions will be originally prepared on mark-sense cards by the foremen, and these cards will be read and punched by a "Reproducer" as an auxiliary machine operation. Purchase order information will be entered on the master file records as part of the processing. The system will use sequential batch processing, so all input cards must be sorted into stock number order before they can be processed.

STORE LEDGER AND VENDOR FILE   Store ledger and vendor files will be consolidated, and the information on them will be stored on magnetic tape in stock number order. Each record on the file will contain the following information arranged by fields:

a. Stock item number
b. Item description
c. Detail of current monthly transactions
d. Current balance on hand
e. Current balance on order
f. Total balance on hand and on order
g. Reorder point
h. Reorder quantity
i. Vendor's name and address

PROCESSING   The master store ledger and vendor file will be updated by the transaction inputs, and a comparison check will be made between the balance on hand and on order and the reorder point. If a new purchase is required, a purchase order is prepared using the vendor's information and the reorder quantity from the master file. If no new order is required, processing of the transaction cards continues. Error messages are printed on the console typewriter if there is any miscoding of stock numbers on the transaction cards.

This batch processing system is shown in Figure 7–4. As in the manual illustration, the flow is from top to bottom. In this system, however, all tasks shown are performed in the EDP department. Moreover, a father-son sequential updating process is used to update both the stock record and the vendor file at the same time. A new master is created, the old one is retained along with the transaction input cards, and an error listing is prepared.

On-Line Interactive Processing

Consider again the same illustration. The Buymore Corporation decides to convert its records to a random access file, so that input is no longer required to be in sequential order by stock number. In addition, receiving information, returns and adjustments, and store requisitions are keyed into the system via teletypes, some of which are at remote locations. Error messages will be displayed on a CRT, and three copies of the purchase order will be distributed and filed as before. A record of transactions will be retained on magnetic tape for future reference. Moreover, management now has access to the information on the master file via remote CRTs which have keyboard input. As in the update process, this inquiry process generates a transaction tape. This on-line random access system is shown in Figure 7–5.

Document Flowchart

Since the objective of flowcharting is to describe the system, it is often advantageous to cast the basic elements of a flowchart in a different form. One of the more common alternatives stresses the flow of documents from one department to another. In Figure 7–6 we illustrate a *document flowchart* for the manual system in Figure 7–3. Across the top or down the side the various departments are noted, and the flow of each document is shown as it moves from its point of origin to its point of final disposition. Often just rectangles or squares are used to represent the documents; here we use the document symbol. In Figure 7–6 we also show the location of the files used in the system. An

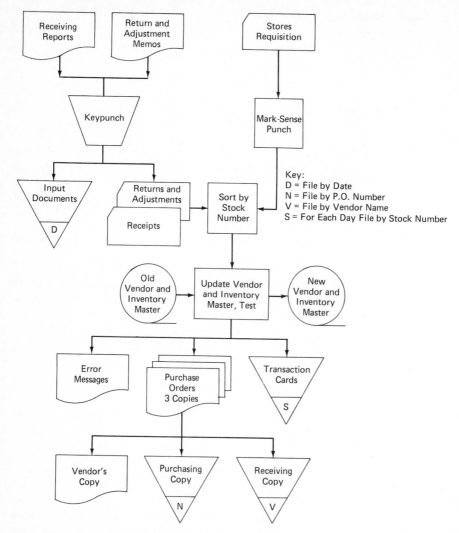

Figure 7–4 Batch Processing

AICPA Staff Level I Training Program — adapted.

accountant or systems analyst generally adds the processing steps to this flowchart. With this last addition, the document flowchart will describe all the attributes of the system as a systems flowchart. A good example of this combined system and document flowchart is shown in Figure 7–7, which describes a raw material purchase function.

SYSTEMS FLOWCHART UTILIZATION

A systems flowchart or an amplified document flowchart that includes files and processing steps will be useful, if not absolutely necessary, for many reasons.

First, it pictorially *describes a system* and shows how all the processing steps, controls, personnel or departments, decisions, documents, reports, files, and processing equipment interrelate to form a system. This is almost impossible to do in a narrative description. This description is useful to auditors, accountants, and systems analysts and, to a limited degree, to management in helping to understand an *existing* or *proposed* system. Moreover, systems flowcharting is most useful in planning new accounting or information systems in which the accountant or systems analyst must integrate all the elements to support the management system effectively. A systems flowchart is also very useful in *documenting* a system. In brief form it describes the essential character of all the elements of the system and their interrelationships.

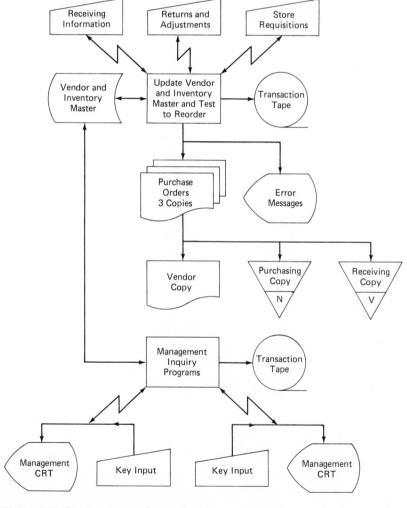

Figure 7–5 Random Access Processing
AICPA Staff Level I Training Program—adapted.

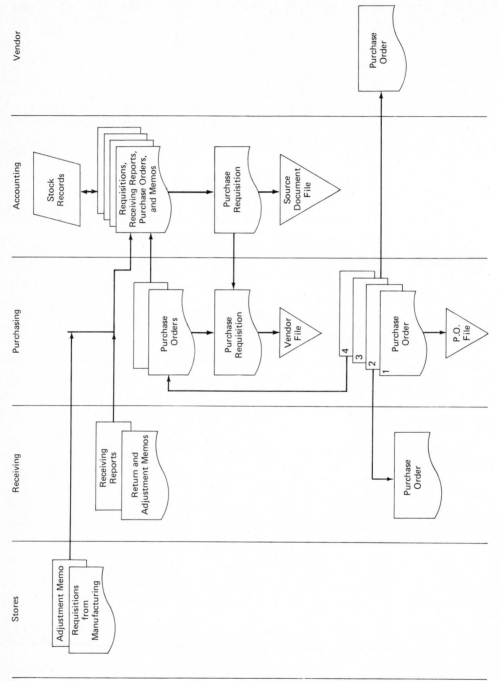

Figure 7-6 Document Flowchart
AICPA Staff Level I Training Program—adapted.

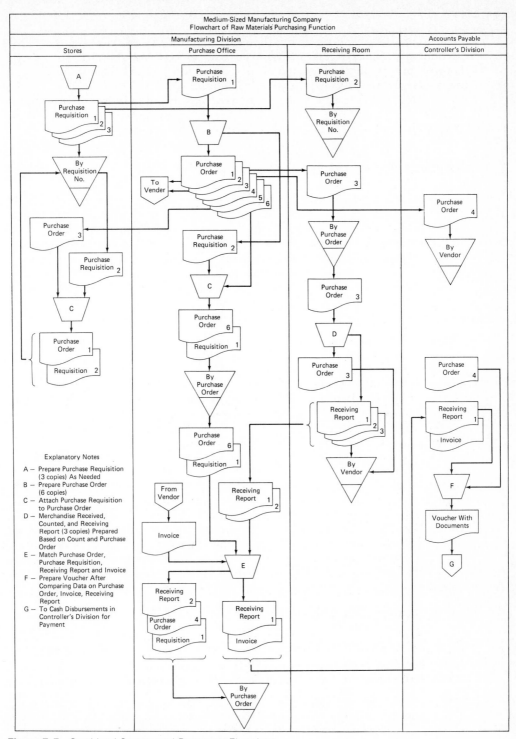

Figure 7–7 Combined System and Document Flowchart
AICPA adapted.

201

In addition to capturing the essence of the system as a whole, auditors, accountants, and systems analysts can use the systems flowchart to describe control, processing, and document flow *detail* for analysis and use by the company's employees as they process information.

In summary, in a series of flowcharts the organization of the system's elements, the movement of data, decisions, controls, processing functions, personnel, and audit trails can be shown for a variety of uses.

SYSTEMS DOCUMENTATION

Documentation consists of workpapers and records which describe the system and procedures for performing a data processing task. It is the basic means of communicating the essential elements of the data processing system and the logic followed by the computer programs. Preparing adequate documentation is a necessary, though frequently neglected, phase of computer data processing. A lack of documentation is an indication of a serious weakness within the management control over a data processing installation.[4]

Documentation is necessary for several reasons. First, as we noted above, it is useful for the *communication* of the essential elements of an automated or manual data processing system to many users who need to know how the system functions. These users are auditors, systems analysts, operators, clerks who prepare input, system designers, programmers, and management personnel. Second, documentation sets forth how the system should operate through statements of policies and procedures, and as such serves as a benchmark for performance comparison by the company or by independent auditors. Third, documentation is very useful for *training* new employees in the operation of the system. Fourth, it is the *basis for future modification* to the system because the modification can affect all elements of the system, including hardware, software, personnel, and procedures. Fifth, documentation is useful for ensuring a high degree of *uniformity* and *consistency* within the system because it is a guideline for all the activities of the system. Finally, it describes the organization of the accounting or information system and shows how that system operates to meet the information requirements of the management system. The types of systems documentation that fill these needs are systems definition, program documentation, and operator instructions. We will examine each of these separately.

Systems Definition

The purpose of systems definition is to communicate to users of the information system how the system and all its elements are organized to accomplish the objective of supporting the management system. This purpose is accomplished through inclusion of the following elements of systems definition.

---

[4] "Systems and Control Questionnaire" developed by Peat, Marwick, Mitchell & Co., adapted for use in W. Thomas Porter and William E. Perry, *EDP Controls and Auditing* (Belmont, Calif.: Wadsworth, 1977), p. 236.

First, the documentation of each system and the modifications to the system must contain *basic descriptive data* such as the name of the system, its purpose, the date of the documentation, the name of the analyst or designer, and the authorization and approval for modification or implementation.

Second, the *purpose of the system* must be summarized. This statement of purpose must include the transaction processing, operational, managerial, and strategic activities that require the information generated by the system and must indicate how the information system proposes to satisfy these information requirements. Critical assumptions must also be included here.

Third, a *systems flowchart* should be included to document the information system, all of its interrelated parts and interfaces, detailed processing controls, and flows of data.

Fourth, a *narrative description* of the system should accompany the flowchart. This should not substitute for the flowchart. It should only complement the flowchart.

Fifth, *input* into the system should be clearly specified. Responsibilities, procedures (including keying, batching, and control procedures), formats, and a complete description of each entry are necessary. Examples of input are the most useful way to clarify the form and content required. Descriptions of input for a general ledger subsystem would include, for example, the description of standard journal entries for recurring transactions, adjustments, and closing entries.

Sixth, as in the case of input, *output* must be clearly specified. Distribution, control, content, and format must all be specified. Examples of output documents and reports are most useful in documenting output of a system.

Seventh, the organization, content, and actual layout of systems *files* and *data base* must be specified. Actual examples of the layouts and data base schema are useful here. Moreover, backup and retention procedures must be described. The company's chart of accounts and coding structure should be specified as part of the description of the data files.

Eighth, a *description of hardware, software,* and *personnel* should be included. Both the specifications and the descriptions of the actual elements are useful for future evaluation or modification of the system.

Ninth, systems and programming *testing, conversion,* and *implementation procedures* are necessary to ensure that these activities are properly carried out for the system and all modifications. Therefore all results of the tests for the initial installation and for each modification should be included with the system documentation. These results enable auditors, management, and systems analysts to know with reasonable assurance that the system is operating as it should. The presence of these test results will also inspire confidence in the system.

Tenth, and perhaps of overriding importance, systems *design* and *development policies* and *procedures* must be spelled out. Adherence to these policies and procedures should be documented. Evidence of compliance with these procedures can go a long way toward ensuring that the information system supports the management system effectively, efficiently, and with a high degree of reliability. Such adherence enhances both accounting and managerial controls. (These concepts are examined in Chapters 9, 10, and 11.)

Program Documentation

Programs must be described in detail so that the systems analysts and programmers can modify and change them. To a limited extent the program documentation is used by auditors when they review the system.

First, as in systems documentation, each program and modification to a program must contain *essential data* such as the name of the program, a date, its purpose, preparer or programmer, authorization, and approval.

Second, each program must be described by a *program flowchart* detailing all input, logic, files, and output of the program.

Third, the flowchart must be accompanied by a *narrative description* to supplement the program flowchart. Decision tables and input/output matrices are useful for this description. Procedural specifications related to the program should be documented in the narrative description.

Fourth, as with systems documentation, *input, output,* and *files* must be fully specified using examples wherever feasible to enhance the description.

Fifth, *test procedures* and *results* should be included to ensure proper testing and give the user confidence in the program.

Sixth, a program *listing* should be included.

Seventh, *run procedures* exactly like those described in the next section should be included.

Operator Instructions

Since the operator of the system should *not* know how files or the data base is organized, how programs work, and how the operating or data base system operates, a special *run book*, or *book of operator instructions*, is prepared so that he or she can operate the programs and procedures that constitute the system.

First, as before, *descriptive data* such as the name of the program, date, preparer, authorization, and approval must be included.

Second, the *time schedules* for running the program and the data files (card, tape, or disk) to be used are noted. Program and file labels are included in this description.

Third, *setup* procedures, including JCL (job-control language) cards, *displays, start* procedures, *restart* procedures, *halt* procedures, *control* and *balancing* procedures, *output* distribution procedures, and *backup* procedures, are clearly spelled out. This generally means that sample card and report formats are included to aid in the description of each run.

The run book should be sufficient for the operator to do all that is necessary to run the program and no more.

Documentation Control and Summary

It is important that procedure manuals and general guidelines be set forth for each organization to ensure proper documentation. Moreover, control must be maintained over the documentation of systems. All documentation must be secure from unauthorized access, and sufficient backup must be retained to reconstruct all the records discussed earlier in this chapter. In addition, all modifications must be appropriately posted to both the main set of documentation records and the backup. Some of the newer word processing systems can be used effectively to facilitate this updating.

Good documentation, consisting of documentation of the system, the program or manual procedures used, and operator or clerical instructions, is very important. It not only affects the administrative and accounting control of the business but also gives auditors, managers, and analysts much needed confidence in the information system. If the system is well designed and properly documented, and if clerical, EDP, and managerial personnel comply with the system as documented, the transactions will be processed, reports generated, and decisions made in accordance with managerial policy. Moreover, good documentation will aid in training users and operators of the system and in designing new systems or modifications of the present system. Good design is the cornerstone of effective and efficient accounting and administrative controls and can affect the information system's support of the management system.

SYSTEMS REPORTING

We have frequently referred to the fact that management is able to use the systems flowchart. However, this is only true if management personnel have had some training. This is not always the case. In this latter situation the narrative description of the system takes on a much more prominent role, and the systems flowchart becomes supplementary information. A typical report to management may therefore adhere to the following general outline:

1. Description of business and decision-making environments
2. Narrative overview of decision cycle and transaction processing cycles
3. For each decision cycle and transaction processing cycle:
    a. A narrative outlining the system and detailing strengths and weaknesses found in the system
    b. Discussion of the consequences of these strengths and weaknesses
    c. Suggestions or recommendations for any problems found in the system
    d. Supporting systems flowchart
4. General closing suggestions and comments

In other words, less reliance is placed on the flowchart if management has not been trained to use it effectively.

SUMMARY

Systems flowcharts and documentation are essential for a well-designed information system that supports the management system of the company. Flowcharting is the means by which the system is described for a variety of users such as systems designers, auditors, the controller, and, to some extent, management. Documentation is the reference and set of instructions for future users, reviewers, and analysts of the system. Systems flowcharting is an integral part of this reference.

SELECTED REFERENCES

AICPA, *Staff Training Program—Level I System Flowcharting Seminar.*

ARENS, ALVIN A., AND JAMES K. LOEBBECKE, *Auditing: An Integrated Approach.* Englewood Cliffs, N.J.: Prentice-Hall, 1980.

BOWER, JAMES B., ROBERT E. SCHLOSSER, AND CHARLES T. ZLATKOVICH, *Financial Information Systems: Theory and Practice.* Boston: Allyn & Bacon, 1972.

BURCH, JOHN G., JR., AND JOSEPH L. SARDMAS, JR., *Computer Control and Audit: A Total Systems Approach.* New York: John Wiley, 1978.

MURACH, MIKE, *Business Data Processing and Computer Programming.* Palo Alto, Calif.: Science Research Associates, 1973.

MURDICK, THOMAS G., THOMAS C. FULLER, JOEL E. ROSS, AND FRANK J. WINNERMARK, *Accounting Information Systems.* Englewood Cliffs, N.J.: Prentice-Hall, 1978.

PEAT, MARWICK, MITCHELL & CO., "Systems Evaluation Approach: Documentation of Controls (SEADOC)." PMM & Co., 1980.

PORTER, W. THOMAS, AND WILLIAM E. PERRY, *EDP Controls and Auditing.* Belmont, Calif.: Wadsworth, 1977.

WEBER, RON, *EDP Auditing: Conceptual Foundations and Practice.* New York: McGraw-Hill, 1982.

WEIL, JOSEPH J., "System Flowcharting Techniques for the Internal Auditor," *Internal Auditor,* 34 (April 1977), 52–58.

REVIEW QUESTIONS

1. What flowchart symbol should be used for:

   a. CRT input
   b. keypunch
   c. video display
   d. EDP processing
   e. a random access file
   f. magnetic tape
   g. connector
   h. a ledger
   i. sales journal
   j. card file of source documents
   k. mechanical card sorter
   l. punched paper tape
   m. data card
   n. communication link
   o. on-line terminal

2. For what purposes is striping used?

3. What should be the focus of the flowchart?

4. What are the advantages of a document flowchart?

5. For what purpose are systems flowcharts used?

6. Why is documentation necessary?

7. Of what does systems documentation consist?

8. What is a *run book* and how does it differ from *program documentation*?

9. Explain what must be done to communicate with management who are not trained in systems flowcharting techniques.

EXERCISES AND CASES

7–1

Following is a description of a simplified cash payment and recording system. There are three inputs to the system:

a. Accounts payable punched cards, which are prepared when invoices are originally received.
b. Punched paper tapes, which are coded to represent all cash payments made from change funds and/or petty cash funds. The punched tape is converted to punched cards by a special device called a punched-tape-to-card converter at the time of petty cash reimbursement.
c. Miscellaneous disbursement requests, which originate in various departments of the company and are prepared manually. These requests are approved by responsible personnel before entering the system. The disbursement requests are keypunched to convert needed information into a form for computer input.

The punched-card output from (1) the cash payments from the change and petty cash funds and (2) the miscellaneous disbursements is combined with (3) the accounts payable punched cards. The entire deck is sorted and merged before being processed by a computer program.

The output from the processing consists of a cash disbursements journal (including distribution information for both cash and check disbursements), a magnetic tape file of all disbursements to be used for further processing, a file of the input cards, and the checks that are required.

REQUIRED: Using as many as needed of the standard flowcharting symbols, prepare a flowchart depicting this system.[1]

7–2

You are reviewing audit work papers containing a narrative description of the Tenney Corporation's factory payroll system. A portion of that narrative follows:

> Factory employees punch time clock cards each day when entering or leaving the shop. At the end of each week the timekeeping department collects the time cards and prepares duplicate batch-control slips by department showing total hours and number of employees. The time cards and original batch-control slips are sent to the payroll accounting section. The second copies of the batch-control slips are filed by date.
>
> In the payroll accounting section, payroll transaction cards are keypunched from the information on the time cards, and a batch total card for each batch is keypunched from the batch-control slip. The time cards and batch-control slips are then filed by batch for possible reference. The payroll transaction cards and batch total card are sent to data processing where they are sorted by employee number within batch. Each batch is edited by a computer program which checks the validity of the employee number against a master employee tape file and the total hours and number of employees against the batch total card. A detail printout by batch and employee number is produced, which indicates batches that do not balance and invalid employee numbers. This printout is returned to payroll accounting to resolve all differences.

In searching for documentation, you found a flowchart of the payroll system that included all appropriate symbols (United States of America National Standards Institute) but was only partially labeled. The portion of this flowchart described by the foregoing narrative is shown in Figure C7–2.

REQUIRED:

a. Number your answers 1 through 17. Next to the corresponding number of your answer, supply the appropriate labeling (document name, process description, or file

---

[1] AICPA, *Staff Level 1 Training Program* (New York: American Institute of Certified Public Accountants).

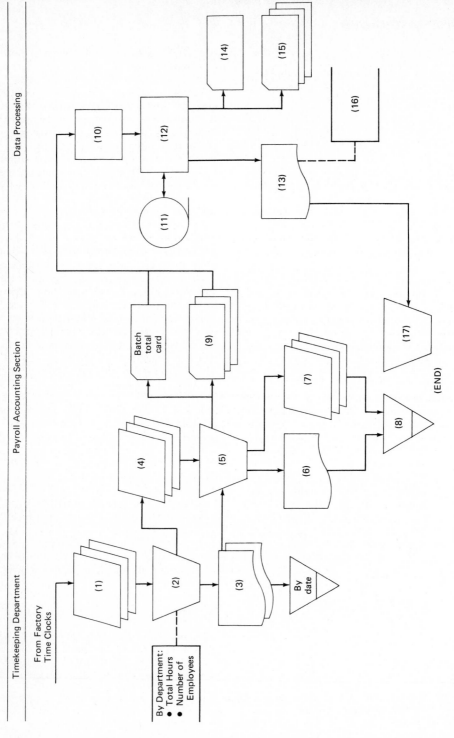

Figure C7–2

Source: CPA Exam.

order) applicable to each numbered symbol on the flowchart.

b. Flowcharts are one of the aids an auditor can use to determine and evaluate a client's internal control system. List the advantages of using flowcharts in this context. (Adapted from the CPA Examination)

7–3

The documentation of data processing applications is an important step in the design and implementation of any computer-based system. Documentation provides a complete record of data processing applications. However, documentation is a phase of systems development that is often neglected. While documentation can be tedious and time consuming, the lack of proper documentation can be very costly for an organization.

REQUIRED:

a. Identify and explain briefly the purposes that proper documentation can serve.

b. Discuss briefly the basic types of information that should be included in the documentation of a data processing application.

c. What policies should be established to regulate access to documentation data for purposes of information or modification for the following four groups of company employees?
   (1) Computer operators
   (2) Internal auditors
   (3) Production planning analysts
   (4) Systems analysts (Adapted from the CMA Examination)

7–4

The independent auditor must evaluate a client's system of internal control to determine the extent to which various auditing procedures must be employed. A client who uses a computer should provide the CPA with a flowchart of the information processing system so that the CPA can evaluate the control features in the system. Figure C7–4(A) shows a simplified flowchart, such as a client might provide. Unfortunately the client had only partially completed the flowchart when it was requested by you.

REQUIRED:

a. Complete the flowchart shown in Figure C7–4(A).

b. Describe what each item in the flowchart indicates. When complete, your description should provide an explanation of the processing of the data involved. Your description should be in the following order:
   (1) "Orders from salesman" to "Run no. 5"
   (2) "From mailroom" to "Run no. 5"
   (3) "Run no. 5" through the remainder of the chart

c. Name each of the flowchart symbols shown in Figure C7–4(B) and describe what each represents. (Adapted from the CPA Examination)

7–5

Charting, Inc., a new audit client of yours, processes its sales and cash receipts documents in the following manner.

a. *Cash receipts.* The mail is opened each morning by a mail clerk in the sales department. The mail clerk prepares a remittance advice (showing customer and amount paid) if one has not been received. The checks and remittance advices are then forwarded to the sales department supervisor, who reviews each check and forwards the checks and remittance advices to the accounting department supervisor.

The accounting department supervisor, who also functions as the credit manager, reviews all checks for payments of past-due accounts and then forwards the checks and remittance advices to the accounts receivable clerk, who arranges the advices in alphabetical order. The remittance advices are posted directly to the accounts receivable ledger cards. The checks are endorsed by stamp and totaled. The total is posted to the cash receipts journal. The remittance advices are filed chronologically.

After receiving the cash from the preceding day's cash sales, the accounts receivable clerk prepares the daily deposit slip in triplicate. The third copy of the deposit slip is filed by date, and the second copy and the original accompany the bank deposit.

b. *Sales.* Salesclerks prepare the sales invoices in triplicate. The original and the sec-

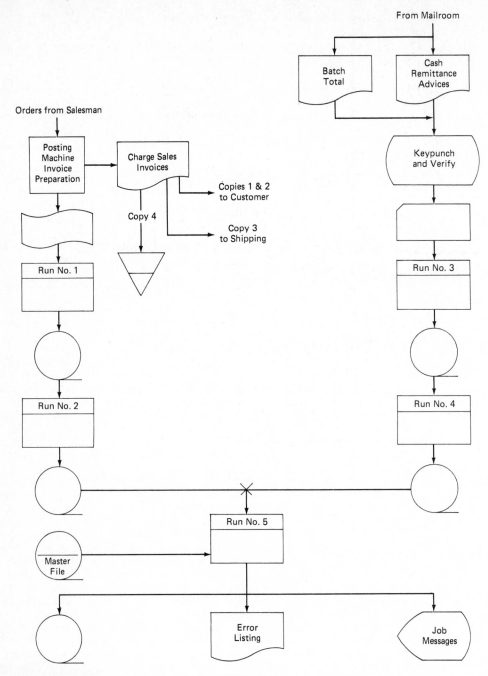

Figure C7–4 (A)

Source: CPA Exam.

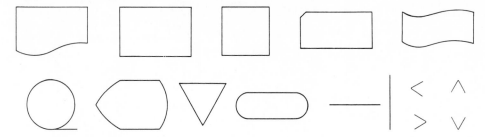

Figure C7–4 (B)

ond copy are presented to the cashier. The third copy is retained by the salesclerk in the sales book. When the sale is for cash, the customer pays the salesclerk, who presents the money to the cashier with the invoice copies.

A credit sale is approved by the cashier from an approved credit list after the salesclerk prepares the three-part invoice. After receiving the cash or approved invoice, the cashier validates the original copy of the sales invoice and gives it to the customer. At the end of each day the cashier recaps the sales and cash received and forwards the cash and the second copy of all sales invoices to the accounts receivable clerk.

The accounts receivable clerk balances the cash received with cash sales invoices and prepares a daily sales summary. The credit sales invoices are posted to the accounts receivable ledger, and then all invoices are sent to the inventory control clerk in the sales department for posting to the inventory control catalog. After posting, the inventory control clerk files all invoices numerically. The accounts receivable clerk posts the daily sales summary to the cash receipts journal and sales journal and files the sales summaries by date.

The cash from cash sales is combined with the cash received on account, and this constitutes the daily bank deposit.

c. *Bank deposits.* Monthly bank statements are reconciled promptly by the accounting department supervisor and filed by date.

REQUIRED: Flowchart the sales and cash receipts functions for Charting, Inc., using good form. Show the segregation of duties. (AICPA adapted)

7–6

Peat, Marwick, Mitchell & Co. has proposed a unique way to flowchart a system where the flow is from the bottom to the top through four zones described in Figure C7–6(A).[2] The left flow lines from documents to ledgers are debits, and the right flow lines are credits. Moreover, controls are indicated and described via symbols in circles next to each process rectangle as shown in Figure C7–6(B), and reconciliations are noted in circles in the base of each "T" or ledger account. Other symbols and details are also shown to facilitate the audit process.

In terms of the annual audit's objective, what is the focus of this type of flowchart? Why, in your opinion, may its construction enhance the efficient completion of the audit process as compared with the systems and document flowcharts described in the chapter?

7–7

During the audit of Carroll Office Supply, a major supplier of office equipment in Fort Apache, a large western city, you have been performing a considerable amount of substantive testing. This has become costly, as the business has grown from one small outlet to ten stores spread throughout the city. You would like to place more reliance on the company's system and spend more time in testing compliance in lieu of substantive testing. You cannot do it, however, because the company's newly acquired microprocessor operates like a "black box." Management bought it, and the company personnel use it in the way in which they were instructed by Micro Data, the vendor who installed it.

[2] Peat, Marwick, Mitchell & Co. *Study Guide Systems Evaluation Approach : Documentation of Controls (SEADOC),* Vol. 1 (New York: Peat, Marwick, Mitchell & Co., 1980).

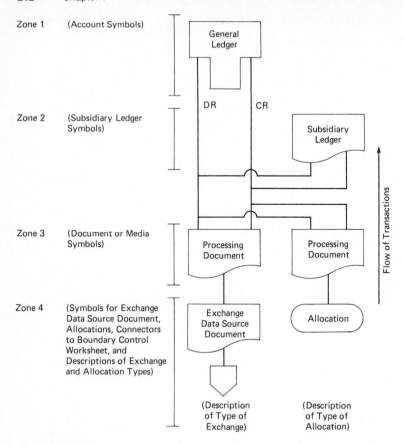

Zone 1 (Account Symbols)

Zone 2 (Subsidiary Ledger Symbols)

Zone 3 (Document or Media Symbols)

Zone 4 (Symbols for Exchange Data Source Document, Allocations, Connectors to Boundary Control Worksheet, and Descriptions of Exchange and Allocation Types)

Figure C7-6 (A)

Adapted with permission from Peat, Marwick, Mitchell & Co., *Study Guide Systems Evaluation Approach: Documentation of Controls (SEADOC)*, Vol. 1 (New York: Peat, Marwick, Mitchell & Co., 1980).

1. Suggest some action Carroll Office Supply can undertake to give you the needed confidence in its accounting system so that you can eventually reduce your audit fee.

2. What benefits will accrue to management from these actions you suggest?

7–8

A company uses sequential batch processing of invoices which are keypunched onto cards and tested by batch prior to processing. Hash, number of transactions, and dollar amount batch totals are used in the verification process. The original invoices are filed numerically. A grandfather-father-son series of tapes is used for control of the updated master file. Punched transaction cards are filed by date.

Exception reports, which are used to reconcile batch totals, good transactions, and exceptions, are generated as a byproduct of updating the master file. The updated master file tape is used in further processing. Prepare a systems flowchart of this processing operation.

7–9

Until recently Consolidated Electric Company employed a batch processing system for recording the receipt of customer payments. The following narrative and the flowchart in Figure C7–9 describe the procedures involved in this system.

The customer's payment and the remittance advice (a punched card) are received in the treasurer's office. An accounts receivable clerk

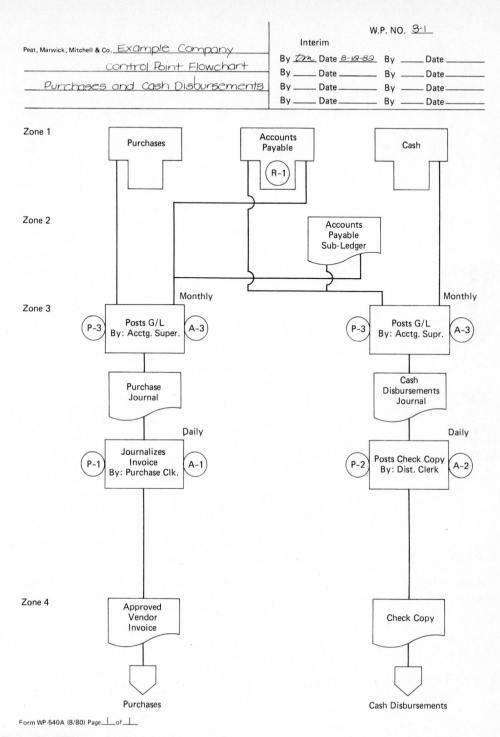

Figure C7–6 (B)

Adapted with permission from Peat, Marwick, Mitchell & Co., *Study Guide Systems Evaluation Approach*, pp. 2–68.

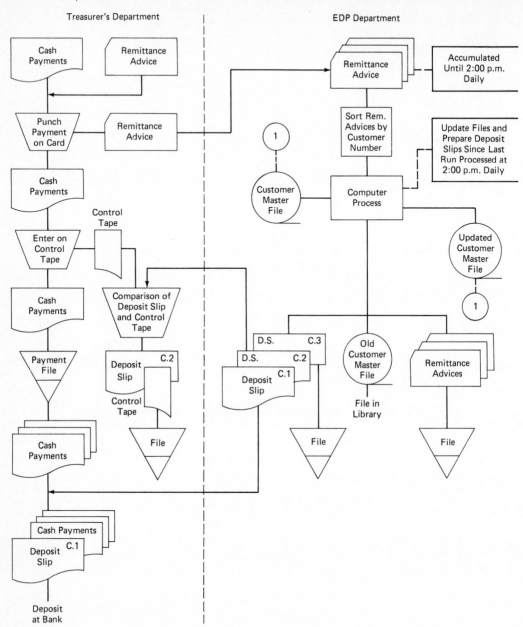

Figure C7-9 Consolidated Electric Company Batch Processing System
Adapted from the CMA Examination.

in the treasurer's office keypunches the cash receipt into the remittance advice and forwards the card to the EDP department. The cash receipt is added to a control tape listing and is then filed for deposit later in the day. When the deposit slips are received from EDP later in the day, the cash receipts are removed from the file and deposited with the original deposit slip. The second copy of the deposit slip and the control tape are compared for accuracy before the deposit is made and are then filed together.

In the EDP department, the remittance advices received from the treasurer's office are held until 2:00 P.M. daily. At that time the customer payments are processed to update the records on magnetic tape and to prepare a deposit slip in triplicate. During the update process, data are read from the master accounts receivable tape, processed, and then recorded on a new master tape. The original and a second copy of the deposit slip are forwarded to the treasurer's office. The old master tape (former accounts receivable file), the remittance advices (in customer number order), and the third copy of the deposit slip are stored and filed in a secure place. The updated accounts receivable master tape is maintained in the system for processing the next day.

The firm has revised and redesigned its computer system so that it has on-line capabilities. The new cash receipts procedures, described below, are designed to take advantage of the new system.

The customer's payment and remittance advice are received in the treasurer's office, as before. A cathode ray tube terminal is located in the treasurer's office to enter the cash receipts. An operator keys in the customer's number and payment from the remittance advice and check. The cash receipt is entered into the system once the operator has confirmed that the proper account and amount are displayed on the screen. The payment is then processed on-line against the accounts receivable file maintained on magnetic disk. The cash receipts are filed for deposit later in the day. The remittance advices are filed in the order in which they are processed; these punched cards will be kept until the next working day and then destroyed. The computer prints out a deposit slip in duplicate at 2:00 P.M. for all cash receipts since the last deposit. The deposit slips are forwarded to the treasur-

er's office. The cash receipts are removed from the file and deposited with the original deposit slip; the duplicate deposit slip is filed for further reference. At the close of business hours (5:00 P.M.) each day, the EDP department prepares a record of the current day's cash receipts activity on a magnetic tape. This tape is then stored in a secure place in the event of a systems malfunction; after ten working days the tape is released for further use.

REQUIRED: Prepare a system flowchart of the new on-line cash-receipts procedure. (Adapted from the CMA Examination)

7–10

Aero Freight, an airline specializing in overnight delivery of freight throughout the continental United States, uses a microprocessor to schedule its thirty-one planes, which converge at a private airport near Oklahoma City, unload their freight, sort it, and fly it to various locations throughout the country. The airline grew rapidly over the years and employed very talented programming assistants who were trained in operations research to maximize throughput on the least number of aircraft at the lowest fuel cost.

One day Aero Freight's programmer (the top systems designer) left the company. Aero Freight operated without problems until it added a thirty-second plane to its fleet and the optimization program failed. No one could find the problem and fix it. Aero Freight therefore operated with thirty-one aircraft for six months until one of its analysts, who had had some training in optimization models, discovered that one of the data fields in an obscure, little-used subroutine only had a dimension of 31 instead of 32. What could have prevented this problem from occurring in the first place?

7–11

Sketch a systems flowchart for an on-line sales order entry system that has an edit routine prior to master file updating and an inquiry provision to make sure sufficient stock is on hand prior to initiating the entry of the sales order. Orders are stored temporarily on a disk pending edit clearance. Sales personnel have access to the EDP system via remote terminals in their field office. Once sufficient stock is deemed to be on hand, the order is cleared and the job-order master file is updated.

7–12

Saxon Company manufactures and sells several product lines. They have a batch processing EDP system. All sales orders received during regular working hours are immediately typed on Saxon's own sales order form. This typed form is the source document for the keypunching of a shipment or back-order card for each item ordered. An order received one day is to be processed that day and night and shipped the next day.

The daily processing that has to be accomplished at night includes the following activities:

1. Preparing the invoice to be sent to the customer at the time of shipment. Cards are sorted by customer number.
2. Updating the accounts receivable file.
3. Updating the finished goods inventory. Cards must be sorted by stock number for this and the next process.
4. Listing of all items back-ordered and short.

Each month the sales department would like to have a sales summary and analysis. At the end of each month, the monthly statements should be prepared and mailed to customers. Management also wants an aging of accounts receivable each month.

REQUIRED: Prepare a system flowchart to reflect the described processing. (Adapted from the CMA Examination)

8

DATA BASE SYSTEMS

INTRODUCTION

In Chapter 5 we examined some of the hardware and software components that make up the data processing elements dimension of an information system (recall that we identified the dimensions of an information system in Chapter 2, Figure 2–4). In Chapter 6 we identified different system structures that can be used to link the dimensions of an information system (i.e., integrated real-time systems versus distributed processing systems). In this chapter we will focus on the data base component of the data processing dimension of an information system. Specifically we will identify what is labeled a *data base management system*, the elements that make up such a system, the advantages as well as the disadvantages of data base processing, the logical as well as the physical structure of a data base, languages applicable in building as well as in using a data base system, and, finally, some of the problems involved in using a data base management system.

Before examining data base systems we will examine the traditional file-oriented approach to data processing and the terminology associated with data processing in general.

TRADITIONAL DATA PROCESSING

Computer data can be organized and maintained to support individual applications. In this arrangement, each application has its own file and generally there is little sharing of data among various applications. The application software (program) for a system built upon this "file-oriented" arrangement is dependent upon the file structure; therefore, if the format of the file changes then the software also has to be changed. Figure 8–1 illustrates this structure of data processing.

The traditional approach to data processing has been the file-oriented arrangement. For scientific applications such an arrangement is acceptable, since in most cases a few separate data items are processed by sophisticated software involving numerous equations and models, and only a few application programs are used. In business data processing a file-oriented approach is not the most desirable structure. In most businesses, processing is quite simple,

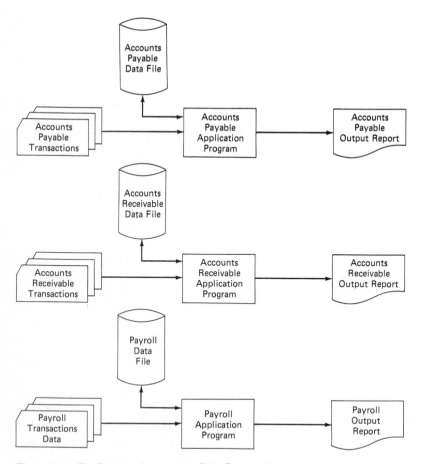

Figure 8–1   File-Oriented Approach to Data Processing

but the number of data items to be processed is often mammoth and the number of different application programs can be substantial.

The file-oriented approach to data processing is used extensively in business, even though data base management systems are becoming more readily available and are the more desirable process for organizing, storing, and accessing data. It is therefore important that we highlight some of the concepts associated with the file-oriented approach. Many of these concepts are also integral parts of data base systems. The specific points we will address include basic terminology (such as data items, records, files), coding schemes, file organization as well as access methods, and weaknesses of the file-oriented approach.

Terminology

Data item, record, file. When viewing data, the smallest unit of data that has meaning to a user is a *data item.*[1] Data items are the basic elements of a data base or a data file. Data items are grouped together, depending on the needs of the user, to form *records*. An application program usually reads and writes records. A user inquiry may access a single data item, a group of data items, and/or a record. A subgroup of data items within a record is often referred to as a *data aggregate*. Records that are grouped together are referred to as a *file*. The grouping of data items into records, and records into files, does not indicate that the items are necessarily physically grouped, as is the case in most file-oriented systems.

A data item can have a *data value* as well as a *data label*. The data label is nothing more than a name used to describe the particular piece of data; the data value is the actual contents of the data item. In a payroll application, data items might appear with such labels as EMPLOYEE NAME, SOCIAL SECURITY NUMBER, GROSS INCOME, STATE INCOME TAX WITHHELD, FEDERAL INCOME TAX WITHHELD, and so forth. The actual data values for this example could be: JOHN DOE, 421-32-6844, $1,192.31, $29.47, $291.87, and so forth. For marketing application data, items with such labels as follows would likely appear: SALESPERSON—NAME, SALES TERRITORY, PRODUCT TYPE, NUMBER OF ORDERS, DOLLARS OF ORDERS, COMMISSION PAID, and so forth. Associated data values in this case could be: JOE JONES, MIDWEST, 10, 218, $7,814.00, $843.21, and so forth. In a large data base it would not be uncommon to have more than ten thousand data items.

Figure 8–2 depicts the relationship between data items, records, and a file. EMPLOYEE ID, NAME, and so forth, are the data labels associated with the respective data items that make up an employee record. The collection of employee records constitutes an employee file. In this example the data items in the record have the same physical as well as logical relationship.

Each data item in Figure 8–2 is a specific *data type*. The *data type* that a data item can handle depends upon the encoding form employed. Data may be represented in a variety of forms such as the following: (1) alphanumeric, (2) numeric, fixed-point (integer) numbers, (3) numeric, floating-point (decimal)

---

[1] A *data item* is made up of *bits* and *bytes*; however, data are only significant to a data base user at the data item level. The relationships between *bits, bytes, characters,* and a *data item* are discussed in Chapter 5.

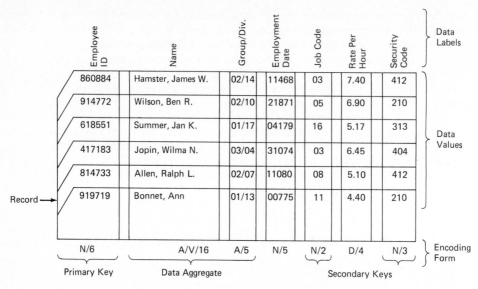

Figure 8–2 Example of *Data Items, Records,* and *Files* with Associated Primary and Secondary Keys

numbers, and (4) binary. Data items may be variable or fixed in length. Alphanumeric data items are usually variable in length, and numeric items are fixed. In the example, the value of the data item EMPLOYEE ID is numeric and six digits in length, (N/6). The NAME data item is alphanumeric, variable in length, up to sixteen characters, (A/V/16). The GROUP/DIV data item is alphanumeric but fixed at five characters, (A/5). The RATE PER HOUR data item is numeric (decimal) and four digits in length, (D/4).

Two additional points are depicted in Figure 8–2; these are *primary key* and *secondary keys.* Any record can have a primary key. This is a unique data item that can be used to access the record directly. EMPLOYEE ID is the primary key for the employee record. Secondary keys may or may not be unique; a record can have one or more such keys. Secondary keys are used to selectively access records. For example, by using JOB CODE as the secondary key, we could selectively retrieve all records with a job code value of 03.

If a secondary key is not unique, the associated file is by definition partitioned into subsets. In Figure 8–2, SECURITY CODE partitions the file into a set of records with codes 412, 210, 313, and 404; the JOB CODE secondary key partitions the file into a set of records with codes 03, 05, 16, 08, and 11. A *set,* therefore, is a group of records that have a common data value in a secondary key data item.

Data Coding

Codes. Data coding is used extensively in file-oriented processing as well as in data base processing. In Figure 8–2 *job code* and *security code* are examples of data coding. Data codes serve two purposes: (1) they uniquely identify a record or identify a record as a member of a file, and (2) they are efficient for information transfer purposes, since they require few characters to convey a given amount of information.

A number of different coding systems exist, such as *serial codes, block sequence codes, hierarchical codes,* and *association codes.* A brief description as well as the advantages and disadvantages of each of these follows.

Serial coding systems employ consecutive numbers (or alphabetic characters) for identifying records, irrespective of the different data items in the record. Thus a serial code uniquely identifies a record, but the code indicates nothing further about the record.

The major advantage of a serial code is the ease with which a new record can be added. It simply requires the selection of the next number in the sequence and assigning it to the record. But this advantage soon weakens when a significant number of records are deleted and added. Deleted records must have their codes reassigned to new records; otherwise gaps occur in the sequence and the code is no longer concise.

Block sequence codes assign blocks of numbers to the particular data items of a record. The primary data items on which records are to be categorized must be chosen and blocks of numbers assigned for each value of the data item. For example, if account numbers for customers are assigned on the basis of the discount allowed each customer, a block sequence code for customer records could be as follows:

701	D. W. Brown	
702	R. K. Allen	5% discount
703	M. M. Moore	
801	S. Elvers	
802	D. D. Rathwell	5¾% discount
803	L. Saunders	
901	M. Lather	
902	L. F. Simmons	6¼% discount

Block sequence codes have the advantage that some information about the record is conveyed by the code; but the disadvantage is in choosing the size of the block. If the block size is too small, an overflow will occur; if too large, wasted characters will occur and the code will no longer be concise.

Hierarchical codes require selection of the set of data items of a record and their ordering in terms of importance. The value of the code for the record is a combination of the values of the codes for each data item of the record. For example, a hierarchical code representing the cost item within a cost center within a department within a division of a company might appear as follows:

APl /	437 /	17 /	9113
Division No.	Department No.	Cost Center No.	Cost Item ID

Hierarchical codes can be very helpful to their users because each code conveys information about the data item to which it is associated. But there are some problems with using hierarchical codes when changes occur. In the above example, if a reorganization in the company occurs and cost center 17 is assigned to another department, then new codes will have to be structured and the master file altered and resequenced.

Association codes have a variety of names and labels, such as *mnemonic codes* and alphabetic *derivation codes*. Regardless of the name or label, however, they can all be classified as association codes. With an associated code the data item of a record is selected, and unique codes are assigned to each data item value. The codes may be alphabetic, numeric, or alphanumeric. The associated code for the record, therefore, is simply a linear combination of the different codes assigned to the data items. The following is an example of an association code assigned to a pair of slacks in a textile plant:

SLM3431DRRAY

where

SL = slack
M   = male
34 = 34″ waist size
31 = 31″ leg inseam
DR = dress
RAY = rayon fabric

Association codes convey a substantial amount of information about the record with which they are associated, but they can quickly become very long.

Charts of Accounts. Coding and classification are basic to accounting systems, regardless of the code involved and regardless of whether a file-oriented or a data base system is employed. The chart of accounts is one area where classification and coding are employed and illustrates the concepts of codes.

An *account* is simply a classification of information. The basic double-entry accounting model contains three major accounts: assets, liabilities, and equity. But a chart of accounts contains more than aggregrate information for these. Each of the major accounts is subdivided into numerous subclassifications. Assets are classified as current or noncurrent and are then further subdivided into cash, inventory receivables, and so forth. Liabilities are subclassified as accounts payable, notes payable, bonds payable, and so forth. Equity can be subdivided into revenue and expense accounts, among others, and each of these can be further subdivided. Thus a chart of accounts is nothing more than a scheme for classifying the firm's accounting information in such a manner that the firm can respond to both the external reporting requirements and the internal information requirements of the firm.

Once the accounts have been selected, they must be grouped or organized into a manageable framework. This can be accomplished by assigning each account a multidigit code in which each digit denotes a particular classification. Traditionally a three-digit code is employed, where each digit represents specific categories of information as follows:

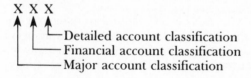

In accounting practice, *major accounts* are often classified 100 through 900 (in hundreds) as follows:

100	Assets
300	Liabilities
400	Stockholders' Equity
500	Sales
600	Cost of Sales
700	Expenses
800	Other Income
900	Summary Accounts

Within the major classifications, *financial subaccounts* are numbered 10 through 90 (in tens). An example of this subclassification would be Inventory, with the code 120. The leftmost digit specifies the major account Assets, the second digit, the subaccount Inventory.

Detailed account classifications are the transaction-level accounts into which data are posted. The subaccounts are generally numbered 1 through 9. An example that illustrates this level of classification or coding would be the bank checking account with code 111. The leftmost digit identifies the major account Assets; the second digit identifies the financial account Cash; and the rightmost digit identifies the specific cash account Checking.

Although there are similarities among all charts of accounts, differences abound in different situations, depending on the nature of the business. Accounting for an electronics firm is similar to, but also certainly different from, accounting for a textile firm. Uniform classifications of accounts have been developed and published by trade associations and numerous other groups to encourage uniform accounting practice. Figure 8–3 illustrates a general chart of accounts.

A hierarchical code can be built by using the chart-of-accounts code. A typical account coding structure might employ a seven-digit code, such as 27-111-01. The first two digits could represent a division, department, or profit center, with the numbering scheme 10 through 99. The following might be a typical example.

10—Consumer Products Division
20—Electronics Division
27—Manufacturing Department in Electronics Division
39—Marketing Department in Military Products Division

The middle three digits would represent the chart-of-accounts code. And, finally, the rightmost two digits could denote a company's product or activities within different subunits. For example, the code 01 could refer to product 1, the code 02 could refer to product 2, and so forth.

File Organization/Access Methods

A topic area that is relevant to both file processing and data base processing, but more so to the former, is file organization and file access methods. Both are examined in this section.

CURRENT ASSETS (100–199)   **Figure 8–3** Chart of Accounts (General)

102   Petty cash
111   Cash in bank
120   Inventory
150   Supplies
155   Prepaid rent

PLANT AND EQUIPMENT (200–250)

201   Land
220   Office equipment

INTANGIBLE ASSETS (280–299)

285   Organization costs

LIABILITIES (300–399)

310   Accounts payable
330   Notes payable

OWNER'S EQUITY (400–499)

450   Capital stock
460   Retained earnings

REVENUES (500–599)

501   Sales—territory 1
502   Sales—territory 2

COST OF SALES (600–699)

610   Salaries
630   Supplies
640   Rent

EXPENSES (700–799)

710   Overhead

SUMMARY ACCOUNTS (900–999)

910   Income summary

File organization refers to the physical arrangement of records on a storage device, and as we noted in Chapter 5, files are organized either (1) sequentially or (2) randomly. *File access* refers to the procedure used to access records from a storage medium, and like file organization this can be achieved (1) in a serial (sequential) manner or (2) directly. (As we will note in the next section, direct accessing of a record from a data base often requires the use of indexes, pointers, or randomizing techniques.)

Though file organization and file access can be viewed separately, they are actually linked in practice by the file arrangement employed. Four basic types of file arrangements exist: (1) sequential, (2) indexed sequential, (3) direct, and (4) random. A *sequential file* employs sequential organization and sequential access. An *indexed-sequential file* has a sequential organization but direct access. A *direct-address file* has records that are arranged randomly and employs a direct-access method. A *random file* employs random organization and random access.

Sequential files. Records in sequential files are organized in numerical or alphabetical order according to a primary key. Given the key of a desired record, sequential reading of each record in the file occurs, beginning with the first, until the desired record is reached. For example, if a file had ten records with the following keys: 713, 415, 714, 215, 445, 833, 554, 023, 244, and 214; and the key 554 was provided as the key for the desired record, seven records would have to be read before locating the desired record.

As we noted in Chapter 5, sequential files are most suitable for magnetic tapes because, by design, such storage media facilitate sequential storage and sequential access. However, as we noted in Chapter 6, sequential access is not conducive to the timely retrieval of data; therefore, for purposes of data base systems, sequential files are generally not employed.

Indexed-sequential files. In this file arrangement the file is organized sequentially; however, records are accessed directly by referring to a table of addresses called an index, or directory. The index contains an entry for either every key or every *n*th key, the latter being the case when *n* records are included in a block. Corresponding to each key in the index is the address of the associated record or the address of the associated block containing the record.

To locate a record stored in an indexed-sequential file requires several steps. First, the index must be accessed from storage, which is usually on the same disk as the indexed file. Second, the index must be searched to locate the key corresponding to the desired record. Third, the address corresponding to the key value is retrieved. Fourth, the record or record block is accessed using the disk address.

Indexed-sequential files are a common type of direct-access file and can be used in both sequential (batch) processing and real-time processing. For sequential processing, the indexed-sequential file is essentially treated as a sequential file. For real-time processing, the direct-access feature of the indexed-sequential file provides a viable access method.

Indexed-sequential files, however, have several disadvantages. First, they cannot be used on magnetic tape. Second, the indexes require added storage space and, in addition, their use is a relatively inefficient direct-access method, since two movements of the read-write head of the direct-access device are required. Third, because of the manner in which new records are added to an indexed-sequential file, a periodic maintenance procedure is required to physically reorder records. An indexed-sequential file does not permit records of the file to be reordered during an update run; therefore new records are put into an overflow area and "pointers" are used to link them to their respective places in the file. Periodically the file must be sorted in order to arrange all the records physically in the proper order, and all linkages must be deleted.

Direct-address files. Unlike sequential and indexed-sequential files, the file organization is random for direct-address files. Also, unlike the indexed-sequential access, which employs indexes, this method employs a record access procedure that accesses the records directly. One method of direct addressing involves establishing record keys that are equivalent to the record addresses. Thus, given the record key, the record can be read directly. However, this form of direct addressing is rarely found in practice, since it is generally not feasible to have record keys that are equivalent to record addresses. Furthermore, changing a set of existing record keys when records are added to or deleted from the file can be very costly.

A second method of direct-address accessing involves the use of a formula to convert keys into record addresses. The disadvantage of this approach is that it is not very suitable for the coding systems from which keys are generated. For example, in most coding systems, all the numbers that could be combined to form keys are not employed. The use of a direct key transformation under this condition is difficult, particularly when it is compounded by records being added to or deleted from the file.

A significant disadvantage of direct-address files is the storage organization process. Since random storage is employed, all available storage may not be employed, particularly when the transformation method is employed. Some record addresses may never be generated.

Random files. Like direct-address files, random files are organized so that records are stored randomly throughout a direct-access storage medium. And like direct-address files, records on random files are accessed directly by ascertaining the storage addresses of the respective records. However, the addressing method for random files differs from that for direct files; a method referred to as *randomizing* is employed.

Randomizing is a procedure often referred to as *hashing*, in which a computation is performed on the record key to convert it into a random number, which in turn is converted into the address of the desired record or the address of a block record containing the desired record. In contrast to direct addressing, this method can be employed with most coding systems. This is possible because the use of random numbers resolves the problems of having a coding system in which some keys are not used and the constant changing of keys when records are added or deleted. This advantage, together with its relative access speed, makes it a popular method of record addressing.

Randomizing does, however, have some drawbacks. As with direct-address files, the full storage capacity of a random file is not used because some addresses are not generated by the randomizing process. Also, the technique may generate identical storage addresses for two or more record keys; when this occurs, the records that encounter occupied storage addresses are placed in an overflow area, with "pointers" linked to their position. Finally, because of the random processing nature of the technique, large batches of transactions cannot be processed efficiently.

Weaknesses of the File-oriented Approach

A key characteristic of the early use of computers in business was the large number of application programs and the many files required to support the programs. This occurred because individual applications focused on their own specific data needs rather than considering the overall information needs of the organization. Many new applications resulted in the sorting and merging of existing files in order to create a new file to satisfy the requirements of the new application program. A tremendous number of application files emerged from this process; and there was usually little compatibility from file to file, since each had been formatted to meet the needs of specific application programs. Also, similar programs and files usually existed because it was more cost efficient and time efficient to create a new program, as well as a new file, than to revise an old one, even when there was only a slight difference between an existing specialized application program and the desired program.

As we noted earlier, file-oriented systems still exist and are being used today. These systems, however, have some key weaknesses, beyond the fact that many files are required to support most of them. The greatest weakness is data redundancy. By *data redundancy* we mean that identical data are stored in two or more files; for example, a "current customer account file" would probably contain some of the same data as an "invoice file." Data editing, maintenance, and storage costs all increase as a result of redundancy. When data are updated, a separate program is required in order to revise each file. If a data item is updated in some files but not in others, then the reports generated from the different files will not agree. Because of data redundancy, additional storage space is required; and therefore storage cost is greater.

Another weakness of a file-oriented approach is that application programs are directly dependent upon the structure of the data file. Since the business records related to an organization must be current, new data must often be added and old data deleted from associated files. Certain changes can be made with little impact on the structure of the file, but some changes may necessitate changes in record formats. (Increasing the number of characters in a part-number code would probably result in such a change.) Necessary changes will not only result in a restructuring of the file, but all the application programs that utilize the file must be changed. The necessity of program modification to reflect changes or additions in data files is a major "maintenance problem" in most file-oriented systems.

Another problem somewhat related to the changing of data within a file is the lack of compatibility of existing application programs to changes in hardware, particularly in storage devices. New technology often results in faster, larger, and less-expensive storage devices. But to take advantage of these changes requires the movement of records or files from the old device to the new one. If the new device has a slightly different storage structure than the old device, which may be the case, then all application programs that accessed the old device will again need to be changed.

An additional weakness of a file-oriented processing approach is the lack of data integration and inability to handle unanticipated information requests. Data on different files can be related, as would be the case for an employee master file and a payroll master file, but unless a specific application program is written to associate the data in the different files, the data will simply be used for the direct application for which they were built. To illustrate this point, assume that a data file and program exist for employee information reporting and that a data file and program exist for generating payroll checks and reports. (Physically the layout would be the same as that represented in Figure 8–1, with the accounts payable or accounts receivable portion being replaced with employee information.) Assume further that management would like to know the salary paid to each employee over thirty-five years of age who has been with the company more than seven years. To obtain this information, a new program must be written that will extract data from both the employee file and the payroll file. But a problem may exist in the extraction process—there is no guarantee that the data files are compatible. The employee information file may be written in assembler binary format, but a record format in COBOL may have been used in storing the payroll data. If this is the case, then one file must be converted to the other file format before the new application program can be written. This process is likely to be time consuming and expensive. By the time the programming has been completed, the information may no longer be required or useful. For many years this has been a key problem in data processing—management knows that the information that is needed is available somewhere in the computer, but no realistic means exists for accessing the data.

DATA BASE PROCESSING

Data base processing or, more specifically, data base management systems (DBMS) emerged as the means to overcome some of the inherent limitations in the traditional file-oriented approach. A *data base management system* is a set of software programs that serve as an interface between application programs and an "integrated" data base, which is a set of coordinated and interlinked physical files. The files of the data base are analogous to the master files of the file-oriented approach; however, the data base is not merely an accumulation of separate files. Rather, it is a collection of data items linked with various pointers and chaining schemes so that a minimum of redundancy of data exists and unanticipated retrieval of related information is possible.

Figure 8–4 illustrates a data base management system. In comparing this figure with Figure 8–1, two changes are apparent. First, the individual master files have been integrated into a data base. (Note that we did not label the data as Accounts Receivable Data File, Accounts Payable Data File, and Payroll Data File, but instead we simply used the term *data*.) Second, a data base management system module has been inserted between the data and the application programs. The accounts receivable, accounts payable, and payroll application programs still perform their original functions, but the data base management system is called upon to retrieve the data from the data base. The data used by these programs have been processed and stored by the data base management

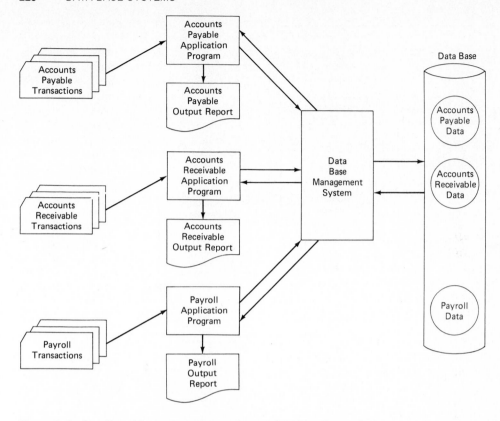

Figure 8-4 Data Base Management System Approach to Data Processing

system prior to being retrieved for use by the respective programs; therefore all the data are integrated and compatible. If a report were desired that called for a combination of and/or integration of accounts receivable and accounts payable data, this could be generated without changing the data base. It would simply require the writing of an application program to access the data base via the data base management system. (We will see shortly that many data base management systems provide a query language whereby it is possible to generate "special reports" on-line without writing a special application program.)

COMPONENTS OF DATA BASE PROCESSING

The data base processing environment involves four components: (1) the user (which includes application programmers as well as the actual programs), (2) the data base administrator, (3) the data base, and (4) the data base management system. The user is involved with the development of application programs, defines the contents of the data base (by specifying the needs of his or

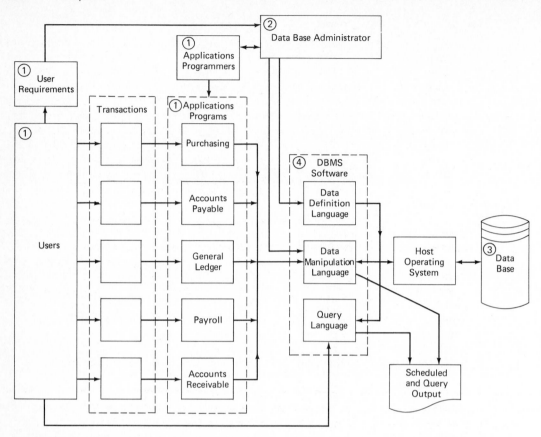

Figure 8–5 Interaction Among DBMS Components

her programs), defines relationships between data items, and by working with the data base administrator brings about modifications to the data base. The data base administrator is the custodian of the data base—this involves creating, adding, and deleting records as well as security and recovery. The data base management system is a set of software programs that operates on the data base (i.e., retrieves data) in accordance with the user commands, and in accordance with commands from the data base administrator, changes data items in the data base (i.e., adds, deletes, and/or modifies). The data base is simply a collection of all the data necessary to support user needs, organized so as to minimize data redundancy, make the most efficient use of storage devices and space, and provide easy retrieval as well as ability to modify. Figure 8–5 illustrates the interrelationships of the components. To better understand the data base processing environment, we will examine each component in detail.

Users

The term *users* generally refers to traditional users, such as departmental managers, accounting personnel, and other individuals outside the data processing area; in data base processing, however, application programmers are also considered key users. This is not to say that other individuals are not involved in or do not interact with the data base management system. For example, the data base administrator directly interacts with the data base management system in maintaining the data base, providing security and error recovery procedures; system programmers work with the data base administrator, the data base management system, and the operating system in physically structuring the data base. In this chapter the term *user* will refer to the application programmers and traditional users whose primary orientation to the data base is utilization.

Users have two means by which they can interact with the data base management system: (1) directly, by using English-like statements known as a query language, or (2) by communicating with an application program, which in turn interacts with the data base management system. The query language is generally used for one-time or ad hoc applications where the particular use does not justify a written program. One benefit of the query language is that it makes the data base accessible for users who have limited or no background in computer programming. In the past the majority of users have interfaced with the data base through application programs rather than through the query mode; however, with the current trend in microcomputers, decision support systems, and terminal technology, this will probably change in the future.

Regardless of how the user interacts with the data base management system, either directly or through an application program, three operations must take place. First, the user defines the logical relationships in the data base, that is, the formats of the data and the relationships among the data items. In our examination of the elements that make up the data base management system later in the chapter, we will identify a data definition language (DDL) that can aid the user (working in conjunction with the data base administrator) in defining certain aspects of the data base. Second, the user may access data. As we have previously noted, this occurs by requesting the data base system to retrieve certain data items from the data base. The data inquiry may be relatively simple, like retrieving the home address of salesperson No. 86088; or it may be complex, like retrieving the name of the salesperson within the organization who sold the largest dollar volume of video device No. 4752 during the first quarter of 1982. Third, the user is responsible for modifying and/or updating that portion of the data base that he or she employs. (This function, like the creation of the data base, is performed in conjunction with the data base administrator.)

Data Base Administrator

The data base administrator (DBA) is, as we have noted, the custodian of the data base and controls the overall structure. Being custodian of the data does not mean that he or she is the owner. The data contained in the data base is neither owned nor used by the data base administrator. The owner of an item of data is the individual, group, or department that creates or assigns values to the item in the data base. The data base administrator will know, for example, that the payroll portion of the data base contains a payroll record that contains a salary data item, but he or she will not know the value recorded in the data item. Unless the owner of the data has so specified, the data base administrator cannot read the values in a given data item. But if the data item must be expanded in order to hold a larger value (for example, if the salary data item noted above needed to be expanded from five digits to seven digits), only the data base administrator has the responsibility and authority for making the change.

The data base administrator is responsible for the overall configuration of the data base. He or she, therefore, encourages standardization of data items and specifies the data structures and layouts that are best for the data users as a group. If an individual user wishes to create a new type of record, change an existing record by including new data items, or expand the size of a data item, application must be made to the data base administrator to make the change. The data base administrator evaluates all requests and modifies the data structure only when it is best for the organization as a whole. An application programmer or any other user working on an individual application is not permitted to change the overall data structure even if the application program can benefit; the data base administrator must take an organizational point of view and also consider the economics of the change.

A key function of a data base administrator is the settling of differences between groups or individuals who have requested the data to be defined, represented, and/or stored differently. A problem that often arises is whether data should be shared between departments who have previously not shared. Also the structuring of a data base from an existing file-oriented system often causes problems because the process necessitates the restructuring of files and the rewriting of programs. Department managers often argue vehemently about these changes—they are reluctant to release control of departmental data and have difficulty understanding why changes are required.

In addition to resolving conflicts over data control and demonstrating the need for certain changes or certain forms of data structure, the data base administrator provides a number of basic services. He or she plans the file-addressing schemes for the data base, the physical data layout, security procedures, and a means for recovery after failures occur. He or she also selects and provides data management software that can aid users in utilizing the data base and provides consulting services to data users. Application programs can be assisted with data definitions; analysts often need help in understanding the structure of the data base, and general users often need support in understanding what data can be made available and the procedures (query language) for accessing.

Figure 8–6 summarizes the major activities and functions of the data base administrator. For a large organization that requires a complex data base, these tasks are not carried out by a single individual. It is unlikely that a single individual would have the technical expertise, the knowledge of the corporation data, and the communication skills to handle all these tasks. However, if there is to be a total integrated system, then a centralized data base is required and these functions must be provided. For a centralized integrated real-time pro-

The data base administrator:

Is responsible for the overall configuration and physical structure of the data base

Is custodian of the data base—provides for updating, deleting, and/or changing data items and records in the data base

Serves as an arbitrator in the sharing of data and provides justification for restructuring of existing files

Performs software and hardware selection to support the operation and use of the data base

Provides and maintains controls for additions or deletions to the data base

Develops control access methods, including the assignment of user access codes, and provides instructional support on the use of the procedures

Is responsible for overall security of the data base and error recovery

Figure 8–6 Major Activities and Functions of the Data Base Administrator

cessing system, a data base administrative *unit* made up of several individuals will be required. This would probably include an overall data base administrator, a data base design analyst, a data definition analyst, a data operations supervisor, and a security officer.

The Data Base

The third component of data base processing is the data base itself (refer to Figure 8–5). As we noted in comparing the structure of a file-oriented system with that of a data base processing system, the data base is not simply a collection of the files that exist in a file-oriented system. Rather, it is a collection of data items linked together to serve a multiple number of applications in an optimal fashion; the data are stored so that they are independent of the application programs and users. Structured and controlled procedures are used to add new data and/or to modify and retrieve existing data within the data base.

To better understand the structure of a data base, we need to examine some basic concepts. In the following subsections we will (1) differentiate between *logical* data and *physical* data, (2) differentiate between *schema* and *subschema* structures used to show logical relationships between items of data, and (3) discuss several data structure concepts.

Logical Data and Physical Data In data base processing, the arrangement of data stored in the data base builds upon the physical organization of files noted in the preceding section. However, the arrangement of data as viewed by the application program or user may differ significantly from how it is physically stored. An application programmer organizes his or her data to fit the needs of a specific program. Data in a data base are organized to maximize storage efficiency, reduce data duplication, and provide ease of access. The two structures differ significantly. The data structure that an application program employs is called a *logical structure*. The data structure employed in storing data, regardless of whether it is in tape, disk, or some other medium, is called a *physical structure*.

To avoid ambiguity, select terms can be used to differentiate between logical data and physical data. A *data base record* refers to a logical record format. A *data base file* is a collection of data base records, viewed logically. We will use the terms *records* and *files* to refer to *logical data base records* and *data base files*. A *physical record* is a contiguous group of characters (bytes) having no logical structure or meaning but having an identifiable physical order. A *physical file* is a collection of physical records. Data base record and data base file have no physical meaning. A data base record may be stored in several physical records, or it may be intermixed with other data base records and stored on a single physical record, depending on the structure of the data base records and the physical records. A data base file may be stored on several physical files, or several data base files may be stored on a single physical file, again depending on the structure of the data.

Figure 8–7 illustrates the difference between logical and physical records. In this figure an application program employs six records. The application program has a logical order in which the records are structured and employed in the program. Physical records are stored in the data base (in this case a disk) in an order different from that viewed by the programmer. To provide the logical (data base) records, the physical records are chained together

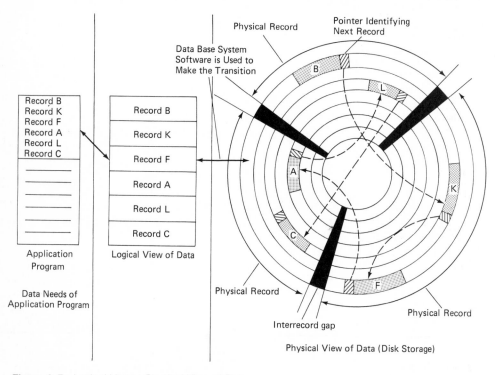

Figure 8–7   Logical Versus Physical View of Data

by a series of pointers. The chaining mechanism is provided by data base system software; therefore the programmer requires no knowledge of the chaining mechanism in order to access data.

Since different application programs will probably require different data base records, the data base system software must be able to handle different types of data structures. Also, since a user operating in a query mode may wish to access specific data items within data base records, the software must have this level of capability.

SCHEMA AND SUBSCHEMAS   To logically describe the data in the data base requires a *schema* and *subschemas*. A *schema* describes the logical view of the entire data base. It is often expressed by means of a *data dictionary*, which lists all the data items in the data base and their associated definitions. A *subschema* is that portion of the schema that is of interest to a particular user. In a sense, a schema is analogous to the map of a city, and the subschema is that portion of the map that includes a given individual's subdivision, neighborhood, and/or area of interest. Figure 8–8 illustrates the relationship between schema and subschemas (the diagram actually shows the relationship between data, physical data base description, schema, subschemas, and application/user programs).

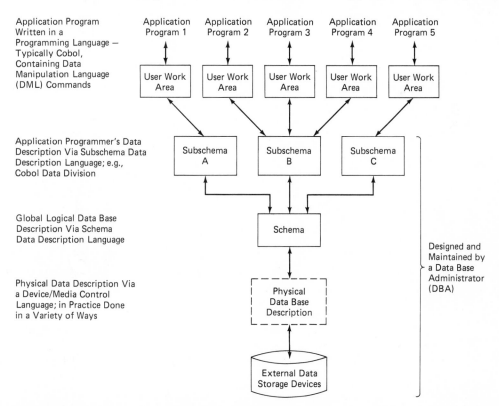

Figure 8–8   Relationship Between Data, Physical Data Base Description, Schema, and Subschemas.
Source: Cardenas, *Data Base Management Systems*, p. 17

The concept of a schema and separate subschemas allows the separation of the descriptions of the entire data base from the descriptions of portions of the data base employed by individual users. This is important for several reasons: (1) since the data base will probably contain data that are relevant to, and shared by, multiple applications, subschemas allow individual users to focus only on that portion of the data base that is relevant to their program—this eases the writing, debugging, and maintaining of programs; (2) the employment of subschemas automatically ensures a certain level of privacy and integrity of the data base, since individual programs access that portion of the data base identified by the subschema; (3) a certain degree of data independence is provided in that certain changes may be made to the schema for the data base, and the data base accordingly will not affect programs that are linked to the data via subschemas; and (4) it allows a common language to be employed in defining the entire data base while a variety of languages, based upon the desires or needs of the individual user, can be used to describe the subportion of the data needed by a given program.

DATA STRUCTURES   As we noted earlier, sequential, indexed-sequential, direct-access, and random files are employed in traditional file-oriented systems. In addition to these file concepts, a variety of data structures are employed in data base processing. These include, to mention a few, (1) trees, (2) networks, (3) linked lists, and (4) inverted lists.

Trees. A tree is a hierarchical, logical data structure consisting of nodes connected by branches. Figure 8–9 illustrates a tree structure. The node at the top of the structure (node 1) is referred to as the root node. The other nodes are referred to as parent nodes, descendent nodes, or both. Tree structures are distinguishable from other structures in that every node with exception of the root node has exactly one *parent* node. Node 2 is the parent of node 4; node 3 is the parent of node 7, and so on. Nodes 4, 5, and 6 are descendants of node 2; nodes 7 and 8 are descendants of node 3. Descendant nodes are often referred to as *children*. A parent node may have an unlimited number of children nodes.

Both *balanced* and *unbalanced* tree structures exist. A balanced tree is one in which every node has the same number of children on the same level. An unbalanced tree violates this requirement. Figure 8–9 illustrates an unbal-

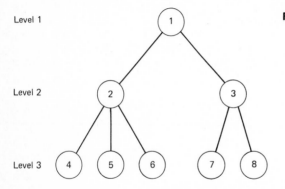

Figure 8–9   Example of a Tree Structure

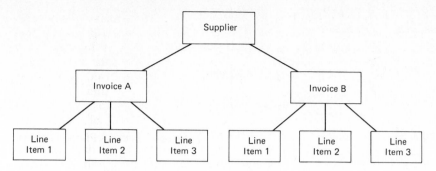

Figure 8–10   Supplier-Invoice-Line Item Tree Structure

anced tree; by adding a node 9 as a descendant of node 3, the structure would become balanced.

A more "real-world" illustration of a tree structure is shown in Figure 8–10. In this example the structure identifies the supplier-invoice-line item relationship. The supplier in this case is the root node; the invoices are children of the supplier; and the line items are children of the respective invoices.

Note that there is no physical relationship implied in the tree structure (which is also the case for the network structure). For example, the physical storage of the data in Figure 8–10 could be three separate records within three separate files. As we will see in our examination of a linked list (in the next section), physical records can be linked together with embedded pointers.

Networks. The second form of a logical structure is a *network*, or *plex structure* as it is often called. A network structure, like a tree structure, is composed of nodes and branches; but unlike a tree, a network can have multiple parents. The relationship from child to parent and from parent to child thus can be one-to-many in a network. Figure 8–11 illustrates a network structure. Node 1 is a parent node and has nodes 3, 4, and 5 as children; however, node 5 (the child node) has two parent nodes—nodes 1 and 2.

To further illustrate the network structure, consider the student-class network shown in Figure 8–12. This particular relationship could represent students (1, 2, 3, . . . , n) and the associated classes (1, 2, 3, . . . , m) in which each student is enrolled. This is not a completely balanced network, since every student is not linked to every class and vice versa.

The relationships of a network structure can be represented by a multiple-tree structure. Figure 8–13 illustrates the multiple-tree structure for the network shown in Figure 8–12. While the multiple-tree structure may reduce complexity, it results in data redundancy. In this particular example, all class information is repeated at least twice; in one case, four times. For a complex

Figure 8–11   Example of a Network Structure

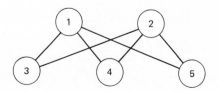

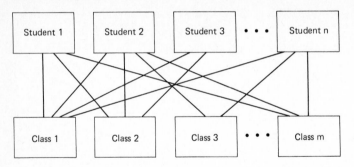

Figure 8–12 Student-Class Network Structure

network, a tremendous amount of data redundancy would probably result if a multiple-tree structure were employed.

Other forms of networks such as cycle networks and loop networks exist; however, this material is beyond the scope of this text. The important point here is that logical relationships can be represented in the form of networks, regardless of the complexity involved.

Linked list. One of the primary means that is used to physically represent trees, networks, and other logical relationships is a *linked list,* which is nothing more than a group of data items linked by pointers within the data items. Most linked lists have a *head* that points to the first item, and a *tail* (which may be a special data item or symbol) that indicates the last item in the list.

To illustrate the use of a linked list, assume that we have an array of records, each of which has a data item that is used to identify the row number (link value) for the next record. Figure 8–14 illustrates the record-array link-data-item relationship. In this example, record A is the first record, since the

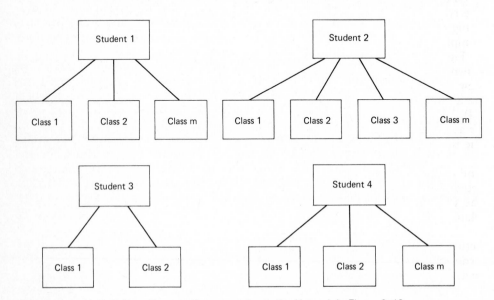

Figure 8–13 Multiple-Tree Structure Corresponding to the Network in Figure 8–12

Row No.	Link No.	Data:
1	3	record M
2	X	record K
3	5	record J
4	6	record A
5	2	record S
6	7	record B
7	1	record Q

[Head: 4]

Figure 8–14 Linked List Structure

head value is 4. The link number associated with record A is 6; therefore record B is the second record. The pointer (link) for record B is 7; therefore record Q follows record B. Following the linking relationship through all records results in the following sequence of records: A–B–Q–M–J–S–K.

Note that the order of the records in the linked list is not the same as the order in the array of records. Several benefits can result from this relationship. First, this means that records can be stored in any physical order and can be linked via a set of embedded pointers (we illustrated this in Figure 8–7). Second, records can easily be inserted into or deleted from a file without a vast reorganization of the file. Third, linked lists can easily be used to represent complex data structures.

To illustrate the ease with which records can be added to or deleted from a file by using a linked list, assume that we physically order a file so that the records are in the sequence order A–B–Q–M–J–S–K (see Figure 8–15). Assume further that we wish to insert a record between records B and Q. To accomplish this without a linked list (with the physically ordered records shown in Figure 8–15) would require that records Q, M, J, S, and K each be shifted down one record and a blank record created between records B and Q. The new record could then be inserted into the blank record. The same results can be accomplished with a linked list in a much easier fashion (refer to Figure 8–14). We simply add the new record to the bottom of the list, change the pointer associated with record B to point to the new record, and set the pointer in the new record to the record location of record Q.

Deleting a record by using a linked list would necessitate changing only one pointer. We would simply locate the record preceding the record to be deleted and change its associated pointer to the location of the record following the record to be deleted. The pointer of the "to be deleted" record is then blanked.

To delete a record from a physically ordered file would necessitate the actual deleting of the record and a shifting of all remaining records. Physically ordered files are therefore much more demanding when adding or deleting records.

Though linked list files have a number of advantages over physically ordered files, they do have some disadvantages. First, an extra data item, or

record A
record B
record Q
record M
record J
record S
record K

Figure 8–15   Physical Ordering of Records

several extra data items in some cases, are required to hold the link pointers. Second, and by far the more critical disadvantage, random retrieval of records in a linked list file is rather slow. To locate the nth record in a file would mean that the pointer route would be traced until the nth record is reached. With a physically ordered file, the record can be accessed directly.

Inverted lists. Lists may be created by using an index which contains pointers indicating the storage address of data rather than placing the pointer in the record. These are called *inverted lists.* Other physical structures and lists exist but are beyond the scope of this text.

Data Base Management System (DBMS)

The fourth component of the data base processing environment is the data base management system (refer to Figure 8–5). A variety of data base management systems exist; however, most systems have at least two common components: (1) a *data definition language* (DDL) and (2) a *data manipulation language* (DML). Some systems also contain an interactive inquiry facility, built around a *query* language. The query language employs a variety of commands for searching the data base and in some cases utilizes complex search strategies to satisfy the data needs of management. This latter feature is in reality a mode of operation rather than a key design element of a data base management system; therefore we will focus most of our comments on the data definition language and data manipulation language and describe how these are employed in the data base management system. We will also examine conceptually how the data base system handles a user data request.

Before we examine the DDL and DML, we need to examine briefly what is termed a *data base manager* (DBM). Every data base management system has a data base manager; however, this is not the data base administrator that we discussed earlier. The DBM is not a person, instead it is software. It is the part of the data base management system that actually controls the data base storage and access. The DBM performs in much the same manner within the data base management system that the operating system does within the computer itself. It controls the data base organization and format storage devices, and it provides storage and retrieval access to the data base. The DBM often utilizes and communicates with the computer's operating system in carrying out these functions. Other labels such as *data management routines* (DMR) and *data manager* (DM) are often used instead of *data base manager* (DBM), but regardless of the label, the task performed by the software is similar.

Figure 8–16 is an expanded version of module 4 in Figure 8–5. Here the data base management system includes the data base manager module. The diagram also includes a teleprocessing monitor, which is required if users are to operate via terminals. A key point that should be noted in the diagram is the role played by the DBM. Since the DBM is the control mechanism for the data base management system, communication must exist between the DBM and the operating system, between the DBM and the DDL and DML languages, and between the DBM and the teleprocessing monitor which is used to input user query commands. Each of these points of communication is depicted by a double directed arrow crossing the respective boundaries.

DATA DEFINITION LANGUAGE (DDL) The DDL is the link between the logical and the physical representation of data. As we noted in the previous section of the chapter, *logical* refers to the manner in which the user views data, and *physical* refers to the manner in which the data are stored. The DDL is employed by the user to describe the logical structure of the data base. Given the DDL, application programs are not constrained or locked into a particular physical representation of data; the physical structure of the data can change, but the DDL remains fixed.

The DDL provides a number of specific functions in serving as the vehicle for describing the structure of the data base. First, it can define the characteristics of each record in the data base, that is, the name and data type of each field. The DDL can also specify the way in which fields are grouped into records and can identify primary and secondary keys. Fourth, the DDL can specify relationships among records such as tree and network structures. Fifth, it can describe the schema and subschemas for the data base. Finally, the DDL

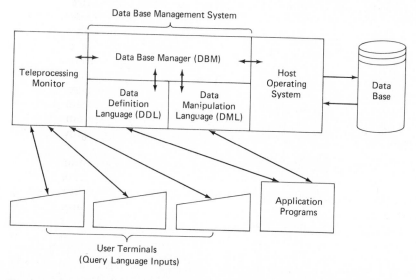

Figure 8–16 Data Base Management System and Associated Components

Adapted from *Management Data Bases,* R. Clay Sprowls, John Wiley & Sons, 1976, p. 73.

SUPPLIER RECORD:

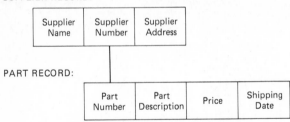

PART RECORD:

Figure 8-17   Two-Record Data Base

can specify the security limits for the data base. In this function the DDL, through inputs from the user, indicates the fields or records that are limited and the type of restrictions (read or write only, or both read and write).

Thus the primary functions of the DDL are as follows:

1. Define the characteristics of each record (the name and data type of each field of a record)
2. Specify the grouping of fields into records
3. Identify the keys of the record
4. Provide a means to specify the relationships among records, such as tree and network structures
5. Describe the schema and subschemas
6. Provide for data security limits and restrictions

To illustrate some of the functions of the DDL more vividly, we will assume that the data base simply consists of the two records shown in Figure 8–17. To describe the data base, we must first use the DDL to develop the schema. Figure 8–18 shows how the schema might appear. Note that the DDL describes the name, type, length, security limits, and key characteristics of both the supplier record and the part record. One item that is not defined in this example is the re-

A. SUPPLIER RECORD

Field Name	Data Type	Length	Security	Key
SUP–NAME	Characters	20	None	Primary
SUP–NUM	Integer	8	None	Secondary
SUP–ADD	Alphanumeric	30	None	None

B. PART RECORD

Field Name	Data Type	Length	Security	Key
PAR–NUM	Integer	10	None	Primary
PAR–DESC	Characters	25	None	None
PRICE	Real	7	Read/write Restricted	Secondary
SHP–DATE	Integer	6	Read only	None

Figure 8–18   Data Definition Language (DDL): Schema Description for Two-Record Data Base

PART RECORD

Name	Data Type	Length	Security	Key
PAR–NUM	Integer	10	None	Primary
PAR–DES	Character	25	None	None
SUP–NAME	Character	20	None	Secondary
PRICE	Real	7	Read/Write Restricted	None

Figure 8–19   Data Definition Language (DDL): Subschema Description for Two-Record Data Base

lationship between the two records. The DDL has this capability, and for a complex tree or network data base, these relationships must be defined. Since the DDL employs such labels as SUP–NAME and SUP–NUM to refer to the different fields of the record, no tie is made to any physical structure or physical file. The records can reside in any order and on any type of storage device (disk, drums, data cell, etc.).

For every application program that accesses the data base, a subschema must be structured. The subschema, as we noted earlier, is the descriptive layout of the record or records employed by the program. Figure 8–19 shows one possible subschema for this data base. The subschema in this case contains only one record, but the data are associated with two records in the schema. When the application program requests the data during execution, the data base system will extract the values of the data items from the appropriate data base record and place them in the order noted by the subschema.

Note that this particular example of a DDL is not structured around a particular data base management system. Since a variety of data base systems exist, the DDL will probably vary from this basic example. The concepts and points, however, are directly applicable.

DATA MANIPULATION LANGUAGE (DML)   The DML is used to describe the manner in which the data base is processed; that is, it provides the techniques for processing the data base, such as retrieval, replacement, sorting, insertion, deletion, and display. To provide these capabilities, the DML employs a variety of manipulation verbs and associated operands for these verbs. Figure 8–20 shows some of the more typical verbs and operands.

The structure of the operand associated with a particular verb depends upon the action taken by the verb (command). The READ verb requires the record type, such as SUPPLIER record for our example; the key name (primary or secondary), such as SUP–NAME; the fields to be read; and associated pass-

VERB	OPERANDS
Delete	Record name, key, field names, passwords
Read	Record name, key, field names, passwords
Sort	Record name, field names
Insert	Record name, key, field names, passwords
Add	Record name, field names
Display	Record name, key

Figure 8–20   Example of DML Verbs and Associated Operands

words (if they exist). The SORT and ADD verbs require only record names and field names for operands.

By employing the manipulation verbs and the associated operands of the DML, a user is able to work with the data base in logical or symbolic terms rather than physical terms. The DML also frees the user from making all the structural changes associated with a modification of the data base. For example, when a record is added to a set, the data base system will make all the necessary changes. The user simply issues the appropriate command.

Most data manipulation languages support a standard symbolic language, such as COBOL, PL/1, and Assembler. To be most suitable, a DML should not be structured around a particular language but should support several languages.

In summary, the DML is designed to do the following:

1. Provide data manipulation techniques such as retrieving, replacing, sorting, and deleting.
2. Provide a means to work with the data base in logical and symbolic terms rather than physical terms.
3. Allow the user to be independent of physical data structure and data base structure maintenance.
4. Provide flexibility in the use of the DML with standard symbolic languages. The DML should support several high-level languages, such as COBOL, PL/1, and Assembler.

CONCEPTUAL VIEW   To better understand how the DDL and DML work in conjunction with the data base management system, we can conceptually examine the steps that would be involved in reading a record from the data base. We will assume that a READ command (verb) has been employed by the user, along with the appropriate operand arguments. Figure 8–21 illustrates the sequence of events. The numbers in the circles indicate the order of the events.

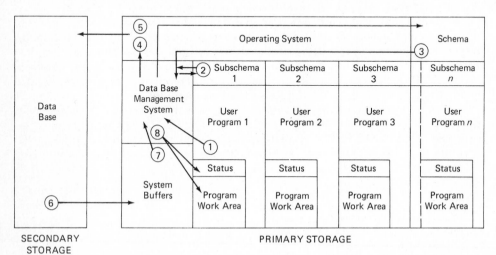

Figure 8–21   Conceptual View of Events That Occur When an Application Program Reads a Record from the Data Base

Adapted from *Management Data Bases,* R. Clay Sprowls, John Wiley & Sons, 1976, p. 81.

A summary of the sequence of events in Figure 8–21 follows:

1.   User program 1 instructs the data base management system to read a record. The program provides the record name and all associated data required to read the record.
2.   The data base management system examines the subschema associated with the user program and examines the record type in question.
3.   The data base management system examines the schema to determine which records are needed.
4.   The data base management system passes control to the operating system after requesting the appropriate records.
5.   The operating system interacts with the storage device on which the data base resides.
6.   The data are transferred from the data base to the system buffer.
7.   By comparing the subschema and the schema, the data base management system extracts the data required by the logical records of the user program.
8.   The data base management system transfers the data to the work area of the user program and reports to the user (through the status area) the results of the call. If errors occur in the process, these are reported to the user; if the read is successful, the user is also notified.

Data Dictionaries

In our initial discussion of data base processing, we did not identify a data dictionary as a processing component. This was not because of oversight; it was simply because all data base systems do not employ data dictionaries. However, we would be negligent if we did not discuss this topic.

A *data dictionary* is a software package that can be used to assist in both the utilization and the management of the total data in the data base. It is a repository of data about data. A data dictionary could easily contain a catalog of the following data:

1.   Data item (field)
2.   Data aggregate
3.   Subschema record (programmer's record)
4.   Schema record (stored logical data base record)
5.   Subschema (program data declaration)
6.   Schema (logical data base description)
7.   Physical data base structure
8.   Source of data (data input)
9.   Output document in which data are used
10.   Program using data
11.   User's name, department, etc.

The data dictionary can be used by the data base administrator, the data processing staff, and the users (managers) and can be accessed by application packages. The dictionary can help the data base administrator educate users about the contents of the data base to ensure that different users will be consistent in their definition of data items and that changes made to the data base will be consistent. It can help staff people determine what data are available for specific applications and the labels and types of data involved. It can help managers determine what types of data are available. And it can also guide a user in interrogation of the data base.

OPERATION AND USE OF DATA
BASE PROCESSING

We have devoted a large portion of this chapter to examining the components that go together to make up a data base processing system, but we have said very little about the use of such systems. In this section we will focus on some factors related to the operation and use of data base processing. Specifically we will examine requirements for data base users, make a brief comment about data base security, and discuss backup and recovery.

Requirements for Data Base Users

Earlier in the chapter we noted that users have two means by which they can interact with the data base management system: (1) directly, by using a query language, or (2) by communicating with an application program. Using a data base system, however, requires more than simply a language or a means of access. In actuality, five elements are involved in a user's interaction with a data base system:

1. Method of access (inquiry versus host language)
2. Mode of access (batch versus on-line)
3. Nature of the request (fixed versus dynamic)
4. Range of data that is referenced (schema versus subschema)
5. Nature of the items to be accessed (data versus data structure)

The *method of access*, as we have noted previously, refers to the method employed to direct the data base system. This may be a query language, or it may involve writing an application program using a host computer language such as COBOL, FORTRAN, or PASCAL.

The *mode of access* refers to whether *batch* or *on-line* (interactive) processing is employed. Some individuals erroneously assume that data base processing involves only on-line processing. Data base processing, however, can be batch, on-line, or a mixture of both. Most systems provide both as well as a mixture of the modes of access.

The third element, *nature of the request*, refers to whether the user's request is *fixed* or *dynamic*. In most systems a user is permitted to make certain specific fixed requests; however, the user also has the flexibility to structure dynamic requests. The dynamic requests are limited only by the constraints of the query and/or host language of the respective system. An airlines ticketing agent making an inquiry to determine the availability of seats, and a bank teller making an inquiry to determine the account balance of a customer, are examples of users making fixed requests. An example of a dynamic-request user would be a marketing manager who is examining different combinations of sales data (i.e., by territory, by salesperson, by product type, by a ratio of product type to salesperson, etc.) in order to fully evaluate the market situation for his or her organization.

The *range of data that is referenced* refers to the extent to which the data base is employed. In some cases the user may need and have approval to access any subpart or all of the data base (schema). In other cases the user may need access to only a select portion of the data base (schema). If a user is given access to a portion (subschema) of the data base, only data in the defined area or areas can be referenced or modified. Security procedures are available to mask data in the data base so that users are restricted to defined subsets of data.

The last element employed in interacting with the data base system is labeled the *nature of the items to be accessed.* This refers to whether the user inquiry involves actual access of data or modification of the data structure (relationships) of the data base. A marketing manager would probably access the data base to retrieve data relating to sales-by-salesperson, sales-by-territory, or some other set of data. However, if the sales territories or the territory-to-salesperson relationships within the organization change, the structure of data base would need to be changed to correspond to the organization. The marketing manager could, if given the proper security clearance, make data structure modifications. However, this responsibility is more appropriately that of the data base administrator.

To illustrate how these five elements are employed by a data base system user, consider the following. Assume that an individual calls an airline office to inquire about the availability of seats on a given flight. The caller talks with a reservations agent who has access to a data base. The agent is the data base system user; more specifically, the agent is a query language access/interactive mode/fixed/subschema/data user. Under this arrangement the agent will utilize query language statements in an interactive mode to access specific items of information. The data base that the agent accesses may contain a vast amount of data relating to the operations as well as financial performance of the airline; however, the agent will only examine a subset of the data base. The agent will only access and modify data in the data base; modifications of data structures and relationships are not required, even if a seat is confirmed and reserved for the caller.

To further illustrate data base system usage, let us consider a second situation. Assume that the top management of a company has decided to provide rebates on all the consumer appliances within one of its divisions; in the past no rebates have been paid on any products. All the product records in the data base corresponding to the consumer appliance division must be modified by adding a field that will indicate the values of the rebates. The data base administrator will be responsible for making such changes; however, the actual changes will probably be made by a programmer who works for the administrator. The programmer in this situation will be the data base user. If the programmer used the host language of the computer and performed the task in a batch mode, then we could say that he or she was a host language/batch mode/dynamic/subschema/data structure user. The changes are dynamic, since the addition of fields to records is not a standard process; and since only a portion of the data base is affected, the subschema concept is applicable.

Data Base Security

Data security is one of the key problems in data base processing, regardless of whether a centralized or a distributed data base is employed, because the data base management system is linked in some manner to all aspects of the data base. Three types of security problems exist in any data base processing environment: (1) illegal access to data, (2) illegal modification of data base software, and (3) illegal modification of data and/or data structures.

If the data in a data base are not coded or password protected, then illegal acquisition can easily result. To obtain data, an offender need only obtain access to the data base system or the data base itself. Most likely the data base system will be protected, even when the data in the data base are not. However, the offender can circumvent the data base system protection by writing software programs to access the data base files directly. To accomplish this requires knowledge of the structure of the data files. If a teleprocessing mode of operation is used in transfiguring data from the data base to the user, then illegal access of data is possible by intercepting the transmissions between the authorized user and the computer. This latter mode of illegal data access is often referred to as *passive tapping*.

The second security problem area relates to the software associated with the data base system. If the offender is unable to obtain data directly from the data base or by intercepting transmission in the teleprocessing operation, then he or she might revert to modifying the data base system software. If the portion of the system's software that provides security protection can be changed, then access to the data is possible. If the offender is unable to change the security software, then other software might be changed so that erroneous data are stored and/or printed on certain output reports.

The actual deleting or modifying of data within a data base can be accomplished by several different means. First, new data can simply be input directly into the data base, assuming the data base system can be bypassed. Second, the data base system itself can be used to make modifications if the data base passwords and protection schemes can be avoided. Third, data can be modified by "active" tapping. Like passive tapping, this occurs in teleprocessing systems. Unlike passive tapping, however, the data are more than intercepted; data are intercepted and changed, and the modified data are forwarded to the computer and/or authorized user.

A number of procedures and operations have been developed to provide data base security. These include passwords, data coding (encryption), audit logs, and edit checks. We will examine these in Chapter 9, along with security procedures in general.

Backup and Recovery

One of the key elements of a successful data base processing operation is a viable backup and recovery procedure. Without this, the data base can become distorted and erroneous results will constantly be produced regardless of the level of sophistication of the data base management system.

A number of problems that require backup and recovery can occur. First, it may be discovered that erroneous data exist in the data base; this may be discovered in a data base inquiry, in an output report, or simply in an edit check of the data base. The origin of the data error is probably unknown; the data error is simply recognized. Second, a mistake in a program modification, an improper use of a program, or the simple inputting of data may result in the loading of erroneous data into the data base. Third, an I/O parity error, a bad disk, a bad tape, as well as failures in hardware storage units, can result in lost data. In such cases the data base is incorrect because parts or all of the data changes were not made. Finally, a power failure or catastrophic machine malfunction can result in partial or complete loss of a data base. This is particularly true if the storage device on which the data are located "crashes."

Fortunately, procedures have been developed whereby recovery can be made from these types of problems. Two distinct and separate items are necessary: (1) a backup data base and (2) a modification activity file. A backup data base can be created by periodically dumping the data base onto an alternate (backup) storage device. The frequency with which the dump is made depends upon how frequently changes are made to the data base and the cost associated with the recovery process. The older the backup data base, the greater the cost will be when recovery is required.

One item that should be checked after the backup data base has been created is the validity of the backup. This sequence of procedures can be employed for this purpose: (1) the data base is dumped onto the backup; (2) the backup data base is used to create (restore) the data base onto a third storage device; (3) a test program is run on the restored data base and the results are compared with the results run on the original data base; (4) if the results of the run are successful, the backup data base is declared valid and the restored test data base is deleted; (5) if the test run is not successful, the entire process, including backup, is repeated.

After the valid backup data base has been created, the second item that is used in a recovery process must be developed; this involves the creation of a "data base modification activity file." The activity file is used to store information associated with data base modifications. When a change or a modification in the data base occurs, data values (images) *before* and *after* the change are recorded in the activity file, along with the date, the time, the area of the data base where the change was made (location), the software program employed in the change, and any other associated information. The more information collected and stored in the activity file, the easier the recovery process will be when restoration is needed. However, the more elaborate the activity file, the greater the operating cost. Larger files take more time to create and require more storage space.

As is obvious from this very brief overview, backup and recovery are an important element in data base processing. The methods discussed here are by no means the only procedures used in practice; however, they are used by a number of organizations. A great deal of research is currently being conducted in this area to find more efficient, more reliable, and less expensive procedures.

ADVANTAGES
AND DISADVANTAGES
OF DATA BASE PROCESSING

From the materials surveyed throughout the chapter, the reader could mistak-enly conclude that data base processing is a complex as well as an expensive process. To avoid this possibility, we will highlight some of the advantages and disadvantages of employing a data base management system.

Advantages

Reduction of data duplication. By employing a data base management sys-tem, duplicate data that traditionally exist in file-processing systems can be re-duced significantly. By employing a data base, data need only be recorded once. This results in lower storage costs; but, more important, it provides a higher level of data integrity. If the same data item exists in two or more places, it is possible to change the data in one place but not the other. If this occurs, conflicting reports can result because one software program may access the updated data item while a second program accesses the incorrect data item. Data base processing minimizes the possibility of this occurring.

Data integration. Because the physical storage and logical storage of data exist in data base processing, a high level of data integration is possible. One of the primary functions of the data base management system is to provide for efficient access of multiple data items, regardless of where the items reside physically in the data base. This means that the system has the ability to pro-cess unanticipated requests for data, an option not available with file-oriented systems.

Program/data independence. Because the data base management system in-terfaces between the data base and the user, physical storage and logical stor-age structures are separated; therefore, software programs and data indepen-dence exist. Programs can be changed without changing data files, and data files can be changed without changing programs. Programs need only be con-cerned with the logical symbolic names of the data, not physical storage. Users (programmers) are freed from the detailed and often complex task of orga-nizing and keeping up with physical storage.

Because changes in the content of the data base do not have an impact on the programs that access it, the overall system is more efficient. Updating and/or reorganizing the data base requires only changes in the data base man-agement system; rewriting of application programs is not required. Also, unlike a file-oriented system, the data base of a data base processing system can constantly grow without having to be reorganized. For example, data fields can readily be expanded or omitted; the only change required is in the logical defi-nition of the information in the data base.

Better data management. When data are centralized (not necessarily physi-cally, but by responsibility), data base processing can lead to better data man-agement. It is more efficient and less expensive to have one department manage the data base than to have several staffs managing a portion of the data. The department can specify data standards and ensure that all data uti-lized in the data base adhere to the standards. With a file-oriented system, several departments or areas might have to be contacted in developing a single application program, particularly if the program cuts across several organizational lines. With data base processing, data requirements can be handled by contacting a single departmental unit.

When an improvement is made in the data base management system for processing any given application program, it will readily be available for use. This type of "software sharing" is not always possible in file-oriented systems. For example, improvements made to a file-oriented payroll system may only benefit that system. By having centralized software in the form of the data base management system, more analysis and programming time and more money can be spent improving the data base system than could be spent on any single file-oriented system. Because of the economies of scale that result from going to data base processing from a file-oriented system, many firms can cost-justify a fairly sophisticated system.

Disadvantages

Complexity. Data base processing is complex because of its very nature. Larger quantities of data, expressed in several different formats, may exist in a data base. Because of the possibility of multiple formats within a single inquiry or single application program, the data base management system must be able to process a variety of data structures and data requests. Sophisticated design and programming skills are required in developing a data base management system. Likewise, because of the complexity of the overall process, application programs may take a lengthy period of time, and highly qualified programming personnel will be required in some cases.

Expense. A major disadvantage of a data base processing system is the expense involved in developing or purchasing the system. Depending on the quantity of data that is to be organized and the number and needs of users, the software cost of a system could be more than $150,000. The software alone, however, may not be the total expense. Since the data base system will reside in memory, additional memory (hardware) may be required; in some cases it may even be necessary to upgrade to a larger computer. If the latter case occurs, additional expenses will be incurred in converting from the existing computer to the new computer. Processing cost with a data base management system will also probably be greater than that for a file-oriented system, not because of the additional hardware but because more complex activities are involved.

Backup and recovery. Because several users may be operating within the data base management system concurrently and because of the complexity in general of the entire system, backup and recovery can be a difficult process. Two general problems exist: (1) when a failure or an error occurs, the status of the data base must be determined; and (2) assuming that the status of the data base can be determined, the task is then to determine what should be done to rectify the error or errors in the data. Both problems can require considerable time and effort.

Vulnerability. Because the data base management system is at the center of data base processing, a malfunction in any component of the system can have an impact on the data base as well as other users and may bring the entire system to a halt. And because several users may access the data base concurrently, an error in one program can create problems in others. For example, if user A attempts to modify several records in the data base but an error occurs in his or her application program, then invalid data may be placed in the data base. If user B reads the records immediately after the modifications take place, then invalid data will be accessed.

Comparison of Advantages and Disadvantages

Figure 8–22 summarizes both the advantages and the disadvantages of data base processing. If we are considering moving to a data base processing environment, these factors should be examined and weighed; however, an additional point should be kept in mind. All the advantages and disadvantages we have noted may not be fully experienced in every system. For example, in our discussion of the data base development earlier in the chapter, we noted that there can be some valid reasons for data duplication; also, in using most commercial data base systems, it will soon become obvious that *all* programs and all data are not necessarily independent. Thus the factors we have noted are not the only reasons why individuals do or do not adopt and employ a data base processing system. Such a system performs a job that is not possible via a file-oriented system. Thus the real question is whether such a system is needed and can it be cost-justified?

SUMMARY

Data base processing is quite different from the traditional file-oriented approach to data processing. In this chapter we have highlighted these differences. In addition, we have identified each of the components that go together to make up a data base processing system; these include the user, the data base administrator, the data base management system, and the data base. In interacting with a data base system, a user incorporates five elements: (1) a method of access, (2) a mode of access, (3) the nature of the request, (4) the range of data referenced, and (5) the nature of the items to be accessed.

Data base processing can reduce data redundancy, provide the ability to retrieve unanticipated data, provide program/data independence, and provide better data management. However, there are some disadvantages to such a system, such as expense and complexity. Because backup and recovery and security are also major problems, we examined these in detail.

ADVANTAGES	DISADVANTAGES
• Reduction of data duplication	• Complexity
• Data integration	• Expense
• Program/data independence	• Backup and recovery
• Better data management	• Vulnerability

Figure 8–22   Advantages and Disadvantages of Data Base Processing

SELECTED REFERENCES

BODNAR, GEORGE H., *Accounting Information Systems.* Boston: Allyn & Bacon, 1980.

CARDENAS, A., *Data Base Management Systems.* Boston: Allyn & Bacon, 1979.

CERULLO, M. J., "The Data Base Concept," *Management Accounting,* 59 (November 1977) 43–47.

CODASYL (CONFERENCE ON DATA SYSTEMS AND LANGUAGES), "Data Base Task Group Report, 1971." New York: Association for Computing Machinery, April 1971.

COHEN, LEO, *Data Base Management Systems.* Wellesley, Mass.: Q.E.D. Information Sciences, 1976.

CURTICE, ROBERT M., "Integrity in Data Base Systems," *Datamation,* May 1977, pp. 64–68.

HICKS, JAMES O., JR., AND WAYNE, E. LEININGER, *Accounting Information Systems.* St. Paul, Minn.: West Publishing, 1981.

KROENKE, DAVID, *Database Processing.* Chicago: Science Research Associates, 1977.

MARTIN, JAMES, *Principles of Data Base Management.* Englewood Cliffs, N.J.: Prentice-Hall, 1976.

NUSBAUM, EDWARD E., ANDREW D. BAILEY, JR., AND ANDREW B. WHINSTON, "Data Base Management Accounting, and Accountants," *Management Accounting,* 58 (May 1978), 35–38.

SPROWLS, R. CLAY, *Management Data Bases.* Santa Barbara, Calif.: Wiley/Hamilton, 1976.

WILKINSON, JOSEPH W., *Accounting and Information Systems.* New York: John Wiley, 1982.

REVIEW QUESTIONS

1. Differentiate between a *file-oriented approach* to data processing and a *data base management system approach.*
2. Identify some of the weaknesses of the file-oriented approach.
3. Differentiate between a *sequential file,* an *indexed-sequential file,* a *direct-address file,* and a *random file.*
4. List the four components of a data base processing system.
5. What functions does the user perform in interacting with the data base management system?
6. What are the functions of the data base administrator?
7. Define the following terms:
   a. Data item
   b. Record
   c. Data aggregate
   d. Data value
   e. Data label
   f. Data type
   g. Primary key
   h. Secondary key
   i. Serial code
   j. Block sequence code
   k. Hierarchical code
   l. Association code
   m. Chart of accounts
8. Differentiate between *logical data* and *physical data.* Give an example to illustrate the concept.
9. Identify two common structures used to organize data logically.
10. Give an example of a tree structure.
11. Give an example of a network structure.

12. Explain the term *multiple tree structure*. How is this type of structure used?

13. Explain how a linked list structure operates. What is the advantage of such structures? What are the disadvantages?

14. What are the two common components of a data base management system?

15. What is a *data base manager*? What is the function of the DBM?

16. What are the functions of the data definition language (DDL)? Give an example.

17. What are the functions of the data manipulation language (DML)? Give an example.

18. Explain how the DDL and the DML work in conjunction with the DBMS to execute a READ command.

19. How are a schema and a subschema utilized within the data base processing environment?

20. What is the purpose of a data dictionary?

21. Identify the five elements involved in a user's interaction with a data base system. Discuss each briefly.

22. Identify three types of security problems that exist in any data base processing environment.

23. Identify four types of coding techniques. Discuss each briefly.

24. What types of problems can occur that require backup and recovery?

25. How would you check the validity of a backup?

26. Explain what is meant by a "data base modification activity file."

27. Explain the steps involved in backup and recovery when erroneous data have been discovered in the data base.

28. How would you recover when a software program has been discovered to have generated bad data?

29. Explain the recovery process for a "system crash."

30. Identify the major advantages and disadvantanges of data base processing.

EXERCISES AND CASES

8–1

Drape Company needs to be able to extract the status of a customer's account from the file at any time during the day. In addition, Drape needs to be able to update the customers' accounts each night. Which one of the following file organizations would be suitable for Drape Company?

a. Linked list file organization
b. Sequential file organization
c. Random file organization
d. Direct file organization
e. Indexed-sequential file organization
   (Adapted from the CMA Examination)

8–2

In a given data base management system (DBMS), all the records pertaining to overdue accounts receivable are physically scattered throughout the data base. However, these same overdue account records may be associated logically by

a. Transaction tags
b. The use of record pointers
c. Randomizing the records
d. The data base schema
e. The implementation of a flat file structure
   (Adapted from the CMA Examination)

8–3

The primary purpose of a data base information system is to

a. Eliminate multiple access to a particular piece of stored data
b. Eliminate redundancy in the data base of a company
c. Lessen the integration of information-pro-

ducing activities so that a given department may easily ascertain its current status

d. Provide each application program with its own fixed data file

e. Make it possible to have data compatible with a variety of computer hardware (Adapted from the CMA Examination)

8–4

For each of the following situations, specify the file arrangement method (sequential, direct, random, indexed-sequential) that best fits. Briefly justify your selection.

a. An inventory file, updated daily, that is employed to determine product availability during daily operations.

b. A sales commission file, used to keep track of each salesperson's commissions. The file is updated at the time of sale from a point-of-sale data-entry terminal.

c. Goodrich Corporation stockholder file, updated weekly; employed for computing dividend checks, quarterly reports, and proxy requests.

d. A payroll file, used weekly to process payroll checks and used quarterly to aid in the processing of tax reports.

e. A customer account file at a major city bank, updated daily based on customer withdrawals and deposits, used monthly to generate monthly statements on each customer account.

8–5

Progress in the design and development of computer-based management information systems has been impressive in the past two decades. Traditionally, computer-based data processing systems were arranged by departments and applications. Computers were applied to single, large-volume applications such as inventory control or customer billing. Other applications were added once the first applications were operating smoothly.

As more applications were added, problems in data management developed. Businesses looked for ways to integrate the data processing systems to make them more comprehensive and to have shorter response times. As a consequence, the data base system composed of a data base itself, the data base management system, and the individual application programs was developed.

REQUIRED:

a. Explain the basic differences between the traditional approach to data processing and the use of the data base system in terms of
   1. File structure
   2. Processing of data

b. Many practitioners have asserted that security in a data base system is of greater importance than in traditional systems. Explain the importance of security and the problems that may arise in implementing security in a data base system.

c. Identify and discuss the favorable and unfavorable issues other than security that a company should consider before implementing a data base system. (Adapted from the CMA Examination)

8–6

Howell and Mitchell, an architecture/engineering firm, currently uses a file-oriented microcomputer system. At the present time it retains separate files (diskettes) for clients or customer receivables, supplies payables, inventory, job specification, job bids and costs payroll, and standard engineering design specifications. To support routine operational and managerial decision making, it needs the following information on a regular basis:

1. Cost data to determine the profit or loss and percent completion for all jobs

2. Cost data to prepare bids on new jobs

3. Job specifications for bidding, cost analysis, and on-the-job instructions

4. Payroll reports and cash disbursements by jobs and by employees

5. Inventory and purchase requests

6. Accounts receivable and collection information for each job and each client

7. Accounts payable analysis disbursements information

8. Cash flow analysis and forecast

9. Financial statements

It has been very awkward and time consuming for the EDP operators to handle the files manually for the preparation of each of these reports, even though there is a straightforward procedures manual and a set of application programs for each report.

The problem is compounded by the need for information on a random basis. The job supervisor or the engineer often has specific requests about the status of an item, cost to date of a project, or other query involving more than one file. For many of these requests, several files must be handled, a program must be written, and a procedural manual must be referenced. However, this is seldom the case and managers must assemble the data from separate files manually to satisfy their needs. The problem has been further compounded during the annual audit when it was discovered that the payroll, the job bid, and the cost files did not reconcile.

Mr. Mitchell has attended a seminar at the national meeting of building contractors and has listened to a discussion of a DBMS for a microcomputer. He has asked you, as his accountant, to advise him on the pros and cons of a DBMS and to explain to him, in language he can understand, how such a system would eliminate the obvious data update problems, the excessive procedural efforts needed to prepare reports, and the need on the part of management to assemble data manually when it requests information involving more than one file.

REQUIRED:

a. Write a brief report to Mr. Mitchell to answer his questions.

b. Also explain to Mr. Mitchell the need to upgrade the microhardware to accommodate the larger data set necessary to support a DBMS and the costs associated with this upgrading.

8–7

The Elkin Corporation of Atlanta, Georgia, is a progressive and fast-growing company. The company's executive board consists of five members: the president, the vice-president of marketing, the vice-president of manufacturing, the vice-president of finance, and the vice-president of computing/information systems.

The marketing department is organized into nine territories and twenty-five sales offices. The vice-president of marketing wants the monthly reports to reflect those items for which the department is responsible and can control. The marketing department also wants information that identifies the most profitable products; this information is used to establish a discount policy that will enable the company to meet competition effectively. Monthly reports showing performance by territory and sales office would also be useful.

The vice-president of finance has recommended that the accounting system be revised so that reports would be prepared on a contribution margin basis. Furthermore, only those cost items that are controlled by the respective departments would appear on their reports. The monthly report for the manufacturing department would compare actual production costs with a budget containing the standard costs for the actual volume of production. The marketing department would be provided with the standard variable manufacturing cost for each product, so that it could calculate the variable contribution margin of each product. The monthly reports to the marketing department would reflect the variable contribution approach; the reports would present the net contribution of the department calculated by deducting standard variable manufacturing costs and marketing expenses (both variable and fixed) from sales.

A portion of Elkin's chart of accounts follows:

ACCOUNT NUMBER	DESCRIPTION
1000	Sales
1500	Cost of sales
2000	Manufacturing expenses
3000	Engineering expenses
4000	Marketing expenses
5000	Administrative expenses

The company wants to retain the basic structure of the chart of accounts to minimize the number of changes in the system. However, the numbering system will have to be expanded in order to provide the additional information that is desired.

REQUIRED: Develop and explain a coding structure that will satisfy the needs of the marketing department management. Add any additional accounts that are needed to the chart of accounts. Be sure to provide some flexibility. Illustrate the new coding structure. (Adapted from the CMA Examination)

8–8

Ollie Mace has recently been appointed controller of a family-owned manufacturing enterprise. The firm, S. Dilley & Co., was founded by Mr. Dilley about twenty years ago, is 78 percent owned by Mr. Dilley, and has served the major automotive companies as a parts supplier. The firm's major operating divisions are heat treating, extruding, small-parts stamping, and specialized machining. Sales last year from the several divisions ranged from $150,000 to over $3 million. The divisions are physically and managerially independent except for Mr. Dilley's constant surveillance. The accounting system for each division has evolved according to the division's own needs and to the abilities of individual accountants or bookkeepers. Mr. Mace is the first controller in the firm's history to have responsibility for overall financial management. Mr. Dilley expects to retire within six years and has hired Mr. Mace to improve the firm's financial system.

Mr. Mace soon decides that he will need to design a new financial reporting system that will

1. Give managers uniform, timely, and accurate reports on business activity. Monthly divisional reports should be uniform and available by the tenth of the following month. Company-wide financial reports should also be prepared by the tenth.
2. Provide a basis for measuring return on investment by division. Divisional reports should show assets assigned to each division and revenue and expense measurement in each division.
3. Generate budget data for planning and decision-making purposes. The accounting system should provide for the preparation of budgets that recognize managerial responsibility, controllability of costs, and major product groups.

4. Allow for a uniform basis of evaluating performance and quick access to underlying data. Cost center variances should be measured and reported for operating and nonoperating units, including headquarters. Also, questions about levels of specific cost factors or product costs should be answerable quickly.

According to Mr. Mace, a new chart of accounts is essential to getting started on other critical financial problems. The present account codes used by divisions are not standard.

Mr. Mace sees a need to divide asset accounts into six major categories (i.e., current assets, plant and equipment, etc.). Within each of these categories, he sees a need for no more than ten control accounts. Based on his observations to date, one hundred subsidiary accounts are more than adequate for each control account.

No division now has more than five major product groups. The maximum number of cost centers Mr. Mace foresees within any product group is six, including operating and nonoperating groups. He views general divisional costs as a non-revenue-producing product group. Altogether, Mr. Mace estimates that about forty-four natural expense accounts plus about twelve specific accounts would be adequate.

Mr. Mace is planning to implement the new chart of accounts in an environment that at present includes manual records systems and one division that is using an EDP system. He expects that in the near future most accounting and reporting for all units will be automated. Therefore the chart of accounts should facilitate the processing of transactions manually or by machine. Efforts should be made, he believes, to restrict the length of the code for economy in processing and convenience in use.

REQUIRED:

a. Design a chart-of-accounts coding system that will meet Mr. Mace's requirements. Your answer should begin with a layout of the coding system. You should explain the coding method you have chosen and the reason for the size of your code elements.

Explain your code as it would apply to asset and expense accounts.

b. Use your chart-of-accounts coding system to illustrate the code needed for the following data:

1) In the small-parts stamping division, $100 was spent by foreman Bill Shaw in the polishing department of the Door Lever Group on cleaning supplies. Code the expense item using the code you developed above.

2) A new motorized sweeper has been purchased for the maintenance department of the extruding division for $3,450. Code this asset item using the code you developed above. (Adapted from the CMA Examination)

8–9

The Convict Savings Bank is a large bank based in Sydney with branches scattered throughout Australia. The bank uses an on-line real-time update system for its customer accounts system. The branches are connected via a telecommunications network to a centralized data base in the head office. The bank uses a data base management system for its data base.

As a member of the external audit firm of the bank, you are reviewing the adequacy of backup and recovery procedures for the on-line real-time update system. During an interview with the data base administrator, she explains to you that when a system crash occurs, the computer operators attempt to restart the system immediately because downtime is intolerable with the system. Since the data base management system used by the bank establishes relationships between entities via pointers, you express your concern to her about the possibility of pointers in the data base not having been updated (that is, an update is in progress when the crash occurs and the data base is in an inconsistent state). The data base administrator concedes this point. Nevertheless, she argues that it is a relatively minor problem. When the system is restarted, tellers are supposed to check whether the last transaction they submitted was posted. If it was not posted, they resubmit the transaction. An inquiry transaction will also identify inconsistent or corrupted pointers. If the data base is in an inconsistent state, since it is unlikely that another transaction will occur for the customer's account during that day, backup and recovery is left until the night shift.

REQUIRED: Write a brief report for your manager commenting on the adequacy of backup and recovery procedures for the on-line system. Make any suggestions that you feel would improve the adequacy of backup and recovery procedures for the system.

8–10

Case 13–11, Delmo, Inc., may be used here.

8–11

Ed Jenkins, data processing manager for the Windfall Corporation, made the following statement: "As manager of data processing in our company, you might say I am also the data base administrator."

Could this be correct? Explain your answer.

8–12

The Thomas Company is a medium-sized manufacturer of high-pressure valves. All products are produced on a job-order basis and are sold on account to other companies which incorporate them into final products. Thomas has been using data processing systems for the past ten years and is generally innovative in terms of applying current computer technology. The company is currently considering the installation of a DBMS in the raw material, production, order shipping, and accounts receivable areas.

a. What factors should the company consider before opting for the DBMS approach?

b. Assuming that Thomas decides to install a DBMS, what physical and logical files would you recommend? What would be the contents of these records with these files? Identify which related records would be associated and show how "pointers" could be used to link the data.

c. How would the DDL of the DBMS be used in setting up the system?

d. What reports would probably be required?

e. Would the DML portion of the DBMS be employed? Give an example.

9
SYSTEM CONTROLS

OVERVIEW OF SECURITY AND CONTROL IMPLICATIONS

Objective of Control Systems

The *Statement on Auditing Standards No. 1* proposes the following definition of *internal control*:

> Internal control comprises the *plan of organization* and *all* of the *co-ordinate methods* and *measures* adopted within a business to safeguard its assets, check the accuracy and reliability of its accounting data, promote operational efficiency, and encourage adherence to prescribed managerial policies.[1]

This definition recognizes the broad responsibility of the public and private accountants for administrative and accounting controls. *Administrative controls* consist of those measures such as budgeting, cash planning, and inventory analysis that help management make sound decisions consistent with the

---

[1] AICPA, *Codification of Auditing Standards and Procedures, Statement on Auditing Standards No. 1*, New York: American Institute of Certified Public Accountants, Inc., copyright© (1972), reprinted with permission.

firm's objectives. *Accounting controls* (usually called internal controls) consist of those measures that are employed to safeguard assets and help ensure reliable financial records. Accounting controls are designed to provide reasonable assurance that

1. Transactions are carried out as authorized.
2. Transactions are recorded accurately.
3. Access to assets is limited to only those authorized.
4. Records of accountability for assets are periodically compared with the existing assets, and appropriate action is taken for differences.

The definition above also implies that the auditor or accountant should consider the organization of the control system. No one control procedure will ensure compliance, but when we view each procedure as part of the network of controls, reasonable reliance and compliance can be ensured.

Assisting management with its accounting controls is one of the accountant's primary tasks.

PUBLIC REPORTING ON INTERNAL ACCOUNTING CONTROLS   As an outgrowth of Watergate and overseas payments by several large corporations, the Foreign Corrupt Practices Act was passed in 1977. This act, along with actions of the Securities and Exchange Commission (SEC), the American Institute of Certified Public Accountants, and the Financial Executives Institute's (FEI) Committee on Corporate Reporting, will have a profound impact on internal control and public disclosure of internal control.

The Foreign Corrupt Practices Act, among other things, amends the Securities and Exchange Act of 1934 to require that:

> (2) Every issuer which has a class of securities registered to section 12 of this title and every issuer which is required to file reports pursuant to section 15(d) of this title shall—(A) make and keep books, records and accounts, which in reasonable detail, accurately and fairly reflect the transactions and dispositions of the assets of the user; and (B) devise and maintain a system of internal accounting controls sufficient to provide reasonable assurances that—

> (i)   transactions are executed in accordance with management's general or specific authorization;
> (ii) transactions are recorded as necessary (1) to permit preparation of financial statements in conformity with generally accepted accounting principles or any other criteria applicable to such statements, and (2) to maintain accountability for assets;
> (iii) access to assets is permitted only in accordance with management's general or specific authorization; and
> (iv) the recorded accountability for assets is compared with the existing assets at reasonable intervals and appropriate action is taken with respect to any differences.[2]

[2] Securities Exchange Commission, *Foreign Corrupt Practices Act* and Arthur Young & Co., *Foreign Corrupt Practices Act, 1977,* (New York: Arthur Young & Co., 1978), p. 24.

These requirements are nothing more than a restatement of the definition of *accounting control* codified in Section 320.28 of the *Statement on Auditing Standards No. 1*. The difference is that the former standards are now required.

The AICPA has broadened the Foreign Corrupt Practices Act requirement, with the recommendation that management's assessment of the company's accounting system (and the controls over it) accompany the financial statements. This recommendation was endorsed by the FEI.[3] The SEC proposed a rule and later withdrew this proposal to require that reports filed with the commission contain a statement that the issuer is in compliance with the Foreign Corrupt Practices Act. Upon withdrawal, the commission said it would look to the private sector to develop methods for voluntary disclosure and monitoring of internal controls. The AICPA then issued the *Statement on Auditing Standards No. 30*, "Reporting on Internal Control," describing the procedures for different types of engagements for reporting on an entity's system of internal control. It further describes the form of the auditor report for such engagements.[4] It should be clear that public reporting of management's assessment of its accounting system and the set of controls it employs is imminent.

IMPLICATIONS OF INTERNAL CONTROL   Both administrative and accounting controls are an integral part of systems design, implementation, and operation and are a function of the firm's business environment. No system should be utilized without adequate controls. The design and implementation of controls requires active participation of the CPA and the controller. Many court cases can be cited in which legal problems resulted when adequate controls were not implemented. In addition, the absence of critical controls has left many organizations open to fraudulent activities. A system that provides unreliable data is also of little use in assisting management in making decisions that are in harmony with the enterprise's objectives. Both administrative and accounting controls are key elements of an information system.

Decision and Processing Network

CONTROL POINTS   All the decision-making information and the transaction processing activities can be viewed as an integrated information and reporting network. There will be critical junctures within this information network where controls need to be established. In a traditional transaction processing cycle, for example, initial recording of the transaction, the transfer of an asset to another individual, and the authorization for payment would be critical points at which some form of control should be established. (Specific control examples for various transaction processing cycles will be reviewed in the application chapters of this text.)

In an EDP system the focus of control shifts from traditional controls consisting of a system of authorization, organizational independence, and supervision to the computer system, but at the same time traditional controls must be maintained.

---

[3] Deloitte, Haskins & Sells, *Internal Accounting Control* (New York: Deloitte Haskins & Sells, 1978).

[4] This sequence of events is outlined in Deloitte, Haskins & Sells, *The Week in Review*, August 15, 1980.

In an EDP system we can characterize the control structure by two broad areas that support EDP operations. Both are important for effective administrative and accounting controls. The classifications, as shown in Figure 9–1, can be summarized as follows:

1. *General controls* which pertain to the actual operation of the computer; the library, hardware, and software; the personnel who operate the sys-

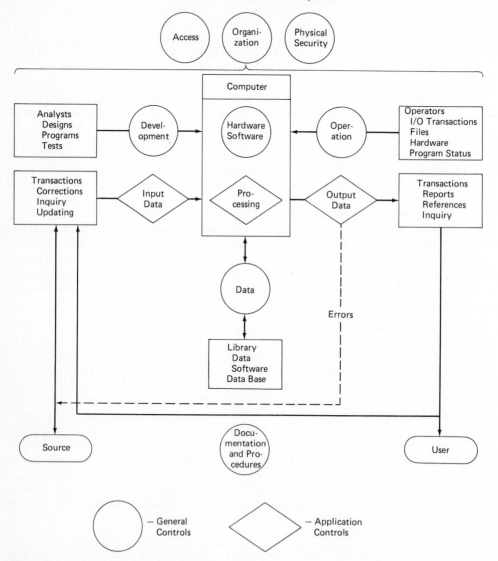

A Structure of Controls for EDP Systems

Figure 9–1 A Structure of Controls for EDP Systems

Adapted from Touche Ross & Co., *Computer Controls and Audit* (New York: Touche Ross & Co., 1972), p. 5 with permission.

tem; the system development; and the activities of systems analysts who are involved in developing systems to meet their user needs

2. *Application Controls* which pertain to the programs that perform a specific activity such as scheduling, billing, payroll, market research, updating receivable, or financial statement preparation

Control points for each of these broad areas are noted in Figure 9–1. These control points are: access, organization, physical security, development, hardware, software, operations (operator), input, processing, output, data (files), procedures, and documentation. The application controls are generally characterized as input, output, or processing controls. All of these controls will be discussed later in this chapter. Note here that the system elements and the system design and development activities constitute an important set of control points and that the EDP system itself is the focal point of the control system.

A well designed and developed system will greatly enhance *both* administrative and accounting controls. It is important that all data be entered correctly and processed in accordance with managerial policies for decision-making needs. In addition, the overall system must be well organized, designed, tested, and implemented to ensure that management obtains the necessary decision-making information and third-party reports.

INTEGRATED SYSTEM OF CONTROLS   An integrated system of controls is essential to support the decision-making and processing network of an organization, to safeguard assets, to ensure the reliability of information, and to obtain compliance with managerial objectives. Consider the administrative controls of the production operation illustrated in Figure 9–2. The assignment of responsibility helps control (a) inventory investment, (b) labor utilization, and (c) production efficiency. The production schedule (a) helps control inventory, since it specifies how many parts will be required for assembly and how many complete units will be produced; (b) helps plan efficient use of labor resources; and (c) helps ensure compliance with the managerial objectives of what, when, and how much to produce. These control features, for example, can aid management in controlling the firm's activities in many ways.

From another perspective, consider inventory activities. Administrative controls can assist management in ensuring compliance with the firm's inventory policies. As we have already observed, the assignment of responsibility and production schedules can be effective. Other controls such as a system of authorization for requisitions and production orders, mathematical EOQ models, and physical inventory can also be effective. Many controls can be used together to promote operational efficiency and to encourage adherence to prescribed managerial policies. These control features should be integrated so that their total effect is synergistic; the controls together produce greater control than the sum of their individual contributions to administrative control. For example, assume that the administrative controls noted in Figure 9–2 each have a 90 percent probability of detecting a certain type of problem. If all five controls were independent, there would result a $1/10 \times 1/10 \times 1/10 \times 1/10 \times 1/10$, or $1/100,000$, probability of not preventing or finding this type of problem. If they are synergistic (each contributes to the other's effectiveness, i.e., they are not independent), the probability of not preventing or finding the problem

Production Activities

Administrative Controls	Inventory	Labor	Production	⋮	Etc.
Assignment of responsibility	X	X	X		X
System of authorization	X		X		
EOQ–ordering system	X		X		
Production schedule	X	X	X		X
Physical inventory	X		X		
. . .					
Etc.	X	X	X		

Figure 9-2 Integrated System of Administrative Controls Illustration

Administrative Controls

Inventory   Labor   Production   Etc.   . . .   . . .

far less. Such a system of controls will provide much better control than one using only individual controls activities.

This same synergistic effect can be accomplished in a system of accounting controls. Consider an input editing and screening system of an advanced computer-based network, as characterized in Figure 9–3. In this system information is entered by using remote terminals; it is then transmitted to the computer center where it is stored in buffer storage awaiting processing. As it leaves the storage area, the information is checked for access authorization, completeness, reasonableness, and accuracy. Any errors in input data are displayed and relayed to a correction process, which may entail feedback to the remote terminal for correction if necessary. The system has several control procedures for detecting several types of potential errors and effecting their correction. The controls complement each other and work as an integrated system to detect and correct potential errors, such as unauthorized, incomplete, unreasonable, and inaccurate input data. For example, an unauthorized user may have a password but may not have all the information necessary to enter a complete transaction and, therefore, what is entered is unreasonable. A transposition error may seem complete, but it may be unreasonable.

In summary, the controls in the system should complement each other and contribute to each other's effectiveness to accomplish the objectives of either administrative or accounting control. The organization of a manual or data processing function and its system of controls should be crucial to the accountant and to the auditor. Both must be concerned with safeguarding the firm's

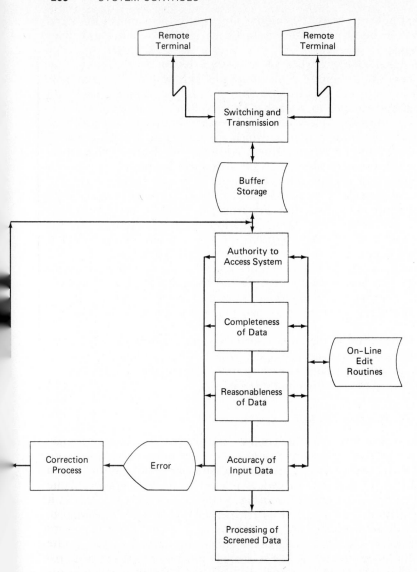

Figure 9–3 Accounting Control System for Editing and Screening of Data Entry

assets, the reliability of information, ensuring compliance with managerial policies, and the requirements of the Foreign Corrupt Practices Act.

MANAGEMENT AND ADMINISTRATIVE CONTROLS

Compliance with Managerial Policies

Accountants and auditors need to be aware of administrative as well as accounting controls in an information system to ensure adherence to prescribed managerial policies. Many techniques are used to accomplish this task. These techniques can be characterized as feedback control systems and planning control systems.

The functional characteristics of a *feedback control system* are (1) an input/output process where input can be compared with output, (2) a standard by which the efficiency of this input conversion process can be measured, and (3) a measurement system such as a standard cost system. Some feedback control systems are dynamic and self-adjusting. An example is an automatic economic-order-quantity inventory system which processes a purchase order whenever a reorder point is reached. Others are less self-adaptive. The cybernetic theory behind this type of system was discussed in Chapter 4.

The accountant or systems analyst must make several decisions regarding feedback control systems. These decisions can be characterized as parameters changing, filtering, and monitoring. For example, consider a responsibility accounting framework. What level of aggregation or detail should exist for each level in its organization? What constitutes a significant variance? What role should internal auditing play in the feedback control system?

The *planning control system* is sometimes regarded as the primary control system for management and is frequently referred to as a *feedforward control system*. Management controls the firm's operations by way of a system of programs, plans, and budgets. These programs, plans, and budgets are used to coordinate the firm's activities so that there is a cohesive effort to achieve its objectives. Techniques used in planning control systems include sales budgets, cash flow forecasts, inventory control models, research development programs, promotion plans, production schedules, corporate planning models, and various mathematical and statistical planning models.

Systems Management Control

As we illustrated earlier in this chapter and in the text, an accountant, an auditor, or a systems analyst should view a system from a decision-making, transaction processing, and reporting network perspective. The auditor is particularly interested in the transaction processing cycles in the network. Thus the management information and accounting system must be well designed, tested, and implemented. The objective of each development and implementation step, such as those suggested by the AICPA and outlined in Chapter 2, must be satisfied. Moreover, the management information and accounting system must satisfy the needs of management. Details for a development and implementation plan are given in Chapters 10 and 11. This plan will ensure management participation, careful consideration of alternatives, inclusion of key decision variables, inclusion of necessary administrative and accounting controls, careful testing, coordinated conversion, and effective review of the system.

Often project controls, such as PERT,[5] can effectively be used to ensure careful scheduling of the necessary development and implementation steps and the allocation of economic and human resources to the system project.

---

[5] Illustrated in Chapter 11. See almost any basic cost, operations research, or production management text.

The development and implementation plan offers milestones that can serve as a set of cost and time standards for control of a systems project. Each cycle of the decision and processing network must be designed to contain a set of controls that will accomplish authorization, accounting, and asset safeguard objectives that promote the overall objectives of internal control as specified by the AICPA and, subsequently, by the Foreign Corrupt Practices Act. (The basic transaction processing cycles will be reviewed in the application Chapters 12 through 17, along with suggested controls.)

ACCOUNTING CONTROLS

Basic Concepts

Accounting controls for EDP systems are commonly classified as general controls and application controls. Several control concepts that are noted in Section 320 of the *Statement on Auditing Standards No. 1* form the basis for both manual and EDP systems; these are reviewed in this section.[6]

First, management has the responsibility for establishing and supervising a system of accounting controls to safeguard the firm's assets and ensure the reliability of data and information generated from the data. The system should provide reasonable, but not absolute, assurance that control objectives are met. Cost-benefit analysis is needed to determine the necessity of further control, as was suggested in the plan for development and implementation (see Chapters 2, 10, and 11). Most often cost-benefit analysis requires the use of judgment. Questions such as the following for a sales order processing system need to be answered and evaluated:

1) What is the average value of individual shipments and the aggregate value of shipment during the specified period?
2) What has been the company's past experience with inventory adjustments or losses?
3) What is the likelihood of shipping tickets not being prepared or being lost or destroyed?
4) What is the likelihood of customers advising that shipments were not billed?
5) What is the likelihood of detecting such errors or irregularities through salespersons' complaints about unpaid commissions?
6) What is the likelihood of detecting such errors or irregularities through reports or other means (for example, by monthly sales comparisons, by the ratio of sales to cost of sales or to shipping expense, by periodic physical inventories, by periodic internal audits, and so forth)?
7) What other potential costs may be involved (for example, damage to customer relations or to the company's reputation)?[7]

---

[6] *SAS No. 1*, copyright© (1972) by the American Institute of Certified Public Accountants, Inc., reprinted with permission.

[7] AICPA, *Report of the Special Advisory Committee on Internal Control*, New York: American Institute of Certified Public Accountants, copyright© (1978), p. 15, reprinted with permission.

In many cases a trade-off among operating efficiency, various risks, and complex control procedure costs must be made. Management judgment must play a key role in internal control cost-benefit analysis where material exposure to loss is present.

Second, a strong system of internal control depends on the employment of competent personnel who have the integrity and competence required to perform their given assignments. Misunderstanding, judgment mistakes, and carelessness on the part of incompetent employees can result in errors. Collusion can circumvent almost any control procedure.

Third, duties should be segregated so that no individual is in a position to perpetrate and to conceal an error or irregularity. This is basically accomplished by segregating (1) transaction authorization, (2) custody and supervision of assets, and (3) maintenance of records.

Fourth, measures should be implemented to give reasonable assurance that transactions have been recorded properly. Examples of such measures would be (1) a cash register for accurate transaction recording, (2) well-designed forms to ensure completeness of input data, (3) prenumbered forms to give reasonable assurance that all transactions have been accounted for and that no forms have been used improperly, (4) a review of transactions by another individual prior to processing, (5) control totals, (6) completeness checks, and (7) a set of standards or budgets to highlight problem areas. The use of standards or budgets is often referred to as a financial control function. Through a set of reports, transactions can be reviewed and compared with plans and budgets for any irregularity.

Fifth, access to assets must be limited to personnel authorized by management. This can be accomplished through a system of physical safeguards, access controls for an EDP system, and limited authority over the acquisition and disposition of assets.

Sixth, asset records, which include records for plant, equipment, inventory, and receivables, should be compared periodically with the actual assets. Someone other than the individuals who have asset custody and record-keeping responsibility should perform this function and reconcile any differences that are found.

Other useful measures of control can be achieved by securing fidelity bonds on employees, rotation of employees, enforced vacations, and utilization of internal and independent auditors. Figure 9–4, an internal control questionnaire, highlights the basic controls frequently used for the major functions of a small business. (More-detailed procedures for major business activities are discussed in the application chapters. Chapter 17, "Small-Business Systems," will review special procedures for small businesses.)

As we noted earlier, the focus of internal control has shifted from a traditional system of separation of duties and authorizations to the computer system. This has occurred because the computer is used to process the entire transaction, to make decisions authorizing the transfer of assets, and to review such transactions and decisions. As in a manual system, the auditor, accountant, or system designer must understand the flow of transactions through the EDP system and the controls required at each control point. These controls are described in the *Statement on Auditing Standards No. 3* as *general controls* and *application controls*.

Figure 9-4   The Smalltime Company Internal Control Questionnaire

	YES	NO

1. General
   a. Are accounting records kept up to date and balanced monthly? ___ ___
   b. Is a chart of accounts used? ___ ___
   c. Does the owner use a budget system for watching income and expenses? ___ ___
   d. Are cash projections made? ___ ___
   e. Are adequate monthly financial reports available to the owner? ___ ___
   f. Does the owner appear to take a direct and active interest in the financial affairs and reports which should be or are available? ___ ___
   g. Are the personal funds of the owner and his personal income and expenses completely segregrated from the business? ___ ___
   h. Is the owner satisfied that all employees are honest? ___ ___
   i. Is the bookkeeper required to take annual vacations? ___ ___
2. Cash Receipts
   a. Does the owner open the mail? ___ ___
   b. Does the owner list mail receipts before turning them over to the bookkeeper? ___ ___
   c. Is the listing of the receipts subsequently traced to the cash receipts journal? ___ ___
   d. Are over-the-counter receipts controlled by cash register tapes, counter receipts, etc.? ___ ___
   e. Are receipts deposited intact daily? ___ ___
   f. Are employees who handle funds bonded? ___ ___
3. Cash Disbursements
   a. Are all disbursements made by check? ___ ___
   b. Are prenumbered checks used? ___ ___
   c. Is a controled, mechanical check protector used? ___ ___
   d. Is the owner's signature required on checks? ___ ___

	YES	NO

   e. Does the owner sign checks only after they are properly completed? (Checks should not be signed in blank.) ___ ___
   f. Does the owner approve and cancel the documentation in support of all disbursements? ___ ___
   g. Are all voided checks retained and accounted for? ___ ___
   h. Does the owner review the bank reconciliation? ___ ___
   i. Is an imprest petty cash fund used? ___ ___
4. Accounts Receivable and Sales
   a. Are work order and/or sales invoices prenumbered and controlled? ___ ___
   b. Are customers' ledgers balanced regularly? ___ ___
   c. Are monthly statements sent to all customers? ___ ___
   d. Does the owner review statements before mailing them himself? ___ ___
   e. Are account write-offs and discounts approved only by the owner? ___ ___
   f. Is credit granted only by the owner? ___ ___
5. Notes Receivable and Investments
   Does the owner have sole access to notes and investment certificates? ___ ___
6. Inventories
   a. Is the person responsible for inventory someone other than the bookkeeper? ___ ___
   b. Are periodic physical inventories taken? ___ ___
   c. Is there physical control over inventory stock? ___ ___
   d. Are perpetual inventory records maintained? ___ ___

Figure 9-4 The Smalltime Company Internal Control Questionnaire (continued)

	YES	NO		YES	NO

7. Property Assets
   a. Are there detailed records available of property assets and allowances for depreciation? ___ ___
   b. Is the owner acquainted with property assets owned by the company? ___ ___
   c. Are retirements approved by the owner? ___ ___
8. Accounts Payable and Purchases
   a. Are purchase orders used? ___ ___
   b. Does someone other than the bookkeeper always do the purchasing? ___ ___
   c. Are suppliers' monthly statements compared with recorded liabilities regularly? ___ ___

   d. Are suppliers' monthly statements checked by the owner periodically if disbursements are made from invoice only? ___ ___
9. Payroll
   a. Are the employees hired by the owner? ___ ___
   b. Would the owner be aware of the absence of any employee? ___ ___
   c. Does the owner approve, sign, and distribute payroll checks? ___ ___
10. Brief Narrative of Auditor's Conclusion as to Adequacy of Internal Control

_____

_____

_____

_____

Adapted with permission from Herbert J. Steltzer, "Evaluation of Internal Control in Small Audits," *The Journal of Accountancy* (Nov. 1964), pp. 55, and Richard C. Rea, "A Small Business Internal Control Questionnaire," *The Journal of Accountancy* (July 1978), p. 54.

General Controls

According to the *Statement on Auditing Standards No. 3*, general controls consist of

1. The plan of organization and operation of EDP activity
2. The procedures for documenting, reviewing, testing, and approving new systems or programs and changes in existing systems or programs
3. Controls built into the equipment by the manufacturer (commonly referred to as "hardware controls") and controls in the operating system
4. Controls over access to equipment and data files
5. Other data and procedural controls affecting overall EDP operations

Each type of general control is discussed in detail below. General controls apply to all the accounting information processing activities and encompass each application.

PLAN OF ORGANIZATION AND OPERATION   A well-planned and properly functioning EDP organization is critical to good accounting control. Several general organizational controls should be present in an EDP system. Segregation of functions between the EDP department and the system user will separate information processing from asset custody, transaction processing, and control activities such as review and error correction. Provision for general authorization over the execution of transactions will prevent the EDP department from initiating and authorizing transactions, having custody over non-EDP assets, having authority for master file changes, and establishing controls.

The major functions within the EDP department should be segregated. These functions are (1) operations, (2) systems analysis and design, (3) control, and (4) librarian. A typical organization chart for small EDP organizations is shown in Figure 9–5. The responsibility for systems analysis and design includes the developmnent and maintenance of program logic, program coding, file record layout, program testing, operating instructions, and error and correction routines. To prevent unauthorized changes, systems and programming personnel must be separate from operations personnel because the former are aware of application program parameters and controls. The library function has custody of the data files and records. Two types of controls are generally part of this function. First, access to files and software is restricted to authorized users at scheduled times. Second, the use of records is monitored and backup files are provided. The control group has the responsibility for controlling the flow and balancing the transactions processed by the computer center. Part of this responsibility often includes the systematic disposition of errors. In a data base management system, another function of data base administration is frequently added to oversee the data base activities dicussed in Chapter 8.

PROCEDURES FOR SYSTEMS DEVELOPMENT AND DOCUMENTATION The auditor and the accountant must also consider controls related to reviewing, testing, and approving a new system, program changes, and documentation to ensure that effective application controls are implemented and executed. Specific procedures for systems development are outlined in Chapters 2, 10, and 11. Several major controls that should be incorporated into this set of procedures are outlined here. Management approval prior to testing and implementation, and complete documentation of the system and all of its elements that

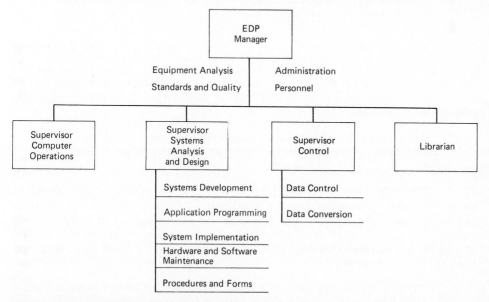

Figure 9–5 Structure of a Small EDP Organization

Adapted from Touche Ross & Co., *Computer Controls and Audit* (New York: Touche Ross & Co., 1972), pp. 3–4 with permission.

were reviewed in previous chapters, are required. A brief list of specific control procedures that will accomplish these objectives follows:[8]

(1)   The procedures for system design, including the acquisition of software packages, should require active participation by representatives of the users and as appropriate the accounting department and internal auditors.

(2)   Each system should have written specifications which are reviewed and approved by an appropriate level of management and applicable user departments.

These specifications serve as a standard for compliance reviews by management and auditors and should be kept up to date.

(3)   System testing should be a joint effort of users and EDP personnel and should include both the manual and computerized phases of the system.

Users should make sure that all the specifications are met and that the interfaces between manual and EDP systems operate smoothly.

(4)   Final approval should be obtained prior to placing the new system into operation.

(5)   All master file and transaction file conversions should be controlled to prevent unauthorized changes and to provide accurate and complete results.

This will help prevent errors, which frequently occur at the time of conversion from an old procedure to a new procedure.

(6)   After a new system has been placed in operation, all program changes should be approved before implementation to determine whether they have been authorized, tested, and documented.

There should be a formal system for requesting, authorizing, approving, testing, implementing, and reconciling changes. Management can run both the old and the new system in parallel using actual data and test data to make sure the new system is working properly and that all differences between old and new results can be explained.

(7)   Management should require various levels of documentation and establish formal procedures to define the system at appropriate levels of detail.

All of the above controls help ensure that the system design, development, and implementation process (outlined in Chapter 2) was executed as planned. This is important because one of the major aspects of good internal control is a well-run EDP system in which all information is processed accurately and in the manner specified by management to meet decision-making and reporting requirements.

[8] With permission from the AICPA Computer Services Executives Committee, AICPA, *Auditor's Study and Evaluation of Internal Control in EDP Systems,* copyright© (1977), pp. 31–36. Many of the controls outlined in this chapter follow those presented in this audit and accounting guide with the permission of the AICPA.

HARDWARE AND SOFTWARE CONTROLS   General controls for the hardware and operating system are usually provided by the vendor and are for the most part quite reliable. These controls are detailed under the heading "Processing Controls" in the application controls discussion. According to the AICPA:

> The control features inherent in the computer hardware, operating system, and other supporting software should be utilized to the maximum possible extent to provide control over operations and to detect and report hardware malfunctions.

Furthermore:

> System software should be subjected to the same control procedures as those applied in installation of and changes to application programs.[9]

A formal control system similar to that proposed in Chapter 2 for application software during system development and implementation should exist for system software packages.

ACCESS AND COMMUNICATION CONTROLS FOR FILE-ORIENTED AND DATA BASE SYSTEMS   To safeguard the EDP system, the records maintained on the system, and communications within the system network (thereby preserving the integrity of the system), it is important that access controls be used. Access controls should help prevent accidental errors, unauthorized use of a program or a data file, improper use of a system's resources such as computer time and storage space, and unauthorized breach of communication within the system. Access controls can be characterized as follows:

(1) Access to program documentation should be limited to those persons who require it in the performance of their duties.
(2) Access to computer hardware should be limited to authorized individuals.
(3) Access to data and programs should be limited to those individuals authorized to process or maintain particular systems.[10]

Access and communication controls can be accomplished in part by physical security of the hardware, software, and data and good organization, specifically the use of a librarian.

Severe problems arise, however, for more complex EDP systems, particularly those with remote terminals and communication networks and those that use a data base management system. Problems in these EDP environments have been increasing because of three significant developments:

(1) More employees than ever have access to corporate computer systems as terminals proliferate throughout offices.
(2) More students learn how to use computers, even in grade schools, and some become sophisticated enough to outwit computer security.

[9] Ibid., pp. 37–38.
[10] Ibid., pp. 40–41.

(3) More consumers have personal computers in their own homes—more than 500,000 at last count—and can dial up data systems at will.[11]

In summary, the risks associated with unauthorized access have been rapidly increasing due to the move toward distributed processing, more widespread knowledge about computer systems, and the presence of thousands of terminals that are a telephone call away.

Several penetration techniques can be used to secure access and enter unauthorized transactions. These are listed in Figure 9–6. Access to terminals is seldom tightly controlled, and the communication network may be entered when outsiders tap transmission lines. Cases have been recorded in which data have been manipulated and merchandise has been fraudulently sent to dummy warehouses for example. In general, a review of the largest computer frauds indicates that the most important area for improvement is the tightening of access controls to prevent manipulation of transactions. This was found to be the most frequent method of perpetrating fraud.[12]

Attempts to improve security have resulted in the use of a system of passwords for authorized users, and restriction of access to certain types of data, such as payroll records, from specific terminals. For a data base system a variety of *passwords* can be used; a single password can be used on the entire data base, file passwords can be used on individual files, record passwords can be associated with each record, or passwords can be placed on specific fields

PENETRATION TECHNIQUE	EXPLANATION
Browsing	Searching through residue such as magnetic tapes and wastebaskets for passwords and other sensitive information to gain access to the system.
Masquerading	Impersonating as a legitimate user of the system to influence transaction processing, reporting or decision-making activities.
Piggybacking	Modifying an intercepted communication by tapping communication lines.
Between Lines Entry	Addition of an unauthorized transaction by tapping lines between gaps in transactions as they are communicated.
Spoofing	Fooling the user into thinking he or she is interacting with the operating system when they are not to compromise the system's security procedures.

Figure 9-6 Operating and Communication System Integrity Penetration Techniques
Adapted from R. Weber, *EDP Auditing: Conceptual Foundations and Practice* (New York: McGraw-Hill, 1982), p. 318, with permission.

[11] Reprinted from the April 20, 1981 issue of *Business Week* by special permission, ©1981 by McGraw-Hill, Inc., New York, N.Y. 10020. All rights reserved.

[12] Brandt Allen, "The Biggest Computer Fraud & Lessons for CPA's," *Journal of Accounting*, May 1977, pp. 52–62.

within records. In addition, the passwords can be set so that only read access, write access, or both read and write operations are possible.

Several modes of operation can be utilized in the password environment. First, a *password matrix* can identify the data base activities (read, delete, modify, etc.) and the areas of the data base to which a user has access. Figure 9–7 illustrates a password matrix for the user with password KRD007. In this example the user can perform only certain functions on certain files or subschema; he or she can read the accounts receivable and payroll files but cannot read the inventory and back-order files, and so forth.

In addition to a password matrix, *passwords by content* or *passwords by combination* can be used. Passwords by content restrict access to certain values of data within a given field. For example, a teller at a bank may be given access to all customer saving accounts that are less than $2,500; accounts greater than this amount are referred to a vice-president. Passwords by combination give a user access to combinations of fields of data. For example, an individual involved with a payroll system might have access to employee name-address data, employee rate-per-hour data, and employee total monthly pay data, on an item-by-item basis but not simultaneously. Developing and maintaining a password by content or password by combination is very expensive; therefore other forms of security are generally adopted before considering this form of data protection. A password, however, can be penetrated by experienced computer personnel because passwords are often found in wastebaskets and codes can be broken. Other methods such as badges, cards, dialogue, voice prints, and signatures of authorization of access to files can be used to overcome this problem. These may be compromised also; for example, by the loss of a card. To make penetration more difficult, the use of minicomputers as "gatekeepers" for the main CPU and data records has been suggested. However, a very experienced system programmer who has designed the system or a similar system, or who has knowledge of a particular vendor control procedure, will be able to circumvent any network of access controls. Hence the minicomputer used as a gatekeeper should be manufactured by a vendor different from the main CPU vendor.

DATA BASE ACTIVITY \ DATA FILE NAME	ACCOUNTS RECEIVABLE	PAYROLL	INVENTORY	BACK-ORDER
Read	YES	YES	NO	NO
Delete	NO	YES	YES	YES
Modify	YES	NO	YES	YES
Merge	YES	NO	NO	YES

Figure 9-7 Password Matrix for User KRD007

Data coding/data encryption. Data coding, or data encryption as it is often called, can be effective in reducing the risk of possible access by means such as those noted in Figure 9–7. It involves the storing and/or transmitting of data in a coded format. Several means of data coding are available. Characters can be shifted between two different fields within a record; a completely separate (new) alphabet can replace the standard one; numeric data can be manipulated by adding a constant or by applying a simple mathematical formula. Data coding is relatively simple to incorporate into data base processing and is effective against tapping and against accessing data directly from the data base. However, the coding scheme itself must be protected if security is to be upheld.

The primary disadvantages of data coding are that it requires additional CPU time and is not effective against access made via a data base management or operating system if one is used by the company. Before data can be stored on the data base they must be coded; and before data from the data base can be used (by an authorized user) they must be decoded. Both processes can be performed by a software package within the operating or data base system; however, the coding and decoding processes require CPU time, which could be avoided if coding and decoding were not employed. Coding and decoding expense can be reduced by coding only one or two fields within a record, particularly if the one or two fields render the uncoded data useless. Since that portion of the data base management system designed to code and decode data will do so on direction from anyone who appears to be an authorized user, data coding does not provide total security. If an offender can bypass the security at the data base or operating system itself, then data coding will not prevent access to the data base.

DATA AND PROCEDURAL CONTROLS Data and procedural controls are necessary to ensure accurate processing of data in compliance with managerial policies. Essentially data controls involve accounting for all transactions and are characterized by a reconciliation function. The AICPA suggests the following controls:

> A control function should be responsible for receiving all data to be processed, for ensuring that all data are recorded, for following up on errors detected during processing to see that they are corrected and resubmitted by the proper party, and for verifying the proper distribution of output.[13]

The use of an EDP structure with segregated functions, such as that illustrated in Figure 9–7, will also aid in this process by establishing control responsibility.

Batch totals. The most common technique used to account for all transactions is the use of *batch totals*. These totals may represent *dollar amounts, number of transactions*, or the *hash totals*. These are illustrated in Figure 9–8. A *hash total* is a nonsense total of account numbers or other numbers to ensure that all the numbers were correctly entered. Accountability is accomplished by a con-

---

[13] AICPA, *The Auditor's Study and Evaluation of Internal Control in EDP Systems*, copyright© (1977), p. 43, reprinted with permission.

TRANSACTION NO.	ACCOUNT NO.	JOURNAL ENTRY	DR.	CR.
1	100	Cash	$1000	
	200	Fixed assets		$1000
2	100	Cash	2000	
	150	Accounts receivable		2000
3	150	Accounts receivable	2500	
	500	Sales		2500
3	1200		$5500	$5500
Transaction Total	Hash Total		Dollar Amount	

Figure 9-8   Batch Total Illustration

trol group's independent reconciliation of all exceptions that usually accompany the processing of large amounts of data.

Procedural controls are characterized by written manuals that provide a step-by-step set of procedures to be followed by computer operators and accounting clerks for the smooth flow of information and the implementation of appropriate control features of the system. To ensure compliance with control and policy directives of management:

(1) A written manual of systems and procedures should be prepared for all computer operations and should provide for management's general or specific authorizations to process transactions.

(2) Internal auditors or some other independent group within an organization should review and evaluate proposed systems at critical stages of development and on a continuing basis internal auditors or some other independent group within an organization should review and test computer processing activities.[14]

The control and librarian functions shown in Figure 9–5 and described earlier are essential to ensuring compliance with prescribed procedures. In data base systems the data base administrator also plays an important role in procedural control. All processing activities should be scheduled, and this schedule is used to route the flow of information and to authorize the use of data files and software packages.

Data Base Controls. All of the general controls discussed above, especially access and communications controls, are useful in maintaining data base integrity and security.

If the data in a data base are not coded or password protected, illegal acquisition can easily result. Most likely, however, the data base system will be protected, even when the data in the data base are not. But an offender can circumvent the data base system protection by writing software programs to access the data base files directly. To accomplish this requires knowledge of the structure of the data files. If a teleprocessing mode of operation is used in

[14] Ibid.

transfiguring data from the data base to the user, then illegal access of data is possible by intercepting the transmissions between the authorized user and the computer. This must be controlled via the communication controls noted earlier.

The second security problem area relates to the software associated with the data base system. If the offender is unable to obtain data directly from the data base or by intercepting transmission in the teleprocessing operation, he or she might revert to modifying the data base system software. If that portion of the system's software that provides security protection can be changed, access to the data is possible. If the offender is unable to change the security software, other software might be changed so that erroneous data are stored and/or printed on certain output reports.

A *transaction log* can be used effectively to control access to the data base. This is a ledger that contains information such as the time, date, name of the user, type of inquiry or access mode, data accessed, location of data within the data base, and name of the specific software programs used to access the data. At least two security procedures can be employed with a transaction log. First, the ledger can be reviewed at random time intervals, and any suspicious accesses or access to high-priority data areas could be investigated. Second, the data base can be dumped at two separate and specific points in time and the ledger entries collected between the dumps. Using the first dump and the transaction log entries, a re-created data base image is generated. If the re-created data base image does not correspond with the second dump of the data base, unauthorized modification may have occurred.

Edit checks, discussed later in this chapter, are also very useful. They are performed to make copies and listings of files, data sets, and software to control for changes by using some form of comparison between the actual and the copy.

Backup and *recovery controls* are discussed in Chapter 8.

Regardless of whether passwords, data coding, transaction logs, edit checks, and/or backup and recovery are made, no data base is completely secure. Also, it is desirable to modify the security procedures periodically, particularly if highly sensitive data are stored in the data base.

PHYSICAL SECURITY   In addition to these reconciliation, balancing, and review procedures, physical security is important. Specifically, a system of physical controls must provide for

1. Prevention measures for physical access (discussed earlier), and malfunctions arising from fire, water, electrical problems, and climate control.

2. Protection to minimize the loss when a problem occurs. This is generally accomplished by keeping duplicates of critical transaction files, data bases, and programs off the premises and physically secured.

3. A plan of recovery to reconstruct the data or to use alternative facilities; this should be tested.

4. Insurance.

In data base management systems, backup and recovery may be quite complex. Procedures that can effectively accomplish security in the data base environment were outlined in Chapter 8.

Application Controls

Application controls apply to specific application input, processing, and output. They are designed to ensure that the recording, classifying, summarizing, and updating of the master files or data base will eventually lead to the generation of accurate and complete information on a timely basis. Four different groups of employees within the organization share the responsibility for adequate application control:

1.   User and data origination functions (groups) must maintain sufficient control to satisfy themselves that they can rely on the quality of data input and the usefulness of the information output.
2.   System designers should ensure that the network of implemented controls is both effective and economical. Furthermore, they should prepare and update procedural manuals for training and consistent application of control procedures.
3.   The EDP control group mentioned earlier is accountable for all the data. They should schedule and log the flow of data and information in the computer operations. They must also secure authorization for input and ensure the reconciliation of any problems occurring during input, processing, and output. In a data base system this function will probably be augmented by a data base administrator.
4.   Data processing operations personnel must comply with the set of instructions set forth in run manuals and other procedural directives.

INPUT CONTROLS   More accurate data input can be ensured through input controls. According to the AICPA's *Statement on Auditing Standards No. 3*:

> Input controls are designed to provide reasonable assurance that data received for processing by EDP has been properly authorized, converted into machine sensible form and identified, and that data (including data transmitted over communication lines) have not been lost, suppressed, duplicated, or otherwise improperly changed. Input controls include controls that relate to rejection, correction, and resubmission of data that were initially correct.[15]

Basically, there are four types of input transactions: (1) updating and transaction entry, (2) file and data base maintenance, (3) inquiry, and (4) error correction. In addition, there are many input methods. The accountant or systems designer must select the appropriate mode of input for each of the types

---

[15] AICPA, *The Effects of EDP on the Auditor's Study and Evaluation of Internal Control, Statement on Auditing Standards No. 3* New York: American Institute of Certified Public Accountants, Inc., copyright© (1972), reprinted with permission.

of transactions based on the organization's processing needs, the control features, and the attributes associated with each input method. Figure 9–9 summarizes these attributes and, as can be seen, some of the attributes can effectively be used to enhance the validity and accuracy of data input. (More details were given in Chapter 5.)

Data entry. Controls such as *standardized forms* designed for ease of data entry and, if possible, machine readability, *tutorial* (question and answer) *on-line input* capability, *sequencing* of input keys, *key verification*, precoded *turnaround documents* where only limited information is entered, and the generation of *machine-readable output at the point of the transaction* are very useful in ensuring more accurate data input.

Validation. Validation of input data is also necessary for accurate transaction input. *Field checks* are designed to assess the validity of the field. Examples would consist of (1) a *master file reference* to ensure that an account number matches one on the master file; (2) a *check digit* (a mathematical combination of the other digits) to give reasonable assurance that transcription and transposition errors were not made; (3) a *completeness* test to ensure that all data in the field are present; (4) a *limit* test, which only allows transactions within specified

INTERNAL CONTROL ATTRIBUTES (DATA-ENTRY METHOD)	KEYPUNCH CARDS	KEY TO TAPE (MAGNETIC)	KEY TO DISK	TURNAROUND DOCUMENT	MAGNETIC INK (MICR)	OPTICAL (OCR)	INTELLIGENT TERMINALS	POINT OF SALE (POS)
Simple and flexible	+	+	+	+	−	−		−
Reduced human intervention					+	+	+	+
Cost		−	−		−	−	−	−
Ease of handling data	+							
Visibility of data	+				+	+		−
Speed	−				+	+		+
Susceptible to damage	−			−				
Buffering		+	+		+	+	+	+
Validation editing and verification		+	+		+	+	+	+
Reliability					+	+	+	+
Machine readable	+	+	+		+	+	+	+
Reduced preparation errors				+	+	+	+	+
Display							+	
Data captured at source							+	+

Figure 9-9 Major Internal Control Advantages (+) and Disadvantages (−) of Data Input Devices

Adapted from Ron Weber, *EDP Auditing: Conceptual Framework and Practice* (New York: McGraw-Hill, 1982) pp. 209–224, with permission.

bounds to be processed—for example, on a typical production day a maximum one thousand units could be processed; and (5) an *alphanumeric* check to ensure that data are either alphabetic or numeric, or both. *Record checks* are designed to ensure that the *logical relationships* among fields are valid. Examples would consist of (1) a *completeness check* to ensure that all input fields were completed—for example, in a material requisition, the part number, job to which the cost should be allocated, number of items, and department should all be completed; (2) a *reasonableness* check to ensure that the interrelationships among the input data are reasonable—for example, each product order should consist of one engine, one handle, and four wheels; (3) a *sign* test—for example, debit or credit, to ensure that the sign is consistent with the nature of the transaction, such as a journal entry; and (4) a *sequence* check to ensure that all fields are properly sequenced for subsequent processing. *Batch checks* are used to establish controls over batches to further assist in controlling accuracy and completeness of fields and records as well as ensuring that all records are input into the processing cycle. *Control totals* such as *dollar amount, number of transactions*, and account number *hash* totals can be used to ensure that all the dollars were entered, all transactions were entered correctly, and account numbers were entered correctly. Examples of these were given in Figure 9–8. The computer or mechanical input device should be programmed to ensure that batch totals agree with those calculated by the individual prior to entry of the data into the system for processing. For large volumes of information, tolerance limits for some discrepancies should be considered to expedite data processing, provided that errors can be cleared up at a later stage of processing, or the subset of data that is in error can be recycled. Other batch checks would entail provision for batch descriptions such as batch number, date, type of transaction, and origin. Internal and external *file labels* and generation numbers can be used to ensure that the correct file or data base is being updated. Another useful control to ensure that the correct file is processed is called an *anticipation control*. The computer is programmed to expect certain transactions and files to be accessed, such as a time card input for each employee and the payroll program run at a certain time during the week. Exceptions to the expectation will be investigated.

Finally, *transaction logs* should be maintained on all input to establish an audit trail.

Other general steps suggested by the AICPA for input control are:[16]

(1) Movement of data between one processing step and another, or between departments, should be controlled.

At each step the *acknowledgement of receipt* is given and a review of balance and control totals is performed.

(2) Correction and resubmission of all errors detected by the application system should be reviewed and controlled.

Error logs are generated by the computer and include complete details such as time, date, and type of error. Corrections are also logged. The computer can be used to keep the track of both errors and subsequent corrections.

[16] AICPA, *The Auditor's Study and Evaluation of Internal Control in EDP Systems*, pp. 54–55. Reprinted with permission.

Input Control Example. Consider the input of credit-card information to the accounts receivable master file of a large oil company (see Figure 9–10). Many of the controls we have just reviewed are present in this system. The input system is designed around two batches. One batch total is prepared for each service station, and another is prepared for each tray of cards processed. First, each station collects a card copy of each credit transaction. Batches of these cards are totaled. The batches are then mailed by several thousand service stations to the credit-card processing center where they are collected in long trays for processing. These trays are used for batch input control and must be balanced. The oil company accumulates totals in dollars from the station batch cards and prepares a batch total card for the tray to be scanned. All cards in each tray are optically scanned. Correction information is coded on the back of the card and stored on a temporary disk file. Incomplete or unreadable cards are rejected for manual processing. Space is reserved on the disk for these cards. They are corrected from the handwritten data on the card and keyed onto a tape. The tape is then merged with the temporary disk file for each tray, and the detail on each transaction card is balanced with each station's batch total. All of these batch totals are compared with the total for the entire tray. Rejected cards are corrected as part of this process so that the tray will be complete. All exceptions are listed. The tray is then sorted so that all the exceptions to the balance run can be reviewed. Corrections are keyed onto a correction tape, the temporary file is updated, and another balance run is performed. Any exceptions are again listed and corrected as before. When the entire tray balances to the tray total and each station's batch total, the accounts receivable master file is updated for future inquiry and cycle billing. Trays are then sorted by billing cycle.

By using control totals, input is edited, completely accounted for, and corrected. Optical scanning equipment is programmed to reject any data that are not complete or are difficult to read. Moreover, such equipment reduces human errors. Trays must balance prior to any update of the accounts receivable master file and sorting of the tray for cycle billing. The result is a high level of assurance, although not absolute assurance, that input will be accurate.

PROCESSING CONTROLS   Processing controls should provide reasonable assurance that processing is performed in compliance with management's specifications. There are basically five types of processing controls. An overview of these controls is given in Figure 9–11 .

Transaction flow and validation controls include the *field, record, batch,* and *file* controls discussed earlier. Note, however, that they are useful throughout the entire information processing cycle including input, processing, and output. In addition, *transaction logs* must be generated for backup and recovery as well as the construction of an audit trail for management decision-making and auditing requirements. Moreover, an *error identification*, reporting, and correction procedure must be present to account for all transactions, isolate errors, and reconcile differences as transactions are being processed.

Processing and logic controls primarily include the assurance that the system complied with the objectives set forth in the *development and implementation procedures* summarized in Chapter 2 and detailed in Chapters 10 and 11. In other words, the system has been well designed and tested. *Programming controls*

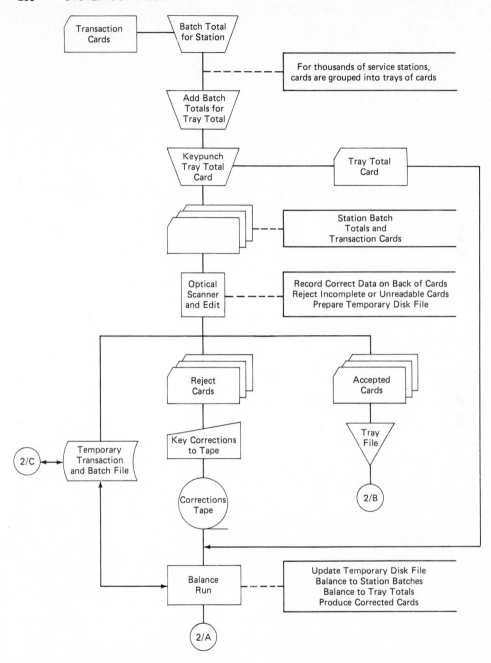

Figure 9–10 Credit-Card Data Input for a Large Oil Company

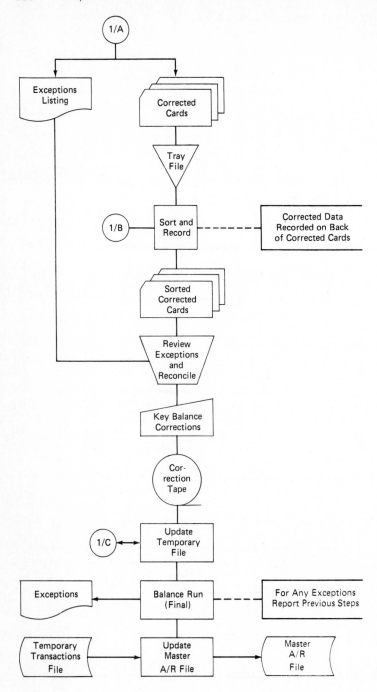

Figure 9–10 (continued)

TYPE	TECHNIQUE
Transaction flow and validation controls (same as input controls)	Data-entry routines Field, record, batch, and file controls Transaction log and audit trail Error identification
Processing and logic controls	Development and implementation Programming controls Logistical relationships Concurrency control
File and data base controls	Installation hardware and software Data base and file access controls File identification
Software controls	Design and implementation Operating and data base systems software access Edit checks Backup, recovery, and restart
Hardware	Dual read and write Parity Overflow Equipment

Figure 9-11 Types and Techniques of Processing Controls

should be present, such as *sequence checks,* to match master and transaction files; *end-of-file* procedures to ensure that entire files are processed; *processing sequences,* such as changing master files prior to updating; and *run-to-run* totals to ensure that each program processed all the data at each stage in the processing cycle. Testing compliance with *logical relationships and limits* such as those noted earlier should be present. Often a *redundancy check* is useful here to *compare* details with control totals. *Concurrency controls,* such as *preempting,* for data base systems must be present to prevent a deadlock when several users attempt to use the same set of data.

   File and *data base controls* ensure that the correct files are processed and that files and data bases are protected from compromise. Files have both *external* and *internal* (header and trailer) *labels* for file identification. For example, a program cannot be run if the label on the tape or disk does not agree with the program. Each file will have *file totals* to ensure that all records have been accounted for. A record of use will be maintained for each file. Other file and data base controls are generally provided through the system hardware and software and access controls noted earlier in this chapter. Finally, *file data base maintenance procedures* will be established for changes to records.

   The most important *processing software control* is the assurance that transactions and information for reporting and decision-making needs are processed in accordance with management's objectives. This assurance is only provided by following a well-planned system for *software development* and *implementation,* such as the one outlined in Chapter 2 and discussed in Chapters 10 and 11. Other software controls restrict *access* to the operating and data base system and provide for *backup, recovery,* and *restart.* These are discussed elsewhere in this chapter. Finally, a useful control for detecting a compromise in software or the operating or data base system is the *edit check.* Programs can be periodically compared with a backup copy for differences, run against a test data base and compared with previously generated reports, and reviewed for size changes to detect any evidence of a software change.

In addition to these processing controls, each manufacturer of hardware will provide for *overflow* and *read and write checks* to ensure that data are not lost and that input and output are accurate and free of transcription errors. *Dual read and write heads, echo checks, parity checks,* and *equipment checks* are also useful for this purpose.

OUTPUT CONTROLS   According to the *Statement on Auditing Standards No. 3:*

> Output controls are designed to assure the accuracy of the processing result (such as account listing or displays, reports, magnetic files, invoices, or disbursement checks) and to assure that only authorized personnel receive the output.[17]

First, output should be *reconciled* with input and processing control totals to help ensure that all transactions have been accounted for and processed in compliance with managerial objectives. Often this reconciliation will involve *procedures for error correction.* At the very least, exception information will be an integral part of the balancing process. Second, output should be scanned and tested to ensure that it has been properly processed. This can be done on a test basis. The extent of this testing will be a function of input and processing controls. Finally, output should be distributed only to authorized users. This latter objective is not difficult to achieve in an on-line system if there are appropriate access controls and the output is displayed on the terminal, but it is very difficult in a processing system where reports are generated. In this latter case controls must be maintained over (1) storage of output media such as payroll checks, (2) the report generating program, (3) the report printing program, (4) the actual printing operation, (5) the output distribution of multiple copies, (6) the review for errors, and (7) the storage and retention of output.[18]

AUDIT OF EDP SYSTEMS

Both external and internal auditors are vitally concerned about effective procedures for auditing EDP systems. The ultimate objective of the external auditor is his or her opinion on the overall fairness of the financial statements. The internal auditor's objective tends to be most concerned with the quality and relevance of management information, data integrity, and the system effectiveness and efficiency of combined management information systems. The advent of EDP has caused several problems for the auditor. First, audit trails, once highly visible, are often an unseen part of the computer system. Second, records such

---

[17] AICPA, *SAS No. 3,* copyright © (1972), reprinted with permission.

[18] For more details, see Ron Weber, *EDP Auditing.*

as tape and disk files are readable only by machine. Third, the EDP controls we have reviewed in this chapter are either founded on system analysis, design, and implementation procedures or based on programmed functions, operating and data base systems, and hardware and software characteristics.

In general, the major steps in an EDP audit parallel those in the audit of a traditional system. The procedures and techniques, however, are very different and must be designed to cope with the EDP system's environment. In general, as in a traditional system, the auditor must first understand the accounting system and obtain an overall view of its associated control system. If this initial estimate of the control system indicates that some reliance can be placed on it, the auditor then conducts a detailed review and evaluation of administration and accounting systems and procedures. The overall objectives of this stage will be to determine the adequacy of the system design from a control perspective. The emphasis here will be dictated by the purpose of the audit —e.g., management or financial. At this juncture an audit strategy should be planned to determine what would be the best approach in auditing the system, what technique to apply, and the overall scope of the investigation.

Once it has been determined that the necessary controls were designed into the accounting EDP system, the next step is to test whether the actual system operates in compliance with these controls. Finally, once the auditor has determined that a reasonable degree of reliance can be placed on the system of administrative or accounting controls, the auditor then applies substantive tests to obtain sufficient evidence to make a final judgment with regard to the audit's objectives.

A wide variety of procedures and techniques are available to help the auditor cope with the challenges of the EDP environment. They each have their advantages and disadvantages, which are very much a function of the nature of the accounting and information system. For example, one procedure will be fine for a batch-oriented production system but will fail to provide the auditor with useful audit evidence for an on-line order-entry system. These procedures and techniques are outlined in Figure 9–12.

PROCEDURE	TECHNIQUE
Audit around the computer	Traditional manual audit techniques
Audit through the computer 　Nonconcurrent audit	Test data Program code comparison Flowchart verification
Concurrent audit	Integrated test facility Tagging and tracing Parallel test facility System control audit review file Reprocessing Simulated attack
Audit with the computer	Generalized audit software

Figure 9-12　EDP Audit Procedures and Techniques

The auditor may audit around the computer. Output is traced to input and vice versa on a test basis, and the computer is treated as a "black box." This approach was common practice ten to twenty years ago. It is still a valid approach today for batch systems that are simple extensions of manual systems. To be effective, these batch systems should have (1) clear audit trails where transactions can easily be traced through the various processing steps by using transaction logs, detailed ledgers, and a good system of referencing; (2) straightforward system logic; and (3) well-defined, tested, and widely accepted software. The major advantage of this procedure is its simplicity. To perform this type of audit, very little specialized training is necessary. The major disadvantage is that it completely ignores the very heart of the EDP accounting and information system, which is the actual data processing and its associated controls.

To assess the actual processing of the information and its associated controls, the auditor needs to audit *through the system* to understand how the "black box" works. This is the only way the auditor can test compliance with specified controls and procedures when the processing logic is complex, large volumes of data are processed, key elements of the internal control system are computerized, and significant on-line random access activity is present.

The auditor can verify system logic by using flowcharts and can assess programming steps by examining the code to ensure that processing is to be performed in accordance with management guidelines and generally accepted accounting principles. Expert knowledge is required to do this, even though the computer may be programmed to generate a flowchart of program logic. These two desk checks are limited, for they do not test compliance.

Several *nonconcurrent* (cannot be implemented concurrently with other computer processing) processing procedures can be used to help the auditor assess system controls. To test the adequacy of the system of controls to prevent fraudulent activities or processing errors, test data (deck) can be used. A data set that includes both good and erroneous transactions is prepared. The controls that should be present as well as those that are supposed to be operating are violated by some of the input. The test data are processed using the system. The results are then compared with a known solution of good and bogus transactions. This method is excellent if the variety of transactions is limited. For larger complex systems, however, the variety of transactions and the number of potential problems that could be encountered become too large to manage by hand. The auditor may also not have the expertise required to test the complex logic of more-advanced on-line random access systems. To handle this problem, *test data generators* have been devised which mechanically produce a wide spectrum of good and bad data. The major advantages of the test data approach are (1) simplicity and (2) a good test of application program controls. The major disadvantages are (1) keeping up with system modifications, (2) the complexity of some systems, and (3) the commingling of test data with actual data in on-line files for a system that cannot be shut down for an audit.

To deal with *concurrency* and increasing complex problems, several additional techniques have been developed. The *integrated test facility*, or "minicompany," is one such technique. The auditor establishes a dummy entity such as a division or cost center in the data base against which data, both good and bad, can be processed along with live transactions. To monitor the system, this technique can be performed without the firm's knowledge. The major advantage is that regular programs are used under ordinary operating circumstances to test the effectiveness of the operating system and to test the adequacy of general and application controls. This concurrent approach is a must for many on-line systems. Another significant advantage is that the flow of data can be tested as transactions are ultimately posted to the dummy entity accounts. The major disadvantages are that, as the auditor reviews these test transactions, he or she runs the risk of reversing real data. Actual data may also be *tagged* and *traced* through the system with the auditor taking *snapshots* before and after each key data processing or control procedure. The major advantage of this latter technique is that the auditor can follow the flow of the information through the system.

Rather than use the actual data base, a *parallel test facility* enables the auditor to test the operating system and its various general and application controls for compliance against a representation of the firm's data base and operation system. *Parallel simulation* of representative programs can also be used on actual data. Results of the simulation would be compared with actual results to test the EDP system. *Reprocessing* is a version of this where the firm's processing is duplicated.

Another approach is to actually embed audit software in the operating or data base system. This technique is called *system control audit review file* (SCARF), or *concurrent processing*.[19] Files are placed at certain key points within the system to monitor the flow of information and to gather data for the audit. Finally, a *simulated attack* may be used to test the EDP system's security and access system.[20]

The external auditor can also use generalized audit software to audit a wide variety of clients. The problem facing the CPA firm is that all of its clients have different accounting systems which must be audited. The auditor's client's systems can range from simple batch file-oriented systems to complex data base systems such as those discussed in Chapters 5, 6, and 8. Generalized audit software is designed to deal with many of these systems. This software helps the auditor to access the system and provides files, reports, and a variety of statistics for the various steps in the audit process. The following functions are performed by the software:

1. *Access and retrieve data.* The auditor can search large files with varied sequential and random structures and extract data necessary to perform other audit steps. Several files may often be read simultaneously to extract data.

2. *Compare, sort, and merge.* Files and the data retrieved in item 1 can be reorganized to facilitate the audit process. Comparisons of key statistics such as ratios can be made.

3. *Arithmetic calculation.* Simple mathematical calculations can be performed, such as addition, subtraction, multiplication, and division, to

---

[19] See Weber, *EDP Auditing,* for a complete discussion of SCARF.

[20] See Tom Alexander, "Waiting for the Great Computer Ripoff," *Fortune,* July 1978, pp. 143–52, for a discussion of simulated attacks and the results.

enable the auditor to prepare data for such analysis as ratio analysis and comparison of control totals.

4. *Statistical.* Several packages provide routines to help the auditor draw a sample and perform statistical sampling procedures. Others support regression analysis and ratio analysis for analytical review.

5. *Reports.* All have provisions for allowing the auditor to specify a wide variety of audit reports.

To use the generalized software, the auditor must prepare a set of specification instructions such as data formats to link the generalized audit software with the characteristics of the system to be audited. Not all generalized audit software packages will operate on all systems. Most are limited because they cannot be used in concurrent auditing and, as a result, cannot effectively be used to audit the processing logic in on-line data base systems. On the other hand, most are very effective in auditing large-batch file-oriented systems. Most of the larger public accounting firms make good use of these packages to simplify the audit process and to reduce the training needed for their auditors to perform EDP audits.

In general, the audit of EDP systems is a challenge to the accounting profession, but procedures and techniques such as those just reviewed are being developed through continued research to meet this challenge. Regardless of the set of techniques and procedures, the auditor must maintain control over their use and the output generated for the audit. Finally, both internal and external auditors should follow traditional practices to verify the results of processing. In the EDP audit these are characterized by compensating procedures such as third-party confirmation of records, comparisons with other records, and review of procedures for reasonableness.

SUMMARY

Both administrative and accounting controls are key elements in an information system. The AICPA and FEI have recommended the inclusion of a statement on the accounting system and internal controls in the annual report.

The objectives of a control system are accomplished by using an integrated network of administrative controls and accounting controls. Management and administrative controls, such as budgets, help ensure reasonable compliance with managerial policy and the implementation of an effective data processing system. Accounting controls are designed to safeguard assets and ensure reliability of information generated from the data gathered during the transaction cycles.

Electronic data processing has had a tremendous impact on accounting controls because the information processing system is now the focal point of control systems. The necessary controls include general controls, organization structures, systems development and documentation, hardware and software controls, access and communication restrictions, data and procedural controls, physical security, and application (input, processing, and output) controls. This network of controls together with the audit function has given management and third parties reasonable assurance that assets are safeguarded, managerial policies are carried out, and the information generated is fair and reliable.

A continued discussion of each of the transaction processing cycles that constitutes a basic part of the firm's information processing network and the control features related to those cycles will be presented in the application Chapters 12 through 17. The AICPA Special Advisory Committee on Internal Accounting Control suggests that such a cycle approach be taken to evaluate internal control procedures and techniques.

SELECTED REFERENCES

ALEXANDER, TOM, "Waiting for the Great Computer Rip-Off," *Fortune* (July 1978), pp. 143–52.

ALLEN, BRANDT, "The Biggest Computer Fraud: Lessons for CPAs," *Journal of Accountancy* (May 1977), pp. 52–62.

American Institute of Certified Public Accountants, Auditing Standards Executive Committee, *Codification of Auditing Standards and Procedures*, Statement on Auditing Standards No. 1, New York: AICPA, Inc., 1972.

American Institute of Certified Public Accountants, Computer Services Executive Committee, *The Auditor's Study and Evaluation of Internal Control in EDP Systems*, New York: AICPA, Inc., 1977.

American Institute of Certified Public Accountants, *Reporting on Internal Control*, Statement on Auditing Standards No. 30, New York: AICPA, Inc., 1980.

American Institute of Certified Public Accountants, *Report of the Special Advisory Committee on Internal Control*, New York: AICPA, Inc., 1978.

ARTHUR YOUNG AND COMPANY, *Foreign Corrupt Practices Act of 1977; Toward Compliance with the Accounting Provisions* (1978).

BANKS, IRA D., "Internal Control of On-Line and Real Time Computer Systems," *Management Accounting* (June 1977), pp. 28–30.

BODNER, GEORGE, "Reliability Modeling of Internal Control Systems," *The Accounting Review*, (October 1975).

BURCH, JOHN G., JR., AND JOSEPH L. SARDINAS, Jr., *Computer Control and Audit: A Total System Approach*, New York: John Wiley & Sons, Inc., 1980.

CUSHING, BARRY E., "A Mathematical Approach to the Analysis and Design of Internal Control Systems," *The Accounting Review* (January 1974), pp. 24–41.

DAVIS, JAMES R., "EDP Control Means Total Control," *Management Accounting* (January 1977), pp. 41–44.

DELOITTE, HASKINS & SELLS, *Internal Accounting Control: Current Developments and Implications of the Foreign Corrupt Practices Act*, (1978).

DELOITTE, HASKINS & SELLS, *The Week in Review* (August 15, 1980).

Financial Executives Research Foundation, *Internal Control in U.S. Corporation: State of the Art*, New York: FEI.

GROLLMAN, WILLIAM K., AND ROBERT W. COLLY, "Internal Control for Small Business," *Journal of Accountancy*, December 1978, pp. 64–67.

LEITCH, ROBERT A., GADIS J. DILLON, AND SUE H. MCKINLEY, "Internal Control Weakness in Small Businesses," *Journal of Accountancy* (December 1981), pp. 97–101.

PORTER, W. THOMAS, AND WILLIAM E. PERRY,   *EDP Controls and Auditing,* 2nd ed., Belmont, California: Woodworth Publishing Company, Inc., 1977.

REA, RICHARD C.,   "A Small Business Internal Control Questionnaire," *Journal of Accountancy* (July 1978).

SCHLOSSER, ROBERT E., AND DONALD C. BRUEGMAN,   "The Effect of EDP on Internal Control," *Management Sciences* (March-April 1967), pp. 44–51.

Securities Exchange Commission,   *Foreign Corrupt Practices Act,* Washington: Securities Exchange Commission, 1977.

STELZER, HERBERT J.,   "Evaluation of Internal Control in Small Audits," *Journal of Accountancy* (July 1978).

———"The Spreading Danger of Computer Crime," *Business Week,* April 20, 1981.

WIBER, RON,   *EDP Auditing: Conceptual Foundations and Practice,* New York: McGraw-Hill, 1982.

REVIEW QUESTIONS

1. Auditors should be familiar with EDP terminology. The following statements contain some of the terminology so employed. Indicate whether each statement is true or false.
   a. An auditor would utilize software if he or she uses the computer to perform audit steps.
   b. A limit test is a test written into a computer program to determine that management's policies are not violated while data are being processed.
   c. A completeness test is an internal equipment control to test whether all transactions have been processed.
   d. The central processing unit of a computer installation does not include peripheral equipment.
   e. One of the characteristics of on-line real-time processing is that inputs are available at random.
   f. An error listing will not be produced as a byproduct of processing by a computer unless provision was made for such a listing in the program.
   g. An internal label is one of the controls built into the hardware by the manufacturer of a magnetic tape system.
   h. The term "grandfather-father-son" refers to a method of computer record security rather than to generation in the evolution of computer hardware.
   i. A control total is an example of a self-checking number within a batch control.
   j. Magnetic tape storage is generally employed with batch sequential processing rather than with random processing of data.
   k. A test deck can be contained on magnetic or paper tape as well as on punched cards.
   l. Field validity tests are employed to determine whether a computer word has the proper parity. (AICPA adapted)

2. What is the difference between *administrative* controls and *accounting* controls? Give some examples.

3. What impact has the Foreign Corrupt Practices Act of 1977 had on the auditor's review of internal control?

4. Describe the control points in a sales transaction processing cycle.

5. What are the key control points in an EDP system?

6. Explain why it is important to consider the system of controls and not individual controls.

7. From an internal control perspective, why is it important that an information

system be well designed and implemented?

8. Describe a set of input controls for an EDP system.

9. When converting a manual system to a batch processing system, is it good practice to maintain the same control procedures? Why or why not?

10. Explain how the information requirements of management are important to internal control.

11. Name and explain the six control concepts outlined in *SAS No. 1*.

12. Explain why there is a shift of internal control from a system of separation of duties and authorizations to the data processing system.

13. According to *SAS No. 3*, what do general controls include?

14. How should an EDP department be organized to promote good internal control?

15. How can the auditor ensure that mandated controls and processing procedures are implemented and operational?

16. Why are program change approvals necessary?

17. What is a *parallel run*? For what is it used?

18. How can access to records be restricted?

19. Why are passwords necessary? Can they be compromised? How?

20. What is the major general control weakness leading to fraud?

21. What basic control procedures are useful in ensuring that all documents have been processed correctly?

22. What physical security steps must be taken with regard to critical files?

23. For what is the EDP control group responsible?

24. Name several EDP input controls and describe how they can be utilized together to promote more effective control.

25. Why must there be a set of procedures for correction of exceptions?

26. What types of controls are useful for ensuring accurate and reasonable processing of information?

27. What controls are necessary to ensure the integrity of a data base?

28. What are some of the advantages of using a CRT that displays a form to be completed and upon completion exhibits summary information on inputs compared with keypunching from handwritten source documents?

29. What controls can be used to protect against unauthorized access to data transmission?

30. Why is the organization of a control system given emphasis in the definition of internal control?

31. What control or controls would you recommend in a computer system to prevent the following situations from occurring?

   a. A computer programmer entered the computer room one night, selected a payroll tape, altered the payroll program, wrote a check for himself, restored the program to its original form to erase the evidence, and left.

   b. The computer programmer left for another job, and no one in the firm could modify his program when the need for a modification was directed by management.

   c. An authorized change to a program was implemented for accounts payable. Upon the next run, checks of the wrong amount were sent to incorrect vendors.

   d. A computer operator was selling mailing lists of a large regional department store.

   e. A systems programmer working for a large software vendor tied into an on-line inventory system via a remote terminal, cracked the password code and generated the appropriate documents to cause the company to ship millions of dollars of merchandise to a warehouse he rented.

   f. In an on-line accounts receivable data base system, account representatives experienced deadlocks when trying to review multiple data sets at the same time that others were trying to access the same data.

g. In an inventory system, items were reordered automatically on occasion after they had been received. A study of the problem revealed that these particular items were always on the exception list generated from the inventory update run.

h. The wrong size of materials often showed up at a work center in the production line. After a schedule was concluded, part numbers were keyed into the system for distribution to work centers.

i. When some invoices were missing, the accounts payable department passed the blame to the mail room.

j. One month the wrong payroll tape was used to issue checks, resulting in many underpayments and payments to terminated employees.

k. Once a critical receivable tape was used to copy an accounts payable transaction file.

l. Transmitted data always balanced when they left the district terminals yet were sometimes out of balance when they were reviewed periodically at the home office.

EXERCISES AND CASES

9–1

George Beemster, CPA, is examining the financial statements of the Louisville Sales Corporation, which recently installed an off-line electronic computer. The following comments have been extracted from Mr. Beemster's notes on computer operations and the processing and control of shipping notices and customers' invoices:

–To minimize inconvenience, Louisville converted without change its existing data processing system, which utilized tabulating equipment. The computer company supervised the conversion and has provided training to all computer department employees (except keypunch operators) in systems design, operations, and programming.

–Each computer run is assigned to a specific employee, who is responsible for making program changes, running the program, and answering questions. This procedure has the advantage of eliminating the need for records of computer operations because each employee is responsible for his or her own computer runs.

–At least one computer department employee remains in the computer room during office hours, and only computer department employees have keys to the computer room.

–System documentation consists of those materials furnished by the computer company—a set of record formats and program listings. These and the tape library are kept in a corner of the computer department.

–The company considered the desirability of programmed controls but decided to retain the manual controls from its existing system.

–Company products are shipped directly from public warehouses, which forward shipping notices to general accounting. There a billing clerk enters the price of the item and accounts for the numerical sequence of shipping notices from each warehouse. The billing clerk also prepares daily adding machine tapes ("control tapes") of the units shipped and the unit prices.

–Shipping notices and control tapes are forwarded to the computer department for keypunching and processing. Extensions are made on the computer. Output consists of invoices (in six copies) and a daily sales register. The daily sales register shows the aggregate totals of units shipped and unit prices, which the computer operator compares with the control tapes.

–All copies of the invoices are returned to the billing clerk. The clerk mails three copies to the customer, forwards one copy to the warehouse, maintains one copy in the numerical file, and retains one copy in an open invoice file that serves as a detailed accounts receivable record.

REQUIRED: Describe weaknesses in internal control over information and data flows and the procedures for processing shipping notices and customer invoices, and recommend improvements in these controls and processing procedures. Organize your answer sheets as follows:

Weakness	Recommended Improvement
	(AICPA adapted)

9–2

VBR Company has recently installed a new computer system that has on-line real-time capability. Cathode ray tube terminals are used for data entry and inquiry. A new cash receipts and accounts receivable file maintenance system has been designed and implemented for use with this new equipment. All programs have been written and tested, and the new system is being run in parallel with the old system. After two weeks of parallel operation, no differences have been observed between the two systems other than keypunch errors on the old system.

Al Brand, the data processing manager, is enthusiastic about the new equipment and system. He reveals that the system was designed, coded, compiled, debugged, and tested by programmers utilizing an on-line CRT terminal installed specifically for around-the-clock use by the programming staff. He claims that this access to the computer saved one-third in programming elapsed time. All files, including accounts receivable, are on-line at all times as the firm moves toward a full data base mode. All programs, new and old, are available at all times for recall into memory for scheduled op-

erating use or for program maintenance. Program documentation and actual tests confirm that data-entry edits in the new system include all conventional data error and validity checks appropriate to the system.

Inquiries have confirmed that the new system conforms precisely to the flowcharts, a portion of which is shown in Figure C9–2. A turnaround copy of the invoice is used as a remittance advice (R/A) by 99 percent of the customers; if the R/A is missing, the cashier applies the payment to a selected invoice. Sales terms are net sixty days, but payment patterns are sporadic. Statements are not mailed to customers. Late payments are commonplace and are not vigorously pursued. VBR does not have a bad debt problem because bad debt losses average only 0.5 percent of sales.

Before authorizing the termination of the old system, Cal Darden, the controller, has requested a review of the internal control features that have been designed for the new system. Security against unauthorized access and fraudulent actions, assurance of the integrity of the files, and protection of the firm's assets should be provided by the internal controls.

REQUIRED: Based upon the description of VBR Company's new system and the flowchart that has been presented:

a. Describe the defects that exist in the system.

b. Suggest how each defect you identified could be corrected. (Adapted from the CMA Examination)

9–3

Simmons Corporation is a multilocation retailing concern with stores and warehouses throughout the United States. The company is in the process of designing a new integrated computer-based information system. In conjunction with the design of the new system, the company's management is reviewing the data processing security to determine what new control features should be incorporated. Two areas of specific concern are (1) the confidentiality of company and customer records and (2) the safekeeping of computer equipment, files, and EDP facilities.

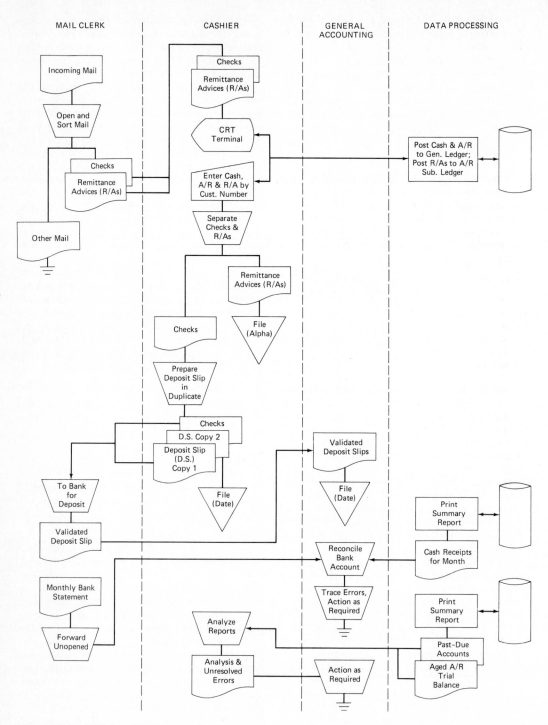

Figure C9–2   VBR Company

The new information system will process all company records, which include sales, purchase, financial, budget, customer, creditor, and personnel information. The stores and warehouses will be linked to the main computer at corporate headquarters by a system of remote terminals. This will permit data to be communicated directly to corporate headquarters or to any other location from each location through the terminal network.

At the present time certain reports have restricted distribution because not all levels of management need to receive them or because they contain confidential information. The introduction of remote terminals in the new system may provide access to this restricted data by unauthorized personnel. Simmons's top management is concerned that confidential information may become accessible and may be used improperly.

The company also is concerned about potential physical threats to the system, such as sabotage, fire damage, water damage, power failure, or magnetic radiation. Should any of these events occur in the present system and cause a computer shutdown, adequate backup records are available so that the company could reconstruct necessary information at a reasonable cost on a timely basis. With the new system, however, a computer shutdown would severely limit company activities until the system could become operational again.

REQUIRED:

a. Identify and briefly explain the problems Simmons Corporation could experience with respect to the confidentiality of information and records in the new system.

b. Recommend measures Simmons Corporation could incorporate into the new system which would ensure the confidentiality of information and records in the new system.

c. What safeguards can Simmons Corporation develop to provide physical security for its (1) computer equipment, (2) files, and (3) EDP facilities? (Adapted from the CMA Examination)

9–4

The Department of Taxation of one state is developing a new computer system for processing state income tax returns of individuals and corporations. The new system features direct data input and inquiry capabilities. Identification of taxpayers is provided by using the Social Security number for individuals and federal identification number for corporations. The new system should be fully implemented in time for the next tax season.

The new system will serve three primary purposes:

1. Data will be input into the system directly from tax returns through cathode ray tube (CRT) terminals located at the central headquarters of the Department of Taxation.

2. The returns will be processed using the main computer facilities at central headquarters. The processing includes

   a. Verifying the mathematical accuracy
   b. Auditing the reasonableness of deductions, tax due, and so forth, through the use of edit routines; these routines also include a comparison of the current year's data with the prior years' data
   c. Identifying the returns that should be considered for audit by revenue agents of the department
   d. Issuing refund checks to taxpayers

3. Inquiry service will be provided taxpayers upon request through the assistance of tax department personnel at five regional offices. A total of fifty CRT terminals will be placed at the regional offices. A taxpayer will be allowed to determine the status of his or her return or get information from the last three years' returns by calling or visiting one of the department's regional offices.

The state commissioner of taxation is concerned about data security during input and processing over and above protection against natural hazards such as fire and floods. This includes protection against the loss or damage of data during data input or processing or the improper input or processing of data. In addition, the tax commissioner and the state attorney general have discussed the general problem of data confidentiality that may arise from the nature and operation of the new system.

Both individuals want to have all potential problems identified before the system is fully developed and implemented so that the proper controls can be incorporated into the new system.

a. Describe the potential confidentiality problems that could arise in each of the following three areas of processing and recommend the corrective action or actions to solve the problem:
    (1) Data input
    (2) Processing of returns
    (3) Data inquiry
b. The State Tax Commission wants to incorporate controls to provide data security against the loss, damage, or improper input or use of data during data input and processing. Identify the potential problems (outside of such natural hazards as fire and floods) for which the Department of Taxation should develop controls, and recommend the possible controls for each problem identified. (Adapted from the CMA Examination)

9–5

Until recently, tapping a data transmission line took the skills of an agent of the Federal Bureau of Investigation or the Central Intelligence Agency—an expertise that went beyond that of even the most talented computer fraud artist. As a result, U.S. banks, which use leased data lines to transfer funds electronically, have added relatively unsophisticated techniques to make such transactions secure from wiretaps. Experience is still on their side; the only known data transmission picked off by an unlawful wiretap involved bonus bids on an oil lease intercepted on an oil company's line between Texas and Alaska.

But unless the banks act quickly to improve the security on their wire fund transfers, it may not be too long before one of them is victimized by a wiretap that could reward a diligent computer thief with millions of dollars. The cause of this changing environment is the personal computer, which may turn out to be as powerful a weapon in staging a bank fraud as a .357 Magnum revolver is in staging a bank robbery.

Breaking in. That, at least, is the message Motorola Inc. is giving to bankers in an effort to sell hardware that would encode bank wire messages and make them less susceptible to theft. In demonstrations that hush audiences, Motorola shows how a wiretap on a data line can be made with only $1,000 worth of equipment bought at any computer store: a $35 wireless microphone (adapted with a capacitor and inductor to keep the mike and the phone line from shorting each other), a $22 AM–FM radio (cassette recorder is optional for $30 more), a $200 modem (modulator-demodulator), and a $750 Model 753 printing computer terminal built by Texas Instruments Inc.

Setting up a wiretap in a bank fraud with this equipment would work as follows: First, a search is made for the bank's data circuit. This is not too difficult, since the main telephone cable runs up and down all floors of most new buildings, and a bank's data line could be tapped in the telephone room on any floor. To find the data line, the wireless mike and radio are set to the same frequency, so that anything coming over a tapped line is broadcast on the radio. The mike monitors the telephone circuits one by one, and when a circuit begins producing a high-pitched whine, the chances are good that it is the bank's data wire. That signal is then recorded on a cassette.

Back in the safety of his home, the wiretapper can replay that recording simply by connecting the radio-recorder to the modem, which converts the purloined telephone analog signals to the digital impulses, which can then be used by the TI terminal to print out a record of the bank's wire transfers.

By making an exhaustive review of these transfers, a criminal can break the code that tells the receiving bank that the message is authentic. In most cases, that code is derived by applying a formula—worked out in advance by two banks—that translates parts of the message into an authentication number. The code, for example, might include the amount of the transfer divided by 18, the date of the transfer, and a number designating the sending bank. Thus a $1.8 million transfer made on Mar. 25 by bank 102 might be coded: 100000325102.

Rerouting dollars. If a wiretapper can break the code, he can then program his personal computer to create bogus transfers of funds to his own bank account. Armed with his computer, the criminal then returns to the telephone room in the bank building, cuts into the bank's data wire, and wires up the computer and modems into the telephone circuit. At that point, he uses his computer to mix the fraudulent messages with the legitimate fund transfers that are then moving through his machine.

In Motorola's demonstrations, only a passive wiretap is made on a line connecting a printing terminal to the company's Phoenix computer center. But when a second terminal—connected to the line via the simplified computer wiretap procedure—begins printing out the very same data that are coming out of the first terminal, it almost never fails to stun observers.

"Bankers had believed that wiretaps of their data lines were very difficult and very expensive to make," says Rod O'Connor, Motorola's marketing manager for secure communications. "Our demonstration opens a lot of eyes."[1]

REQUIRED: In what ways can a bank secure its funds transfer transmissions and its data base which is updated via these fund transfers?

9–6

You have been engaged by Central Savings and Loan Association to examine its financial statements for the year ended December 31.

In January of the current year the association installed an on-line data base system. Each teller in the association's main office and seven branch offices has an on-line input/output terminal. Customers' mortgage payments and savings account deposits and withdrawals are recorded in the accounts by the computer from data input by the teller at the time of the transaction. The teller keys the proper account by account number and enters the information in the terminal keyboard to record the transaction. The accounting department at the main

[1] Reprinted from the April 20, 1981 issue of *Business Week* by special permission, ©1981 by McGraw-Hill, Inc., N.Y. 10020. All rights reserved.

office has both punched card and typewriter input/output devices. The computer is housed at the main office.

In addition to servicing its own mortgage loans, the association acts as a mortgage-servicing agency for three life insurance companies. In this latter activity the association maintains mortgage records and serves as the collection and escrow agent for the mortgagees (the insurance companies), who pay a fee to the association for these services.

REQUIRED:

a. You would expect the association to have certain application controls in effect because an on-line real-time computer system is employed. Classify these as data entry, input, processing, and output.

b. Also list the access controls you would expect Central Savings and Loan to have to protect the data base. (AICPA adapted)

9–7

The customer billing and collection functions of the Robinson Company, a small paint manufacturer, are attended to by a receptionist, an accounts receivable clerk, a general ledger clerk, and a cashier who also serves as a secretary. The company's paint products are sold to wholesalers and retail stores.

The following list describes *all* the procedures performed by the Robinson Company's employees pertaining to the customer billings and collections:

1. The mail is opened by the receptionist, who gives the customers' purchase orders to the accounts receivable clerk. Fifteen to twenty orders are received each day. Under instructions to expedite the shipment of orders, the accounts receivable clerk immediately prepares a five-copy sales invoice form which is distributed as follows:

   a. Copy 1 is the customer billing copy and is held by the accounts receivable clerk until notice of shipment is received.

   b. Copy 2 is the accounts receivable department copy and is held for ultimate posting of the accounts receivable records.

c. Copies 3 and 4 are sent to the shipping department.

d. Copy 5 is sent to the storeroom as authority for release of the goods to the shipping department.

2. After the paint ordered has been moved from the storeroom to the shipping department, the shipping department prepares the bills of lading and labels the cartons. Sales invoice copy 4 is inserted into a carton as a packing slip. After the trucker has picked up the shipment, the customer's copy of the bill of lading and copy 3, on which are noted any undershipments, are returned to the accounts receivable clerk. The trucker retains a copy of the bill of lading. The company does not "back-order" in the event of undershipments; customers are expected to reorder the merchandise. The Robinson Company's copy of the bill of lading is filed by the shipping department.

3. When copy 3 and the customer's copy of the bill of lading are received by the accounts receivable clerk, copies 1 and 2 are completed by numbering them and inserting quantities shipped, unit prices, extensions, discounts, and totals. The accounts receivable clerk then mails copy 1 and the copy of the bill of lading to the customer. Copies 2 and 3 are stapled together.

4. The individual accounts receivable ledger cards are posted by the accounts receivable clerk by a bookkeeping machine procedure whereby the sales register is prepared as a carbon copy of the postings. Postings are made from copy 2 which is then filed, along with staple-attached copy 3, in numerical order. Monthly the general ledger clerk summarizes the sales register for posting to the general ledger.

5. Since the Robinson Company is short of cash, the deposit of receipts is also expedited. The receptionist turns over all mail receipts and related correspondence to the accounts receivable clerk, who examines the checks and determines that the accompanying vouchers or correspondence contains enough detail to permit posting of the accounts. The accounts receivable clerk then endorses the checks and gives them to the cashier, who prepares the daily deposit. No currency is received in the mail and no paint is sold over the counter at the factory.

6. The accounts receivable clerk uses the vouchers or correspondence that accompanied the checks to post the accounts receivable ledger cards. The bookkeeping machine prepares a cash receipts register as a carbon copy of the postings. Monthly the general ledger clerk summarizes the cash receipts registers for posting to the general ledger accounts. The accounts receivable clerk also corresponds with customers about unauthorized deductions for discounts, freight or advertising allowances, returns, and so forth, and prepares the appropriate credit memos. Disputed items of large amount are turned over to the sales manager for settlement. Each month the accounts receivable clerk prepares a trial balance of the open accounts receivable and compares the resultant total with the general ledger control account for accounts receivable.

REQUIRED:

a. Flowchart the customer billing and collection system for Robinson Company. Use a document systems flowchart.

b. Discuss the internal control weaknesses in the procedures related to customer billings and remittances and the accounting for these transactions. In your discussion, in addition to identifying the weaknesses, explain what could happen as a result of each weakness. (AICPA adapted)

9-8

The accounting and internal control procedures relating to purchases of materials by the Branden Company, a medium-sized concern manufacturing special machinery to order, have been described by your junior accountant in the following terms:

After approval by manufacturing department foremen, material purchase requisitions are forwarded to the purchasing department supervisor, who distributes such requisitions to the several employees under his control. The latter employees prepare prenumbered purchase orders in triplicate, account for all numbers, and send the original purchase order to the vendor. One copy of the purchase order is sent to the receiving department where it is used as a receiving report. The other copy is filed in the purchasing department.

When the materials are received, they are moved directly to the storeroom and issued to the foreman on informal requests. The receiving department sends a receiving report (with its copy of the purchase order attached) to the purchasing department and sends copies of the receiving report to the storeroom and to the accounting department.

Vendors' invoices for material purchases, received in duplicate in the mail room, are sent to the purchasing department and directed to the employee who placed the related order. The employee then compares the invoice with the copy of the purchase order on file in the purchasing department for price and terms and compares the invoice quantity with the quantity received as reported by the shipping and receiving department on its copy of the purchase order. The purchasing department employee also checks discounts, footings, and extensions and then initials the invoice to indicate approval for payment. The invoice is then sent to the voucher section of the accounting department, where it is coded for account distribution, assigned a voucher number, entered in the voucher register, and filed according to payment due date.

On payment dates prenumbered checks are requisitioned by the voucher section from the cashier and prepared except for signature. After the checks have been prepared they are returned to the cashier, who puts them through a check-signing machine, accounts for the sequence of numbers, and passes them to the cash disbursements bookkeeper for entry in the cash disbursements book. The cash disbursements bookkeeper then returns the checks to the voucher section, which then notes payment dates in the voucher register, places the checks in envelopes, and sends them to the mail room. The vouchers are then filed in numerical sequence. At the end of each month one of the voucher clerks prepares an adding machine tape of unpaid items in the voucher register and compares the total thereof with the general ledger balance and investigates any difference disclosed by such comparison.

REQUIRED: Discuss the weaknesses, if any, in the internal control of Branden's purchasing and subsequent procedures and suggest supplementary or revised procedures for remedying each weakness with regard to

a. Requisition of materials
b. Receipt and storage of materials
c. Functions of the purchasing department
d. Functions of the accounting department (AICPA adapted)

9–9

In connection with his examination of the financial statements of the Olympia Manufacturing Company, a CPA is reviewing procedures for accumulating direct-labor hours. He learns that all production is by job order and that all employees are paid hourly wages, with time-and-one-half for overtime hours.

Olympia's direct-labor-hour input process for payroll and job-cost determination is summarized in the flowchart shown in Figure C9–9.

Steps A and C are performed in timekeeping, step B in the factory operating departments, step D in payroll audit and control, step E in data preparation (keypunch), and step F in computer operations.

REQUIRED: For each input process step (A through F):

a. List the possible errors or discrepancies that may occur.
b. Cite the corresponding control procedure that should be in effect for each error or discrepancy.

Note: Your discussion of Olympia's procedures should be limited to the input process or direct-labor hours, as shown in steps A through F in the flowchart. Do not discuss personnel procedures for hiring, promotion, termination, and pay rate authorization. In step F do not discuss equipment, computer program, and general computer operational controls.

Organize your answer for each input-processing step as follows:

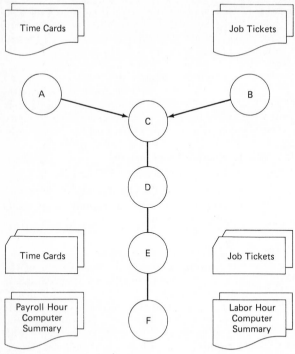

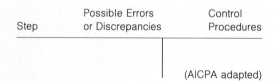

Figure C9-9 Olympia Manufacturing Direct Labor Input Process

Step	Possible Errors or Discrepancies	Control Procedures

(AICPA adapted)

9-10

Roger Peters, CPA, has examined the financial statements of the Solt Manufacturing Company for several years and is making preliminary plans for the audit of the year ended June 30. During this examination, Mr. Peters plans to use a set of generalized computer audit programs. Solt's EDP manager has agreed to prepare special tapes of data from company records for the CPA's use with the generalized programs.

The following information is applicable to Mr. Peters' examination of Solt's accounts payable and related procedures:

1. The formats of pertinent tapes are shown in Figure C9–10.
2. The following monthly runs are prepared:
   a. Cash disbursements by check number

b. Outstanding payables
c. Purchase journals arranged (1) by account charged and (2) by vendor

3. Vouchers and supporting invoices, receiving reports, and purchase order copies are filed by vendor code. Purchase orders and checks are filed numerically.
4. Company records are maintained on magnetic tapes. All tapes are stored in a restricted area within the computer room. A grandfather-father-son policy is followed for retaining and safeguarding tape files.

REQUIRED:

a. Explain the grandfather-father-son policy. Describe how files can be reconstructed when this policy is used.
b. Discuss whether company policies for retaining and safeguarding the tape files provide adequate protection against losses of data.
c. Describe how the CPA could use a generalized computer audit program to audit Solt's accounts payable system. (AICPA adapted)

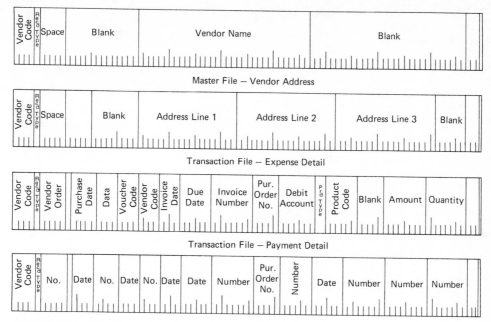

Figure C9–10 Tape Format for Audit of Solt Manufacturing Company
(AICPA adapted)

9–11

Peterson Electronics has just computerized its old manual accounting system. The management thought it was about time and acted quickly and decisively when the salesperson for Matrix Systems called and described the features of Matrix Systems' new material requirements planning system. This was just what Peterson thought it needed to get control of its inventory and production system, which had become unmanageable. It implemented the system cold because the old system was so bad that comparisons were meaningless.

REQUIRED: As Peterson's auditor, how much faith can you put in the inventory data generated by this material requirements planning system? Why? What *general* control steps are not indicated above?

9–12

Boos & Baumkirchner, Inc., is a medium-sized manufacturer of products for the leisure-time-activities market. The company has been quite successful and operates three shifts, twenty-four hours, seven days a week. During the past year a computer system was installed, and inventory records of finished goods and parts were converted to computer processing. Each record of the inventory master file, which is stored on a magnetic disk, contains the following information:

Item or part number
Description
Size
Unit-of-measure code
Quantity on hand
Cost per unit
Total cost of inventory on hand
Date of last sale or usage
Quantity used or sold this year
Economic order quantity
Vendor code

In preparation for the year-end physical inventory, the client prepares two identical sets of preprinted and prepunched inventory-count cards. One set is for the inventory counts, and the other is to be used by the CPA in test counts. The following information has been keypunched into the cards and interpreted on their face.

In taking the year-end inventory, the firm's personnel will write the actual counted quantity on the face of each card. When all counts are complete, the counted quantity will be keypunched into the cards. The cards will be processed against the random access disk file, and quantity-on-hand figures will be adjusted to reflect the actual count. A computer listing will be prepared to show missing inventory-count cards and all quantity adjustments of more than $100 in value. These items will be investigated, and all required adjustments will be made. When adjustments have been completed, the final year-end balances will be computed and posted to the general ledger.

The CPA has available a general purpose audit software package that will run on the client's computer and can process random access files.

REQUIRED:

a. Describe how the auditor can make effective use of generalized audit software in this case.
b. Is there a need for concurrent audit procedures for this client? What techniques seem to be applicable to the audit of inventory in this case? (AICPA adapted)

9-13

Cash register sales in the Super Bird food chain stores are recorded as follows: Sales are entered by keying into an intelligent terminal the dollar amount of each item and the category (meat, produce, canned goods, etc.). The tax and total are calculated and a receipt is given to each customer, and correct change is issued. A cassette tape is generated to record transactions, and when the register is cleared, totals are keyed in and recorded on the tape. Tape from each register is transmitted that night over telephone lines to the regional office for its reporting and information needs. Super Bird uses a minicomputer data base system at each regional office to service each region's network of states.

REQUIRED:

a. Flowchart the system.
b. Describe several control policies and procedures that should be incorporated to ensure accurate data input. Indicate the purpose of each.
c. Describe several control procedures that should be incorporated into the transmission of the data and the integrity of the data base.

9-14

The Y Company, a client of your firm, has come to you with the following problem. It has three clerical employees who must perform the following functions:

1. Maintain general ledger
2. Maintain accounts payable ledger
3. Maintain accounts receivable ledger
4. Prepare checks for signature
5. Maintain disbursements journal
6. Issue credits on returns and allowances
7. Reconcile the bank account
8. Handle and deposit cash receipts

Assuming that there is no problem as to the ability of any of the employees, the company requests that you assign the above functions to the three employees in such a manner as to achieve the highest degree of internal control. It may be assumed that these employees will perform no other accounting functions than the ones listed and that any accounting functions not listed will be performed by persons other than these three employees.

REQUIRED: State how you would distribute the above functions among the three employees. Assume that, with the exception of the nominal jobs of the bank reconciliation and the issuance of credits on returns and allowances, all functions require an equal amount of time. (AICPA adapted)

9-15

Design and development progress in computer-based management information systems has been impressive in the past two decades. Traditionally, computer-based data processing systems were arranged by departments and applications. Computers were applied to single, large-volume applications such as inventory control or customer billing. Large files were built for each application.

As more applications were added, problems in data management developed. Many files contained redundant data. Businesses looked for ways to integrate the data processing systems to support management needs for decision making and on-line inquiry. As a consequence, the data base system composed of the data base itself, the data base management systems, and the individual application programs were developed. Moreover, distributed processing systems have been developed where managers can interact with their own data base or the corporate data base via communication lines.

REQUIRED:

a. Identify special control features a company should consider incorporating into its data base system.
b. Identify special control features a company should consider to prevent access to its telecommunications. (Adapted from the CMA Examination)

9–16

Oxford Pharmaceutical Company has the following system for billing and recording accounts receivable:

1. An incoming customer's purchase order is received in the order department by a clerk who prepares a prenumbered company sales order form in which is inserted the pertinent information, such as the customer's name and address, customer's account number, and quantity and items ordered. After the sales order form has been prepared, the customer's purchase order is stapled to it.
2. The sales order form is then passed to the credit department for credit approval. Rough approximations of the billing values of the orders are made in the credit department for those accounts on which credit limitations are imposed. After investigation, approval of credit is noted on the form.

3. Next the sales order form is passed to the billing department where a clerk keys in the customer's invoice on a microcomputer system. The computer cross-multiplies the number of items and the unit price, and it then adds this automatically extended amount for each line to obtain the total amount of the invoice. The unit prices for the items are stored in the computer on a diskette and do not need to be keyed in unless they change. All information is posted to an accounts receivable file during a daily computer run, and transaction lists are provided for the sales department.

The computer program automatically accumulates daily batch totals of customer account numbers and invoice amounts. After the sales orders have been processed by the computer, they are placed in files and held for about two years. The following copies of the invoice are printed on prenumbered forms during the daily billing run:

a. "Customer's copy"
b. "Shipping department copy," which serves as a shipping order

4. The shipping department copy of the invoice and the bills of lading generated by another computer run are then sent to the shipping department. After the order has been shipped, copies of the bill of lading are returned to the billing department. The shipping department copy of the invoice is filed in the shipping department.
5. In the billing department a copy of the bill of lading is attached to the customer's copy of the invoice and both are mailed to the customer. The other copy of the bill of lading, together with the sales order form, is then stapled to the invoice file copy and filed in invoice numerical order.
6. The microcomputer system uses this sales input for preparation of the sales journal, subsidiary ledger, and perpetual inventory records. Invoice information may be referenced by management at any time from the micro computer system using the invoice and number.

REQUIRED:

a. Flowchart the billing system as a means of understanding the system.

b. List the internal controls that should be present over sales data input. (AICPA adapted)

9–17

Until recently, Consolidated Electricity Company employed a batch processing system for recording the receipt of customer payments. The narrative is given in Case 7–9 in Chapter 7, and Figure C 7–9 describes the procedures involved in the batch processing system.

REQUIRED:

a. Using the symbols provided in Chapter 7, prepare a systems flowchart of Consolidated Electricity Company's new on-line cash receipt procedures.

b. Have the new cash receipt procedures as designed and implemented by Consolidated Electricity Company created any internal and systems control problems for the company? Explain your answer. (Adapted from the CMA Examination)

9–18

The following multiple-choice questions have been adapted from questions on CPA and CMA exams. Select the best answer.

A. Sample CPA Exam Questions
 1. Some electronic data processing accounting control procedures relate to all electronic data processing activities (general controls) and some relate to specific tasks (application controls). General controls include
    a. Controls designed to ascertain that all data submitted to electronic data processing for processing have been properly authorized
    b. Controls that relate to the correction and resubmission of data that were initially incorrect
    c. Controls for documenting and approving programs and changes to programs
    d. Controls designed to assure the accuracy of the processing results
 2. Parity checks, read-and-write checks, and duplicate circuitry are electronic data processing controls that are designed to detect
    a. Erroneous internal handling of data
    b. Lack of sufficient documentation for computer processes
    c. Illogical programming commands
    d. Illogical uses of hardware
 3. Program controls, in an electronic data processing system, are used as substitutes for human controls in a manual system. Which of the following is an example of a program control?
    a. Dual read
    b. Echo check
    c. Validity check
    d. Limit and reasonableness test
 4. Where computers are used, the effectiveness of internal accounting control depends, in part, upon whether the organizational structure includes any incompatible combinations. Such a combination would exist when there is no separation of the duties between
    a. Documentation librarian and manager of programming
    b. Programmer and console operator
    c. Systems analyst and programmer
    d. Processing control clerk and key-punch supervisor
 5. The primary purpose of a generalized computer audit program is to allow the auditor to
    a. Use the client's employees to perform routine audit checks of the electronic data processing records that otherwise would be done by the auditor's staff accountants
    b. Test the logic of computer programs used in the client's electronic data processing systems
    c. Select larger samples from the client's electronic data processing records than would otherwise be selected without the generalized program.
    d. Independently process client electronic data processing records
 6. In an electronic data processing system, automated equipment controls or hardware controls are designed to
    a. Arrange data in a logical sequen-

tial manner for processing purposes

b. Correct errors in the computer programs

c. Monitor and detect errors in source documents

d. Detect and control errors arising from use of equipment

7. In its electronic data processing system a company might use self-checking numbers (check digits) to enable detection of which of the following errors?

a. Assigning a valid identification code to the wrong customer

b. Recording an invalid customer's identification charge account number

c. Losing data between processing functions

d. Processing data arranged in the wrong sequence

8. A customer inadvertently ordered part number 12368 rather than part number 12638. In processing this order, the error would be detected by the vendor with which of the following controls?

a. Batch total

b. Key verifying

c. Self-checking digit

d. An internal consistency check

9. Which of the following is an example of application controls in electronic data processing systems?

a. Input controls

b. Hardware controls

c. Documentation procedures

d. Controls over access to equipment and data files

10. The grandfather-father-son approach to providing protection for important computer files is a concept that is most often found in

a. On-line, real-time systems

b. Punched-card systems

c. Magnetic tape systems

d. Magnetic drum systems

B. Sample CMA Exam Questions

1. The data control group of Burch Company has determined upon investigation that a large portion of the errors in processing payroll result from incorrectly recorded employee numbers. What method of control should Burch Co. install to reduce the chance of error?

a. Sequence check

b. Reasonableness test

c. Check digit verification

d. File protection ring

e. Batch total

2. The management of Kusbar Co. has reason to suspect that someone is tampering with pay rates by entering changes through the company's remote terminals located in the factory. The method Kasbar Co. should implement to protect the system from these unauthorized alterations to the system's files is

a. Batch totals

b. Checkpoint recovery

c. Passwords

d. Record counts

e. Parity checks

3. A source document with an invalid number of hours worked for one week, i.e., 93 hours instead of 39, would be best detected by

a. Key punching controls

b. A limit test in an edit run

c. Hash total of hours worked

d. Record count total

e. Key verifying control

4. A transaction involving a charge to a nonexistent customer account was entered into an accounts receivable and billing system that was batch processed. This error should be detected by the computer system and appear in

a. The sort run error printout

b. The edit run error printout

c. The customer statements printout

d. The master file update run error printout

e. Some error printout other than those mentioned above

5. A company's computer facilities and computer room conceivably could be destroyed completely by fire. The most appropriate action a company could take in an attempt to prepare for and protect itself from such a disaster as this would be

a. To have backup computer facilities at the same site
b. To have off-site backup computer facilities
c. To have a reconstruction and recovery plan which outlines the procedures for reconstruction of files and use of alternate facilities
d. To have a contractual agreement with the manufacturer or another company to use its facilities
e. To have the grandfather-father-son concept implemented for all files stored on magnetic tapes

6. Transactions which were erroneous and had been previously rejected by the computer system apparently were not being reentered and reprocessed once they had been corrected. This erroneous condition is best controlled by
a. Comparing a record count of transactions input into the system
b. A comparison of the batch controls totals
c. Scanning the error control log
d. Scanning the console log
e. Desk checking

7. An operator inadvertently has mounted the wrong master tape file. Which one of the following controls is most likely to detect such an error?
a. Password control procedures
b. Header label control procedures
c. Library control procedures
d. Trailer label control procedures
e. Control procedures of the input/output control group

8. In an on-line real-time system which of the following would be most likely to be used as backup for an application's master file maintained on magnetic disk?
a. At specified periods the disk files would be dumped to (copied on) magnetic tape along with the period's transactions
b. A duplicate disk file would be maintained and all activity would be copied on magnetic tape continuously
c. The grandfather-father-son technique would be employed to retain disk files

d. All source documents for transactions would be retained
e. The disk files would be copied to magnetic tape continuously

9. Jonkers, Inc., a large retail chain, is installing a computerized accounts receivable system employing a batch mode of processing with sequential files. The program which will process receipts on account should include an input edit routine to assure
a. Proper sequencing of data
b. Header and trailer label accuracy
c. The amount received is recorded correctly
d. The existence of control totals
e. Proper operator intervention

10. The internal auditors of the Zebra Company have expressed concern that the new computerized purchase order system does not permit them to trace through the system from the source document to the final report. The item about which the auditors have expressed concern is the nonexistence of
a. Test data
b. Operations manuals
c. System flowcharts
d. Internal file labels
e. Audit trails

9–19

Your firm has been retained by Mr. E. H. Green to perform an audit of his financial statements. Mr. Green, who devotes his full time and attention to it, operates a small retail hardware store with an annual gross income of about $200,000. In addition to the owner, the personnel consist of two salespersons and the owner's assistant who is the bookkeeper.

Because this is your first audit of this client and because the client is so small, your firm is very concerned that the review of internal control be a most careful one. Therefore you must (1) flowchart each system, (2) describe any internal weaknesses you find, and (3) recommend any improvement you deem necessary.

A member of your firm has interviewed Mr. Green regarding the procedures used. The interview notes are given below. You are to assume that gaps in the notes indicate the lack of a formal system and procedures for that particular activity.

CASH RECEIPTS (Cash Sales and A/R Payments) The store has two cash registers. Every cash sale, credit sale, and accounts receivable payment is recorded in the cash register by the owner, bookkeeper, or salespersons. Payments are usually made at the store, not by mail. Each cash register is prominently and conveniently located for best protection and customer service.

The bookkeeper or the owner approves each payment on account, and each payment on account is posted by the owner, bookkeeper, or salespersons to an accounts receivable ledger, which consists of a card file of customer accounts.

At the end of each day the cash registers are cleared by the bookkeeper. Credit and cash sales totals from the registers are posted to the sales journal daily by the bookkeeper. The bookkeeper then compares the total from the cash register with the adding machine tape of cash and checks in the drawers; the tape is then destroyed. The bookkeeper then prepares the deposit. The owner makes the deposit daily. The bookkeeper reconciles the bank statement.

CREDIT SALES Either the bookkeeper or the owner approves and records all credit sales and payments.

At the time of sale, prenumbered sales invoices are posted directly to the customer's account by the owner, bookkeeper, or a salesperson. The sale is recorded in the register. The bookkeeper posts to the sales journal from a cash register total daily.

At the end of each month, the bookkeeper prepares a proof tape of credit sales invoices for comparison with the sales journal. The bookkeeper also prepares an aged accounts schedule for past-due accounts in the card file of customer accounts. The proof tape is destroyed.

PURCHASING AND RECEIPT OF MERCHANDISE Most merchandise is ordered by the owner. Any merchandise ordered by the sales personnel is approved by the owner in advance. All orders are prepared on prenumbered purchase order forms by the bookkeeper in triplicate and signed by the owner. Two orders are filed, to be used by the bookkeeper when the merchandise arrives. The third purchase order is sent to the vendor.

When the merchandise is received, it is checked in by one of the sales personnel with the help of the bookkeeper. Then the receiving report is written up in duplicate. The original receiving report is checked against a copy of the purchase order by the bookkeeper and filed with the vendor's invoice and the purchase order. The extra copies of the purchase order and receiving report are destroyed.

DISBURSEMENTS FOR PURCHASE The bookkeeper verifies all quantities, prices, terms, extensions, and footings on the invoice before posting to a remittance form. Often the remittance form supplied by the vendor is used. The bookkeeper determines that the amount being paid is consistent with the merchandise ordered and received from a comparison with purchase orders and receiving report.

After verification of the invoice, the bookkeeper makes out the check. The vendor's invoice and remittance form are attached to the check. The owner then signs the check.

10
SYSTEM DESIGN CONCEPTS: Analysis and Definition of the System

SYSTEMS ANALYSIS

As a resource, information should be used effectively to help management achieve the firm's objectives. This can be accomplished by designing an information system that supports the management decision-making, reporting, and transaction processing systems of the organization. Design of an information system, however, is not a simple task; management should have a master plan for system design. We can begin the design process by using Anthony's management function criteria and by carefully assessing where the information system ends and the decision-making system it supports begins.[1] It is also necessary to recognize that a well-designed information system requires careful planning, organizing, staffing, coordinating, directing, and controlling of all the elements that will be integrated to form the system, including personnel, hardware, software, and procedures.

Designing an information system involves much more than physical design aspects and requires steps other than those just noted. The system design process is traditionally divided into two segments: *systems analysis and definition*

[1] See R. N. Anthony, *Planning and Control System: A Framework for Analysis* (Boston: Harvard University School of Business Administration, 1965).

and *system design and implementation (synthesis)*. The American Institute of Certified Public Accountants, in its *Guidelines for Development and Implementation of Computer-Based Application Systems*,[2] includes two phases in the systems analysis and definition segment: (1) Requirements Definition and Alternative Approaches, and (2) General Systems Design, as shown in Figure 10–1. Systems design and implementation is the process of actually creating the new system or redesigning the existing system. In each case design and implementation builds from the systems analysis and definition. Systems design and implementation should not be confused with the collective use of the term *systems design*. Many authors use the term *systems design* to refer to both *analysis* and *design* of an information

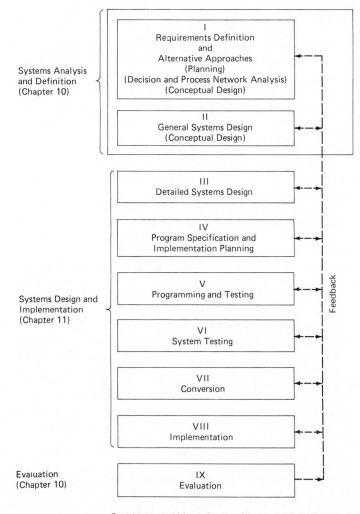

Systems Analysis and Definition (Chapter 10)

I
Requirements Definition and Alternative Approaches (Planning)
(Decision and Process Network Analysis)
(Conceptual Design)

II
General Systems Design
(Conceptual Design)

Systems Design and Implementation (Chapter 11)

III
Detailed Systems Design

IV
Program Specification and Implementation Planning

V
Programming and Testing

VI
System Testing

VII
Conversion

VIII
Implementation

Evaluation (Chapter 10)

IX
Evaluation

Feedback

Figure 10–1 Information System Development and Implementation Life Cycle

(Adapted with permission from the AICPA *Guidelines for System Development and Implementation.* © 1976, AICPA.)

[2] AICPA, *Guidelines for Development and Implementation of Company-Based Application Systems*, Management Advisory Services Guideline Service No. 4 (New York: American Institute of Certified Public Accountants, copyright © 1976).

system. These are the two segments of the overall design process. In this chapter the procedures and steps for systems analysis and definition will be developed.

SYSTEMS ANALYSIS AND THE LIFE CYCLE FRAMEWORK[3]

In Chapter 2 the analysis, definition, design, and implementation of an information system were described in terms of a life cycle framework. The framework is divided into nine phases. Phase I, Requirements Definition and Alternative Approaches, and Phase II, General Systems Design, can be viewed collectively as systems analysis and definition. Often a combination of these two phases is referred to as a *feasibility study*. Phases I, II, and IX are the areas on which we will focus in this chapter. Phase IX is Evaluation. The remaining phases of the framework can be viewed collectively as systems design and implementation and will be examined in Chapter 11.

Systems analysis is primarily concerned with *defining* the system that already exists or should exist within the firm. This is true regardless of whether the system is manual or a sophisticated on-line data base system. As suggested by the AICPA guidelines, several possible alternatives may be conceived at this juncture in the life cycle. Within this framework, some authors use the term *systems definition* or *definition phase* to designate the activities associated with systems analysis. In this chapter we will use the term *systems definition* interchangeably with *systems analysis* to refer to the activities included in the first two phases of the life cycle framework (Figure 10–1). Some authors limit analysis and definition to the analysis of the existing system; we take a broader perspective and apply the concepts of analysis to proposed new systems as well. This means that the analyst can and perhaps should view systems analysis from a fresh perspective without being tied to past processing and decision-making procedures.

The need for systems analysis has been widely accepted as an integral part of systems design and development. However, there is continuing debate regarding the approach or procedures with which the activities of systems analysis are conducted. One approach is the *bottom-up*, or *data analysis* approach— i.e., systems activities are defined by beginning with transaction data and summing upward through the organization. This approach also suggests that the analysis and definition procedures start with the analysis of the existing decision-making, reporting, and transaction processing system. Another approach is the *top-down*, or *decision analysis*, approach to systems definition, where information needs associated with the various levels of decision making are the starting point in defining a new or modified system. Using this decision analysis philos-

---

[3] The life cycle framework used in this chapter is adapted with permission from AICPA, *Guidelines for Development and Implementation of Computer-Based Application Systems.* Phase I, II, and IX are discussed in this chapter. Phases III through VIII are discussed in the next chapter. Copyright © (1976) by the American Institute of Certified Public Accountants, Inc. The discussion is supplemented extensively with permission from Charles L. Biggs, Evan G. Birks, and William Atkins, *Managing the System Development Process* (Englewood Cliffs, N.J.: Touche Ross & Co. and Prentice-Hall, (1980).

ophy, the accountant or systems designer does not start with the existing system and its related data and information flows; he or she begins with an analysis of the decisions needed to control the various activities of the organization and their related reporting and transaction requirements.

The approach presented in this chapter will show that *data analysis* can be an integral part of the *decision analysis* approach. Figure 10–1, the life cycle framework, can be used to describe both approaches, and the term *integrated systems analysis* will be used to describe the combination of the two approaches. The specific approach involved will be shown to be a function of the management activity under review and the level of support the information system gives to the management (decision-making) system. We will use the term *decision-making system* interchangeably with *management system* for emphasis on that aspect of the management process in this chapter.

SYSTEMS BOUNDARIES

Before beginning our review of systems analysis, the *boundaries* of the system or subsystem under review must be defined. The boundaries of the firm's information system, the management (decision-making) system, and the environment must be specified. The boundaries between the environment and the information and decision systems were discussed in Chapters 2 and 4; we will focus on information system boundaries in this chapter.

Since the object of systems design should be to structure a well-planned, coordinated system, attention must be given to the procedures for *factoring* the firm's system into manageable modules or subsystems. If each subsystem, its associated boundaries, and the resulting interfaces are not identified and clearly defined, coordination of the resulting subsystems will be difficult. Figure 10–2, for example, shows that sales will interface with all other subsystems of the firm. As can be seen in the figure, the number of interfaces in-

Figure 10–2 Subsystem Coordination

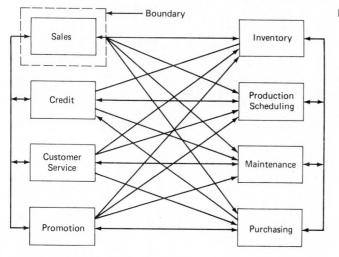

creases geometrically with the number of subsystems. Design problems can quickly become unmanageable.

The system shown in Figure 10–2 is said to be tightly *coupled*. It requires precise coordination for all factors or components to operate efficiently. The system can be simplified, however, by *clustering* the marketing subsystems and the production subsystems, as illustrated in Figure 10–3. Close coordination can be maintained within each cluster, but not between a subsystem of one cluster and that of another cluster. There will be *one* interface between clusters. Clustering, therefore, results in *decoupling*. Sales, for example, will no longer be tightly coordinated with inventory; sales will be loosely coordinated with production activities via the marketing-production cluster interface.

In the process of defining a system and in the detailed design phase, the cost of tight coordination should be compared with the cost of the resources necessary to decouple subsystems. This comparison should be made before selecting the final design framework for the proposed system. The cost comparison must, however, also consider the cost of communication hardware and software. As we noted in Chapter 2, the firm's accounting system can be used as the focal point for each cluster interface. Therefore either the planning and budgeting system or the transaction processing system, with its various reports and files, can serve as a reasonable structure upon which to build an interface between organizational units. Profitability and responsibility accounting systems with their accompanying data organization structures also can serve as a basis for clustering various functions within the organization.

Regardless of the philosophical approach to systems analysis and definition used by the firm, the system will need to be factored into subsystems so that the scope of the analysis and design process will be manageable. Each subsystem must be clearly defined. The systems analysis and design activities must further describe the boundaries as well as the specification of requirements, decoupling resources, and interfaces with all subsystems.

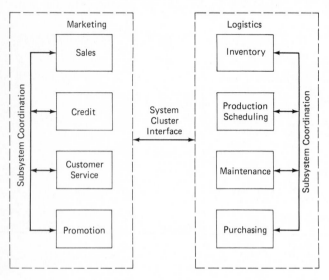

Figure 10–3 System Cluster Interface and Subsystem Coordination

SYSTEMS DEFINITION: DECISION
ANALYSIS APPROACH

The basic precept of the decision analysis, or top-down, approach to systems analysis is that an information system should provide management with relevant information for making decisions and for the various reporting requirements set forth by agencies such as the Securities and Exchange Commission, Interstate Commerce Commission, Internal Revenue Service, and Public Service Commission and by investors. This is a lofty goal which requires careful planning and analysis.

Ackoff suggests that this goal can be accomplished using the following procedure:[4]

1. Analysis of the Decision Systems—"Each (or at least each important) type of managerial decision required by the organization under study should be identified and the relationships between them should be determined and flow charted."

2. Analysis of Information Requirements—"Decisions for which models can or cannot be constructed to support the decisions, need to be analyzed and the type of system (as detailed in Chapter 4) with its related requirements needs to be determined."

3. Aggregation of Decisions—"Decisions with the same or largely overlapping informational requirements should be grouped together as a single manager's task. This will reduce the information a manager requires to do his job and is likely to increase his understanding of it."

4. Design of Information Processing—"Now the procedure for collecting, storing, retrieving and treating information can be designed."

5. Design of the Control System—". . . it is necessary to identify the ways in which it [systems] may be deficient, to design procedures for detecting its deficiencies, and for correcting the system so as to remove or reduce them."

The focus of the decision analysis philosophy must therefore be on the decision-making and transaction processing networks of the firm. Special emphasis must be given to those decisions that are critical to the firm's success. Eventually all system expenditures will be justified by management's needs.

It should be pointed out that Phases I and II can be used, given a bottom-up philosophy; the difference is in the relative emphasis of certain key steps. Figures 10–4, 10–6, and 10–7 outline suggested Phase I and Phase II tasks for the two analysis and design approaches.

Steering Committee

There must be a master plan for any systems analysis and definition. To develop a master plan, management must participate in, understand, and render full support to the decision analysis approach. Chapters 3 and 4 empha-

[4] Russel L. Ackoff, "Management Misinformation Systems," *Management Science*, 14, No. 4 (December 1967), B147–56.

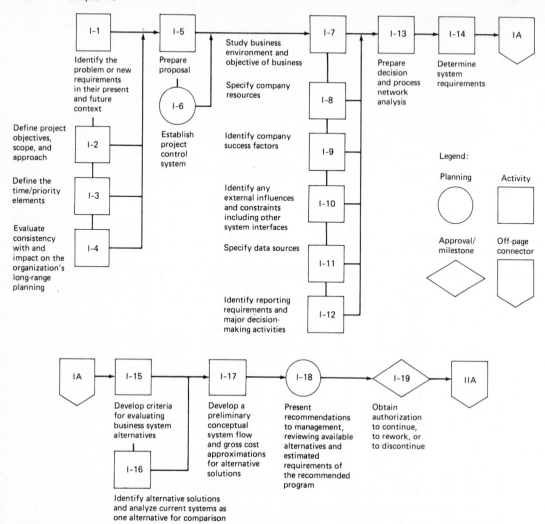

Figure 10-4 Phase I—Requirements Definition and Alternative Approaches

(Adapted with permission from AICPA, *Guidelines for Development and Implementation of Computer-Based Application Systems*, ©1976, AICPA)

sized the need for this cooperation. Typically this is done by a top-level steering committee which guides the planning, development, and implementation of systems. Members of this committee should include top management and other managers with relevant experience, as outlined in Chapter 3. Moreover, the members must have (1) knowledge of strategic, managerial, and operational plans to assess the project's compliance with these plans, (2) objectivity in assessing corporate priorities, and (3) considerable experience. [5]

[5] Biggs, Birks, and Atkins, *Managing the Systems Development Process*, p. 51.

Requirements Definition
and Alternative Approaches

First the analyst or a project team and the steering committee must lay a foundation for the systems analysis and definition phases. The project team generally consists of the decision makers or their representatives who are involved, technical system personnel, and a liaison with the steering committee which in turn represents top management. The AICPA suggests steps I–1 through I–6, concluding with a project proposal. Paralleling the AICPA suggested guidelines, the project team or analyst must first identify the current problem or future requirements of the organization. Frequently this information is set forth in a letter from a manager who needs the new or revised system. In addition, the need for a revision or modification may come from a periodic operational review of the system such as the one described later in this chapter.

As an important part of this initial step the project team, systems analyst, or even the controller—if this is the controller's area of responsibility—must do some fact finding to follow up on the expressed need for modification or revision of the system. Interviews must be conducted with top and middle managers who initiated the request and who will be affected by any change. The fact-finding interviews should clarify the problems, the information needs, the organizational units affected, the current procedures used to provide the information, and the relationship between the proposed project and the long-range goals of the organization. Top management, generally through the steering committee, must be informed of the scope, objectives, benefits, and general nature and cost of the project. Particular attention must be given to the boundaries of the system and the interfaces with other systems. Deadlines and priorities should be detailed with respect to completion of various phases of the project. Techniques such as PERT may be useful for scheduling. Moreover, the project's objectives need to be reconciled with the long-range objectives of the organization. Often the steering committee must help with the reconciliation.

Concluding this set of steps, a project proposal is prepared by the project team or analyst or in some instances by a CPA firm if it has been engaged to perform the systems analysis. Concurrently with the proposal, and before any study commences, project controls—such as projected times, project task analysis, personnel assignment and work load analysis, and project status reports—must also be formalized to help manage the system development project. These plans will be useful for checking compliance with design schedules, assessing staff requirements, and determining project check points, which evolve as development progresses.

The next sequence of steps leading to a determination of system requirements will differ depending on the philosophy adopted by the organization and its steering committee, the project team, the analyst, the controller, or in some cases the CPA firm. The original steps suggested by the AICPA are more appropriate for a *data analysis approach* to systems analysis and definition (we will elaborate on this point later). To employ a decision analysis approach, steps I–7 through I–13 as shown in Figure 10–4 should be followed. Some of these new steps can be characterized as planning; others can be characterized as decision and process network analysis activities.

Assuming management adopts the decision analysis approach, the project team, analyst, or accountant must acquire a complete understanding of not only the firm's objectives, policies, and resources but also the nature of the business in which the firm is operating. Environmental questions such as the following should be examined to assess the critical decisions, reports, and transaction flows:

1. What are the organization's structural, behavioral, and decision-making characteristics?
2. What are the firm's objectives?
3. Who are the customers and how can they be characterized demographically?
4. What are the products and how are they distributed with regard to sales and types of customers?
5. What are the firm's market characteristics, such as competition and price elasticity?
6. What is the demand forecast?
7. What are the firm's resources, such as capital, goods, personnel, customer goodwill, research capabilities, reputation, and financial management?
8. How are these resources being used and allocated?
9. What are management's policies?
10. What is the firm's interface with government and regulatory agencies?
11. What factors are key to success, given the nature of the firm and the business environment?

DECISION AND PROCESS NETWORK ANALYSIS   The next stage of the decision analysis approach requires an analysis of the management decision-making activities and the reporting requirements of the firm as suggested by Ackoff earlier in the chapter. To accomplish this, decision-making activities or nodes must be identified, information requirements for the activities must be specified, and the characteristics of each type of information must be spelled out. Sometimes a brief overview (not an analysis) of the existing system will aid in a general understanding of the decision process at this point.

Inputs such as documents, records, files, and data, as well as characteristics such as volume, media, origin, and location of this input, should be identified. In addition, in steps I–11, I–12, and I–13 in Figure 10–4 and eventually in step I–14, input such as the following (which relate to the Decision and Process Network Analysis and the Conceptual Design) must be obtained:

1. Major decision-making activities
2. Information requirements for these decisions
3. Information generated by decisions
4. Other reporting requirements
5. Transaction records necessary to support

      both information and reporting requirements
6. Sensitivity analysis of information requirements
7. Aggregation requirements
8. Timing requirements
9. Economic analysis
10. Model specifications
11. Data source specifications

    From an analysis of these requirements, a minimum set of objectives for the proposed or modified system also should be developed to provide a baseline. All alternatives must meet these minimum requirements.

    For a better understanding of these activities, consider the production scheduling decision network in Figure 10–5. The specified decision nodes denoted as processing steps in the systems flowchart are (1) the production schedule for the plant (what should be manufactured on which machine at what time and in what sequence), (2) quantities to be manufactured of a particular product, (3) the best assembly or production sequence method of manufacturing for each product, (4) materials requirements quantities and schedules, and (5) the completion date for shipping.

    The information set for the production scheduling decision will include, in this illustration, information from other decision nodes: assembly sequence, optimal run size, completion date, and material availability. Statistics relating to manpower and other jobs-in-process are also a necessary part of the required information set. Some of the needed information will be available in the present system on tape or cards, and some will be entered into the system for only this decision process. In this example information is input from all of these sources. In other systems information will be in the form of managerial reports; in more complex on-line systems it will be on random access disks. In most situations, such as the one illustrated, the information set for one decision will be composed of information generated from other decisions. Thus it is important that the entire network be analyzed for the subsystem under review.

    All the information needs will be a function of the business environment and the type of decision algorithm employed. The algorithm may be a very sophisticated linear-programming scheduling model or an informal heuristic judgment. The characteristics and the parameters of the various needed information sets must be explicitly identified. For example, it is necessary to identify the exact nature of the assembly sequence information required by the scheduling algorithm. This specification must be made for each alternative to be considered.

    Necessary characteristics of information sets can be determined by asking questions such as the following: Should the information be machine readable? Is random access to be used? Should the information be updated frequently because of production and specification changes? Is the information contingent upon the type of materials available? (No provision for obtaining this last coupling of information is shown in Figure 10–5, but it may be required.)

    At the conclusion of this process, I–14 system requirements should be specified. These requirements should include the functions and decisions to be

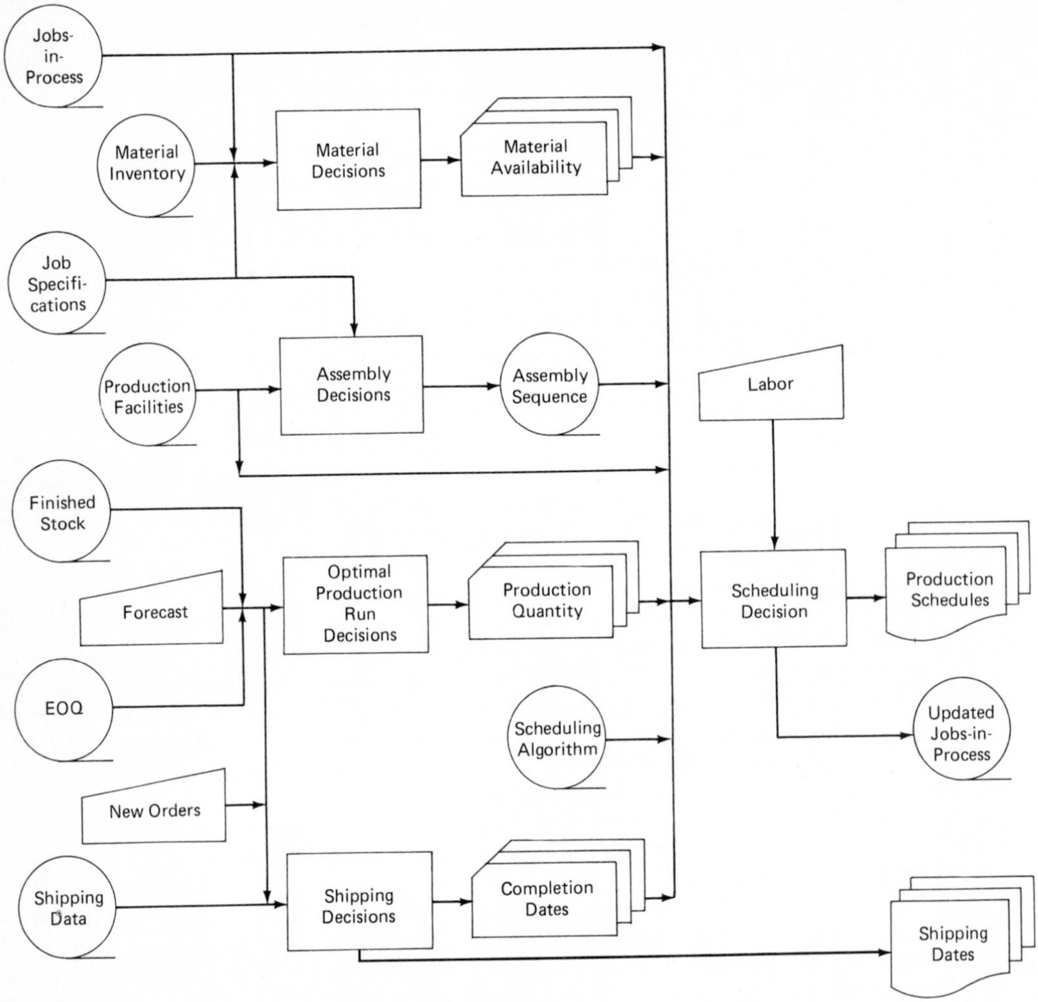

Figure 10–5 Production Scheduling Decision Network

supported, service levels to be obtained, processing approaches, and models to be utilized.

Next the criteria should be specified for evaluation of alternatives.

CONCEPTUAL DESIGN After a thorough analysis of decision requirements and corresponding reporting and transaction processing needs, several alternative designs should be identified. This must be a very creative process. Many ideas should be pursued. Consideration should be given to each of the following:

1. Decision model specification (matching requirements and sources)

2. Development of integrated or distributed network of information flow

3. Coordination of subsystems

4. Interface with other systems

Those alternatives that meet the specified criteria should be identified. At this juncture the overall type of system required to support management decision-making activities should become clearer. Each proposed modification or change will often require organizational, decision-making, and reporting changes. The behavioral impact of these expected changes, as detailed in Chapter 3, should be considered and summarized in each alternative's description.

At this juncture it may also be useful to conduct an analysis of the current system, assess its cost, and outline its problems so that it may serve as a benchmark for comparison with other alternatives.

Given this information set, the analyst must next develop a *preliminary conceptual design for each alternative* (I–17, Figure 10–4). Each design must integrate all information flows into a coordinated system that will interface with all the other systems of the firm (see Figure 10–3). In the production scheduling example, particular attention must be given to the marketing, inventory, and personnel systems interfaces. Systems flowcharts should be utilized in this step.

In addition to developing information specifications, an economic analysis (step I–17) and sensitivity analysis should be performed on each major decision, information set, and alternative. If an information set is to be employed, a cost-benefit analysis should demonstrate that some initial savings result. The information must also alter management's assessment of outcome probabilities; it must make a difference in the resulting decisions, as noted in Chapter 4. From the example, information provided on assembly sequence, optimal production run size, and other jobs in process will result in a tightly coupled production scheduling network with good communication and coordination between the functions of the system. The cost of decoupling resources, on the other hand, would include buffer inventory, potential obsolete inventory, idle time, and idle equipment.

In the example discussed, the sensitivity of the algorithm to each item of information must also be analyzed. It may be such that the scheduling model is not sensitive to daily fluctuations in labor levels. Information on weekly levels rather than daily levels may suffice. In addition to supplying information for the decision network, transaction records must be provided for the preparation of many reports. In the production scheduling illustration, a cost accounting network to support pricing decision and inventory valuation will parallel the scheduling information network.

From model specification, interface descriptions, and information matrices an integrated information flow network can be conceptually designed. All the elements of the system, decision algorithms, personnel, computer hardware and software, data base, and so forth, must be integrated. The resulting conceptual information flow networks must provide management with the information and reports it needs to manage the affairs of the business effectively. Recommendations are presented to management, and these recommendations outline the alternative conceptual designs and requirements for each, as well as cost and benefits. A work program including specific tasks, personnel required, and a schedule should also be presented to management.

At this juncture in the systems development process, management or the steering committee must decide whether to continue or terminate the project. This decision will primarily be a function of the potential of the proposed alternatives for providing management with decision-making and transaction processing information at a reasonable cost.

General Systems Design

Given authorization by management to continue, Phase II—General Systems Design—can begin. At the end of this phase, one of the conceptual designs is recommended to management. Completion of this phase will terminate what is often called the feasibility study. Based on a detailed study of the alternatives, the objective of this phase is to recommend the adoption of one of the conceptual designs. The detailed study of alternatives follows the steps outlined in Figure 10–6.

First the systems requirements, such as those illustrated in the production scheduling example, should be spelled out in detail. Particular attention should be given to input, storage, processing, communication, and personnel requirements.

Technical support for each alternative should be specified. For larger, more complex systems this will involve specifications for data management such as structures and updating requirements. The mode of processing proposed will also lead to hardware and software requirements. Finally, for some systems such as the distributed processing systems, communication requirements will need to be specified in greater detail. For some systems an alternative may be the purchase of an existing package. Any package must at least meet the minimum objectives of the system for consideration. Consideration of such a package means that it should be evaluated, designed, developed, and implemented as any other alternative. Attention should also be directed to internal control features of the proposed alternatives. General system flowcharts of each alternative should be prepared.

At this point resources and specifications for conversion, implementation, operation, and maintenance of each alternative should be estimated. Next the costs, benefits, and limitations of each alternative should be explored. Estimated tangible as well as intangible costs and benefits should be made. These should include current as well as future estimates.

Given this analysis of each conceptual design, a final recommendation should be prepared and presented to management for approval. This report is the culmination of the creative effort of the project team, analyst, or CPA firm and great care should be taken to present its recommendations. Moreover:

> . . . the project team should refrain from giving the steering committee [management] only one alternative. While a clear and unambiguous recommendation is necessary, it is also important to ensure that all major alternatives are presented fairly in a way that permits easy comparison.[6]

[6] Biggs, Birks, and Atkins, *Managing the Systems Development Process,* p. 44.

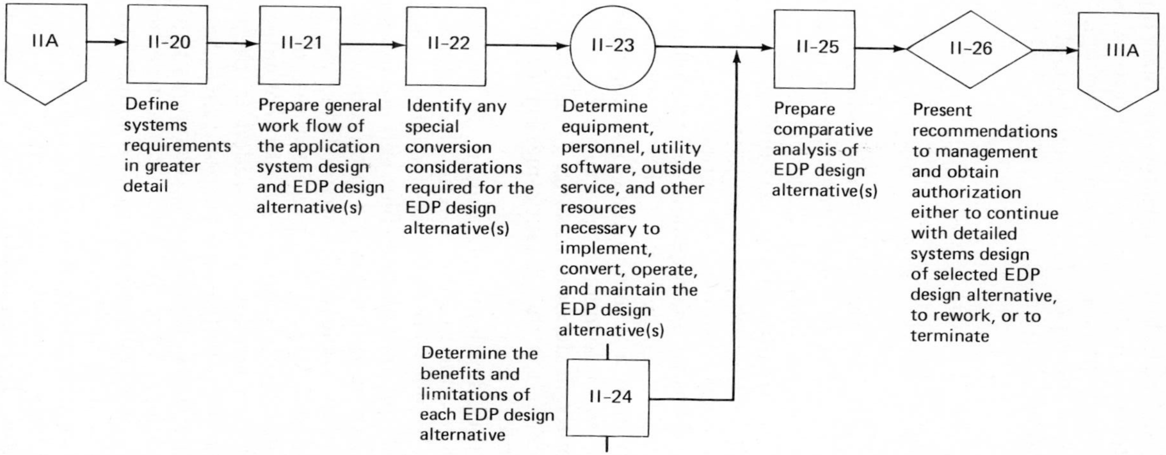
IIA
II-20
Define systems requirements in greater detail
II-21
Prepare general work flow of the application system design and EDP design alternative(s)
II-22
Identify any special conversion considerations required for the EDP design alternative(s)
II-23
Determine equipment, personnel, utility software, outside service, and other resources necessary to implement, convert, operate, and maintain the EDP design alternative(s)
II-24
Determine the benefits and limitations of each EDP design alternative
II-25
Prepare comparative analysis of EDP design alternative(s)
II-26
Present recommendations to management and obtain authorization either to continue with detailed systems design of selected EDP design alternative, to rework, or to terminate
IIIA

Figure 10–6 Phase II—General Systems Design

(Adapted with permission from the AICPA, *Guidelines for Development and Implementation of Computer-Based Application Systems*, © 1976, AICPA)

This last step ends the system definition and analysis phase of systems development. The final product at this juncture is a *conceptual systems definition*. The Actual Physical Design (Detailed Systems Design, Programming and Testing, and Conversion) and Implementation phases will be discussed in the next chapter. These phases include the introduction of economic, behavioral, and technological constraints on the conceptual design recommended at this juncture in the development process. Chapters 12 through 17 will illustrate these theoretical concepts, with respect to the functions and the managerial activities of the firm discussed in Chapter 1.

SYSTEMS DEFINITION: DATA ANALYSIS APPROACH

Due to natural growth patterns in business, many information systems have evolved over time. Computers were programmed to support various transaction processing operations; many of these operations were in accounting because of the formal structure of the accounting process. Examples of early functions supported by the computer are payroll, perpetual inventory, and accounts receivable systems. As businesses grew, complex data processing equipment became less expensive, management became more familiar with computer operations, and data files formerly used only to support transaction processing operations were put into a common data base for management use. Management began to use the information generated by transaction processing and stored in the computer in decision making. (This level of support provided by the information system for the decision-making or management system was outlined in Chapter 4.)

Following this development, simple decision models that used data base information were added to the system. Operational activities such as sales, inventory, and purchasing were integrated so that a single transaction, such as a sales order, would update inventory files and accounts receivable records and possibly initiate a purchase order via a programmed decision model. Operational control was thus achieved by many firms as their respective systems evolved from a data bank system to a predictive and decision-making system.

More complex models, such as those that integrated marketing, planning, and production scheduling, were added to these operational activities. This enabled management to plan production schedules based on incoming orders and sales projections, thereby enhancing management's control of the business. Finally, attempts were made to use the transaction processing system and the data and reports generated from it to support long-range planning and strategic policy formulation activities.

The philosophy of this evolutionary data analysis[7] approach is most appealing; a system is built from what is currently in use in the way of transaction processing procedures, decision models, and data files. The literature is replete with discussions that support a data analysis or bottom-up approach. A summa-

[7] See Gordon B. Davis, *Management Information Systems: Conceptual Foundations, Structure, and Development* (New York: McGraw-Hill, 1974) for a more complete description of the evolutionary process which is summarized above.

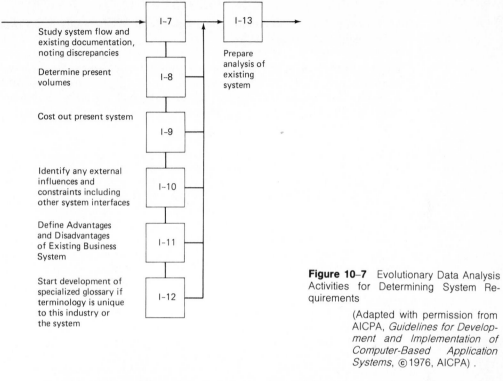

Figure 10–7 Evolutionary Data Analysis Activities for Determining System Requirements

(Adapted with permission from AICPA, *Guidelines for Development and Implementation of Computer-Based Application Systems*, © 1976, AICPA) .

ry statement would read as follows: Before designing a new system or adding to an old system, the analyst must understand the current system. Therefore the analyst proceeds to study documents, reports, data files, information flows, and organization charts in order to understand and build upon the current system. This is precisely the sequence of systems development tasks (I–7 through I–13) suggested by the AICPA in Figure 10–7.

SYSTEMS DEFINITION: COORDINATED MASTER PLAN

Neither the decision nor the data analysis approach to system analysis and definition will suffice; an integrated plan that includes the best of both is needed. Management cannot start from scratch for every modification of the system as suggested by decision analysis. The piece-by-piece evolutionary process, which is used in data analysis to add continually to the current system, is dangerous. In the latter case several key factors are overlooked. More than likely irrelevant data will be collected, processed, and reported. Previously used data will become useless as business changes. Provisions to add new and relevant data will be founded on current practice rather than on managerial needs for decision making. Moreover, technology will quickly outdate past transaction processing modes, data collection methods, communication procedures, and storage media. For example, consider the advent of microcomputers and their impact on small businesses.

The problem associated with the evolutionary data analysis approach has been expressed as follows:

> The corporate MIS did not deliver the full promise of management support. Instead, MIS printed seemingly endless stacks of reports that managers were supposed to use in decision making. Overwhelmed by data not directly usable by them, managers lost interest and MIS became synonymous with EDP.[8]

And:

> Most MIS designers "determine" what information is needed by asking managers what information they would like to have. This is based on the assumption that managers know what information they need and want.
>
> For a manager to know what information he needs he must be aware of each type of decision he should make (as well as does) and he must have an adequate model of each. These conditions are seldom satisfied. Most managers have some conception of at least some of the types of decisions they must make. Their conceptions, however, are likely to be deficient in a very critical way, a way that follows from an important principle of scientific economy: the less we understand a phenomenon, the more variables we require to explain it. Hence, the manager who does not understand the phenomenon he controls plays it "safe" and, with respect to information wants "everything." The MIS designer, who has even less understanding of the relevant phenomenon than the manager, tries to provide even more than everything. He thereby increases what is already an overload of irrelevant information. . . .
>
> The moral is simple: one cannot specify what information is required for decision making until an explanatory model of the decision process and the system involved has been constructed and tested. Information systems are subsystems of control systems. They cannot be designed adequately without taking control into account.[9]

We propose an integrated design master plan. Such an integrated planning procedure is not a universally new concept; it builds upon several approaches, including the evaluation phase in the life cycle (Figure 10–1).

The key elements are

1. The philosophy that a firm's information system should be founded on decision making, reporting, and transaction processing needs.
2. A feedback structure that signals the need for an operational review and evaluation, leading to possible modification or complete redesign of the system.

---

[8] G. R. Wagner, "The Future of Corporate Planning and Modeling Software Systems" (unpublished paper presented at the Corporate Planning Model Conference at Duke University, Dallas: Execucom, 1981 June 1981).

[9] Ackoff, "Management Misinformation Systems."

3.   A framework that allows for minor modification of the system using the data analysis approach within the decision analysis overall approach.

4.   Decision making and reporting needs must provide the basic justification for every element of the system.

The last element is perhaps the most important aspect of the integrated approach. Every expenditure should result in some identifiable benefit to the organization. All programs and activities, including information processing, should be coordinated by a steering committee or top management to achieve the organization's goals. As we have already emphasized, this will not happen by chance; an integrated master plan is needed, and it is the role of the steering committee or top management to oversee this plan. Figure 10–8 illustrates a master plan that will enable a firm to react to changes in the business envi-

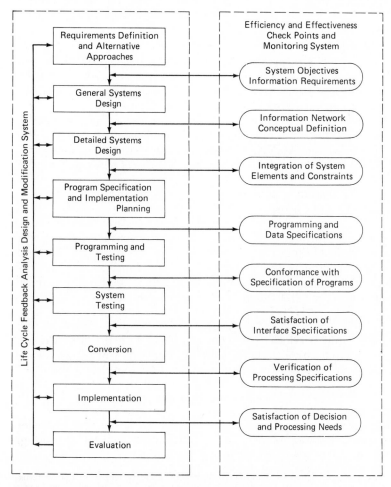

Figure 10–8   Master Plan: System Analysis and Design
(Adapted with permission from the AICPA, *Guidelines for Development and Implementation of Computer-Based Application Systems*, © 1976, AICPA)

ronment and meet the ever-increasing needs of management for operational, managerial, and strategic planning and control. Two key elements are required in the framework. The first is a feedback structure that signals the system's efficiency and effectiveness. The second is a modification provision that allows for minor revisions within the decision analysis framework.

The objective is to have a functioning information system that is both effective and efficient. An *effective system* is one that (1) provides management with necessary information for planning and control, (2) stores sufficient historical information for future decision and reporting needs, and (3) processes transactions necessary for ongoing business operations. An *efficient system* is one that utilizes all the system's elements and the most up-to-date technology to accomplish these tasks in the most economical and expedient manner. A set of check points, shown in Figure 10–8, provides a structure for measuring a system's effectiveness and efficiency.

SYSTEMS EVALUATION

Even though this chapter is primarily concerned with the analysis and definition phase of systems design and development, the entire feedback evaluation structure is presented here along with a brief explanation of the need for check points. Check points can be periodically audited or continually monitored by management, the controller's department, the systems design organization, or the steering committee. This monitoring and audit process is often referred to as an operational review. The AICPA, in a special report entitled *Operational Review of the Electronic Data Processing Function,* defines *operational review* as follows:

> It is a systematic study conducted by experienced and technically competent personnel of an organization's EDP activities (or of a stipulated segment of them) in relation to specific objectives for the purpose of (1) assessing performance, (2) identifying opportunities for improvement, and (3) developing recommendations for improvement. Its scope may include all aspects of the data processing function, from overall planning and organization procedures to specific operating procedures, as well as the EDP department's relationship with users and with top management.[10]

A regular schedule is suggested for such a review, but the need will clearly be a function of organizational circumstances. Certain situations will dictate examination of isolated check points in the systems life cycle. Examples of these situations noted by the AICPA are

1. Costs of EDP services that appear excessive
2. A major shift in corporate plans
3. A proposal for a major hardware or software upgrade or acquisition
4. An inability to attract and retain competent EDP executives

[10] American Institute of Certified Public Accountants, a Management Advisory Services Special Report, *Operational Review of the Electronic Data Processing Function,* (New York: Copyright © 1978 AICPA), used with permission.

5. A new EDP executive's need for an intensive assessment
6. An inordinate amount of personnel turnover within the EDP department
7. A proposal to consolidate or distribute EDP resources
8. Major systems that appear unresponsive to needs or are difficult to enhance or maintain
9. An excessive or increasing number of user complaints[11]

In other words, when a system ceases to be effective and efficient an operational review is in order. The objective of the review is to determine which objectives (check points) are no longer being met. This may lead to either a modification or a complete revision of the system. According to the AICPA the scope of the review may include the following:

1. Administrative control including organization planning, budgeting, and control of EDP functions
2. EDP organizational and communication structure and personnel policies
3. Systems development and implementation policies (outlined in this Chapter, Chapter 2, and Chapter 11)
4. Computer operations and related activities including
    (a) Data input and output internal control
    (b) Data-entry procedures
    (c) Computer processing (scheduling, hardware, software, and operator procedures)
    (d) File library
    (e) Security of facilities, equipment, and data
    (f) Technical support for systems, data files, and teleprocessing
5. Responsiveness of application systems in meeting the needs of the organization and users[12]

The feedback loop will help in the review process; management need only examine the check points that do not comply with the effective and efficiency guidelines. In other cases the impetus for the change may come from a manager of a user department. Such a letter should contain (1) the objectives of the modification, (2) the expected economic and operational, managerial, and strategic decision-making benefits, and (3) the subset of the organization that will be affected by the proposed change.

Sometimes only minor modification will be required, and data analysis procedures will probably be used. As an illustration of this situation, many organizations require that requests from management for system changes be initially routed to the systems department to determine if the proposed modification can be achieved by a simple enhancement such as an additional terminal for the existing system.[13] In other situations the entire system will have to be redesigned, and new decision analysis procedures will have to be implemented.

For example, if the production decision network no longer satisfies specific management needs, a minor modification, such as a report design simplification and addition of a tape drive, may satisfy the need for more understandable reports and increased model specification storage requirements. In this case the basic set of decisions and the conceptual information network

---

[11] Ibid.

[12] Ibid.

[13] Biggs, Birks, and Atkins, *Managing the Systems Development Process.*

remain effective and efficient. On the other hand, if the firm acquires a new-product line that requires continual rescheduling of production to serve customers in the new market, it is likely that most of the current checkpoint criteria will not be satisfied because the old system is no longer effective. Under these conditions the firm must redesign the entire system. To add to the old system would probably result in an ineffective and inefficient system because the general nature of the business has undergone a substantial change. A new system scheduling algorithm may be much more complex and may even provide "what if" feedback for sales personnel so that customers can be informed on the feasibility of order expediting. The new decision-making system may be interactive rather than batch, and the level of support the information system gives the management system (decision maker) may change from data and prediction-inference to a decision-support system as discussed in Chapter 4.

These check points provide a convenient monitoring procedure for systems definition and analysis, and for the design and implementation process. However, a phase should not be started before the preceding phase is complete. For example, management in its haste often errs in starting with the actual detailed physical design phases before the analysis of the decision requirements and the business environment is complete. In the AICPA's *Guidelines for Development and Implementation of Computer-Based Application Systems*, the review process is characterized as an evaluation phase (Phase IX). This phase and its corresponding steps are illustrated in Figure 10–9. As can be observed, Phase IX is essentially the same as the institute's suggested "operational review" procedures.

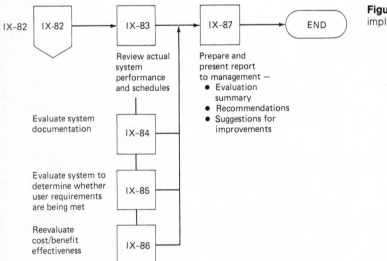

Figure 10–9 Phase IX—Post-implementation Evaluation

(Adapted with permission from AICPA, *Guidelines for Development and Implementation of Computer-Based Application Systems*, © 1976, AICPA)

SUMMARY

Systems analysis requires careful planning and coordination. The conceptual definition of a system will not occur by chance. Information requirements and alternatives must be developed through careful examination of a firm's objectives, resources, boundaries, and environmental factors and through careful specification of the decision and transaction processing network. Furthermore, general conceptual system design must be developed and the alternative selected. The system may be an existing system or a new system; the same concepts apply. During the analysis and the subsequent design stages, each step can be monitored to ensure compliance with management objectives. Moreover, check points between the stages of the life cycle can be used to signal a need for an operational review. The review may lead to a revision or redesign of the system. Either data or decision analysis procedures can be used to implement revisions, depending on the nature of the problem. For complete redesign, decision analysis procedures will be necessary if the system is to be effective and efficient.

The recommended conceptual definition of the system must specify appropriate boundaries, information requirements, interfaces with other systems, and a decision and process transaction information flow network. Detailed physical design, programming, testing, and implementation procedures follow. These are discussed in Chapter 11.

SELECTED REFERENCES

ACKOFF, RUSSELL L., "Management Misinformation Systems," *Management Science*, 14, No. 4 (December 1967), B147–56.

American Institute of Certified Public Accountants, *Guidelines for Development and Implementation of Computer-Based Application Systems.* Management Advisory Services Guideline Series Number 4, 1976.

———, *Operational Review of the Electronic Data Processing Function,* Management Advisory Services Special Report, 1978.

ANTHONY, R. N., *Planning and Control System: A Framework for Analysis.* Boston: Harvard University Graduate School of Business Administration, 1965.

BELL, THOMAS E., "Twenty-one Money-Saving Questions," *Management Controls,* May–June 1977, pp. 2–8.

BIGGS, CHARLES L., EVAN G. BIRKS, AND WILLIAM ATKINS, *Managing the Systems Development Process.* Englewood Cliffs, N.J.: Prentice-Hall, 1980.

BLACKMAN, M., *The Design of Real Time Application.* New York: John Wiley, 1975.

BURCH, JOHN G., FELIX R. STRATER, AND GARY GRUDNITSKI, *Information Systems: Theory and Practice.* Santa Barbara, Calif.: Hamilton Publishing Company, 1979.

CUSHING, BARRY F., *Accounting Information Systems and Business Organization.* Reading, Mass.: Addison-Wesley, 1978.

DANIEL, RONALD D., "Management Information Crisis," *Harvard Business Review,* September–October 1961.

DAVIS, GORDON B., *Management Information System Conceptual Foundation, Structure, and Development.* New York: McGraw-Hill, 1974.

DAVIS, K. ROSCOE, AND BERNARD W. TAYLOR, "System Design through Gaming," *Journal of Systems Management*, September 1975.

DONALDSON, HAIMISH, *A Guide to Successful Management of Computer Projects*. New York: John Wiley, 1975.

GODFREY, JAMES J., AND THOMAS R. PRINCE, "The Accounting Model from an Information System," *Accounting Review*, January 1971, pp. 75–89.

GORRY, G. ANTHONY, AND MICHAEL S. SCOTT MORTON, "A Framework for Management Information Systems," *Sloan Management Review*, Fall 1975, pp. 55–70.

HERSHANER, JAMES, "What's Wrong with Systems Design Methods?" *Journal of Systems Management*, 29 (April 1978), 25–29.

KING, WILLIAM R., AND DAVID I. CLELAND, "The Design of Management Information Systems: An Information Analysis Approach," *Management Science*, 22 (November 1975), 286–97.

KINGER, JOHN G., "A Model for System Design," *Journal of System Management*, October 1972.

LUSK, EDWARD J., AND ARTHUR E. WOLF, "The Planning Dimension of a Data Base Information System," *Managerial Planning*, 23 (January–February 1975), 36–40.

MARTIN, MERLE P., "System Analysis Strategy," *Journal of System Management*, May 1974.

MARTINO, R. L., "The Development and Installation of a Total Management System," *Data Processing for Management*, April 1963, pp. 31–37.

MASON, RICHARD O., "Concepts for Designing Management Information Systems." AIS Research Paper No. 8, October 1969.

MCFARLAND, F. WARREN, "Problems in Planning the Information System," *Harvard Business Review*, March–April 1971, pp. 75–88.

MCFARLAND, F. WARREN, RICHARD L. NOLAN, AND DAVID P. NORTON, *Information Systems Analysis*. New York: Holt, Rinehart & Winston, 1973.

NOLAN, RICHARD L., "Managing the Crises in Data Processing," *Harvard Business Review*, March–April 1979, pp. 15–26.

NUSBAUM, EDWARD F., ANDREW D. BAILEY JR., AND ANDREW B. WHINSTON, "Data-Base Management, Accounting and Accountants," *Management Accounting*, 58 (May 1978), 35–38.

PARETTA, ROBERT L., "Designing Management Information Systems: An Overview," *Journal of Accountancy*, 129 (April 1975), 42–47.

PESCOW, JEROME K., ed., *Encyclopedia of Accounting Systems*, Vols. 1, 2 and 3. Englewood Cliffs, N.J.: Prentice-Hall, 1976.

PHYRR, PETER A., "Zero Based Budgeting," *Harvard Business Review*, November–December 1970.

Price-Waterhouse, "Do It Yourself Rating Guide;" *Price Waterhouse Review* No. 1, 1980, pp. 25–26.

PRINCE, THOMAS R., *Information Systems for Management Planning and Control*. Homewood, Ill.: Richard D. Irwin, 1975.

RADFORD, K. J., "Information Systems and Management Decision Making," *Omega*, 2, No. 2 (1974), 235–42.

ROCKART, JOHN F., "Chief Executives Define Their Own Data Needs," *Harvard Business Review*, March–April 1979, pp. 81–93.

SCHLOSSER, ROBERT E., "Accounting System Review Techniques," *Journal of Accountancy*, December 1962, pp. 45–48.

SETH, RAYMOND E., "Smooth Roads to Systems That Yield Profits," *Management Controls*, May–June 1977, pp. 12–17.

SHAW, JOHN C., AND WILLIAM ATKINS, *Managing Computer System Projects*. New York: McGraw-Hill, 1970.

TREAT, ROBERT H., AND THOMAS L. WHEELER, *Developments in Management Information Systems*. Encino, Calif.: Dickenson, 1974.

WALSH, MYLER E., "The Fictional Demise of Batch Processing," *Infosystems*, 28 (March 1981), 64–68.

WAGNER, G. R., "The Future of Corporate Planning and Modeling Software Systems." Paper presented at the Conference on Corporate Planning Models at Duke University, June 1981.

WILKINSON, JOSEPH W., "Specifying Management's Information Needs," *Cost and Management*, 48 (September–October 1974), 7–13.

REVIEW QUESTIONS

1. What costs associated with integrated systems are tightly coupled? How can these costs be reduced?

2. Should a systems analyst review an entire system at one time? If not, what must the analyst do to structure the review?

3. How should the existence of a system be justified using the decision analysis approach?

4. Describe the steps involved in the decision analysis approach to general systems design.

5. Contrast the steps in AICPA Phase I (Requirements Definition and Alternative Approaches) for decision analysis and data analysis.

6. What must be completed before the initial conceptual design of the system is started?

7. What must be completed before the physical design of the system is started?

8. What is the basic philosophy behind decision analysis?

9. What are the advantages and disadvantages of the decision analysis and data analysis approaches?

10. Explain how the integrated design approach incorporates both decision analysis and data analysis design concepts.

11. How can a firm's controller monitor a system to ensure compliance with the firm's decision needs and economic objectives?

12. What are the nine phases of the procedure suggested by the AICPA for information systems development and implementation?

13. What is meant by a decision and transaction processing network?

14. Give several examples of environmental considerations for systems definition. Why is each important in the context of a management (decision) system supported by an information system?

15. What pitfall is involved in starting the definition of a system with an analysis of the current system?

16. What are the key elements of the integrated master plan for systems analysis and design? Why is each important?

EXERCISES AND CASES

10-1

Consider again the Wright Manufacturing Company (Case 4–1). From a systems definition perspective, what steps were missing in the initial analysis and subsequent modifications which may have led to the general demise of the system? Would an operational review have helped? How? (Adapted from the CMA Examination)

10-2

Greenway Manufacturing experiences a very seasonal demand for the products in its lawn mower division. Most mowers are purchased in the early spring. Greenway's plant is highly automated, and a large portion of its manufacturing costs are fixed. The labor required is skilled, and training workers is expensive. The current practice in the industry is to sell to distributors, who then either sell or consign merchandise to retail hardware or discount stores. Due to the bulky nature of the product, warehouse costs at either Greenway or its distributors is high.

You have been engaged to develop a production-scheduling algorithm for Greenway Manufacturing. As part of this assignment, you must specify the interface between production and marketing. What issues are involved?

10-3

Nashville Recording Company operates a mail-order division. Nashville purchases country music albums and tapes in volume. The savings are passed on to its country music club members. Club members are solicited via direct mail, newspapers, selected publications, and radio and television advertising. New members are offered six tapes or albums for one dollar, providing they purchase at least six tapes or albums during a two-year period. After that they are given a bonus selection on the purchase of four recordings at the regular club price. On occasion, special discounts are offered to club members on slow-moving recordings.

Each month a club member is sent an IBM card stating the regular monthly selection along with alternative selections. The member

indicates on the card whether the regular selection, an alternative, or no selection is desired that month. Upon receipt of this card, Nashville Recording then sends the appropriate selection. No recording is sent unless a card is received; a positive response is required from the customer. The customer may return the recording if it has not been opened.

Your firm has been engaged to design a computerized billing inventory system.

1. What key managerial or operating decisions will influence the success of the firm?
2. How can a computerized billing and inventory system support these decisions?
3. Identify the master data files required to support these decisions.
4. Identify the sources from which these files can be compiled.
5. Prepare a systems flowchart for your conceptual view of the billing and inventory systems.
6. Briefly identify the hardware configuration you envision to be necessary to support your conceptual view of the system. (Refer to Chapters 5, 6, and 8 for this step.)

10-4

Audio Visual Corporation of Wooster, Massachusetts, manufactures and sells visual display equipment. Most sales are made through seven geographical sales offices located in Los Angeles, Seattle, Minneapolis, Cleveland, Dallas, Boston, and Atlanta. Each sales office has a warehouse located nearby to carry an inventory of new equipment and replacement parts. The remaining sales are made through manufacturers' representatives.

Audio Visual's manufacturing operations are conducted in a single plant, which is highly departmentalized. In addition to the assembly department, there are several departments responsible for various components used in the visual display equipment. The plant also has maintenance, engineering, scheduling, and cost accounting departments.

Early in 1981, management decided that its management information system (MIS) needed upgrading. As a result, the company ordered an advanced computer in 1981, and it was installed in July 1982. The main processing equipment is still located at corporate headquarters, and each of the seven sales offices is connected with the main processing unit by remote terminals.

The integration of the new computer into the Audio Visual information system was carried out by the MIS staff. The MIS manager and the four systems analysts who had the major responsibility for the integration were hired by the company in the spring of 1982. The department's other employees—programmers, machine operators, and keypunch operators—have been with the company for several years.

During its early years, Audio Visual had a centralized decision-making organization. Top management formulated all plans and directed all operations. As the company expanded, some of the decision making was decentralized, although the information processing was still highly centralized. Departments had to coordinate their plans with the corporate office, but they had more freedom in developing their sales programs. However, as the company expanded, information problems developed. As a consequence, the MIS department was given the responsibility for improving the company's information processing system when the new equipment was installed.

The MIS analysts reviewed the information system in existence prior to the acquisition of the new computer and identified weaknesses. To overcome the weaknesses, they redesigned old applications and designed new applications. During the eighteen months since the acquisition of the new equipment, the following applications have been redesigned or developed and are now operational: payroll, production scheduling, financial statement preparation, customer billing, raw material usage in production, and finished goods inventory by warehouse. The operating departments of Audio Visual that were affected by the systems changes were rarely consulted or contacted until the system was operational and the new reports had been distributed to the operating departments.

The president of Audio Visual is very pleased with the work of the MIS department. During a recent conversation with an individual who was interested in Audio Visual's new system, the president stated: "The MIS people are doing a good job and I have full confidence in their work. We paid a lot of money for the new equipment and the MIS people certainly cost enough, but the combination of the new equipment and new MIS staff should solve all of our problems."

Recently two additional conversations regarding the computer and information system have taken place. One was between Jerry Adams, plant manager, and Bill Taylor, the MIS manager; the other was between Adams and Terry Williams, the new personnel manager.

TAYLOR-ADAMS CONVERSATION

Adams: Bill, you're trying to run my plant for me. I'm supposed to be the manager, yet you keep interfering. I wish you would mind your own business.

Taylor: You've got a job to do but so does my department. As we analyzed the information needed for production scheduling and by top management, we saw where improvements could be made in the work flow. Now that the system is operational, you can't reroute work and change procedures because that would destroy the value of the information we're processing. And while I'm on that subject, it's getting to the point where we can't trust the information we're getting from production. The mark sense cards we receive from production contain a lot of errors.

Adams: I'm responsible for the efficient operation of production. Quite frankly, I think I'm the best judge of production efficiency. The system you installed has reduced my work force and increased the work load of the remaining employees, but I don't see that this has improved anything. In fact, it might explain the high error rate in the cards.

Taylor: This new computer costs a lot of money and I'm trying to be sure that the company gets its money's worth.

Adams: My best production assistant, the one I'm grooming to be a supervisor when the next opening occurs, came to me today and said he was thinking of quitting. When I asked him why, he said he didn't enjoy the work anymore. He's not the only one who is unhappy. The supervisors and department heads no longer have a voice in establishing production schedules. This new computer system has taken away the contribution we used to make to the company planning and direction. We seem to be going way back to the days when top management made all the decisions. I have more production problems now than I used to. I think it boils down to a lack of interest on the part of my management team. I know the problem is within my area but I think you might be able to help me.

Williams: I have no recommendations for you now but I've had similar complaints from purchasing and shipping. I think we should get your concerns on the agenda for our next plant management meeting.

REQUIRED:

a. Apparently the development of and transition of the new computer-based system has created problems among the personnel of Audio Visual Corporation. Identify and briefly discuss the apparent causes of these problems.

b. How could the company have avoided the problems? What steps should be taken to avoid such problems in the future?
(Adapted from the CMA Examinations)

10–5

Channel 7 in Center City, an affiliate of a national television network, broadcasts both local and national shows. The primary source of Channel 7's revenue is spot advertising, and the station's inventory consists of ten-, twenty-, and thirty-second advertising time slots. Management has two primary objectives: to maximize profits and to provide a service to the community.

It is the practice of the industry to place different values on different time slots. A thirty-second commercial, for example, will cost less at two o'clock in the morning than during prime time. Shows with higher ratings command a higher price for their associated commercial time slots than do less-popular programs. Moreover, it is the practice of the industry to have a priority system for guaranteeing time slots. A higher price is paid for a ten-second guaranteed slot during the six o'clock news than for a ten-second slot at the same time that is not guaranteed which may be bumped by another commercial. A commercial may be bumped for another that costs more or by a public service announcement. Because of the diversity in changes in time slots, the station salespeople are constantly trying to obtain the greatest amount of revenue for the array of time slots available.

Currently the station does all the scheduling of commercials and public service announcements by hand using a large spread sheet that eventually becomes a report for the FCC. Records of each time slot's usage must be filed with the FCC, and each customer must have a record of his or her actual commercial time and cost.

Channel 7 must cut off sales one week prior to broadcast time in order to prepare the programming schedule, optimize revenue, and satisfy programming constraints, such as the same time each night for some spots and sufficient time duration between conflicting spots. Due to this time delay, sales that could increase the station's profits are lost. Moreover, prior to the cutoff, salespeople are often not aware of available time.

You have been engaged to assist station management in reducing this time lag and to assist sales personnel with timely information. Describe the management information system you would conceptualize. In general, follow the system definition steps in this chapter for *one* alternative conceptual system. Be sure to include a description of the reporting requirements, major decision-making activities, information processing modes, and general hardware and software requirements. Refer to Chapters 4, 5, 6, and 8 if necessary. Do not provide detailed system controls at this point.

10–6

Citizens' Gas Company, a medium-sized gas distribution company, provides natural gas service to approximately two hundred thousand customers. The customer base is divided into three revenue classes. Data by customer class are as follows:

CLASS	CUSTOMERS	SALES IN CUBIC FEET		REVENUES
Residential	160,000	80	billion	$160 million
Commercial	38,000	15		25
Industrial	2,000	50		65
		145	billion	$250 million

Residential customer gas usage is primarily for residence heating purposes and consequently is highly correlated to the weather— i.e., temperature. Commercial and industrial customers, on the other hand, may or may not use gas for heating purposes, and consumption is not necessarily correlated to the weather.

The largest twenty-five industrial customers of the two thousand total account for $30 million of the industrial revenues. Each of these twenty-five customers uses gas for both heating and industrial purposes and has a consumption pattern that is governed almost entirely by business factors.

The company obtains its gas supply from ten major pipeline companies. The pipeline companies provide gas in amounts specified in contracts that extend over periods ranging from five to fifteen years. For some contracts the supply is in equal monthly increments, while for others the supply varies in accordance with the heating season. Supply over and above the contract amounts is not available, and some contracts contain take-or-pay clauses—i.e., the company must pay for the volumes specified in the contract, whether or not it can take the gas.

To assist in matching customer demand with supply, the company maintains a gas storage field. Gas can be pumped into the storage

field when supply exceeds customer demand, and gas can also be obtained when demand exceeds supply. There are no restrictions on the use of the gas storage field except that the field must be filled to capacity at the beginning of each gas year (September 1). Consequently, whenever the contractual supply for gas for the remainder of the gas year is less than that required to satisfy projected demand and replenish the storage field, the company must curtail service to the industrial customers (except for quantities that are used for heating). The curtailments must be carefully controlled so that an oversupply does not occur at year-end. Similarly, care must be taken to ensure that curtailments are adequate during the year to protect against the need to curtail commercial or residential customers in order to replenish the storage field at year-end.

In recent years the company's planning efforts have not provided a firm basis for the establishment of long-term contracts. The current year has been no different. Planning efforts have not been adequate to control the supply during the current gas year. Customer demand has been projected only as a function of the total number of customers. Commercial and industrial customers' demand for gas has been curtailed excessively. This has resulted in lost sales and has caused an excess of supply at the end of the gas year.

In an attempt to correct these problems, the president of Citizens' Gas has hired a new director of corporate planning and has instructed the director to develop a conceptual design of a system that can be used to analyze the supply and demand of natural gas. The system should provide a monthly gas plan for each year for the next five years, with particular emphasis on the first year. The plan should provide a set of reports that will assist in the decision-making process and contain all necessary supporting schedules. The system must provide for the use of actual data during the course of the first year to project demand for the rest of the year and the year in total. The president has indicated to the director that he will base his decisions on the effect on operating income of alternative plans.

REQUIRED:

a. What planning reports should be generated by the system and what type of on-line inquiry should be feasible to support decision requirements?

b. Identify the major data items that should be incorporated into Citizens' Gas Company's new system to provide adequate planning capability.

c. In general what hardware configurations and software systems do you as director expect to utilize? (Adapted from the CMA Examination)

10–7

You have been called upon to assist the administrative services branch of your accounting firm with a client whose business is warehousing and distributing frozen seafood. As an initial step to automating this warehouse operation, you are to study the firm's business environment. Briefly note the environmental characteristics you might find that would be important to the scope of your firm's engagement. Flowchart the decision network you might use for processing sales orders, assuming that the firm sells to both retail and institutional customers. Describe the data base as well as the processing mode, along with its related hardware and software necessary to support a sales processing system alternative that can be used to support these decisions.

10–8

A large international tire manufacturing firm is considering expanding and locating several plants in the United States. You have been engaged as a management consultant to develop an information system to support the firm's long-range policy-making decision. Briefly outline how you would proceed.

10–9

Interstate Transfer is a regional moving and storage firm located in the Midwest. It has been growing at a rapid rate over the past several years and has been having increasing difficulty scheduling its trucks. Customers have had to wait several days for delivery of their furniture, and trucks have frequently been operating with partial loads. A management consultant was hired by the firm to help resolve this scheduling problem. The consultant decid-

ed that the firm could schedule its operations much more effectively by using a linear-programming algorithm. To support this model, Interstate would need to lease a small computer. To further justify the computer cost, the firm would automate its current billing, payroll, and payables systems. Using this computerized accounting system, management could make better decisions because information would be readily available.

Comment on the appropriateness of the system analysis approach used here.

10–10

Cite two or three critical decisions for each of the following businesses:

a. Large department store
b. Television broadcasting station
c. Building contractor
d. Small retail druggist
e. Oil refinery
f. Local welfare agency
g. University admissions office
h. General Motors automative design division
i. Fishing fleet
j. Furniture manufacturing firm

What data sources are available to satisfy the information requirements of the decisions?

10–11

For several years Brown's Department Store has been using magnetic tape to store its accounts receivable records. The credit department has been complaining about the increase in bad debts over the past year. The company has one location, and its computer is on the premises. You have been called upon to help Brown's Department Store with its problem. How would you proceed? Comment on the sensitivity of credit decisions to any change in information storage and processing modes.

10–12

Columbia County has an estimated population of thirty-seven thousand. It is for all practical purposes contiguous to River City, which has a population of two hundred thousand and is one of the fastest-growing cities in the state. The county budget and accounting system can be described as follows.

BUDGET PROCESS A cumulative computer printout prepared in August is transmitted to each department for use as a basis for next year's budget. Five budget items are shown, along with cumulative variances from the budget through the end of July. Each department makes its requests on the basis of this information, and these requests are approved or revised by the county commissioners after department heads have been given the right to defend their requests at public hearings.

Monthly variances are used to control expenditures. These are generated on a monthly basis by the computer service provided by River City.

CASH RECEIPTS There are nine offices that generate revenue for the county from the following sources:

1. Engineer's office: street light assessments, paving assessments, and landfill fees
2. Planning and zoning commission: occupational tax (business licenses), building permits, trailer permits, and plumbing inspectors
3. Ambulance service: fees
4. Probate Court: fees
5. Clerk of Superior Court: fines
6. Sheriff's office: overdue taxes
7. Tax commissioner: taxes
8. Water department: sales and federal grants
9. Federal grants: revenue sharing

These offices are distributed throughout the county at various locations.

EXPENDITURES A Burroughs L-3000 is used to generate payroll reports and checks. No attempt is made to break down employees by department, and withholdings are summarized by hand.

Capital outlays and other expenditures are approved by the commissioners as part of the annual budget. Commissioners review all invoices prior to signing checks.

DATA PROCESSING SYSTEM The county uses a Burroughs L-3000 machine to print checks, update employee payroll cards, and make general ledger entries for issued checks. The machine has a limited memory and can accumulate minor summary totals during each payroll run.

Other computer services are purchased from River City:

1. Trial balance report: assets, liabilities, reserves
2. Financial report: monthly and cumulative transactions
3. Budget report: by department, monthly charges, allotment, variances, and remaining budget
4. Expenditure report: by department

The input is prepared by one clerk at the county courthouse.

EXISTING PROBLEMS The following problems, discovered during an audit, exist with the current system:

1. Bank accounts have not been reconciled during the year.
2. Cash book contained entries that did not agree with the bank statement.
3. The engineer's office and the planning and zoning offices have separate bank accounts not under the commissioners' control.
4. Several invoices have been paid twice.
5. Numerous clerks in various offices collect fees.
6. Computer printouts currently received by the commissioners do not provide clear, timely, current information. Generally they are two months old.
7. There is no chief financial officer or controller.
8. Expenditures exceeded the budget projection for 1982 by a substantial margin.
9. Books are not balanced except during the annual audit, and therefore current cash pictures are difficult to obtain.
10. Mileage reimbursement rates have not changed since 1968, even though the county has grown by over 40 percent.

NEW TECHNOLOGY Another county in the state, Spalding, recently installed an IBM System 32 (minicomputer). Spalding County uses the System 32 to develop a budget, print out monthly budget reports, maintain a general ledger and double-entry books, write checks, generate encumbrance reports, keep inventory, and indicate where idle funds can be invested. The computer keeps the county so well informed about cash flows that it earned $16,000 on interest from idle funds in the first year.

The System 32 uses a keyboard terminal and has external data storage on diskettes. An optical screen is used to assist input. All input is edited. The operation is so simple that it took Spalding County only two days to train employees, and no new employees were hired.

In addition to the operations mentioned earlier, the System 32 will

1. Process all revenue and expenditure transactions immediately
2. Provide detailed expenditure reports by line item
3. Develop budget forecasts
4. Provide automated payroll support
5. Keep property inventories
6. Make assessments
7. Do all tax digest computations and billing

The cost of the System 32 is approximately $1,073 per month, with an initial outlay of $5,500.

REQUIRED:

a. Using this description of the system and the results of the annual audit, perform an operational review of the system.
b. What objectives are not being met?
c. Why, in your opinion, have the problems developed? Can they be related to the system design and modification practice used in the past? Why?
d. Assume that Columbia County is much larger than Spalding County. Should Columbia acquire a System 32? What management and information system analysis and design issues are involved in this decision?

10–13

Five assumptions commonly made by designers of management information systems are . . .

1. the critical deficiency under which most managers operate is the lack of relevant information,
2. the manager needs the information he wants,
3. if a manager has the information he needs his decision making will improve,
4. better communication between managers improves organizational performance, and
5. a manager does not have to understand how his information system works, only how to use it.[1]

These five assumptions are from a classic MIS article entitled "Management Misinformation Systems." In your opinion, how can each of these seemingly valid assumptions lead to *mis*information?

10–14

Business organizations are required to modify or replace a portion or all of their financial information system in order to keep pace with their growth and to take advantage of improved information technology. The process involved in modifying or replacing an information system, especially if computer equipment is utilized, requires a substantial commitment of time and resources. When an organization undertakes a change in its information system, a series of steps or phases is taken. The following steps or phases are commonly included in a systems study:

1. Survey of the existing system
2. Analysis of information collected in the survey and development of recommendations for corrective action
3. Design of a new or modified system
4. Equipment study and acquisition
5. Implementation of a new or modified system

These steps or phases tend to overlap rather than be separate and distinct. In addition, the effort required in each step or phase varies from one systems change to another depend-

[1] Ackoff, "Management Misinformation Systems."

ing upon such factors as the extent of the changes or the need for different equipment.

REQUIRED:

a. Explain what problems may exist by starting with an analysis of the existing system. What step would you replace it with and why? When would you suggest starting with the existing system?

b. Identify and explain the general activities and techniques that are commonly used during the systems analysis phase of a systems study conducted for a financial information system.

c. The system analysis phase of a financial information systems study is often carried out by a project team composed of a systems analyst, a management accountant, and other persons in the company who would be knowledgeable and helpful in the systems study. What would be the role of the management accountant in these phases of a financial information systems study? (Adapted from the CMA Examination)

10–15

In your opinion in the George Beemster CPA Case (9–1), did the Louisville Sales Corporation use an evolutionary data analysis or a decision analysis approach in designing its system? What problems resulted and what effectiveness and efficiency opportunities were overlooked by Louisville Sales Corporation?

10–16

In many important ways a banking system differs from a system found in a manufacturing environment. Students may wish to refer to other literature on the subject for background information to use in answering the following requirements:[2]

1. Briefly describe a bank operation and some of the problems that may be encountered by bank management.
2. How would a systems analyst approach the analysis of an interactive MIS system for a medium-sized bank, emphasizing decision analysis and output processing controls?
3. a. Discuss the internal control of teller operations in connection with input/output processing.
   b. Flowchart the teller operations, assuming these input/output controls.

10–17

Blue Ridge General Contractors erects commercial buildings in western Virginia, North Carolina, and eastern Tennessee. The firm has grown to the point where it needs to structure its information system. Specify the information needs that would be encountered in this type of firm.

One of these needs is that of cost allocation and accumulation on existing jobs. What are the characteristics of an information system required to support costing decisions?

Describe appropriate internal controls for this type of cost system. Flowchart the system controls, the processing steps, and the movement of information through the system.

To answer these requirements, students may wish to refer to outside references on the construction industry and cost accounting.[3]

[2] Jerome K. Pescow, *Encyclopedia of Accounting Systems*, Prentice-Hall, Inc., 1976, presents a good overview of accounting systems and decision-making and reporting needs.

[3] Ibid. Also consult any standard cost accounting text.

11

SYSTEM DESIGN CONCEPTS: Design and Implementation

OBJECTIVE OF SYSTEMS DESIGN AND IMPLEMENTATION[1]

The overall objective of the design and implementation of accounting information systems is the ultimate satisfaction of decision, transaction, and reporting needs. This objective must dominate all the work and discussion by the accountants and systems analysts as they interact with management to improve the information system. Accomplishment of this objective requires careful planning, organizing, staffing, coordinating, directing, and controlling of all the elements that will be integrated into the information system, which in turn will support the management system of the organization.

[1] This entire chapter is adapted with permission from the life cycle framework developed by the AICPA and discussed in detail in AICPA, *Guidelines for Development and Implementation of Computer-Based Application Systems*, Management Advisory Services Guidelines Series Number 4, (New York: American Institute of Certified Public Accountants, 1976). Phases III through VIII are discussed in this chapter; Phases I, II, and IX were discussed in Chapter 10. The discussion is supplemented extensively with permission from Charles L. Biggs, Evan G. Birks, and William Atkins, *Managing the Systems Development Process* (Englewood Cliffs, N.J.: Touche Ross & Co. and Prentice-Hall, Inc., 1980).

In Chapter 10 we focused on the first two phases of the process, shown in Figure 11–1, which must be followed to accomplish the overall design and implementation objective. These phases constituted the systems analysis and definition steps of the overall process. The objective of these two phases, regardless of whether they follow the data analysis or decision analysis approach, is a recommended conceptual systems design. The conceptual design represents, in the case of the decision analysis approach, a detailed investigation of management's decision network. In the data analysis approach, a careful review of the existing system forms the basis for the conceptual design. The recommended conceptual systems design also requires a rough investigation of the resources necessary to implement, convert, operate, and maintain each alternative conceptual design and a comparison of several alternative designs. The most important output of these first two phases is a careful analysis and

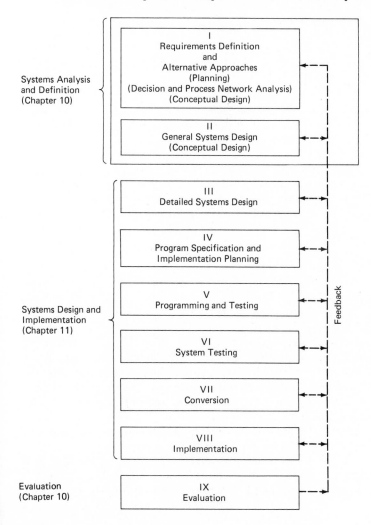

Figure **11–1** Information System Development and Implementation Life Cycle

(Adapted with permission from the AICPA *Guidelines for System Development and Implementation.* © 1976, AICPA.)

Systems Analysis and Definition (Chapter 10)

I
Requirements Definition and Alternative Approaches (Planning) (Decision and Process Network Analysis) (Conceptual Design)

II
General Systems Design (Conceptual Design)

III
Detailed Systems Design

IV
Program Specification and Implementation Planning

V
Programming and Testing

Systems Design and Implementation (Chapter 11)

VI
System Testing

VII
Conversion

VIII
Implementation

Feedback

Evaluation (Chapter 10)

IX
Evaluation

definition of the requirements and specifications of the system needed by management.

In this chapter we will review the key aspects of the actual physical design and implementation phases of the design shown in Figure 11–1. This review will carefully consider *economic, behavioral,* and *technological constraints,* which were also discussed in earlier chapters of this text. For example, the actual detailed design of the system may require a slightly different configuration of hardware for economic and technological reasons. Moreover, certain behavioral problems may lead to a slightly different organization of the data structure.

From the auditor's perspective, it is important that these sequential phases be followed. In Chapter 9 we pointed out that one of the most important facets of good internal control is the set of procedures used to develop and implement the accounting and, in a larger sense, the information system of the organization.

STRATEGY FOR CHANGE

Strong consideration must be given to the factors that affect the social environment of the organization in the physical design and implementation of information systems. Organizational, behavioral, and decision-making concepts are extremely important. For this reason, the accountant or systems analyst should not attempt to change or modify the management system and supporting information system without the active participation of management. Furthermore, it is much easier to change segments of the system successfully rather than the entire system, although this approach does have its drawbacks, as will be noted later.

Project Teams

Perhaps the best way to alleviate many of the problems cited in Chapter 3 and achieve many of the decision-making requirements cited in Chapter 4 is to involve all the key personnel who will be affected by the system. This team will consist of a key representative of top management (for support and direction), the managers who will eventually use the information to make decisions and issue reports, the controller, the manager of information systems, technical advisers (operations research, EDP, training, and accountants, for example), and, if feasible, the firm's independent auditors. As a matter of practice, these individuals may send their representatives to routine meetings, but they must themselves be involved in all key decisions if the systems development and implementation process is to be successful. In larger organizations these teams will probably report to an executive steering committee.

In summary, all parties who are involved in the decision making and reporting process supported by the system must participate in its design and implementation phases. Moreover, all phases must have top-management support.

Modular Concept

System boundaries were reviewed in Chapter 10. We noted that it is often infeasible to modify or change an entire system at one time; management should change only a subset of the system at one time. In this way the project is made more manageable. Clear objectives can be set, and design and implementation can proceed in an orderly fashion under the direction of the project team and steering committee.

There is a cost associated with this procedure, however, and it should be recognized. Any time a subset of the entire system is considered, the interface with other systems and the slack resources that will probably be required to accommodate this interface must be considered, if the modules are loosely coupled. Moreover, if the modules modified are too small, management will probably get the impression that the system will be in a continuous state of change. This will lead to disenchantment with the system.

As a matter of practice, it is necessary in an organization of any size to use the modular approach, but there are financial, organizational, and behavioral limits to its application.

Planning Change

The change conceptualized in the first two phases of systems development and implementation must be well planned and organized. In the network proposed by the AICPA, there are many planning steps in the first two phases. The same is true of the remaining detailed design and implementation phases. The number of steps emphasizes the careful planning required in conversion, programming, staff training, testing, coding, and implementation activities. Moreover, the whole process must be carefully planned and organized from its very inception. Network analysis such as the *Program Evaluation Review Technique* (PERT) is most useful in this overall process. This procedure will be reviewed in the Appendix to this chapter after all the necessary activity, planning, and decision steps have been reviewed.

SYSTEMS DESIGN
AND IMPLEMENTATION PHASES

In this section AICPA systems design and implementation Phases III through VIII will be reviewed, along with the equipment, site selection, and preparation activities necessary to finally implement the system conceptualized in Chapter 10. In several cases a planning step will be noted. The various options related to this step will *not* be reviewed at the planning point, but at the implementation point in the development and implementation network.

Detailed Systems Design—Phase III

Phase III represents all the planning and preparation necessary to go from a conceptual definition of an information network in Phase II to an operational system design. At this juncture, careful consideration must be given to economic, technological, and social constraints that have, or will have, an impact on the accounting information system.

According to the AICPA guidelines, the principal objectives of this phase are to (1) design a network of information flows and decision-making activities, specify the interfaces with other systems, and begin the specific selection of software and hardware; (2) establish the specifications for files, processing, and control; and (3) make plans for programming, conversion, and training.

The detailed steps of Phase III are outlined in Figure 11–2. These represent a slight modification of the original AICPA guidelines for Phase III.

First a plan and schedule for design and implementation must be prepared. This plan is based on the recommended conceptual design developed in Phase II and the documented requirements associated with the chosen design. Next this plan, along with all its prescribed conventions, standards, and restrictions, should be communicated in a memo to all personnel involved in the project. A summary should also be forwarded to all company personnel who will be affected to keep them informed.

User decision-making, reporting, and transaction processing requirements must be defined more precisely than they were in the conceptual design phases. There must be a thorough definition of each decision model (III–29), report, and transaction to be processed to ensure that alternative technical approaches can be evaluated on how effectively and efficiently they meet these requirements. One of the major accounting firms suggests that the preparation of a requirements manual include the following:

–Functions that are to be part of the new system are identified, described in terms of their operation and impact on the users, and related to the functions of the current system.
–Information to be maintained and reported by the new system is described in terms of outputs, inputs, data elements, and data structures.
–The workflow associated with the new system is documented by a flow diagram with supporting narrative descriptions.
–Internal and external assumptions and constraints on the new system are identified and documented.
–The impact of the new system on its target organizations is described in terms of new, revised, and eliminated functions or positions.[2]

Outputs to be generated by the system must be described in terms of their purpose, frequency, and distribution. Data elements required must be defined by a system-wide identification, format, source, content, and edit criteria.[3] Inputs required must be described as follows:

–Source, including form name and responsibility for completing the form.
–Data elements included.
–Method of data collection (e.g., remote terminals, OCR, etc.).

[2] Charles L. Biggs, Evan G. Birks, and William Atkins, *Managing the Systems Development Process* (N.J.: 1980), pp. 92–95.
[3] Ibid., pp. 94–95.

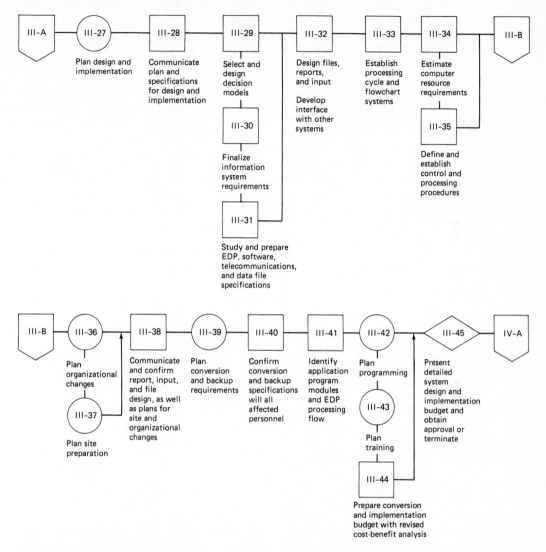

Figure 11–2 Detailed Systems Design

(Adapted with permission from AICPA, *Guidelines for Systems Development and Implementation*, ©1976, AICPA)

    –Manual processing, including edit procedures and distribution.
    –Controls required, both manual and automated.[4]

Behavioral consideration should be given to the user's interface with the system input and output. Futhermore, the preliminary organization of required data el-

    [4] Ibid.

ements into logical records should be established. Finally, volumes of transactions now and in the future should be estimated.

After the general requirements have been formalized (III–30), the project team, analyst, or accountant should study (III–31) various software approaches, with supporting EDP hardware, and specify the needs of the system with respect to the hardware and software. Various communication networks, file and data base structures, and types of operating and data base systems that meet the general requirements specified above should be considered. Detailed information from prospective vendors may be sought at this juncture for firms and companies with limited technical expertise.

In addition, consideration should be given here to "package" software that meets the requirements of the recommended conceptual decision-making, reporting, and transaction processing systems. Requests for proposals should be prepared for these packages so that they can be evaluated. These should be evaluated using the criteria noted later for all system components. The objective here is simply to obtain a description of prepackaged software that may meet the requirements of the system.

Given this analysis of feasible communication, data or file structures, software (including packages), and hardware, the specifications (III–32) need to be detailed for data base, input, processing, and output design as well as vendor proposals.

Next the data base is designed, as detailed in Chapter 8. Often it is useful to assemble a data base on an on-line operating system to verify operating assumptions prior to any applications programming.[5] Reports and other output media are designed along with distribution specifications. Input methods and procedures may furthermore be designed in detail at this juncture given the preliminary specifications of hardware and software that have been developed thus far.

After input and output formats, decision models, and files and data structures have been designed, and EDP hardware, software, and communications equipment have been specified, systems interfaces must be specified. This includes manual interfaces as well as systems interfaces.

Systems flowcharts (III–33) must be prepared to indicate the flow of transactions and information through the transaction processing and decision-making network of the organization at this point to describe the system and its various interfaces with management and other systems.

Using this description and set of systems flowcharts, the processing cycle can be described in terms of frequency, time, data, and reports. From this detail, estimates (III–34) can be made for the computer, software, and telecommunication resources that will be required for the system. Advice from prospective vendors may be helpful here for many firms that do not have a great deal of technical expertise.

At this juncture in the detailed systems design stage, these resource requirement estimates must be carefully reviewed by the project team, the steering committee (management), the systems analyst, and the accounting personnel to ensure that the computer, software, and storage and telecommunication resources exist and that they are economical, serviceable, effective, and

---

[5] Ibid., p. 146.

easy to use given the availability of personnel. In other words, strict attention must be given to the technological and behavioral constraints mentioned in the earlier chapters on computer equipment and data bases.

Next, control and processing procedures can be designed (III–35) in accordance with the basic principles and concepts outlined in Chapter 9. General control procedures need to be developed for users so that they can effectively use the new system. Input and output controls such as batching, verification, correction, resubmission, and balancing must be specified for users. Procedures for maintenance of data base and data file integrity, including backup procedures, must be developed. Procedures must be designed to process transactions in accordance with the desires of management and generally accepted accounting principles. Finally, access controls such as passwords and physical access to terminals must be developed.

When all of these specifications have been completed, the project team should prepare for any organizational changes (III–36). It is important that the project team quickly and accurately communicate the nature of these changes, along with the compelling reasons for the changes, to personnel. In Chapter 3 we noted that these systems changes can often alter the social structure of the organization and cause a great deal of frustration and anxiety. Therefore consideration must be given to the behavioral constraints and principles.

With the essence of the system designed and considerable thought given to the nature of the hardware, site planning or preparation may be necessary at this time, especially if more space, different air conditioning, fire protection, or special security is required.

At this point the project team should communicate the results of these decisions to all management personnel. Management personnel should confirm that these decisions and plans are consistent with the information and decision-making requirements set forth during the general systems design phase. This confirmation must be obtained because the conceptual definition that emerged from Phase II has now been altered, in some cases substantially, by the introduction of economic, behavioral, and technological constraints.

Given this confirmation that the detailed systems design conforms to the general systems concept authorized by management, the project team, accountant, or systems designer should then plan systems conversion (III–39) and backup systems. The precise details of the conversion plan and schedule must be specified. PERT may be used extensively here. The backup plan must detail recovery and alternative processing plans for the proposed system. These must also be confirmed with management.

Next, program requirements for each application module should be specified and plans should be made to schedule all programming tasks for each module needed in the system. At this time, with the detailed design nearly accomplished, plans should be made for training. Personnel requirements, location, duties, and topics to be covered must be communicated. (Training procedures will be discussed later.)

The last step in the detailed design phase is the preparation of an updated conversion and implementation budget, along with a cost-benefit revision for the system. The system must ultimately be justified on a cost-benefit basis. As illustrated in Chapter 4, all benefits must be considered in light of the potential value of the information obtained from the accounting system. The value of the system to the firm includes impact on both the reporting and information needs and the management decisions. The benefits to be derived must be compared with the estimated cost of the system. If the cost exceeds the expected benefits, then a revision in the detailed systems design is necessary before the design and implementation phases of the system can continue. In other words, in terms of the economic constraint, the benefits (value) of the information derived from the system must exceed the cost. The plans, design, and cost-benefit budget analysis set forth in this detailed systems design must then be approved by management. The completion of this phase will result in an integration of systems elements and constraints.

Program Specification and Implementation Planning—Phase IV

The objective of Phase IV is to (1) develop program specifications, (2) prepare test plans, (3) plan actual implementation, and (4) select software and hardware equipment vendors. The last objective assumes sufficient expertise exists on the part of the accountant, CPA firm, or company to justify waiting until after the total system has been specified to select a vendor. In cases where this expertise does not exist, this step must be exercised earlier, at step II–23 or III–31, to utilize the vendor's expertise in the design process. Vendor-selection principles will be similar regardless of the point at which the choice is made.

First, the program, system, and volume test plans must be described and planned. These plans should outline the testing philosophy, procedures to be used, responsibilities, and evaluation criteria.

VENDOR SELECTION   Vendor selection should proceed next. There are a wide variety of vendors and procedures for vendor selection. In this sequence of development and implementation phases, it is assumed that the client or company has sufficient expertise to propose a specific configuration to several vendors and to request bids from these vendors. Moreover, it is assumed that the vendor will be selling, renting, or leasing the hardware and software to the company. Depending on the company's EDP expertise, there are many other alternatives to this scenario.

In the computer industry there are many types of vendors. An impression of vendors and their products and services should have been obtained in steps III–31 and III–34 as the company studied and estimated EDP hardware, software, and communication requirements. There are *large computer* manufacturers such as IBM, Honeywell, Univac, NCR, CDC, and DEC that manufacture, sell, rent, and lease CPUs and a wide variety of peripheral equipment. For smaller clients and companies and for distributed processing systems, there are many (including some of the large computer manufacturers mentioned above) *mini* and *micro computer* manufacturers and distributors. In addition, there are many *peripheral equipment* manufacturers and distributors as well as *supply* vendors. Finally, there are data base, operating systems, and application systems *software vendors*; many have products designed for specific business markets and specific hardware manufacturers.

Much of this hardware, peripheral equipment, and software can be made available to a firm through *leasing companies, service bureaus,* and *time-sharing* arrangements. In the latter two cases, the hardware will probably be located off the user's premises. Service bureaus are an excellent means by which companies can begin to move toward computerization of a data processing system. In most cases service bureaus specialize in batch processing of transaction information. Time sharing, on the other hand, offers the power of large-scale configurations for file storage and problem solving to organizations at a fraction of the cost that would be incurred if the equipment were rented, leased, or purchased by the business. (This concept was reviewed in Chapter 6.) Finally, to help a client or company with all of the phases of systems development and implementation or just a few steps, such as equipment selection, there are many systems *consulting firms*. These include all the large CPA firms.

There are several ways in which the vendors can be approached. These approaches will take place at different points in the system development and implementation network. First, as was suggested in the preceding procedure, a client or company should approach vendors with *specific configuration proposals* that will satisfy the company's systems design. Configuration and financial arrangement bids should be sought for specific requirements for input, output, storage, interface, processing cycles, volume of processing, input and output communication activity, controls, communications, conversion, training, testing, and backup systems. This solicitation of bids should take place as suggested at design stage IV–47, shown in Figure 11–3.

Another alternative, which might give vendors more creative latitude in using their hardware and software expertise, would be to translate the compa-

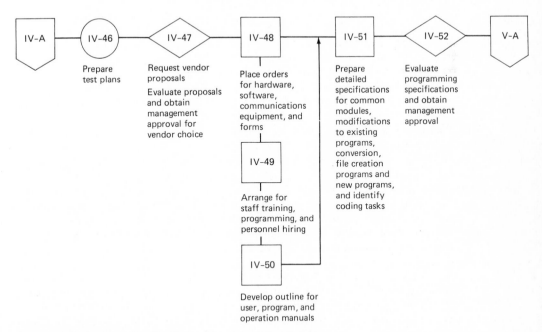

Figure 11–3 Program Specification and Implementation Planning

(Adapted with permission from AICPA, *Guidelines for System Development and Implementation*, © 1976, AICPA)

ny's requirements into *performance objectives* and obtain configuration proposals on this basis. This may be done earlier in the design stage (Phase III) and be based on the conceptual design requirements.

Finally, a company with little in-house expertise and without access to the expertise of an accountant or other consultant may choose to work closely with *one vendor* from the outset of the general design process. The vendor should be contacted at step II–23, or beginning with the detailed design process, step III–31 in this case.

EVALUATION OF VENDOR PROPOSALS   First, only those vendors who meet the specified systems requirements directly or with reasonable alternative configurations and software packages should be considered. Second, all key aspects of a vendor's hardware and software should be evaluated. Criteria can include such items as (1) price, (2) lease or rent payments, (3) maintenance contracts, (4) storage capacity in each storage device, (5) access speed for each storage device, (6) processing speed, (7) speed of input and output devices (CRT, printer, card reader, etc.), (8) number of input and output terminals that can be supported, (9) hardware controls, (10) backup systems, (11) compatibility with other manufacturers in terms of hardware and software programs, (12) software support, (13) vendor support, (14) modularity to enable additional components and peripheral support to be added, (15) reliability statistics on downtime, (16) implementation support, (17) testing and conversion support, (18) initial and continued training, (19) documentation flowcharts and operation manuals, and (20) reputation of the vendor.

It is useful to lay out a table, such as the one shown in Figure 11–4, for vendor comparisons. Selection should be based on an array of variables, with key variables being given more weight. As indicated in Figure 11–4, which represents three microcomputer configurations, the task of vendor selection is not easy because there are so many intangible factors.

The *equipment should be tested prior* to final vendor selection. Two basic procedures are used. Typical *benchmark* problems and sets of transactions can be run on the configuration suggested by the vendor to test input/output devices, controls, software, operating systems, data base systems, and utility packages for the handling of transaction volume and anticipated problems. This testing can usually be done at the vendor's location and is excellent for evaluating batch processing systems. As an alternative, models may be used to evaluate storage, access, and processing structures. Based on these models, *simulation* may be used to predict response time, transaction processing time, and turnaround time for an on-line system. Following this evaluation and testing of hardware, software, and other critical characteristics of vendors' systems, the best vendor is selected after receiving management's approval.

POSTSELECTION ACTIVITIES   Once a vendor has been selected, a mode of financing must be selected. Consideration must be given to such variables as the ability to change equipment, expected value of the equipment at the end of the time period, risk of obsolescence, life of hardware and software relative to the company's needs, availability of lease and rental contracts clauses, cancelability, maintenance provided, and, finally, cost. A capital budgeting approach, using present value to assess cash flows for hardware, software, maintenance,

CRITERION	VENDOR		
	A	B	C
1. Price	$12,000	$8,000	$6,000
2. Lease payments	$ 3,000/yr.	$3,000/yr.	$1,500/yr.
3. Maintenance	$ 100/mo.	$ 150/mo.	$ 50/mo.
4. Storage (diskettes)	32K	16K	16K
5. Access	Same	Same	Same
6. Processing speed	N/A	N/A	N/A
7. Input speed			
Card readers	Same	Same	Same
CRT	Tutorial (slow)	Faster	Faster
Output			
CRT	Same	Same	Same
Printer	150 CPS	80 CPS	80 CPS
8. Number (multiprocessing)	3	1	3
9. Hardware controls	Excellent	Good	Good
10. Backup system	Not local	Local	Not local
11. Compatibility	Yes	No	Yes
12. Software support	Good	Good	Poor
13. Vendor support	Excellent	Excellent	Good
14. Modularity	Yes	No	Yes
15. Reliability	Excellent	Excellent	Excellent
16. Implementation	Fair	Good	Fair
17. Testing and conversion	Fair	Good	Fair
18. Training	Good	Good	Little
19. Documentation	Poor	Poor	Poor
20. Reputation	Nationally known	New company	Good locally

Figure 11–4   Vendor Selection Criteria

installation, training, conversion, implementation, programming, testing, personnel, and the overall development and implementation process, is useful here.

Generally speaking, purchase arrangements are superior if equipment will be kept for five years or more. Cancelable leases offer more flexibility and often have purchase clauses at the end of the lease period; cash outflows may be higher here than with a purchase. A company may also opt for the most flexible of all arrangements: renting the equipment from month to month. Renting will result in the highest cash outflow. Another alternative is to rent, lease, and purchase various components based on their expected life and flexibility attributes.

After financial arrangements have been made, hardware, software, communication equipment, and forms should be ordered. Arrangements should be made with the vendor and within the firm for staff training and programming. A training schedule should be finalized so that all personnel, not only programmers, will be familiar with objectives, software, standards, documentation, procedures, data organization, and testing and conversion requirements. At this time an outline should be given to the vendor spelling out any requirements the company has regarding a user's manual. If increases in staff are required, new personnel should be selected. Great care should be taken to obtain well-qualified personnel. A company should beware of individuals who have changed jobs frequently, as is often the case with EDP and systems personnel. The reason for any change in job must be determined.

Finally, in this phase detailed program specifications should be made. These specifications must include the (1) purpose, (2) logic, (3) coding specifications, (4) testing specifications, and (5) criteria and conversion specifications. Specification must be done in terms of the logic, input, output, files, decision tables, formulas, and algorithms. Sometimes the actual test of vendor configuration must wait until after any needed in-house program development has been accomplished.

At the end of this phase, management must approve all programs and data specifications.

Programming and Testing—Phase V

In Phase V, hardware should be installed and tested to ensure that all maintenance, operating, utility, and other routines provided by the vendor are functioning as specified. After all programs and data files have been specified and hardware and vendor software have been installed,[6] programs must be coded and program and string tested, as shown in Figure 11–5. This phase requires active participation on the part of the ultimate decision makers and auditors to ensure that the results conform to the requirements of the information system and that adequate controls are present in the process.

First, programming logic must be finalized and documented with descriptions and program flowcharts, which are keyed to the systems flowcharts developed in Phase III. Modules must be assigned to programmers and assigned a priority. It may be most effective to program and test the higher-level, more frequently used application modules first. Programs must then be coded, desk checked, and compiled.

Concurrent with this test, procedures must be derived to ensure that each program functions as specified by itself as well as in conjunction with oth-

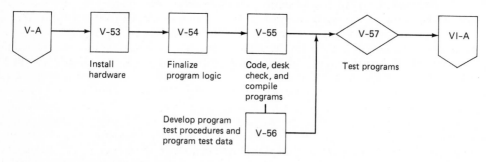

Figure 11–5 Programming and Testing

(Adapted with permission from AICPA, *Guidelines for Systems Development and Implementation,* © 1976, AICPA)

[6] Often programs may be tested on the vendor's equipment, but the system should be tested on the client's or the firm's (user's) equipment.

er programs and files with which it interfaces. There are several types of test procedures, each with its positive and negative attributes:

1. Desk check: review of program logic
2. Debugging: use of vendor hardware and software to debug program logic as programs are being compiled and run on test data
3. Random transactions and inquiries: selection of a sample of transactions and inquiries to make sure the program logic is functioning
4. Actual data: use of live groups of data to make sure all data are being processed as planned
5. Parallel: volume testing of actual data, which may be current or old, to make sure all data are being processed as planned
6. Controlled test data: testing of all possible permutations of transactions and inquiries that are good and bad to test actual processing and control procedures

These are noted in their order of increasing cost and reliability. Moreover, each *program*, as well as combinations (*strings*) of programs and data files that are tightly coupled or integrated, must be tested via one of these procedures.

If test data are required, they must be developed. As we noted above and especially in Chapter 9, the data can be a set of random transactions, an actual group of transactions, or a set of controlled fictitious good and bad transactions.

Given the programs, procedures, and test data, the programs and strings can now be thoroughly tested. As we noted in Chapter 9 on internal control, this testing is an important aspect of the overall system of controls. These test results are an important part of the system's documentation.

Systems Testing—Phase VI

Finally, all programs and strings of programs and data files must be tested together as an entire system to ensure compliance with management's expectations and control procedures, as shown in Figure 11–6. Emphasis here is on the interface between strings of programs, the operating system, data base systems, internal controls, and the various other systems of the organization.

Procedures and assignment of responsibility for obtaining data must be prepared. The operations manual and documentation must then be reviewed with computer operators and control personnel to assure that utility program support, operating rules, restart procedures, processing options, and systems controls are clear. The data base or master files must then be tested for the handling of input, processing, and output. Transaction data representing a full range of valid and invalid operational possibilities must be prepared with the full cooperation of users, auditors, and management. The limits of the system must be determined here, including (1) the capacity such as throughput, turnaround, access time; (2) its ability to handle stress without blowing up or going down; and (3) its ability to restart and recover when it does crash.

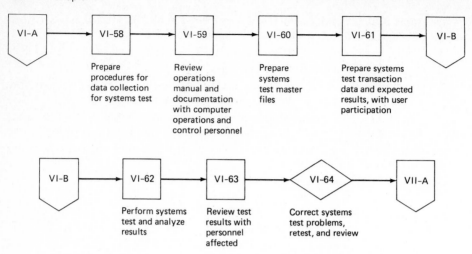

Figure 11–6 Systems Testing
(Adapted with permission from AICPA, *Guidelines for Systems Development and Implementation*, ©1976 AICPA)

After all procedures are working well, the data are available, and the programs have been tested, the systems test is performed. The results are thoroughly reviewed by decision makers, systems personnel, accountants, and outside auditors to assure everything is functioning in accordance with definition and design specifications. All problems are reconciled, and corrections to programs and procedures are made. The system is retested as often as necessary, for it must satisfy the requirements of management for effectiveness and efficiency and maintain data integrity through good controls.

Conversion and Volume Testing— Phase VII

Phase VII is the transition stage between the old way and the new way information is provided to management for decision-making, transaction processing, and reporting requirements. The principal objectives of this phase are to

1. Complete and validate systems documentation and training manuals
2. Convert and verify files
3. Perform volume and final testing
4. Obtain user approval

First, the conversion plan must be finalized, as shown in Figure 11–7. Objectives must be communicated and responsibilities assigned. Time tables for file and program conversion must be prepared. Error and reconciliation procedures must be detailed. Moreover, specific rules for maintenance of old and new file and program integrity must be set forth.

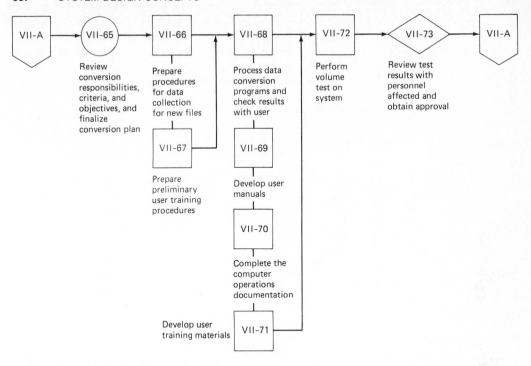

Figure 11-7 Conversion and Volume (or Final) Testing

(Adapted with permission from AICPA, *Guidelines for System Development and Implementation*, © 1976, AICPA)

The actual conversion approach may vary depending on the situation. A *direct approach* to stopping the old system and implementing the new system may be applicable when the differences between the old and the new information system are so great that any comparison would be meaningless.

Most often, however, a *parallel conversion* is used where both old and new systems are operated simultaneously, results are compared and reconciled, and the new system is corrected for differences if necessary. This parallel operation may be run on old or current inquiries and transactions. This procedure is costly, but it offers considerable protection for the company and its records.

Another approach is to use a branch or small subset of the organization in which to implement the new system as a *pilot* system. Using this method, all risk is localized and problems can be corrected in the pilot situation prior to organization-wide implementation.

Finally, *phase in conversion* can be used where small subsystems are implemented one at a time. This method has the major disadvantage of dealing with too many subsystem interfaces and the perpetual lack of a complete system. The job will never be finished, and a piecemeal system is likely to result.

After the conversion plan has been finalized, procedures for the creation of new files must be determined and prescribed. Regardless of the approach used, careful attention must be given to data files. They must be free of problems prior to conversion. The integrity of all the old files must be preserved while new ones are being created. After the procedures have been outlined for data conversion, the file conversion programs are run and the results are thoroughly checked.

At this time, computer operations documentation must be completed with specific instructions for operating the system. Data base and file requirements, hardware and software constraints, restart procedures, paper requirements, file labeling, and retention requirements must be detailed.

User training procedures and schedules should also be completed. Personnel to be trained should also be chosen by this time. This training can be accomplished in many ways, as will be noted later in our discussion of Phase VIII. A major part of training will involve complete familiarization with the user's manual. The user's manual should be completed at this stage in systems development. It should provide:

1. A flowchart of the system describing all flows, documents, and procedures
2. Operating instructions for each system, including input, data processing, and output reports
3. Time schedules for input submission, processing, and output generation
4. Control and security procedures
5. Assignment of responsibility
6. Description of all files and data to be used by each system
7. Instruction for completion of operating forms
8. Complete documentation of each program

Finally, a *volume test* is performed, applying one or more of the approaches noted earlier, to test the system in a live environment using all the converted files. All deficiencies are reconciled and corrected at this point. The test stage may run for several months before the new information system is finally approved and implemented. Before approval is given, all problems must be resolved and the system must function in accordance with the design specifications.

Implementation—Phase VIII

The objective of final implementation should be to complete user training; start operating the system; make any final changes to programs, the system, and documentation; and, in the case of management advisory service practitioners, turn the system over to the user after obtaining the user's written acceptance.

First, as noted in Figure 11–8, the final *implementation plan* and schedule should be prepared. This plan should be reviewed by users and operators, and any revisions should be made at this time.

User training should be completed. This training may take the form of group *seminars*, individual study of *procedure manuals*, individual *tutorials* for more complex and complicated procedures (such as using the CRT for the first

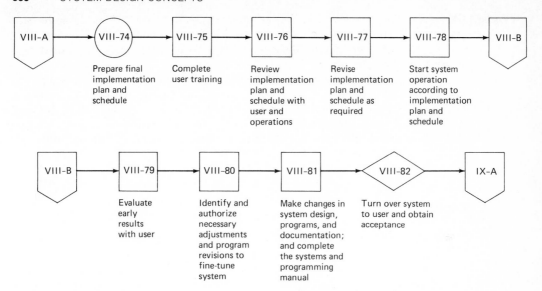

Figure 11–8 Implementation

(Adapted with permission from AICPA, *Guidelines for Systems Development and Implementation*, ©1976, AICPA)

time), *games* or *simulation* for problem-solving routines, and *on-the-job training*. It is important that this training continue throughout the use of the system.

Next, the operations of the new information system should be started and the use of the old system should cease according to schedule. The early results should be evaluated with users who no longer rely on the old system. Any adjustments to fine-tune the system should be made at this point. After these minor modifications, the system should be turned over to the users and, as time passes, should go through a postimplementation evaluation, as described in Chapter 10.

MODIFICATION AND MAINTENANCE PROCEDURES

Periodically the system must be audited by the management, the steering committee, the internal auditors, the controller, or the company's accountants. The audit should ensure that all the checkpoints noted in Chapter 10 are complied with.

If a minor modification will resolve the problem, data analysis techniques will suffice; if not, the decision analysis procedures must be replicated to the extent necessary to modify the system. In either case, technological, behavioral, and economic constraints must be considered in the modification.

It is imperative that Phases V through VIII be followed for each program change, no matter how small. Each modification must be completely tested. Moreover, complete records and documentation are necessary for each modification.

SUMMARY

All the design, specification, testing, conversion, and implementation phases have certain objectives that have to be met to lead ultimately to user satisfaction. These effectiveness and efficiency checkpoints were noted in Figure 10–8. Management's ability to make decisions dealing with a wide variety of problems and opportunities and to provide the necessary reports to third parties will be greatly enhanced if these phases suggested by the AICPA and adapted here are followed, because a well-designed and carefully implemented system will result. Such a system will also be the cornerstone of good internal control, as shown in Chapter 9.

SELECTED REFERENCES

ACKOFF, RUSSELL L., "Management Misinformation Systems," *Management Science*, December 1967, pp. B147–56.

American Institute of Certified Public Accountants, *Guidelines for Development and Implementation of Computer-Based Application Systems.* Management Advisory Services Guidelines Series Number 4, 1976.

BELANGER, L. R., "The Evaluation of Software Packages," *Canadian Charted Accountant*, 101 (December 1972), pp. 57–58.

———"The Evaluation of Software Packages—Part 2," *Canadian Charted Accountant*, 102 (February 1973), pp. 71–74.

BERLINER, HAROLD I., AND MARVIN GOLLAND, "Minicomputer Systems: A Practical Approach to Computer Implementation," *Financial Executive*, 48 (November 1980), pp. 24–29.

BIGGS, CHARLES L., EVAN G. BIRKS, AND WILLIAM ATKINS, *Managing the Systems Development Process.* Englewood Cliffs, N.J.: Prentice-Hall, 1980.

BURCH, JOHN G., FELIX R. STRATER JR., AND GARY GRUDNITSKI, *Information Systems: Theory and Practice.* New York: John Wiley, 1979.

CHERVANY, NORMAN L., AND GARY W. DICKSON, "Economic Evaluation of Management Information Systems: An Analytical Framework," *Decision Sciences*, July–October 1970, pp. 296–308.

CLELAND, DAVID I., AND WILLIAM R. KING, *Systems Analysis and Project Management* (2nd ed.). New York: McGraw-Hill, 1978.

CUSHING, BARRY F., *Accounting Information Systems and Business Organizations.* Reading, Mass.: Addison-Wesley, 1978.

DEARDEN, JOHN, "MIS Is a Mirage," *Harvard Business Review*, January–February 1962, pp. 90–99.

DONALDSON, HAIMISH, *A Guide to Successful Management of Computer Projects.* New York: John Wiley, 1978.

EIN-DOR, PHILLIP, "A Dynamic Approach to Selecting Computers," *Datamation*, 23 (June 1977), pp. 103–8.

FOSS, W. B., "Guidelines for Computer Selection," *Journal of Systems Management*, 27 (March 1976), pp. 36–39.

GREEN, GARY I., AND EARL A. WILCOX, "Find the Right Software through Specifications," *Management Accounting*, January 1982, pp. 43–49.

HARTMAN, W., H. MATTHES, AND A. PROEME, *Management Information Systems Handbook.* New York: McGraw-Hill, 1968.

LUCAS, HENRY C., JR., "Unsuccessful Implementation: The Case of a Computer-Based Order Entry System," *Decision Sciences*, 9 (1978), pp. 68–79.

McFARLAND, F. WARREN, "Problems in Planning an Information System," *Harvard Business Review*, March–April 1971, pp. 75–89.

McFARLAND, F. WARREN, RICHARD L. NOLAN, AND DAVID P. NORTON, eds., *Information Systems Administration.* New York: Holt, Rinehart & Winston, 1973.

MUMFORD, ENID, AND DON HENSHALL, *A Participative Approach to Computer Systems Design.* New York: John Wiley, 1979.

PARETTA, ROBERT L., "Designing Management Information Systems: An Overview," *Journal of Accountancy*, April 1975, pp. 42–47.

RAPPAPORT, ALFRED, "Management Misinformation Systems—Another Perspective," *Management Science*, December 1968, pp. B133–36.

ROCKART, JOHN F., "Chief Executives Define Their Own Data Needs," *Harvard Business Review*, March–April 1979, pp. 81–93.

SHAW, JOHN C., AND WILLIAM ATKINS, *Managing Computer System Projects.* New York: McGraw-Hill, 1970.

WEINGARD, MARVIN, "The Rockford Files: A Case for the Computer," *Management Accounting*, April 1979, pp. 36–38.

APPENDIX: SCHEDULING THE ANALYSIS, DEFINITION, DESIGN, AND IMPLEMENTATION OF INFORMATION SYSTEMS—PERT

The analysis, definition, design, and implementation process outlined in Chapter 10 and in this chapter considers a series of activities and decision nodes. The various figures in Chapters 10 and 11 outlined the general sequence of these activities and decisions. More than once, planning activities were noted where the next sequence of activities and plans were to be scheduled.

A technique developed during the 1950s that has proved useful in scheduling this type of problem consists of a sequence of activities and nodes, the start of each depending on the completion of others. This procedure is called PERT (Program Evaluation Review Technique). PERT is especially useful where there is a large network of tasks, such as the one suggested by the AICPA which has been slightly modified in this text. This network has eighty-seven such nodes and activities, and each activity unit precedes or follows other activities. A node begins and completes each activity, such as programming.

Consider a subset of the major activities and their expected times of completion in Phases III through VIII shown in Figures A11–1 and A11–2. Activities are designated by a letter, and the nodes denoting the beginning and ending of activities are numbered. For each activity to commence, another activity or set of activities must be completed. This is denoted in the preceding activity column. For example, to begin activity *O* (writing of programs), *N*, *I*

DESCRIPTION	ACTIVITY	TIME (IN WEEKS)	PRECEDING ACTIVITY
Design the decision model	A	4	General design
Design the input and report formats	B	2	A
Design the file	C	2	B
Develop the interface	D	2	C
Establish control procedures	E	2	D
Prepare the site	F	10	E
Plan conversion and backup	G	1	E
Plan training	H	3	E
Plan programming	I	1	J
Identify program module and flow	J	1	E
Prepare specifications and budget	K	2	E,G,H,I,J
Select vendor	L	4	K
Outline user, operation, and program manuals	M	1	L
Prepare detailed program specifications	N	3	L
Write programs	O	8	N,I,F
Test programs	P	1	O
Review operations manual documentation	Q	1	M
Test the systems	R	2	P,Q
Collect data for conversion	S	1	C,G
Convert data files	T	2	S
Conversion volume test (parallel runs)	U	12	R,T
Complete user training	V	8	J,M
Implement system	W	1	V,U

Figure A11–1   Activities and Their Expected Time of Completion

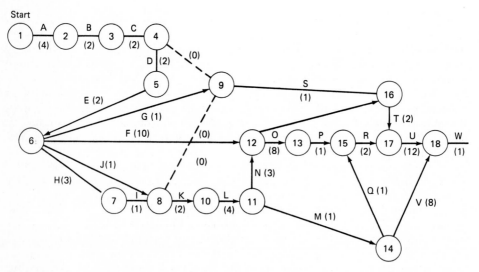

Figure A11–2   PERT Diagram

and *F* must be complete. Note also that estimated times are shown in Figure A11-1. These can be calculated by taking the most pessimistic time, *a*, the expected time, *m*, and the most optimistic time, *b*, and calculating an expected time $(a + 4m + b)/6 = 4$. For example, for activity *A*, $a = 2$, $m = 3$, $b = 10$; or the estimated time is equal to 4.

As these activities are being completed, comparisons can be made between planned times and actual time. Moreover, these times and their network can be used to compute the critical path. The *critical path* is the path through the network with the longest time estimated for completion. Any delay along this path will delay implementation of the entire system. In this example, the critical path is A B C D E H K L N O P R U W, which takes a total of 48 weeks to complete. Any activity not on this path has some slack time. For example, item *F* has a three-week slack time, for the longest time along the critical path from node 6 to node 12 is twelve weeks and activity *F* is ten weeks. Management could start *F* two weeks late and still not delay the entire project. If, however, *F* is started three weeks late, then it becomes part of a new critical path.

Using this scheduling procedure, the accountant, systems designer, and managers involved in the systems development project can track the progress of the development and implementation steps. They can pay particular attention to the activities on the critical path and be more flexible with those items where slack is present. In summary, PERT has proved useful for the design and development of large complex information systems.

REVIEW QUESTIONS

1. What constraints should be considered in the final detailed design of an accounting information system?

2. What should a project team consist of and why?

3. Why is the modular concept necessary?

4. At what point in the systems design and development phases must the decision models be fully specified and why?

5. At what point in the systems design and development phases must the data files be specified and why?

6. Where are systems flowcharts used in the systems design and development phases? How are they used?

7. When are detailed accounting and administrative controls considered in the design process? Why?

8. Discuss the variety of vendor options available to the potential EDP user.

9. When would you use a benchmark problem in vendor selection?

10. Discuss the pros and cons of the various test procedures.

11. What is meant by systems testing?

12. What are the advantages and disadvantages of the various conversion procedures? What is a volume test?

13. What should be included in the user's manual?

14. What methods may be used for user training?

EXERCISES AND CASES

11-1

Easy Way Builders, a regional building and supply retailer with outlets in several southeastern states, recently decided to install small microprocessors (intelligent terminals) at each location and to tie these via telephone lines to the home office. Sales data were transmitted once each day for the day's activities after closing. The microprocessors accumulated local sales statistics and kept a perpetual inventory of building supplies better than the old manual system previously used by each location. With this new system, billing was handled out of the home office instead of from each location. This relieved each manager of a large volume of paper work.

Initially, considerable cost savings were realized. Lower stock levels were achieved with the new perpetual inventory system and better sales forecasting due to the superior sales data available. Problems developed, however. Easy Way started to lose its market share. Managers complained that many of their larger customers (builders) had a difficult time in communicating and resolving problems related to their monthly statements. Moreover, these builders detested paper work and preferred to resolve problems and misunderstandings on a face-to-face basis. Generally these problems arose because the supplies ordered were excessive or the wrong items were delivered. Returns and exchanges were common.

What problems in the detailed systems design and ultimate testing could lead to this loss of business? How would you, as the accountant suggest that the company resolve this problem?

11-2

As a CPA advising a client in the design and development of a new system, how would you explain to the client the need to follow the phases in systems design suggested by the AICPA and slightly modified in this chapter? Keep in mind that the client is not impressed with academic reasons for all this effort and wants to know why he just can't go and lease an accounting system like his friend at the Rotary Club. Also, keep in mind that you will need to justify your billing time.

11-3

After deciding that its decision-making, transaction processing, and reporting needs required a new microprocessing system, Platte River Contractors purchased a system, well suited to its needs, from a leading supplier of such systems for Platte River's type and size of business. All programs and their combinations were well tested by the software supplier. Given their lack of expertise, Platte River's managers clearly decided to select a proven vendor for general contractors of their size.

Given their confidence in the system and its ease of operation, they terminated their bookkeeper. The receptionist was given the user's manual and told to enter the information on the CRT during her free time, which averaged six to seven hours per day. Moreover, the day the system arrived, Platte River's management personnel ceased operations of the old manual payroll, accounts receivable (contracts), purchasing and inventory, equipment scheduling, and asset systems. They immediately started using the new system.

Within a month, the company's auditors (one of the "big eight") were called in to send out confirmations to its suppliers to clean up an awful mess. Platte River had completely lost track of its accounts payable records and was in the embarrassing position of having to ask each of its suppliers for the information.

What went wrong? What should the company have done to prevent this problem?

11-4

Soft and Tender Footware, a manufacturer of bedroom slippers for ladies, recently fired its controller and EDP manager, who had been with the company for several years. To take his place, it sent one of its operations managers to school to learn all about the DEC hardware it was using. The company justifiably felt that, aside from the transaction processing and report generation of the DEC equipment and supporting software, most of which had been programmed by the former controller, all accounting needs could be handled by several bookkeepers and the advice of a local CPA.

Subsequent to this, the CPA began to ask various questions about some of the output from the system, and the new EDP manager could not answer these questions. In fact, every time the EDP manager needed to find out how a program worked or how it interfaced with other programs, he had to request a code listing and proceed from there. On each of these listings he found a considerable amount of what he termed "excess baggage," or programming steps without apparent use. Upon hearing all of this, the president of the company was furious and threatened to "chuck" the EDP system, hire several bookkeepers, and return to an old manual system where the mode of transaction processing was clear-cut and easy to see.

What action on the part of the former controller would have prevented this problem? Why? Other than scrapping the EDP system, what should management first do to get its system in order?

11–5

Ross and Montgomery, CPAs, are advising one of their clients about the acquisition of a new data processing system. To assist in scheduling the major tasks involved in design and development, they are using PERT. Their estimation of their client's major activities and the weeks required to accomplish these activities is shown in Figure C11–5.

Figure C11–5 Estimated Times for Each Design and Implementation Activity.

ACTIVITY		TIME (IN WEEKS)
A	Select vendor	2
B	Prepare site	7
C	Define system requirements	4
D	Determine specifications for system	3
E	Analyze decision and transaction processing network	6
F	Determine general approach to data processing	5
G	Write programs	5
H	Install hardware	2
I	Purchase hardware and software	1
J	Test (programs and systems)	6
K	Design data base	3
L	Parallel conversion	8
M	Switch from old to new system	1
N	Train employees	4

REQUIRED: What is the earliest date for the completion of system implementation? Where is the slack in the system? What assumptions did you make in your analysis?

11–6

A computer software vendor has contracted with a small business to design, install, and test a microcomputer system for basic accounting applications. These applications include payroll, sales analysis, accounts receivable, accounts payable, inventory, fixed assets, cash receipts and disbursements, and general ledger accounting. In order to complete the project on time, and in order to establish deadlines for receipt of information from the client and for various steps in the design and development process, the vendor used PERT (Program Evaluation Review Technique). The network shown in Figure C11–6 was developed, where the expected days for each activity were those noted on the network between nodes.

REQUIRED:

a. The critical path for the design and development project shown in Figure C11–6.

b. The slack time (time the activities on this path can be delayed and not delay the entire project) on path 1-9-6.

c. If all other paths are operating on schedule but path segment 1-3 has an unfavorable variance of 2.5 days, what will happen to the critical path?

11–7

Washington Farm Supply, a farm supply distributor for the upper Midwest, has decided to acquire a microprocessor to process its accounting transactions, post the general ledger, and prepare stock status reports, accounts receivable, and purchase activity reports on a daily basis for management's decisions needs. It can rent or purchase or lease the equipment and software. The following information is given on the four available alternatives:

1. Rent for $4,000 per year.
2. Lease for $2,000 per year for three years with an option to purchase at the end of three years for $4,000. Maintenance contract $1,500 per year for life of lease, and

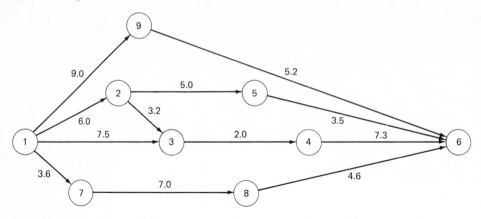

Figure C11–6

$1,000 per year if purchase option is exercised at the end of three years. The option to purchase is not exercised.

3. Alternative 2, with the option to purchase at the end of three years for $4,000 exercised.

4. Purchase for $8,000, with a maintenance contract costing $1,200 per year. The cost of capital is 10 percent. Other costs will be the same.

What is the most desirable contract if Washington intends to keep the hardware and software from one to eight years, and the exact number of years is unknown at the present time? Due to rapid technology changes, salvage value will be negligible.

11–8

West Coast Apparel Manufacturing Company sells ready-to-wear men's clothing. Division A specializes in men's sports clothes, and Division B sells the company's original line of men's clothing.

Sales representatives for the firm cover territories throughout the United States selling to retail stores, who in turn sell to the buying public. Division A, the smaller of the two, was formed more recently and is staffed primarily with former employees of Division B. There are several significant differences between sales representatives in the two divisions. Sales representatives in Division A are on the average younger and have been with the firm for less time than sales representatives from Division B. Due to the smaller size of the division, the sales representatives in Division A also average more accounts than those in Division B.

The company's original order input form is keypunched onto cards, which become the input for a computer system. This is a lengthy process that results in slow order entry and customer order acknowledgment. At the beginning of the new sales season, sales representatives in Division A began using a *new order input form*. This new form is read by an OCR optical scanner, which prepares a computer tape for input to order-entry processing. The firm hoped the new OCR form would speed order processing by eliminating the keypunching step.

The new order input form represents a major change in job content for the sales force, since a significant amount of each sales representative's time is spent writing orders. The use of the scanner also requires major changes in the method of processing input orders. Previously all orders had been processed at regional warehouses. However, because of economies of scale, order processing became centralized. In addition, a new automated warehouse serving the Division A sales force was opened concomitantly with the change to the new order-entry procedures. (There was no technological connection between the warehouse and the new order input form; they both happened to be scheduled for implementation at the same time.)

During the initial operation period the firm's hopes were not realized. The quality of information processing service was low. The firm rented time on another company's OCR scanner. Because of logistics problems in using a scanner at another location and difficulties with the new, automated warehouse, improvements in computer service were minimal or nonexistent. A good argument could be made that computer problems actually reduced the quality of information.

From the standpoint of costs, sales representatives had to print more carefully and familiarize themselves with a new form. Writing orders is a significant part of a sales representative's daily activity, so these added requirements for the new system were time consuming. Similar problems existed before with an earlier attempt to use a mark sense version of an input form. This earlier attempt was abandoned when field test results were highly unfavorable.

Based on the analysis above, it is predicted that the implementation of the new OCR system will not be highly successful. Based on the steps of this chapter and Chapter 10 as well as the behavioral concepts in Chapter 3, why?[1]

11-9

Quasar Air, a freight company, guaranteed overnight delivery of all packages in the continental United States. It would pick up and deliver door-to-door in select U.S. cities, place packages on the plane, fly the planes to an old air force base south of St. Louis, sort all packages, fly to select destinations, and deliver packages the next morning at these various cities.

The company started out with a few major cities and eventually gained an excellent reputation. Its stock joined the list of other glamour companies on Wall Street. It easily raised more equity and expanded rapidly. Soon its scheduling and delivery routing problem became a nightmare. It began to have some trouble and frequently fell short of its goal of 100 percent overnight delivery because of scheduling and delivery problems.

Management was beginning to consider deleting some routes in order to assign more aircraft to high-volume traffic areas. The problem here was that the company controller could

[1] Adapted with permission from Henry C. Lucas, "Unsuccessful Implementation: The Case of a Computer-Based Order Entry System," *Decision Sciences*, 9 (1978), pp. 68–79.

not determine the contribution to profit (if any) each route made because the cost system was so full of allocation assumptions and other dependent cost relationships.

Management had heard of some new operations research procedures that could resolve the company's traffic routing problems and had read about some new cost-allocation schemes that could help it get a better handle on contribution to actual profit of the various routes. Management decided to engage the services of Operations Research Systems. Operations Research Systems' managers recommended a software package they had used before, called Traffic Scheduler—III, and a flexible standard cost system that they had sold to a wide variety of clients.

Mr. Blake, president of Quasar Air, decided that these two systems would meet the company's needs, so he purchased the systems and instructed Mr. Simmons, his controller who was responsible for all data processing, to install the systems and begin using them. This was done as soon as each had been compiled and run on Quasar's computer system. The programs worked well.

The conversion step was skipped because the programs ran so smoothly, and they were immediately implemented. Disaster struck next.

1. The schedule was fairly good from a distribution perspective under normal circumstances but resulted in costly mistakes such as routing one plane for St. Louis to Miami to San Francisco to Toronto and back.

2. The schedule could not handle adverse weather conditions, which frequently socked in upper Midwest airports.

3. The schedule algorithm broke down when no solution was feasible and the "best" alternative was needed because it was a linear-programming optimization model. This occurred when more than one plane was in maintenance and a peak traffic load occurred.

4. The cost system did not interface with the scheduling algorithm to cost and various routes over a range of potential routing patterns. The cost system did not interface with the general ledger system. Input actually had to be keyed into the general ledger package from reports generated by the cost system. The maintenance system did

not interface with the scheduling algorithm, and there was no way to determine an optimal maintenance program for the fleet.

5. The amount of time needed to input delivery location data into the delivery algorithm on busy days took three hours at some locations and it was nine o'clock before the trucks could leave to deliver the packages, resulting in many late deliveries.

The president, given these and many more problems, fired Mr. Simmons for failing to implement the new systems properly.

REQUIRED:

a. List any weaknesses in systems development implementation and state what should have been done to correct the weaknesses. Use the following format:

WEAKNESS	WHAT SHOULD HAVE BEEN DONE

b. As Quasar's accountant, where do you suggest it begin to clean up this mess? Outline your suggestions step by step and briefly explain the reason for each step.

11–10

Consider again E. H. Green Hardware (Case 9–19). Mr. Green's volume of business is beginning to overwhelm the manual system described in Chapter 9. He has requested your services in designing a new system using a small microcomputer. Propose a detailed design alternative that includes a flowchart, suggested hardware and software, suggested records and data files, and suggested internal control. Also propose any organizational changes.

11–11

Robinson Company (Case 9–7) is considering computerizing its manual system. Prepare a systems flowchart of a conceptual alternative using random access on-line software and a microcomputer. (AICPA adapted)

11–12

The Reed Company of Winnipeg, Manitoba, has yearly sales close to $40 million. All of its business activities are conducted from one location. Currently, office workers manually perform all operations in accounts payable, accounts receivable, general ledger, and invoicing. The amount of work that the office staff performs is increasing each year and the staff, which now numbers 15 people, is finding it difficult to keep up with the excess work load. Reporting deadlines are often missed. Additional clerical help is not the solution and the manager recognizes that automation of the firm's procedures is essential.

In the existing system, orders are received through the mail. Clerks pull customers' records to check for poor credit risks and delinquent accounts. These are then referred to the manager.

Each customer record is updated manually and an entry is made in the sales summary. An invoice and bill of lading are made up and the latter is sent to the warehouse for assembly of the order. The products are picked from the inventory and product cards are changed to reflect the change in inventory. If a product is not in stock, the office is notified and the invoice is adjusted. The return of a copy of the bill of lading to the office to advise that the order has been filled serves as authorization for sending the invoice to the customer.

At present, there are 6000 customers for whom records are kept (200 characters of data per customer) and 500 products for which product ledger cards are kept (100 characters of data per product).

The design objectives are that the proposed system must be able to handle the existing order entry and invoicing applications as well as an improved inventory control function. It would also be desirable if some other basic functions could be handled. Moreover, the system must be designed to operate without a team of exponsive EDP personnel. No in-house programming or operation talent is available and training such a staff is not planned.

After a study of the system requirements and the potential benefits, two alternative system designs are proposed. One approach is to use a small business computer system that handles the several applications. The applications will be handled sequentially, and no internal processing interfaces are needed between applications. All essential functions can be handled, although some cannot be handled as completely as desired. The back-order and future-order functions, for example, cannot be satisfactorily handled automatically, and so they will be maintained manually. Commissions and accounts payable will not be handled initially. Also, there is no possibility of handling the sales analysis requirements of the company.

In this first alternative, magnetic ledger cards are used as the storage medium. There is a magnetic ledger card for each customer and for each product. Processing is performed one application at a time. When the accounts receivable or invoicing program is loaded into the computer, only that application can be run. Input to the program is provided by the magnetic ledger cards and by transaction data keyed-in at the keyboard. Output is produced on the printer as the magnetic ledger cards are processed (e.g., updated). The supplier provides developed basic business programs with this machine and charges $3 per instruction when deviations from the standard program are required. It appears that approximately 2500 instructions will need to be modified in these programs. The hardware configuration—consisting of a keyboard/printer terminal, card reader, card punch, and ledger card reader/writer—has a purchase price of $32,000. On a five-year purchase plan the monthly payments

are $800. Monthly maintenance is $100. Installation can be accomplished in three months. The supplier will supply four additional weeks of programmer training for the user, at any time the user desires. This system requires 100 square feet of space.

The other proposed system uses a relatively sophisticated minicomputer with disk files. In this system, orders will be entered via a series of keyboard CRT display units. When an order arrives at a CRT unit the operator enters the customer's identification. The program will validate this identification, check the customer's credit, and then notify the input clerk at the CRT whether to proceed with the first product ordered or to take the order to the manager to be handled manually. Assuming that the customer has a good credit rating, the operator will then enter the product number and the quantity desired, wait for the program to check if enough inventory is available to fill the order, and then enter the next product ordered. This procedure is repeated until the entire order is entered. The input clerk is notified if special action is required (such as excluding an item from the order because of insufficient inventory). Items which must be reordered are printed daily. Invoicing for all deliverable items is performed automatically, as is the preparation of shipping documents. The preceding procedures initiate other functions which interface with the system.

The proposed minicomputer system includes the processor, three CRT units, two printers, and a disk drive. This hardware costs $36,000, or $900 per month on a five-year monthly installment plan. Maintenance is $250 per month. Application software will have to be developed in its entirety to make the integrated approach work. This cost is estimated to be $90,000, despite the use of much of the manufacturer's software. It is estimated that the installation time for such a system would be nine months. Also, this minicomputer would require 200 square feet of space.

The manufacturer of the small business computer provides, at a $750 charge, the means to convert Reed's customer and product files to magnetic ledger card media. With respect to the minicomputer system, the software developed for processing the sales data also can be used to convert the data to disk storage. (However, the data in the present files

ACTIVITY CODE	DESCRIPTION OF ACTIVITY	EXPECTED ACTIVITY DURATION (DAYS)	CODES OF PREDECESSOR ACTIVITIES[a]
A	Prepare System Requirements	10	
B	Plan Design Phase	3	A
C	Design System	20	B,F
D	Verify Feasibility	2	C
E	Organize Project	5	A
F	Establish Plans and Controls	3	E
G	Prepare Design Specifications	2	C
H	Prepare Audit and Control Specifications	4	G
I	Prepare Job Descriptions for New Employees	3	H
J	Prepare Training Guides	3	I
K	Prepare Logic Diagrams and Programs	20	D
L	Prepare Test Data	4	K
M	Perform Program Testing and Debugging	5	L
N	Select and Order System Resources	20	D
O	Install Computer System	12	N
P	Perform System Testing and Debugging	5	M,O
Q	Prepare Program Documentation	5	M,O
R	Prepare System Documentation	3	J,Q
S	Plan for System Support	2	R
T	Perform Final Checkout and Cutover	3	Q

[a] Activities that must be completed *prior* to starting the listed activity.

Figure C11–13 St. Anne's Hospital

will still need to be keyed into the computer system via the CRT units.)

Current space costs are $2 per square foot per month. Keypunching and key-verifying rates are $7 per hour at a rated speed of 10,000 keystrokes per hour.

REQUIRED: Which alternative system should the manager choose? Justify your answer in quantitative and qualitative terms. Use a three-year horizon. (SMAC adapted)

11–13

The St. Anne Hospital of Ottawa, Ontario, has decided to develop and implement a computer-based information system as soon as it is feasible. St. Anne's controller has identified the following activities, with their expected durations and interdependencies, that would be involved in the undertaking.

REQUIRED:

a. Prepare a network diagram and specify the activities on the critical path.

b. What is the minimum number of days required to design and implement this system?

Hint: Refer to Appendix.
(SMAC adapted)

11–14

Case 17-5 (ABC Leasing) may be used here.

12

LOGISTICS SYSTEMS

OBJECTIVE

The objective of a logistics information system is to support the decision-making, transaction processing, and reporting requirements of inventory, production, and purchasing management. These requirements are a function of the management system's objectives. Production management needs inventory to absorb fluctuations in the supply of raw material and subassemblies and to meet the demand for finished goods. Economical production runs and production balancing need inventory to support long-run efficient operation. Marketing management needs inventory to smooth fluctuations in its distribution system and in sales demand in order to better serve customers. Inventory is also useful in decoupling parts of an organization such as marketing and production. It serves as a buffer between those areas that would be too costly and impractical to couple tightly or coordinate.

In developing an inventory system the level of service provided as well as the cost of that service is very important. The cost of service can increase astronomically; therefore the inventory system must be designed to enhance management's control over inventory levels and costs. Inventory systems vary in complexity from those using simple status reports, reorder points, and economic lot sizes to those using mathematical and statistical models. Regardless of the inventory system's complexity, it must be designed to provide information to support the various activity levels within each function (primarily the logistics and marketing functions in this illustration), and it must link all the elements of the system in the most efficient way.

The basic objective of the production system is to support efficient production operations through the efficient use of company resources such as plant and equipment, financial, raw material, labor, and supporting overhead. This system must support planning and controlling activities. To accomplish this objective, management needs accurate, timely, and relevant information including production orders, the demand for products, product and quality specifications, manufacturing sequence specifications, labor efficiency data, and resource availability information.

The basic objective of the purchasing system is to ensure that production and inventory systems have sufficient raw material, supplies, equipment, and inventory to operate effectively and efficiently.

Planning objectives are generally executed using budget or responsibility accounting systems, scheduling procedures, or mathematical models such as those reviewed in Chapter 4. Cost control objectives are often reached through a system of overhead budgets and through the use of standard costs and the subsequent variance feedback information. Quality control objectives are accomplished using a series of checkpoints throughout the plant. Either an integrated or a distributive system can be used to accomplish these objectives. The systems must, however, be well designed and effectively implemented in order to achieve these objectives.

DECISION AND TRANSACTION PROCESSING CHARACTERISTICS

Environmental Considerations

We cannot easily generalize specifications for an accounting system for production and inventory management because each firm operates in a unique and often vastly different environment. Thus, as we noted in Chapters 2 and 10, environmental characteristics play a major role in information system development and implementation. An accountant, as a system designer and auditor, therefore, must understand the decision-making, reporting, and transaction processing environment of the business. Figure 12–1 outlines some characteristics that have a bearing on typical logistics management systems. For example, an accountant who is advising a utility organization must be cognizant of such key environmental characteristics as governmental regulations, public rate-making activities, the assets involved and the effect of technology on these assets, classes of customers, electrical distributive systems and backup capabilities, supplies of fuel, and capital requirements for future expansion. The information system must be designed to satisfy decision-making, processing, and reporting needs in this context. Therefore studies of the economic decision-making environment must precede an analysis of decision-making and transaction processing networks.

Plant capacity
Competitive environment
Resource availability
Financial capability
Product life cycle
Product options
Obsolescence
Variety of products
Styles and colors
Inventory policy

Customer characteristics
Distribution system
Labor requirements
Technology level
Uniqueness of product
Economy
Government regulation
Government influence
Seasonality
Ownership

Figure 12–1 Environmental Characteristics

In traditional manufacturing and inventory systems, the environment may be such that scheduling and ordering decisions are made weekly. In these cases daily economic activities have little effect on management decisions. Changes in plans are very infrequent. Weekly stock reports on material, work in process, and finished goods suffice for most decision-making requirements. Prices and costs are relatively stable and can be published once a week for marketing decisions. A batch processing or manual system that generates reports following traditional lines of authority and responsibility will be likely to satisfy management's information needs.

In a highly competitive environment, however, prices, costs, and demand fluctuate daily. Profitability and forecasting decisions are more difficult to make. A system is required that can constantly monitor the environment and alert managers to changing economic events in order to allow timely production, scheduling, and inventory decisions. This type of environment will often require a manager to cut across traditional management functions. To support these coordinated activities, an information system must be able to support a product or matrix organization structure. Moreover, the system may require on-line data processing capability, as well as a complex data base management system such as the systems outlined in Chapters 6 and 8.

In either example above, the set of system elements, their organization, and the decision network are a function of the business environment.

Decision Network

The objective of a logistics and production information system is to provide management with the information necessary to make operational, planning, and strategic decisions, report the results of operations to third parties, and process transactions. These transactions undergird the information system because summaries of transaction data are often used to make decisions. However, such information is often irrelevant for decision making or is in a form not useful for levels of management other than the operations level. The accountant and the system analyst must therefore design the system around the decision and reporting network and not around the flow of transactions, although transactions are necessary to value inventory and subsequently help in the preparation of financial statements. A typical transaction processing network used to support many of these decisions is outlined later in this chapter.

As outlined in Chapters 2 and 10, the economic, business and information environment must also be reviewed in designing the system. The organization within which the system must function is a key facet of this environment. A typical organization chart is illustrated in Figure 12–2. The production vice-president is responsible for providing corporate headquarters with information for strategic planning. The vice-president also needs information for managerial decisions and for working with the marketing and finance organizational units. Each plant manager and each staff manager is responsible for supplying the production vice-president with sufficient information for these decision-making and reporting requirements. Department supervisors and various department heads in turn supply information to the plant managers.

Depending on the firm and its economic environment, the department heads may be responsible for such activities as production, maintenance, inventory control, engineering, cost accounting, personnel, and scheduling. The department heads need information for operational decisions, and they must also supply information to the plant manager for decisions and reporting needs. The logistics information system must therefore satisfy the information requirements of all levels within the organization. Figure 12–3 outlines the various operational decisions that must be made for a typical plant.

Logistics Subsystems

Basically, there are three types of logistics subsystems: purchasing, inventory, and production. Each has a characteristic set of information sources, data files, decisions, and information requirements.

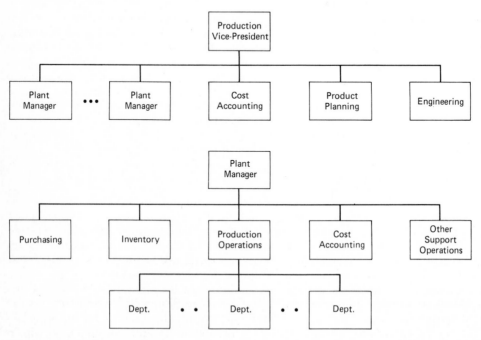

Figure 12–2 Logistics Organization

ACCOUNTING—PRODUCTION

Inventory Levels
Cost Standards
    Material
    Labor
    Overhead Application Rates
Analysis of Variances
Budgets
    Each Production Department

PRODUCTION PLANNING AND SCHEDULING

Planning
    Production Sequence
    Inventory
        Finished Goods
        Sub-assemblies
        Raw Material
    Work Force
    Factory Layout
        Departments
        Work Stations
    Quality
    Mix of Products
Processing Customer Orders
Scheduling
    Production Orders
    Balancing
    Materials
    Sub-assemblies
    Work Force
    Work Stations and Departments
Expediting
Coordination
Controlling
    Resources
    Time
    Cost

ENGINEERING—PRODUCTION

Product Design Specifications
    Material
    Sub-assemblies
    Quality
Manufacturing Specifications

    Operations Sequence
    Material Quantity
    Labor Requirements
Cost Standards
    Material
    Labor

PLANT MANAGER

Planning, Scheduling and
    Coordination
Cost Decisions
Purchasing
Quality Control
Engineering Design and
    Manufacturing
Maintenance
Inventory
Personnel

DEPARTMENT FOREMAN

Job Scheduling
Machine Usage
Repairs
Labor Usage

PURCHASING

Vendor Selection
Quantity
When to Order (reorder point
    or time)
Price
Methods of Shipment

MAINTENANCE

Schedule of Preventative
    Maintenance
Schedule of Repairs
Manpower
Equipment
Supplies
Sub-contracting

Figure 12-3 Logistical Decisions

PURCHASING   The objective of a purchasing system is to ensure that production operations either have available or can readily obtain the necessary raw material components, supplies, and equipment. Because purchasing is related to inventory, it is subject to all the financial constraints associated with carrying costs. The purchasing department is charged with selecting the order quantities, vendors, prices, and mode of shipment.

Decision models used in purchasing can range from the visual scanning of production schedules, parts requisitions, stock status reports, and the stock itself, to complex mathematical and statistical models for reorder quantity. When more-sophisticated models are used, purchase orders are usually generated automatically once inventory reaches a certain reorder point. Inventory records, vendor price, product availability, delivery schedules, history, economic forecasts, and cash forecasts are some of the prime sources of the information needed as input for these decision models.

An example of an inventory purchase order and vendor record is shown in Figure 12–4. Generally the record is identified by part number, but it may be sorted by vendor name or number for accounts payable information.

Even a small microcomputer system, for example, has available the following random access data and reports to facilitate the purchasing manager's decision process:

1. Inventory listing
2. Inventory analysis: item code, description number in stock, purchase price, unit list price, total purchase price, unit profit, total profit, and percent profit
3. Inventory by vendor: item code, description, purchase price, list price, maximum discount allowed, vendor level, number in stock, number ordered, number sold, and number returned
4. Inventory vendor list: item code, description, reorder level, number in stock, status (vendor, back order depleted), vendor number ordered
5. Inventory on order list: item code, description, vendor, date ordered, lead time, when overdue, number ordered, unit price, total price
6. Inventory by vendor overdue report: item rank and code description, date ordered, lead time, when overdue, days late, number ordered, unit price, total price
7. Inventory value by vendor: item code, description, number in stock, unit cost, total cost, unit list price, total list price, gross profit, percent gross profit
8. Accounts payable account
9. Accounts payable aging report[1]

With this information, purchasing should be able to make more intelligent decisions with regard to what, from whom, and when to order. Transaction records and simple economic order quantity models can also be used to supply much of this information.

---

[1] OS-AMCAP, *Small Business Accounting System*, (Aurora, Ohio: Ohio Scientific, 1978) with permission of American Intelligent Machines, Lincolnshire, Ill.

INVENTORY STOCK, PURCHASE ORDER, AND VENDOR RECORD

Part Description
    Part Number—key field for
      identification
    Part Name and Description
    Price
    Cost
    Location
Order Information
    Vendor Name and Number
    Lead Time
    Order Frequency
    Order Quantity
    Reorder Point
    Safety Stock
    Forecast
    Purchase Price
    Maximum Discount Allowed

Current Activity
    Quantity on Hand
    Quantity on Order
    Purchase Order Numbers
    Dates
    Vendors
    Receiving Report Number
    Number Received
    Dates Received
Historical Detail
    Quantity Purchased in Last 12
      Months
    Purchase Order Numbers
    Quantity Per Order
    Vendor Delivery Information
    Number Received
    Profit Per Item

FINISHED GOODS INVENTORY RECORD

Production Order (Job)—Key
Production Number
Cost
    Material
    Labor
    Overhead Applied

Price
Location
Quantity Completed
Requirements
Shipment Date
Production Quantity

Figure 12-4   Inventory, Purchase Order, and Vendor Record and Finished Goods Inventory Record

INVENTORY   The objective of the inventory management subsystem is to ensure that an adequate stock of raw material, parts, subassemblies, and buffer stock exists; to support production operations adequately; and to make finished goods available at convenient locations in the company's distribution system. Since this objective is constrained by the investments in inventory and other carrying costs, a balance must be achieved between these costs and the costs of production interruptions, lost sales, and late deliveries.

Decision models can be used to aid in balancing service with inventory costs. Regardless of the inventory model, all decision models are directly or indirectly based on the traditional ABC system in which inventory items are classified as A (High cost $\times$ High volume = High total cost); B (High cost $\times$ Low volume or Low cost $\times$ High volume = Medium total cost); and C (Low cost $\times$ Low volume = Low total cost).

The level of sophistication of the inventory system is a function of the amount of inventory in each of the above classifications as well as the size of the firm's inventory. For a large firm all inventory may be in Class A. For a very small firm most of the inventory may be in Class C where inventory control systems may be relatively simple. In the typical firm all three types of inventory will be present. Mathematical and statistical models can be used to control those items with a high total cost, such as engines and transmissions in a firm that manufactures garden tractors. Casual inspection or periodic ordering, based on the department supervisor's requisitions, can be used for small cost items such as hand tools. Complex systems can only be justified where they can economically help management control costs and provide service.

There are a wide variety of inventory models based on production line balancing, economic order quantity, and simulation techniques. Most economic order quantity models are derivations of the traditional Economic Order Quantity (EOQ) model in which management inputs the following:

A (the annual quantity used in units),
S (setup costs for production or the cost of placing an order),
U (unit cost), and
I (inventory carrying charges expressed as a percentage of cost).
Q (the economic order quantity or production run size) can then be determined by using the following optimization equation:[2]

$$Q = \sqrt{\frac{2AS}{UI}}$$

For example, assume that the annual requirement is 10,000 items, setup cost is $1000 per production run, unit cost is $20, and inventory carrying charges are 25 percent of the unit cost. In that case

$$Q = \sqrt{\frac{2\,(10,000)\,(\$1000)}{\$20\,(.25)}} = \sqrt{4,000,000} = 2,000 \text{ units}$$

The optimal production run order quantity is therefore 2,000 units.

Determining the quantity of inventory that should be ordered is part of the decision process. Management needs to know when to order or produce as well. Reorder points need to be set so that when stock reaches a certain level, a new production run is scheduled or purchase orders are initiated. This type of timing decision is a function of demand, seasonal fluctuations, suppliers' lead time, and desired safety stock levels. However, since some of these factors are often uncertain, sophisticated models based on statistical decision theory are often used to determine reorder points.[3]

In addition to using decision models, management can often use status reports similar to those outlined in the purchasing discussion. These reports are based on the types of records outlined in Figure 12–4. They are often the only reports that small firms use in decision making. In those firms the data sources for decisions are day-to-day transaction and production records. Other information can be calculated and extracted from basic source documents such as receiving reports and purchase orders. However, it should be clear that these sources do not always provide enough information for sophisticated models, which often require marketing information.

PRODUCTION OPERATIONS The objective of the production subsystem of a logistics system is to effectively and efficiently schedule production opera-

---

[2] See any basic production management or cost accounting text for a full explanation of the equation.

[3] Elwood S. Buffa, *Modern Production Management* (New York: John Wiley, 1970), p. 493.

tions. Given a set of constraints on equipment, personnel, supplies, and financial resources, management must meet sales and distribution system stock demands. Management can use a variety of decision models to accomplish this objective.[4] As in the economic order quantity models, allocation models can vary from a review of inventory status reports to sophisticated mathematical models such as linear programming.

To demonstrate the concepts of a decision model applied to production, consider the following problem. Assume that a production process exists in which three separate and distinct products can be produced. The only limited resource is labor; 400 labor-hours are available. From prior experience it is known that product 1 requires eight hours of labor per unit of product output, product 2 requires four hours per unit of output, and product 3 requires two hours per unit of output. Product 1 contributes $12 per unit to profits, product 2 contributes $10 per unit, and product 3 contributes $8 per unit. Based upon these data, we might conclude that as many units as possible of product 1 should be produced because this product contributes the most per unit to profit. Upon examining the labor requirements, however, we can see that product 1 has the highest per unit labor requirement.

A decision model approach to the problem would be to express the problem as a linear-programming model and solve via the SIMPLEX method.[5] Expressed mathematically, the problem is:

Maximize: $z = 12x_1 + 10x_2 + 8x_3$
Subject to: $8x_1 + 4x_2 + 2x_3 \leq 400$

where x_1 = number of units of product 1 to produce
x_2 = number of units of product 2 to produce
x_3 = number of units of product 3 to produce
z = total profits resulting from the production of x_1, x_2, and x_3

The optimal solution to the problem, resulting from employing the SIMPLEX algorithm, is $x_1 = 0$, $x_2 = 0$, $x_3 = 200$ units, and $z = \$2,400$.

The decision network and set of cost accounting transaction requirements in a particular production allocation subsystem must be supported by the information system. Several records are often necessary to support this information subsystem. In addition to inventory records, such as those shown in Figure 12–4, production records (Figure 12–5) such as the production order record, production information record, production schedule, and performance record are often required. Remember that even though all the records here are set up for traditional file storage, each element of each record could be assigned a location in a data base system and accessed randomly. This organization logic was described in Chapter 8.

As in the purchasing and inventory information subsystems, day-to-day transactions provide the source of much of the information required for production operation decisions. However, daily transactions are not sufficient for

---

[4] Everett E. Adam, Jr. and Ronald J. Ebert, *Production and Operations Management—Concepts, Models and Behavior,* 2nd ed. (Englewood Cliffs, N.J.: Prentice-Hall, 1982).

[5] SIMPLEX is a mathematical algorithm for solving linear-programming models.

PRODUCTION ORDER

Key—Production Order Number (Job Number)
Product Cost Detail
    Standard Cost
    Standard Price
    Standard Times
Bill of Materials
    Sub-assembly Numbers
    Sub-assembly Components
    Sub-assembly Locations
    Component Location
Shop Schedule Information
    Work Sequence
    Work Centers—Departments
Status
    Scheduled
    Cleared for Scheduling
    Not Cleared for Scheduling
Quantity
    Required
    Completed
    In Process
    Not Started

PRODUCTION INFORMATION RECORD

Key—Product Number
Product Cost Detail
    Standard Cost
    Standard Price
    Standard Times
Bill of Material
    Sub-assembly Numbers
    Sub-assembly Components
    Sub-assembly Locations
    Component Location
Shop Schedule
    Work Sequence
    Work Centers

PRODUCTION SCHEDULE

Key—Department (Work Center) Number
Production Order (Job Number)
Product Number
Product Description
Sub-assembly Number (if applicable)
Sub-assembly Information (if applicable)
Quantity to be Manufactured
Quantity Required for Order
Standard Time
Standard Cost
Work Sequence
Work Centers
    Origination
    Destination
Material Requirements
Sub-assembly Requirements
Material Location
Sub-assembly Locations
Schedule Work Date
Scheduled Completion Date
Actual Time
Actual Cost
Material Requisitions

PERFORMANCE RECORD

Key—Department (Work Center) Number
Material Standard
Cost Standard
Time Standards
Material Requisitions
Actual Cost
Actual Time

Figure 12-5 Production Records

more complex systems. Planning information in the form of standard cost data, work sequences, production requirements, expected selling prices, and standard times and standard material requirements is, for example, required to support logistical decisions. Moreover, it may be necessary to draw from other functions in order to generate a data base that can support the logistical decisions of many companies. For example, a production order (number, quantity, and completion dates) may be generated by the marketing function.

SUPPORT SYSTEMS In addition to the purchasing, inventory, and production subsystems, a logistics management system requires supporting subsystems such as maintenance, engineering, cost accounting, and personnel.

The objective of the maintenance system is to keep the logistics system operating. Decisions concerning the timing and amount of maintenance to be performed must be made periodically as well as when breakdowns occur. As before, an information system must be designed and implemented to support the decision-making network of the maintenance system. Maintenance is often planned, but an information system must clearly monitor the logistics (operations) process so that management can react when problems exist. Performance records, such as the one shown in Figure 12–5, can be used to generate variances that may serve as early warning signals.

Cost accounting systems, which compare planned operations with actual results by using a set of standards and resulting variances, provide a key role in supporting logistical operations. The objective of a cost accounting support system is twofold. First, it is an effective control device because it provides production standards with which production and purchasing personnel can control their costs. Second, through a comparison of standards and production data, problem areas can be detected. With this information, logistics management can take corrective action. For example, excessive labor variances may signal the need for increased maintenance for a particular type of machine in the manufacturing process. Performance records consisting of data such as those shown in Figure 12–5 generally form the basis for such a system. The cost system is also used to value inventory and determine the cost of goods sold.

The production operations subsystem of a logistics system may have an engineering support subsystem. The objective of an engineering support subsystem is to provide product specifications and design effective production sequences, prepare bills of material, specify quality controls, determine subassembly requirements, and specify a scheduling algorithm. Information from this support system is often key input information for operations decisions.

Transaction Processing Networks

A logistical transaction processing network is necessary (1) to support the decision-making requirements of a logistical system, (2) to supply key data elements for many of the records noted in this chapter, and (3) to provide information necessary for financial reporting and inventory evaluations.

In a typical logistics transaction processing network, management must record quantities and costs and must apply a share of the overhead to the product or service rendered. The flow of transactions generally proceeds as follows. First, a sales order is received. After it has been determined that all the necessary subassemblies, parts, and materials are on hand, the order is approved for production. Often the production components are stocked in anticipation of future sales orders. Parts, subassemblies, and materials are generally accounted for as follows:

Materials, stores, parts inventory	XXX	
Accounts payable		XXX

An inventory record is kept for each of these components, by part or subassembly number, for reference, control, and accountability.

In a typical job shop,[6] cost and quantity are charged to the job (production order) that requires the particular component part, through the use of a material requisition such as the one illustrated in Figure 12–6. The following journal entry is used to support this transaction:

Work in process (Job #102)   XXX
        Inventory (parts, material, subassemblies, etc.)   XXX

In a similar fashion, labor is charged to various jobs, based upon the amount of time spent for both direct and indirect labor. An example of a time card used to charge labor to various jobs is shown in Figure 12–7. The following journal entry is typically used to support this labor charge transaction:

Work in process (Job #102)   XXX
        Accrued payroll   XXX

Overhead is generally applied to departments, work centers, or plants, using either departmental or plant-wide rates. Generally the application rate is predetermined because of the lack of knowledge of actual overhead, the timing of overhead charges, and the need to apply overhead to jobs as they pass through the various departments. The following journal entries are used to accumulate the *actual* overhead charges for each department:

Overhead control department XYZ   XXX
        Accrued payroll   XXX
        Inventory—indirect supplies   XXX
        Sundry accounts (rent, taxes, deductions, etc.)   XXX

Entries for charges for overhead applied to the job are usually of the following form:

Work in process (Job #102)   XXX
        Overhead applied department XYZ   XXX

Figure 12–6 Material Requisition

Department	Assembly			
Date	1/15/82			
Authorization	RAL			

Description	Quantity	Unit Cost	Amount	Job No.
Brackets	60	1.50	90	102
"	40	1.50	60	105
Nuts	100	.50	50	102

[6] See Charles T. Horngren, *Cost Accounting: A Managerial Emphasis*, 5th ed. (Englewood Cliffs, N.J.: Prentice-Hall, 1982), for a discussion of process and standard cost accounting transaction systems.

```
┌─────────────────────────────────────────────────────────────┐
│                    EMPLOYEE TIME CARD                        │
├─────────────────────────────────────────────────────────────┤
│ Employee Number __206_____                              │
│ Department _____10_____                               │
│ Operation _____Inspect_____                              │
│ Date _____1/17/82_____                              │
├──────────────────┬─────────┬──────────┬─────────┬───────────┤
│                  │   Job   │  Pieces  │  Start  │   Stop    │
│ Job Description  │ Number  │Completed │         │           │
├──────────────────┼─────────┼──────────┼─────────┼───────────┤
│ 18" Mower        │  101    │   20     │  8:00   │  12:00    │
│ 21" Mower        │  102    │   10     │  1:00   │   3:00    │
│ 26" Snow Blower  │  109    │    5     │  3:00   │   5:00    │
└──────────────────┴─────────┴──────────┴─────────┴───────────┘
```

Figure 12–7   Employee Time Card

All costs, direct (or standard) and applied, are accumulated by job on job cost sheets (Figure 12–8) or on a computerized record (Figure 12–9). Either medium would contain the same information. This is also the work-in-process inventory record. In a standard cost system, actual and standard usage and the associated costs are accumulated by department or job for variance analysis.

```
┌─────────────────────────────────────────────────────────────┐
│                     JOB COST SHEET                           │
├─────────────────────────────────────────────────────────────┤
│ Production Order No. _____ Page _____      │
│ Product _____                      │
│ Date Started _____                      │
│ Date Completed _____                      │
│ Routing Departments _____      │
├─────────────────────────────────────────────────────────────┤
│                  Department _____                        │
├──────────────────┬────────────────────┬─────────────────────┤
│    Material       │       Labor        │      Overhead       │
├──────┬─────┬──────┼──────┬─────┬───────┼──────────┬──────────┤
│ Date │Ref. │Amount│ Date │Ref. │Amount │   Date   │  Amount  │
├──────┼─────┼──────┼──────┼─────┼───────┼──────────┼──────────┤
│      │     │      │      │     │       │          │          │
│      │     │      │      │     │       │          │          │
│      │     │      │      │     │       │          │          │
├──────┴─────┴──────┴──────┴─────┴───────┴──────────┴──────────┤
│                  Department _____                        │
├──────────────────┬────────────────────┬─────────────────────┤
│    Material       │       Labor        │      Overhead       │
├──────┬─────┬──────┼──────┬─────┬───────┼──────────┬──────────┤
│ Date │Ref. │Amount│ Date │Ref. │Amount │   Date   │  Amount  │
├──────┼─────┼──────┼──────┼─────┼───────┼──────────┼──────────┤
│      │     │      │      │     │       │          │          │
│      │     │      │      │     │       │          │          │
└──────┴─────┴──────┴──────┴─────┴───────┴──────────┴──────────┘
```

Figure 12–8   Job Cost Sheet

Product Number

Description

Shop Schedule or Routing
    Work sequence

Standards for Each Work Center (if applicable)
    Material
    Labor
    Overhead

Actual Applied Costs (Actual or Standard) (for work center)
    Material (date, reference, amount)
    Labor (date, reference, amount)
    Overhead (date, amount applied)

Completion Date

Production Order Number

Figure 12-9 Job Cost Sheet: Work-In-Process Inventory Record

Costs are accumulated by job as the job moves from work center to work center. Upon completion, the total costs are transferred to finished goods inventory as follows:

Finished goods	XXX	
Work in process (Job #102)		XXX

Finally, the sale is recorded by the following entry:

Cost of goods sold	XXX	
Finished goods		XXX

At the very least, a logistics information system must contain the necessary features to record the flow of costs through a job cost system, maintain the inventory records, and generate reports for inventory valuation and cost control. Thus the information set shown in Figure 12–9 is basic to any production inventory system if management is to properly record the transactions that relate to the flow of costs through a job cost system. Accounting for a process cost system will be similar to accounting for a job cost system.

Information Retrieval Considerations

Information retrieval needs will be a function of the type of logistic management activity. Strategic, managerial, and operational and transaction processing activities have major impact on these needs in terms of frequency of use, level of aggregation, scope, and accuracy of information. In many situations periodic status reports can be used to meet these decision-making, reporting, and transaction processing needs; in other situations managers will need on-line, up-to-date information on inventory and production status in order to react to environmental changes. In some situations this quick response may be required at all three managerial activity levels.

Microcomputer and minicomputer hardware was discussed in Chapter 6. Rapid information retrieval is possible at a reasonable cost with these systems. This will be illustrated in Chapters 14 and 17. For example, in a small microcomputer system a manager can display a menu of accounting packages available and then a menu of inventory packages. The manager can then select the desired status report from the inventory menu quickly and easily. Information such as this is up-to-date and accurate and not a week old. This type of system should enable a manager to make better decisions regarding purchasing, inventory management, and production scheduling.

Planning and Control of Logistical Functions

Management, with the aid of the controller, must plan and control all the different types of logistical functions including purchasing, inventory, and production operations, and all their supporting systems. Management's objective should be to coordinate all functions and managerial activities within each type of function in order to create an effective and efficient managerial system. Thus the manager must design, develop, and implement an effective and efficient information system. The management information system should approach that which was conceived in the conceptual framework in Chapter 2 and discussed in Chapters 10 and 11.

In this chapter we focus on the logistics function. In Chapter 16 all organizational functions will be integrated to form an integrated or a distributed information system. The same principles apply here, however, because common inventory records and transaction processing systems are used for the logistical functions of purchasing, inventory, production scheduling, and support.

MANUAL SYSTEM ILLUSTRATION

To illustrate the flow of transactions, the records generated from this flow, internal control considerations, and the information used to make operational decisions, a *manual* purchasing, receiving, and inventory system is described in this section. The system flowchart is shown in Figure 12–10.

The manager reviews the sales forecast and the stock records that contain information similar to, but not as extensive as, that illustrated in Figure 12–4. Here it is assumed that the records consist of the following:

1. Stock number
2. Name
3. Number on hand
4. Number on order

From this information, the manager manually prepares prenumbered purchase requisitions. These are batched by the manager, and control totals are run on the dollar amount and number of requisitions. From the purchase requisitions, the purchasing department then prepares five copies of prenumbered purchase orders, using separate vendor records consisting of the following:

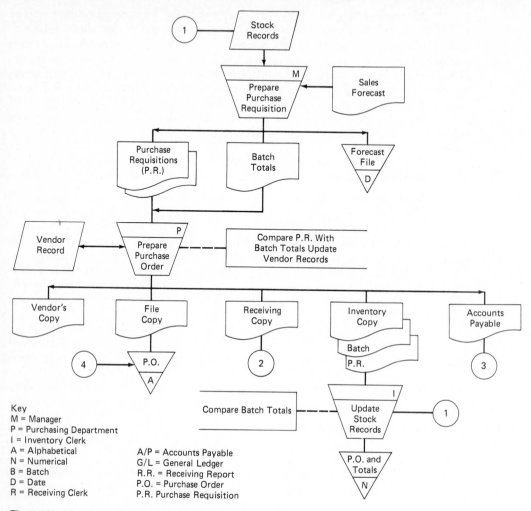

Figure 12-10 *Manual* Purchasing, Receiving, and Inventory System

1. Vendor number
2. Vendor name
3. Types of materials supplied
4. List of most recent prices
5. Number on order from each vendor
6. Possibly some note pertaining to delivery time and financial terms

The purchasing department compares the total number and dollar amounts of the purchase orders with the batch totals forwarded from the manager. The purchasing department updates these vendor records to reflect the new purchase orders.

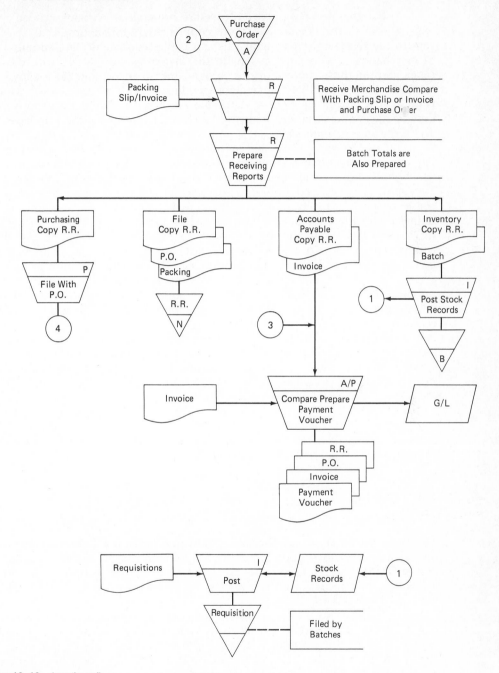

Figure 12–10   (continued)

The five purchase order copies are distributed as follows: (1) a vendor copy is sent to the vendor, (2) a file copy is filed alphabetically, (3) a copy is sent to the receiving department where it is filed alphabetically pending receipt of merchandise, (4) a copy is sent to the inventory clerk along with the batch totals and purchase requisitions to update stock records, and (5) a copy is sent to the accounts payable department pending receipt of an invoice from the vendor. The inventory clerk updates the stock records to reflect items on order, reconciles the changes with the batch totals, and files the purchase order and requisitions numerically.

Upon receipt of the merchandise, a receiving clerk compares the packing slip or invoice that accompanies the shipment with the purchase order file, which is in alphabetical vendor order. Four copies of the prenumbered receiving report are prepared. One copy goes to purchasing for an alphabetical purchase order file by vendor. A file copy is kept in receiving and is filed numerically with the related purchase orders and packing slips. A third copy is forwarded, along with the invoice (if it accompanies the shipment), to the accounts payable department. The last copy, along with batch totals, is sent to the inventory manager for posting stock records and reconciliation of totals.

In the accounts payable department a comparison is made between purchase orders, invoices, and receiving reports. Payment vouchers are prepared upon receipt of invoices which are supported by the purchase order and receiving report. Provisions can be made here for partial shipments and payments if necessary. The payment voucher, invoice, purchase order, and receiving report are all forwarded to the manager or owner for payment. The general ledger accounts are posted to reflect payment at this point in time. Numerical control is maintained on the payment vouchers. These last three payment steps are not shown in Figure 12–10.

In addition to updating inventory records for purchase orders and merchandise receipts, the inventory department also receives requisitions, which are used to update stock records when items are issued. These are batched for stock record control and filed by batches.

BATCH PROCESSING ILLUSTRATION

The flow of transactions, information, and internal control considerations, and the records used to support operational and managerial control activities in a typical batch processing system, are illustrated in this section. A production scheduling system is flowcharted in Figure 12–11. Weekly production scheduling runs are assumed.

First, the production planning department prepares production orders based on finished goods stock status, customer orders, sales forecasts, and the current production schedule. These orders are batched, keypunched onto cards, and filed by date. Next, the cards are sorted and processed by the computer. After a comparison with the production information specification file and the materials inventory records, these new production orders are analyzed, along with those previously submitted but not yet scheduled, to determine whether or not to schedule them. There may be a delay in the scheduling of

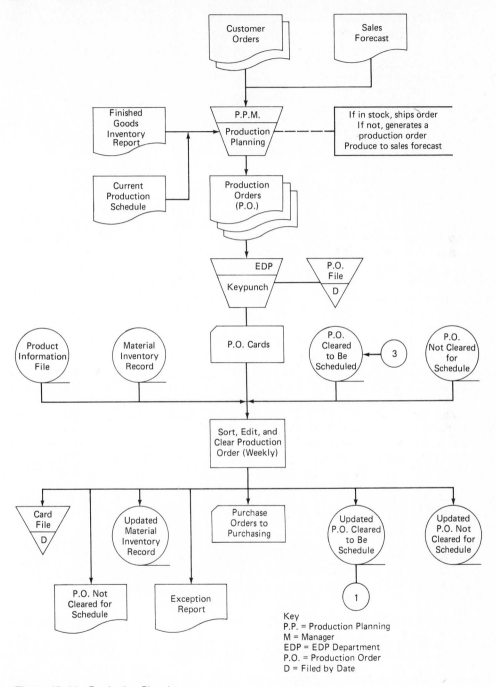

Figure 12-11 Production Planning

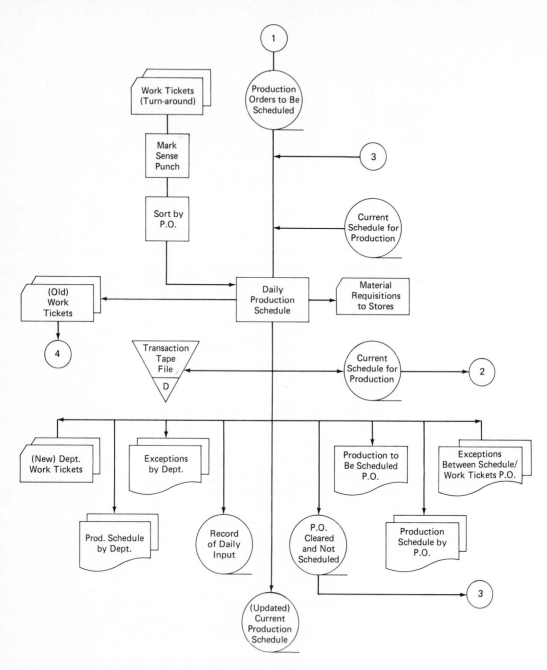

Figure 12–11 (continued) Production Scheduling

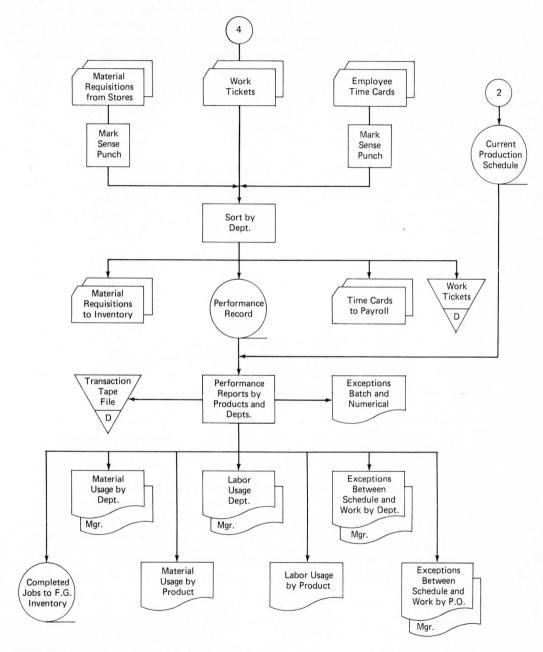

Figure 12–11 (continued) Production Control

production orders (P.O. not cleared for schedule) because all the material is not on hand. If this is the case, purchase orders are generated for the purchasing department for those items not already on order. Some production orders are not scheduled because they have longer lead times and can wait until the next scheduling run. This analysis and comparison results in updated (1) materials inventory records, (2) files of production orders cleared for scheduling, and (3) files of production orders not cleared for scheduling. All scheduling records are sequenced by production order number. Reports are also prepared on orders not scheduled and processing exceptions arising from reconciliation of batch totals, missing input, or product information. The production order data cards are filed by date. In essence, the computer run verifies that all the needed information and materials are available prior to scheduling production and that only those requiring production before the next run are scheduled. The production order run results in production to be scheduled the following week.

The production scheduled is run daily. Input includes work tickets that detail the preceding day's progress, the current production schedule, and all production orders cleared but not yet scheduled that detail product specifications.

Machine-readable work tickets serve as turnaround documents for collecting production data. Work tickets are accumulated each day from the shop, batched, and keypunched using a mark sense off-line punch. From each daily updating run, the following information is generated for shop supervisors and production management:

1. New work tickets for each production department. These will be used as turnaround documents for the next day's production.
2. A daily production schedule for each department, explaining what, when, and how much to produce.
3. An updated master production schedule sorted by production order number.
4. Reports listing (a) the production orders scheduled and (b) those pending scheduling for production management.
5. A record of daily input on tape for backup and audit trail.
6. Exceptions between the current schedule, work tickets, and production orders. These are reviewed and corrected, if necessary, by management, keypunched, and reentered during the next production run.
7. Material requisitions to be forwarded to the warehouse so that only those parts and materials necessary for each day's activities are issued from stores to the production departments.
8. Production orders cleared but not scheduled.

After the work tickets have been used in the daily production run, they are processed and sorted by department using the computer, along with employee time cards and material requisition cards, which are also machine-readable. The output of this processing procedure is a daily performance record tape. A hard copy input is filed for backup security measures and for audit purposes. Given this performance record and the current (not the updated) production schedule which details what should have been done, a daily control run is made for operational and management control activities.

In addition to a transaction tape file and an exception listing, the following information is generated:

1. Completed production orders, which are sent to finished goods inventory.
2. Material usage reports for each department and manager.
3. Material usage by production order or product.
4. Labor usage reports for each department and manager.
5. Labor usage reports by production order or product.
6. Reconciliation and resulting exceptions between the current schedule, the materials requisitioned, and employee time cards. The reconciliation and exceptions are produced by department and by product.
7. A reconciliation of the number and batch totals of work tickets, material requisitions, and time cards and the issuance of a report for correction and follow-up action.

By careful management planning at the outset of the process, and by employing a production schedule and turnaround documents, effective control of operational activities can be exercised. Feedback control is obtained through the various exception reports and comparisons. From a data processing perspective, effective control is achieved through a system of record retention, transaction records, keypunch verification, comparison of data and batch totals, and turnaround documents such as requisitions and work tickets.

REAL-TIME ILLUSTRATION

The production scheduling problem can be reconsidered from the standpoint of an on-line real-time system. Suppose the business environment has changed so that more and more production orders need to be expedited, customer sales representatives are increasingly calling to check on the status of production orders, and the business environment has become such that the plant needs to clear production orders for scheduling as soon as possible, not weekly as is the current practice. It has become apparent to management that more-rapid response, more-sophisticated algorithms, and instantaneous feedback are required for planning and dealing with customers.

A real-time system that will satisfy the information requirements of the management system might look like the one shown in Figure 12–12. The system is essentially a set of on-line programs that will edit input, generate transaction records, periodically dump all files for control and security, clear orders for production when all materials are on hand, generate daily production schedules with the appropriate work tickets and material requisitions, update the status of materials and parts as supplies are received, and answer inquiries as they are received from management personnel. This set of programs will interface with a set of random access files for the production schedule, materials inventory, product information, production orders, and finished goods invento-

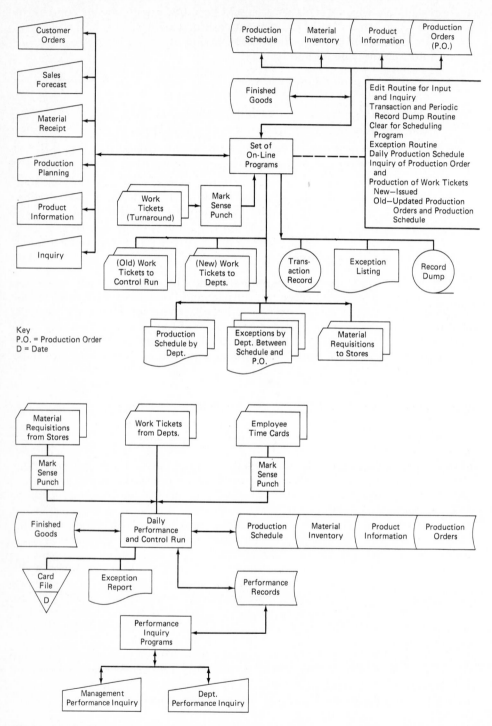

Figure 12-12 Production Scheduling and Control (Real Time)

ry. The data elements that comprise these files can also be logically organized into a common data base. This system should permit on-line input of customer orders, sales forecast changes, materials receipt, production plans, and expediting decisions. It should also, at any time, permit management to inquire into the status of materials production orders, product information, finished goods, and the current date for scheduled production of a product. As in the batch system, work tickets and material requisitions can be generated as turnaround documents for the control of material flow in the plant. Any number of reports can be generated, such as the exception listings and the production schedules shown in the batch illustration.

In addition to faster input and inquiry capability, another advantage of the real-time system is that changes to the schedule can be made daily rather than weekly. Moreover, management can use the system in a simulation mode in order to experiment with different schedules, product configurations, manufacturing procedures, and size of production runs. Many "what if" questions can be asked.

As with the batch system, a daily control run is feasible. The difference is that unsorted input is used in conjunction with the random access records to generate a random access performance record. This record can be used to generate reports like those discussed in the batch system or to support on-line inquiries related to differences between plans or standards and actual departmental output.

INTERNAL CONTROL

The current state of the art in auditing emphasizes the flow of transactions through cycles. The logistics function contains a large subset of the expenditure and the conversion cycles suggested for review by the AICPA in its "Special Advisory Report on Internal Control."[7] From the perspective of a hypothetical manufacturing entity, the AICPA outlines a set of control procedures for three broad control objectives: (1) authorization, (2) accounting, and (3) asset safeguarding. Criteria for meeting these objectives and examples of selected control procedures and techniques for logistics systems are presented in the Appendix to this chapter. Controls for other cycles can be found in other applications chapters.

SUMMARY

In this chapter we have highlighted the framework involved in designing and developing a logistics system. This framework integrates all the subfunctions, levels of management activity, and data processing elements associated with the logistics function of a firm. A manual purchasing, receiving, and inventory system, and a batch and a real-time production scheduling system were described in detail in order to illustrate the integration of the different dimensions of a logistics system.

[7] AICPA, *Special Advisory Report on Internal Control,* (New York: American Institute of Certified Public Accountants, 1978).

SELECTED REFERENCES

American Institute of Certified Public Accountants, *Special Advisory Report on Internal Control*, New York: AICPA 1978.

BOEING CO. AND HEWLETT-PACKARD, "A Production Management System at Boeing," *Management Accounting*, April 1979, pp. 33–35.

BRIVIO, D., "On-Line Production Control in an Integrated Steel Mill," *Control Engineering*, October 1971.

BURCH, JOHN G., FELIX R. STRATER, AND GARY GRUDNITSKI, *Information Systems: Theory and Practice.* Santa Barbara, Calif.: Hamilton Publishing Company, 1978.

CARBONE, FRANK J., "Automated Job Costing Helps Mulack Steel Stay Competitive," *Management Accounting*, June 1980, pp. 29–31.

CUSHING, BARRY F., *Accounting Information Systems and Business Organization.* Reading, Mass.: Addison-Wesley, 1978.

DAVIS, GORDON B., *Management Information System Conceptual Foundation, Structure, and Development.* New York: McGraw-Hill, 1974.

ELIASON, ALAN L., AND KENT D. KITTS, *Business Computer Systems and Applications.* Palo Alto, Calif.: Science Research Associates, 1978.

GRAZIANO, VINCENT J., "Integrated Logistics Planning and Control," *Management Control*, 19 (February 1972), pp. 26–32.

HAX, ARNOLD C., "Planning a Management Information System for a Distribution and Manufacturing Company," *Sloan Management Review*, 15 (Spring 1973), pp. 85–98.

MURDICK, ROBERT G., AND JOEL E. ROSS, *Information Systems for Modern Management.* Englewood Cliffs, N.J.: Prentice-Hall, 1971.

NCR MISSION, "Complete Business System for Manufacturing," 1978.

PRINCE, THOMAS R., *Information Systems for Management Planning and Control.* Homewood, Ill.: Richard D. Irwin, 1975.

REMBOLD, ULRICH, K. SETH MAHESH, AND JEREMY S. WEINSTEIN, *Computers in Manufacturing.* New York: Marcel Debber, 1977.

SAMUEL, G. H., "On-Line Computer Boosts Steel Mill Output," *Control Engineering*, June 1967.

SULLIVAN, RAYMOND, "Transformation from Batch to Timesharing," *Infosystems*, 23 (February 1976), pp. 37–40.

APPENDIX: CRITERIA
AND EXAMPLES OF SELECTED
CONTROL PROCEDURES
FOR LOGISTICAL SYSTEMS[1]

THE PRODUCTION OR CONVERSION CYCLE

The production or conversion cycle covers the functions involved in production planning and control, inventory planning and control, property and deferred cost accounting, and cost accounting.

[1] Reprinted with permission from AICPA, *Special Advisory Report on Internal Control*, (New York: AICPA 1978).

"Authorization" in the production or conversion cycle encompasses the types and quantities of goods to be manufactured or services to be provided, the methods and materials to be used, the inventory levels or service capabilities to be maintained, the scheduling of goods to be produced or services to be provided, adjustments and policies with respect thereto, such as provisions for obsolete inventory or write-downs of deferred costs, and dispositions of property, scrap, and obsolete or excessive inventory.

"Accounting" encompasses the procedures and techniques used to control the recording and classification of transactions that relate to resources used, completed production, and inventory, and includes depreciation, amortization, and gain or loss on the sale or disposition of property.

"Asset Safeguarding" relates (a) to protecting the company from loss of inventory or property and (b) to protecting important records.

Authorization Objectives

CRITERIA	EXAMPLES OF SELECTED CONTROL PROCEDURES AND TECHNIQUES
1. The types and quantities of goods to be manufactured or services to be provided, the methods and materials to be used, the inventory levels or service capabilities to be maintained, and the scheduling of goods to be produced or services to be provided should be properly authorized.	• Preparation and review of sales forecasts. • Establishment of a production control function. • Approval of an overall production and inventory control plan, and of changes thereto. • Bills of material for goods to be produced. • Requirement for capital expenditure requests over a specified amount to include a documented cost-benefit analysis.
2. Adjustments to inventory, property, deferred cost, and cost of sales should be properly authorized.	• Policies for determining excess or obsolete inventory quantities. • Assigned responsibility for review and approval of adjustments, including adjustments to standard costs. • Periodic review of the reasonableness of lives assigned to classes of property and to deferred costs, and of the methods of depreciation and amortization.
3. Disposition of property, scrap, and obsolete or excessive inventory should be properly authorized.	• Requirement for all movements or shipments of merchandise and assets out of the physical facility to be accompanied by appropriate documentation. • Periodic follow-up on disposition of inventory identified as obsolete or excessive.

Accounting Objectives

CRITERIA	EXAMPLES OF SELECTED CONTROL PROCEDURES AND TECHNIQUES

4. Resources used and completed production should be properly recorded on a timely basis.

- Inventory released to production based on bills of material which are used as sources for postings to inventory records.
- Additional inventory transfers to production based on documents approved by a designated employee, which would include review of scrap reports.
- Physical transfer of completed production on hand to a storeroom.
- Independent check of quantities transferred to storerooms and quantities shipped.
- Comparison of quantities transferred to storerooms to production reports.
- Perpetual inventory records.
- Periodic physical inventories or cycle counts.
- Reconciliation of payroll costs to labor charged to inventory.
- Investigation of significant amounts of over- and under-absorbed overhead.
- Periodic physical inventory (where existence cannot be determined by other means) of property and equipment.

5. Inventory, production costs, depreciation of property, and amortization of deferred costs should be properly classified in the accounts.

- Inventory pricing policies that are in conformity with generally accepted accounting principles.
- Policies and procedures covering accounting routines and related approval procedures for the major functions within the conversion cycle, including sales or other dispositions of property.
- Use of a cost system (job cost, process cost) that accumulates and allocates production costs in an appropriate manner (by cost center, department, and/or product) and that provides information adequate for pricing inventories, appropriate to the manufacturing process.
- Use of standard costs with investigation of variances.
- Periodic comparison of standard costs to actual costs (comparison of material

costs to vendor invoices, comparison of labor rates and hours to actual rates and results of time studies, analysis of over- or under-absorbed overhead).

- A suitable chart of accounts and standard journal entries.
- Written, properly communicated cut-off procedures on transfers among inventory accounts, and review of compliance with procedures. (Purchase and sales cut-offs are covered in the expenditures and revenue cycles.)
- Review of priced inventory listings for conformity with established pricing policies.
- Individual records for items of property that include description, location, cost, depreciation, tax, and investment credit information.
- Maintenance of appropriate records to support amortization of deferred charges.
- Periodic review of appropriateness of depreciation and amortization rates.

6. All costs of sales should be recorded at the appropriate amounts and in the appropriate periods and should be properly classified in the accounts.

- Procedures that provide for the same document (e.g., a sales invoice) to serve as the source document for the recognition of revenue and the related receivable and for the recognition of cost of sales and the related reduction of inventory.
- Reconciliation of inventory records to the general ledger on a regular basis.
- Physical inventories at the end of annual reporting periods and/or on a cycle basis.

Asset Safeguarding Objectives

CRITERIA

EXAMPLES OF SELECTED CONTROL PROCEDURES AND TECHNIQUES

7. Inventory should be protected from unauthorized use or removal.

- Physical controls (fences, restricted-access storerooms, guards, inspection of personnel, independent storeroom clerks).
- Physical control procedures that vary with the individual dollar value of inventory items and with the volume of transactions.

8. Items of property should be properly controlled.

- Identification tags affixed upon acquisition.
- Physical security procedures in plants and offices (fences, guards, etc.).
- Periodic physical inventories of items susceptible to removal, giving due regard to the cost and lives of such items.

9. Access to inventory, property, cost, and production control records should be suitably controlled to prevent or detect within a timely period improper dispositions of inventory and property.

- Segregation of duties between those who have access to inventories and those responsible for inventory, cost and production control records. ("Access to inventories" includes those who physically receive, handle, and ship; it also includes those who prepare shipping orders or other disposal authorizations.)
- Periodic physical inventories under the supervision of personnel other than those who have access to inventories.
- Investigation of significant physical inventory shortages by those who do not have access to inventories.
- Segregation of duties between those who have custody of movable property and those who maintain the property records.

EXPENDITURES CYCLE

PURCHASING FUNCTION

Authorization Objectives

CRITERIA

EXAMPLES OF SELECTED CONTROL PROCEDURES AND TECHNIQUES

1. The types of goods, other assets, and services to be obtained, the manner in which they are obtained, the vendors from which they are obtained, the quantities to be obtained, and the prices and other terms

- Use of purchase requisitions.
- Guidelines for vendor acceptability, based on considerations such as past performance, reputation and credit standing, ability to meet delivery, quality and service specifications, price competitiveness, legal restrictions, and policies on related party transactions.
- Use of an approved vendor list based on established guidelines.

of sale should be properly authorized.

- Use of priced purchase orders.
- Procedures for prior review of contracts with vendors.
- Established procedures for approval of purchase requisitions and purchase orders, and changes thereto, including the establishment of reasonable limitations on the approval authority of specific individuals or classes of individuals.
- Assigned responsibility for effecting compliance with purchasing policies.

2. Adjustments to vendor accounts and account distributions should be properly authorized.

- Use and approval of debit memos to notify vendors of goods returned to them and other adjustments to their accounts.
- Assigned responsibility for approval of changes in the classification of purchases.

Accounting Objectives

CRITERIA

EXAMPLES OF SELECTED CONTROL PROCEDURES AND TECHNIQUES

3. All goods, other assets, and services received should be accounted for properly on a timely basis.

- Use of receiving reports.
- Timely review of all unmatched receiving reports and purchase orders.
- Accounting for all issued vouchers.
- Policies and procedures covering accounting routines and related approval procedures for the major purchasing functions.
- Review of vendor statements for past-due items.
- Comparison of vendor invoices to receiving reports and purchase orders.
- Clerical check of vendor invoices.

4. Amounts payable for goods and services received should be recorded as the appropriate amounts and in the appropriate period and should be properly classified in the accounts.

- Written, properly communicated cut-off procedures and review of the cut-off.
- Procedures for making appropriate financial statement accruals based on unmatched receiving reports and, where appropriate (certain other assets and services), unmatched purchase orders.
- A suitable chart of accounts and standard journal entries.

- Insertion of account distribution on purchasing documents.
- Reconciliation of accounts payable subsidiary ledger to the general ledger on a regular basis.
- Independent follow-up of vendors' statements, payment requests, complaints, etc.

Asset Safeguarding Objectives

CRITERIA	EXAMPLES OF SELECTED CONTROL PROCEDURES AND TECHNIQUES
5. Access to purchasing, receiving, and accounts payable records should be suitably controlled to prevent or detect within a timely period duplicate or improper payments.	• Cancellation of supporting documents upon payment. • Approval of vouchers and supporting documents prior to payment. • Segregation of duties between access to cash disbursements (issuing checks or handling signed checks) and keeping purchase and accounts payable records.
6. Only authorized goods, other assets, and services should be accepted and/or paid for.	• Receiving procedures that provide for an independent count of quantities received. • Comparison of specifications and quantities of goods, other assets, and services received to approved purchase orders. • Testing procedures appropriate in the circumstances for goods, other assets, and services received.

REVIEW QUESTIONS

1. What are the objectives of the various logistics subsystems?
2. Why is the production environment important in logistics system design?
3. Can logistics systems be used to support operational, managerial, and strategic decisions?
4. Why is it important to consider the decision-making activities of the various levels of management in the design of inventory data bases?
5. Outline the basic flow of transaction information in a logistics system.
6. Discuss the role of the job cost sheet in an EDP batch processing system.
7. From the text and your previous course work, discuss the production decision models with which you are familiar and their information requirements.
8. Why are ABC inventory classification procedures important in system design?
9. How can linear-programming models be used in production scheduling and planning?

10. What information would you expect to find in a typical inventory record?

11. For cost accounting information requirements, what data must be included in the set of records for production operations?

12. Contrast the records, processing operations, internal control features, and information attainable for a manual, a batch processing, and a real-time inventory system.

EXERCISES AND CASES

12–1

In the manual illustration in the chapter, assume that the volume of paper work was becoming so large that more information, such as lead time and reorder points, was required to make purchasing decisions. Flowchart and describe appropriate internal control procedures for a batch processing procedure to replace the manual system illustrated.

12–2

Assume that you are a member of the management advisory service department of a large CPA firm and that you are knowledgeable about the new and rapidly developing microcomputer field. You believe that the firm illustrated in Case 12–1 could make excellent use of an inventory system that would give management up-to-date, on-line inventory status information to support field sales personnel in placing orders. Conceptualize, flowchart, and describe internal control procedures for a random access system using a microcomputer.

12–3

Beccan Company, a discount tire dealer, operates twenty-five retail stores in the metropolitan area. Beccan sells both private brand and name brand tires. The company operates a centralized purchasing and warehousing facility and employs a perpetual inventory system. All purchases of tires and related supplies are placed through the company's central purchasing department to take advantage of quantity discounts. The tires and supplies are received at the central warehouse and distributed to the retail stores as needed. The perpetual inventory system at the central facility maintains current inventory records, designated reorder points, optimum order quantities, and continuous stocktakings for each type of tire and size and other related supplies.

Beccan uses the following documents in its inventory control system:

- *Retail Stores Requisition.* This document is submitted by the retail stores to the central warehouse whenever tires or supplies are needed at the stores. The shipping clerks in the warehouse department fill the orders from inventory and have them delivered to the stores.

- *Purchase Requisition.* The inventory control clerk in the inventory control department prepares this document when the quantity on hand for an item falls below the designated reorder point. The document is forwarded to the purchasing department.

- *Purchase Order.* The purchasing department prepares this document when items need to be ordered. The document is submitted to an authorized vendor.

- *Receiving Report.* The warehouse department prepares this document when ordered items are received from vendors. The receiving clerk completes the document by indicating the vendor's name, the date the shipment is received, and the quantity of each item received.

- *Invoice.* An invoice is received from vendors specifying the amounts owed by Beccan.

The following departments are involved in Beccan's inventory control system:

- *Inventory Control Department.* This department is responsible for the maintenance of all perpetual inventory records for all items carried in inventory. This includes current quantity on hand, reorder point, optimum order quantity, and quantity on order for each item carried.

- *Warehouse Department.* This department maintains the physical inventory of all items carried in inventory. All orders from vendors are received (receiving clerk) and all distributions to retail stores are filled (shipping clerks) in this department.

–*Purchasing Department.* This department places all orders for items needed by the company.

–*Accounts Payable Department.* This department maintains all open accounts with vendors and other creditors. All payments are processed here.

REQUIRED:

a. Prepare a document flowchart to show how these documents should be coordinated and used among the departments at the central facility of Beccan Company to provide adequate internal control over the receipt, issuance, replenishment, and payment of tires and supplies. You can assume that the documents have a sufficient number of copies to ensure that the perpetual inventory system has the necessary basic internal controls.

b. (optional) Using a system flowchart and the information above, describe the flow of information that would be involved if you were designing a new system that made use of random access microcomputer software for inventory. (Adapted from the CMA Examination)

12–4

You have been engaged by the management of Alden, Inc., to review its internal control over the purchase, receipt, storage, and issue of raw materials. You have prepared the following list, which describes Alden's procedures:

–Raw materials, which consist mainly of high-cost electronic components, are kept in a locked storeroom. Storeroom personnel include a supervisor and four clerks. All are well trained, competent, and adequately bonded. Raw materials are removed from the storeroom only upon written or oral authorization of one of the production supervisors.

–There are no perpetual inventory records; hence the storeroom clerks do not keep records of goods received or issued. To compensate for the lack of perpetual records, a physical inventory count is taken monthly by the storeroom clerks, who are well supervised. Appropriate procedures are followed in making the inventory count.

–After the physical count, the storeroom supervisor matches quantities counted against a predetermined reorder level. If the count for a given part is below the reorder level, the supervisor enters the part number on a materials-requisition list and sends this list to the accounts payable clerk. The accounts payable clerk prepares a purchase order for a predetermined reorder quantity for each part and mails the purchase order to the vendor from whom the part was last purchased.

–When ordered materials arrive at Alden, they are received by the storeroom clerks. The clerks count the merchandise and compare the counts with the shipper's bill of lading. All vendors' bills of lading are initialed, dated, and filed in the storeroom to serve as receiving reports.

REQUIRED: Describe the weaknesses in internal control and recommend improvements of Alden's procedures for the purchase, receipt, storage, and issue of raw materials. Organize your answer sheet as follows:

WEAKNESSES	RECOMMENDED IMPROVEMENTS

(AICPA)

12–5

Anthony, CPA, prepared the flowchart shown in Chapter 7, Figure 7–7, which portrays the raw materials purchasing function of one of Anthony's clients, a medium-sized manufacturing company. The flowchart shows the preparation of initial documents through the vouching of invoices for payment in accounts payable. The flowchart was a portion of the work performed on the audit engagement to evaluate internal control.

REQUIRED: Identify and explain the systems and control weaknesses evident from the flowchart. Include those resulting from activities performed or not performed. All documents are prenumbered. (AICPA adapted)

12–6

Wekender Corporation owns and operates fifteen large departmentalized retail hardware stores in major metropolitan areas of the Southwest United States. The stores carry a wide variety of merchandise, but the major thrust is toward the weekend "do-it-your-selfer." The company's business has almost doubled since 1970.

Each retail store acquires its merchandise from the company's centrally located warehouse. Consequently the warehouse must maintain an up-to-date and well-stocked inventory ready to meet the demands of the individual stores.

Wekender Corporation wishes to maintain its competitive position with similar type stores of other companies in its marketing area. Therefore Wekender must improve its purchasing and inventory procedures. The company's stores must have the proper goods to meet customer demand, and the warehouse in turn must have the goods available. The number of company stores, the number of inventory items carried, the volume of business—all are providing pressures to change from basically manual data processing routines to mechanized data processing procedures. Recently the company has been investigating three different approaches to mechanization—unit-record equipment, computer with batch processing, and computer with real-time processing. No decision has been reached on the approach to be followed.

Top management has determined that the following items should have high priority in the new system procedures:

1. Rapid ordering to replenish warehouse inventory stocks with as little delay as possible
2. Quick filling and shipping of merchandise to the stores (this involves determining whether sufficient stock exists)
3. Some indication of inventory activity
4. Perpetual records in order to determine inventory level by item number quickly

A description of the current warehousing and purchasing procedures is given below.

WAREHOUSE PROCEDURES The stock is stored in bins and is located by an inventory number. The numbers are generally listed sequentially on the bins to facilitate locating items for shipment; frequently this system is not followed and, as a result, some items are difficult to locate.

Whenever a retail store needs merchandise, a three-part merchandise request form is completed—one copy is kept by the store and two copies are mailed to the warehouse the next day. If the merchandise requested is on hand, the goods are delivered to the store accompanied by the third copy of the request. The second copy is filed at the warehouse.

If the quantity of goods on hand is not sufficient to fill the order, the warehouse sends the quantity available and notes the quantity shipped by the warehouse. At the end of each day all the memos are sent to the purchasing department.

When the ordered goods are received, they are checked at the receiving area, and a receiving report is prepared. One copy of the receiving report is retained at the receiving area, one is forwarded to the accounts payable department, and one is filed at the warehouse with the purchase memorandum.

PURCHASING DEPARTMENT PROCEDURES When the purchase memoranda are received from the warehouse, purchase orders are prepared. Vendor catalogs are used to select the best source for the requested goods, and the purchase order is prepared and mailed. Copies of the order are sent to the accounts payable department and the receiving area; one copy is retained in the purchasing department.

When the receiving report arrives in the purchasing department, it is compared with the purchase order on file. The receiving report is also checked with the invoice before forwarding the invoice to the accounts payable department for payment.

The purchasing department strives periodically to evaluate the vendors for financial soundness, reliability, and trade relationships. However, because of the tremendous volume of requests received from the warehouse, this activity currently does not have a high priority.

Each week a report of the open purchase orders is prepared to determine if any action should be taken on overdue deliveries. This report is prepared manually from scanning the file of outstanding purchase orders.

REQUIRED:

a. Wekender Corporation is considering three possible automated data processing systems: unit-record system, batch processing system, real-time computer system.
   (1) Which of these three systems would best meet the needs of Wekender Corporation? Explain your answer. Flowchart your suggested system.
   (2) Briefly describe the basic equipment configuration that Wekender would need for the system recommended in Question 1.
b. Regardless of the type of system selected by Wekender Corporation, data files will have to be established.
   (1) Identify the data files that would be necessary
   (2) Briefly indicate the type of data that would be contained in each file.
c. (optional; refer to Chapter 8) Assume Wekender acquires a data base management system. How would you organize (structure) and access the files to generate a set of reports and support management inquiries you expect Wekender to need and make? (Adapted from the CMA Examination)

12-7

Peabock Company, a wholesaler of softgoods, has an inventory composed of approximately thirty-five hundred different items. The company employs a computerized batch processing system to maintain its perpetual inventory records. The system is run each weekend so that the inventory reports will be available on Monday morning for management use. The system has been functioning satisfactorily for the past fifteen months and has provided the company with accurate records and timely reports.

The preparation of purchase orders has been automatic as a part of the inventory system to ensure that the company will maintain enough inventory to meet customer demand. When an item of inventory falls below a predetermined level, a written record is made of the inventory item. This record is used in conjunction with the vendor file to prepare the purchase orders.

Exception reports are prepared during the update of the inventory and the preparation of the purchase orders. These reports identify any errors or exceptions identified during the processing. In addition, the system provides for management approval of all purchase orders exceeding a specified amount. Any exceptions of items requiring management approval are handled by supplemental runs on Monday morning and are combined with the weekend results.

A system flowchart of Peabock Company's inventory and purchase order procedure is shown in Figure C12–7.

REQUIRED: The illustrated system flowchart of Peabock Company's inventory and purchase order system was prepared before the system was fully operational. Several steps important to the successful operations of the system were inadvertently omitted. Indicate in narrative terms where the omissions have occurred. The flowchart does not need to be redrawn. (Adapted from the CMA Examination)

12-8

Wooster Company is a beauty and barber supplies and equipment distributorship servicing a five-state area. Management has generally been pleased with the company's overall operations to date. However, the present purchasing system has evolved through practice rather than having been formally designed. Consequently it is inadequate and needs to be redesigned.

The present purchasing system can be described as follows. Whenever the quantity of an item is low, the inventory supervisor phones the purchasing department and gives the item description and quantity to be ordered. A purchase order is prepared in dupli-

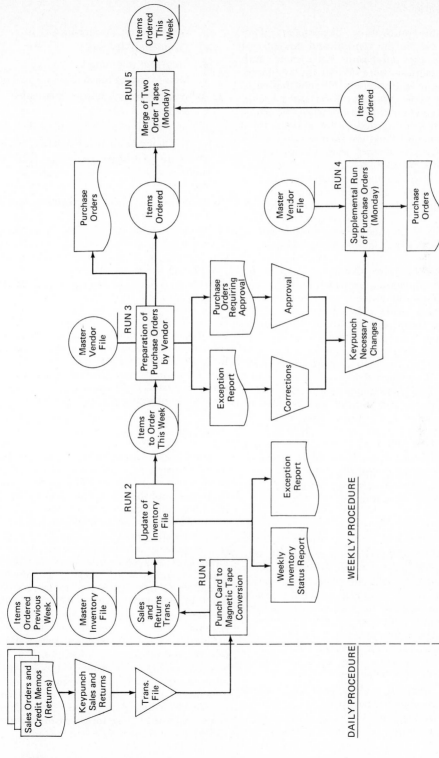

Figure C12–7 Peabock Company's Inventory and Purchase Order Procedure

cate in the purchasing department. The original is sent to the vendor, and the copy is retained in the purchasing department and filed in numerical order. When the shipment arrives, the inventory supervisor sees that each item received is checked off on the packing slip that accompanies the shipment. The packing slip is then forwarded to the accounts payable department. When the invoice arrives, the packing slip is compared with the invoice in the accounts payable department. Once any differences between the packing slip and the invoice have been reconciled, a check is drawn for the appropriate amount and is mailed to the vendor with a copy of the invoice. The packing slip is attached to the invoice and is filed alphabetically in the paid invoice file.

REQUIRED: Wooster Company intends to redesign its purchasing system from the point in time when an item needs to be ordered until payment is made. The system should be designed to ensure that all the proper controls are incorporated into the system.

a. Identify the internally and externally generated documents that would be required to satisfy the minimum requirements of a basic system and indicate the number of copies of each document that would be needed.

b. Explain how all of these documents should interrelate and flow among Wooster's various departments, including the final destination or file of each copy. (Adapted from the CMA Examination)

12–9

Specialty Steel Corporation is a small rolling mill in Sandusky, Ohio, which produces special steel alloy slabs and plates. It is considering the implementation of a computer-based information system to support its logistics management system from order entry through shipping of customer orders.

The objectives of the system are to

1. Generate work schedules
2. Track work through production, inspection, and shipping facilities
3. Have on-line
   a. Order entry

b. Order status monitoring
   c. Production planning
   d. Shipment planning
   e. Monitoring of finished goods inventory
4. Achieve processing improvements by
   a. Reducing waste
   b. Increasing equipment utilization
   c. Reducing labor requirements
5. Optimize slab-making throughputs while meeting specifications as closely as possible
6. Minimize the slabs not meeting specifications
7. Monitor customer orders, control processing, ensure correct routing, minimize delivery times, and provide for status inquiry in the heavy plate facility
8. Use the computer to plan weekly and daily schedules

Discuss in general the data base requirements for transaction, operational, and managerial control of Specialty Steel's logistics function. Refer to Chapter 8 for details of data base design to support your general discussion. Prepare a systems flowchart of the on-line function in objectives 3a and 3b above.

12–10

Lawn Care Lawn Mower Company has a policy of using its distribution system to stock finished goods inventory. The company effectively accomplishes this objective by offering discounts and delayed invoice payments from its distributors to smooth its production over slack sales months. In the lawn mower industry, seasonality is a big problem. As a result, Lawn Care has very little space for finished goods inventory in its plant. The industry in recent years has suffered from large fluctuations in material prices, which are putting pressure on management to speculate in material purchases. To compound the logistics planning problems, sales often follow the pattern of housing starts. Competition is in terms of price, service, and quality. Thus Lawn Care must carefully plan and schedule its logistics operations. It must be able to act fast in response to changing supply and demand problems while producing for a season six months in the future at minimum cost.

Lawn Care manufactures three basic products: walk-behind lawn mowers, riding lawn mowers, and rototillers. Each machine is produced in three sizes for a total of nine basic products. Various options are added to these basic products, and many parts are common among the products.

Production orders are received from distributors and approved by management as follows. Each week the production and sales management personnel review the production schedule for the next year. They prepare a list of changes and new production orders at this time. They also review the raw material status report weekly and override the automatic reorder system with an authorization to purchase so that the company can take advantage of lower costs or anticipated cost increases. The changes, new production orders, and purchase authorizations are keypunched and entered into the next daily production scheduling run.

Lawn Care uses a small IBM 370/40 with several disk drives for its programs and records. It uses a mathematical optimization model to maximize throughput in the proper mix of products while minimizing in-house inventory of raw material and finished goods and delivery time to the distributors.

The daily production run accesses an operations specification list for each product and an open production order file, which indicates when each production order is to be scheduled for the next year. The mathematical algorithm then generates two copies of the production orders for the day, for the department supervisor and management. At the same time, production schedules are generated for each department and the plant for the day's activities. Also, an update of the yearly production schedule is prepared for management. At the same time, operation cards are punched to be distributed to the factory departments. Material requisition cards are sent to the warehouse for the distribution of the raw materials to each department for that day's production. After the materials have been sent to the departments, these requisition cards are returned to data processing with a signature of compliance. The operation cards are marked as to what actually occurred in terms of number of units produced, time consumed, and materials used in each department. They are returned each day to EDP to be mark sensed and punched.

Along with these three outputs of the daily scheduling run, an assembly order is generated for each mower to be assembled. This is used to ensure that the mower (tiller) is assembled to specifications. The assembly order is attached to each mower through the assembly process. When the mower is finished, the assembly order is removed and sent to EDP.

REQUIRED:

a. Itemize the operational, managerial, and strategic control decision activities required for the operation of the firm.

b. Prepare a systems flowchart for all operations above.

c. Discuss several control policies and procedures that should be incorporated.

12–11

ABS Wholesalers distributes food products. The firm uses a perpetual inventory system with automated reorder points. Sales orders are received from salespeople and are approved for credit and stock availability. A stock status inquiry system is used for this purpose. On-line terminals interface with a random access inventory status file. Sales personnel also call the warehouse to write up a purchase order on an item they believe to be in short supply.

Sales orders are keyed into the terminal and processed. At this time, stock status data are updated. A shipping card, an invoice, and a packing slip are generated and used by warehouse personnel to process the order. Upon completion of the order, the shipping card is signed and returned to a data processing for stock status update. The packing slip and invoice are sent to the customer with the merchandise.

Purchase orders are generated as necessary each time a stock status update run is made. Due to the size of the operation, stock status runs are made each hour.

REQUIRED:

a. Prepare a systems flowchart of the operations described above.

b. Describe several control policies and procedures that should be incorporated into this computerized system.

c. Describe the stock status inventory record.

12–12

Ready Build General Contractors has the following information needs:

1. Information that will allow a competitive bid to be submitted for a construction job
2. Internal accumulation and control of costs related to a specific job
3. Planning and budgeting information for scheduling job and resource allocation

The initial information requirement in the estimation process is a knowledge of the construction jobs that are "up for bid." This knowledge is gathered primarily from trade journals. Ready Build utilizes the Dodge Report, which offers a weekly listing of new construction jobs in the metropolitan area. This report provides a brief description of the job. Specialized blueprints for the job must then be obtained from the architect (or owner) for a specified charge. Next the actual bid is prepared by an estimator. The estimator will consider the amount of materials needed, the amount of labor needed, the bids received from the various subcontractors, and an appropriate allowance for overhead and profit. An important factor to be considered is the price of materials: Supplies used in the building industry are sometimes subject to violent fluctuation on a daily basis. For this reason, the estimator will not compute the material costs until moments before the bid is telephoned in. The most recent prices available are used for the bid. If the bid is accepted, the estimator will immediately place an order with suppliers for the amount of materials needed. This establishes the price for the materials at the price quoted in the bid.

Cost information in the contruction industry is of primary importance for three types of users. Estimators need relevant information on past costs of completed contracts in order to make estimates for bidding on future contracts. Managers use cost information in order to monitor the progress of the contract by comparing estimated cost figures with actual cost figures. Cost figures are also important in preparing income tax returns.

If the analysis of costs is to be useful, it is important to know how they are allocated to each job. Direct costs are a function of subcontractors' costs, direct labor, direct materials, and equipment charges. Subcontractors' costs are allocated on the basis of the contract price and are readily verified. Direct labor is a function of time spent on a job by the contractor's employees and the rate of pay. This information is assembled on time cards that show (1) how long the employee worked, (2) which job was worked on, and (3) the rate of pay. Direct materials are purchased for a specific job following the estimator's analysis. Materials are charged to the job for which they were purchased. Equipment charges are divided into three categories: durable and standard equipment, special equipment, and perishable equipment. Durable and standard equipment charges for trucks, cranes, and bulldozers are made to each job on the basis of the fair amount of rent that would be paid to an outside equipment rental concern less any profit that would be incurred. Special equipment is equipment that can be used only on a particular project. This equipment would be rented and the rental payments would be charged to the job for which it was used. Perishable equipment (hammers and nails) is charged to the job for which it is used less any residual value remaining after the job has been completed.

Indirect costs are charged on the basis of a fixed overhead rate. Costs of the estimating department are recorded on the basis of time spent on a successful bid. Costs of unsuccessful bids are considered general administrative expense and are charged out using the fixed overhead rate.

The division of costs by elements is important as a guide in future construction of the same nature. Also, if analyzed on a fairly current basis, these unit costs can indicate whether the contract is running in excess of the estimate. It is important that a periodical accumulation of actual costs on each project be submitted by the accounting department. These reports should be analyzed by cost classifications on each job and compared with the total bid estimate using the same classifications.

REQUIRED:

a. From the above information, indicate what records may be useful in the estimation and bidding process.

b. Flowchart this process for Ready Build General Contractors.

c. Indicate the internal controls necessary in the manual computation of the above bid and estimation information to ensure a reasonable degree of accuracy.

d. Describe in general how a microcomputer using on-line programs can be used in this business environment to enhance management's decision making.

12-13

A description of NCR's Material Requirements Planning (MRP) system, which is part of NCR MISSION's "Complete Business System for Manufacturing," follows.

MISSION's Material Requirements Planning System (MRP) takes advantage of the speed and accuracy of electronic data processing to:

–Calculate material requirements on the basis of sales forecasts, current and projected orders, and other future-demand information.

–Update master schedule details instantly as new orders are added, as forecasts are changed, or as delivery dates are rescheduled.

–Interact with other systems to translate material requirements into real-world deadlines, order release, storage requirements, and production schedules.

Major Functions of MRP

Gross-to-Net Calculation. MRP converts Gross Requirements into Net Requirements, helping you produce precise, timely purchase orders and shop orders. The Gross-to-Net Calculation "subtracts" available inventory from Gross Requirements, and then takes net requirements and adjusts for lead-time.

The Gross-to-Net Calculation interfaces with the MISSION Bill of Material System. Gross-to-Net explodes all levels of product structures, generating requirements and deadlines down to the level of purchased parts and assemblies.

Planned orders are developed by the MRP Gross-to-Net Calculation by using multiple lot-sizing techniques—for example, lot-for-lot, periods of supply, minimum buy quantities, etc.

Item Master Maintenance. You can inquire, add, change, or delete MRP information in your system's data base through the real-time Item Master Maintenance program. Security codes prevent unauthorized tampering with lines.

Master Schedule Requirements File Maintenance. The Master Schedule Requirements File Maintenance function gives you real-time access to files on all forecasts and requirements for end units, assemblies, and parts.

The Master Schedule Requirements File Maintenance function also reports on schedule variance. MRP reports the early filling of purchase orders to save inventory costs. When order release is past due, MRP generates an "expedite" report.

Regeneration of Scheduled Receipts. MRP records all data on scheduled deliveries for Purchased Parts and all shop orders. This report summarizes data from other files on order delivery and completion from the MISSION data base.

Regeneration of Dependent Demand. The Regeneration of Dependent Demand function summarizes all requirements generated by Gross-to-Net processing and builds information on Dependent Demand: the total demand for an item which accrues through product explosion.

Data Base Inquiry Function. This function produces information from the data base on on-line CRT's or printers.

Maintenance Error and Audit Function. The Maintenance Error and Audit function of MRP checks all data and prints error reports to identify input problems. The function also generates a report to describe the flow and consequences of valid transactions. The Maintenance Error and Audit function performs both field analysis and logical validation of data.[1]

---

[1] NCR MISSION's "Complete Business System for Manufacturing," courtesy of NCR Corporation, 1978.

In the design of a new on-line system to replace the batch-processing system described in the text, will this package satisfy the needs outlined in the introductory notes in the chapter on the need to move to a real-time on-line system? In other words, is it a viable alternative? Why, in terms of decision-making, reporting, and transaction-processing requirements?

12–14

A description of Boeing Company's Commercial Electronic Manufacturing Divisions Production Management System (PMS) follows.

Keeping track of every assembly being manufactured, not to mention every hex nut and cap screw going into it, can be an overwhelming task in a manufacturing plant. Even with huge computers such detailed information is difficult to keep current. Yet one plant in the Boeing Company's Commercial Electronic Manufacturing Division, with sales of $12 million a year, tracks not only every assembly but where every part is located, what has been purchased and received for it, for whom it is being built, what inspections have been performed on it, how many more parts can be built out of current inventory and each payroll hour chargeable to any part or assembly constructed.

What It Needed. In establishing the PMS, Boeing management determined that it had to have an on-line system that could keep track of inventory and work-in-process while updating bills of materials, performing material requirements planning and handling several accounting functions, including payroll accounting by job and contract from each work area. The decision was to use a dedicated computer with a magnetic tape update of the firm's larger mainframes to avoid the excessive costs of programming for complete interaction with the mainframe and to avoid delays of batch transaction.

The guidelines under which the PMS was written demanded that the system:

1. Justify its cost through measurable production cost reductions,
2. Prevent—or at least accurately predict—late end-item deliveries,

3. Function on-line, so as to respond to spares manufacturing needs, as well as routine production, and spot shop flow bottlenecks early in either operation,
4. Respond to inquiries into any level of a bill of materials—whether full assembly, subassembly or part—as end-items in themselves, in order to fill spares order requirements,
5. Require minimum training for use by noncomputer people, including such things as providing displayed lists of options and resisting failure under operator error, and
6. Provide complete front-end error checking to preserve data base integrity.

According to Graeber Jordan, Automated Data Systems manager for Electronics Manufacturing, the criteria used for selection included processing speed, size of on-line storage, and operating system characteristics, with particular emphasis on after-sales support. "We researched small computers thoroughly before deciding the Hewlett-Packard Model 3000 was the one to implement the system. The HP operating system provided greater flexibility to do what we had in mind than any other we looked at. And the HP data base can be interrogated in almost any fashion to supply the answers people who use the system need. Most of those people don't know anything about a computer, but they have to get data quickly in a form they can use. The HP system supplies it well."

What It Got. The Boeing department uses a complete HP 3000 Computer System with a 128K byte memory. The computer system includes three 47 megabyte disc drives, two tape drives to record data for the company's System 370 accounting and payroll functions, a machine readable interface with Boeing's central procurement facility, and a line printer. A total of 29 terminals, both hardcopy and video tape, are connected with the computer, although normally about 22 are running at once.

The HP 3000 system includes a multiprogramming executive operating system and an on-line text editor as well as file-copy and sort and merge utilities. These features provided the power Boeing needed to develop the system.

The data base management system is HP's IMAGE/QUERY. The combination permits on-line access to the data base in almost any fashion to dig out information for nonroutine as well as regular reports without having to redesign the application program. With the magnetic disk drives, the system provides a virtual memory so that large programs can be executed without overrunning the main memory.

80% Use by Production. To ensure that the needs of those who generate the data are met (production people account for 80% of the data demands made on the system), production personnel at every level were consulted during the system's development. From their input, flowcharts showing every step in manufacturing were developed. These formed the basis of the program and highlighted the edits and error checks that would be needed.

The system was fully developed before it was put on-line to encourage user confidence in the program's capabilities from the outset.

To protect each portion of the data base against unintentional or unauthorized entry, PMS includes password protection for user groups. The bill of materials, for instance, cannot be modified by quality control people, nor the inventory altered by production control employees.

PMS addresses most of the manufacturing aspects of the CEMD's inventory, bills of materials, master schedules, planning and ordering of parts, monitoring open job orders, recording and accumulating shop labor charges, measuring job standards performance, and monitoring shipping requirements and dates.

The material requirements planning module considers all on-hand inventories and open orders and plans additional orders so that both "make" and "buy" parts will be available at the proper time. Records of lead times are constantly updated by the module. Planning for any assembly follows a complicated path in which the computer spots any difficulty that might result in a late order shipment.

An accounting interface subsystem of PMS updates Boeing's larger financial accounting system. Data processed by the subsystem accumulate from other modules which monitor work flow on the factory floor. Daily, the accounting subsystem transmits actual labor hours to the payroll system, transmits data on material dollar transfers resulting from contract-to-contract transfer of purchased parts, and notifies the financial department of transactions concerning assemblies.

In addition to handling payroll accounting for employees on the floor, the system supplies daily reports to cost center foremen. These reports tell the foreman which jobs are in the shop and what priorities they have, what jobs will flow into the shop in the next five days along with their priorities, and what the performance has been on jobs just completed by the shop. All rework time and assemblies scrapped are logged and reported to foremen weekly to assist them in evaluating their own performance.[2]

REQUIRED:

a. From the description above, comment point by point on how the new system satisfies its stated requirements.

b. What internal control features were built into the system?

c. What report generation features are present in the system? Why are these features important for management decision making?

d. What is the interface with Boeing's accounting and payroll functions?

e. Given the system development phases outlined in Chapters 10 and 11, briefly discuss this system's compliance with those phases.

---

[2] With permission, this case is based on and quoted from Boeing Company and Hewlett-Packard, "A Production Management System at Boeing," *Management Accounting,* April 1979, pp. 33–35.

13

MARKETING SYSTEMS

OBJECTIVE

The objective of a marketing system is to support the decision making, reporting, and transaction processing requirements of marketing and sales management. These requirements are a function of the management system's objectives. The major objective of the marketing management system is to develop, promote, distribute, sell, and service the products of the organization and return a profit that is sufficient to justify the organization's investment in the product.

To accomplish this objective, marketing management needs to make effective marketing decisions in a dynamic environment that is often characterized by intense competition and technological change. These decisions span product planning and development, advertising and promotion, sales and distribution, and market research and customer service functions, as well as all three managerial activities. They must often be made on the basis of market research, accounting information, and a wide variety of externally generated information.

In general, a marketing information system must be designed to support a marketing management organization such as the one shown in Figure 13–1.

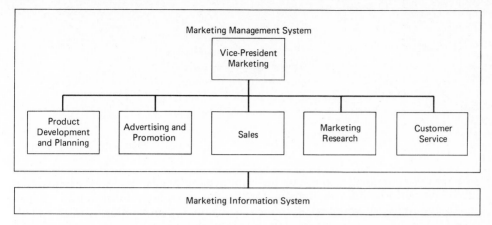

Figure 13–1   Marketing Organization Subsystems and Supporting Information Systems

Other organization structures, such as product organization, are also common for marketing (product) management. The specific objectives of each of the subsystems noted in Figure 13–1 are described later in this chapter.

DECISION AND TRANSACTION PROCESSING CHARACTERISTICS

Environmental Considerations

Over the past several years management has become increasingly aware that (1) the success of an organization is largely a function of marketing success, and (2) marketing success requires management to focus on customer needs and market demands and not to focus on the product. The major implication of this development for accounting information systems is in the increase in the flow of information to and from the marketplace. In other words, intensive interaction with the environment is critical to the accomplishment of the objectives of marketing and sales management. This interaction is illustrated in Figure 13–2, in which three general flows of environmental and transactional information are indicated.

First, there is a continual monitoring of the environment through a marketing intelligence system. The system must gather information on trends that may have an impact on sales, competition, pricing, promotion activities, suppliers' activities, market trends, distribution problems, new developments stemming from technology changes with respect to markets and products, changes in cultural values and norms, legal requirements, and potential substitute products.

One of the earliest market intelligence systems was established at the Mead Johnson Nutritional Division of Mead Johnson and Company. This company's system continually monitored the environment, integrated a network of data sources, and effectively used data processing to provide management with

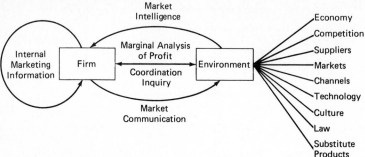

Figure 13–2 Marketing Information Flows

the necessary reports to meet its decision-making needs.[1] Its monitoring system gathered periodic information on store audits, sales accounting reports, supermarket warehouse withdrawal reports, consumer panel reports, sales call reports, advertising expenditure data, syndicated panel audits of inventory sales, and consumer surveys of awareness, attitudes, and usage of competing products. Mead Johnson also commissioned advertising pretests, product tests, and special studies of marketing opportunities and product placement. From all this activity, the system provided periodic reports to management on consumer awareness and attitudes, product purchase and use, factory sales, wholesale withdrawal rates, retail sales, prices, inventory, distribution, and advertising-sales relationships. Moreover, the data base provided by its intelligence system enabled management to secure reports on advertising quality, product quality, basic consumer wants and needs, market segments, and consumer and market reaction to promotion and package stimuli.

A marketing intelligence system such as the one just described involves a large volume of data, and as we noted in Chapters 1 and 10, an attempt must be made to transform the data into information. The design process for such a system starts with an analysis of success factors for the industry and the organization, and decision and transaction processing networks.

In addition to obtaining intelligence from the environment, the organization must be able to interact with the environment to perform marginal analysis on products and coordinate the activities of the organization. Negotiation of contracts for delivery, price, and quality specifications requires sales personnel to be able to coordinate their activities with logistical and production management in terms of inventory, production schedules, and cost data in order to determine the feasibility of the terms of the sale and the potential profitability of the contract. This coordination may require changes in production and shipment schedules. An assessment of the costs associated with such a change, for example, should consider a marginal analysis of the contract. For some organizations, this type of marginal analysis and production and marketing coordination may be so intense that on-line systems and mathematical models may be required. For other organizations, current cost data coupled with an occasional

---

[1] This description is used with the permission of the Mead Johnson Nutritional Division and is reprinted by permission of the Harvard Business Review from "Systems Approach to Marketing," (May–June 1967), pp. 105–18. Copyright©1967 by the President and Fellows of Harvard College; all rights reserved.

phone call to the production manager to review an upcoming production schedule may suffice.

Finally, marketing management and sales management must be able to make inquiries with respect to the availability of inventory and the status of sales or production orders to be able to service customers. Customers need to know when they can expect delivery and the status of their orders that are being manufactured. These inquiries again require coordination of marketing and logistical systems.

In addition to these intelligence and inquiry flows, marketing management requires an internal information system that is effective and efficient in supporting management decision-making, reporting, and transaction processing activities. Marketing functions can generally be classified as sales, product development, promotion and advertising, customer service, and market research. Within each of these functions, and for marketing management as a whole, information is required for operational, managerial, and strategic decision-making activities. Moreover, the accounting transaction processing and cost analysis subsystems must be designed to contribute to a transaction history, accounts receivable, credit, and cost analysis data base to support the marketing information system. These transaction data can be obtained from credit data (generally part of the treasurer's function), the inventory subsystem, sales order transaction processing, and accounts receivable records and billing activities. We noted in Chapter 2 that the source of information for managerial and strategic decisions increasingly tends to be environmental and follow from market research and intelligence. Operational decisions tend to rely more on the analysis of internal transaction sources.

In addition to the information flows from the environment and internal information flows used to satisfy decision-making needs, an organization must also consider its requirements for communication to the environment, as shown in Figure 13–2. Some of this communication is in the form of reports to third parties (including financial statements), reports to consumer agencies on product characteristics, and reports to various trade associations. Other information may be required to communicate to the organization's customers and the general public the merits of the firm's products and services through promotion and advertising. The information system must be capable of generating data to support all these information flows to the environment.

The nature of the business will dictate the extent of the information flows outlined above. The nature of the business will in turn be a function of the organization's products and markets, the nature of the competitive environment, the size of the organization, the resources available from subsystems, and, finally, the management's expertise in the use of the information. These environmental characteristics are summarized in Figure 13–3. In general, however, marketing systems require intensive *monitoring* of the environment and complex *retrieval systems* to support intensive *inquiry* and *coordination* activities.

Decision Network

The overall objective of a marketing and sales order processing information system is to provide marketing management with the information nec-

Organization structure

Volume and frequency of information flows

Competitive environment

Resource availability

Financial capability

Product attributes

Product life cycle

Product seasonality

Substitute products

Product line and variety

Obsolescence and uniqueness

Styles and colors

Customer characteristics

Promotion activity

Credit and collection practice

Advertising media

Inventory policy

Distribution system

Technology level of product

Service requirements

Mathematical and statistical expertise

Pricing policies

Logistical support

Cultural norms

Legal requirements

Economic conditions

Government influence and regulation

Figure 13–3 Environmental Characteristics

essary to make operational, planning, and strategic decisions and to report the results of the operations to third parties. In a functional organization such as the one illustrated in Figure 13–1, the vice-president is primarily responsible for the strategic planning activities and, in smaller organizations, the managerial planning, coordinating, and control of marketing activities. These activities must interface with logistical and financial activities and are often critical to the firm's overall success.

At the strategic level, marketing decisions primarily involve the setting of marketing objectives, new-product introduction and development, and determination of policies to be followed by the firm in its approach to sales, pricing products, inventory levels, distribution channels, promotion, and levels of customer service. In addition, some allocation of scarce resources to accomplish these objectives within the firm's policies is done by the vice-president of marketing.

Each of the managers of the functional areas of product development and planning, advertising and promotion, sales, market research, and customer service is responsible for providing the vice-president with sufficient information, via the information system, for decision making and reporting. In turn, each of the managers of a functional area will have a staff or organization that will be responsible for providing sufficient information to him or her for managerial and operational decision-making activities.

Transaction systems, which process sales and accounts receivable transactions, and credit systems, which establish credit for customers, must support these decisions. Sufficient data must be obtained at the point of sale, upon credit application, and upon the exercise of credit over time to support many of these decisions. (The major transaction processes that support the majority of marketing information systems are examined in the latter part of this chapter.)

Summaries and analyses of these transaction flows are often used to make decisions. The accountant, systems analyst, or project team must, however, design the system around decision, reporting, and transaction processing needs and not just around the flow of transaction necessary to process sales, survey customers and competitors, and prepare the financial statements, for these data may often be irrelevant and insufficient for many decisions at all levels of managerial activity.

Consider, for example, a marketing information system for a retail store. The system should (1) support managerial and operational decisions about customer service, stock turnover, profitable stock balances, markdown frequency and amount, and increasing salesperson productivity; (2) help in receivables collection; (3) help in financial and inventory management; (4) help in the control of inventory, accounts receivable, and credit; and (5) make it relatively easy to collect this information at the point of sale. Many hardware and software vendors as well as public accounting firms offer this type of system.[2] NCR, for example, uses a microprocessor and its associated software to generate the reports shown in Figure 13–4 for retail management decision making in small to medium-sized companies. The external, interactive, internal, and communication information flows outlined earlier undergird this information system.

Marketing Subsystems

SALES   The objective of the sales manager is to coordinate the sales effort so that the long-run profitability of the company is maximized. Decisions must be made and implemented by the sales management system to ensure adequate stock, effective distribution channels, effective motivation of sales personnel, promotion of more-profitable products or product lines, profitable pricing of products, and good customer relations. These managerial decisions all require careful planning, given the strategic objectives of the firm, its marketing plan, and its supporting sales forecast. Each decision of sales management must consider new products and product development, advertising and promotion activities, market research information, and customer service. Moreover, as we noted earlier, these decisions often require intensive interaction with the marketplace and coordination with logistical operations of inventory and production. Mathematical models may be used to assist with these decisions, but often they are not. In any case, the decision must be made by sales management; it is often based in part on a set of internal reports.

One of the most useful of these reports is the *stock status report*, which indicates the number of items in stock, the price, and the cost (fixed and variable) if possible. This is most useful for marginal analysis of the profitability of sales.

A *sales analysis report*, such as the one shown in Figure 13–5, is also quite useful because it details unit and dollar sales for the current period and the year-to-date, by location (department, store, or territory), and by salesperson. Budgeted sales and last year's sales are often noted for comparison. Other analyses, such as sales by product, are also feasible given the basic transaction data gathered at the point of sale. This sales analysis information

---

[2] See the NCR systems listed in the "Selected References" section of this chapter and Price Waterhouse & Co.'s RM/80 for examples.

SALES REPORTS

Sales Analysis
Sales, Tax, and Nonmerchandise Report
Salesperson Productivity

INVENTORY MANAGEMENT REPORTS

Retail Inventory Management Report
Cost/Direct Cost Inventory Management Report

OPEN-TO-BUY REPORTS

Open Order Summary
Preseason Merchandise Plan
Postseason Merchandise Plan
Open-to-Buy Season Report

AUDIT AND BALANCING REPORTS

NCR . . . Retail Terminal Validation Report
Store Balance Report
Detail Summary

FINANCIAL REPORTS

General Journal Listing
Trial Balance
Income Statement
Balance Sheet
Vendor Accounts Payable Summary
Merchandise Stock Ledger
Physical Inventory Difference Report

ACCOUNTS RECEIVABLE REPORTS

Aged Trial Balance
Selective Trial Balance
Customer Statements
Credit Authorization
Selective Accounts Analysis
Collection Report
Accounting Activity Report
Accounts Receivable Summary
Receivables Maintenance and Exception Report
Maintenance and Update Recap

Figure 13–4   Retail Management Information Reports

NCR
PROFITABLE STORE — SALES ANALYSIS — STORE NO. 1 — (CN123456) — 9/30/8-

Class Sku/Sty Cl Sz S	Desc		Current				Month to Date						Year to Date					
		Net Units	Net Sales	%Sls /Tot	%Ret /Sls	Net Units	Net Sales	%Sls Tot	%Ret Sls	%Diff Unit	Ty/Ly Dollar	Net Units	Net Sales	%Sls /Tot	%Ret /Sls	%Diff Unit	Ty/Ly Dollar
1643	Merchandise A	2	42	3.7	.3	6	125	3.6	.9	−5.1	−6.0	80	1080	5.1	1.0	.7	.6
1645	Merchandise B	2	15	1.3	.0	2	15	.4	.0	−2.5	−3.0	16	118	.6	.0	−2.9	−4.7
1759	Merchandise C	6	123	10.9	3.5	14	282	8.0	2.7	6.9	8.0	111	2313	10.9	2.5	1.5	2.3
1761	Merchandise D	11	78	6.9	.0	32	224	6.4	.0	1.2	2.0	220	1540	7.3	.0	6.8	5.3
1773	Merchandise E	17	181	16.1	1.2	96	1031	29.3	1.6	4.7	5.2	598	6362	30.0	1.7	5.8	6.4
1775	Merchandise F	12	96	8.5	.0	45	360	10.2	.0	1.4	1.0	333	2664	12.5	.0	3.0	2.1
1784	Merchandise G	10	90	24.1	.0	27	243	16.4	.0			123	1107	15.4	.0		
916120	BL/34/2	4	48	12.9	.0	23	276	18.6	.0			213	2556	35.7	.0		
916126	A B C Co.	2	20	5.4	.0	14	140	9.5	.0			124	1240	17.3	.0		
916127	X Y Z Co.	1	5	1.3	.0	2	46	3.1	.0			5	114	1.6	.0		
916128	Promotion	14	210	56.3	.9	41	615	41.5	.8			92	1380	19.3	.6		
916129	Bad Goods	0	0	.0	.0	3	161	10.9	.0			15	762	10.6	.0		
Class 1784 TOT		31	373	33.2	.9	110	1481	42.1	.8	3.7	4.0	572	7159	33.7	.6	4.8	5.0
Dept. 12 TOT		81	1123	25.7	.8	305	3518	19.4	.9	2.7	3.6	1930	21236	26.0	.9	2.8	2.4
x				x				x						x			
x				x				x						x			
x				x				x						x			
Div. 5 TOT		693	4365	28.3	1.2	2596	18095	53.1	1.4	4.8	5.1	12491	81745	33.1	1.0	1.8	2.3
x				x				x						x			
x				x				x						x			
x				x				x						x			
Store 1 TOT		1289	15430	100	.8	3806	34102	100	1.0	2.6	3.5	23461	246698	100	1.0	2.9	3.1

Reprinted with permission NCR— *Retail Management Information System* (Dayton: NCR Corporation)

Figure 13–5 Sales Analysis Report

may be merged with cost accounting and inventory records to prepare profitability analysis reports by location, salesperson, product, or any other category of interest as long as the raw data are collected.

As we can see, much of the information on these management reports, which are used for decision making, is generated by the sales order and accounts receivable transaction processing system, which will be examined later.

PRODUCT DEVELOPMENT AND PLANNING   The product development and planning manager must provide marketing management with packaging, promotion, pricing, and style recommendations throughout the product's life cycle. This life cycle includes the test marketing of new products, the introduction of new products, the maintenance of each product, and, finally, the phasing out of products or the substitution of alternative products. Often the product life cycle dominates marketing management. If it does, a project organization may be preferable to a functional organization.

Decisions that support these product recommendations may be based on marketing models,[3] but as in sales management, a series of inventory, sales, and profitability analysis reports often provide basic input into the decision. Marginal analysis of sales revenue and costs is often quite useful in assessing the potential contribution of a product to the overall profitability of the organization. Environmental information is also critical to these decisions. Information on changing styles, customer demand, competitor actions, new products, and so forth, is very useful in assessing the strengths and weaknesses of an organization's products and recommending various courses of action to marketing management.

Therefore the data base needed here includes not only internal information gathered at the point of sale and through the cost accounting system but also considerable external information, which is needed by product planning and development managers. Market research can be quite instrumental in satisfying this need.

ADVERTISING AND PROMOTION   The objective of the advertising and promotion manager is to plan, coordinate, execute, and evaluate advertising and promotion policy. Given a limited budget, advertising and promotion management must allocate resources in the most effective manner through a variety of media to products and locations (territories, regions, stores, etc.) to accomplish the overall sales objectives of marketing management. These decisions require careful planning and coordination of sales and product development. They are generally a function of a market's response to the various media, exposure to those media over time, and the product and market strategy of the organization. Mathematical models have been used effectively for a number of years in helping advertising and promotional management to select the best type of media and exposure for various products. A subsequent evaluation of the impact of these efforts is necessary to refine these models for future use. The *sales analysis report* shown in Figure 13-5 can be used effectively in this evaluation process. It is essential that key sales statistics be collected at the point of sale

---

[3] See David B. Montgomery and Glen L. Urban, "Marketing Decision—Information Systems: An Emerging View," *Journal of Marketing Research*, 7 (May 1970), pp. 226–34.

or during the sales transaction process if advertising and promotion management is to make intelligent decisions on allocating the advertising and promotion budget. To further assist advertising and promotion management, the array of sales statistics on salespeople, locations (department, store, territory, etc.), products, styles, sizes, and so forth, should be in a random access file so that planned and actual promotional efforts can be matched with their respective target populations to facilitate future decision making and the evaluation of past decisions.

As with product planning, promotional decisions require a considerable amount of external information, such as that noted earlier, which is often gathered by market research. The data base, therefore, not only must contain information about customers, competition, and the economic and legal environment but also must be organized in such a way that it can facilitate retrieval either in report form or via random inquiry as needed by decision makers (see Chapter 8).

MARKETING RESEARCH   The objective of marketing research is to investigate problems confronting the other managers in the marketing organization. These problems may involve sales, product development, advertising and promotion, customer service, or general marketing management needs.

To satisfy these decision-making and reporting requirements, the market research department must, either periodically or upon demand, gather information for specifically commissioned assignments by a general scanning of the environment and by retrieval from the firm's data base. This information must then be processed. This may entail evaluation of the various signals received and an abstraction of the relevant signals from a large set of data. This set of currently or potentially relevant data must be planned, indexed (coded), and logically organized for retention and retrieval purposes for responses to inquiries, solutions to problems, analysis of information, and generation of periodic reports to be disseminated to the appropriate decision makers or users.

The decision maker can use the information provided by marketing research in a number of ways, which generally parallel those used by the types of information systems outlined in Chapter 4. The information may be of value in its own right for decision making; it may be analyzed using statistical, economic, or psychometric models; or it may be used in conjunction with models to enable marketing management to pursue "what if" questions. Moreover, it may be used in corporate planning models such as those outlined in Chapter 15. Market research management will probably utilize all the mathematical and statistical techniques it can to provide the best possible information to the other areas of marketing management.

The data base used by market research will include sales, inventory, and accounts receivable statistics which are generated from transaction data of the kind described later in this chapter. It will, moreover, require the set of external data noted earlier which is gathered via a continual monitoring of the environment through a marketing intelligence system. In fact, the management of this intelligence system may very well be the responsibility of marketing research.

CUSTOMER SERVICE   The goal of customer service is to serve the customer in such a way that he or she will be satisfied with the product. To do this, the objective of customer service management is to provide customers technical assistance and product maintenance. Decisions must be made pertaining to the maintenance organization, training of service personnel, capabilities of equipment, and location of facilities to serve customers and assist in the dissemination of technical information to these customers. These management decisions must be congruent with the marketing management strategy regarding customer satisfaction and service.

Again, the basic sales, inventory, and accounts receivable transaction information is useful for customer service management. In addition, information on sales returns, customer complaints, and frequency and cause of repair by location, salesperson, and product is useful for making decisions and evaluating customer service policies. Most of these reports can be generated periodically. An on-line system may be needed for parts inventory and maintenance activities.

Supporting Transaction Processing Network and Systems

All marketing information systems are supported by a revenue cycle that includes the processing of sales transactions and the subsequent collection of receivables. This sales and collection cycle represents the prime source of internally generated data for the decision-making and reporting needs of marketing management.

Two major subsystems generally provide this basic transaction information and serve as prime inputs into the data base or files utilized by product development, promotion, sales, market research, and customer service. These subsystems are the *sales order processing and accounts receivable system* and the *credit authorization and management system.*

Moreover, at the point of sale a considerable amount of information must often be gathered in addition to the dollar amount of the transaction. Due to the tremendous volume of this information, special point-of-sale systems that can capture large volumes of data economically and effectively have been developed.

SALES ORDER PROCESSING AND ACCOUNTS RECEIVABLE During the processing of the sales transaction a large volume of data can be captured by using either a sales invoice or a point-of-sale (POS) system. POS systems are frequently used in retail firms. (A configuration of this type of system will be reviewed later in this chapter.) A typical sales invoice will contain information similar to that shown in Figure 13–6. In particular, the information captured will consist of the customer order, sales order, or invoice number for control, the customer account number to interface with the accounts receivable system, the salesperson number, the item or part number and description, the quantity of each item, the price of each item, any applicable discounts, the date, the date to be delivered, delivery instructions, freight charges, and credit authorization (if applicable). Also included is pertinent information about the company, such as name, address, and telephone number. (An example of a simple sales order entry and invoicing system is given later in this chapter.)

In addition to being recorded as a debit to the accounts receivable control or cash account, and a credit to sales, information related to this transac-

Company Information
    Name
    Address
    Telephone number
    Store number
    Department number
Order (Sales or Invoice) Number—for control and accountability
Customer Account Number
Credit Authorization
Salesperson Number
Item (for each)
    Number
    Description
    Quantity
    Price
    Discount
    Total
Freight Charges
Grand Total
Date
Date to Be Delivered
Delivery Instructions

Figure 13–6 Sales Order Information

tion is used to update three key files used by marketing management. These are the finished goods inventory, accounts receivable and credit history file, and sales summary files. The typical content of finished goods and inventory files was shown in the preceding chapter in Figure 12–4.

The accounts receivable and credit history file will normally contain the kind of data shown in Figure 13–7. There are three basic types of accounts receivable systems. One is an *open item system* in which there is a complete accounting of customer activity for all unpaid or uncontested invoices. Credits are made either to specific invoices or to the oldest invoice as cash is remitted. Simpler systems such as the one shown in Figure 13–7 retain detail for the current month's activity and bring forward only the balance and past-due charges from previous months' activity. This type of system is called a *balance forward system*. Other systems record only the balance. This type of *balance only system* is frequently used by retail stores and is supported by copies of the original invoice.

A typical sales summary file will contain the kind of data shown in Figure 13–8, all of which can be obtained manually at the point of sale, on the sales invoice, or via a POS system.

CREDIT AUTHORIZATION AND MANAGEMENT   Prior to the authorization of credit and the determination of the amount of credit, the firm's credit and collection department must review the credit history of old customers. This history is contained in the accounts receivable file (illustrated in Figure 13–7). For

Customer Account Number
Name
Address
Credit Authorization
Credit Limit
Credit History and Frequency of Late
  Payments and Letters (if any)
Prior Balance Due
Finance Charges
Current Activity for Each Transaction
Invoice
    Number
    Department
    Salesperson number
    Store location
    Date
    Amount dollars
    Number ordered
    Item number
Payments

Figure 13–7 Accounts Receivable and Credit Record (Balance Forward)

new customers, the application for credit must be reviewed and the credit-worthiness of the potential customer assessed. Mathematical models such as multiple regression and discriminant analysis (a special case of multiple regression) are often used to forecast and classify a potential customer's credit risk. Multiple regression must be used because of the multiplicity of variables, most of which are gathered on the application and contribute to the overall credit rating of the potential customer. Examples of these variables are salary, age, education, marital status, outstanding debt, and other charge account numbers.

Credit management systems are important to retailers. The vast increase of the use of credit has expanded sales volumes throughout the country, but it has also led to increased collection problems, fraud, and bad debts. The retailer must therefore have a good system for scrutinizing credit purchases so that these problems can be reduced. This system must not interfere with customer service and must not cost more than the benefits derived from the system. There are many such on-line systems available today. For example, NCR has a credit management system that[4]

1. Allows interaction between the sales personnel, credit, and customer data files.

2. Permits quick retrieval of customer records by the credit department.

3. Generates messages to sales personnel for credit authorization decisions. This relieves the sales personnel of this decision.

4. Protects the integrity and confidentiality of the data files via several levels of security and access codes.

[4] Reprinted with permission NCR—*Credit Management System* (Dayton: NCR Corporation).

CURRENT ACTIVITY

Location Code (Department, Store, Territory, etc.)
    Salesperson number (for each employee)
        Sales detail (for each sale)
            Invoice number
            Date
            Product or item number
            Number sold
            Dollar amount
            Customer number
    Returns

BUDGET

Location
    Product budget (units and dollars)
    Salesperson budget (may be by product also)

HISTORY

Location
    Product history (units and dollars)
    Salesperson history (sales and returns)

Figure 13–8 Sales Summary File

    5. Provides dynamic file updating to ensure that the credit authorization file is current via
      a. Data generated from an accounts receivable system
      b. On-line changes in customer records
      c. Point-of-sale transactions
    6. Permits the use of a negative file for restricted checking accounts.
    7. Monitors check-cashing activity via number of checks and dollar amount.

DATA INPUT AND POINT-OF-SALE SYSTEMS Data entry can be very costly when either the amount of sales analysis detail to be collected for each transaction or the volume of these transactions is large. This is particularly true of many retail firms and food chains. There are numerous small transactions, and for each transaction, data must be collected and subsequently be used to prepare sales analysis and inventory reports and to support random inquiry by marketing personnel. As we noted earlier, these reports and the need for such inquiry are essential for many marketing decisions.

    There are seven basic steps to data entry:[5]

    1. Record data at source
    2. Convert to machine-readable form
    3. Transfer to intermediate memory
    4. Verification, error checking, and validation

---

[5] "Data Entry: A Cost Giant," *Datamation*, August 1973.

5. Preprocessing, editing, merging, and sorting
6. Transfer to storage for processing
7. Control statistics and report generation

A simple sales invoice that must subsequently be keypunched and processed only accomplishes step one. During the past decade, however, equipment and procedures have been developed that can automate most of these steps in a cost-effective way. Cash registers can generate machine-readable output, such as paper tape, magnetic tape, and tape that can be optically scanned. Hand-held optical scanning wands and other optical equipment have been developed to read codes directly from the merchandise tags or boxes. Universal product codes have been developed and printed on the merchandise by the manufacturer for many items typically sold through supermarkets. Product codes, coupled with salesperson and location codes, enable a small microprocessor located in the store to perform all seven data-entry steps, including the local generation of sales and inventory reports. Moreover, many locations that formerly used registers are now using intelligent terminals.

The general differences between POS systems for supermarkets and retail stores follow from the business environment for which they were designed.[6] The major impetus for supermarket POS systems was checkout productivity, whereas in retailing, inventory and other managerial support systems dominated. In a supermarket universal product codes and descriptions are used and are maintained on a random access file where they are matched with prices, which may vary from store to store and day to day. The universal product code is read by a scanner built into the checkout counter. Prices need only be posted on shelves and not on the merchandise. Price and descriptive information is displayed and printed for customer use. The checkout clerk basically stays in one place and checks out large volumes of merchandise.

This is in contrast to a traditional department store where the salesclerk spends a considerable amount of time assisting customers and, when a sale is consumated, a multitude of options such as sales discounts, charge, COD, layaway, and partial payments are available. Moreover, salesclerks are often temporary and need assistance in processing transactions. In addition, ticket marking or coding merchandise descriptions and possibly prices on sales tickets is a major task for retail stores compared with supermarkets that use a universal product code. As a result of these characteristics, POS systems for retail stores tend to be intelligent terminals that "walk" salesclerks through a transaction by requesting a sequence of data input activities—i.e., they are tutorial. Moreover, they may also have hand-held wands that can optically or magnetically read the merchandise and price codes printed on the sales tickets.

An example of an intelligent terminal is the NCR 2151, which can incorporate up to 48,000 bytes of random access memory. It utilizes a transaction sequence control and guides the cashier or operator through the steps of the transaction by using a sequence of messages. Moreover, it is fully programma-

---

[6] This discussion is based on P. V. McEnroe, H. T. Huth, E. A. Moore, and W. W. Morris III, "Overview of the Supermarket and the Retail Store System," *IBM Systems Journal,* 15, No. 1 (1975), pp. 3–15.

ble by the user for many retail point-of-sale applications. Its features include the following:

1. Customized keyboard arrangement
2. Transaction prompter display
3. 3-station matrix printer
4. Keylock program control
5. Expanded programming flexibility
6. Change computation
7. High amount limit lockout
8. Lay away previous balance features
9. Merchandise tag reading
10. Transaction sequence control
11. Print format control
12. Printing of store name
13. Check digit verification
14. Fully buffered keyboard
15. Programmable alpha printing
16. Enforced document validation
17. Enforced sales check insertion
18. Enforced deposit payment
19. Enforced fee payment
20. Tax calculation
21. Selective itemization
22. Multiple price extension
23. Deposit calculation
24. Automatic check endorsement
25. Automatic department number entry.[7]

Other terminals can be further programmed to obtain a customer credit rating if the firm's equipment and software configuration permit random access of accounts receivable records.

Several equipment configurations may be used with these intelligent terminals and supermarket checkout scanners and registers. First, they may be on-line and directly interface with the company's central processing unit, enabling the sales clerk to interact with the company's random access files such as accounts receivable and inventory. Second, the terminals may be pooled in each store to periodically, often daily, transmit sales statistics electronically to the company's CPU to update accounts receivable, inventory, and sales analysis records. Third, each terminal may stand alone and generate machine readable output, such as a cassette tape, which is transmitted or sent to the home office where the company's master files are subsequently updated. Fourth, each store

[7] NCR, *NCR 2151 Retail Terminal System* (Dayton: NCR Corporation).

may have its own microprocessor (sometimes referred to as a controller) to which its terminals are connected.[8] The microprocessor is used to generate reports for local management and, if needed, transmit (computer to computer) information to a home office. In all of these configurations, each terminal must be able to stand alone or have sufficient backup—even from other stores if necessary—so that transactions can continue to be processed when a malfunction occurs in the system to which the POS terminal is connected.

Coordination of Subsystems and Supporting Systems

All of these decision-making and supporting transaction processing systems must be coordinated by marketing management to achieve the goals and policies set forth by the general management of the firm. To accomplish this, the management information system must be designed to communicate objectives and policies to and among the various marketing managers, such as those for the areas of responsibility illustrated in Figure 13–1. Generally this is part of the budgeted process, and the controller plays a key role in this process. The coordination of the management subsystems can be further enhanced by using an integrated data base (see Chapter 8). The result will be one common set of data from which each report is generated and to which inquiry is made. Finally, the centralization of the market intelligence activities under market research will aid in the coordination of these activities.

Interface with Logistical Systems

An interface between the marketing and logistical systems is often necessary at all levels of management activity. Strategic planning must obviously consider marketing as well as logistical capabilities and constraints. Managerial activities must often cut across marketing and logistical, as well as financial, functions. This is the case when a manager is responsible for the coordination of all activities for one product, project, or location. As we noted in Chapter 3, this type of product matrix is quite common. If the organization is to function smoothly, the marketing and logistical activities must be coordinated to produce a product, meet sales forecasts or demands, and eventually ship to the customer. The budgeting process can be particularly effective in this type of situation.

A good example of the coordination necessary at the operational decision-making and transaction processing level is found in a typical *order entry system*. A batch processing and a manual system are illustrated in this chapter. An example of such a system for a microcomputer is given in Chapter 14. More-advanced systems often employ direct data entry, random file access, and interactive processing for (1) order entry, (2) on-line inquiry and credit authorization, (3) on-line invoicing, (4) on-line inventory control, (5) shipment processing, (6) price changes, (7) cost changes, order statistics, and inquiry, (8) customer payment entry, (9) posting stock orders, and (10) posting stock receipts. In addition to having inquiry capability, advanced systems can generate several reports.

---

[8] For a more complete discussion of configurations like these see "Retail Terminals a POS Survey," *Datamation*, July 15, 1971, pp. 22–31.

These may include order statistics, orders received, orders shipped, orders canceled, out of stock, credit limit exceeded, inventory stock status, buyer's report, customer status and delivery, customer master file, accounts receivable, trial balance aging report, and back order reports.

Internal Control

The sales order transaction processing cycle, like the logistical cycle discussed in the preceding chapter, has a unique set of authorization, accounting, and asset-safeguarding objectives. Criteria for examples of selected control procedures and techniques used for accomplishing these objectives are noted in the Appendix to this chapter. These reflect the current state of the art in auditing, which emphasizes the flow of transactions.

APPLICATIONS

Manual System Illustration:
Order Entry

To illustrate a manual system, a simple order entry and invoicing system is shown in Figure 13–9. Assume that all sales are on account. An invoice is mailed once a month for the sales during the current month and any past-due balance. All of these data are recorded on a card for each customer and filed alphabetically. After credit approval, one copy of the sales order is filed in a numerical file for future sales analysis and numerical control. A second copy is used by the accounting clerk to update the perpetual inventory records. This copy is then sent to shipping where the order is prepared. The second copy becomes the packing list for the shipment and is subsequently sent to the customer. The third copy is forwarded to accounting where the accounts receivable and general ledgers are posted. It is then temporarily filed alphabetically. At the end of the month, the third copy and the accounts receivable detail ledger are used to prepare two copies of the invoice (statement) which indicates current activity and any past-due amounts with appropriate interest. The third copy of the sales order and the second copy of the invoice are then filed alphabetically in a permanent file for reference. The original invoice is mailed to the customer.

Batch Processing Illustration:
Order Entry, Accounts Receivable,
and Sales Analysis

To illustrate batch processing concepts and issues in a marketing system, consider the simple order entry, accounts receivable, and sales analysis shown in Figure 13–10. This type of system will be required when the volume of transactions involving sales, inventory, and accounts receivable exceeds that which can be processed manually. A batch processing system is also required when the volume of detail collected during the transaction process exceeds that which can be processed manually on an economical basis. A batch processing system is also necessary to support product, location, and salesperson analysis

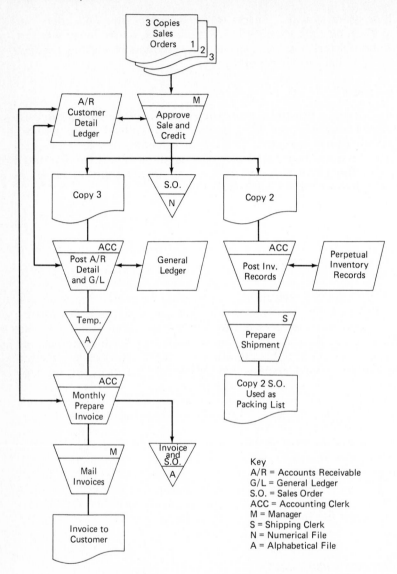

Key
A/R = Accounts Receivable
G/L = General Ledger
S.O. = Sales Order
ACC = Accounting Clerk
M = Manager
S = Shipping Clerk
N = Numerical File
A = Alphabetical File

Figure 13–9 Order Entry and Invoicing System

for marketing decisions, when the volume of detail required for those decisions exceeds that which can be processed manually on an economical basis.

In the system illustrated, approved sales orders are batched using dollar amount and transaction totals. They are sent to the data processing department for keypunching onto cards and key verification. The original orders are filed by sales order number for future reference and accountability. Each sales order contains the type of information shown in Figure 13–6. The sales order card deck is then sorted mechanically by customer number. These cards are processed to update both the current monthly sales tape and the accounts receivable master file. Cash sales (if any) are noted separately on the sales report

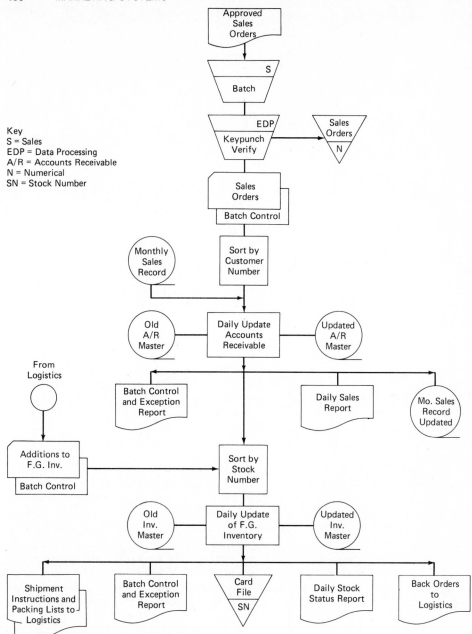

Key
S = Sales
EDP = Data Processing
A/R = Accounts Receivable
N = Numerical
SN = Stock Number

Figure 13–10 Daily Sales Order Processing Cycle

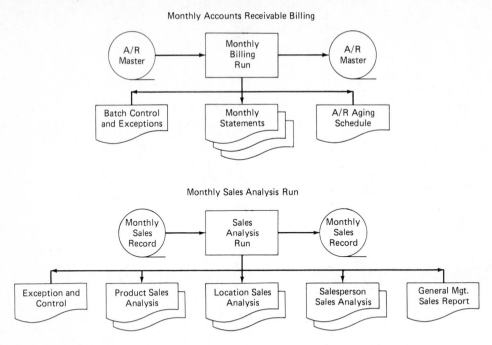

Figure 13–10   (continued)

and tape. In many other systems this update of the accounts receivable records will include the update of a daily cash receipts file. For credit sales, accounts receivable records are posted. For all sales, the monthly sales record is updated for future analysis. Batch control totals and exceptions are reported to management for control and possible follow-up of errors. A daily sales report is generated for marketing management.

Sales order cards are then sorted by stock number along with batch control cards indicating additions to finished goods inventory from the logistical system. Once these cards have been sorted (finished goods additions are on tape in many batch processing systems), the old inventory master file is then updated to reflect additions to and reductions in inventory. As part of this update run, shipping instructions and packing lists are sent to the shipping department, batch control and exception reports are forwarded to management for review, cards are filed numerically by stock number for reference, daily stock status reports are given to marketing and production management for decision making and review, and a listing of back orders is forwarded to the production and sales departments.

In this illustration, billing is done once a month for all customers. In some firms, billing is done on a daily basis where statements are prepared for customers for certain billing cycles (segment of the accounts receivable master file) each day. The accounts receivable master file is run to prepare statements to be sent to customers. Aging reports of current and past-due accounts are also prepared for credit and sales management decision needs. For all runs, an exception and control report is given to management for review.

In addition to processing transactions and generating reports, this system is capable of taking the monthly sales record, which is updated daily, and sorting these data in a number of different ways to generate reports for management decision making. In this illustration, product, location, salesperson, and overall sales statistics are generated each month. These monthly sales statistics could be aggregated once a year and could be compared with monthly or yearly budget and historical data. This type of comparison is much more feasible and economical with a batch system than with a manual system. More details, a larger volume of data, and greater information needs are more easily handled because the data, in this case the monthly sales records, are easily sorted, aggregated, and compared because they are in machine-readable form.

In this batch processing illustration, cards and magnetic tape were used as the storage media. The same systems could use magnetic disks to store the data in files and still process all data the same way.

Real-Time Illustration: Accounts Receivable and Cycle Billing

A real-time on-line accounts receivable system is illustrated in Figure 13–11. The specific system illustrated here is that used by the same major oil

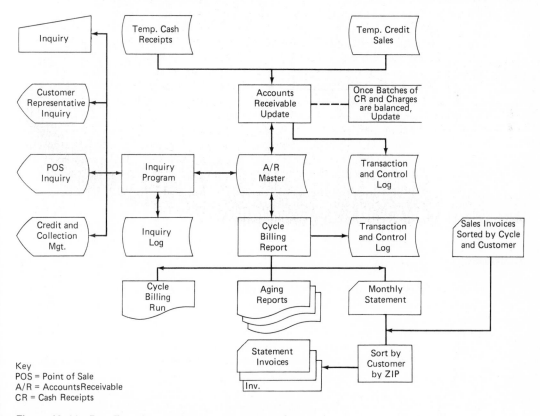

Figure 13–11   Real-Time On-Line Accounts Receivable System

company whose data input procedures are described in Chapter 9; many large credit-card operations would be similar.

First, in contrast with the manual and batch systems illustrated in Figures 13–9 and 13–10, there is a requirement for an on-line inquiry. Thus the data must be stored on a random access media such as a disk. Customer representatives respond to customer questions pertaining to statements, and perhaps to letters sent out by the credit and collection department, from a point-of-sale system. The POS system used here is for major purchases on credit as service station personnel call in for credit authorization. Credit and collections managers use the system as they reference customer activity records in attempting to collect delinquent account balances. On-line inquiry is necessary in this type of system because the accounts number a million or more.

In the system illustrated, a temporary cash receipts file and a temporary sales file are credited as transactions are being processed. Not shown here are the procedures used to balance these files. The credit sales transaction processing procedure for this system was illustrated in Chapter 9. After these files have been balanced, they are used to update the accounts receivable master file. A transaction and control log is retained on disk for security, review, processing any exceptions, and an audit trail. The accounts receivable master file is then used for the inquiries from customer representatives, point-of-sale credit authorization, and credit and collection reference information. Additional procedures in the system, not shown here, are on-line file maintenance procedures for adjustments, address changes, and credit information. Again, a transaction and control log is created on disk for future review.

Part of the accounts receivable master file is processed daily according to the cycle to be billed that day. The total receivables file is divided into approximately twenty billing cycles for the month. Each billing run updates the credit information on the accounts receivable master; produces a cycle billing report for management; produces an aging report for management, credit and collections, and customer representatives; and generates monthly statements. Statements are sorted by ZIP code and customer number, and are merged with the original sales invoice received from the service stations (see Chapter 9). After this sorting, the statements, along with their attached sales invoices, are mechanically stuffed into an envelope and mailed to the customer.

SUMMARY

Marketing information systems must be carefully planned, designed, and implemented if they are to succeed in satisfying the varied decision-making and reporting needs of marketing management. To compound this problem, there is a further need for extensive coordination with other functions, a need for very intensive interactive inquiry, and a need to search the environment for relevant data that will be transformed into information useful for strategic, managerial, and operational decision making and reporting. As a result, marketing systems tend to require more complex hardware and software in order to support the management system for which they are designed.

SELECTED REFERENCES

ADLER, LEE, "Systems Approach to Marketing," *Harvard Business Review*, May–June 1967.

AKRESH, ABRAHAM D., AND MICHAEL GOLDSTEIN, "Point-of-Sale Accounting Systems: Some Implications for the Auditor," *Journal of Accountancy*, December 1978, pp. 68–74.

American Institute of Certified Public Accountants, "Tentative Special Advisory Report on Internal Control," 1978.

CARDENAS, ALFONSO F., "Data Entry: A Cost Giant," *Journal of Systems Management*, August 1973, pp. 35–42.

CUSHING, BARRY E., *Accounting Information Systems and Business Organizations.* Reading, Mass.: Addison-Wesley, 1978.

ELIASON, ALAN L., AND KENT D. KITTS, *Business Computer Systems and Applications.* Palo Alto, Calif.: Science Research Associates, 1979.

"Information Processing: Market Research by Scanner," *Business Week*, May 5, 1980, pp. 113–16.

KOTLER, PHILIP, "A Design for the Firm's Marketing Nerve Center," *Business Horizons*, Fall 1966.

Management Science America, Inc., *Accounts Receivable II: Commercial System.* Atlanta, 1980.

———, *Realtime, Online Accounts Receivable*, Atlanta, 1980.

McENROE, P. V., H. T. HUTH, E. A. MOORE, AND W. W. MORRIS III, "Overview of the Supermarket System and the Retail Store System," *IBM Systems Journal*, 15, No. 1 (1975), pp. 3–15.

MITCHELL, WILLIAM G., AND JOSEPH W. WILKINSON, "POS Systems Revolutionize Retailing," *Journal of Systems Management*, 27 (April 1976), pp. 34–41.

MONTGOMERY, DAVID B., AND GLEN L. URBAN, "Marketing Decision—Information Systems: An Emerging View," *Journal of Marketing Research*, 7 (May 1970), pp. 226–34.

NCR Accounts Receivable System for Retailers. Dayton: NCR Corporation, 1975.

NCR Credit Management System. Dayton: NCR Corporation.

NCR Online Retail System. Dayton: NCR Corporation.

NCR SPIRIT Online Order Entry System. Dayton: NCR Corporation.

NCR 250 Electronic Cash Register. Dayton: NCR Corporation, 1974.

NCR 2135 Food Store System. Dayton: NCR Corporation.

NCR 2151 Retail Terminal System. Dayton: NCR Corporation, 1978.

NCR 2160 Food Service System. Dayton: NCR Corporation, 1978.

Retail Management Information System. Dayton: NCR Corporation.

Price Waterhouse & Co., *A Retailer's Guide to Accounting Controls.* New York: Price Waterhouse, 1979.

———, *RM/80 A New Retail Management Information System for the 80's.* New York: Price Waterhouse & Co., 1980.

PRINCE, THOMAS R., *Information Systems for Management Planning and Control.* Homewood, Ill.: Richard D. Irwin, 1975.

"Retail Terminals: a POS Survey," *Datamation*, July 15, 1971, pp. 22–31.

SULLIVAN, RAYMOND, "Transformation: From Batch to Timesharing," *Infosystems*, 23 (February 1976), pp. 37–40.

APPENDIX: CRITERIA
AND EXAMPLES OF SELECTED
CONTROL PROCEDURES
FOR THE REVENUE CYCLE[1]

THE REVENUE CYCLE

The revenue cycle covers the functions involved in receiving and accepting requests for goods or services, delivering or otherwise providing the goods or services, credit granting, cash receipts and collection activities, billing, and accounting for revenues, accounts receivable, commissions, warranties, bad debts, returned goods, and other adjustments.

"Authorization" in the revenue cycle encompasses the types of products and services provided, classes of customers serviced (including related and foreign parties), distribution channels used, prices, credit and other terms of sale, individual customer acceptance, sales-related adjustments and policies (such as policies on acceptance of returned goods), services furnished to customers (including warranty policies), billing and collection practices, and sales compensation policies.

"Accounting" encompasses the procedures and techniques used to control the recording and classification of transactions that relate to revenue and cash receipts, deductions from revenue (for example, sales taxes, commissions, bad debts), and the distribution of such transactions to individual accounts receivable records and other subsidiary records.

"Asset Safeguarding" relates primarily to controls that safeguard cash receipts and protect important records.

Authorization Objectives

CRITERIA	EXAMPLES OF SELECTED CONTROL PROCEDURES AND TECHNIQUES
1. The types of goods and services to be provided, the manner in which they will be provided, and the customers to which they will be provided should be properly authorized.	a. Procedures for acceptance and approval of orders for nonstandard goods or services and for unusual delivery arrangements.
	b. Policies on export sales and sales to related parties.
	c. Policies on customer acceptance, including policies on acceptance and approval of checks and credit cards.
	d. Use of an approved customer list.
	e. Assigned responsibility and established procedures for approval of customer

---

[1] Reprinted with permission AICPA, "Special Advisory Report on Internal Control," (New York: AICPA, ©American Institute of Certified Public Accountants, 1978), pp. 18–20.

Accounting Objectives

CRITERIA	EXAMPLES OF SELECTED CONTROL PROCEDURES AND TECHNIQUES
	orders (customer acceptance, credit-worthiness, prices, and other terms of sale).
2. Credit terms and limits should be properly authorized.	a. Established credit policies. b. Policies for investigating credit-worthiness of prospective customers. c. Periodic review of credit limits.
3. The prices and other terms of sale of goods and services should be properly authorized.	a. Approved sales catalogs or similar documents containing current price information and policies on matters such as discounts, sales taxes, freight, service, warranties, and returned goods. b. Use of appropriate contract forms. c. Procedures for approval of individually priced sales.
4. Sales-related deductions and adjustments should be properly authorized.	a. Approved commission schedules. b. Procedures for approval of "no charge" service invoices and services performed under a warranty. c. Procedures for approval of bad debt write-offs and other credits to customer accounts, including credits given for returned goods.
5. Deliveries of goods and services should result in preparation of accurate and timely billing forms.	a. Shipping and billing procedures that provide for the means to account for all goods shipped or services delivered and comparisons of shipments to billings, perhaps individually or through a form of batch control. b. Policies covering the types of "memo billings" that may be issued and approval procedures over such billings. c. Check of quantities of goods shipped by, for example, independent counts by common carrier or double counting of shipments. d. Independent follow-up on customer complaints.
6. Sales and related transactions should be recorded at the appropriate amounts and in the appropriate period and should be	a. Policies and procedures covering accounting routines and related approval procedures for the major functions within the revenue cycle. b. A suitable chart of accounts and standard journal entries.

Accounting Objectives

CRITERIA	EXAMPLES OF SELECTED CONTROL PROCEDURES AND TECHNIQUES
properly classified in the accounts.	c. Written, properly communicated sales (and cost of sales) cut-off procedures and review of the cut-off. d. Reconciliation of the accounts receivable subsidiary ledger to the general ledger on a regular basis. e. Independent mailing of statements to customer on a monthly basis.
7. Cash receipts should be accounted for properly on a timely basis.	a. Comparison of initial record of cash receipts to bank deposits and accounting entries and investigation of any unusual delays in depositing receipts.

Asset Safeguarding Objectives

CRITERIA	EXAMPLES OF SELECTED CONTROL PROCEDURES AND TECHNIQUES
8. Access to cash receipts and cash receipts records, accounts receivable records, and billing and shipping records should be suitably controlled to prevent or detect within a timely period the interception of unrecorded cash receipts or the abstraction of recorded cash receipts.	a. Independent control of cash upon receipt (through, for example, lock box arrangements, cash registers, prenumbered cash receipt forms). b. Restrictive endorsement of checks upon receipt. c. Segregation of duties between access to cash receipts and keeping records of sales customer credits, cash receipts, and accounts receivable.

REVIEW QUESTIONS

1. In terms of "success factors," what should be the focus of a marketing system? What are the implications of this for designers of accounting information systems?

2. What information flows are characteristic of a marketing information system? Contrast these with a logistical system.

3. What are some prime sources of internally generated information in typical marketing information systems?

4. Contrast the three types of accounts receivable systems.

5. Why are mathematical models useful in assessing a customer's credit risk?

6. For what decisions would sales analysis reports be useful?

7. List the objectives of the various functions, or subsystems, of marketing management.

8. What role does market research play in the company's information system and decision network?

9. How can the budget system be used to coordinate marketing management activities?

10. Why is a highly automated point-of-sale system useful for retail stores and supermarket food chains? What internal control advantages does it have?

11. What can an intelligent terminal be programmed to do to assist a clerk who enters the sales data into the marketing information POS system?

12. What equipment configurations can be used with intelligent terminals? In what business environments would you suggest each be used?

EXERCISES AND CASES

13–1

A partially completed document flowchart is shown in Figure C13–1. The flowchart depicts the charge sales activities of the Bottom Manufacturing Corporation.

A customer's purchase order is received and a six-part sales order is prepared therefrom. The six copies are initially distributed as follows:

Copy 1—Billing copy: to billing department

Copy 2—Shipping copy: to shipping department

Copy 3—Credit copy: to credit department

Copy 4—Stock request copy: to credit department

Copy 5—Customer copy: to customer

Copy 6—Sales order copy: file in sales order department

When each copy of the sales order reaches the applicable department or destination, it calls for specific internal control procedures and related documents. Some of the procedures and related documents are indicated on the flowchart. Other procedures and documents are labeled letters *a* to *r*.

REQUIRED: List the procedures or the internal documents that are labeled letters *a* to *r* in the flowchart of Bottom Manufacturing Corporation's charge sales system. (AICPA adapted)

13–2 (This question draws upon the student's background from other courses.)

Bundt Foods Company produces and sells many products in each of its thirty-five different product lines. From time to time a product or an entire product line is dropped because it has ceased to be profitable. The company does not have a formalized program for reviewing its products on a regular basis to identify those products that should be eliminated.

At a recent meeting of Bundt Foods Company's top management, one person stated that there probably were several products or possibly a product line that was unprofitable or producing an unsatisfactory return on investment. After considerable discussion, management decided that Bundt Foods should establish a formalized product discontinuance program. The purpose of the program would be to review the company's individual products and product lines on a regular and ongoing basis to identify problem areas.

The vice-president of finance has proposed that a person be assigned to the program on a full-time basis. This person would work closely with the marketing and accounting departments in determining (1) the factors that indicate when a product's importance is declining and (2) the underlying data that would be required in evaluating whether a product or product line should be discontinued.

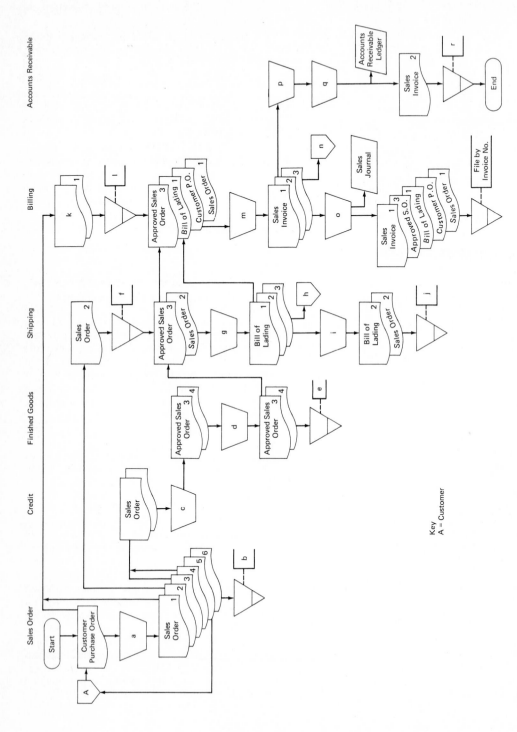

Figure C13–1 Bottom Manufacturing Corporation: Flowchart of Credit Sales Activities

REQUIRED:

a. Identify and explain briefly the benefits, other than the identification of unprofitable products or product lines, that Bundt Foods Company can derive from a formalized product discontinuance program.

b. In developing Bundt Foods Company's product discontinuance program:

(1) Identify the factors that would indicate that a product's or product line's importance is diminishing.

(2) Identify the data that the accounting department would be able to provide for the purpose of evaluating a product or product line. (Adapted from the CMA Examination)

13–3

Smith & Smith, a national mail-order house, is designing a new warehouse facility in Texas to serve the Southwest. Customer orders come in from retail outlets throughout the geographical territory and from customers via mail. The retail outlets each have a microprocessor that transmits these orders directly to the warehouse facility. Orders that come in through the mail are keyed onto a disk file, edited, and verified for current stock numbers.

Both sources of orders are then compared with an on-line inventory file to ensure that the item, style, and quantity are in stock. If the item is out of stock an out-of-stock memo is generated, a copy of which is mailed to a mail-order customer or transmitted electronically to the retail outlet's microprocessor for subsequent memo generation for a customer at a retail outlet. Out-of-stock reports are generated concurrently with both sets of memos.

Those orders that can be filled are cleared Reports are generated by the computer for each department indicating the sequence of order filling and the time at which each order is to be filled. A route slip is also printed to accompany each item of an order as it is pulled from stock. The route slips serve as a packing list and follow pulled items through the actual shipment to the store or individual. Clerks pull items to fill each of these orders and place the items on long conveyors that converge in a packing area. The orders are sequenced and timed so that all the items ordered by a store or by an individual arrive at the packing area at the same time. Items pulled for shipment are compared with the customer or store order to make sure that all goods "cleared" are included in the order. A listing of the order number and detail (items ordered, customer name, customer number, and store name and number, if applicable) was sent to each packing station at the beginning of each shift for this comparison. If the items and the order do not reconcile, the order is set aside and a call is made to the stock area from which the items should have been sent. If the error occurred there, the needed item is immediately sent to packing. If the error is in the order itself, an exception is noted on the order listing and these listings are returned to EDP where they are keyed into an error file. From these data an exception memo is transmitted to either the retail store or the mail-order customer, the packing manager, the warehouse stock manager, the EDP manager, and general management. A report that summarizes the substance of these exception memos is also prepared for management.

It is the objective of the distribution center to process these orders as effectively and efficiently as possible. The center's management strives for a 1 percent or less exception ratio.

REQUIRED:

a. Flowchart the system using a document flowchart to show the movement of documents as well as processing steps.

b. Describe the internal control procedures that should be used throughout the order processing cycle.

c. Describe the organization and content of a data base (1) needed to operate the transaction processing system described above, and (2) needed to support sales, promotion, and customer service management decisions. (*Note*: It is useful to first outline these decisions assuming Smith & Smith's competitors are J. C. Penney and Sears.)

13–4

Henderson, Inc., a distributor of institutional food to hospitals, schools, and restaurants in the metropolitan area, distributes an entire line of products including meat, fruit, fresh vegetables, canned goods, dairy products, and frozen food. Some of these items must be handled with special care; they are frozen and perishable, and special equipment is required to distribute and store these items. Henderson is particularly known for its large variety of fresh vegetables, and many customers buy from Henderson for this reason.

All of Henderson's sales are negotiated by ten salespeople, who use daily stock status reports to see what is on hand at the beginning of the day. Negotiated sales contracts (invoices) are based on monthly price and cost statistics for each food item stocked.

Fair Value Foods, a small, aggressive distributor, has been rapidly gaining in market share in the metropolitan area. Its gains have hurt several of Henderson's competitors and are beginning to attract some of Henderson's best customers. From inquiries, Henderson's sales personnel have received the following comments:

1. "Fair Value can give us a better price."
2. "Their meat, fruits, vegetables, and dairy products are fresher."
3. "Their variety is not as large, but it meets 95 percent of my needs."
4. "They never need to substitute a product [a common practice in this business] because they always know exactly what is on hand. All they do is call the office to find out the current stock status."
5. "Their service is as good as yours."

To compound this competitive problem, Henderson has been experiencing slow inventory turnover in the past several years, resulting in more spoilage. This spoilage has caused some pressure to negotiate higher prices. Currently Henderson uses a small batch processing system with input/output media consisting of cards and tapes to control inventory and generate reports.

From a technological and reporting perspective, what would you suggest, as their CPA, that Henderson consider to become competitive again? Why?

13–5

Describe the content and organization of the data base and the nature of the internal control needed for a point-of-sales system for the sales order process shown in Figure 13–10. Describe and flowchart the system. Assume that all data are consolidated in a common data base. All files are random access to facilitate the generation of management reports and random inquiry regarding sales, inventory, and receivables information. Clerks who process sales will have access to inventory and accounts receivable for stock status and credit inquiry. Management will have access to all data for graphical analysis and display of sale, inventory, and receivable statistics.

13–6

A credit authorization system is used by a large regional department store. Credit applications are submitted to the credit office, and responses to the questions listed below are weighted. Weights are determined by using discriminant analysis. Discriminant analysis assigns weights to factors, such as those in the following table, so that good and bad credit risks can be assessed with a high degree of statistical significance. The higher the score, the better the credit risk.

FACTOR	WEIGHT
1. Age over twenty-five	7
2. Own home	20
3. Own automobile	3
4. Employed with present company over three years	25
5. Has bank reference—account number	8
6. Lived at present address over two years	6
7. Married	5
8. Fewer than four children	5
9. Income over $20,000	15
10. Income over $10,000	6

a. Will these weights be appropriate a year from now? If not, what data must be maintained in the firm's data base to reassess the credit granting model?

b. How can the data be obtained to update these weights for processing applications next year?

c. What subset of input data for a and b can be collected via transaction processing and what subset must be obtained from other sources?

13–7

Huron Company manufactures and sells eight major product lines with fifteen to twenty-five items in each product line. All sales are on credit, and orders are received by mail or telephone. Huron has a computer-based system that employs magnetic tape as a file medium.

All sales orders received during regular working hours are typed on Huron's own sales order form immediately. This typed form is the source document for the keypunching of a shipment or back-order card for each item ordered. These cards are employed in the after-hours processing at night to complete all necessary record keeping for the current day and to facilitate the shipment of goods the following day. In summary, an order received one day is to be processed that day and night and shipped the next day.

The daily processing that has to be accomplished at night includes the following activities:

1. Preparing the invoice to be sent to the customer at the time of shipment
2. Updating the accounts receivable file
3. Updating the finished goods inventory
4. Listing of all items back-ordered and short

Each month the sales department would like to have a sales summary and analysis. At the end of each month, the monthly statements should be prepared and mailed to customers. Management also wants an aging of accounts receivable each month.

REQUIRED:

a. Identify the master files that Huron Company should maintain in this system to provide for the daily processing. Indicate the data content that should be included in each file and the order in which each file should be maintained.

b. Employing the symbols shown in Figure C13–7, prepare a systems flowchart of the daily processing required to update the finished goods inventory records and to produce the necessary inventory reports (assume that the necessary magnetic-tape devices are available). Use the annotation symbol to describe or explain any facts that cannot be detailed in the individual symbols.

c. Describe (1) the items that should appear in the monthly sales analysis report or reports that the sales department should have and (2) the input data and master files that would have to be maintained to prepare these reports. (Adapted from the CMA Examination)

13–8

TuneFork, Inc., is a large wholesaler of sheet music, music books, musical instruments, and other music-related supplies. The company acquired a medium-sized tape-oriented computer system last year, and an inventory control system has already been implemented. The systems department is now developing a new accounts receivable system.

The flowchart in Figure C13–8 is a diagram of the proposed accounts receivable system as designed by the systems department. The objectives of the new system are to produce current and timely information that can be used to control bad debts, to provide information to the sales department regarding customers whose accounts are delinquent, to produce monthly statements for customers, and to provide notices to customers regarding a change in the status of their charge privileges.

Input data for the system are taken from four source documents—approved credit ap-

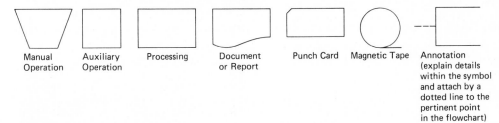

| Manual Operation | Auxiliary Operation | Processing | Document or Report | Punch Card | Magnetic Tape | Annotation (explain details within the symbol and attach by a dotted line to the pertinent point in the flowchart) |

Figure C13–7 Huron Company

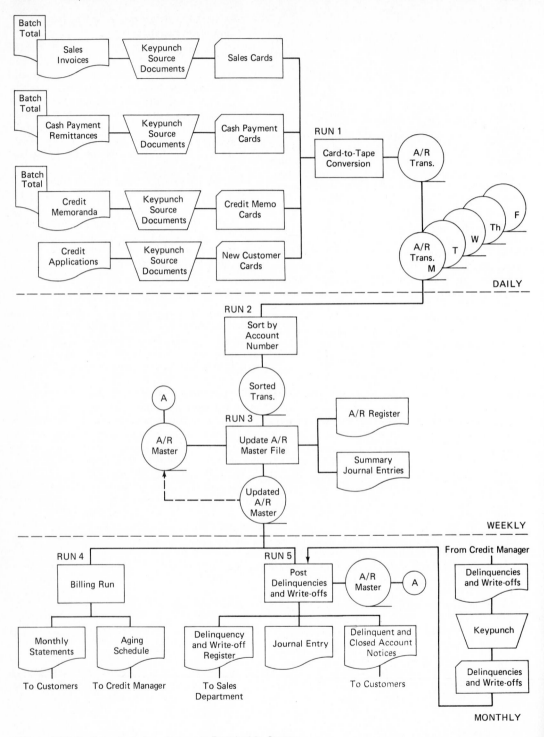

Figure C13–8 Tune Fork, Inc. Accounts Receivable System

plications, sales invoices, cash payment remittances, and credit memoranda. The accounts receivable (A/R) file is maintained on magnetic tape by customer account number. The record for each customer contains identification information and the last month's balance, current month's transactions (detailed), and current balance. Some of the output items generated from the system can be described as follows:

–Accounts receivable register (weekly)—a listing of all customers and account balances included in the accounts receivable file

–Aging schedule (monthly)—a schedule of all customers with outstanding balances detailing the amount owed by age classifications—0–30 days, 30–60 days, 60–90 days, over 90 days

–Delinquency and write-off registers (monthly)—(1) a listing of those accounts that are delinquent and (2) a listing of customers' accounts that have been closed and written off; related notices are prepared and sent to these customers

REQUIRED:

a. TuneFork's systems department must develop the system controls for the new accounts receivable system. Identify and explain the system controls that should be instituted with the new system. When appropriate, describe the location in the flowchart where the control should be introduced.

b. The credit manager has indicated that the department receives frequent telephone inquiries from customers regarding their accounts. The manager has asked if the department could have a cathode ray tube (CRT) terminal connected to the main computer. Can a CRT terminal be used with the new accounts receivable system as proposed to satisfy the needs of the credit manager? Explain your answer. (Adapted from the CMA Examination).

13–9 (This case requires the student to draw upon his or her marketing course work.)

Daizy Shoes, a merchandiser of stylish and casual ladies' shoes, must order several lines of shoes from at least two dozen domestic and foreign manufacturers and ensure distribution to several hundred retail shoe stores located in shopping centers throughout the United States. Due to long lead times and the great risk of high-style items not selling, Daizy requires all its sales personnel to keep accurate records of sales at each retail outlet and report this to the home office in Sunnyville, Florida. Using these sales statistics, Daizy uses an exponential smoothing forecasting model which quickly adapts to changing trends and seasonal changes to give sales management guidance in reordering more of certain styles. This model was provided by the company's accounting firm and works extremely well. Daizy's management employees, most of whom have recent M.B.A. degrees from well-known universities, have a great deal of faith in this forecasting technique.

Management, however, is still unhappy with the number of styles that must be marked down at the end of each season. Management has asked you, as the accountant who provided the model it uses, what other information it needs to improve its forecasting and inventory control. Outline the information requirements, sources of the data procedures for obtaining the data, and methods of data storage for rapid retrieval of information for management decisions. Pay specific attention to the point-of-sale transaction date in your assessment of the problem.

13–10

D and D Catalog Sales has retail and catalog outlets throughout the South. It has been using a cash register system for several years where the cashier rings up the department, salesperson number, item stock number, and dollar amount of sales. The registers are equipped to generate a punched paper tape as each sale is processed, and a total summary punched paper tape for reconciliation of the cash at the end of each salesperson's shift. This latter tape is read mechanically and compared with cash on hand at the end of the day.

These punched paper tapes are placed in metal canisters each day and are mailed to D and D's office in Memphis where they are used to update inventory records, post sales journals, and generate several reports. In some locations they are mailed the following day when the post office opens. These reports include stock status and sales statistics. Reports are mailed back to each store for management's use. Each store normally receives these reports in two days. Purchasing is done centrally to obtain the most leverage with suppliers.

Most transactions are processed adequately with this system, but occasionally a clerk forgets to enter an item number and management has no idea of what was sold. Consequently it is not unusual for the internal auditors to make numerous year-end adjustments to inventory. Moreover, other missing or incorrect information creates many exceptions when the data are edited for completeness and reasonableness at D and D's Memphis office.

As D and D's CPA, you have been asked to advise management on a revision of its system. First, outline step-by-step the approach it should take in modifying its sales processing system. Note why each step is important. Second, contrast briefly the various equipment configurations that management can use to resolve its obvious data input problems. To the extent feasible, without extensive research, contrast the pros and cons of each configuration. Third, without extensive research, comment to the extent feasible on the pros and cons of centralization and decentralization in light of new developments in computer hardware and software. Fourth, recommend a revised system. Flowchart the revised system.

13–11

Delmo, Inc., a wholesale distributor of automotive parts, serves customers in the states east of the Mississippi River. During the past twenty-five years the company has grown from a small regional distributorship in Michigan to its present size. It is still located in East Lansing, Michigan, where it was founded.

To service Delmo customers adequately, the states are divided into eight separate territories. Delmo salespersons regularly call upon current and prospective customers in each of the territories. Delmo customers are of four general types:

1. Automotive parts stores
2. Hardware stores with an automotive parts section
3. Independent garage owners
4. Buying groups for garages and filling stations

Because Delmo must stock such a large variety and quantity of automotive parts to accommodate its customers, the company acquired its own computer system very early and implemented an inventory control system first. Other applications such as cash receipts and disbursements, sales analysis, accounts receivable, payroll, and accounts payable have since been added.

Delmo's inventory control system is comprised of an integrated purchase-ordering and perpetual inventory system. Each item of inventory is identified by an inventory code number; the code number identifies both the product line and the item itself. When the quantity-on-hand for an item falls below the specified stock level, a purchase order is automatically generated by the computer. The purchase order is sent to the vendor after approval by the purchasing manager. All receipts, issues, and returns are entered into the computer daily. A printout of all inventory items within product lines showing receipts, issues, and current balance is prepared weekly. However, current status for a particular item carried in the inventory can be obtained daily if necessary.

Sales orders are filled within forty-eight hours of receipt. Sales invoices are prepared by the computer the same day that the merchandise is shipped. At the end of each month, several reports that summarize the monthly sales are produced. The current month's and year-to-date sales by product line, territory, and customer class are compared with the same figures from the previous year. In addition, reports showing only the monthly figures for product line within territory and customer class within territory are prepared. In all cases the reports provide summarized data—i.e., detailed data such as sales by individual customers or product are not listed. Terms of 2/10, net 30 are standard for all of Delmo's customers.

Customers' accounts receivable are updated daily for sales, sales returns and allowances, and payments on account. Monthly statements are computer prepared and mailed following completion of entries for the last day of the month. Each Friday a schedule is prepared showing the total amount of accounts receivable outstanding by age—current accounts (0–30 days), slightly past-due accounts (31–90 days), and long overdue accounts (over 90 days).

Delmo, Inc., recently acquired Wenrock Company, a wholesale distributor of tools and light equipment. In addition to servicing the same type of customers as Delmo, Wenrock sells to equipment rental shops. Wenrock's sales region is not as extensive as Delmo's, but the Delmo management has encouraged Wenrock to expand the distribution of its products to all of Delmo's sales territories.

Wenrock Company uses a computer service bureau to aid in its accounting functions. For example, certain inventory activities are recorded by the service bureau. Each item carried by Wenrock is assigned a product code number that identifies the product and the product line. Data regarding shipments received from manufacturers, shipments to customers (sales), and any other physical inventory changes are delivered to the service bureau daily, and the service bureau updates Wenrock's inventory records. A weekly inventory listing showing the beginning balance, receipts, issues, and ending balance for each item in the inventory is provided to Wenrock on Monday morning.

Wenrock furnishes the service bureau with information about each sale of merchandise to a customer. The service bureau prepares a five-part invoice and records the sales. This processing is done at night, and all copies of each invoice are delivered to Wenrock the next morning. At the end of the month the service bureau provides Wenrock with a sales report classified by product line showing the sales in units and dollars for each item sold. Wenrock's sales terms are 2/10, net 30.

The accounts receivable function is still being handled by Wenrock's bookkeeper. Two copies of the invoice are mailed to the customer. Two of the remaining copies are filed—one numerically and the other alphabetically by customer. The alphabetic file represents the accounts receivable file. When a customer's payment is received, the invoice is marked "paid" and placed in a paid invoice file in alphabetical order. The bookkeeper mails monthly statements according to the following schedule:

10th of the month	A–G
20th of the month	H–O
30th of the month	P–Z

The final copy of the invoice is included with the merchandise when it is shipped.

Wenrock has continued to use its present accounting system, and it supplies Delmo management with monthly financial information developed from this system. However, Delmo management is anxious to have Wenrock use its computer and its information system because this will reduce accounting and computer costs, make Wenrock's financial reports more useful to Delmo management, and provide Wenrock personnel with better information to manage the company.

At the time that Delmo acquired Wenrock, it also hired a new marketing manager with experience in both product areas. The new manager wants Wenrock to organize its sales force using the same territorial distribution as Delmo to facilitate the managing of the two sales forces.

The new manager also believes that more useful sales information should be provided to individual salespersons and to the department. Although the monthly sales reports currently prepared provide adequate summary data, the manager thinks that additional details would aid the sales personnel.

The acquisition of Wenrock Company and the expansion of its sales to a larger geographic area have created a cash strain on Delmo, Inc., particularly in the short run. Consequently, cash management has become much more important than in prior years. A weekly report that presents a reliable estimate of daily cash receipts is needed. The treasurer heard that a local company had improved its cash forecasting system by studying the timing of customers' payments on account to see if a discernible payment pattern existed. The payment pattern became the model that was applied to outstanding invoices to estimate the daily cash receipts for the next week. The treasurer thinks that this is a good approach and wonders if it can be done at Delmo.

Required:

a. Identify and briefly describe the additional data Wenrock Company must collect and furnish in order to use the Delmo data processing system. Also identify the data, if any, currently accumulated by Wenrock which will no longer be needed due to the conversion to the Delmo system.

b. Using only the data currently available from the Delmo data processing system, what additional reports could be prepared that would be useful to the marketing manager and the individual salespersons? Briefly explain how each report would be useful to the sales personnel.

c. If Delmo, Inc., were to use a cash forecasting system similar to the one suggested by the treasurer, describe

   (1) The data currently available in the system that would be used in preparing such a forecast

   (2) The additional data that must be generated

   (3) The modifications, if any, that would be required in the Delmo data processing system

d. (optional) Develop codes for identifying inventory items and customers.

e. (optional) What advantages would there be to Delmo-Wenrock to replacing the current system with a data base management system? Describe the content of the data base, the basic organization schema, the internal controls necessary for such a system and flowchart the system. Assume Delmo, Inc., plans to implement a cash forecasting system similar to the one described. (Adapted from the CMA Examination)

13–12

Forward Corporation is a progressive and fast-growing company. The company's executive committee consists of the president and the four vice-presidents who report to the president—marketing, manufacturing, finance, and systems.

The company has ordered a new computer for use in processing its financial information. Because the computer acquisition required a substantial investment, the president wants to make certain that the computer is employed effectively.

The new computer will enable Forward to revise its financial information system so that the several departments will get more useful information. This should be especially helpful in marketing because its personnel are distributed widely throughout the country.

The marketing department is organized into nine territories and twenty-five sales offices. The vice-president of marketing wants the monthly reports to reflect those items for which the department is responsible and which it can control. The marketing department also wants information that identifies the most profitable products; this information is used to establish a discount policy that will enable the company to meet competition effectively. Monthly reports showing performance by territory and sales office would also be useful.

The vice-president of finance has recommended that the accounting system be revised so that reports would be prepared on a contribution margin basis. Furthermore, only those cost items that are controlled by the respective departments would appear on their reports. The monthly report for the manufacturing department would compare actual production costs with a budget containing the standard costs for the actual volume of production. The marketing department would be provided with the standard variable manufacturing cost for each product so that it could calculate the variable contribution margin of each product. The monthly reports to the marketing department would reflect the variable contribution approach; the reports would present the net contribution of the department calculated by deducting standard variable manufacturing costs and marketing expenses (both variable and fixed) from sales.

A portion of Forward Corporation's chart of accounts follows:

Required:

a. Given that Forward Corporation's EDP system is file oriented, describe the contents of the sales and finished goods inventory files which are necessary to prepare the marginal analysis desired by management.

b. Describe the processing steps necessary to merge these files to produce the marketing reports.

c. Would Forward Corporation have been better off purchasing an on-line random access computer system to meet the requirements of management above? Would an increased awareness of the potential of on-line random access hardware and software alter the information requirements above? How and why?

d. Is there some potential for the use of a distributed EDP system in this case? Why?

e. How could a data base management system contribute to the ability of the marketing vice president to manage the marketing function for Forward Corporation? (Adapted from CMA Examination)

13–13

Nelson's Pharmacy is a sole proprietorship owned by a practicing pharmacist. Nelson's offers a small lunch counter, an extensive line of cosmetics, and a wide range of sundry items in addition to its prescription service. Nelson's employs three pharmacists and six full-time sales clerks.

Mr. Nelson's wife and his son, Gordon, work in the business also. Mrs. Nelson posts accounts receivable and handles all billing. Gordon Nelson opens all mail, deposits the daily cash receipts, and reconciles the monthly bank statements. A local CPA firm does write-up work for Nelson's at year-end and handles all tax matters. Gordon sometimes prepares monthly financial statements. The accounting system is manual and double entry. A chart of accounts is used.

Short-term budgeting is used on an informal basis. Weekly cash flow projections are made and compared with actual results. Monthly estimates of sales, stock levels, markups, and expenses are made by Mr. Nelson working with the personnel employed in the various departments of the business. These figures are compared with actual results and with industry averages.

The pharmacy has four cash registers: a register near the front door and one each in the lunch counter, cosmetic, and prescription departments. A base amount of cash is kept in each drawer to use in making change. All reg-

isters except the one near the door are closed out one hour before the business shuts down for the evening. The final register is closed out after business hours. Deposits are made each morning, and receipts are kept in a safe in the back of the store overnight. The base amount of money for change always stays in the drawer and never exceeds $30 per register.

When the cash registers are closed out for the day, all sales totals are broken down into cosmetics, food, sundry, prescriptions, and nonprescription drugs on a summary tape. The total amount of sales tax collected is also shown. If the contents of the register approximately equal the amount of cash sales rung up, the employee in the department in question places the cash and register tape in a bank bag and gives the bag to Mr. Nelson, who places it in the safe. Bank credit-card sales are also totaled, and the charge slips are placed in the safe. Credit-card sales are rung up using a special key on the cash registers, and therefore they are included in the sales totals recorded on the cash register tape.

The next morning, Gordon Nelson removes all bank bags from the safe. He counts the money for deposit and sees that the total approximately agrees with the cash register tapes. He then enters cash, bank card and charge sales totals into a sales journal, fills out a deposit slip, and makes the deposit. Bank charge-card slips are accumulated for a week and then mailed to the appropriate banks.

Mr. Nelson feels that a definite problem exists with customers' checks being returned from the bank for lack of funds. He has established a lenient check-cashing policy and is reluctant to change this policy because he wants to maintain a good relationship with the local residents. At the present time two-party checks, payroll checks, and checks for more than the amount of purchase are accepted. Identification is required.

Mr. Nelson is also very lenient regarding the extension of credit to local customers. No credit check is performed. Uncollectible accounts are usually one percent of total sales. When a customer makes a credit purchase, a pre-numbered credit invoice is signed. There are two copies of this invoice, both of which are filed alphabetically. The sale is keyed into the cash register using a special key. All credit sales are posted the next day to the sales journal and accounts receivable ledger card by

Mrs. Nelson. Once a month, customers are sent statements and the original credit invoice is enclosed. Payment is received by mail or in person and is posted to the customer's account by Mrs. Nelson. The second copy of the credit invoice is permanently filed alphabetically by customer.

In all departments, vendors come to the store periodically and take a physical inventory of the supply of their products on hand. They then suggest purchases to the employees on duty. The vendor prepares the order using his or her own order form and it is approved by the employee on duty. For prescription drugs, Mr. Nelson assists in the inventory and the drugs are purchased through wholesalers. Narcotic drugs are purchased and inventoried, as required by law. No shopping around is done to get better prices on purchases. The employees analyze the profitability of their lines to see if maximum profit is being obtained for the shelf space used. Markdowns are used for promotions and to move slow items. No list is kept of goods marked down.

Order forms are filed by vendor. When goods are received, a clerk will count them and give the order form to Mrs. Nelson in most cases. Some items are paid for by cash directly from the cash register using the appropriate key. Checks are prepared for other vendors twice a month by one of the clerks. Either Mr. Nelson or Mrs. Nelson must sign all checks. The Nelsons trust their employees and feel that this procedure is adequate. Order forms are thrown out after the check has been prepared. Suppliers' statements are discarded when received because all payments are made from order forms after the goods have been received.

REQUIRED: From the limited notes above, flowchart the system and describe the internal control weaknesses. Suggest how you might make use of intelligent terminals to help control sales, cash receipts, and inventory.

13–14

West Montana Wire, Inc., (WMW) is a manufacturer of electrical wire and cable. Copper and aluminum are the two primary raw materials used in the production process and account for about fifty percent of the total cost of the finished goods. Because of the importance of these raw materials, a separate department has been set up to manage the contracts. To further control the cost of its copper input, WMW vertically integrated by constructing a copper refinery in Butte. The refinery smelts and refines copper scrap and virgin ore into pure copper, or copper cathode. In the remainder of the production process, the copper cathode is melted down, cast into continuous copper rod, drawn into wire, and finally stranded into cable or building wire. Some of the wire is then insulated.

The Copper Management Department of West Montana Wire is responsible for the procurement of copper, inventory, and contracts until the copper is cast or reaches the drawing machines. Organizationally Copper Management is directed by a corporate vice-president. The department seems very small to be under the control of a high ranking official, but its importance stems from the fact that it oversees nearly half of West Montana Wire's total annual expenditures of $400 million. The organization chart is shown in Figure C13–14. No formal job descriptions exist for the specific positions. All four managers and the two assistant managers can write sales orders, approve contracts, and approve release documents for shipment of copper from the refinery.

Copper is traded internationally as a commodity and as such experiences dramatic fluctuations in market price. Copper Management uses several types of contracts to stabilize this price fluctuation. The manner in which a transaction is processed through West Montana Wire's information system depends on the type of contract. The most common type of contract is a simple purchase contract, usually for thirty-day delivery. Conversion contracts, on the other hand, involve changing the form of copper owned by another party, and charging a fee for this service without ever taking title to the copper. Purchased conversion contracts are the opposite of conversion contracts; to alleviate a capacity shortage WMW sends its metal to another smelter to be converted but retains title to it. Exchange contracts are used to trade one type of metal for another to save freight charges or correct a temporary inventory imbalance. Sales contracts are infrequently used; they involve the disposi-

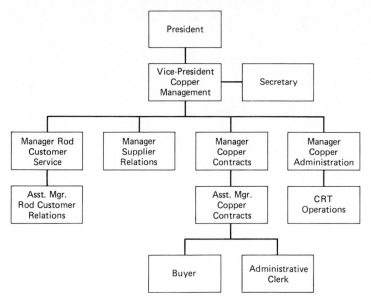

Figure C13-14 Organization Chart for Copper Management

tion of surplus raw materials when a favorable price can be obtained.

Copper Management uses an on-line real time computer system for almost all of its information requirements. The information system is very specialized and was developed at West Montana Wire specifically for the Copper Management Department.

The Copper Management information system operates as follows. Copper management personnel negotiate contracts with suppliers. The pertinent contract information, including the type of contract, is given a unique contract number. The CRT operator then keys this information into the system. Purchase, Conversion, Purchase Conversion, Exchange, and Sales contracts carry prefixes of P, C, O, E, and S, respectively. Each contract is numbered sequentially by type, using a 5-digit code. An additional 2 digits are also added to indicate multiple batches for a contract. Eight additional spaces in the code allow for a contract date and batch receipt date if applicable. Other pertinent information is also coded for reporting purposes. The type of contract code indicates the types of transactions which can validly be posted to that contract. The order entry system is real time, on-line, and automatically updates the Copper Management information system for new contracts. All input data are

edited and totals are logged in, as will be described later.

Upon receipt of copper ore, or scrap, a transaction is required to update the quantity of metal received. A metals receipt document is created daily for receipt of each load of copper. These transactions, called assay transactions, specify the composition and tonnage of each batch of metal received. Each assay transaction must use the appropriate contract and batch code. If a purchase contract is involved, a payment authorization will be automatically generated. These authorizations are numbered sequentially. For other types of contracts, the perpetual inventory balance of metal due to or from the other party is updated.

Once a contract is received and a batch of metal has been assayed and a batch number is assigned and after a review of the various status reports (described later), smelting operations are scheduled by the Refining Department. Any member of Copper Management can determine at any time, through inquiry to its data base, the status of any contract or batch or any transaction related to a contract. Examples of information which can be accessed through inquiry of the contract master file include information on all open contracts and batches along with all pertinent information on a specific contract and batch, shipping dates, inventory levels by location, and information on a specific receipt of inventory.

Several hardcopy reports are output from the Copper Management information system. The vendor listing provides trend analysis and demographic information about suppliers. The standard pricing report projects the expected costs for the next month. This information is used for determining the material costs in setting prices for finished goods. The metals position report compares the aggregate demand and supply expected for a particular type of copper input material. The active contract and batch report indicate the status of each contract in the refinery. An analysis of copper purchases report determines whether weekly procurement targets are being met. The conversion position report indicates the status of each conversion contract, including the balance due to or from a customer when the metal is due, and the particular form in which it is due.

The Copper Management system data base includes the following random access files: contract master file, vendor master file, daily summary file, daily control totals file, inventory master file, and file of standard costs.

The system controls used include: checks for valid codes, characters, field size and sign, transactions, and field combinations. Transactions are also checked for missing date fields. Limit checks, check digits, and passwords are used.

Totals (dollars, tons, and number transactions) are prepared by CRT operators to ensure the ultimate posting of transactions to reports and entering of all transactions, i.e., the system will not accept out-of-balance input where details do not match control tables. The control totals are kept in the temporary daily totals file. These totals are compared to a log book kept by the CRT operator at the end of the day, when the CRT operator enters number of transaction by type of contract, assay documents, and release documents. Dollar and tonnage totals are also entered for reconciliation at the end of the day. Errors are corrected before the nightly update of interfacing files. An audit tape is produced by the CPU for all transactions.

The Copper Management system interfaces with accounts payable and a separate batch system at the copper refinery, which maintains a perpetual refinery inventory of contract batches and their progress through the refinery. The accounts payable system is run once a day, in a batch processing mode, and the accounts payable vendor file is updated from the Copper Management information system daily transaction file.

REQUIRED:

a. Flowchart the system.

b. Describe the internal control strengths.

c. Describe the internal control weaknesses.

d. Describe the data content of each file necessary to generate the reports generated by the system.

e. How do these reports support operational, managerial, and strategic decision-making needs?

f. Should West Montana Wire consider a data base management system? What would be the advantages of such a system to West Montana Wire?

14

FINANCIAL ACCOUNTING SYSTEMS

OBJECTIVE

The objective of a financial accounting system is to support the decision-making, transaction processing, and reporting requirements of the financial, marketing, logistics, and personnel functions of the organization. This support must be furnished for operational, managerial, and strategic decisions. The pervasiveness of the accounting system was illustrated in Figure 2–4, in which the financial accounting system is shown to undergird all the other functional aspects of the information system.

In this chapter we focus on the financial accounting system. A state-of-the-art system for the Apple II™ microcomputer is illustrated. Day-to-day transaction processing requirements of the organization are emphasized. In Chapter 15 we will discuss corporate planning and budgeting systems and review their use in decision making, planning, and controlling the organization.

DECISION AND TRANSACTION
PROCESSING CHARACTERISTICS

Environmental Considerations

It is difficult to specify a general financial accounting system for all organizations because each operates in its own unique environment. This diversity has posed a real challenge to the numerous software houses as they have attempted to develop and market computer packages for the financial accounting. As a result, many focus on various fields and professions such as medical, construction, real estate, retailing, and education in an effort to achieve some commonality. It can readily be observed that the widely used financial accounting system for small businesses illustrated later in this chapter would not meet the needs of management in many situations.

The accountant, in assuming the role of systems designer, must understand the decision-making, reporting, and transaction processing environment of the organization. Environmental factors will have a definite impact on the management system of the organization. In turn, these factors should be considered in the design of the financial accounting system which supports all aspects of the management system. For example, one firm may have many credit customers with whom a high degree of interaction is necessary. Such a firm may need an on-line accounts receivable system such as that illustrated in Chapter 13 for a large oil company. Another firm may have one primary customer, such as the U.S. Air Force, and thousands of employees working on various large complex jobs. In this latter case the accounts receivable system will be very different and a complex job-order cost accounting system will be very important. Diversity of needs is found even in small businesses.

The financial accounting needs of a building contractor with many employees, many vendors, and a considerable capital investment are vastly different from those of a retail shoe store with one vendor, two employees, and cash or credit-card customers. The accountant must be able to advise or assist clients in a wide variety of situations with the selection of financial accounting systems that meet their information processing requirements.

Decision Networks and Information Requirements

The accountant must design an information system around the decision and reporting needs of the firm, *not* around the flow of transactions. Nevertheless the reports and summaries that are common to many financial accounting systems do provide considerable information that is useful in management decision making.

We will therefore take a slightly different approach in this chapter and address common information requirements as they relate to a financial accounting information system, recognizing that these form the core of what may be required for decision-making needs. Controls for financial accounting systems are detailed in Appendix B of this chapter and in Chapters 12 and 13.

Transaction Processing Network

The typical financial accounting transaction processing network is composed of all the financial transactions of the organization. The centerpiece of this network is the general ledger system. The general ledger accounts represent control accounts and are supported by detailed subsidiary ledgers, which are necessary for management's use in dealing with vendors and customers, and in making day-to-day operating decisions, such as the granting of credit, payment of invoices, and ordering of inventory. These accounts and their supporting transactions and resulting reports will be detailed in this chapter. In general, the general ledger and the journal entries (transactions) from which it is created are the very heart of the management information system of the business organization.

REPORTING NEEDS AND GENERAL LEDGER   Most business firms require financial statements. The balance sheet and income statement are useful for many internal decision-making needs. Often these are required on a monthly basis, and by division, for management decisions. These two statements, along with the statement of changes in financial position, are required by stockholders, creditors, the Internal Revenue Service, the Securities and Exchange Commission, and many other third parties, depending on the nature of the business. Moreover, many derivatives of these statements, such as the 10–K and quarterly reports, are often required. These statements, along with many other reports that are useful for decision making and third-party reporting, all come from a general ledger system that is the heart of the financial accounting system.

A typical general ledger system will interface with all the other financial accounting systems and management information systems, as illustrated in Figure 14–1. General ledger and financial systems can be completely integrated using a large complex data base, or they can be modular so that they may be adapted to many types of business conditions and information requirements. An example of a modular software design can be found in the MSA (Management Science America, Inc.)[1] General Ledger Accounting System. It has the following modules, which can be adapted for a wide variety of organizations:

1. General Ledger Module: records and reports accounting transactions in accordance with generally accepted accounting principles.
2. Budget and Planning Module: provides an organized approach to the budget and planning process.
3. Cost Allocation Module: distributes actual or planned amounts to departments, profit centers, products, functions, or services.
4. Custom Reporting Module: provides a means for extracting any information in the General Ledger data base to produce management and accounting reports easily designed to [the firm's] specification.

---

[1] MSA, *General Ledger Accounting System* copyright 1981, Management Science America, Inc. (Atlanta: Management Science America, Inc. 1981), p. 6. MSA is one of the largest business software houses in the world. This particular general ledger system is used by over 1,200 organizations. The discussion of this example general ledger system which follows is reprinted with MSA's permission.

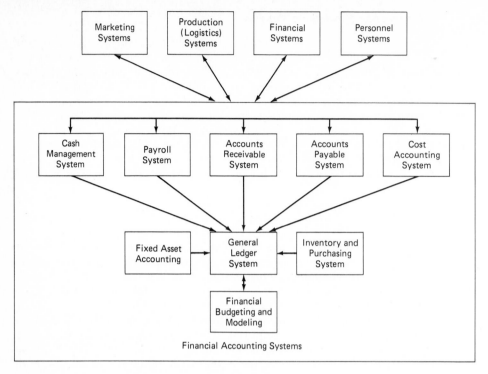

Figure 14-1 General Ledger Interface with Other Accounting and Information Systems

5. Encumbrance Recording Module: tracks requisitions, commitments, and obligations for available funds for not-for-profit organizations.
6. Fund Evaluation Module: develops internal transfer charges and credits for funds used and supplied.
7. Easy-Plan: provides extended planning and forecasting capabilities using general ledger budget information.
8. On-line Module: provides online entry, edit, and validation of journals, online input of file maintenance, inquiry into the General Ledger database, online display of management reports, and inquiries into detailed transactions.
9. Easy-Screen: an on-line screen generator that lets you create your own online inquiry screens to access existing General Ledger information.

The General Ledger, Budget and Planning, Cost Allocation, and Custom Reporting Modules comprise the central General Ledger Accounting System. All other modules are implemented optionally, depending on an organization's requirements.

This general ledger system has a segmented data base, where all information pertinent to one particular function is stored in the same segment. These are the general ledger, budget, and cost-allocation segments. The general ledger segment is shown in Figure 14-2. Any entity requiring a balanced set of books is defined as a *company*. It may be a legal entity, a division, a fund, a

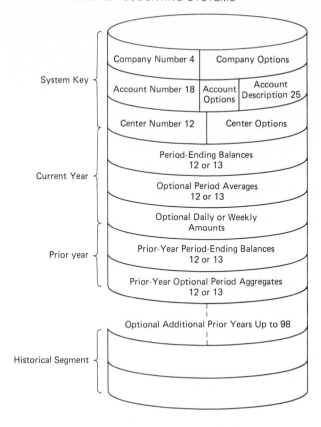

System Key

Current Year

Prior year

Historical Segment

Company Number 4	Company Options
Account Number 18	Account Options	Account Description 25
Center Number 12	Center Options

Period-Ending Balances
12 or 13

Optional Period Averages
12 or 13

Optional Daily or Weekly Amounts

Prior-Year Period-Ending Balances
12 or 13

Prior-Year Optional Period Aggregates
12 or 13

Optional Additional Prior Years Up to 98

Figure 14–2 MSA General Ledger Data Base

MSA, *General Ledger Accounting System*. Copyright 1981 Management Science America, Inc. Reprinted with permission.

subsidiary, or an individual plant. It is identified by a four-digit code. A *chart of accounts* is defined for *each* company, where each account may be defined with up to eighteen alphanumeric positions and twenty-five positions for an account name. A *center* is the lowest level of detail for which detailed accounts are accumulated. It may be a cost center, a department, a shift, or even a person. To identify the center, twelve alphanumeric characters and forty name positions are available. All data are stored at this lowest level of detail for ease and flexibility of reporting. Thus the system key may have up to thirty-four positions: four for the company, eighteen for the account, and twelve for each center. In addition, processing and control options such as the following are available:

1. *Company options*
   a. Years of history to be retained for each company. This may be from one to ninety-eight.
   b. Update procedure. This may be random or sequential depending on the needs of each "company." This may differ for each division in the organization.
   c. Edit controls. These may be built in and user designed.
   d. Average balances may be calculated in addition to end-of-period balances. This may be more useful information for decision making.

       e.   Each "company" may have a different fiscal calendar.

       f.   Daily or weekly reporting is feasible.

2. *Account options* within each company

       a.   Each account may contain either financial or nonfinancial information, such as units sold.

       b.   Exception or alert criteria along with the automatic processing or exception reports are available.

3. *Center options*

       a.   Exception criteria are available and may be user defined.

The system also maintains prior-year balances and may accommodate either twelve or thirteen period-ending balances depending on the nature of the business.

To define the logistical relationship between centers, accounts, and "companies" for the organization, the user begins with the organization chart and chart of accounts for each "company." The user then defines valid combinations for each company.

Using this system, multiple organizational entities can be maintained on the same data base. In addition, the flexible data base structure offers automatic consolidation capabilities including standard elimination and adjusting entries.

Data entry to the general ledger system can be made via card, tape, key-to-tape, disk, or key-to-disk or by using an on-line CRT. Transactions generated by other accounting systems such as those shown in Figure 14–1 can also be entered directly without manual intervention. The following journal entries are feasible:

    Direct entries

    Recurring entries

    Standard journal entries

    Accrual entries

    Reversing entries

    Intercompany transactions

    Statistical entries

    MSA and non-MSA automated system interfaces

    Adjusting entries

    Future-dated entries

    Maintenance transactions

These entries can be batched or entered individually.

All editing and validating is accomplished prior to updating the data base. All errors and out-of-balance conditions are reported. Exceptions can be determined by user-specified rules and validity comparison with active account and center numbers. Distributions can be predefined to allocate costs, and a translation provision is present to translate one account number to another account number with a different number of digits.

Moreover, a wide variety of control reports are available with provision for effective audit trails. This is accomplished using a descriptive feature to allow precise input identification including date, source, project, and application.

Many reports are generated by the system, and even more are optional and easy to design by the user. During posting procedures, the general ledger activity is detailed and a trial balance is prepared along with an exception report. Other reports may include posting journals, reconciliation reports, expense reports, account analysis, and cash flow reports. In addition, this particular general ledger system (this is common for most new systems) has a report-writing feature where the user may access the data base any way he or she wants and design a custom report. The report organization is independent of the data base organization because it uses the unique center, account, and company key for each dollar or nonfinancial amount. This makes it easy to prepare responsibility reports and even track projects. The user has a great deal of flexibility in formatting these reports, as can be seen in Appendix A of this chapter. For example, comparisons, ratios, graphics, mathematical calculations, and ranges are feasible for communicating the information in the reports to management.

This particular general ledger system even has provisions with several options for cost allocation. Allocations or distributions may be made either at the time of the transaction or at the end of the period. Five common techniques are available:

1. Percent distribution: predetermined or fixed
2. Percent to total: percentage of distribution based on some base such as square feet or hours used
3. Weighted percent to total: to add weights to the above allocation technique
4. Volume times a standard cost
5. Direct fixed allocation

These allocations may be either sequential using a step-down procedure or simultaneous.

Finally, this particular general ledger system contains a budget and planning system that incorporates several of the simple corporate planning model features detailed in Chapter 15. Moreover, this general ledger model interfaces with larger, more complex planning models similar to those reviewed in Chapter 15.

This overview of a general ledger system should clearly demonstrate that this is the heart of the financial accounting system, the general accounting system, and the entire information system of the firm. (A microcomputer version of a general ledger system is illustrated later in this chapter.)

ACCOUNTS RECEIVABLE   When there are a large number of credit customers, a formalized accounts receivable system is useful for basic transaction processing needs and compiling reports to assist management in many operational and managerial decisions. (Accounts receivable systems are reviewed in Chapter 13.) These decisions involve cash management, credit, customer relations, collections, customer maintenance, and promotion. Some of the more useful reports are customer lists, customer status reports, aging reports, and summary journal entries. Automatic transaction-by-transaction posting of sales, collections, returns and adjustments, and the generation of customer statements is a great help in dealing with volumes of paper work common to businesses with many credit customers. (Examples of accounts receivable customer files are given later in this chapter and in Chapter 13.)

These systems interface with the general ledger system, sales order processing systems, and cash management systems, as shown in Figure 14–1. The basic transactions involve debiting cash and crediting the corresponding or oldest receivable for each customer upon collection as follows:

Cash	XXX	
Accounts receivable		XXX

and crediting sales and debiting accounts receivable for each credit sales transaction as follows:

Accounts receivable	XXX	
Sales		XXX

ACCOUNTS PAYABLE Where many vendors supply an organization with goods or services, a formalized accounts payable system will often be useful in decision making and transaction processing. Some of the more common operational and managerial decisions that may be supported by the information from the accounts payable system are cash planning, bank relations, expense allocation or distribution, invoice payment selection, and purchasing. Some of the typical reports generated by these systems to assist in the decisions are vendor lists with pricing information and status data, transaction lists, open voucher reports, cash requirement reports, aged payable reports, check registers, payment selection lists, and summarized general ledger posting entries. Automatic transaction-by-transaction posting of vouchers and all their corresponding changes, and the printing of checks for vouchers selected for payment, are essential for many firms with a large number of vendors. Examples of basic vendor files are given later in this chapter and previously in Chapter 12. These files are useful for queries by management on vendor status. The essential features of an accounts payable system are fully illustrated later in this chapter.

The typical accounts payable system must interface with the general ledger, procurement and inventory, purchasing, and cash management systems of the organization. A specific example of such an interface is shown in Figure 14–1. The fundamental transactions involve debiting accounts payable and crediting cash for payment of merchandise invoices and debiting the appropriate asset or expense account and crediting accounts payable for the amount of the purchase. These can be summarized as follows:

Accounts payable	XXX	
Cash		XXX
Asset or expense account	XXX	
Accounts payable		XXX

INVENTORY   Inventory systems and their relationship to production and material requirement planning systems were examined in Chapter 12. Examples of reports and files were given in that chapter and are detailed later in this chapter for small microcomputer systems. As shown in Figure 14–1, inventory systems interface with the general ledger, accounts payable, payroll, cash management, and fixed asset systems.

PAYROLL   Where an organization has many employees, such as a labor-intensive manufacturing company, or the mode of payment or the reporting requirements are complex, a formalized payroll system will prove useful for personnel management and daily transaction processing. Information from this system will be useful for strategic and managerial activities such as personnel planning, performance and employment policies, safety standards, and collective bargaining.

Generally the system will interface with the other financial accounting systems, as illustrated in Figure 14–1. For example, consider a typical payroll and labor distribution system for production operations. This system is shown in Figure 14–3. The employee master file is updated and remains current through on-line entry of personnel and payroll changes from the respective departments. This master file is used along with the production schedule, generated from systems such as those illustrated in Chapter 12, and is used to prepare prepunched time cards and daily production schedules for employees and departments, respectively. The time cards are sent to timekeeping, and each employee punches in upon arrival at work and punches out upon termination of work for that day. The department foreman uses the production schedule to assign jobs to employees. Upon completion of each job, the employee keys in a set of information to a temporary disk file. This information includes his or her employee number, department, job-order number, number of units that he or she completed, and time in hours spent on each job. Idle time and setup time are also reported, to account for all the time an employee spends in the plant. These data are edited and verified to ensure that all numbers are valid, logical (the employee is assigned to that department and the job is scheduled for that department), and reasonable. These data are stored on a temporary disk file, and at the end of the shift they are merged with completed time cards to reconcile employee time—i.e., the hours must match for each employee, and the job assignments must match with the labor distribution data reported by the employee. Exceptions are reported and followed up by plant auditors and management. Major exceptions are corrected at this time, before any further processing. Once the input data have been reconciled, job cost distributions are made and the employee master file is updated. Moreover, labor distribution along with other reports is issued to production supervisory personnel. Periodically the payroll is processed in a method similar to that illustrated later in this chapter. Checks and a check register are prepared at that time. Both the job cost data and the payroll data are subsequently used to update the general ledger.

The following basic journal entries are related to payroll distribution:

Direct labor	XXX
Indirect labor—factory	XXX

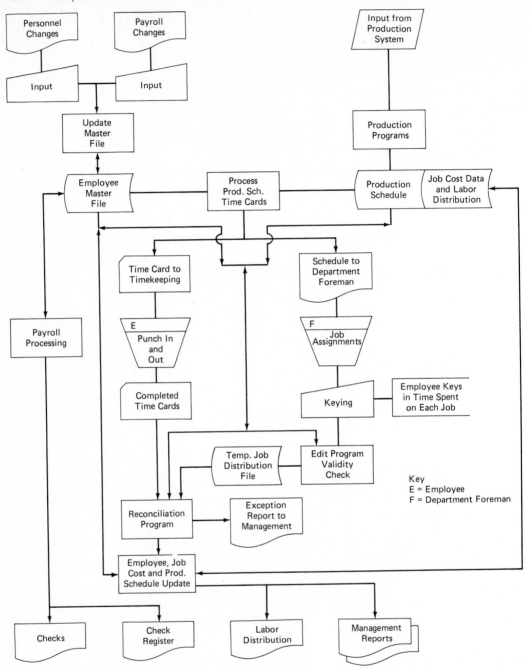

Figure 14–3 Payroll and Labor Distribution System for Production

General and administrative expense	XXX	
Accrued payroll		XXX
Deduction liabilities		XXX

where direct labor is applied to each job, as outlined in Chapter 12. Upon payment the entry is

Accrued payroll	XXX	
Cash		XXX

The corresponding employer tax liability is also recorded as follows:

Factory overhead	XXX	
General and administrative expenses	XXX	
Liability for taxes		XXX

For many organizations, numerous reports are needed to help management control personnel activities and labor costs. At the operational level, the data collected can often be transformed into useful information for such management and accounting needs as career development, training, job scheduling, performance evaluation, medical and safety records, turnover problems, job costs, employee benefit programs, profit sharing, group insurance, ERISA compliance, employee selection, and affirmative action.

MSA's Payroll Accounting System provides a good example of the type of reports that can be generated by payroll systems:

1. A Transaction Validation Report which provides a detailed analysis of all items processed and an explanation of any rejected items.
2. An Input Balancing Proof List Report which provides a permanent audit trail of current pay action transactions with system-produced totals and may be used by the Payroll Department to balance adding machine totals.
3. A W–2 Audit Report which provides a printout of W–2 data by employee, enabling management to audit tax records prior to printing W–2's on the specified form.
4. An Employee Master Profile Report which provides computer printouts of employee information that include administrative data and the frequency of specific deductions and/or other earnings.
5. A File Maintenance Report which furnishes an audit trail of all subsidiary and employee master file changes, including those generated by the system.
6. A Reversal Update Report which provides detailed and summary information on transactions entered to reverse specific checks and deposit records.
7. A Worker's Compensation Report which provides compensation information that makes compliance with state reporting requirements easier.
8. A Tax Distribution Summary Report which furnishes accrued federal, state, county, city, and provincial (Canadian) tax figures, which facili-

tates the necessary function of filing required tax reports to taxing authorities.

9. A W–2 Report which provides a wage and tax statement that complies with federal requirements.

10. A Form 1099 which reports compensation that is not required on either the W–2 or the W–2P Report to employees.

11. A Payroll Register which provides a recap of payment transactions for each employee and serves as an important part of the system audit trail.

12. A Check/Deposit Notification which provides an employee with check and deposit notification records when all or a portion of net pay is deposited to one or more banks or bank services.

13. An Hours Register which furnishes a listing of various hours categories, as well as available vacation and sick leave, by employee.

14. A Deductions/Earnings List which details individual employee deductions and other earnings in a user-defined format.

15. A Deductions/Other Earnings Register which details employee deductions and other earnings, providing a permanent employee record and supporting the totals provided on the Payroll Register.

16. A Labor Distribution Report which provides meaningful cost/labor distribution information for management and Accounting Department use.

17. An Earnings History Report which provides a listing of an employee's history of payment of earned wages. The detail of this report is an essential component of an employee's permanent records.[2]

In addition, many user-defined reports are possible because of the data base management system, the report generator, and on-line capabilities of the system.

It is essential that the employee file or data base be comprehensive and flexible so that these decision-making and reporting requirements can be satisfied. This file can include such items as pay rates, tax information, benefit data, and as much history, skill, and performance data as management deems necessary. In addition, it is essential that current, monthly, and year-to-date pay records be complete and interface, if necessary, with the sales and manufacturing systems to efficiently capture commission, pay rates, overtime, and cost distribution information. An example of a limited transaction processing system for a microcomputer is given later in this chapter. However, much more employee information than that provided by the system described later may be necessary to manage this key business asset.[3]

FIXED ASSETS   For many firms, a formalized system for fixed asset accounting is necessary for property control, financial accounting, journal entries, tax accounting, and reporting to third parties and regulatory agencies. Fixed

---

[2] MSA, *Payroll Accounting System* copyright 1981, Management Science America, Inc., Atlanta, Ga. Reprinted by permission.

[3] For example, see any large software package description, such as *NCR General Payroll and Personnel Reporting*.

asset systems must enable management to make replacement decisions, forecast future expenditures, plan maintenance operations, and purchase new assets. Moreover, the system should be detailed enough to help management decide on the various modes of asset financing and their impact on cash flow and on the financial statements of the business. At a minimum (1) locational and descriptive information for property control, (2) depreciation information for multiple sets of books (tax and financial reporting), (3) lease accounting, (4) constant-dollar accounting information, and (5) tax information for various governmental and regulatory agencies must be incorporated into the system. All information should be complete, timely, accurate, and flexible.

Management Science America Inc.'s fixed asset accounting system is a good example of the software available for a wide variety of businesses in managing and reporting their fixed assets. It provides information for the requirements listed above. To help management control property, the system is designed with up to fourteen levels of locational and descriptive information and up to seven separate sets of books for each asset. The system has provisions for insurance revaluation based on historical cost, net book value, current replacement costs, and current insurable value. Moreover, it provides maintenance and repair cost statistics (including service contract information) for each asset. It also provides construction-in-progress reporting. The system can report on such data items as quantity, status, condition, serial number, vendor or manufacturer name, model name, and purchasing authority. All transfers of location can also be detailed. From a financial accounting perspective, the system will automatically—via a general ledger interface—generate journal entries for depreciation expense, additions, transfers, adjustments, and retirements. Many depreciation methods are provided, and these may even be projected for planning needs. The system will also assist management in the necessary calculation so that the company can comply with *FASB 13*.

From a tax accounting perspective, the most recent depreciation tax laws are incorporated, the system will calculate investment tax credit and recapture information for management's needs, and gains and losses on the disposition of property can be calculated in accordance with the current tax regulations. In addition, the system is designed to assist management in accounting for inflation via current value, replacement cost, or price-level adjustments as required. Input is simple, audit trails are maintained, and a report generator is available for custom reporting to satisfy management's needs for decision making, reporting, and transaction processing.[4]

CASH RECEIPTS AND DISBURSEMENTS   All organizations must maintain effective control over their cash resources. The nature of this control ranges from physical control to investment and borrowing decisions. In addition, the cash receipts and disbursements system interfaces with all other accounting and information systems, as seen in Figure 14–1. Here only a simple cash receipts and disbursements system is reviewed. A cash receipts system is outlined in Figure 14–4, and a cash disbursement system for a small microcomputer is discussed as part of the accounts payable system later in this chapter.

---

[4] MSA, *Fixed Asset Accounting System*, copyright 1981, Management Science America, Inc., Atlanta, Ga. Reprinted with permission.

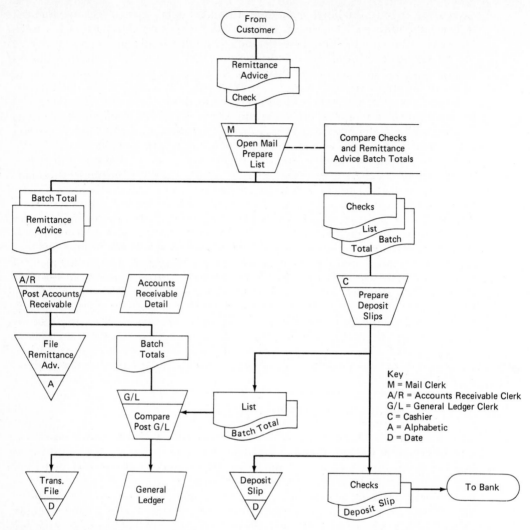

Figure 14–4 Cash Receipts System

In this example, remittance advices, along with checks, are received and opened by a mail clerk. The mail clerk compares the advice with the checks and makes any corrections, lists all remittances, and prepares a batch total containing the number of transactions and dollar amounts. All remittance advices are forwarded to accounts receivable along with the batch totals. These are posted to customer accounts and filed alphabetically. Batch totals are then sent to the general ledger clerk after this detailed posting. All checks, the list, and the batch totals are forwarded to the cashier, who prepares two copies of a deposit slip. One copy is filed by date for future reconciliation, and the checks and the original are deposited in the bank. The general ledger clerk receives the list and the batch totals from the cashier, compares them with the totals received from accounts receivable, and posts the general ledger. All transactions are then filed by date.

Financial Accounting Transaction Network

All of these systems—the general ledger, accounts receivable, accounts payable, inventory, payroll, and fixed assets—are integrated either through manual journal entries, automatic transfer of summary information from one system to another, or the use of general ledger control accounts as illustrated in Figure 14–1 and in the discussion of the general ledger system. All of these systems are basic to the operations of most organizations. Clearly, all need not be complex or even EDP systems. On the other hand, some may be very complex and serve as the vehicle for gathering large volumes of data for other management needs. These should use EDP systems. Regardless of the system used, however, these financial accounting systems will always be the focal point or cornerstone of the organization's management information system. As a result, the accountant or systems designer must be cognizant of interfaces with other systems. In particular, the systems designer must know how to use this transaction processing framework to gather needed data for various operational, managerial, and strategic decision needs of management, as shown in Figure 14–1.

MICROCOMPUTER SYSTEM ILLUSTRATION

Overview

We illustrate here an example of the type of general financial accounting software packages now available for microcomputers such as the Radio Shack TRS–80™, the Apple II™,[5] or the IBM personal computer. The particular system we illustrate was designed by Peachtree Software™,[6] a division of Management Science America, Inc.,[7] for the Apple II™ computer.[8] It requires the following hardware: an Apple II™ computer with 48K of RAM (random access memory), two Apple II™ disk units, an additional 16K RAMCARD, a 40-character-by-24-line CRT, and a 132-column printer. In addition, some spe-

---

[5] See E. S. Walker, "Accounting Packages: Selection and Management," *Datamation*, August 1981, pp. 76–122, for a complete listing of accounting software packages for both large and small systems.

[6] All figures and discussion unless otherwise indicated in this section are adapted from Peachtree Software, Inc.™ *Accounting Series 40, Apple II™ Edition* (Atlanta: Management Science America, 1980). Peachtree's dealer network exceeds 1000 with an installed base exceeding 40,000 packages. IBM chose Peachtree Software's™ accounting packages for their personal computer.

[7] The world's largest independent supplier of packaged computer applications software programs.

[8] Others for which liaison has been established for using Peachtree Software™ (version of the same basic package base) are IBM, Vector Graphic, Apple Computer, Inc., Zenith Data Systems, Osborne, and Hewlett Packard.

cial systems software is required to make the Apple II™ computer compatible with the package.

The overall package described here consists of five modular systems: (1) accounts receivable, (2) accounts payable, (3) inventory management, (4) payroll, and (5) general ledger. The complete system discussed here is outlined in the flowchart shown in Figure 14–5. The major inputs originate from sales, purchases, payroll, and other transactions; other input and query features are shown in the detailed system flowcharts that follow. As shown in Figure 14–5, the complete financial system consists of five major files: (1) the customer and transaction file, (2) the vendor file, (3) the inventory file, (4) the employee and payroll file, and (5) the general ledger account file. Each of these systems can be used to generate a wide variety of reports which are useful for managerial and operational decision making and financial reporting. Moreover, all the systems have random access files for management's use in decision making and inquiry. As can be seen in Figure 14–5, an automatic interface is feasible between the accounts receivable, accounts payable, payroll, and general ledger system. In summary, an end-of-month program generates journal entries that are recorded in a transfer file which is used to update the general ledger. This is *not* the case for inventory; all transactions here must be entered using the CRT and a keying operation. Other journal entries are entered to the general ledger in this manner. The major output apart from the managerial reports is an updated general ledger and a set of monthly and year-end financial statements, as shown in Figure 14–5. These systems can be used either together (as shown here), separately, or in any combination depending on the needs of the business.

The capacity is such that a large number of firms can readily adapt the system. The approximate number of records for each of these modular systems is as follows:

> Accounts Receivable: 500 customers in customer file
> Accounts Payable: 350 vendors in vendor file
> Payroll: 250 employees in employee file
> Inventory: 700 items in inventory file
> General Ledger: 500 accounts in chart of accounts
> Mailing List: 700 name and address records

Accounts Receivable System

To support the minimum information needs of a wide variety of business firms, an accounts receivable system should have the following capabilities:

1. Maintenance of customer records (additions, changes, and deletions)
2. List of customer records
3. Query certain customer files
4. Preparation of invoices and statements
5. Production of reports such as
   a. An aging schedule
   b. An invoice register

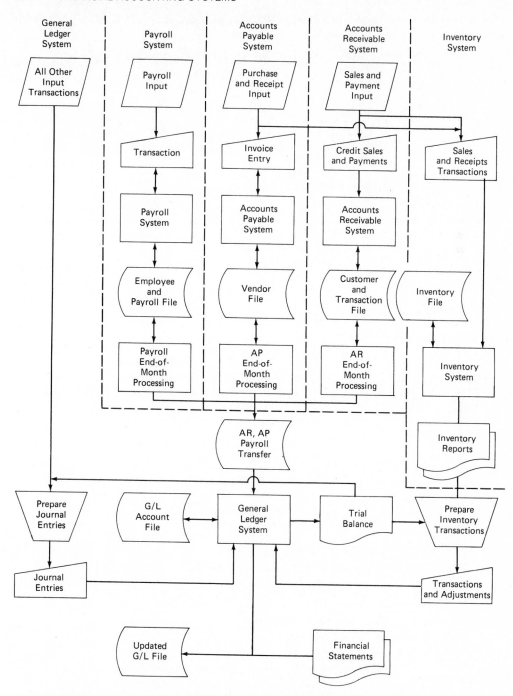

Figure 14–5 Overview of Peachtree Software's™ Financial Information System for a Microcomputer Peachtree Software™, *Accounting Series* 40, *Apple II*™ *Edition*, Copyright 1980 Peachtree Software, Inc. Reprinted with permission.

    c. Payment, credit, and adjustment register
    d. Customer status

6. Automatic posting or generation of monthly journal entries for
    a. Invoice sales
    b. Freight charges
    c. Sales tax
    d. Service charge income
    e. Cash payments
    f. Discounts allowed
    g. Returns and audits
    h. Income adjustments
    i. Accounts receivable

7. Exercise of reasonable control over input and records via
    a. File backup
    b. Recovery routines
    c. Control reports for audit trails
    d. Editing procedures and error messages
    e. Transaction listings (logs)
    f. Self-instructing user documentation
    g. Instructor menu driven system
    h. Automatic totaling and extension procedures
    i. Training procedures

The Peachtree Software™ system illustrated here for the Apple II™ is a good example of a widely used system that possesses these basic attributes. Figure 14–6 illustrates the flow of various processes encompassed by the system. The system is designed to maintain a file for each customer using the *customer maintenance* program. This particular *customer file* consists of the following data:

    Customer number
    Customer name, address, and phone number
    Type of account
    Credit terms and limit
    Tax rate
    Discount rate
    Date and amount of last credit and debit
    Current balance
    High balance
    Year-to-date sales and payments
    Automatic billing amount

The customer maintenance program can also be used to change, add to, or delete from the file.

The *print invoice* program allows the user to enter the information for each credit sale. The information is entered in a question-and-answer format, as shown in Figure 14–7. Items of information to be entered, such as date, customer ID, shipping date, customer order number, and salesman ID, will appear

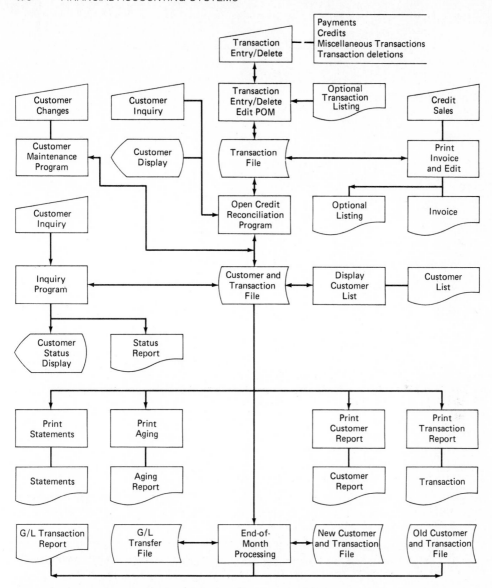

Figure 14–6 Accounts Receivable System Flow

Peachtree Software™, *Accounting Series* 40, *Apple II™ Edition*, Copyright 1980 Peachtree Software, Inc. Reprinted with permission.

on the CRT menu. Information initially set up on customer records, such as the tax rate, is displayed as a default value for many of these questions. It may be overridden by entering a new value for this particular transaction. For each line item, information such as item number, number ordered, number shipped, description, and current price will be entered and a total will be calculated. At the end, the question "Are these fields correct (Y or N)?" will be asked to prompt the user to edit the data entered. Several line items can be added to

TRANSACTION ENTRY

STEP _____ VIDEO PROMPT/DISPLAY _____

(10)   _____NAME_____   _____DEFAULT_____
        SALE, PAYMT, OR OTHER: S

(11)   DUE DATE   :   MM/DD/YY
        TERMS OR REF   :   NET 30
        SALES   :   0.00
        FREIGHT   :   0.00
        TAXES   :   0.00
        SER. CH.   :   0.00
        MISC. DB   :   0.00
           TOTAL DB   :   0.00

        ARE THESE FIELDS CORRECT (Y OR N)?

(12)   TERMS OR REF   :
        PAYMENTS   :   0.00
           TOTAL CR   :   0.00

        ARE THESE FIELDS CORRECT (Y OR N)?

(13)   DUE DATE   :   MM/DD/YY
        TERMS OR REF   : NET 30
        CODE (0-9)   :   0.00
        SALES   :   0.00
        FREIGHT   :   0.00
        TAXES   :   0.00
        SER. CH.   :   0.00
        MISC. DB   :   0.00
           TOTAL DB   :   0.00
        PAYMENTS   :   0.00
        CREDITS   :   0.00
        RETURNS   :   0.00
        DISCOUNT   :   0.00
        MISC. CR   :   0.00
           TOTAL CR   :   0.00
              TRANS BALANCE :   0.00

        ARE THESE FIELDS CORRECT (Y OR N)?

Figure 14–7 Example Video Display Menu

Peachtree Software™, *Accounting Series* 40, *Apple II*™ *Edition*, Copyright 1980 Peachtree Software, Inc. Reprinted with permission.

one invoice and subtotals can be calculated. Provisions for freight, tax, service charge, deposits, and discounts are available on the system menu. Finally, an invoice total is calculated and displayed. When the user concludes that the information is correct, it is printed on an invoice, such as that shown in Figure 14–8, and is stored in the customer record. The record, or *transaction file*, consists of the transaction type, data, and amount and an invoice file consisting of the invoice number, date, amount, and credit terms. An optional listing is available. The operator can then switch back to the main accounts receivable menu.

Once invoices have been generated, the payments, credits, or other transactions for that particular customer or invoice can be applied using the

```
                              ********************************
                              ***                        ***
HOWELL ENTERPRISES, INC.      ***      I N V O I C E     ***
4783 ROSWELL RD., N.E.        ***                        ***
ATLANTA, GEORGIA 30326        ********************************
```

ACCOUNT NUMBER: EVER

INVOICE NO.   1449

INVOICE DATE: 08/19/80

PAGE   : 1

```
       ------------------------              ------------------------
       ------------------------              ------------------------
SOLD   EVERREADY HARDWARE CO.       SHIP     EVERREADY HARDWARE CO.
TO     2041 CHAMBLEE-TUCKER RD.     TO       2041 CHAMBLEE-TUCKER RD.
       DORAVILLE, GA. 30340                  DORAVILLE, GA. 30340
       ------------------------              ------------------------
       ------------------------              ------------------------
```

```
SHIP VIA : UPS               YOUR ORDER NO.: 00236549
DELIVERY : COD               OUR ORDER NO. : PO 80-0015678
SHIP DATE : 08/19/80         ORDER DATE    : 08/17/80
DUE DATE  : 9/18/80          SALESMAN      : PHILLIPS
TERMS    : NET 30
```

ITEM	ORD	SHP	DESCRIPTION	PRICE	AMOUNT
98-0023401	24	24	FELT-TIPPED PENS	0.79	18.96
88-0045602	12	12	LEGAL TABLET	0.95	11.40
92-0078201	6	6	16 IN. RULER, METAL	1.89	11.34
28-00567	2	2	WEBSTER COLLEGIATE DICT.	12.56	25.12
38-0987602	36	24	BIC PENS, BLUE	1.80	43.20

```
                                               SUBTOTAL    110.02

FREIGHT   TAX     SERV. CH  MISC. DB  DEPOSIT  DISCOUNT     TOTAL
--------  -----   --------  --------  -------  --------    --------
 2.50     4.40      0.00      0.00     0.00      0.00
                                                            116.92
```

Figure 14–8 Sample Invoice

Peachtree Software™, *Accounting Series* 40, *Apple II*™ *Edition*, Copyright 1980 Peachtree Software, Inc. Reprinted with permission.

transaction enter program. Invoice and transactions both become part of the customer file. The transaction enter program can be used to enter sales, receipts, and miscellaneous transactions. For each transaction, the user will enter the customer ID, transaction date, invoice number, sale, payment, or other code. If a zero is entered instead of an invoice number an open credit can be entered. These credits are subsequently reconciled through the Open Credit Reconciliation program. At that time they can be applied to a specific invoice or to the oldest invoice first. Each transaction is edited as it is keyed in using the menu prompts. An optional but recommended control report is available for a back-up audit trail.

The *transaction delete* program permits the user to delete any transaction from a specified customer's account. Each account is displayed before the delete option is exercised, and a control report is available for an audit trail. No transaction can be deleted from the system if it has already been posted to the general ledger; in those cases a reversing entry is necessary. This is accomplished by using the same invoice number and entering a transaction with a negative sign.

This illustrative system also provides an *open credit reconciliation* program, which allows a payment or credit to be applied directly to a particular invoice or to the oldest invoices for each customer. In other words, this particular microcomputer software system is open item and balance forward. Again, a control report (not shown in Figure 14–6) is available for an audit trail. The user simply enters the customer ID, displays on the screen a list of unpaid invoices, and, if appropriate, selects the mode of application of any open credit amount that originated in the transaction processing program. In addition, the program is used to reconcile differences and clean up customer files.

In addition to the transaction processing and maintenance procedures noted above, this particular microcomputer software package has provisions for the generation of several reports besides the control listings. These reports are designed to assist the firm's management in making decisions, for they report customer and transaction information.

First, to respond to numerous and varied inquiries, the *display customer status* program provides the user with all current information in the customer file, all current entries made to that customer account, and open transactions from prior periods. The user of this small microcomputer system has access to information similar to that generated by the large oil company system illustrated in Chapter 13. All customer accounts can be listed in alphanumeric order and displayed individually on the CRT or printed. Printed output is illustrated in Figure 14–9.

The *print statements* program allows the user to print a customer statement like the one illustrated in Figure 14–10. This can be either an itemized listing of all invoices and all transactions this period or merely the balance forward plus this period's transactions. Provisions are available for preparation of statements for a single customer, cycle (automatic) billing of some customers, or statements for all customers. Provisions are even available for a dun message for selected customers.

Three more reports can be generated from the customer file. The *aged receivables* program gives the user the option of obtaining either a detailed (Fig-

```
                          HOWELL ENTERPRISES INC.                    PAGE 1
                            ACCOUNTS RECEIVABLE
                          QUERY CUSTOMER ACITVITY
                                 08/18/80


ADCOCK                                        DATE LAST DB:    5/28/80
                         TYPE      :  REGULAR   AMT LAST DB :    133.35
ADCOCK BUSINESS PRODUCTS CUR. BAL  :   157.73  YTD SALES   :    237.35
4431 LOWER ROSWELL RD.   BAL. FWD. :     0.00  DATE LAST CR:    5/28/80
MARIETTA, GA. 30360      AUTO. BILL:     0.00  AMT LAST CR :      2.54
(404) 255-9999           TAX RATE  :   4.000%  YTD PAYMENTS:     79.62

INVOICE   CODE     DATE   TERMS OR REF.   DEBITS    CREDITS    BALANCE
-------  --------  ------  -------------  ---------  ---------  ---------
    812  SALE      5/ 4/80  2-10-NET 30    104.00      2.08     101.92
    812  PAYMENT   5/16/80  CHECK 11031      0.00     75.00      26.92
    884  SALE      5/28/80  2-10-NET 30    133.35      2.54     157.73


DAVIS                                         DATE LAST DB:    7/30/80
                         TYPE      :  BAL FWD   AMT LAST DB :     49.02
DAVIS TEMPORARIES, INC.  CUR. BAL. :  3316.89  YTD SALES      2446.34
23 MARIETTA ST. NW       BAL. FWD  :   870.55  DATE LAST CR:    2/14/79
ATLANTA, GA. 30301       AUTO. BILL:     0.00  AMT LAST CR :      0.00
(404) 394-6666           TAX RATE  :   4.000%  YTD PAYMENTS:      0.00

INVOICE   CODE     DATE   TERMS OR REF.   DEBITS    CREDITS    BALANCE
-------  --------  ------  -------------  ---------  ---------  ---------
   1257  SALE      7/19/80  NET 30        1146.37      0.00    2016.92
   1269  SALE      7/23/80  NET 30        1250.95      0.00    3267.87
   1288  SERV. CH  7/30/80  NET 30          49.02      0.00    3316.89


EVER                                          DATE LAST DB:    7/15/80
                         TYPE      :  REGULAR   AMT. LAST DB:     22.76
EVERREADY HARDWARE CO.   CUR. BAL  :    71.73  YTD SALES   :     92.75
2041 CHAMBLEE-TUCKER RD. BAL. FWD. :     0.00  DATE LAST CR:    6/15/80
DORAVILLE, GA. 30340     AUTO. BILL:     0.00  AMT  LAST CR:     21.02
(404) 939-8888           TAX RATE  :   4.000%  YTD PAYMENTS:     21.02

INVOICE   CODE     DATE   TERMS OF REF.   DEBITS    CREDITS    BALANCE
-------  --------  ------  -------------  ---------  ---------  ---------
   1030  SALE      6/10/80  NET 30          42.49      0.00      42.49
   1030  PAYMENT   6/15/80  CHECK 3711       0.00     21.02      21.47
   1066  SALE      6/22/80  NET 30          27.50      0.00      48.97
   1245  SALE      7/15/80  NET 30          22.76      0.00      71.73


FGINS                                         DATE LAST DB:    7/30/80
                         TYPE      :  AUTO BILL AMT. LAST DB:    180.00
FANNING & GULF INS. CO.  CUR. BAL. :    36.39  YTD SALES   :    336.39
3781 W. PEACHTREE ST. NE. BAL. FWD. :    0.00  DATE LAST CR:    8/14/80
ATLANTA, GA. 30309       AUTO. BILL:   180.00  AMT. LAST CR:    180.00
(404) 238-1212           TAX RATE  :   4.000%  YTD PAYMENTS:    360.00

INVOICE   CODE     DATE   TERMS OF REF.   DEBITS    CREDITS    BALANCE
-------  --------  ------  -------------  ---------  ---------  ---------
```

Figure 14–9 Customer Accounts List

Peachtree Software™, *Accounting Series* 40, *Apple II*™ *Edition*, Copyright 1980 Peachtree Software, Inc. Reprinted with permission.

HOWELL ENTERPRISES, INC.
4783 ROSWELL RD. N. E.
ATLANTA, GEORGIA 30326

```
*****************************
***                       ***
***   S T A T E M E N T   ***
***                       ***
*****************************
```

STATEMENT DATE: 08/19/80

ACCOUNT NUMBER: SAN

PAGE   1

```
===========================
SANTINI & ASSOCIATES
47 PEACHTREE CIRCLE
ATLANTA, GA. 30309
===========================
```

DON'T FORGET TO TAKE ADVANTAGE OF OUR MID-SUMMER SPECIALS!!

INVOICE	DATE	TERMS OR REF	CODE	DEBITS	CREDITS	BALANCE
1206	3/ 3/79	OC RECONCIL	9		111.05	-111.05
1206	7/ 2/80	NET 15	0	159.95		48.90
1251	7/17/80	CHECK 1019	5		150.00	-101.10
1271	7/23/80	NET 30	0	38.95		-62.15
1292	7/30/80	NET 30	0	39.98		-22.17
				238.88	261.05	

```
CODE
  0 - SALE      5 - PAYMENT          ============
  1 - FREIGHT   6 - CREDIT      CREDIT        -22.17
  2 - TAX       7 - RETURN           ============
  3 - SERV. CH. 8 - DISCOUNT
  4 - MISC. DB  9 - MISC CR
```

Figure 14–10 Customer Statement

Peachtree Software™, *Accounting Series* 40, *Apple II*™ *Edition*, Copyright 1980 Peachtree Software, Inc. Reprinted with permission.

HOWELL ENTERPRISES INC.
ACCOUNTS RECEIVABLE
DETAILED AGING REPORT
08/15/80

ACCOUNT	CUSTOMER NAME	PHONE	INVOICE	DUE DATE	CURRENT	1-30	31-60	OVER 60	TOTAL	OPEN CR
ADCOCK	ADCOCK BUSINESS PRODUCTS	(404)255-9999	812	6/ 3/80			130.81	26.92		
			884	6/27/80						
					0.00	0.00	130.81	26.92	157.73	0.00
DAVIS	DAVIS TEMPORARIES, INC.	(404)394-6666	----	7/30/80					3316.89	
EVER	EVERREADY HARDWARE CO.	(404)939-8888	1030	7/10/80		27.50	21.47			
			1066	7/22/80		22.76				
			1245	8/14/80						
					0.00	50.26	21.47	0.00	71.73	0.00
FGINS	FANNING & GULF INS. CO.	(404)238-1212	1260	8/19/80	36.39					
					36.39	0.00	0.00	0.00	71.73	0.00
GWIN	GWINETT LUMBER SUPPLY	(404)262-2555	0	7/ 8/72						-20.13
			1263	8/20/80	36.75					
			1275	8/24/80	102.98					
					139.73	0.00	0.00	0.00	139.73	-20.13
ING	INGLES, MARKHAM, & DADE	(404)634-1555	----	8/ 9/80					582.72	
LMR	LANCE MOTOR REPAIRS	(404)237-2323	----	8/ 7/80					2263.30	
PACK	PACKETT & SONS	(404)634-6666	----	7/30/80					162.58	
PDI	PEAVY DIST., INC.	(404)233-7777	0	8/ 5/80	90.00					
			1000	7/30/80		90.00				
			1219	8/ 5/80		33.49				
			1236	8/11/80		39.95				
			1395	8/29/80						-90.00
					90.00	163.44	0.00	0.00	253.44	-90.00
RIGHT	RIGHTMOVE MOVERS	(404)763-3333	1084	7/28/80		36.36				
			1242	8/13/80		365.25				
					0.00	401.62	0.00	0.00	401.62	0.00
SAN	SANTINI & ASSOCIATES	(404)633-5555	1206	4/ 2/79				48.90		
			1251	8/16/80	38.95					
			1271	8/22/80	39.98					
			1292	8/29/80						-150.00
					78.93	0.00	0.00	48.90	127.83	-150.00

Figure 14–11 Detailed Aging Report

Peachtree Software™, *Accounting Series 40, Apple II*™ *Edition*, Copyright 1980 Peachtree Software, Inc. Reprinted with permission.

ure 14–11) or a summary (not shown here) aging schedule. A *transaction report* (not shown here) also lists the customer ID, all invoices for that customer, and up to ten possible debit and credit categories that can be tailored to each user. Finally, a *customer report* is available which summarizes in one line the account ID, customer name, address, phone, account type, and balance.

This particular microcomputer software package also has an end-of-month processing system that accumulates the necessary data to be transferred to the general ledger and removes paid invoices from the system to prepare for a new month's processing. This program creates a data diskette for the next month, allowing the current diskette to be retained for history and backup. If it is the end of the year, all records are prepared for year-end processing. Moreover, a *general ledger transfer file* is created on the new diskette and printed on paper. This provides the basis for the automatic transfer to the general ledger, which will be detailed later in this chapter. To accomplish this, the *system setup* program for this package requires the following account numbers for the general ledger: sales, freight, sales tax, service charges, miscellaneous debits, payments, credits, returns, discounts, miscellaneous credits, and accounts receivable.

In addition to the above program and controls, a series of error messages such as "invalid entry," "customer does not exist," and "systems error (6)" are built into the system to edit the input of data and file maintenance procedures.

Procedures and reports found in other, larger, accounts receivable systems may include cash management, credit inquiry, exception reports, dunning letters, automatic collection correspondence, and cash forecasting. (Several of these features, along with more comprehensive files, were discussed in Chapter 13.)

Accounts Payable System

A basic set of minimum capabilities for an accounts payable system to provide management with reporting, transaction processing, and decision-making information includes the following:

1. Vendor file maintenance (additions, deletions, and changes) procedures
2. Records listing procedure
3. Vendor status query
4. Vendor entry procedures
5. Procedures for determining which vendor to pay
6. Check printing and check register preparation procedures
7. Reporting procedures for
   a. Open voucher report
   b. Accounts payable aging report
   c. Cash forecast requirements
8. Automatic interface with the general ledger
9. Control procedures such as
   a. Automatic file backup once a month
   b. Recovery routines for hardware breakdowns
   c. Interactive menu-driven system
   d. Self-instructing documentation

   e. Editing and error procedures
   f. Control reports
   g. Transaction listings (logs)

The Peachtree Software™ system illustrated here for the Apple II™ computer is widely used and has these attributes. Figure 14–12 describes this system's flow of transactions, processing procedures, and reports.

The accounts payable system shown in Figure 14–12 maintains a record for each vendor setup using the *vendor maintenance* program. The *vendor file* consists of the following data:

Vendor code (up to six alphanumeric characters) and name
Address and phone

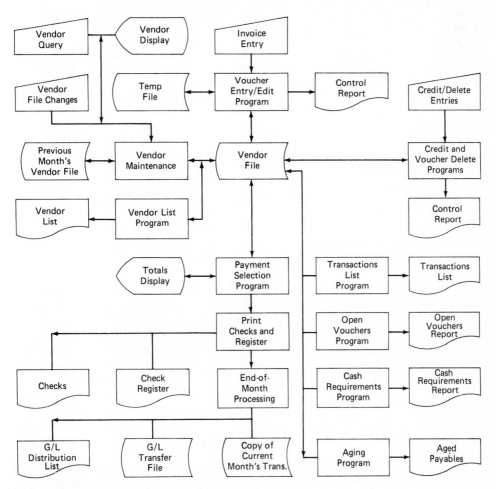

Figure 14–12 Accounts Payable System Flow

Peachtree Software™, *Accounting Series 40, Apple II™ Edition*, Copyright 1980 Peachtree Software, Inc. Reprinted with permission.

Detailed voucher record

Year-to-date purchases and payments

Current balance

Last payment date and amount

Monthly entry flag

Due date of month

Debit account number

Amount (debit)

Month last paid

Information for automatic payment of voucher such as rent and bank payments

This program is also used to add, delete, change, and query data. No vendor can be deleted until all vouchers in that vendor's record have been paid and removed from the system. Figure 14–13 illustrates the *vendor query* report (only the display option is shown in Figure 14–12). The vendor query is used by management for daily decision making and communication with the vendor. A *vendor list* program is also available.

Invoices are entered into the system through a *voucher entry* program. From this a temporary *voucher record* is set up which contains the following:

Voucher code

Voucher date

Amount and date due

Discount percent, amount, and date

Invoice number (vendors in most cases) and date

Status

General ledger account number and account fields (up to six) for account distribution

This program permits the user to enter both automatic (regular monthly payments) vouchers and voucher information from invoices as they are received from vendors. These vouchers (up to ninety-nine) are stored in a temporary file on a disk. The menu system requests the data above for each entry. A provision is available for prepaid invoices. No data are actually entered into the system until the user reviews the entire entry for each voucher and indicates that it is correct. A control report (transaction log) is available and is recommended.

Two other programs are provided for special handling of vouchers. The *credit entry* program allows the user to apply credit either against a specific open voucher or to a vendor record for a voucher already paid and removed from the system. When the first happens, the amount due for that invoice is reduced. If the *end-of-month* program has been run, this cannot be done. In this case the user gets an error message and must enter the transaction as an open credit to the vendor's record, which will be applied against the total due the vendor the next time a check is prepared for that vendor. The other special

HOWELL ENTERPRISES, INC.
ACCOUNTS PAYABLE
QUERY VENDOR
08/31/80

VENDOR ID	NAME / ADDRESS	PHONE	AMOUNTS	LAST CHECK
ANDER	ANDERSON OFFICE EQUIPMENT 4889 INDUSTRIAL COURT EAST POINT, GA. 30303	404-262-2555	YTD PURCH: $16,633.88 YTD PAYMT: $7,600.00 CURR. BAL.: $9,033.88	NO.: 753 AMT.: $7,600.00 DATE: 07/25/80

INVOICE NUMBER / DATE	AMOUNT DUE / DATE DUE	DISCOUNT AMOUNT / DATE	ACCOUNT - AMOUNT	ACCOUNT - AMOUNT	AUTO VOUCHER ENTRY ACCOUNT - AMOUNT	TAKEN	PAY
10016 08/05/80	$4,025.12 09/05/80	$80.50 08/15/80	41101 $4,000.00 $0.00	42101 $25.12 $0.00	$0.00 $0.00	NO	NO
10022 08/03/80	$5,008.76 09/03/80	$100.18 08/13/80	41102 $4,950.00 $0.00	42102 $58.76 $0.00	$0.00 $0.00	NO	YES

VENDOR ID	NAME / ADDRESS	PHONE	AMOUNTS	LAST CHECK
NATWID	NATION-SIDE DISTRIBUTORS 696 BOULDER CREEK ROAD LYNWOOD, CA 90262	213-820-1948	YTD PURCH: $29,020.27 YTD PAYMT: $3,000.00 CURR. BAL.: $26,020.27	NO.: 766 AMT.: $3,000.00 DATE: 07/25/80

INVOICE NUMBER / DATE	AMOUNT DUE / DATE DUE	DISCOUNT AMOUNT / DATE	ACCOUNT - AMOUNT	ACCOUNT - AMOUNT	AUTO VOUCHER ENTRY ACCOUNT - AMOUNT	TAKEN	PAY
XY0076 08/01/80	$5,013.95 09/01/80	$100.28 08/11/80	41101 $4,086.38 $0.00	42101 $927.57 $0.00	$0.00 $0.00	NO	YES
XY0078 08/03/80	$4,000.00 09/03/80	$80.00 08/13/80	41102 $4,000.00 $0.00	$0.00 $0.00	$0.00 $0.00	NO	NO
XY0065 07/05/80	$2,088.99 08/05/80	$41.78 07/15/80	41101 $2,088.99 $0.00	$0.00 $0.00	$0.00 $0.00	NO	YES
XY0080 08/07/80	$8,095.33 09/07/80	$161.91 08/17/80	41101 $3,095.95 41102 $3,095.95	42101 $951.72 $0.00	42102 $951.71 $0.00	NO	NO

Figure 14-13 Vendor Query

Peachtree Software™, *Accounting Series 40, Apple II™ Edition*, Copyright 1980 Peachtree Software, Inc. Reprinted with permission.

voucher-handling program is the *vendor delete* program. This enables the user to remove vouchers that are no longer valid from the system. This program deletes all the data from the records and adjusts the year-to-date purchase and current balance fields accordingly. This must be done prior to running the end-of-month program. Management has the option in the system to prevent the use of this program and to generate an error message if it is inadvertently used. With both of these programs, optional control reports are available for an audit trail.

Three report programs are available to assist management in its decisions regarding which vendors to pay and how much to pay. These three reports also assist the user in cash management, which is so critical in today's business environment. The first of these is the *open voucher* report illustrated in Figure 14–14. This program lists all open vouchers in the system. As can be seen in Figure 14–14, this report will indicate the voucher number and date, due date and amount, discount date and amount, net due, and whether the voucher has been marked by the *pay selection* program to be paid. For each open voucher, a second useful report may be generated. This is the *cash requirement* report illustrated in Figure 14–15. The report can be printed by due date or by available discount date. In both cases vouchers will be ordered by their respective dates (either due or discount date).

An *aged payables* report is also available. After the user selects an effective aging date, vendors are listed by their ID (alphabetical or numerical) order. For each vendor, payables that are current, and aged 1 to 30, 31 to 60, 61 to 90, and over 90 days, credits and total net due are printed. Totals are also printed for each category.

After analyzing these reports and cash availability, management can then select the vendors to pay using the *payment selection* program. This program allows the user to (1) select a specific vendor, or vendors, to be paid (as indicated above) or (2) pay all vouchers within a specific due or discount date. If the automatic mode is used, all the vendors with the range from today's date to either the specified date or the discount date are marked to be paid. Upon completion of this marking process, the following totals are displayed to make sure sufficient cash is on hand to pay the vouchers: vouchers marked to pay, applied open credit, and cash requirement total. Unused open credit is also noted. At this juncture the user can elect to (1) scan all vendors in ID order to make payment adjustments (mark more or fewer vouchers to be paid), (2) scan specific vendors and make adjustments, or (3) end, upon which the user can print an *open voucher* report for review. For options 1 and 2, the cash requirements total will automatically be updated and displayed for management's use. When the payment decision is made for specific vouchers, the menu system will display each voucher. Only those vouchers or vendors (all vouchers) marked to be paid will be paid when checks are printed.

After the payment selection program has been run, the *print checks* and *register* program can be run. A check will be printed listing all vouchers paid by this check. The user has the option of printing check registers upon completion of the check-printing program (see Figure 14–16).

A *transaction list* program can be run at any time to provide a listing (log) of all transactions processed in this accounting period. The list is by vendor ID code (see Figure 14–17). After this, a listing of general ledger distribu-

HOWELL ENTERPRISES, INC.
ACCOUNTS PAYABLE
OPEN VOUCHERS
08/31/80

VENDOR ID	VOUCHER DATE	INVOICE NUMBER	INVOICE DATE	DUE AMOUNT	DUE DATE	DISCOUNT AMOUNT	DISCOUNT DATE	NET	PAY?
ANDER	08/31/80	10016	08/05/80	$4,025.12	09/05/80	$80.50	08/15/80	$3,944.62	NO
	08/31/80	10022	08/03/80	$5,008.76	09/03/80	$100.18	08/13/80	$4,908.58	YES
				$9,033.88		$180.68		$8,853.20	
ARMOND	08/31/80	A10034	08/10/80	$14,378.20	09/10/80	$287.56	08/20/80	$14,090.64	NO
	08/31/80	A10056	08/10/80	$3,576.59	09/10/80	$71.53	08/20/80	$3,505.06	NO
				$17,954.79		$359.09		$17,595.70	
BANKS	08/31/80	AB102	08/01/80	$350.00	09/01/80			$350.00	NO
BARNES	08/31/80		08/07/80	$900.00	08/17/80			$900.00	YES
	08/31/80	B#3384	08/02/80	$14,793.58	09/02/80	$295.87	08/17/80	$14,497.71	NO
	08/31/80	B#3738	08/15/80	$7,503.64	09/15/80	$150.07	08/30/80	$7,353.57	NO
	08/31/80			-$111.00	08/31/80			-$111.00	
				$23,086.22		$445.94		$22,640.28	
COHN	08/31/80	264	08/20/80	$5,000.00	09/20/80	$100.00	08/30/80	$4,900.00	NO
	08/31/80	1287	08/31/80	$4,436.73	09/30/80	$88.73	09/15/80	$4,348.00	NO
				$9,436.73		$188.73		$9,248.00	

Figure 14–14 Open Voucher Report

Peachtree Software™, *Accounting Series 40*, *Apple II*™ *Edition*, Copyright 1980 Peachtree Software, Inc. Reprinted with permission.

HOWELL ENTERPRISES, INC.
ACCOUNTS PAYABLE
CASH REQUIREMENTS
08/31/80

** DATA SORTED BY DUE DATE

PAY DATE	VENDOR	INVOICE NUMBER	INV. DATE	AMOUNT	DISCOUNT	NET	DAILY TOTAL	REQ. TO DATE
08/01/80	MENSER		07/01/80	$900.00	$0.00	$900.00	$900.00	$900.00
08/15/80	WALLST		08/01/80	$100.00	$0.00	$100.00	$100.00	$1,000.00
08/30/80	FRTSC		08/15/80	$4,250.73	$0.00	$4,250.73		
	GOFORT	CD1101	08/15/80	$2,108.59	$0.00	$2,108.59	$6,359.32	$7,359.32
09/01/80	BANKS	AB102	08/01/80	$350.00	$0.00	$350.00	$350.00	$7,709.32
09/02/80	BARNES	B#3384	08/02/80	$14,793.58	$295.87	$14,497.71	$14,497.71	$22,207.03
09/03/80	NATWID	XY0078	08/03/80	$4,000.00	$80.00	$3,920.00	$3,920.00	$26,127.03

Figure 14–15 Cash Requirement Report

Peachtree Software™, *Accounting Series 40, Apple II*™ *Edition*, Copyright 1980 Peachtree Software, Inc. Reprinted with permission.

HOWELL ENTERPRISES, INC.
ACCOUNTS PAYABLE
CHECK REGISTER
08/31/80

VENDOR ID	VENDOR NAME	CHECK NUMBER	CHECK DATE	NUMBER	I N V O I C E DATE	AMOUNT	DISCOUNT	NET / TOTAL
ANDER	ANDERSON OFFICE EQUIPMENT	900	08/31/80	10022	08/31/80	$5,058.76	$0.00	$5,058.76
				CREDITS ON ABOVE	INVOICE=	$50.00	$0.00	-$50.00
					TOTAL THIS CHECK =			$5,008.76
BARNES	BARNES EQUIPMENT COMPANY	901	08/31/80		08/31/80	$900.00	$0.00	$900.00
					08/31/80	-$111.00	$0.00	-$111.00
					TOTAL THIS CHECK =			$789.00
NATWID	NATION-WIDE DISTRIBUTORS	902	08/31/80	XY0076	08/31/80	$5,013.95	$0.00	$5,013.95
				XY0065	08/31/80	$2,088.99	$0.00	$2,088.99
					08/31/80	-$178.00	$0.00	-$178.00
					TOTAL THIS CHECK =			$6,924.94
				NUMBER OF CHECKS WRITTEN	3	TOTAL CHECKS WRITTEN =		$12,722.70

Figure 14-16 Check Register

Peachtree Software™, *Accounting Series 40, Apple II™ Edition*, Copyright 1980 Peachtree Software, Inc. Reprinted with permission.

HOWELL ENTERPRISES, INC.
ACCOUNTS PAYABLE
TRANSACTION REGISTER
08/31/80

TRANSACTION LIST

VENDOR	INVOICE NUMBER	INVOICE DATE	DEBIT ACCT.	DISTRIBUTION AMOUNT	CREDIT ENTERED VOUCHERS	DEBIT PAYMENTS	CREDIT DISCOUNTS TAKEN	CREDIT CASH
ANDER	10016	08/05/80	41101	$4,000.00				
			42101	$25.12	$4,025.12			
	10022	08/03/80	41102	$4,950.00				
			42102	$58.76	$5,058.76			
	CREDIT ON ABOVE	08/03/80			-$50.00			
	CK. NO. 900	08/31/80				$5,008.76	$0.00	$5,008.76
ARMOND	A10034	08/10/80	41101	$7,525.50				
			42102	$189.11				
			42102	$188.34				
			41102	$6,475.25	$14,378.20			
	A10056	08/10/80	41102	$3,028.14				
			42102	$548.45	$3,576.59			
BANKS	AB102	08/01/80	52100	$350.00	$350.00			
BARNES		08/07/80	53300	$900.00	$900.00			
	B#3384	08/02/80	41101	$14,000.00				
			42101	$793.58	$14,793.58			
	B#3496	08/07/80	41102	$2,800.00				
			42102	$31.95	$2,831.95			
	PRE-PAID VOUCHER	08/07/80				$2,831.95	$56.64	$2,775.31
	B#3738	08/15/80	41101	$3,522.25				
			42101	$355.55				
			42102	$239.26				
			41102	$3,386.58	$7,503.64			
			20100	-$111.00	-$111.00			
	CK. NO. 901	08/31/80				$789.00	$0.00	$789.00

Figure 14-17 Transaction List
Peachtree Software™, *Accounting Series 40, Apple II™ Edition*, Copyright 1980 Peachtree Software, Inc. Reprinted with permission.

```
                          HOWELL ENTERPRISES, INC.
                             ACCOUNTS PAYABLE
                           TRANSACTION REGISTER
                               08/31/80
                                                              PAGE   3
                      GENERAL LEDGER TRANSACTION REGISTER

ACCOUNT NUMBER   DATE       DESCRIPTION     SC      DEBIT         CREDIT
--------------   --------   ----------------  --   ------------   ------------

     20100      08/31/80                    A                      $289.00
     21300      08/31/80                    A     $4,250.73
     21400      08/31/80                    A     $2,108.59
     41101      08/31/80                    A    $60,658.10
     41102      08/31/80                    A    $48,974.94
     42101      08/31/80                    A     $3,551.79
     42102      08/31/80                    A     $2,565.22
     52100      08/31/80                    A       $450.00
     53300      08/31/80                    A       $900.00
     20100      08/31/80   ENTERED VOUCHERS A                    $123,170.37
     20100      08/31/80   PAYMENTS         A    $29,554.65
     10200      08/31/80   CASH             A                     $29,218.01
     20100      08/31/80   DISCOUNTS TAKEN  A                        $336.64
                                                 ------------   ------------
                                    TOTAL    $153,014.02   $153,014.02
```

Figure 14–18   Transaction Transfer Register

Peachtree Software™, *Accounting Series* 40, *Apple II™ Edition*, Copyright 1980 Peachtree Software, Inc. Reprinted with permission.

tions by account number is printed (see Figure 14–18). This listing, coupled with the end-of-month automatic disk copying procedure, provides good record security and a valuable audit trail. The files can be reconstructed through the time of the last listing.

Finally, the *end-of-month* program accumulates the debit and credit transactions and prints a transfer register like the one in Figure 14–18. If the general ledger system (described later in this chapter) is available, a temporary file is set up for later transfer. This program removes all paid vouchers from the system. It also creates a backup diskette of the current month's transactions before removing them from the system. If it is year-end, the year-to-date purchase and payment fields will be cleared. As with the *accounts receivable system*, this system has data-entry controls for invalid entries.

Larger *accounts payable systems* would have provisions for additional reports for management, such as check reconciliation, 1099 report information, other tax reports, and more-detailed and longer-term vendor history.

Inventory Management System

Businesses have many needs, and management information requirements vary a great deal with respect to inventory. Generally speaking, however, the essential requirements can be met by a system that has the following capabilities:

1. Inventory file maintenance system (add, delete, and change)
2. Listing procedure
3. Sales, receipts, returns, and adjustment procedures

4. Procedures for
   a. Detailed inventory status reports
   b. Department summary reports
   c. Reorder report
   d. Year-to-date and month-to-date reports
   e. Physical inventory worksheet reports
   f. Inventory price lists
5. On-line query
6. Multiple pricing levels
7. Control procedures such as
   a. Automatic file backup
   b. Recovery routines for hardware failure
   c. Interactive menu-driven system for input editing
   d. Self-instructing documentation
   e. Editing and error procedures
   f. Transaction entry log

Because of their unique requirements, many businesses cannot use an inventory software package. The Peachtree Software™ system for the Apple II™, however, at least has the attributes listed above and is a good example of the type of package now available that can be used to provide basic inventory information for management decision-making needs. This system is illustrated in Figure 14–19 and can be described as follows.

All transactions are entered into a *master inventory record* through a *transaction entry* program or the *inventory maintenance* program. For transaction entry, the user selects the type of transaction: sales, returns, merchandise receipts, or adjustments. For a sale, the menu will require a valid department ID and a valid item ID, quantity, unit price (up to three may be used), and unit cost (entered automatically for standard cost option and defaults to average cost for average cost option). The program will calculate total price and total costs. The same information is required for a return. A receipt or adjustment only requires the ID (departmental and item), quantity, and cost data. A *control report* option is available and may be required by management when the program is initially set up. Figure 14–20 illustrates this control report and typical transaction data for the system. The *inventory maintenance* program gives the user the option of adding new inventory items, changing an existing record, deleting an existing record, modifying a field, or querying an existing record. The menu system requests all the following data, which constitute the inventory record for each item:

Department ID code (3 characters)
Item ID (15 characters)
Description
Units
Vendor ID
Vendor item number
Current average cost

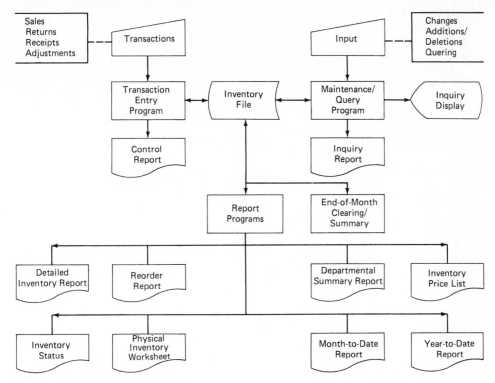

Figure 14–19 Inventory System Flow

Peachtree Software™, *Accounting Series* 40, *Apple II*™ *Edition*, Copyright 1980 Peachtree Software, Inc. Reprinted with permission.

> Last cost/item
> Prices A (normal price), B, and C
> Reorder level and quantity
> Last reorder date
> Period-to-date and year-to-date sales
> Period-to-date and year-to-date cost of goods sold
> Year-to-date number of units sold

In addition, the number of units sold, received, and returned and the adjustments for this period are entered. Changes and modifications are made by keying in the department and item ID, reviewing each field as it is displayed, and entering adjusted values. Control reports for an audit trail can be mandated by management or selected as an option for the inventory maintenance system. A query is simply made by entering the department and item IDs to display the desired information.

Several reports (some of which are illustrated) are available in this system for management's use in stock analysis, maintenance, and forecasting. The first is the *detailed inventory* report shown in Figure 14–21, which is a complete listing of the master file for all items or by department. This report can be ei-

HOWELL ENTERPRISES INC.
INVENTORY MANAGEMENT
ENTER TRANSACTIONS

DATE	T/C	DEPT-ITEM ID	P C	TRANSACTION QUANTITY	SALES AMOUNT	CA LC	COMMENT	EFFECT ON INV. QTY.	EFFECT ON INV. VALUE	WARNING MESSAGE
8/28/80	SAL	BDR-12000HEA	H	1.00	199.99		FULL PRICE	1.00-	92.00-	
8/28/80	SAL	LVR-10030OTT	L	2.00	253.32		DISC	2.00-	180.00-	
8/28/80	SAL	MIS-10000VAS	M	2.00	50.00			2.00-	17.00-	
8/28/80	SAL	MIS-10020PIC	M	1.00	99.00		10% DISC	1.00-	48.00-	
8/28/80	SAL	DNR-10050PED	T	1.00	800.00		FULL PRICE	1.00-	360.00-	
8/28/80	RET	BDR-10000TWI	C	1.00	87.99-		NOT NEEDED	1.00	40.00	
8/28/80	RED	BDR-12020HEA	H	1.00	229.99-		RET SCRATCH	1.00	150.00	
8/28/80	ADJ	APP-10010REF	B	1.00				1.00	152.80	
8/28/80	SAL	BDR-12020HEA	H	1.00	224.99		REPLACE SALE	1.00-	150.00-	
8/28/80	SAL	DNR-1003OCHI	T	1.00	1100.00			1.00-	440.00-	
8/28/80	SAL	DNR-10020SIL	T	1.00	600.00			1.00-	399.00-	

SALE TOTALS					3,327.30			10.00	1,686.00-
RETURN TOTALS					317.98-			2.00	190.00
RECEIPT TOTALS								0.00	0.00
ADJUSTMENT TOTALS								1.00	152.80
GRAND TOTALS					3,009.32			7.00-	1,343.20-

*** END OF ENTER TRANSACTIONS ***

Figure 14–20 Transaction Control Report

Peachtree Software™, *Accounting Series 40, Apple II™ Edition*, Copyright 1980 Peachtree Software, Inc. Reprinted with permission.

HOWELL ENTERPRISES INC.
INVENTORY MANAGEMENT
DETAIL INVENTORY REPORT

DEPARTMENT DNR

ITEM ID : DNR-10000BUF	: DNR-10010MOB	: DNR-10020SIL	: DNR-10030CHI	: DNR-10040OVA	
PRODUCT CODE : T	: T	: T	: T	: T	
DESCRIPTION : BUFFET	: MOBILE SERVER	: SILVER CHEST	: CHINA CABINET	: OVAL TABLE	
UNITS : EA	: EA	: EA	: EA	: EA	
VENDOR ID : BASSET	: BASSET	: BASSET	: BASSET	: BROYHL	
VENDOR ITEM # : EAM110	: EAM510	: EAM560	: EAM420	: 752DN	
CURR AVG COST : 300.00000000	: 220.00000000	: 399.00000000	: 440.00000000	: 140.00000000	
LST COST/ITEM : 500.00	: 450.00	: 400.00	: 550.00	: 350.00	
PRICE A : 1000.00	: 900.00	: 800.00	: 1100.00	: 700.00	
PRICE B : 750.00	: 676.00	: 600.00	: 825.00	: 525.00	
PRICE C : 666.66	: 600.00	: 533.33	: 733.33	: 466.66	
REORDER LEVEL : 4.00	: 15.00	: 10.00	: 9.00	: 18.00	
REORDER QTY : 4.00	: 15.00	: 10.00	: 9.00	: 20.00	
RO REPRT DATE : 8/25/80	: 8/25/80	: 8/25/80	: 8/25/80	: 8/25/80	
YTLP $ SALES : 29653.75	: 7125.00	: 10850.00	: 130475.00	: 6200.00	
PTD $ SALES : 0.00	: 0.00	: 600.00	: 1100.00	: 0.00	
YTLP CST SOLD : 14500.63	: 3750.00	: 5099.00	: 62940.00	: 3041.00	
PTD CST SOLD : 0.00	: 0.00	: 399.00	: 440.00	: 0.00	
YTLP # SOLD : 34.00	: 11.00	: 17.00	: 31.00	: 10.00	
BEGINNING BAL : 14.00	: 4.00	: 14.00	: 9.00	: 3.00	
PTD # SOLD : 0.00	: 0.00	: 1.00	: 1.00	: 0.00	
PTD # RECVD : 0.00	: 0.00	: 0.00	: 0.00	: 0.00	
PTD # RETURNS : 0.00	: 0.00	: 0.00	: 0.00	: 0.00	
PTD # ADJMTS : 0.00	: 0.00	: 0.00	: 0.00	: 0.00	
BAL. ON HAND : 14.00	: 4.00	: 13.00	: 8.00	: 3.00	

ITEM ID : DNR-10050PED	
PRODUCT CODE : T	
DESCRIPTION : PEDESTAL TABLE	
UNITS : EA	
VENDOR ID : BROYHL	
VENDOR ITEM # : 772DN	
CURR AVG COST : 360.00000000	
LST COST/ITEM : 400.00	
PRICE A : 800.00	
PRICE B : 600.00	
PRICE C : 533.33	
REORDER LEVEL : 4.00	
REORDER QTY : 4.00	
RO REPRT DATE : 7/14/80	
YTLP $ SALES : 14400.00	
PTD $ SALES : 800.00	
YTLP CST SOLD : 7060.00	
PTD CST SOLD : 360.00	
YTLP # SOLD : 18.00	
BEGINNING BAL : 3.00	
PTD # SOLD : 1.00	
PTD # RECVD : 0.00	
PTD # RETURNS : 0.00	
PTD # ADJMTS : 0.00	
BAL. ON HAND : 2.00	

DEPARTMENT TOTALS
TOTAL VALUE: 14,927.00   NUMBER OF ITEMS: 6.00   NUMBER OF UNITS: 44.00

** END OF DEPARTMENT DNR **

Figure 14-21 Detail Inventory Report

Peachtree Software™, *Accounting Series 40, Apple II™ Edition*, Copyright 1980 Peachtree Software, Inc. Reprinted with permission.

ther displayed or printed or both. The second is the *reorder* report which lists in vendor number order all items whose in-stock quantity is below the reorder level. This will indicate to management which items to purchase. The third is the *inventory status* report shown in Figure 14–22, which indicates the basic item information plus the activity during the current period. A *physical inventory worksheet* is available which indicates the item number, description, vendor ID, vendor item number, and calculated book balance. Provision is made for both actual counts and comments. Again, the report can be produced by department. An *inventory price list* is available with a multiple pricing provision for marketing and selling decisions. The sixth report is the *departmental summary* shown in Figure 14–23. This report summarizes in one line the key statistics for each department, such as sales, investment, cost of sales, and margin. Finally, *month-to-date* and *year-to-date* activity reports are available which indicate for each item per department the units sold, the amount sold, the cost of goods sold, the cost of goods sold as a percent of sales, the margin, and the average selling price. The year-to-date report is shown in Figure 14–24.

The inventory system also has an *end-of-month* program to summarize, update current balances, and clear previous balances. No provision is made in this software to automatically update the general ledger at the end of the month because, to conserve space, no cumulative records are kept of all transactions. The control reports only list current transaction input. These entries originate in sales and purchasing. They can be reconciled with the month-to-date and year-to-date reports from the accounts receivable and accounts payable systems.

Larger systems often have provisions for manufacturing cost accounting systems, actual or standard costs, general ledger, accounts receivable, accounts payable, and payroll reconciliation as well as the capabilities discussed in Chapter 12.

Payroll System

As in the other three basic financial accounting systems discussed thus far in this chapter, it is difficult to specify a general payroll system because the needs and operating environments of businesses vary so much. A basic set of requirements may read as follows, however:

1. Employee file maintenance procedures (additions, deletions, and changes)
2. Listing procedures
3. Ability to modify tax information
4. Ability to support hourly, salaried, and commissioned pay types
5. Ability to support weekly, monthly, biweekly, and semimonthly pay periods
6. For each pay period
   a. Calculate pay
   b. Print checks
   c. Print payroll register

RUN DATE   8/29/80

HOWELL ENTERPRISES INC.
INVENTORY MANAGEMENT
INVENTORY STATUS REPORT

DEPARTMENT: BDR

ITEM NUMBER	DESCRIPTION	BEGINNING BALANCE	SALES	RETURNS	RECEIPTS	ADJMTS.	CURRENT BALANCE	CURRENT AVG. COST	TOTAL VALUATION
BDR-10000TWI	TWIN MATTRESS	1.00	0.00	1.00	0.00	0.00	2.00	40.000	80.00
BDR-10010TWI	TWIN FOUNDATION	11.00	0.00	0.00	0.00	0.00	11.00	45.000	495.00
BDR-10020TWI	TWIN SET	6.00	0.00	0.00	0.00	0.00	6.00	60.000	360.00
BDR-10040FUL	FULL MATTRESS	9.00	0.00	0.00	0.00	0.00	9.00	95.000	855.00
BDR-10050FUL	FULL FOUNDATION	7.00	0.00	0.00	0.00	0.00	7.00	78.830	551.81
BDR-10060FUl	FULL SET	13.00	0.00	0.00	0.00	0.00	13.00	90.000	1170.00
BDR-10070QUE	QUEEN SET	9.00	0.00	0.00	0.00	0.00	9.00	150.000	1350.00
BDR-10080KIN	KING SET	8.00	0.00	0.00	0.00	0.00	8.00	200.000	1600.00
BDR-11000BED	BED FRAME	11.00	0.00	0.00	0.00	0.00	11.00	39.000	429.00
BDR-12000HEA	HEADBOARD, 5'	5.00	3.00	0.00	0.00	0.00	2.00	92.000	184.00
BDR-12010HEA	HEADBOARD, 6'	13.00	0.00	0.00	0.00	0.00	13.00	112.790	1466.27
BDR-12020HEA	HEADBOARD, 6'6"	14.00	1.00	1.00	0.00	0.00	14.00	150.000	2100.00
BDR-12030HEA	HEADBOARD, 4'6"	9.00	0.00	0.00	0.00	0.00	9.00	89.530	805.77
BDR-12040HEA	HEADBOARD, 3'6"	6.00	0.00	0.00	0.00	0.00	6.00	80.000	480.00

DEPARTMENT BDR TOTALS   VALUE =   11,926,850   NUMBER OF ITEMS =   14   NUMBER OF UNITS =   120.00

*** END OF INVENTORY STATUS REPORT ***

Figure 14-22 Inventory Status Report

Peachtree Software™, *Accounting Series 40, Apple II™ Edition*, Copyright 1980 Peachtree Software, Inc. Reprinted with permission.

HOWELL ENTERPRISES INC.
INVENTORY MANAGEMENT
DEPARTMENTAL SUMMARY REPORT

DEPT	CURRENT INVENTORY VALUE	% TOTAL INVENTORY VALUE	YTD SALES AMOUNT	YTD SALES % TOTAL	COST OF SALES YTD AMOUNT	COST OF SALES % TOTAL	YTD MARGIN AMOUNT	% TOTAL MARGIN
APP	16526.24	29.65	57394.03	15.94	28945.32	16.46	28448.71	15.44
BDR	11926.85	21.40	49679.93	13.79	21396.87	12.17	28283.06	15.35
DNR	14927.00	26.78	201203.75	55.87	97589.63	55.49	103614.12	56.22
LVR	11604.00	20.82	48681.55	13.52	26404.61	15.01	22276.94	12.09
MIS	753.50	1.35	3195.45	0.89	1530.00	0.87	1665.45	0.90
GRAND TOTALS	55,737.59		360,154.71		175,866.43		184,288.28	

*** END OF DEPARTMENTAL SUMMARY REPORT ***

Figure 14-23 Departmental Summary Report.

Peachtree Software™, *Accounting Series 40, Apple II*™ *Edition*, Copyright 1980 Peachtree Software, Inc. Reprinted with permission.

RUN DATE 8/29/80

HOWELL ENTERPRISES, INC.
INVENTORY MANAGEMENT
YEAR-TO-DATE REPORT

DEPARTMENT BDR

ITEM ID	P C	DESCRIPTION	NET SALES UNITS	NET SALES AMOUNT	COST OF GOODS SOLD AMOUNT	COST OF GOODS SOLD % SALES	MARGIN AMOUNT	MARGIN % SALES	AVERAGE SELLING PRICE
BDR-10000TWI	C	TWIN MATTRESS	19.00	1604.93	170.00	10.59	1434.93	89.41	84.47
BDR-10010TWI	C	TWIN FOUNDATION	18.00	1516.43	135.00	8.90	1381.43	91.10	84.25
BDR-10020TWI	C	TWIN SET	3.00	437.97	340.00	77.63	97.97	22.37	145.99
BDR-10040FUL	C	FULL	16.00	1700.32	220.00	12.94	1480.32	87.06	106.27
BDR-10050FUL	C	FULL FOUNDATION	20.00	2172.28	183.33	8.44	1988.95	91.56	108.61
BDR-10060FUL	C	FULL SET	4.00	818.57	485.00	59.25	333.57	40.75	204.64
BDR-10070QUE	C	QUEEN SET	43.00	11748.62	5500.00	46.81	6248.62	53.19	273.22
BDR-10080KIN	C	KING SET	9.00	2352.93	1100.25	46.76	1252.68	53.24	261.44
BDR-11000BED	C	BED FRAME	50.00	2742.57	1425.00	51.96	1317.57	48.04	54.85
BDR-12000HEA	H	HEADBOARD, 5'	30.00	5399.70	2410.50	44.64	2989.20	55.36	179.99
BDR-12010HEA	H	HEADBOARD, 6'	11.00	10007.88	5001.79	49.98	5006.09	50.02	909.81
BDR-12020HEA	H	HEADBOARD, 6'6"	12.00	2724.88	1358.00	49.84	1366.88	50.16	227.07
BDR-12030HEA	H	HEADBOARD, 4'6"	20.00	4568.15	2159.00	47.26	2409.15	52.74	228.41
BDR-12040HEA	H	HEADBOARD, 3'6"	10.00	1884.70	909.00	48.23	975.70	51.77	188.47
DEPARTMENT BDR TOTALS				49,679.93	21,396.87	43.07	28,283.06	56.93	

*** END OF YEAR-TO-DATE REPORT ***

Figure 14-24 Year-to-Date Inventory Management Report

Peachtree Software™, *Accounting Series 40, Apple II™ Edition,* Copyright 1980 Peachtree Software, Inc. Reprinted with permission.

7. Monthly
   a. Print monthly summary
   b. Print unemployment tax report
   c. Prepare general ledger transfer file automatically
8. Distribute pay to several departments
9. Print 941-A at end of quarter
10. Print W–2 at end of year
11. User-generated or precomputed tax tables for state and local taxes
12. Control procedures such as
    a. Self-instructing user documentation
    b. Interactive, easy-to-use menu-driven programs
    c. Editing and error messages and procedures
    d. Check registers and numerical control over checks
    e. Hard copy backup via payroll register
    f. A disk backup system

The Peachtree Software™ package for the Apple II™ has these basic attributes and is illustrated in Figure 14–25. This particular software package maintains an *employee master file*, which contains the following data for each employee:

Name and address
Local and state codes
Marital status
Number of federal and state exemptions
Social Security number
Pay period, type, and rate
Insurance deductions
Miscellaneous deductions
Date employed and terminated
Last check information
Current, month-to-date, quarter-to-date, and year-to-date totals for
    Regular earnings
    Overtime hours and earnings
    Other hour rate and earnings
    Commission earnings
    Miscellaneous income
    FICA, federal, state, and local deductions
    Insurance and miscellaneous deductions

These records, along with a *tax file* containing federal, state, and local tax tables, are used to calculate the payroll, print checks, and prepare a basic set of payroll reports. The *employee maintenance* program is used to enter, delete, or change employee records. A deleted employee record is retained in the file until year-end. A menu system is used to edit entries. The same program is also used to *query* an employee record; personnel and current, month-to-date,

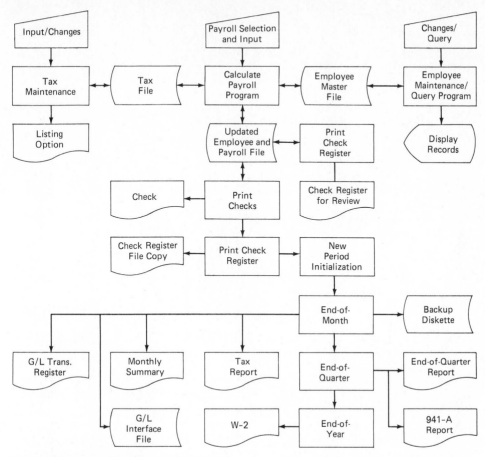

Figure 14–25 Payroll System

Peachtree Software™, *Accounting Series* 40, *Apple II™ Edition*, Copyright 1980 Peachtree Software, Inc. Reprinted with permission.

quarter-to-date, or year-to-date data may be queried. At any time an *employee* listing like the one illustrated in Figure 14–26 can be run. It can be used to print all employee information, personal information only, or personal information only for selected employees. A *tax maintenance* program allows the user to set up and maintain tax files for federal, state, and local withholding. Unemployment taxes and limits can also be set up for federal and state reporting. These are automatically calculated. The program has options for listing, creating new files, and updating tax files. Using the employee and tax files, the *calculate payroll* program is run for each pay period. The operator selects a weekly, biweekly, monthly, or semimonthly pay period. A "paid through" date is selected, and the operator indicates whether or not to pay a specific employee or all the employees. Provisions are available through the menu system to enter regular hours (different from standard), overtime hours, other and miscellaneous hours as well as commissions and miscellaneous income. This whole data-entry

HOWELL ENTERPRISES, INC.
PAYROLL SYSTEM
EMPLOYEE LIST
08/31/80

101/JMS MICHAEL S. JAMESON   MARITAL ST. =M   DATE EMP. =05/01/74   STATUS=A
        24 MAIN STREET   FED. EXEMPT =3   DATE TERM. =//0
        DECATUR, GA 30343   ST. EXEMPT =3   PAY PERIOD = S   PAY TYPE = S
        231-72-4343   CITY=00   ST. =10   PAY RATE = $760.000
CURRENT:HOURS OVERTIME OTHER DATE CHECK NO.   DEDUCTIONS:INSURANCE   MISC #1   MISC #2
        0   0   0   //0 $12.50 $1.50 $0.00

                  CURRENT   MONTH   QUARTER   YEAR
EARNINGS -REGULAR $0.00 $2,020.00 $2,020.00 $2,020.00
          -OVERTIME $0.00 $0.00 $0.00 $0.00
          -OTHER HRS. $0.00 $0.00 $0.00 $0.00
          -COMMISSIONS $0.00 $0.00 $0.00 $0.00
          -MISC. $0.00 $0.00 $0.00 $0.00
DEDUCTIONS-FICA $0.00 $122.21 $122.21 $122.21
          -FEDERAL $0.00 $252.05 $252.05 $252.05
          -STATE $0.00 $48.54 $48.54 $48.54
          -LOCAL $0.00 $0.00 $0.00 $0.00
          -INSURANCE $0.00 $37.50 $37.50 $37.50
          -MISC. #1 $0.00 $4.50 $4.50 $4.50
          -MISC. #2 $0.00 $0.00 $0.00 $0.00

Figure 14-26 Detailed Employee Listing

Peachtree Software™, *Accounting Series 40, Apple II™ Edition,* Copyright 1980 Peachtree Software, Inc. Reprinted with permission.

procedure is interactive and menu driven for editing and review of data completeness.

After the payroll has been calculated, the *print register* program *may* be run to review and verify all items that will appear on the employee's check. The *print check* program is then run. Preprinted and computer-assigned check numbers may be used for security. An example of the check and stub containing the deduction and pay information is shown in Figure 14–27. As in the preceding program, the operator selects the type of payroll and either specific or all employees. The operator enters the number to appear on the first check. After that the numbers are incremented. After the checks have been printed, the file copy of the payroll register is run (see Figure 14–28). On this run the check numbers will appear. Totals are accumulated by department, and grand totals are calculated. The payroll register should be saved and filed in a safe place for backup of payroll records.

Following this, the *new period initialization* program may be run. This is done only after the operator is certain that all checks have been correctly printed. Management may even adopt a policy of not running the program until right before the calculate payroll program is run for the next pay period. This program adds current information to the month, quarter, and year-to-date fields and clears the current information by setting up the employee records for a new pay period. Again, the type of payroll is selected for processing.

At the end of the month, the *end-of-month* program is run. This program produces several reports (not shown here). A *monthly summary* lists total active and inactive employees and total dollars in month, quarter, and year-to-date fields for all earning and deduction classifications. An *unemployment tax report* is prepared. Finally, a *general ledger transaction register* listing all general ledger journal entries is printed. A file is created for automatic transfer of the general ledger posting journal entries if the company's system uses the general ledger system described in the following section. Moreover, a diskette is created as a backup in the process of running this program. Here the monthly fields are cleared.

In addition to these reports, an *end-of-quarter* program is used to prepare an end-of-quarter payroll listing by employee. A 941 tax report is also prepared. Here the quarter-to-date fields are cleared. Finally, an *end-of-year* program clears year-to-date fields and prints an employee W–2 form. This program also purges the file of inactive employees.

As in the other systems, data-entry controls with appropriate error messages are present to prevent the user from making a variety of entry errors, such as nonexistent employee numbers and invalid pay codes. Larger payroll systems may have some additional provisions such as direct bank deposits, check reconciliation, labor cost distribution, vacation accrual, time card reconciliation, and more earnings history.

General Ledger System

The most widely used financial accounting system is the basic general ledger system. Following are some basic requirements of such a system:

1. Flexible chart of accounts designed for varied business needs
2. Provisions for adding, deleting, and changing master file records

101JMS

MICHAEL S. JAMESON

	--HOURS WORKED--		------YOU EARNED------		
--YOUR--					
PAY RATE	REGULAR	PREMIUM	REGULAR	PREMIUM	OTHER	***GROSS***
760.000	0.0	0.0	760.00	0.00	0.00	760.00

--GOVERNMENT TAX DEDUCTIONS--				--OTHER DEDUCTIONS--		
FICA	FEDERAL	STATE	LOCAL	INSUR.	MISC 1	MISC 2	****NET***
46.59	96.78	20.52	0.00	12.50	1.50	0.00	582.11

	--------YEAR TO DATE TOTALS--------			
PAID THRU	EARNINGS	FICA	FEDERAL	STATE	LOCAL
08/31/80	2,780.00	168.80	348.83	69.06	0.00

No.   3002

| DATE | AMOUNT |
| 08/31/80 | ****$582.11 |

**** FIVE HUNDRED EIGHTY TWO & 11 /100 DOLLARS

V O I D

PAY
TO THE
ORDER   MICHAEL S. JAMESON
OF   24 MAIN STREET
           DECATUR, GA 30343

Figure 14-27 Sample Check

Peachtree Software™, *Accounting Series 40, Apple II*™ *Edition,* Copyright 1980 Peachtree Software, Inc. Reprinted with permission.

HOWELL ENTERPRISES, INC.
PAYROLL SYSTEM
PRINT REGISTER
08/31/80

101JMS   MICHAEL S. JAMESON   TYPE=S   RATE= 760.00

---HOURS---	---EARNINGS-		------DEDUCTIONS------		---TOTALS---
REG= 0.000	REG= 760.00	FIC= 46.59	INS= 12.50	EARN= 760.00
OT = 0.000	OT = 0.00	FED= 96.78	MI1 1.50	DEDU= 177.89
OH = 0.000	OH = 0.00	STA= 20.52	MI2= 0.00	
	COM= 0.00	CIT= 0.00		
	MIS= 0.00			

CHECK NUMBER: 3002
CHECK AMOUNT: 582.11

101ZKD   KAREN D. ZAMANGIL   TYPE=S   RATE= 350.00

---HOURS---	---EARNINGS-		------DEDUCTIONS------		---TOTALS---
REG= 0.000	REG= 350.00	FIC= 21.46	INS= 4.00	EARN= 350.00
OT = 0.000	OT = 0.00	FED= 43.25	MI1= 1.50	DEDU= 76.88
OH = 0.000	OH = 0.00	STA= 6.67	MI2= 0.00	
	COM= 0.00	CIT= 0.00		
	MIS= 0.00			

CHECK NUMBER: 3003
CHECK AMOUNT: 273.12

*** TOTALS - DEPARTMENT 101

---EARNINGS---	------DEDUCTIONS------		---TOTALS---
REG 1,110.00	FIC 68.05	INS 16.50	EARN 1,110.00
OT 0.00	FED 140.03	MI1 3.00	DEDU 254.77
OH 0.00	STA 27.19	MI2 0.00	
COM 0.00	CIT 0.00		
MIS 0.00			

TOTAL CHECKS (NET) :   855.23

Figure 14-28 Payroll Register

Peachtree Software™, *Accounting Series 40, Apple II™ Edition*, Copyright 1980 Peachtree Software, Inc. Reprinted with permission.

3. Listing provision for chart of accounts
4. A transaction file (log)
5. Listing provision for transaction file
6. Automatic interface (entries) during end-of-period processing of other systems, such as accounts receivable, accounts payable, and payroll
7. Reports
   a. Trial balance
   b. Transaction register
   c. Departmental accounting
   d. Comparative financial statement
   e. Budgeting provision for financial planning
8. Control procedures
   a. Interactive menu system
   b. Self-instructing documentation
   c. Control reports for audit trail (transaction log)
   d. Automatic month-end file backup
   e. Data-entry error messages and control
   f. Recovery routines for hardware failure
   g. Automatic interface with other systems

The Peachtree Software™ General Ledger System is a good example of a system that has these characteristics. Figure 14–29 outlines the various file-updating and report-generating procedures of the system. The general ledger system operates with a G/L account file and a transaction file. The *G/L account file* consists of

Account number, description, and type

Balance sheet format code

Current and year-to-date amount

Budget and prior year monthly amounts for comparison

The *transaction file* of journal entries consists of

Account number and description

Source code and reference

Date and amount

The accounts contained in the account file are queried, updated, changed, and deleted through the *account maintenance* program. Provisions are made for budget amounts and monthly comparisons with the preceding year. Moreover, provisions are made for formatting the balance sheets through the type of account code. The types are (1) title account, (2) detail posting accounts (only these will accept journal entries), and (3) level indicators used for subtotals and totals. An account can be specified as a master or a subsidiary account. At any time any account may be queried by management. To list these files, the *master file list* program is run, and a listing such as that shown in Figure 14–30 is printed. Provisions are available to list only report formatting in-

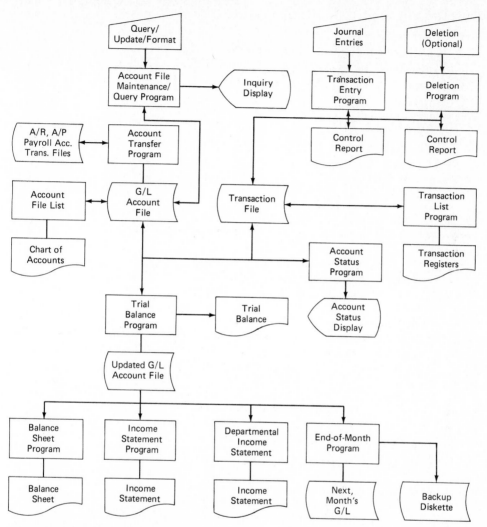

Figure 14–29 General Ledger System

Peachtree Software™, *Accounting Series* 40, *Apple II*™ *Edition*, Copyright 1980 Peachtree Software, Inc. Reprinted with permission.

formation and to extend the list to include dollar amounts for the twelve previous months for trend and seasonal analysis.

Journal entries are added to the transaction file through a *transaction entry* program. They are stored in a temporary file on the disk. After entry has been completed, the temporary file is edited for valid account numbers and is then used to update the general ledger master file. A control report listing of each transaction is available. Once entered on the master file it cannot be changed. Transactions can, however, be reversed and deleted through the *transaction delete* program. It is good policy to reverse the entry and not delete it

HOWELL ENTERPRISES, INC.
GENERAL LEDGER
MASTER FILE LIST
08/31/80

PAGE 1

ACCOUNT	DESCRIPTION	TYP	M/S	COL	CURRENT	Y-T-D	BUDGET
100	ASSETS	1		1			
10009	CURRENT ASSETS	1		1			
101	CASH	2	M	1			
102	CASH - OPERATING	2	S	1	655.42	2,835.56	0.00
109	CASH ON HAND	2	S	1	0.00	150.00	0.00
111	ACCOUNTS RECEIVABLE	2		1	10,070.20	37,441.45	0.00
121	PREPAID EXPENSES	2		1	0.00	490.00	0.00
131	INVENTORY	2		1	0.00	19,731.99	0.00
170	TOTAL CURRENT ASSETS	4		2			
17009	FIXED ASSETS	1		1			
171	FURNITURE & EQUIPMENT	2		1	0.00	4,255.37	0.00
172	ACCUMULATED DEPRECIATION	2		1	-180.40	-966.40	0.00
180	DEPOSITS	2		1	0.00	750.00	0.00
198	TOTAL FIXED ASSETS	5		2			
199	TOTAL ASSETS	6		3			
200	LIABILITIES & CAPITAL	1		1			
20009	CURRENT LIABILITIES	1		1			
201	ACCOUNTS PAYABLE	2		1	-2,046.56	-7,650.11	0.00
210	TAXES PAYABLE	2	M	1			
211	EMPLOYEE TAXES PAYABLE	2	S	1	-127.60	-759.95	0.00
212	FEDERAL TAX APYABLE	2	S	1	-374.30	-1,756.51	0.00
213	STATE TAX PAYABLE	2	S	1	-74.28	-304.14	0.00
214	SALES TAX PAYABLE	2	S	1	-239.12	-1,143.08	0.00
250	TOTAL CURR LIABILITIES	4		2			
251	NOTE PAYABLE-BANK	2		1	800.00	-1,600.00	0.00
289	TOTAL LONG TERM LIAB	4		2			
290	TOTAL LIABILITIES	6		3			
291	CAPITAL STOCK	2		2	0.00	-25,000.00	0.00
296	RETAINED EARNINGS	2		2	0.00	-8,773 26	0.00
297	CURRENT EARNINGS	2		2	0.00	0.00	0.00
298	TOTAL CAPITAL	6		3			
299	TOTAL LIAB & CAPITAL	8		3			
300	INCOME	1		1			
301	SALES	2	M	1			
30101	SALES	2	S	1	-11,618.00	-34,854.00	-208,100.00
30102	SALES	2	S	1	-5,647.00	-9,180.00	-203,100.00
311	SERVICE	2	M	1			
31101	SERVICE	2	S	1	0.00	0.00	-14,100.00
31102	SERVICE	2	S	1	0.00	0.00	-15,100.00
321	RETURNS & ALLOWANCES	2	M	1			
32101	RETURNS & ALLOWANCES	2	S	1	0.00	0.00	2,800.00
32102	RETURNS & ALLOWANCES	2	S	1	0.00	0.00	3,100.00
399	NET SALES	4		1			
400	COST OF GOODS SOLD	1		1			
411	COST OF SALES - PURCHASES	2	M	1			
41101	COST OF SALES - PURCHASES	2	S	1	1,560.32	4,680.96	212,000.00
41102	COST OF SALES - PURCHASES	2	S	1	2,008.00	6,024.00	216,700.00
421	FREIGHT	2	M	1			
42101	FREIGHT - DEPT 1	2	S	1	56.00	168.00	4,600.00
42102	FREIGHT - DEPT 2	2	S	1	0.00	0.00	4,000.00
431	OTHER COST OF SALES	2	M	1			

Figure 14-30 General Ledger Master File List

Peachtree Software™, *Accounting Series* 40, *Apple II*™ *Edition*, Copyright 1980 Peachtree Software, Inc. Reprinted with permission.

so that an audit trail is maintained. For each transaction, all the data noted in the file above will be requested. A reference field is provided to refer to source documents for an effective audit trail.

For control purposes, a *transaction register* listing or log is provided. This listing can be requested either sequentially by the account number of entry or by the particular source code. Figures 14–31 and 14–32 show examples of these respective listings with the source code of each disbursement. Good control is provided through a zero balance in the listing and dollar amounts and transaction number totals for each source.

HOWELL ENTERPRISES, INC.
GENERAL LEDGER
TRANSACTIONS REGISTER
08/31/80

ACCOUNT	DESCRIPTION	REFER	S	DATE	AMOUNT
102	TOM WILSON	30628	1	08/05/80	625.00
102	H. BAKER	30645	1	08/05/80	582.40
102	DANIEL JOHNSON	30639	1	08/30/80	3,640.00
102	GEORGE JONES	30634	1	08/30/80	2,587.00
102	STEVENS - B5044	429	2	08/15/80	-1,560.32
102	NOTE - FIRST ATLANTA	430	2	08/15/80	-882.00
102	SOUTHERN BELL	431	2	08/15/80	-120.00
102	GEORGIA POWER	432	2	08/15/80	-25.00
102	FEDERAL EXPRESS	433	2	08/15/80	-56.00
102	CASCADE REALITY	428	2	08/30/80	-500.00
102	SALARIES	435-439	2	08/30/80	-1,524.30
102	RYDER TRUCK RENTAL	450	2	08/30/80	-1,420.00
102	BANK CHARGE - JULY	STMT	6	08/12/80	-5.16
102	METCALF & FRIX, CPA	434	2	08/15/80	-125.00
102	SIMS SANDING COMPANY	451	2	08/30/80	-561.20
111	SALE - JAMES WILSON	30641	6	08/16/80	561.60
111	TOM WILSON	30628	6	08/05/80	-625.00
111	BAKER HARDWARE	40642	6	08/12/80	133.12
111	T. J. WRIGHT & SON	30643	6	08/12/80	2,600.00
111	BROWNS CLEANING SERVICE	30644	6	08/15/80	2,340.00
111	DANIEL JOHNSON	30639	6	08/15/80	-3,640.00
111	ADJUSTMENT TO BAKER	30642	6	08/08/80	0.48
111	JASPER & HARDING	30645	6	08/21/80	8,700.00
172	JULY DEPRECIATION	531	3	08/30/80	-180.40
201	ANDERSON OFFICE SUPPLY	10074	6	08/07/80	-38.56
201	STEVENS - EQUIP PURCHASE	6114	6	08/19/80	-2,008.00
211	FICA TAX PAYABLE	PAYROLL	6	08/19/80	-127.60
212	FEDERAL TAX PAYABLE	PAYROLL	6	08/19/80	-374.30
213	STATE TAX PAYABLE	PAYROLL	6	08/19/80	-74.28
214	GA SALES TAX UNIT	S/J	6	08/30/80	-239.12
251	NOTE PAYABLE - FIRST ATL	430	3	08/30/80	800.00
30101	SALE - JAMES WILSON	30641	6	08/16/80	-540.00
30101	BAKER HARDWARE	40642	6	08/12/80	-128.00
30101	BROWNS CLEANING SERVICE	30644	6	08/15/80	-2,250.00
30101	JASPER & HARDING	30645	6	08/21/80	-8,700.00
30102	T. J. WRIGHT & SON	30643	6	08/12/80	-2,500.00
30102	H. BAKER	30645	6	08/05/80	-560.00
30102	GEORGE JONES	30634	6	08/15/80	-2,587.00
41101	EQUIPMENT PURCHASE	B5044	6	08/15/80	1,560.32
41102	STEVENS - EQUIP. PURCHASE	6114	6	08/19/80	2,008.00
42101	FEDERAL EXPRESS	433	6	08/15/80	56.00
43101	RYDER TRUCK RENTAL	450	6	08/30/80	1,420.00
43102	SIMS SANDING COMPANY	A2014	6	08/30/80	561.20
50101	SALARIES	435-436	6	08/30/80	900.00
50102	SALARIES	437-439	6	08/30/80	1,200.00
511	CASCADE REALITY	428	7	08/30/80	500.00
512	ANDERSON OFFICE SUPPLY	10074	6	08/07/80	38.56
513	SOUTHERN BELL	431	7	08/15/80	120.00
514	GEORGIA POWER	432	6	08/15/80	25.00
523	METCALF & FRIX, CPA	434	7	08/15/80	125.00
531	DEPRECIATION - JUNE	531	3	08/15/80	180.40
532	NOTE INTEREST - FIRST ATL	430	3	08/15/80	82.00
533	BANK CHARGE - JULY	STMT	7	08/12/80	5.16

** TOTAL TRANSACTIONS IN LIST = 53

TOTAL DEBITS $31,351.24
TOTAL CREDITS $31,351.24

BALANCE   .00

Figure 14-31 General Ledger Transaction Register

HOWELL ENTERPRISES, INC.
GENERAL LEDGER
CASH DISBURSEMENTS
08/31/80

ACCOUNT	DESCRIPTION	REFER	S	DATE	AMOUNT
102	STEVENS - B5044	429	2	08/15/80	-1,560.32
102	NOTE - FIRST ATLANTA	430	2	08/15/80	-882.00
102	SOUTHERN BELL	431	2	08/15/80	-120.00
102	GEORGIA POWER	432	2	08/15/80	-25.00
102	FEDERAL EXPRESS	433	2	08/15/80	-56.00
102	CASCADE REALITY	428	2	08/30/80	-500.00
102	SALARIES	435-439	2	08/30/80	-1,524.30
102	RYDER TRUCK RENTAL	450	2	08/30/80	-1,420.00
102	METCALF & FRIX, CPA	434	2	08/15/80	-125.00
102	SIMS SANDING COMPANY	451	2	08/30/80	-561.20

** TOTAL TRANSACTIONS IN LIST = 10

TOTAL DEBITS	0.00
TOTAL CREDITS	-6,773.82

OUT OF BALANCE	-6,773.82

Figure 14–32 Cash Disbursements Listing

Peachtree Software™, *Accounting Series* 40, *Apple II*™ *Edition*, Copyright 1980 Peachtree Software, Inc. Reprinted with permission.

To review each account's activity, management is provided with a *display account status* program. For each account, the beginning balance, all transactions, and current-to-date balance can be listed. If the accounts receivable, accounts payable, and payroll programs discussed earlier are part of the system, the user has the option to generate the necessary information for posting these entries to the general ledger. This information can be transferred automatically from the other system diskettes to the general ledger system prior to the trial balance calculation by using the *account transfer* program.

The key program in this system is the *trial balance* program, which matches the general ledger with the appropriate entries in the transaction file and performs the calculations. As can be seen in Figure 14–33, it gives the beginning balance, lists all transactions, and calculates the ending balance for each account and level total. This program then updates the account file by posting the transaction totals to current-month field.

Balance sheets, income statements, and departmental income statements can be generated each month from the updated general ledger. The balance sheet is shown in Figure 14–34 with the preceding year's comparative monthly figures. Options are available to not print the comparative figures. The income statement is shown in Figure 14–35 with budget figures and the preceding year's comparative figures. Again a statement without these two options is feasible. A special departmental income statement is also available but is not shown here.

Finally, the *end-of-month* program is run to update year-to-date amounts and clear the current amount fields. It also erases all transactions except those that are retained because they are repeating journal entries. These carry an

HOWELL ENTERPRISES, INC.
GENERAL LEDGER
TRIAL BALANCE
08/31/80

ACCOUNT NUMBER	ACCOUNT DESCRIPTION	BEGINNING BALANCE	TRANSACTION DATE	SRC	REFERENCE	DESCRIPTION	AMOUNT	ENDING BALANCE
100	ASSETS							
10009	CURRENT ASSETS							
101	CASH	0.00					0.00 *	0.00 *
102	CASH - OPERATING	2,835.56						
			08/05	1	30628	TOM WILSON	625.00	
			08/05	1	30656	H. BAKER	582.40	
			08/30	1	30639	DANIEL JOHNSON	3,640.00	
			08/30	1	30634	GEORGE JONES	2,587.00	
			08/15	2	429	STEVENS - B5044	1,560.32—	
			08/15	2	430	NOTE - FIRST ATLANTA	882.00—	
			08/15	2	431	SOUTHERN BELL	120.00—	
			08/15	2	432	GEORGIA POWER	25.00—	
			08/15	2	433	FEDERAL EXPRESS	56.00—	
			08/30	2	428	CASCADE REALITY	500.00—	
			08/30	2	435-439	SALARIES	1,524.30—	
			08/30	2	450	RYDER TRUCK RENTAL	1,420.00—	
			08/12	6	STMT	BANK CHARGE - JULY	5.16—	
			08/15	2	434	METCALF & FRIX, CPA	125.00—	
			08/30	2	451	SIMS SANDING COMPANY	561.20—	
							655.42 *	3,490.98 *
109	CASH ON HAND	150.00					0.00 *	150.00 *
111	ACCOUNTS RECEIVABLE	37,441.45						
			08/16	6	30641	SALE - JAMES WILSON	561.60	
			08/05	6	30628	TOM WILSON	625.00—	
			08/12	6	40642	BAKER HARDWARE	133.12	
			08/12	6	30643	T. J. WRIGHT & SON	2,600.00	
			08/15	6	30644	BROWNS CLEANING SERVICE	2,340.00—	
			08/15	6	30639	DANIEL JOHNSON	3,640.00—	
			08/08	6	30642	ADJUSTMENT TO BAKER	0.48	
			08/21	6	30645	JASPER & HARDING	8,700.00	
							10,070.20 *	47,511.65 *
121	PREPAID EXPENSES	490.00					0.00 *	490.00 *
131	INVENTORY	19,731.99					0.00 *	19,731.99 *
170	TOTAL CURRENT ASSETS						10,725.62 **	71,374.62 **
17009	FIXED ASSETS							

Figure 14-33 General Ledger Trial Balance

Peachtree Software™, *Accounting Series 40, Apple II™ Edition*, Copyright 1980 Peachtree Software, Inc. Reprinted with permission.

```
                           HOWELL ENTERPRISES, INC.
                               GENERAL LEDGER
                               BALANCE SHEET
                                  08/31/80

               ** THIS MONTH THIS YEAR **          ** THIS MONTH LAST YEAR **

                              ASSETS

CURRENT ASSETS
CASH                      $3,640.98                    $2,871.21
ACCOUNTS RECEIVABLE      $47,511.65                   $27,371.25
PREPAID EXPENSES            $490.00                      $490.00
INVENTORY                $19,731.99                   $19,731.99
  TOTAL CURRENT ASSETS                 $71,374.62                  $50,464.45

FIXED ASSETS
FURNITURE & EQUIPMENT     $4,255.37                    $4,255.37
ACCUMULATED DEPRECIATION $1,146.80-                      $786.00-
DEPOSITS                    $750.00                      $750.00
  TOTAL FIXED ASSETS                    $3,858.57                   $4,219.37

    TOTAL ASSETS                       $75,233.19                  $54,683.82
                                      ============                ============

                         LIABILITIES & CAPITAL

CURRENT LIABILITIES
ACCOUNTS PAYABLE          $9,696.67                   $12,000.01
TAXES PAYABLE             $4,778.98                    $3,148.38
  TOTAL CURR LIABILITIES               $14,475.65                  $15,148.39

NOTE PAYABLE-BANK           $800.00                    $1,400.00
TOTAL-LONG TERM LIAB.                     $800.00                   $1,400.00

  TOTAL LIABILITIES                    $15,275.65                  $16,548.39

CAPITAL STOCK            $25,000.00                   $25,000.00
RETAINED EARNINGS         $8,773.26                    $4,273.26
CURRENT EARNINGS         $26,184.28                    $8,862.17
  TOTAL CAPITAL                        $59,957.54                  $38,135.43

    TOTAL LIAB. & CAPITAL             $75,233.19                   $54,683.82
                                     ============                 ============
```

Figure 14-34 Balance Sheet

Peachtree Software™, *Accounting Series 40, Apple II™ Edition*, Copyright 1980 Peachtree Software, Inc. Reprinted with permission.

HOWELL ENTERPRISES, INC.
GENERAL LEDGER
INCOME STATEMENT
08/31/80

	THIS YEAR					LAST MONTH	
	THIS MONTH	RATIO	YEAR-TO-DATE	RATIO	BUDGET	THIS MONTH	YEAR-TO-DATE
INCOME							
SALES	$17,265.00	100.0	$61,299.00	100.0	$411,200.00	$14,678.00	$66,638.30
SERVICE	$0.00	0.0	$0.00	0.0	$29,200.00	$0.00	$4,200.00
RETURNS & ALLOWANCES	$0.00	0.0	$0.00	0.0	$5,900.00-	$0.00	$0.00
NET SALES	$17,265.00	100.0	$61,299.00	100.0	$434,500.00	$14,678.00	$70,838.30
COST OF GOODS SOLD							
COST OF SALES - PURCHASES	$3,568.32	20.7	$14,273.28	23.3	$428,700.00	$3,568.32	$47,218.32
FREIGHT	$56.00	0.3	$224.00	0.4	$8,600.00	$56.00	$394.00
OTHER COST OF SALES	$1,981.20	11.5	$7,912.96	12.9	$27,200.00	$1,485.00	$1,485.00
GROSS PROFIT	$11,659.48	67.5	$38,888.76	63.4	$30,000.00-	$9,568.68	$21,740.98
SALARIES	$2,100.00	12.2	$3,400.00	13.7	$49,300.00	$2,100.00	$8,700.00
PAYROLL TAXES	$0.00	0.0	$0.00	0.0	$4,400.00	$0.00	$423.20
RENT	$500.00	2.9	$2,000.00	3.3	$10,200.00	$500.00	$1,600.00
OFFICE EXPENSES	$38.56	0.2	$154.24	0.3	$2,400.00	$38.56	$234.53
TELEPHONE	$120.00	0.7	$480.00	0.8	$1,900.00	$120.00	$435.10
UTILITIES	$25.00	0.1	$100.00	0.2	$2,300.00	$25.00	$232.68
ADVERTISING	$0.00	0.0	$0.00	0.0	$12,400.00	$0.00	$450.00
INSURANCE	$0.00	0.0	$0.00	0.0	$600.00	$0.00	$324.00
PROFESSIONAL FEES	$125.00	0.7	$500.00	0.8	$1,300.00	$125.00	$125.00
DEPRECIATION	$180.40	1.0	$721.60	1.2	$1,700.00	$180.40	$229.30
INTEREST EXPENSE	$82.00	0.5	$328.00	0.5	$200.00	$82.00	$102.34
MISCELLANEOUS EXPENSES	$5.16	0.0	$20.64	0.0	$400.00	$5.16	$22.76
TOTAL EXPENSES	$3,176.12	18.4	$12,704.48	20.7	$87,100.00	$3,176.12	$12,878.81
NET INCOME	$8,483.36	49.1	$26,184.28	42.7	$117,100.00-	$6,392.56	$8,862.17

Figure 14-35 Income Statement

Peachtree Software™, *Accounting Series 40, Apple II™ Edition*, Copyright 1980 Peachtree Software, Inc. Reprinted with permission.

identification code. The end-of-year option clears current and accumulated amounts. With both the end-of-month option and the end-of-year option, the twelve prior-period accumulators will be updated appropriately. Moreover, in each case the old diskette can be retained for backup data.

The system also has provisions for master file verification and recovery as well as input controls for invalid entries, such as nonexistent account numbers. Larger general ledger systems may have some additional provisions and report-generating capabilities such as better batch controls, exception reports for deletions and erroneous entries, codes or passwords for operators who make entries, cost-allocation procedures, more financial ratios, and more extensive budgeting provisions.

SUMMARY

In this chapter we reviewed the basic financial accounting system. A detailed description of accounting procedures was not given because it can be found in all elementary accounting texts. The current state of the art in microcomputer financial accounting software was illustrated, and the reports generated by the software were discussed. The financial accounting system is often the heart of the organization's management information system. In most cases all other systems interface with the type of system illustrated in this chapter.

SELECTED REFERENCES

Apple Computer Company, *Apple in Depth*, 1980.

ELIASON, ALAN L., *Business Information Processing*. Palo Alto, Calif.: Science Research Associates, 1980.

HICKS, JAMES O., AND WAYNE E. LEININGER, *Accounting Information Systems*. St. Paul, Minn.: West Publishing, 1981.

HIMROD, BRUCE W., "Microcomputers for Small Businesses," *Journal of Accountancy*, December 1979, pp. 44–50.

McGLYNN, DANIEL R., *Personal Computing: Home, Professional and Small Business Applications*. New York: John Wiley, 1979.

Management Science America, *Fixed Assets Accounting*. Atlanta, 1981.

———, *General Ledger Accounting System*. Atlanta, 1981.

———, *Payroll Accounting System*. Atlanta, 1981.

———, *Accounting Series 40, Apple II Ed.*. Atlanta, 1980.

———, *Personnel Management and Reporting Systems*. Atlanta, 1981.

NCR, *General Accounts Payable*. Dayton: NCR Corporation.

———, *NCR General Payroll and Personnel Reporting*. Dayton: NCR Corporation.

———, *NCR Interactive Financial Management System*. Dayton: NCR Corporation, 1979.

Price Waterhouse & Company, *FRS/80*. New York: Price Waterhouse, 1980.

ROBINSON, L. A., J. R. DAVIS, AND C. W. ALDERMAN, *Accounting Information Systems: A Cycle Approach*. New York: Harper & Row, Pub., 1982.

SCHWARTZ, DONALD A., "Microcomputers Take Aim on Small Business Clients," *Journal of Accountancy*, December 1979, pp. 57–62.

Tandy Corporation, *TRS–80 Computer Catalog No. RSC-5.* Fort Worth, Tex., 1981.

WALKER, EWING S., "Accounting Packages: Selection and Management," *Datamation*, August 1981, pp. 76–122.

APPENDIX A: CUSTOM REPORTING ILLUSTRATION FROM MSA GENERAL LEDGER ACCOUNTING SYSTEM[1]

Custom Reporting is generally an easy process. In this example three steps are required. They are

1. Define the organization
2. Select the report format or design your own report
3. Direct the data

STEP 1: DEFINE THE REPORTING ORGANIZATION Defining the reporting organization is straightforward (see Figures A14–1 and A14–2). To define a typical reporting organization to Custom Reporting, relate Centers 101, 102, 103, and 104 to a report center Plant B. A report center is a grouping of one or more cost centers. By the same method, Plants A, B, and C report to the Manufacturing Division. This process is repeated until the reporting organization is defined. With the flexibility of Custom Reporting, any number of reporting organizations may be established. For example, one may have reporting by product line, business segment, responsibility, or any other reporting hierarchy.

STEP 2: SELECT THE REPORT FORMAT When using one of the system's more than eighty formats, one only need fill in the line descriptions of the organization. The Custom Report Line Form and Custom Report show the form and the results (see Figure A14–3). If one decides to use one's own format, one only need specify the columns and lines necessary for the report.

STEP 3: DIRECT THE DATA Directing the data to the report center and report format is the third and final step in building a Custom Report. One specifies that a certain account or group of accounts must appear on a particular line of a report. Illustrated in Figure A14–4 is the Account Range Report Record one uses to direct data from the Chart of Accounts to the Custom Report.

[1] MSA, General Ledger Accounting System, copyright 1981, Management Science America, Inc. Reprinted with permission.

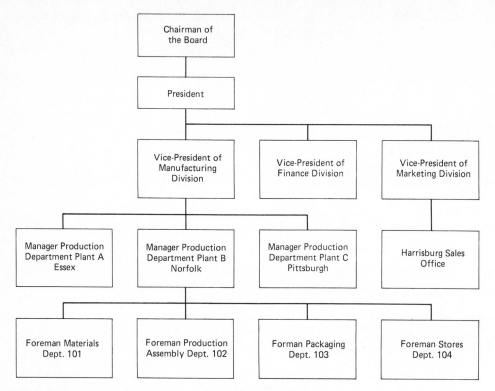

Figure A14–1   Responsibility Reporting Relationships by Levels

MSA General Ledger Accounting System, Copyright 1981, Management Science America, Inc. Reprinted with permission.

Tran Code		ID	A C	Responsibility Center												Report Center												Report Group Codes												
1	2	3	4	5	6	7	8	9	10	11	12	13	14	15	16	17	18	19	20	21	22	23	24	25	26	27	28	29	30	31	32	33	34	35	36	37	38	39	40
M	2	J	2						D	E	P	T	1	0	1							P	L	A	N	T	B	1											
M	2	J	2						D	E	P	T	1	0	2							P	L	A	N	T	B	1											
M	2	J	2						D	E	P	T	1	0	3							P	L	A	N	T	B	1											
M	2	J	2						D	E	P	T	1	0	4							P	L	A	N	T	B	1											
M	2	J																																					
M	2	J																																					
M	2	J																																					
M	2	J																																					
M	2	J																																					
M	2	J																																					

Figure A14–2   The Organization Definition Form Shows How Centers Are Assigned to Report Centers

MSA General Ledger Accounting System, Copyright 1981, Management Science America, Inc. Reprinted with permission.

SELECT THE REPORT FORMAT

The structure of any report has these parts:

Headings and descriptive information

Columns

Lines

T C R O A D N E	I D C	A	CUSTOM REPORT NUMBER	HEADER PAGE/LINE NUMBER	REPORT FORMAT CODE
1 2	3 4	5	6 7 8 9	10 11 12 13 14	15 16 17
C 1	1 2	5	7 0 0 / 1	0 0 0 0 0	0 4

T C R O A D N E	I D C	A	CUSTOM REPORT NUMBER	PAGE/LINE		L T	SHORT DESCRIPTION		WIDE DESCRIPTION (45 CHARACTERS)				
				PAGE	LINE NUMBER		HEADING / DETAIL / TOTAL / SAVE		USER DEFINED FIELD FOR OUTPUT RECORDS				O P R
									USER FIELD SDC7	USER FIELD SDC8	USER FIELD SDC9		
							S D C F				S D C G		
1 2	3 4	5	6 7 8 9	10 11	12 13 14	15	16 17 18 19 20 21 22 23 24 25 26 27	28 29 30 31 32 33 34 35 36 37 38 39 40 41 42 43 44 45 46 47 48 49 50 51 52 53 54 55 56 57 58 59 60					
C 1	2	2 5 7 0 0 / 1	0 0 1	0 /	L A B O R E X P E N S E								
C 1	2	2 5 7 0 0 / 1	0 0 2	0 3	L A B O R P R O D U C T I O N - D I R E C T								
C 1	2	2 5 7 0 0 / 1	0 0 3	0 3	L A B O R P R O D U C T I O N - I N D I R E C T								
C 1	2	2 5 7 0 0 / 1	0 0 4	0 3	O V E R T I M E P R E M I U M P A Y								
C 1	2	2 5 7 0 0 / 1	0 0 5	0 3	E M P L O Y E E B E N E F I T S								
C 1	2	2 5 7 0 0 / 1	0 0 6	0 1								
C 1	2	2 5 7 0 0 / 1	0 0 7	0 6	T O T A L L A B O R E X P E N S E								
C 1	2	2 5 7 0 0 / 1	0 0 9	0 1	O T H E R P R O D U C T I O N E X P E N S E								
C 1	2	2 5 7 0 0 / 1	0 1 0	0 3	R E P A I R A N D M A I N T - E Q U I P								
C 1	2	2 5 7 0 0 / 1	0 1 1	0 3	S A F E T Y E Q U I P M E N T								
C 1	2	2 5 7 0 0 / 1	0 1 2	0 3	U N I F O R M S								
C 1	2	2 5 7 0 0 / 1	0 1 3	0 3	T O O L S								
C 1	2	2 5 7 0 0 / 1	0 1 4	0 3	O T H E R P R O D U C T I O N S U P P L I E S								
C 1	2	2 5 7 0 0 / 1	0 1 5	0 1								
C 1	2	2 5 7 0 0 / 1	0 1 6	0 1	T O T A L O T H E R P R O D E X P E N S E								
C 1	2											
C 1	2											
C 1	2											
C 1	2											

Figure A14–3 Report Specification

MSA General Ledger Accounting System, Copyright 1981, Management Science America, Inc. Reprinted with permission.

APPENDIX B: CRITERIA AND EXAMPLES OF SELECTED CONTROL PROCEDURES FOR THE EXPENDITURE, FINANCING, AND EXTERNAL REPORTING CYCLES[2]

THE EXPENDITURES CYCLE

The expenditures cycle is subdivided into purchasing, payroll, and disbursement functions.

Purchasing covers the functions involved in initiating requests for goods, other assets, and services ("goods"); obtaining information as to avail-

[2] Reprinted from AICPA, "Special Advisory Report on Internal Control," 1978.

MCF ACCOUNT RANGE REPORT RECORD

FORM NO.	GFM530

				FROM			THRU								
TRAN CODE	ID	AC	*CT	ACCOUNT/ ACN	*CL	*CT	ACCOUNT/ ACN	*CL	REPORT NUMBER	PAGE/LINE		CC	BASE NO.	PYR	EC
M2	L			50010			50030		57001	10100					
M2	L			50110			50130		57001	10110					
M2	L			50201			50200		57001	10120					
M2	L			50310			50330		57001	10130					
M2	L			50410			50400		57001	10140					
M2	L														
M2	L														
M2	L														
M2	L														
M2	L														
M2	L														
M2	L														
M2	L														
M2	L														
M2	L														
M2	L														
M2	L														
M2	L														
M2	L														
M2	L														
M2	L														
M2	L														
M2	L														
M2	L														

Figure A14–4 Account Range Specification

MSA General Ledger Accounting System, Copyright 1981, Management Science America, Inc. Reprinted with permission.

able vendors, prices and other specifications; placing orders for goods; receiving and inspecting or otherwise accepting the goods delivered or provided; accounting for amounts payable to vendors, including freight-in, cash discounts, returned goods, and other adjustments. Payroll covers the functions involved in hiring employees and deciding their compensation, direct and indirect; reporting attendance and work performed; accounting for payroll costs, payroll deductions, employee benefits, and other adjustments. Disbursement covers the functions involved in preparing, signing and issuing checks, or distributing cash.

"Authorization" in the expenditures cycle encompasses the types and specifications of goods to be obtained; vendors used (including related parties); prices, specifications, credit, and other terms of purchase; the selection, hiring, termination and promotion of employees; wages, salaries and commission rates; types and amount of employee benefits; signing and issuance of checks; adjustments to vendor, payroll and cash accounts, and policies with respect thereto, such as quality control policies for goods accepted, and policies for termination pay and other special employee payments.

"Accounting" encompasses the procedures and techniques used to control the recording and classification of transactions that relate to purchases, payroll and cash disbursements, including accounts payable, purchase discounts lost, freight-in, gross payroll, payroll deductions, accruals related to such accounts, and the distribution of such transactions to the appropriate accounts, including individual payroll records.

"Asset Safeguarding" relates primarily to controls that provide reasonable assurance that payments are made only for authorized goods and authorized employees and that protect important records.

PURCHASING FUNCTIONS

[See Chapter 12.]

PAYROLL

Authorization Objectives

CRITERIA	EXAMPLES OF SELECTED CONTROL PROCEDURES AND TECHNIQUES
Employees, employee benefits, and perquisites should be properly authorized.	• Procedures for hiring and terminating employees. • Policies on vacation pay, overtime pay, sick pay, and other similar benefits. • Establishment by the board of overall policies for employee benefits and perquisites, such as company cars and use of company airplane. • Approval by the board or a committee thereof of significant individual benefits or perquisites. • Assigned responsibility for effecting compliance with company guidelines.
Compensation should be made at authorized rates for services rendered, and payroll deductions and adjustments to payroll-related accounts should be properly authorized.	• Assigned responsibility for approval of wages, salaries, and commission rates. • Assigned responsibility for approval of additions, deductions, and other changes to basic payroll information. • Maintenance of personnel files, including support for payroll deductions. • Supervisory approval of time cards or sheets. • Periodic comparison, possibly on a test basis, of rates paid to (a) individual approvals or (b) overall approvals, such as a union contract or commission policy statement.

CRITERIA	EXAMPLES OF SELECTED CONTROL PROCEDURES AND TECHNIQUES
	• Assigned responsibility for approval of adjustments of specific types (for example, accounting errors, termination payments, special payments).

Accounting Objectives

Recorded payroll should be work actually performed.	• Policies and procedures covering accounting routines and related approval procedures for the major payroll functions. • Use of time clocks or timekeepers. • Reconciliation of payroll records to production records when employee pay is based on output. • Review of payroll register by individuals at a responsible level of management. • Comparison of actual payroll to budgeted amounts.
Payroll and related withholdings should be correctly computed and remitted when due.	• Reconciliation of payroll register to independent controls (such as hash totals) over source data. • Assigned responsibility for preparation of payroll tax returns.
Payroll costs should be recorded at the appropriate amounts and in the appropriate period and should be properly classified in the accounts.	• Review of payroll source data by supervisors. • Reconciliation of payroll distribution to gross pay. • Guidelines for determining account distribution (capital vs. expense, inventory vs. expense, etc.). • A suitable chart of accounts and standard journal entries. • Procedures for making appropriate financial statement accruals.

Asset Safeguarding Objectives

Access to personnel and payroll records should be suitably controlled to prevent or detect within a timely period duplicate or improper payments.	• Institution of physical security measures over these records. • Segregation of duties between personnel, timekeeping, and payroll preparation and distribution.

CRITERIA	EXAMPLES OF SELECTED CONTROL PROCEDURES AND TECHNIQUES
Payments should be made only to authorized employees.	• Periodic independent distribution of signed payroll checks, possibly on a test basis or by rotating employees. • Assigned responsibility for custody of follow-up on unclaimed payroll checks.

DISBURSEMENT FUNCTIONS

Authorization Objectives

Disbursements should be made only for properly authorized expenditures.	• Formal designation of authority to sign checks, including establishment of requirements for dual signatures. • Examination by individuals authorized to sign checks of documentation, possibly on a test basis in accordance with established criteria, supporting proposed cash disbursements. • Independent mailing of signed checks. • Use of imprest bank accounts and comparison of the deposits to such accounts to expenditures. • Investigation of unusual amounts charged to "purchase discounts lost."
Adjustments to cash accounts should be properly authorized.	• Assigned responsibility for review of bank reconciliations and for approval of adjustments to cash accounts.

Accounting Objectives

Disbursements should be recorded at the appropriate period and should be properly classified in the accounts.	• Policies and procedures covering accounting routines and related approval procedures for the major disbursement functions. • Accounting for all checks issued. • A suitable chart of accounts and standard journal entries.

Asset Safeguarding Objectives

Access to cash and cash disbursements records should be suitably con-	• Segregation of duties between the accounts payable and cash disbursements functions; segregation of duties

CRITERIA	EXAMPLES OF SELECTED CONTROL PROCEDURES AND TECHNIQUES

<table>
<tr>
<td>

trolled to prevent or detect within a timely period duplicate or improper payments.

</td>
<td>

within the cash disbursements function between the issuance of checks or disbursement of cash and the maintenance of cash disbursements records.

- Safekeeping procedures for blank checks and facsimile signature plates.
- Safekeeping procedures over the signing of checks (dual signatures, control over signing equipment and signature plates).
- Reconciliation of the number of checks issued on a facsimile signature machine to the number of checks prepared.
- Mutilation and retention of spoiled checks.
- Independent bank reconciliations, including (a) comparison, possibly on a test basis, of paid checks with cash disbursements records and (b) examination, possibly on a test basis, of paid checks for alterations, unauthorized signatures, and unusual endorsements.
- Surprise counts of cash funds on hand.

</td>
</tr>
</table>

THE FINANCING CYCLE

The financing cycle covers the functions involved with the issuance and redemption of capital stock and the recording of transactions therein; the payment of dividends; the investigation and selection of appropriate forms of financing, including lease transactions; debt management, including monitoring compliance with covenants; investment and management and physical custody of securities.

"Authorization" in the financing cycle encompasses the sources, nature, and terms of equity and debt financing and any changes therein, and the nature and terms of investments, dividends, and other transactions affecting capital accounts. "Accounting" encompasses the procedures and techniques used to control the recording and classification of those transactions.

"Asset Safeguarding" relates primarily to safekeeping procedures and segregation of duties with respect to investments, debt, and capital stock.

CRITERIA	EXAMPLES OF SELECTED CONTROL PROCEDURES AND TECHNIQUES

Authorization Objectives

The sources, nature, and terms associated with equity and debt financings (including lease transactions) and any adjustments or changes therein should be properly authorized.

- Approval by the board of guidelines for selection among financing alternatives based upon such factors as covenants of existing financial arrangements, rating agency considerations, existing banking relationships, internal cost of capital, and corporate financial objectives.
- Approval by the board of significant financial objectives.
- Assignment of approval authority for less significant financing transactions to specific members of management.
- Maintenance and review of loan covenant checklists.
- Preparation and review of projected cash requirements with respect to payouts relating to existing loans and equity securities.
- Preparation and regular review of key financial ratios and statistics.
- Legal reveiw of all loan agreements prior to signing.

The nature and terms of investments, dividends, and other transactions affecting capital accounts and related adjustments should be properly authorized.

- Approval by the board of guidelines for selection among investment alternatives based upon such factors as corporate charter and bylaws, legal restrictions, required rates of return, risk, cash flow, and portfolio diversification.
- Preparation and review of financial forecasts including cash flow analyses.
- Preparation and review of lease versus buy analyses.
- Approval by the board of dividends, stock splits, treasury stock transactions, and significant investments.
- Assignment of approval authority for less significant investments to specific members of management.

Accounting Objectives

| CRITERIA | EXAMPLES OF SELECTED CONTROL PROCEDURES AND TECHNIQUES |

CRITERIA

EXAMPLES OF SELECTED CONTROL
PROCEDURES AND TECHNIQUES

Financing, investing, and capital transactions should be promptly recorded and properly classified in the accounts.

- Policies and procedures covering accounting routines and related approval procedures for the major functions within the financing cycle.
- Schedules of notes, interest payable, and commitments.
- Schedules of marketable securities, including certificate numbers and tax and dividend information.
- Procedures to accumulate and review financial data of investees on a regular basis.
- A suitable chart of accounts and standard journal entries.
- Policies governing the valuation of investments and treasury stock.
- Reconciliation of interest accruals on debt and interest and dividends earned on investments with terms of individual notes or securities.
- Comparison of recorded transactions with minutes of meetings of the board or a committee thereof.
- Review of interest income and expense and cash flow analyses by reference to budgets and prior period amounts.
- Procedures to account for the registration and transfer of issued shares.
- Utilization of banks, brokers, independent registrars and transfer agents, and other third parties to account for changes in investments, changes in the company's capital stock accounts, and changes in ownership of the company's issued shares.
- Prompt review of broker's advices.

Asset Safeguarding Objectives

Access to debt, equity, and investment records and to investment securi-

- Segregation of custody of marketable securities from accounting for marketable securities.

CRITERIA	EXAMPLES OF SELECTED CONTROL PROCEDURES AND TECHNIQUES
ties and capital stock records should be suitably controlled to prevent or detect within a timely period improper dispositions of investments or of funds from debt or equity transactions.	• Use of independent safekeeping custodians. • Physical controls (safes, safe deposit boxes, etc.). • Procedures requiring two individuals to be present whenever such documents are inspected. • Maintenance of a log showing securities added to or removed from safekeeping. • Periodic comparison of securities to a schedule of marketable securities. • Segregation of duties between access to cash receipts from investments, debt, and equity, and keeping the related cash receipts records.

THE EXTERNAL FINANCIAL REPORTING CYCLE

The external financial reporting cycle covers the functions involved in preparing journal entries and posting transactions to the general ledger (to the extent such functions are not performed within other cycles); deciding the generally accepted accounting principles that the company should follow; gathering and consolidating the information required for the preparation of financial statements and other external historical financial reports, including related disclosures; preparing and reviewing the financial statements and other external reports.

"Authorization" in the external financial reporting cycle encompasses the company's accounting policies; major valuation, adjustment and estimation decisions; decisions with respect to the proper accounting for unusual or nonrecurring transactions or events.

"Accounting" encompasses a supervisory or review responsibility with respect to the procedures followed within other cycles as well as direct responsibility for the preparation of financial statements and reports and the accounting procedures and routines used in their preparation.

"Asset Safeguarding" relates primarily to controls that restrict access to important records and to appropriate physical safekeeping procedures.

Authorization Objectives

Accounting policies, including selection among alternative accounting principles, should be properly authorized.	• Written policy statements. • Written procedures manuals. • Assigned responsibility for approval of accounting policies. • Timely review of the selection of accounting principles with independent auditors.

CRITERIA	EXAMPLES OF SELECTED CONTROL PROCEDURES AND TECHNIQUES
Adjustments to account balances, including valuation estimates and write-offs, should be properly authorized.	• Assigned individuals to approve adjustments and write-offs. • Requirements for documentation, including supporting calculations, of adjustments and write-offs. • Assigned responsibility for independent review and approval of adjustments and write-offs.
Journal entries should be properly authorized.	• Use of standard journal entries. • Assigned responsibility for approval of standard and nonstandard journal entries.
The accounting recognition given to unusual or nonrecurring transactions and events not specifically covered in existing policy statements or procedures manuals should be properly authorized.	• Policies requiring the reporting of significant unusual or nonrecurring transactions or events to top management. • Timely review of the accounting recognition appropriate for such transactions and events with independent auditors. • Approval of the accounting treatment for such transactions or events by a senior financial officer.
Financial statements, including related disclosures, and other external financial reports should be prepared in conformity with management's authorization.	• Assigned responsibility for advising management of requirements of existing and new accounting rules and regulations of appropriate regulatory bodies. • Assigned responsibility for accumulating information for disclosure. • Assigned responsibility for review of all external financial reports. • Policies and procedures governing the preparation and presentation of financial statements. • Requirement for written representations on financial statement matters from responsible employees. • Review by management and the board of decisions relative to the presentation and disclosure of external financial reports.

Accounting Objectives

CRITERIA	EXAMPLES OF SELECTED CONTROL PROCEDURES AND TECHNIQUES
Financial statements, including related disclosures, should be prepared in conformity with generally accepted accounting principles or any other criteria applicable to such statements.	• Written financial statement closing schedule with assignment of specific responsibilities, including review responsibilities. • Forms that identify for subsidiaries, branches, departments, etc., the data that are to be reported. • Overall review of the consolidated and consolidating financial statements, including comparisons to the prior year and budgeted amounts. • Reconciliation of general ledger balances to subsidiary ledgers or records. • Standard elimination, currency translation, and reclassification entries. • Procedures for an independent comparison of the financial statement working papers to source data and a comparison of elimination, currency translation, and reclassification entries to those made in prior periods. • Examination by internal and external auditors.
Other external financial reports, including other information included in documents containing financial statements, should be prepared in conformity with generally accepted accounting principles or any other criteria applicable to such reports, and should be consistent with the financial statements, where applicable.	• Designation of individuals permitted to discuss financial results with individuals outside of the company. • Assigned responsibility for preparation of government and regulatory reports and for preparation procedures (similar to those mentioned above) to the extent necessary. • Assigned responsibility for reviewing all financial information presented outside of the financial statements.

Asset Safeguarding Objectives

Adjustments and write-offs made to the account	• Use of contra accounts for valuation adjustments.

CRITERIA	EXAMPLES OF SELECTED CONTROL PROCEDURES AND TECHNIQUES
balances should not impair the accountability for actual amounts.	• Use of memorandum accounts to control adjustments such as bad debt write-offs.
Access, direct and indirect, to accounting and financial records used in the preparation of external financial reports should be suitably controlled to guard against physical hazards and to prevent or detect within a timely period unauthorized entries.	• Suitable restrictions on access to work papers used in preparing financial statements. • Suitable safekeeping facilities for work papers, supporting documentation, etc., to guard against physical hazards. • Suitable records retention program. • Assigned responsibility for approval of all changes in policies and procedures covering accounting routines and related approval procedures.

REVIEW QUESTIONS

1. What basic characteristics would you expect software packages to have for the following?
   a. Fixed assets
   b. Accounts receivable
   c. Accounts payable
   d. Inventory
   e. Payroll
   f. General ledger
2. Note (a) the strong control features in the system illustrated in this chapter, and (b) the internal control weaknesses. Why are more features not included?
3. What files are expandable (i.e., more than one diskette can be used) in the Peachtree system and why?
4. What is a good feature about a variable format for a general ledger?
5. What is the control strength of the menu system of data input?
6. Why is a single financial accounting system not suitable for all businesses? Would you recommend the modification of packages such as the one illustrated here? Why or why not?
7. What is the relationship between the decision analysis approach to systems design and the adoption of a software system such as the one presented in this chapter?

EXERCISES AND CASES

14–1

A CPA's audit working papers contain a narrative description of a segment of the Croyden, Inc., factory payroll system and an accompanying flowchart as follows.

NARRATIVE   The internal control system with respect to the personnel department is functioning well and is *not* included in the accompanying flowchart (see Figure C14–1).

At the beginning of each workweek payroll clerk No. 1 reviews the payroll department

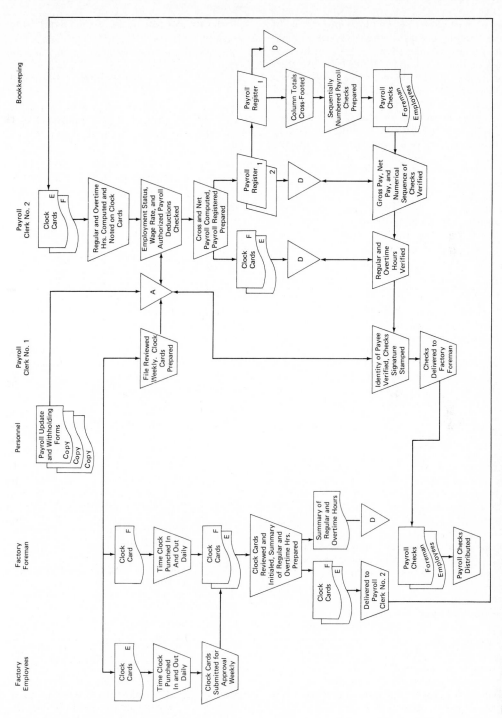

Figure C14-1 Croyden, Inc., Factory Payroll System

files to determine the employment status of factory employees and then prepares time cards and distributes them as each individual arrives at work. This payroll clerk, who is also responsible for custody of the signature stamp machine, verifies the identity of each payee before delivering signed checks to the foreman.

At the end of each workweek, the foreman distributes payroll checks for the preceding workweek. Concurrent with this activity, the foreman reviews the current week's employee time cards, notes the regular and overtime hours worked on a summary form, and initials the aforementioned time cards. The foreman then delivers all time cards and unclaimed payroll checks to payroll clerk No. 2.

REQUIRED:

a. Based upon the narrative and the flowchart in Figure C14–1, what are the weaknesses in Croyden's system of internal control?

b. Based upon the narrative and the flowchart, what inquiries should be made with respect to clarifying the existence of *possible additional* weaknesses in Croyden's system of internal control? (*Note:* Do not discuss the internal control system of the personnel department.) (AICPA adapted)

14–2

Deake Corporation in Eugene, Oregon, is a medium-sized, diversified manufacturing company. Fred Richards has recently been promoted to manager of the Property Accounting Section. Richards has had difficulty in responding to certain requests from individuals in some of Deake's other departments for information about the company's fixed assets. Some of the requests and problems Richards has had to cope with are as follows:

1. The controller has requested schedules of individual fixed assets to support the balances in the general ledger. Richards has furnished the necessary information, but he has always been late. The manner in which the records are organized makes it difficult to obtain information easily.

2. The maintenance manager wants to verify the existence of a punch press which he thinks was repaired twice. He has asked Richards to confirm the asset number and location of the press.

3. The insurance department wants data on the cost and book values of assets to include in its review of current insurance coverage.

4. The tax department wants data that can be used to determine when Deake should switch depreciation methods for tax purposes.

5. The company's internal auditors have spent a significant amount of time in the Property Accounting Section recently, attempting to confirm the annual depreciation expense.

The property account records that are at Richards's disposal consist of a set of manual books. These records show the date the asset was acquired, the account number to which the asset applies, the dollar amount capitalized, and the estimated useful life of the asset for depreciation purposes.

After many frustrations, Richards has realized that his records are inadequate and that he cannot easily supply the data when they are requested. He has decided to discuss his problems with the controller, Jim Castle.

Richards: Jim, something has got to give. My people are working overtime and can't keep up. You worked in Property Accounting before you became controller. You know I can't tell the tax, insurance, and maintenance people everything they need to know from my records. Also, that internal auditing team is living in my area and that slows down the work pace. The requests of these people are reasonable, and we should be able to answer these questions and provide the needed data. I think we need an automated property accounting system. I would like to talk to the information systems people to see if they can help me.

Castle: Fred, I think you have a good idea, but be sure you are personally involved in the design of any system so that you get all the information you need.

REQUIRED:

a. Identify and justify four major objectives that Deake Corporation's automated property accounting system should attain in order to provide the data necessary to respond to the company personnel's requests for information.

b. Identify the data that should be included in the computer record for each asset included in the property account.

c. From the brief discussion of the MSA Fixed Asset Accounting System in the chapter, would that system be an option for Deake Corporation given the problems noted above? Why? (Adapted from the CMA Examination)

14-3

Fort Loudon Furniture has used a manual accounting system for many years. It has been advised by its accountant that it could make good use of a budget system, a system that would give it departmental income statements, and a system that would give it comparisons with last year's results on a month-to-month basis. Its accountant asserts that these reports would enable Fort Loudon Furniture to better plan and monitor its progress with respect to its plans and last year's results. Would the Peachtree Software™ general ledger system illustrated in this chapter provide this information? If it would, what reports would be useful?

14-4

Given the Howell Enterprises, Inc., payroll system illustrated in this chapter, assume that during the calculate payroll program the updated employee payroll file was compromised. This was discovered when the bookkeeper reviewed the check register prior to printing the checks. She found that many fields were filled in with meaningless data. Given that all control reports are utilized, how would you propose that Howell Enterprises reconstruct its employee master file?

14-5

Henderson's Hardware has approximately 300 credit customers, 200 vendors, 25 employees, 6,000 inventory items, 250 general ledger accounts, and 10 departments. The company is in need of a new inventory system to handle the volume of inventory. It would like to have a system where each clerk would inquire as to the quantity-on-hand and either retail or contractor prices prior to processing a sales invoice. It would also like the system to accommodate tight control over cash in the payment of vendors. Moreover, it would like the system to respond to inquiries about a contractor's activity—i.e., history of purchases and payments—prior to authorizing large credit sales.

Would the version of Peachtree Software™ presented in this chapter accommodate all these requirements? Which ones and how? If not, how would you suggest that Henderson's Hardware modify its specifications so that the software can be used without any costly programming modifications?

14-6

Quick and Easy Office Equipment Supply purchased the system illustrated in this chapter. The company, however, has had difficulty tracing sales transactions to support various line items on customer statements. On several occasions items have shown up and were contested, and no record was found to support the original entry. Moreover, upon physical inventory several items were on hand, but there was no record of the item in the inventory file. In each of the above cases indicate where effective use of the system illustrated could have aided in the control of these deficiencies had Quick and Easy taken the time and effort to use only what the system offered in the way of control.

14-7

The Vane Corporation, a manufacturing concern, has been in business for the past eighteen years. During this period the company has grown from a very small family-owned operation to a medium-sized organization with several departments. Despite this growth, many of the procedures that Vane uses have been in effect since the company was founded. Just recently Vane computerized its payroll function.

The payroll function operates in the following manner. Each worker picks up a weekly time card on Monday morning and writes in his or her name and identification number. These blank cards are kept near the factory entrance. The workers write on the time card the time of their daily arrival and departure. On the following Monday, the factory foremen collect the completed time cards for the previous week and send them to data processing.

In data processing the time cards are used to prepare the weekly time file. This file is processed with the master payroll file, which is maintained on magnetic tape according to worker identification number. The checks are written by the computer on the regular checking account and imprinted with the treasurer's signature. After the payroll file has been updated and the checks have been prepared, the checks are sent to the factory foremen, who distribute them to the workers or hold them for the workers to pick up later if they are absent.

The foremen notify data processing of new employees and terminations. Any changes in hourly pay rate or any other changes affecting payroll are usually communicated to data processing by the foremen.

The workers also complete a job time ticket for each individual job they work on each day. The job time tickets are collected daily and are sent to cost accounting where they are used to prepare a cost distribution analysis.

Further analysis of the payroll function reveals the following:

1. A worker's gross wages never exceed $300 per week.
2. Raises never exceed $0.55 per hour for the factory workers.
3. No more than twenty hours of overtime is allowed per week.
4. The factory employs 150 workers in ten departments.

The payroll function has not been operating smoothly for some time, but even more problems have surfaced since the payroll was computerized. The foremen have indicated that they would like a weekly report indicating worker tardiness, absenteeism, and idle time so that they can determine the amount of productive time lost and the reason for the lost time. The following errors and inconsistencies have been encountered during the past few pay periods:

1. A worker's paycheck was not processed properly because he had transposed two numbers in his identification number when he filled out his time card.
2. A worker was issued a check for $1,531.80 when it should have been $153.81.
3. One worker's paycheck was not written, and this error was not detected until the paychecks for that department had been distributed by the foreman.
4. Part of the master payroll file was destroyed when the tape reel was inadvertently mounted on the wrong tape drive and used as a scratch tape. Data processing attempted to reestablish the destroyed portion from original source documents and other records.
5. One worker received a paycheck for an amount considerably larger than he should have. Further investigation revealed that 84 had been punched instead of 48 for hours worked.
6. Several records on the master payroll file were skipped and were not included on the updated master payroll file. This was not detected for several pay periods.
7. In processing nonroutine changes, a computer operator included a pay rate increase for one of his friends in the factory. This was discovered by chance by another employee.

REQUIRED: Identify the control weaknesses in the payroll procedure and in the computer processing as they are now being conducted by the Vane Corporation. Recommend the changes necessary to correct the system. Arrange your answer in the following columnar format:

CONTROL WEAKNESSES	RECOMMENDATIONS

(Adapted from the CMA Examination)

14–8

Consider again E. H. Green Hardware (Case 9–19). As the accountant for E. H. Green Hardware, design a new computerized inventory system using the Peachtree Software™ system illustrated in this chapter. Include in your design a flowchart, description of the inventory file, general report content, and internal controls.

14–9

Consider Clayton County News (Case 17–3). As the accountant for Clayton County News, write a brief explanation of the applicability of the Peachtree Software™ accounts receivable system to the subscription systems outlined in the case. In other words, is the software illustrated in this chapter a viable alternative for computerizing the subscription receivables subsystem of Clayton County News?

14–10

Consider again the Robinson Company (Case 9–7). Adapt Peachtree Software's™ accounts receivable system to Robinson Company's billing and collection system. Robinson's management is flexible and will agree to slight procedural modifications in its system to accommodate standardized software because it is less expensive than a customized system. (AICPA adapted)

14–11

Rockmart Construction Company needs an accounts payable system that will let it manage its cash disbursements. It needs to know when to pay certain invoices to take advantage of discounts, and it needs a suspense system that will pay all invoices by their due date. It also needs to be able to make partial payments and select individual invoices to pay so that payments will not exceed available cash.

Considerable changes must be made to invoices because of the nature of the contruction business. Rockmart needs to be able to implement these changes as they occur using an on-line system. Rockmart also needs to be able to document these changes so misunderstandings can be resolved by tracing transactions via the managerial audit trail. What on-line information is required? What reports will give management this accounts payable information? Is this information available given the system illustrated in this chapter?

14–12

Consider again TuneFork, Inc. (Case 13–8). The frequency of customer inquiries has become so great that the credit manager has asked you, as TuneFork's controller, to consider an alternative design using a microcomputer with random access to the customer files via an on-line terminal. As controller, flowchart an alternative design, describe the controls you would implement, outline the content of the data files you would use, and indicate the reports you would use for such an on-line system. Also indicate any behavioral considerations TuneFork should consider prior to making such a shift to an on-line system. You may consider Peachtree Software™ if it is applicable to this case. (Adapted from the CMA Examination)

14–13

Owl Manufacturing produces a line of novelty goods. It distributes its products throughout the West Coast region. It uses the Peachtree Software™ inventory management package and denotes each sales territory as a department. It would like to reward each manager on his or her contribution to profit so that each manager would be motivated to stress sales of high-contribution-margin items. It has been using the departmental summary report to accomplish this, but the results have not been as good as those forecast. Does this report convey to management the necessary information so that it can assess each manager's contribution to profit? Discuss briefly.

15

CORPORATE PLANNING AND MODELING SYSTEMS

INTRODUCTION

Today several thousand corporations are using, developing, or experimenting with some form of corporate planning model; more than a dozen computer software companies now specialize in corporate planning and modeling; and there are more than fifty planning and modeling software packages. (These include systems such as CUFFS, EMPIRE, BUDPLAN, IFPS, EXPRESS, SIMPLAN, REVEAL, and MODPLAN.) Corporate planning and modeling thus is a viable topic that should be studied by every individual dealing with or studying accounting systems.

For the accountant, the attractive features of corporate modeling are the budgetary planning and control and financial analyses that can be used to support management decision making. However, corporate modeling involves much more than the generation of financial statements. Depending on the structure and breadth of the modeling activity, a variety of capabilities and analyses are available. Our objective in this chapter is to provide an understanding of corporate planning and modeling systems and how they may be used to support management decision making.

This chapter is organized into five somewhat distinct segments.[1] The first section gives a formal definition of *corporate modeling*, along with the types of analyses that can be performed. The section also summarizes some of the major uses and decision support applications of such models over the past ten years. The second section focuses on the three basis elements that go together to form a planning and modeling system: (1) the planning system, (2) the information system, and (3) the modeling system. The third section gives a brief overview of the different types of models that can be and have been developed. A fairly detailed case example in the fourth section illustrates consolidations and "what if" analysis. The final section of the chapter surveys a number of existing software packages that support the planning and modeling process.

OVERVIEW OF CORPORATE MODELING[2]

Before examining the basic elements that make up a formal planning and modeling system, it is necessary to define what is meant by *corporate modeling*, identify some types of questions and analyses addressed by such models, and examine some of the prior uses of corporate models.

Definition

Numerous corporate models exist in the literature, but in general, these models are quite heterogeneous. Therefore, as Gershefski remarks, ". . . no generally accepted definition of a corporate model exists."[3] For purposes of this chapter we will define *corporate model* as a description, explanation, and interrelation of the functional areas of a firm (accounting, finance, marketing, production, and other organizational units) expressed in terms of a set of mathematical and logical relationships so as to reproduce the behavior of the subunits, or the firm as a whole.

Expressed in a more formalized and "general model" framework, *corporate model* can be defined as a set of relationships, notably equations, that relate so-called input variables to output variables. An evaluation method or algorithm is used to calculate the values of the output variables, based on a given set of input variables.[4] Figure 15–1 represents this general form of the model.

Within this general model framework, the output variables are referred to as endogenous variables, and the input variables are classified as either ex-

---

[1] The primary material for this chapter has been adapted by permission from two sources: (1) "Elements of a Planning and Modeling System" by Thomas H. Naylor (AFIPS Conference Proceedings, Montvale, N.J., 1976), Vol.45; and (2) *An Introduction to Corporate Modeling* by Friedrich Rosenkranz (Durham, N.C.: Duke University Press, 1979). The section "Elements of a Planning and Modeling System" relates to the Naylor reference. All other sections relate to the Rosenkranz reference.

[2] Rosenkranz, *Introduction to Corporate Modeling*, pp. 2–40.

[3] G. W. Gershefski, "What's Happening in the World of Corporate Models?" *Interfaces*, 1 (April 1971), 43.

[4] R. H. Day, *Adaptive Processes and Economic Theory* (New York: Academic Press, 1975), pp. 17–18.

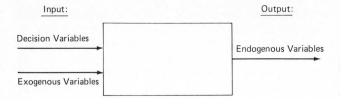

Figure 15–1 General Form of a Corporate Model (Input and Output Variable Relationship)

ogenous or decision (policy) variables. During the modeling (evaluation) process, the values of the exogenous variables are known and are held constant. The decision variables are chosen by the model user to determine their influence on the endogenous variables.

The values of the decision variables represent managerial or user decisions. Exogenous variables, on the other hand, are set by a firm's environment (which cannot be influenced by the decision maker). The values of the endogenous variables provide the answers to "what if" and other questions that can be addressed by the model.

Types of Analysis

A number of factors influence the type of corporate model and the investigation it is designed to support, such as the goals and the environment of the firm, the organizational unit or user within the firm for which the model is built; the background and organizational status of the model builder; and the intended use of the model. In general, however, three types of model investigations can be provided.

The first type of investigation focuses on "what is" or "what has been" questions, such as the relationship between variables of the firm and extrapolated macroeconomic variables like GNP or certain raw material prices. The goal in this type of analysis generally is to obtain a specific (or best) answer based on a defined or developed set of relationships.

The second type of investigation focuses on "what if" questions. This analysis often takes the following form: "What happens under a given set of assumptions if the decision variables are changed in a prescribed manner?" An analysis of this type is supposed to provide a quantitative answer to hypothetical entrepreneurial decisions.

The answers to "what if" questions are determined by either analysis or experimentation (simulation). With an analytical solution, the output variables of the model would be directly expressed by equations as a function of the decision variables. In many cases, however, it is impossible to develop an analytical solution because of the mathematical complexity of the model relationships. When this occurs, experimentation or simulation can be used to generate values for the endogenous variables, based on the values of input decision variables. (This is the form in which most output is presented in corporate modeling.) In those cases where some decision variables or parameters are probabilistic in nature, a so-called stochastic simulation will be required.

The third type of investigation that can be addressed via corporate modeling takes the following form: "What has to be done in order to achieve a given output?" Under this arrangement, the decision maker sets target values for the endogenous variables and uses the model to determine which decisions will provide the predefined target values.[5] This "target" type of analysis is more restrictive than the "what if" analysis because the range of values for the output or target values may be limited. If the model user chooses a target value that is outside the feasible range, then an infeasible solution would result. In the cases where feasible values for the output variables exist, the solutions to the input (decision variables) can be found by analysis or by experimentation (simulation); but it should be recognized that with either solution process the solution can be affected by the initial values of the exogenous input variables and the target values of the endogenous output variables.

From these brief descriptions it is difficult to provide the depth of analysis that is available via corporate modeling. These descriptions only provide the logical framework for the analysis. By examining some of the specific questions addressed in previous modeling analyses, we can gain a more in-depth perspective. Following is a list of questions compiled by Rosenkranz from a group of corporate modeling conference proceedings and from published articles in the literature that deal with model development and usage:

> What is the effect of different interest rates and currency exchange rates on the income statement and balance sheet of the firm?
>
> What effects with respect to the financial position of the firm could an acquisition or merger with another firm have?
>
> Should the firms produce and sell a certain product, purchase and sell the product or not get involved at all?
>
> How will the income statement, the balance sheet, and cash flow develop for several operating divisions? What will be their net profit contributions?
>
> In which range will the return on investment on various projects and units lie?
>
> What is the nature of the conditions that must be fulfilled if the total sales of the firm at a certain time are supposed to be higher than a certain budget value?
>
> How do certain states of the national or world economy influence sales of the firm on the one side and purchase price of the production factors on the other?
>
> What do price demand or supply relations on the output or input side of the firm look like? What are the effects of price/cost changes on sales?
>
> What is the effect of advertising and distribution expenditures on sales? What marketing strategy can and should the firm follow?
>
> What will the absence and fluctuation rates of the employees of the firm be and what effect will they have?
>
> What will be the demand for the end products of the firm at various locations and different times?
>
> What is and will be the unit marginal income for certain production, transportation, and sales allocations?
>
> What are the effects of different pricing policies?

---

[5] Rosenkranz, *Introduction to Corporate Modeling*, p. 37.

How will future raw material prices and quantity restrictions imposed on the availability of the production factors influence output by quantity and value?

Where should the firm construct a new plant?

What impact can a future change in production technology have?

How should the firm set inventory levels?[6]

Uses of Corporate Models

From the preceding list of questions we could quickly conclude that corporate models are frequently used to support financial analyses. This is correct. Most often corporate models are used to support managerial planning activities in the financial area. Thus the core of most corporate models tends to be budget simulation, largely based on financial and accounting identities. But corporate models are obviously not limited to the financial area. As we indicated in our definition earlier, the scope of the modeling task can incorporate the financial area, marketing, production, and other functional areas of the firm. To get a perspective on the prior use of corporate models, we can examine some of the previous studies made in the area.

Survey information on the breadth of application of corporate models is available from three primary sources. In 1969 Gershefski surveyed 1,900 U.S. companies and received a 17 percent response rate.[7] From the study, he identi-

APPLICATION	PERCENTAGE OF COMPANIES (%)
(A) Financial:	
Financial planning (up to 1 year)	38
Financial planning (up to 5 years)	78
Financial planning (over 5 years)	45
Cash flow analysis	75
Financing	14
(B) Non-financial Planning:	
Aid marketing decisions	65
Market share forecasting	8
Aid production decisions	60
Aid distribution decisions	38
Aid purchasing decisions	11
Manpower planning	12
(C) Evaluation of Special Projects:	
Project evaluation	45
New venture evaluation	14
Acquisition studies	12
Computer evaluation (rent or buy)	5

Figure 15-2 Major Use of Corporate Models

Source: Grinyer and Wooller, "Corporate Models Today," p. 12.

[6] Ibid., p. 31.

[7] G. W. Gershefski, "Corporate Models—The State of the Art," *Management Science*, 16 (June 1970), B303–21.

fied 63 companies who indicated that they had used or were using a corporate modeling system. In 1973 Grinyer and Wooller surveyed the "Times 1000" firms in the United Kingdom and found that 9 percent of these companies had developed or were developing corporate models.[8] In 1974 Naylor and Schauland surveyed some 1,880 select firms in the United States and Europe.[9] From a response rate of 19 percent, they identified 240 companies that either employed or were in the process of developing a corporate model.

Figure 15–2 summarizes the findings of the Grinyer and Wooller study relating to "major uses of models." Figure 15–3 summarizes the "application of corporate models" as noted in the Naylor and Schauland study. Both of these studies support our earlier statement that accounting and financial-based analyses are the most frequently employed in corporate modeling. But the studies also show that marketing- and production-related analyses equally have a high usage rate. Nothing in either study, however, indicates whether the companies were successful in developing an integrated model of all three areas.

Figure 15–4 summarizes some additional information from the Grinyer and Wooller survey. This information relates to the "output reports" produced

APPLICATION	PERCENTAGE OF COMPANIES (%)
Cash flow analysis	65
Financial forecasting	65
Balance sheet projections	64
Financial analysis	60
Proforma financial reports	55
Profit planning	53
Long-term forecasts	50
Budgeting	47
Sales forecasts	41
Investment analysis	35
Marketing planning	33
Short-term forecasts	33
New venture analysis	30
Risk analysis	27
Cost projections	27
Merger-acquisition analysis	26
Cash management	24
Price projections	23
Financial information systems	22
Industry forecasts	20
Market share analysis	17
Supply forecasts	13

Figure 15–3 Applications of Corporate Models

Source: Naylor and Schauland, "Survey of Users of Corporate Planning Models," p. 932.

[8] P. H. Grinyer and J. Wooller, "Corporate Models Today" (London: Institute of Chartered Accountants, 1975).

[9] Thomas H. Naylor and H. Schauland, "A Survey of Users of Corporate Planning Models," *Management Science*, 22 (September 1976), 927–36.

REPORT	TOTAL COMPANY (%)	SUBSIDIARIES (%)	DIVISIONS (%)	OPERATING UNITS (%)
Profit and loss	98	43	40	22
Balance sheet	79	37	25	12
Cash flow	77	37	28	15
Financial ratio analysis	68	31	23	18
Source and use of funds statement	55	28	20	11
Marketing operation	34	25	31	23
Project evaluation	34	25	12	15
Production	34	22	28	22
Distribution	29	17	20	17
Purchasing	11	8	8	6
Manpower	9	6	9	6
Financing	8	2	2	2
New Venture	3	2	3	2

Figure 15–4 Output Reports Produced by Models: Percentage of Companies with Each Report

Source: Grinyer and Wooller, "Corporate Models Today," p. 13.

by the models studied. From this summary information we can note that in many cases corporate models focus not only on the total company activities but on subsidiaries, divisions, and, in some cases, operating units as well. Again, however, nothing is indicated as to the extent of organizational and/or functional model integration.

In all three studies it is apparent that a variety of decisions are supported by these models.

ELEMENTS OF A PLANNING AND MODELING SYSTEM[10]

A full-blown corporate planning model will probably encompass several subunits within the corporation and may well be an integrated model of the firm. To begin to understand how one goes about structuring or developing such models, we can break the problem into a number of manageable components or elements. For discussion purposes, we will subdivide the corporate modeling process into three basic elements: (1) the planning system, (2) the information system, and (3) the modeling system. Each of these systems is made up of subcomponents or subelements. In the following sections we will examine these major systems and their associated subelements.

Planning System

The focal point of any corporate planning model is the planning system. Unless there is a formal planning system, there is probably little need to consider the modeling process.

[10] Naylor, "Elements of a Planning and Modeling System," pp. 1017–26.

Obviously the planning system for any firm or corporation will be tailored to the particular needs of the organization. For illustrative purposes, however, we can assume that most firms will have financial, production, and marketing functions and that these must be linked somehow in the planning process. As a general example, we will assume that the company we will examine is a large decentralized firm with multiple divisions or strategic business units. Furthermore, we will assume that each business unit is autonomous and thus is responsible for its own marketing and production activities. The financial planning and cash management activities for the firm are handled at the corporate level, but each division is responsible for its own balance sheet and income statement.

At the beginning of the planning process, corporate goals and objectives are set by top management of the firm. These are conveyed to the divisional business units by the corporate planning manager. The corporate goals may be specific target objectives for the company as a whole, which would require breaking them down to the individual business unit level, or they may be target levels for specific business units. Typical target variables could include return on investment (ROI), market share, sales growth, and cash flow. Target objectives might also include environmental, social, and political functions.

Regardless of whether there is a formal modeling process, the corporate planning department should design the final report formats to be employed by the business units in formulating their plans. Standardized reporting at the business unit level greatly facilitates the generation of a consolidated plan at the corporate level. Individual business units are allowed to make their own marketing, production, and other activity assumptions as long as these do not conflict with external assumptions about market activity or policies of the firm in general. Financial plans at the business unit level must obviously follow from given assumptions about revenues and costs.

For our hypothetical example, we will assume that during the formal planning process, plans from the business units are transmitted to the corporate planning department for consolidation, review, and evaluation. In the initial stages of the process, individual business unit plans will probably be returned to the respective unit for modification and/or reformulation. This iterative process will be replicated until all the business unit plans have been approved and consolidated into the corporate plan.

As we indicated earlier, the modeling process can only occur if a planning system exists; however, the modeling process should coincide directly with the planning process. But it should not be concluded that the only time the modeling process is undertaken is during the formal planning process.

If we were to sketch a flow diagram for the relationship between the planning process and the modeling process, we would note that the modeling activities are closely linked with the iterative procedures used in reviewing and revising the respective business plans and with the consolidation activities necessary to generate summary corporate reports. Rather than trying to sketch these complementary relationships, we will only lay out the modeling framework. The flow diagram in Figure 15–5 depicts the corporate modeling framework for our hypothetical firm.

Just because this framework is presented in a hierarchical form does not mean that corporate modeling systems are structured this way. To the contrary, a more typical arrangement would be something along the lines of the "systems approach" framework shown in Chapter 2, Figure 2–3, particularly if we recognized that a corporate modeling system contains not only the planning system element but also the information system element and the modeling system element. To avoid confusion at this point, we will employ the basic framework shown in Figure 15–5.

For this particular example, a group of business planning models (finance, marketing, and production) exist for each individual business unit. These models can either be used on a stand-alone basis at the business unit level or be used to generate information that can be consolidated and used at the corporate level. The objective of the business unit models is to generate alternative scenarios and plans based on various assumptions about business unit policies and the external environment of the corporation.

To get a better idea of the overall corporate model framework, we can examine each of the respective business-level models. A summary of each of these follows.

BUSINESS-LEVEL FINANCIAL MODELS Each business unit financial model can be used to produce its own pro forma income statement. In cases where the business unit is actually a subsidiary unit of the parent company, it may be desirable to produce a pro forma balance sheet and a statement of changes in financial position.

Basically, the financial models at the business unit level can be used to simulate the effects on net profits of alternative business strategies for a given business unit. The results generated by a given business-level financial model, however, will be a function of the assumption relating to revenue and product cost projections, which are inputs to the model.

BUSINESS-LEVEL MARKETING MODELS For our example, as well as for most firms, revenue projections must be made during the formal planning process. The marketing model for each of the business units can be used, among

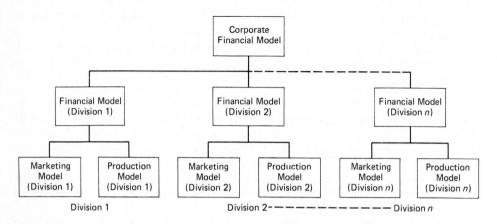

Figure 15–5 A Conceptual Framework for Corporate Modeling

other things, to accomplish this task. Two alternative projection methods are available: (1) forecasting models and (2) econometric models. *Forecasting models* are time-series techniques that attempt to forecast next-period sales in terms of the preceding period's sales, sales of the period before that, and the period before that, and so on. Forecasting is useful for trend analysis and can be used for for "data fitting," but it cannot be used for "what if" analyses. Alternative marketing strategies or the impact of the changing economy on sales and market share cannot be evaluated with forecasting models.

Econometric models can be used for "what if" analyses. Such models can be used to simulate the effect on sales volume or market share of alternative pricing and advertising strategies. In addition, such models can be used to link market forecasts to the national and regional economics. But the forecast and/or results from such models are no better than the accuracy of the policy assumptions and the assumption about the firm's external environment. (Additional comments relating to forecasting and econometric models will be made in the section entitled "Modeling System.")

BUSINESS-LEVEL PRODUCTION MODELS An effective production model can provide management with the production cost associated with a given level of demand. Given a forecast for a particular business unit, the production model can generate the "cost of goods sold" associated with the forecast. An extended analysis, linked with this basic analysis, would even generate the minimum cost production plan associated with a set of demand levels that match all the products in the business unit. We will note in the "Modeling System" section, later in the chapter, that this latter alternative is accomplished by a mathematical optimization technique (such as linear programming).

CORPORATE-LEVEL FINANCIAL MODELS The term *corporate financial model* is somewhat misleading; the corporate-level model should be able to handle more than the consolidated corporate plans. It should be such that it can perform "what if" experiments with any of the business-level models either on a stand-alone basis or as part of the consolidated corporate financial plan.

The output reports at the corporate level typically include pro forma income statements, balance sheets, and statements of changes in financial position. Some of the application programs employed at this level include (1) cash flow analysis, (2) profit planning, (3) budgeting, (4) investment analysis, and (5) merger-acquisition analysis.

Information System

In Chapter 2 we noted that an information system is linked to the organizational function and managerial activities dimensions of a firm; an information system likewise is an integral part of a corporate planning and modeling system. The elements that make up the information system for the latter, however, specifically support the analysis and modeling activities. These elements are (1) data and the associated data base, (2) a data base management system, (3) access control, (4) a report generator, and (5) graphics.

DATA AND THE ASSOCIATED DATA BASE Before a solution of a corporate model can be determined, the variables and the structure of the model must be specified, the numeric values for the input variables (exogenous and decision) of the model must be supplied, and the values of model parameters and the initial or target values of the endogenous variables must be identified. Symbolic information related to input variables, parameters, and initial or target values is called input data to a model. Information dealing with values of endogenous variables or internally estimated parameters is called output data. Both types of data are in most cases arranged in series (normally time series or cross sections). The main difference between input data and output data is that the numeric values of the latter are calculated, measured, or sampled within a model, whereas the numeric values of input data are collected, calculated, measured, and determined by the user outside of the model.

Numeric input data are obtained by measurement or forecasts or decisions of the model user. Measurements are typically used if historical data are available for model variables and parameters. Forecasts have to be employed if future values of variables are needed.

In using measurements and/or forecasts, statistical sampling is often used in collecting and generating data. Examples of data that follow from statistical sampling are the values of macroeconomic exogenous variables or the values of marketing variables that follow from consumer panel data.

The amount of data required to support a corporate modeling system will depend on the variables involved and the type of model. A minimum of three or four years of historical financial data is required, or even more if the model is involved in generating monthly or quarterly reports. Econometric marketing models should have twenty-five to thirty observations of historical data.

Although most firms have little difficulty in meeting the data requirements for financial modeling, data problems are often severe in the cases of marketing and/or production modeling. One means for augmenting this problem is to rely on external sources for data. A number of service bureaus offer national historical macroeconomic data and econometric forecasts to their clients. The major disadvantages of these services, however, are that they are quite expensive and in most recent past have not been consistently accurate. An inexpensive alternative is to subscribe to the historical data base of the National Bureau of Economic Research (NBER). The cost associated with the NBER data base is nominal, and the data base includes over twenty-two hundred economic and time series and is available through most time-sharing bureaus. The data base can also be installed on a user's in-house computer.

DATA BASE MANAGEMENT SYSTEM   Regardless of the source of the data for a planning and modeling system, the data should be organized in such a way that they are "user oriented." To support this objective, a modeling system should have a flexible easy-to-use data base management system for reading data into the system, storing them, and making them readily available for both modeling and report generation.

Most commercially available software modeling languages employ and utilize a data base management system that meets the above objectives; however, there are some differences in the internal structure of the data base systems. At least three different structures have emerged: (1) a matrix structure, (2) a row-column structure, and (3) a record-file structure.

Many FORTRAN-based planning and modeling systems use matrices in reading data into the system. The data base management and modeling functions are likewise carried out using matrix manipulations. This type of structure creates no problem for a scientific programmer; however, for corporate planners, accountants, and financial analysts who are neither mathematicians nor scientific programmers, the matrix structure of data handling and manipulation may be cumbersome and difficult, if not impossible, to use.

A number of planning and modeling systems make use of row numbers and column numbers in formulating models, creating and loading data bases, and generating reports. This row-column type of structure is much easier to work with than the matrix arrangement, particularly for accountants who are accustomed to working with financial spread sheets. However, the disadvantages of this structure are that the user must keep track of the row and columns numbers and that econometric and production data do not necessarily lend themselves to this arrangement.

The third type of data base management structure employs a record-file arrangement. Under this structure, a record is the basic unit of data. Time series data such as sales, costs, and profits are stored in a record. Each record has a name, an abbreviation, a value, units, and a security level (which is used in determining who has access to the record). Records are collected together to form a file.

Under a record-file arrangement, each model may have one or more files. For example, for a given model, one file may contain actual historical data; another file, budgeted data; and a third file, simulated data. Variance reports as well as a number of special user reports are particularly easy to implement with the record-file structure.

ACCESS CONTROL A key element of the information system component of a planning and modeling system is security. Some means must exist for controlling who has access to different files, records, models, and reports. Division managers should be able to access their own models and reports and should have access to certain data bases, but they should be restricted from accessing such data from other divisions or the entire corporation. Corporate managers, on the other hand, should be able to access corporate-level data bases as well as all division-level data bases, models, and reports. An internal control system similar to that described in Chapters 8 and 9 can be designed to provide these capabilities.

REPORT GENERATOR The report generator should be an integral part of any planning and modeling system. To be most effective, the report generator should be flexible and easy to use and should not impose any restrictions on the type of report produced by the system. If the planning system is to be used effectively to support a wide variety of decisions such as those summarized earlier in this chapter, the generator should be able to produce any type of report format desired.

Of the fifty or more modeling software packages available today, two-thirds are little more than report generators. The packages that fall into this category can produce financial reports and can perform financial consolidations, but they have very limited data base management, modeling, and econometric features. While financial reporting generation and consolidations are important factors in a planning and modeling system, other factors are needed to support many management decisions. Users of these limited report generator systems have frequently found that once they were committed to using the system and began to expand the modeling activities, they needed additional data base management modeling, econometric, and forecasting features which were not available. In the initial development stages when a firm is beginning to develop a planning and modeling system, simple financial consolidation and report generation capabilities are adequate. But a serious user should be aware that these software packages that can only provide report generation capabilities. These packages are not able to support a wide variety of management decisions.

GRAPHICS The tabular form of presenting information, particularly financial information, is traditionally employed throughout industry. However, with recent developments in graphic technology it is now possible, and in many cases more cost effective, to employ full-color charts and graphs to present the data. Graphics can be particularly important in planning and modeling systems because results displayed from different types of analyses are easier to comprehend in a bar-chart graph or pie-chart form as opposed to actual numbers, particularly if rapid "what if" types of analyses are being conducted.

Figures 15–6 and 15–7 are sample illustrations of an income statement and a balance sheet, respectively, presented in a graphic display mode.

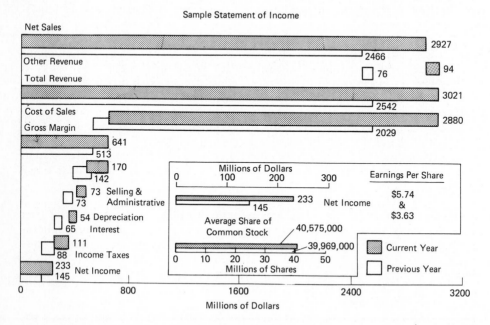

Figure 15–6 Graphic Display of a Sample Income Statement

Source: Irwin M. Jarrett, "Computer Graphics: A Reporting Revolution," *Journal of Accountancy*, May 1981, p. 53. Copyright © 1981 by the American Institute of Certified Public Accountants, Inc.

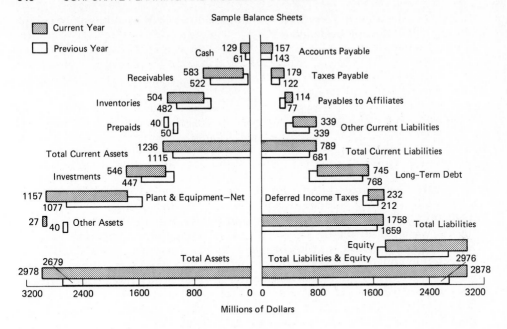

Figure 15–7 Graphic Display of a Sample Balance Sheet

Source: Irwin M. Jarrett, "Computer Graphics: A Reporting Revolution," *Journal of Accountancy*, May 1981, p. 54. Copyright © 1981 by the American Institute of Certified Public Accountants, Inc.

Modeling System

Almost every corporate planning model consists at least partially of a set of finite difference equations. The solution to these difference equations is often the basic solution to the analysis being conducted. However, the modeling system component of a corporate model involves more than solving difference equations. A number of features should be available to support the modeling effort. These include (1) recursive modeling capabilities, (2) ability to handle simultaneous equations, (3) logical models, (4) risk analysis, (5) optimization, (6) forecasting, and (7) econometric modeling. We will discuss each of these briefly.

RECURSIVE MODELING A number of the financial models that have been developed to date are recursive models. A *recursive model* is one in which, by placing the equations of the model in the proper order, it is possible to solve each equation individually in a step-by-step fashion by substituting the solution values of previous equations into the equation being solved. The advantage of recursive models is that matrix inversion or some other simultaneous equation solution technique is not required in order to solve the model.

SIMULTANEOUS EQUATION MODELS Ideally, every corporate model should have a recursive structure. Unfortunately, this is not always the case. For this reason a corporate modeling system should include the capabilities for handling the solution of simultaneous equations.

To illustrate the need for a simultaneous equation solution technique, consider the following basic model:

EQUATION NO.	EQUATION
1	$PROFIT_t = REVENUE_t - CGS_t - INT_t - TAX_t$
2	$INT_t = 0.16 * DEBT_t$
3	$DEBT_t = DEBT_{t-1} + NDEBT_t$
4	$CASH_t = CASH_{t-1} + PROFIT_t + NDEBT_t$
5	$NDEBT_t = MBAL_t - CASH_t$

For this case, equation 1 defines profit during the current time period t (PROFIT$_t$) as revenue for the period (REVENUE$_t$) less cost of goods sold (CGS$_t$), interest (INT$_t$), and taxes (TAX$_t$) for the period. While cost of goods sold and taxes (CGS$_t$, TAX$_t$) could be inputs, interest for the time period (INT$_t$) depends on total indebtedness for the period (DEBT$_t$), as defined by equation 2. But indebtedness for the period (DEBT$_t$) is dependent upon indebtedness from the prior period (DEBT$_{t-1}$) plus new debt for the current period (NDEBT$_t$), as expressed in equation 3. New debt for the period (NDEBT$_t$) is defined in equation 5 as the firm's minimum required cash balance for the period (MBAL$_t$) less the cash balance for the period (CASH$_t$). In equation 4, cash balance for the period (CASH$_t$) is defined as the cash balance for the previous period (CASH$_{t-1}$) plus profits and new debt for the period (PROFIT$_t$, NDEBT$_t$).

Although this is a rather simple model, it is impossible to solve the model recursively by simply ordering the equations. To solve the model requires the use of a technique capable of solving simultaneous equations. Most of the more-sophisticated modeling software packages have the capabilities for solving simultaneous systems of equations. Some can handle linear as well as nonlinear simultaneous equations.

LOGICAL MODELS In some modeling situations the user must sometimes be able to determine whether a variable has dropped below some predetermined minimum level. An example would be to determine whether or not a cash balance or an inventory level has dropped to a previously established critical level. Logical commands such as an IF statement and a GOTO statement can be used to design logical submodels within the overall model.

RISK ANALYSIS Obviously some of the variables in the real world are probabilistic in nature and should be treated as such in the modeling process. Risk analysis is the formal process used in modeling to handle such situations. Risk analysis is also useful in testing the sensitivity of the model to random variations, developing confidence intervals, and testing hypotheses.

Though risk analysis can be used to address a number of different statistical and probabilistic questions, it is only used in a limited way. This lack of use is undoubtedly based on a number of factors. First, any type of probabilistic analysis is very time consuming; thus the use of risk analysis, even via a computer, is very costly. Second, because of its stochastic or probabilistic nature, risk analysis is often viewed with doubt or trepidation by management. Management is usually more comfortable with a deterministic model, even though it may not well represent the situation being studied, than with the uncertain nature of a probabilistic model.

OPTIMIZATION   In the Naylor and Schauland study that was conducted in 1976, it was found that only 4 percent of the users of corporate planning models employed an optimization type model.[11] Those firms who did tended to do it in conjunction with business-level production systems or marketing systems. Little emphasis was placed on employing global optimization models to optimize the entire business or corporation as a whole.

Overall the use of optimization models in corporate planning and modeling has been limited. This is not to say that optimization techniques have not been employed in business. On the contrary, virtually every major oil refinery in the world uses optimization techniques to schedule its operations. Likewise, every major airline in the world uses optimization methods for route design and scheduling. The use of optimization techniques in corporate planning models, however, has not been this far reaching. The usage tends to be limited to submodels within the overall corporate model.

The disadvantage with using optimization techniques to develop optimal plans for a corporation as a whole is that problems are difficult to define and the corporation has multiple objectives. If a company is to be successful, it must deal with a whole host of variables such as profits, ROI, market share, sales growth, and cash flow, as well as all the line items of the income statement and balance sheet. To develop a model that incorporates these and other variables requires a lot of assumptions about conditions and interrelationships. Even if the model can be developed, the problem of multiple objectives must be addressed. Goal programming and utility theory are two optimization techniques that can be used to aid in examining multiple objectives; however, these techniques are only available in a limited number of corporate modeling software systems.

In terms of the decision-making process outlined in Figure 4–2 the choice criteria (objectives) and the relationships are hard to specify. Thus optimization systems are rare at the corporate level.

The use of optimization models in corporate modeling will probably continue to be focused at the business unit level. Production planning, resource utilization, advertising, scheduling, and other problems can be addressed with optimization techniques. Limited use will probably be made of such techniques as global optimization for overall corporate planning.

FORECASTING   As we indicated earlier, forecasting cannot be used for "what if" analysis, but the ability to generate short-term forecasts for variables that appear to have reasonably stable relationships with respect to time is useful in planning and modeling systems. Such techniques can be used for marketing planning models, financial forecasting, and determining trends in variable performance.

A variety of forecasting methods exist, although all are not available in every software modeling package. The most basic forecasting models are simple linear, quadratic, exponential, or logarithmic time trends. For the user who wishes to employ a weighted forecasting method, exponential smoothing is available. This method employs a set of weighting schemes that assign the greatest weight to the most recent historical observation. Adaptive forecasting

---

[11] Naylor and Schauland, "Survey of Users of Corporate Planning Models," pp. 927–36.

models provide methods whereby the models themselves have the ability to "self-correct" if the forecast is not tracking the actual occurrences. Box-Jenkins techniques are the most versatile and most sophisticated forecasting models, but they are also the most difficult to use.

ECONOMETRIC MODELING   The majority of corporate modeling systems employ recursive models and/or utilize simultaneous equation solution techniques; however, the in-depth modeling capabilities are available only through econometric modeling. Pricing, advertising, and competitive strategies can be evaluated via such techniques; and a better understanding of the market behavior of specific products or groups of products can be obtained by employing such models.

Econometric modeling, however, is much more detailed, complex, and time consuming than most other modeling tools. The methodology for the process involves a four-step framework: (1) model specification, (2) parameter specification, (3) validation, and (4) simulation. Data for building such models are vast and are likely to be in the form of a market or economic data base. Fortunately many of the existing corporate modeling software packages are flexible enough to support the methodology steps necessary to link together the required data bases. Thus it is possible for a user to move in a step-by-step fashion to design, test, and implement a model, all within the corporate modeling system. Some systems even contain commands that enable the user to save the structural specifications and parameter estimates of submodels. With this feature, it is much easier to integrate marketing, production, and financial submodels.

TYPES OF MODELS[12]

From the materials covered thus far, we could easily conclude that every corporate model is complex, detailed, and tailor-made for each firm. This is not necessarily the case; a variety of model types exist, depending on the planning problem to be solved, the type of user, and the available computing facilities. There are two types of model classifications: (1) ready-made models and (2) tailor-made models. Within the tailor-made classification, however, there are three subclassifications: (a) ad hoc or throwaway models, (b) fixed-structure models, and (3) integrated models.

A ready-made model has a predefined structure that is not specifically designed for a particular company. Such models do not depend on special planning, accounting, or controlling conventions for a firm, but rather are built around standard procedures. Examples of such models include balance sheet statements, investment analyses that employ standardized discounted cash flow methods and internal rate-of-return calculations, and forecasting methods such as trend analysis and smoothing.

Because of their predefined structure, ready-made models are generally developed and made available by software houses or consultants. Such models are often programmed in ASSEMBLER language, rather than a software lan-

---

[12] Rosenkranz, *Introduction to Corporate Modeling*, pp. 98–107.

guage specifically developed for corporate modeling, since a key objective is to make the execution of the models very efficient.

Tailor-made models are exactly what their name implies; they are tailor made for a specific firm. With very few exceptions, such models are not transferable to other firms. Even when firms are in the same industry, such as electronics, textiles, or foods, it is unlikely that a tailor-made model could be transferable between firms.

Ad hoc tailor-made models generally are small, in terms of both data requirements and size of the coded programs. Such models are usually designed to solve nonroutine, nonrepetitive planning problems. Quite often the demand for such models is on a "quick turnaround" basis; therefore it is desirable to have a software modeling language that will enable users to formulate and develop the model themselves, if possible. The development of such models generally requires on-line interactive hardware facilities. Typical examples that fall into the ad hoc classification include the following:

1. Isolated investment studies, such as new ventures or research and development, whose objective is to evaluate the effects that the investment has on the profit-and-loss statement and the balance sheet of a firm or organizational unit
2. Product line analysis and forecasting, for cases involving a small number of variables
3. Marginal income analysis for a given product or product line

A fixed structure tailor-made model is made up of programs or modules that perform specific planning activities for a given firm. Because the structures of the task or activity focused upon by such model is fairly rigid, the software is generally very inflexible. Fixed structure models do not include decision analyses, environmental analysis, or simulation analysis, but rather deals with routine automatic calculations such as the following:

1. Consolidation of financial statements, plans, and budgets
2. Evaluation of changes in the planning and budget data base
3. Report writing associated with different activities of the planning process

An integrated tailor-made model links the planning, information, and modeling elements of the overall planning/modeling process and provides a means for interaction between the different submodels (marketing, production, financial, etc.). However, few, if any, corporate models are totally integrated. A number of interlinked models exist whereby the sharing of data bases exists, consolidations are possible, and common financial analyses can be performed, but in most cases limited "what if" analyses are possible.

The structure of an integrated tailor-made model, although not necessarily complex, may contain several thousand equations and relationships. To be fully operable and to be able to fulfill heterogeneous requirements, such models must be very flexible. Interlanguage communication facilities will probably be needed in order to link submodel programs; dialogue programs may be needed in order to interactively use specific econometric models. The system may also require interactive programming as well as execution. The most flexible and more desirable arrangement is to be able to operate such models in a conversational, remote batch or batch mode; obviously the most versatile arrangement is the conversational mode.

Figure 15–8 depicts the relationship between ready-made and tailor-made models.

TYPES OF EQUATIONS

Regardless of the type of model developed, most will be made up of structural equations.[13] For design purposes, we can classify the structural equations into the following four categories: (1) behavioral relations, (2) identities or definitions, (3) technological or institutional relations, and (4) equilibrium relations or boundary conditions.

Behavioral relations are used to express a hypothesis about the economic behavior of the entity (firm) being modeled or its environment. Equations that contain decision variables or random variables can be classified as behavioral equations. An example of a behavioral equation is a demand function (equation). It expresses a relationship about the reaction of a market (demand) to a firm's price decisions.

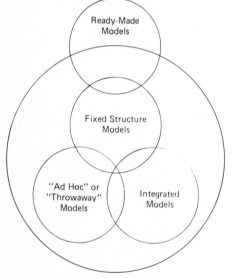

Figure 15–8   Different Types of Corporate Models

Ready-Made Models

Fixed Structure Models

"Ad Hoc" or "Throwaway" Models

Integrated Models

Tailor-Made Models

---

[13] Corporate models may also contain parameter equations or restrictions. Parameter equations constrain the values of the objective function; typically nonlinear mathematical-programming techniques are required in solving models with such restrictions. This material is beyond the scope of this chapter; only structural equations will be examined.

Identities or definitional equations, are usually employed in the financial portions of a corporate model. For example, an identity would be used to equate total assets and total liabilities in a balance sheet. Following are two simple examples of identities:

$$\text{NET INCOME}_t = \text{SALES}_t - \text{COSTS}_t$$

and

$$\text{CASH}_t = \text{CASH}_{t-1} + \text{CASH INCREASE}_t - \text{CASH DECREASE}_t$$

Technological equations are used to describe how various production factors are combined in the production process to provide a given quantity of finished product or service. It is assumed that the combination is accomplished in such a way that some objective of either optimization or satisfaction is attained. The objective to a large degree prescribes the quantities of substitutional factors to be employed in production. Technological equations do not contain decision variables.

Institutional relations, like technological equations, only relate endogenous and exogenous variables of a model (refer to Figure 15–1). They describe the relationship between model variables that is set by a given firm's environment. Examples of structural equations that can be classified as institutional relations are expressions that describe sales and functions used to describe taxes or insurance that a company must pay.

Equilibrium or boundary conditions are equations that restrict the values of endogenous variables in time. Equilibrium equations relate endogenous variables at any point in time to other endogenous or exogenous variables. A typical short-term equilibrium condition would be the following:

$$I_t = \frac{\Sigma\, S_t}{12}$$

where

$$I_t = \text{inventory at time } t$$

$$S_t = \text{sales for month } t$$

This equation states that at time t (yearly), the firm adjusts its inventory level I_t so that it is equal to average monthly sales (total sales divided by twelve—$\Sigma\, S_t/12$).

Boundary conditions correspond to short- or medium-range equilibrium conditions; however, they differ from general equilibrium conditions in that they are expressed as inequalities. Very often they appear as nonnegativity constraints or conditions. They restrict the values of the endogenous variables in a solution only when the strict equality in an inequality is approached.

A CASE EXAMPLE[14]

It is impossible to demonstrate with a single example all the concepts examined thus far in the chapter; however, we can provide an overview of some modeling activities. In this section a case example of the Redding Company, an electrical parts manufacturer, will be used to describe the development of model equations, consolidation, and "what if" analysis.

The Redding Company consists of the parent organization and a subsidiary group. For illustration purposes, we will use the letter A to refer to the parent organization and the letter B for the subsidiary group. Simplified versions of the balance sheets and income statements for the two units are shown in Figures 15–9 and 15–10, respectively.

Upon careful examination of the balance sheet portion of Figure 15–9, we can see that the parent company makes a loan to the subsidiary group (line 5). The associated line item on the balance sheet of the subsidiary group, Figure 15–10, is line 12.

Lines 18 and 21 in Figure 15–10 show that the subsidiary group manufactures and ships products to the parent company. Line 21 in Figure 15–9 is the associated entry on the income statement of the parent company.

The income statement of the subsidiary group (Figure 15–10) also indicates that ten monetary units of profits result from sales to the parent company, and the *balance sheet* indicates that five monetary units of its receivables result from deliveries to the parent company (line 3).

Consolidations

To develop consolidated balance sheet and income statements for Redding only requires the use of accounting and structural identity equations. To begin, we will let XA_{it} denote the line variables of Figure 15–9, where i designates the line number, and t designates time. (For example, $XA_{7,1978}$ would indicate the total assets of the parent company at time 1978.) Similarly, we will let XB_{it} be the corresponding variables for the subsidiary group (Figure 15–10).

Since the balance sheet and income statement for both the parent company (A) and the subsidiary group (B) must be adjusted before consolidation can occur, auxiliary variables must be employed. We will let YA_{it} represent the auxiliary variables associated with the parent company and YB_{it} be those corresponding to the subsidiary group. Once the values of the auxiliary variables have been computed, the value of the consolidated variables, Y_{it}, can be computed by summing YA_{it} and YB_{it} as follows:

$$Y_{it} = YA_{it} + YB_{it}; \; i = [1,24]$$

Since the consolidated variables only express the financial status of the firm with respect to its environment, intercompany capital and product trans-

---

[14] This example is a modification of the case study reported by Rosenkranz in *An Introduction to Corporate Modeling*, pp. 157–73.

fers have to be eliminated. Therefore the associated variables must be set to zero, as follows:

$$YA_{5t} = 0 \qquad YB_{3t} = 0$$
$$YA_{9t} = 0 \qquad YB_{12t} = 0$$
$$YA_{21t} = 0 \qquad YB_{18t} = 0$$
$$YB_{21t} = 0$$

BALANCE SHEET PARENT COMPANY (A)

LINE		1978	1979	1980	1981
1	Cash	80	90	100	110
	Receivables:				
2	Third parties	160	200	240	280
3	Intercompany	0	0	0	0
4	Total receivables	160	200	240	280
5	Loan subsidiary company	20	20	20	20
6	Inventories	500	600	700	800
7	Total assets	760	910	1060	1210
	Short-term liabilities:				
8	Third parties	40	50	60	70
9	Intercompany	5	5	5	5
10	Total short-term liabilities	45	55	65	75
11	Long-term liabilities	140	220	185	240
12	Loan parent company	0	0	0	0
13	Share capital	300	360	400	400
14	Reserves	160	160	260	360
15	Profits	115	115	150	135
16	Total liabilities	760	910	1060	1210

INCOME STATEMENT (A)

LINE		1978	1979	1980	1981
	Sales:				
17	Third parties	950	1000	1500	1700
18	Intercompany	0	0	0	0
19	Total sales	950	1000	1500	1700
	Variable costs:				
20	Third parties	715	715	1130	1295
21	Intercompany	20	20	20	20
22	Total variable costs	735	735	1150	1315
23	Variable expenses	100	150	200	250
24	Profits	115	115	150	135

Figure 15–9 Balance Sheet and Income Statement for Parent Company

BALANCE SHEET SUBSIDIARY GROUP (B)

LINE		1978	1979	1980	1981
1	Cash	20	30	40	50
	Receivables:				
2	Third parties	5	5	5	5
3	Intercompany	5	5	5	5
4	Total receivables	10	10	10	10
5	Loan subsidiary company	0	0	0	0
6	Inventories	50	75	100	130
7	Total assets	80	115	150	190
	Short-term liabilities:				
8	Third parties	10	35	60	80
9	Intercompany	0	0	0	0
10	Total short-term liabilities	10	35	60	80
11	Long-term liabilities	10	30	50	80
12	Loan parent company	20	20	20	20
13	Share capital	0	0	0	0
14	Reserves	0	0	0	0
15	Profits	40	30	20	10
16	Total liabilities	80	115	150	190

INCOME STATEMENT (B)

		1978	1979	1980	1981
	Sales:				
17	Third parties	80	130	180	230
18	Intercompany	20	20	20	20
19	Total sales	100	150	200	250
	Variable costs:				
20	Third parties	40	90	140	190
21	Intercompany	10	10	10	10
22	Total variable costs	50	100	150	200
23	Variables expenses	10	20	30	40
24	Profits	40	30	20	10

Figure 15–10 Balance Sheet and Income Statement for Subsidiary Group

Because of intercompany loans and intercompany sales, adjustments must be made in line items 7, 10, 16, and 22 for the parent company. These identities are as follows:

$$YA_{7t} = XA_{7t} - XA_{5t}$$
$$YA_{10t} = XA_{10t} - XA_{9t}$$
$$YA_{16t} = XA_{16t} - XA_{9t}$$
$$YA_{22t} = XA_{22t} - XA_{21t}$$

For all remaining line items, the existing value of the variable remains unchanged. Therefore:

$$YA_{it} = XA_{it}; \; i = [1,24]$$

and

$$i \neq (5,7,9,10,16,21,22)$$

Adjustments for the subsidiary group, because of intercompany loans and transfers, occur in line items 4, 7, 16, 19, and 20. The identity equations for these are as follows:

$$YB_{4t} = XB_{4t} - XB_{3t}$$
$$YB_{7t} = XB_{7t} - XB_{3t}$$
$$YB_{16t} = XB_{16t} - XB_{12t}$$
$$YB_{19t} = XB_{19t} - XB_{18t}$$
$$YB_{20t} = XB_{20t} - XB_{21t}$$

For all remaining line items, no adjustments are necessary. Therefore:

$$YB_{it} = XB_{it}; \; i = [1,24]$$

and

$$i \neq (3,4,7,12,16,18,19,20,21)$$

After all these calculations have been made, the consolidated values can be computed by aggregating the YA_{it} and YB_{it} variables, as noted earlier. In terms of modeling, the XA_{it} and XB_{it} are treated as exogenous, or input, variables and Y_{it} are endogenous, or output, variables. (The YA_{it} and YB_{it} are, as we noted, auxiliary variables.) Figure 15–11 shows the consolidated balance sheet and income statement.

"What If" Analysis

To illustrate a "what if" type of analysis, we will employ the subsidiary group only. Beginning with the balance sheet and income statement in Figure 15–10 we would like to answer the question, If total sales in each year are increased by 10 percent, what is the impact on the balance sheet and income statement?

Obviously we could easily step through the computational process to determine the impact of a 10 percent change in sales. Expressing this in a general model form, however, is rather complex. We can begin by defining the exogenous, decision, and endogenous variables:

EXOGENOUS VARIABLES

$X\Delta_{it} = 0,1 \; ; \; i = [17,18]$ — Absolute sales growth rate

$XI_{it} = 0,1 \; ; \; i = [1,4]$ — Interest rate for liquid funds, short- and long-term liabilities, parent company loan

XB_{it} — Variables and values of Figure 15–10

DECISION VARIABLES

$\theta_{it} = 0,1$ — Terms of payment($\hat{=}$ 36 days)

$\theta_{2t} = 1,0$ — Liquidity coefficient

$\theta_{3t} = \theta_{4t} = 0,5$ — Relative fractions to finance

$\theta_{5t} = \theta_{6t} = 0$ — Additional financial requirements; (3) cash, (4) short-term liabilities, (5) long-term liabilities, (6) parent company loan

ENDOGENOUS VARIABLES

YF_t — Additional financial requirements

YLW_t — Short-term liquidity variable without financing

YL_t — Short-term liquidity ratio

YB_{it} — Variables and values of output balance sheet and income statement

The structural equation set for the model consists of identities, equilibrium relations, restrictions, and behavioral equations. These are as follows:

IDENTITIES

$$YB_{4t} \equiv YB_{2t} + YB_{3t}$$

$$YB_{7t} \equiv YB_{1t} + YB_{4t} \quad + YB_{5t} + YB_{6t}$$

$$YB_{10t} \equiv YB_{8t} + YB_{9t}$$

$$YB_{16t} \equiv YB_{10t} + YB_{11t} + YB_{12t} + YB_{13t} + YB_{14t} + YB_{15t}$$

$$YB_{19t} \equiv YB_{17t} + YB_{18t}$$

$$YB_{22t} \equiv YB_{20t} + YB_{21t}$$

$$YB_{24t} \equiv YB_{19t} - YB_{22t} - YB_{23t}$$

$$YB_t \equiv \frac{YLW_t}{YB_{10t}}$$

$$YB_{it} \equiv XB_{it} + X\Delta_{it}; \; i = (17,18)$$

$$YB_{it} \equiv XB_{it}\left(1 + \frac{X\Delta_{(i-3)t}}{XB_{(i-3)t}}\right); \; i = (20,21)$$

Variable product costs increase at the same rate as sales.

$$YF_t \equiv (YB_{6t} - XB_{6t}) + (YB_{4t} - XB_{4t})$$

$$YB_{5t} \equiv YB_{9t} \equiv Y_{13t} \equiv Y_{14t} \equiv 0$$

CONSOLIDATED BALANCE SHEET

LINE		1978	1979	1980	1981
1	Cash	100	120	140	160
	Receivables:				
2	Third parties	165	205	245	285
3	Intercompany	0	0	0	0
4	Total receivables	165	205	245	285
5	Loan subsidiary company	0	0	0	0
6	Inventories	550	675	800	930
7	Total assets	815	1000	1185	1375
	Short-term liabilities:				
8	Third parties	50	85	120	150
9	Intercompany	0	0	0	0
10	Total short-term liabilities	50	85	120	150
11	Long-term liabilities	150	250	235	320
12	Loan parent company	0	0	0	0
13	Share capital	300	360	400	400
14	Reserves	160	160	260	360
15	Profits	155	145	170	145
16	Total liabilities	815	1000	1185	1375

CONSOLIDATED INCOME STATEMENT

		1978	1979	1980	1981
	Sales:				
17	Third parties	1030	1130	1680	1930
18	Intercompany	0	0	0	0
19	Total sales	1030	1130	1680	1930
	Variable costs:				
20	Third parties	765	815	1280	1495
21	Intercompany	0	0	0	0
22	Total variable costs	765	815	1280	1495
23	Variable expenses	110	170	230	290
24	Profits	155	145	170	145

Figure 15–11 Consolidated Balance Sheet and Income Statement

INSTANTANEOUS EQUILIBRIUM RELATIONS

$$YB_{6t} = 0,5 \cdot YB_{19(t+1)} \quad t < 1981$$

$$YB_{6(1981)} = XB_{6(1981)} \left[1 + \frac{(YB_{19(1981)} - XB_{19(1981)})}{XB_{19(1981)}} \right]$$

Inventories by value are set to be a six-month average of future sales.

RESTRICTIONS

$$YB_{it} \geq 0 \qquad i = [1,24]; \; i \neq (15,24)$$

BEHAVIORAL EQUATIONS

$$YB_{it} = \theta_{1t} \cdot YB_{i+15t} \qquad i = (2,3)$$
$$YB_{12t} = XB_{12t} + \theta_{6t} \cdot YF_t$$
$$YB_{8t} = XB_{8t} + \theta_{4t} \cdot YF_t$$

If all interests and a proportion θ_{3t} of the additional financial requirements YF_t are paid in cash, the cash position would be

$$YLW_t = XB_{1t} + X\Delta_{17t} + X\Delta_{18t} - (YB_{20t} - XB_{20t}) - (YB_{21t} - XB_{21t})$$
$$- [\theta_{3t}(1 + XI_{1t}) + \theta_{4t} \cdot XI_{2t} + \theta_{5t} \cdot XI_{3t} + \theta_{6t} \cdot XI_{4t}] \, YF_t.$$

Provided that the liquidity coefficient θ_{2t} is not endangered, short-term financing is expressed as follows.
If

$$YL_t \geq \theta_{2t}$$
$$YB_{1t} = YLW_t$$
$$YB_{11t} = XB_{11t} + \theta_{5t} \cdot YF_t$$
$$YB_{23t} = XB_{23t} + [XI_{1t} \cdot \theta_{3t} + XI_{2t} \cdot \theta_{4t} + XI_{3t} \cdot \theta_{5t} + XI_{4t}\theta_{6t}] \, YF_t.$$

If the liquidity position is not good enough, the cash position is set in such a way that the liquidity condition is exactly fulfilled and all cash requirements are financed by long-term liabilities. This is expressed as follows.
If

$$YL_t < \theta_{2t}$$
$$YB_{1t} = \theta_{2t} \cdot YB_{10t}$$
$$YB_{23t} = XB_{23t} + \frac{1}{1 - XI_{3t}} \cdot [- XI_{1t} \cdot (YB_{1t} - XB_{1t}) + XI_{2t} \cdot (YB_{10t} - XB_{10t})$$
$$+ XI_{3t}(\theta_{3t} \cdot YF_t) + \theta_{5t} \cdot YF_t + (YB_{1t} - XB_{1t}) - (YB_{19t} - XB_{19t})$$
$$+ (YB_{22t} - XB_{22t}) + XI_{4t}(YB_{12t} - XB_{12t})]$$
$$YB_{11t} = XB_{11t} + (YB_{23t} - XB_{23t}) + \theta_{3t} \cdot YF_t + \theta_{5t} \cdot YF_t + (YB_{1t} - XB_{1t})$$
$$- (YB_{19t} - XB_{19t}) + (YB_{22t} - XB_{22t}).$$

The last two complex relations result from the consideration of the interest rates for long-term liabilities in the same period in which they are incurred.

The model equations are recursive; therefore, to actually generate the balance sheet and income statement simply requires successive solution of the equations. Figure 15–12 summarizes this activity for a 10 percent change in sales.

Two points should be noted about this model and the resulting analysis. First, the model is solely related to the subsidiary group; no linking is provided to the parent company. Second, the intended use of the model

BALANCE SHEET (B)

LINE		1978	1979	1980	1981
1	Cash	21.4	42.0	71.0	95.25
	Receivables:				
2	Third parties	8.8	14.3	19.8	25.30
3	Intercompany	2.2	2.2	2.2	2.20
4	Total receivables	11.0	16.5	22.0	27.50
5	Loan subsidiary company	0.0	0.0	0.0	0.00
6	Inventories	55.0	82.5	110.0	143.00
7	Total assets	87.4	141.0	203.0	265.75
	Short-term liabilities:				
8	Third parties	13.0	42.0	71.0	95.25
9	Intercompany	0.0	0.0	0.0	0.00
10	Total short-term liabilities	13.0	42.0	71.0	95.25
11	Long-term liabilities	10.0	45.0	89.0	138.50
12	Loan parent company	20.0	20.0	20.0	20.00
13	Share capital	0.0	0.0	0.0	0.00
14	Reserves	0.0	0.0	0.0	0.00
15	Profits	44.4	34.0	23.0	12.00
16	Total liabilities	87.4	141.0	203.0	265.75

INCOME STATEMENT (B)

		1978	1979	1980	1981
	Sales:				
17	Third parties	88.0	143.0	198.0	253.0
19	Intercompany	22.0	22.0	22.0	22.0
19	Total sales	110.0	165.0	220.0	275.0
	Variable costs:				
20	Third parties	44.0	99.0	154.0	209.0
21	Intercompany	11.0	11.0	11.0	11.0
22	Total variable costs	55.0	110.0	165.0	220.0
23	Variable expenses	10.6	21.0	32.0	43.0
24	Profits	44.4	34.0	23.0	12.0

Figure 15–12   Results of "What If" Analysis for Subsidiary Group

determines to a large extent how the model variables and equations are classified. If a different type of "what if" question were asked, the equations and variables would change to reflect the new analysis. This, however, does not mean that a total new model is developed; only modifications are required. We can quickly see, however, that a totally flexible "what if" analysis can require a great variety of relationships.

SOFTWARE SUPPORT
FOR PLANNING AND MODELING
SYSTEMS

Overview

The corporate models that exist today have usually been developed for given firms; however, most are built around common software packages that support the model building, data analysis, data retrieval, and communication tasks. In general, software that is designed to support corporate planning and modeling will consist of a language supervisor and a number of ready-made building blocks. The supervisor program, which will probably be coded in a general-purpose language (FORTRAN, PASCAL, etc.) or assembler language, controls the building blocks, which, among other things, allow access to a model's data base and perform user-defined calculations and operations. Overall the modeling software consists of macroinstructions, built-in functions, and subroutines which perform frequently encountered modeling tasks. Apart from being used to actually code the model structure, the software is used to call the data base, to link to other available software, and to communicate with the model user via input/output instructions. Ideally, statements, commands, and routines of the software package allow a faster, more flexible, and transparent coding of a model, thus reducing the costs of programming, testing, documentation, and changing.

More than fifty software packages that support corporate planning and modeling systems are now available in the market. Because so many packages are available, one needs to be cautious in selecting software and make certain that the software will indeed support the modeling effort. Two key factors that should be considered in evaluating any software package are whether the package supports a modular design structure and whether it is adaptive. A corporate model is often likely to be a large model. To facilitate the control and debugging of such a model, a structured and modular program design is needed. The same is true of the modeling software. In addition, in today's world it is unlikely that a firm's internal structure and/or its external environment and market will remain fixed for a very long period of time. Thus a corporate model must be adaptive in the sense that it can track and represent such changes. This, together with the fact that a decentralized firm may want to build corporate models for different organizational subunits, means that the modeling software package must be adaptive. This latter point also reinforces the need for a modular structured set of software.

Adaptability and modularity are the key factors that should be considered in examining modeling support software; however, these are by no means the only factors. Rosenkranz states that hardware requirements, mode of operations, cost of the system, flexibility of input and output, ability to handle nonnumeric data, the variety of available macro-instructions, and a number of other factors should be considered.[15] Specifically, Rosenkranz suggests that the points in Figure 15–13 be used as a checklist for comparison purposes.

---

[15] Rosenkranz, *Introduction to Corporate Modeling*, p. 396.

1. Main Application Area
   - Corporate modeling
   - Financial modeling
   - Marketing modeling
   - Production modeling
2. Type of System
   - Fixed structure
   - Flexible, modular structure
3. Hardware Requirements
   - Main storage
   - External storage
   - Input-output facilities
4. Software Requirements
   - Compilers and source languages
   - Interfaces
   - File organization, data access methods
5. Mode of Operation
   - Batch
   - Real time
   - In-house
   - Service bureau
6. Costs of System
   - Purchasing, leasing
   - Consulting, training
   - Storage
   - Operation
7. Type of Language
   - Free format-fixed format
   - Compiler-interpreter
   - Restrictions
   - English-like or symbolic text
8. Flexibility of Input and Output
   - Choice and number of formats
   - Sequence
   - Graphics and histograms
9. Type of Data Base
   - File and data set structure
   - Internal, external data base
   - Connection and hierarchies of data bases and files
10. Basic Time Intervals
    - Maximum number
    - Specific periods
    - Interval transformations
11. Maximum Size of Model
    - Statements
    - Number and Size of
      - Arrays
      - Matrices and tables
      - Files and number of data, variables/file

12. Arithmetic
    - Operators
    - Column arithmetic
    - Line arithmetic
    - Table arithmetic
    - Built-in functions
13. Systems Logic
    - Linear sequential
    - Logical branching
    - Index calculations
    - IF, GOTO
    - DO Loop, END
    - Forward, backward iterations
    - Labels
    - Subroutines
    - Table access methods
14. Handling of Nonnumeric Data
    - Character string operations
    - List and tree processing
    - Set statements
15. Macro-Instructions
    - Practitioner methods
      - Interpolation, extrapolation
      - Financial indicators
    - Short-term forecasting
    - Trend forecasting
    - Econometric methods
    - Specification and verification testing
    - Random numbers and stochastic simulation
    - Matrix algebra and linear programming
    - Nonlinear solution and optimization methods
    - Sensitivity analysis
    - Experimental designs
    - Graph analysis
16. Security System
    - Physical security of data base, model and CSPS
    - Authorization codes and passwords for data base, files, models—privacy
17. Documentation and Support
    - Users and systems manuals
    - Debugging and error tracing
    - Menu programs, prompting, and "help" explanations
    - Computer-aided instruction
    - Consulting support

Figure 15–13   Factors to Consider in the Evaluation of Modeling Software

Available Software Packages

A systematic and exhaustive description of all software packages/systems commercially available to support corporate planning and modeling is beyond the scope of this chapter. However, in the following pages we will give a brief overview of several such packages.

In June 1981 a conference entitled "The Future of Corporate Planning and Modeling Software Systems" was held at Duke University. At that conference a number of developers as well as users of existing software systems presented their products and demonstrated some current applications. Following is a summary of a select group of software systems discussed at the conference These include CUFFS, EXPRESS, IFPS, SIMPLAN, and XSIM, among others.

CUFFS   CUFFS (the Combs Unangst Financial Forecasting System) is a financial planning, modeling, forecasting, and analysis language. CUFFS was developed in 1973 by Cuffs Models and Planning Ltd. and is currently being marketed through a number of time-sharing companies including ADP Network Services, Boeing Computer Services, CompuServe Inc., Informatics, and Landart Systems, Inc.

CUFFS can be used to create simple or sophisticated models. The planning and forecasting applications of the language are very broad. Pro-forma balance sheets and income statements, depreciation analysis, cash requirement forecasts, credit analysis, lease or buy decisions, mergers and acquisition analysis, and short as well as long-term financing analysis—all can easily be modeled. The language, however, does not contain an econometric modeling feature, nor does it have the ability to handle risk analysis or optimazition calculations.

The language does have the ability to reorder the logic statement automatically during the model building process. Thus the user can design the model in whatever sequence is most natural, and CUFFS will arrange the logic in a "top-to-bottom" calculation sequence. Automatic reordering also means that the user can make small or drastic changes in the model without having to rearrange the model by hand or invalidate it entirely.

CUFFS accepts data in a variety of ways. If the data values for an account are known, they can be entered directly into the model as vectors. If the values are to be calculated, a formula can be entered. Values can be entered from the terminal during execution, simply by inserting a question into the formula or in place of the formula. Account data may come from a data file when a formula is omitted.

The CUFFS report format allows a user to generate any number of required reports during one pass through a model. This means that the user need only run the model one time to generate required reports. Reports can be sent to either the user's terminal or a data file, or a combination of the two.

The system also allows the user to link data automatically to Executive Information Services (EIS), a large data service bureau. This means that the user can utilize the EIS computer graphics capabilities as well as financial and statistical libraries and report writers without having to reenter data manually.

EXPRESS   EXPRESS was developed in 1969 by Management Decision Systems. It was one of the first software systems specifically designed to support financial and marketing modeling. Since its conception, it has been expanded to include a full spectrum of modeling capabilities including an integrated financial structure.

EXPRESS is built around four main components or modules: (1) the data base, (2) report and display capabilities, (3) analytical capabilities (including financial and statistical utilities), and (4) modeling (financial and operational).

The data base module in EXPRESS allows the storage of data in structures. This means that multiple-dimension storage is possible. The user specifies the detail and the number of dimensions required. Instead of storing yearly line item information for each subunit of a company, the user thus has the flexibility of storing additional, monthly line item data or information organized by product, month, division, and so forth.

The data base module also contains the security features for the system. Two types of protection are available: (1) the data can be examined but not changed, and (2) the data can be made totally inaccessible. Either of these types of protection can be applied to the entire data base or to specified partitions (particularly line items or all the data for a certain division).

The display module for EXPRESS contains the report generator and display features for the system. All the display capabilities are integrated with the system's data management, analysis, and modeling routine; therefore a variety of calculations and operations can be performed and reported.

The system has full graphic display capabilities. Graphic displays in bar chart, scatter plot, and pie plots are available. The user has control over the specifications of each graph including titles, labels, symbols used, size, scale, and type of grid. All graphic displays can also be immediately produced on plotters and other graphic output devices.

EXPRESS contains a variety of analytical and statistical features. Besides the standard mathematical capabilities, the system has the following automatic built-in calculations: sorting, percent difference, lags and leads, minimum/maximum of a set of numbers, year-to-date, and rounding. The statistical features include a number of time series analysis and forecasting routines (exponential smoothing, linear extrapolation, compound total extrapolation, curve fitting, deseasonalization, and others). Advanced statistical features such as multiple linear regression, best possible regression, cluster analysis, and factor analysis are also available.

EXPRESS provides the standard set of financial planning and analysis features including the generation of pro forma statements, budgeting, analysis, projections, target analysis, and consolidations. One of the special modeling features of the system is risk analysis (including Monte Carlo simulation).

EXPRESS is operational on three different computer mediums: (1) time-sharing systems, (2) mainframe computers, and (3) large-scale minicomputers.

IFPS IFPS is EXECUCOM's interactive financial planning system.[16] This system is designed to support the construction of ad hoc planning and

---

[16] EXECUCOM, "Interactive Financial Planning System User's Manual" (Austin, Tex.: EXECUCOM Systems Corporation, 1976).

budgeting models. In a record and table line-oriented fashion, it mainly supports the formulation, evaluation, and solution of financial identities and statements.

IFPS incorporates five subsystems: (1) executive, (2) modeling language, (3) report generator, (4) data file, and (5) command file.

The executive subsystem is used to call the other subsystems by EXECUTIVE commands. In addition, it contains commands to specify and consolidate data files and to list, delete, copy, combine, and consolidate IFPS models and reports. The latter two commands are of sufficient flexibility to allow tree calculations and hierarchical modeling.

The modeling language subsystem is used to create, edit, solve, and print the results from IFPS models. Models consist of statements of the IFPS language. They are written, processed, and stored in a linewise fashion.

The language possesses a number of built-in functions and subroutines to perform frequently encountered modeling tasks. Examples are commands to perform totaling; built-in functions to calculate specific functions, perform financial calculations, and generate random numbers for a well-developed risk analysis; and subroutines to calculate depreciation schedules. The analyst may call on user-written FORTRAN functions and subroutines from an IFPS program.

The language subsystem incorporates commands to experiment with a model. The modeling steps of equation specification and solution are separated. The latter can be specified by a SOLVE command. IFPS incorporates algorithms to handle the sequencing of recursive equations, an iterative process to handle the solution of simultaneous linear equations, a Monte-Carlo simulation process, and a procedure to determine goal-oriented solutions. Several "what if" investigations of a model can be formulated by using a specific "what if" command and statements of the language.

The IFPS report generator subsystem incorporates commands to specify, format, and print customized reports that cannot be written using statements of the modeling language subsystems.

The data file subsystem allows the creation, updating, deleting, and editing of permanent IFPS data files. The subsystem contains commands that permit the storage of alternative model solutions.

The command file subsystem operates with permanent files on which IFPS commands and directives can be stored. The execution of the stored commands can be initiated by other IFPS commands, thus reducing the effort needed to specify operations that use many commands.

SIMPLAN   SIMPLAN is a corporate modeling system developed and offered by the SIMPLAN Group of Social Systems, Inc.[17] SIMPLAN models can be run in either interactive or batch mode. Its application is not restricted to small "ad hoc" models only. Its data base structure and management system, modeling language, and software allow the construction of financial, marketing, production, and integrated corporate models. The system operates in the following six modes: (1) control, (2) data, (3) analysis, (4) report, (5) user, and (6) edit.

[17] Social Systems, Inc., "SIMPLAN—Command Descriptions" (Chapel Hill, N.C., 1976).

The SIMPLAN control mode is employed to enter the other modes of operation. The data mode supports the creation and maintenance of the SIMPLAN data base. In addition, it incorporates commands that support data aggregations and consolidations as well as the selection of groups of data series in the data base.

The edit mode is entered if a user wants to either specify or modify a SIMPLAN model or report. The SIMPLAN simulation language and modeling commands are used for the first purpose, whereas report commands are used for the specification of customized reports. Both models and reports can be stored in a SIMPLAN text library.

The report mode is entered for the actual report generation, but additional definitions and modifications of reports can be defined in the edit mode. Models that have been defined in the edit mode are evaluated in the analysis mode. It supports the modeling steps of model estimation, solution, and validation.

SIMPLAN has a well developed internal security system. In the user mode, the operator can define and store security levels for data, models, functions, and reports together with the levels a given user may access. This helps prevent unauthorized use of the system. A company may thus construct an integrated model (i.e., one consisting of several divisional models) where central management can experiment with the total model and system, but users in the divisions can only control and experiment with their appropriate submodel or submodels.

The system offers a large amount of software to support the model-buiding process. Practitioner methods are available to extrapolate data series and to perform frequently encountered financial calculations. Descriptive forecasts can be calculated by smoothing methods or trend calculations. The single-stage and two-stage least squares methods are available for the estimation of econometric models. Risk analysis models can be constructed by using random number generators, and both recursive and simultaneous linear and nonlinear models can be solved. Measures of goodness of fit and predictive accuracy can be calculated in order to discriminate between alternative models.

XSIM XSIM is an on-line corporate modeling system developed by Dynamics Associates.[18] It is among the furthest-developed systems available today and can, like SIMPLAN, be characterized as a planning information system with analytical capabilities. With the exception of optimization methods and experimental design techniques, it offers almost all the corporate modeling techniques and methods. It does not possess automatic language intercommunication facilities, which is only a disadvantage if the user wants to call PL/I or FORTRAN programs from an XSIM program. The simulation and modeling languages incorporated by the system are rich in structure. They should require the use of higher-level problem-oriented languages only for very specific applications.

XSIM is offered through one of the commercial time-sharing networks and incorporates fully integrated commands by which a user can directly access

[18] Dynamics Associates, "XSIM, a Reference Manual" (Cambridge, Mass., January 1977).

several macroeconomic data bases and models. They may, in an integrated fashion, directly be used together with XSIM corporate models.

Except for the macroeconomic data bases, XSIM has access to two other types of files: a random access XSIM data base, which is used to store data mainly in the form of series or records for on-line modeling purposes; and an indexed sequential XSAM data base, which can be used to store large sequences of series as contained in data matrices.

Data entry to XSIM is in free format mainly using terminals. However, special XSAM files may independently be created, using special bridge programs and batch mode. Data series and parameters can be distinguished. These two separate categories conceptually facilitate experimentation with alternative parameters of a model—especially for time series data, where additional attributes allow the identification of their starting and termination date together with their periodicity.

The system, in principle, incorporates two simulation languages: The XSIM language, for interactive use, processes command after command in a sequential fashion. The FORTRAN-like general programming language XTASK allows the construction of programs consisting of blocks of statements.

The modeling software available in XSIM can be used to construct integrated corporate models as well as a variety of marketing, finance, and production submodels. Many statistical procedures for data analysis are available. The specification, estimation, verification, and solution of econometric models is also possible. Estimation methods such as multiple-linear regression, step-

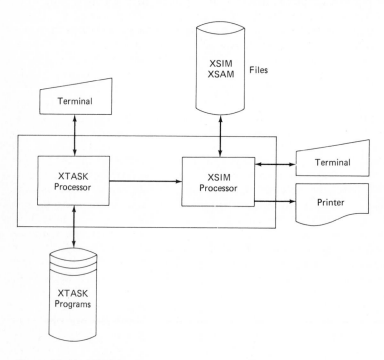

Figure 15–14 XSIM System

wise regression, and nonlinear regression can be used with Box-Jenkins and a combination of traditional econometric and Box-Jenkins models. Random number generators are available for the construction of risk analysis models. Special financial functions can be employed for financial submodels. Solution methods allow the solution of single equations and also large systems of nonlinear simultaneous systems of equations. Methods are also available to sequence, check, and form subgroups of model equations. Special software allows the continuous and discrete graphical representation of data and modeling results. Report generator commands permit the formulation of output reports tailored to the needs of the user.

Summary of Software Package Capabilities

The preceding summaries of software packages described some of the capabilities available with a specific package. A further comparison of the packages can be made by examining the software in light of the planning system, the information system, and the modeling system activities discussed earlier in the chapter.

SUMMARY

This chapter has provided an overview of the corporate planning and modeling process. Although the reader may not actually be able to develop a corporate model after reading the chapter, enough details have been given so that he or she will have a sound understanding of the components involved in the development and use of such models.

More than two thousand companies have been or are now experimenting with some form of a corporate planning and modeling system to support managerial and strategic decision making. From previous studies it was noted that most applications have tended to be financially based, such as cash flow analysis, generation of pro forma financial reports, profit planning, and budgeting. This trend will probably continue. However, with the software and hardware currently available, it is likely that companies will move more toward integrated models that link marketing production, as well as the financial areas. More emphasis will undoubtedly be placed on the use of econometric modeling, since this subelement of the overall planning and modeling process is closely tied to the marketplace and the economy.

One area that may be a potential problem for companies just entering the modeling arena is the differences that exist between the software packages available in the market. Quite often there is a tendency for a company to select and begin using a particular modeling system without giving much thought to the long-run implications of the system. It is possible, even by employing externally developed software, to make effective use of in-house computer hardware and data bases. An effective modeling system does not necessarily imply an outside time-sharing system or an external economic data base. The design and selection of a company's planning and modeling system must follow the system design concepts outlined in Chapters 10 and 11.

SELECTED REFERENCES

BOULDEN, J. B., AND E. S. BUFFA, "Corporate Models: On-Line, Real-Time Systems," *Harvard Business Review*, July–August 1970, pp. 65–83.

DAVIS, K. ROSCOE, AND ROBERT A. LEITCH, "Improving Marketing Production Coordination Through On-Line Modeling," *Production and Inventory Management*, 17 (Second Quarter 1976), pp. 56–72.

DAY, R. H., *Adaptive Processes and Economic Theory*. New York: Academic Press, 1975.

Dynamic Associates, *XSIM, A Reference Manual*. Cambridge, Mass., 1977.

EXECUCOM, *Interactive Financial Planning System User's Manual*. Austin, Tex.: Execucom Systems Corporation, 1976.

GERSHEFSKI, G. W., "Building a Corporate Financial Model," *Harvard Business Review*, July–August 1969, pp. 61–72.

———, "Corporate Models—The State of the Art," *Management Science*, 16 (June 1970), pp. B303–21.

———, "The Development and Application of a Corporate Financial Model." Oxford, Ohio: Planning Executives Institute, 1968.

———, "What's Happening in the World of Corporate Models?" *INTERFACES*, Vol. 1, April 1971.

GRINYER, P. H., AND J. WOOLLER, "Corporate Models Today." London: Institute of Chartered Accountants, 1975.

KOTLER, P. H., "Corporate Models: Better Marketing Plans," *Harvard Business Review*, July–August 1970, pp. 135–49.

LEITCH, ROBERT A., "Marketing Strategy and the Optimal Production Schedule," *Management Science*, 21 (November 1974), pp. 302–12.

MAYO, R. B., *Corporate Planning and Modeling with SIMPLAN*. Reading, Mass.: Addison-Wesley, 1979.

NAYLOR, THOMAS H., "Elements of a Planning and Modeling System." Proceedings of the AFIPS National Computer Conference, AFIPS Press, Montvale, N.J., 1976, pp. 1017–26.

NAYLOR, THOMAS H., AND H. SCHAULAND, "A Survey of Users of Corporate Planning Models," *Management Science*, 22 (September 1976), pp. 927–36.

ROSENKRANZ, FRIEDRICH, *An Introduction to Corporate Modeling*. Durham, N.C.: Duke University Press, 1979.

——— "Methodological Concepts of Corporate Models." Proceedings of the Conference on Computer Simulation versus Analytical Solutions for Business and Economic Models, Göteborg, Sweden, 1973.

——— "Status and Future Use of Corporate Planning and Simulation Models: Case Studies and Conclusions," *Computer Assisted Corporate Planning*. SRA Lectures and Tutorials, Chicago, 1977, pp. 143–79.

Social Systems, Inc., "SIMPLAN—Command Descriptions." Chapel Hill, N.C.: 1976.

SPRAGNE, RALPH H., JR., AND ERIC D. CARLSON, *Building Effective Decision Support Systems*. Englewood Cliffs, N.J.: Prentice-Hall, 1982.

WHEELWRIGHT, STEVE C., AND SPYROS G. MAKRIDAKIS, *Computer-Aided Modeling for Managers*. Reading, Mass.: Addison-Wesley, 1972.

REVIEW QUESTIONS

1. Define the term *corporate model* as given in the chapter. Give the more "general model" definition also.

2. Identify the different types of analyses that can be performed via corporate modeling.

3. Explain the difference between a "what if" analysis and a "what has to be done" analysis.

4. Identify some of the typical questions that can be addressed via corporate modeling.

5. What are some of the key applications that have been made of the corporate model in the past?

6. Identify the three basic elements or components associated with the corporate modeling process.

7. Describe in detail the planning system component of corporate modeling.

8. What are the five subelements that support the information system component of corporate modeling?

9. Differentiate between *input data* and *output data*.

10. What quantity of data is required to support a corporate modeling system?

11. What sources are available for obtaining external data?

12. Differentiate between a *matrix structure*, a *row-column structure*, and a *record-file structure* used in data bases that can be employed to support modeling.

13. What are some of the limitations of a modeling software package that is primarily a report generator?

14. What role does graphics play in corporate modeling systems?

15. Differentiate between *recursive modeling* and *simultaneous equation models*.

16. Identify seven basic subelements that can be associated with the modeling component of corporate modeling.

17. Explain how risk analysis and optimization are used in modeling.

18. Explain the difference between *forecasting* and econometric modeling.

19. Differentiate between a *ready-made model* and a *tailor-made model* as related to corporate planning models.

20. Differentiate between the following three types of tailor-made models: (1) ad *hoc*, (2) *fixed-structure*, and (3) *integrated*.

21. Identify five software packages that support corporate planning and modeling systems.

22. Identify at least ten factors that should be considered in selecting a modeling software package.

23. Identify a unique feature that each of the following software packages contains: (1) CUFFS, (2) EXPRESS, (3) IFPS, (4) SIMPLAN, and (5) XSIM.

24. From Chapter 4, corporate planning models are characteristic of what type of information system? Why?

EXERCISES AND CASES

15-1

Alpha Video Systems is a small manufacturer and distributor of video games and equipment. The company began as a small operation five years ago but has grown significantly over the past two years. For the fiscal year ending June 30, 1982, two thousand systems were sold. Figure C15–1(A) shows the company's financial statements for the year-end. For the past two years sales volume has grown about 20 percent per year. Bill Blakely, controller of Alpha, anticipates that the business will continue to grow at this same rate for the next couple of years.

Alpha has fourteen employees: two salesmen, eleven production/manufacturing personnel, and a production foreman. Blakely assumes all management responsibility for the company.

ALPHA VIDEO SYSTEMS
BALANCE SHEET AS OF JUNE 30, 1982
(DOLLAR FIGURES IN THOUSANDS)

ASSETS			LIABILITIES AND EQUITY	
Cash		69.0	Accounts payable	48.0
Accounts receivable		0.0	Bank loan	129.0
Inventory			Equity	400.0
Materials	48.0			
Finished goods	320.0	368.0		
Fixed assets		140.0		
		577.0		577.0

ALPHA VIDEO SYSTEMS
INCOME STATEMENT FOR YEAR ENDING JUNE 30, 1982
(DOLLAR FIGURES IN THOUSANDS)

Sales (2,000 systems at $400/system)		800.0
Cost of goods sold		656.0
Gross profits on sales		144.0
Expenses		
Selling	24.0	
General and administrative	48.0	
Depreciation	14.0	86.0
Net income before taxes		58.0
Taxes (52%)		30.2
Net profit		27.8

Figure C15–1(A) Financial Statements for Alpha Video Systems for Year Ending June 30, 1982

PRODUCTION   Alpha's production operations are such that 250 systems can be produced in a single month. The shipment of video systems is highly seasonal—starting in September or October, rising to a peak in December, and declining to almost zero in May. (Figure C15–1(B) depicts this variation in sales.) Production is scheduled evenly throughout eleven months of the year even though variability in sales exists. Production is shut down for June, during which time production employees take their vacations.

According to Blakely:

The company does not have to have level production to be efficient, but it sure makes scheduling a lot easier. Besides it builds up the inventories before the major selling season starts, so if we get some early sales that we have not planned, we will have the systems ready to ship.

For the first five months of 1982 (January through May), the production level has been two hundred systems per month.

Blakely's comments relating to material and labor costs are as follows:

Materials account for a large portion of the cost of manufacturing a video system. The standard cost for manufacturing a system is $320; of this cost approximately $240 is for materials, but the material costs tend to fluctuate at times. Competition keeps us from raising the sales price above $400. If the costs go down, we can have a real good year; but if they get too high, we get squeezed. However, I think the $240 figure will hold for this production year. Direct labor cost is about $80 per system.

MONTH	MONTHLY VOLUME
July	3
August	22
September	152
October	274
November	440
December	570
January	262
February	117
March	88
April	41
May	21
June	10
	2,000

Figure C15–1(B) Monthly Shipping Profile for Alpha Video Systems

Purchases are made each month for materials that will be needed the following month. The terms that we have with the suppliers are net thirty days. This is the same arrangement we have with our receivables, but they generally take two months to get their checks in. Because of competition we are willing to accept this delay.

The company has recently upgraded its production facilities, and therefore no capital expenditures are anticipated in the next three or four years unless sales outstrip production capacity. The existing $140,000 in fixed assets is being depreciated on a ten-year, straight-line basis.

MARKETING The majority of the selling for Alpha is done by a two-person sales force calling on retail distributors. The competition in video systems is very fierce, and therefore it is important that the salespeople constantly call on their distributors.

In 1982 each salesperson received $12,000 salary per year. But in addition to this, each operates under a bonus method. A bonus of $20 is paid for each system sold above the 20 percent growth rate for the company. Currently the company has an $80 profit margin on each video system; for all extra systems sold, the profits would be $60 before taxes.

FINANCE According to Blakely:

The only financial problem that we have is drumming up enough cash to finance our operations while we are waiting for our sales revenues. Fortunately we have been getting credit from the local banks. They have allowed us a line of credit up to 90 percent of the equity in the business. The interest is 1.2 percent per month on the amount borrowed during the month. The only restrictions are that we must be completely paid up for at least one month a year and we have to maintain a cash balance of at least 20 percent of the loan. The cash balance is not a problem because I keep enough cash on hand to cover next month's cash requirements.

I have been approached several times by investors who want to buy into the business. However, since the company's growth is not being restricted by lack of equity, I see no reason to bring in outsiders.

REQUIRED:

a. Alpha Video Systems is not the typical-size firm that would be involved with corporate planning and modeling; however, it can effectively be used to illustrate some basic concepts. Given the following balance sheet account codes and transaction account codes, develop the set of recursive equations that can be used to generate a balance sheet for July 1982:

BALANCE SHEET ACCOUNT CODES	TRANSACTION ACCOUNT CODES
BC_t = Cash	TCR_t = Collection of receivables
BR_t = Accounts receivable	TCL_t = Borrowing
BI_t = Inventory	TPC_t = Payment of accounts payable
BF_t = Fixed assets	
BP_t = Accounts payable	TFC_t = Purchase of fixed assets
BL_t = Loan	TLC_t = Repayment of loan
BE_t = Equity	TRI_t = Cost of goods sold
	TRE_t = Gross profit on sales
	TIP_t = Purchase of materials
	TIE_t = Direct labor costs
	TEF_t = Depreciation
	TEP_t = Expenses of the period

b. Generate the income statement for the period ending July 1982.

c. Explain how risk analysis and/or forecasting might be used in support of requirements *a* and *b*.

d. A natural extension of a balance sheet model is a target-type model, that is, a model that can be used to determine what the values of the transactions will be, given a desired ending balance sheet. Whereas in the case of a balance sheet model transactions are used as inputs and the account balances are outputs (computed), a transaction or target model would have the desired (as well as beginning) account balances as inputs and the transaction values would be output (computed).

Using the following event, the decision codes, the discussion above, and accounting identities, develop a transaction model for the firm:

EVENT AND DECISION CODES

TV = Total annual sales volume (in systems), July 1, 1982–June 30, 1983

P_t = Percentage of total orders (systems) shipped during month t when t = 1 for July

V_t = Production volume in month t

SP = Selling price per system (assumed constant for the year)

MP = Material cost per system (assumed constant for the year)

DL = Direct labor costs per year

SC = Selling costs per year, excluding any bonuses that might be given

GA = General and administrative cost per year

Hint: Eleven transaction equations will be required in the model.

15–2

The planning process at the Best Company consists of a network of interrelated decisions that can be summarized in the form of budgets. These budgets are related to each other in a manner similar to that shown in Figure C15–2.

A synopsis of the budgeting process follows: Long-range sales forecasts and corporate policies are determined. Capital projects are then outlined in a capital planning budget; afterward a periodic sales budget is prepared. The sales budget is then used as a basis for determining inventory levels. Based on the inventory levels, the production requirements are established. From the production requirements, direct material requirements and purchases can be planned, labor needs can be determined, and overhead needs can be budgeted. Also, given the sales budget, cash receipts can be estimated. And given the capital budget, the production budget for material, labor, and overhead, for planned selling and expenditures, and for cash disbursements can be estimated. From estimated receipts and disbursements, a cash budget can be prepared. The cash budget allows the organization to plan for effective use of cash resources and prepare effectively for the acquisition of additional cash resources as the need arises. Given the sales, inventory, production, selling, and administrative expense, along with capital and cash budgets, a pro forma income statement and balance sheet can be prepared.

Best's budget process for the first quarter of 19X4 is as follows: First, a *sales forecast* is prepared from historical sales patterns and from an assessment of the economic and competitive outlook for Best's product. Best's sales were 30,000, 20,000, and 10,000 units in October, November, and December 19X3, respectively. It has forecast that sales will be 20,000, 25,000, 30,000, 50,000, 50,000, and 40,000 for the next six months. Best anticipates no change in price over the next six months, which has been $4 per unit for the past six months. Furthermore, based on last year's experience, Best forecast that its collection pattern would be 60 percent in the month of the sale, 20 percent the following month, and the remaining 20 percent the month after that.

REQUIRED:

a. From these data prepare a *Sales Budget* and *Cash Collection Budget* for the first quarter of 19X4. The accounts receivable from November and December 19X3 sales is as follows:

		19X4	
	12/31	JANUARY	FEBRUARY
November sales	16,000	16,000	
December sales	40,000	8,000	8,000

b. Following the preparation of the sales budget, the *Production Budget* can be prepared, but several decisions must be made prior to this. First, an inventory policy must be set, based on the degree of uncertainty in the sales forecast and production operations and on the need for a buffer stock of finished goods. Best has decided that to avoid lost sales and ensure adequate distribution to retail centers, the company should end each month with at least 50 percent of next month's sales inventory. From this information, the balance on December 31, 19X3, and the sales budget, production requirements for the next three months can be planned. Develop the production requirements portion of the Production Budget.

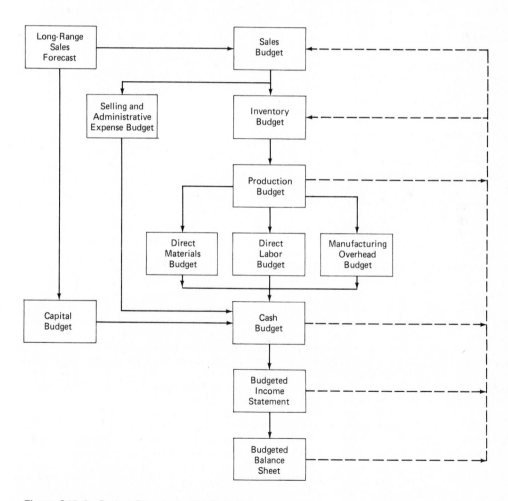

Figure C15–2 Budget Process for the Best Company

c. Given (1) the production requirements, (2) an estimated need of two pounds of material (per unit) at $0.25 per pound, and (3) the same 50 percent ending inventory policy, the monthly *acquisition of raw material* (expressed in terms of units) and *cash disbursements* for these purchases can be determined. Prepare this portion of the budget. Assume that all materials will be paid for in the month following the purchase.

d. Best uses an industrial engineering study and concludes that it will take one-quarter of an hour of labor at $6.00 per hour, or $1.50 per unit, to manufacture its product. Given the number of units to be produced in the production requirements portion of the Production Budget, *labor costs* and *disbursements* can be completed, assuming that cash disbursements for labor are made for all practical purposes in the same month in which the labor cost is incurred. Compute this portion of the budget.

e. Best uses direct labor hours to allocate variable factory overhead at $1 per direct labor hour. Therefore, upon completion of the direct labor requirement (in part *d* above), *variable overhead* expenses can be determined. To these, estimated fixed overhead expenses can be added. Assuming that overhead expenses are paid for in the month in which they are incurred (by subtracting depreciation from the *budgeted overhead*), *cash disbursements* for manufacturing overhead can be determined. Compute the manufacturing overhead portion of the Production Budget.

f. Given the sales patterns, the behavior of selling and administrative cost based on these patterns, and the planned discretionary expenses for promotion and other expenditures, the *selling and administrative expense budget* can be computed. Develop this budget by assuming that variable selling/adminstrative expenses are $0.25 per unit and all selling and administrative expenses are paid in the month in which they are incurred.

g. Prepare a cash budget for the Best Company. In January, February, and March 19X4, no capital additions are planned. Assume that Best has a policy of borrowing and repaying in $500 increments with a 12 percent annual interest rate. The interest paid monthly is on the maximum balance during the month, and all borrowing takes place at the beginning of the month and all repayments are made at the end of the month. A $5,000 minimum cash balance is required by Best as a contingency against uncertainties. The cash budget is prepared as follows: (1) expected cash receipts from the cash collection schedule (prepared in part *a* are added to the beginning balance to determine the total cash available, (2) all disbursements from the Production Schedules Budget and the Selling and Administrative Expense Budget are added to capital expenditures and cash dividend payments to obtain total cash disbursements, (3) any excess or deficiency is adjusted by a minimum balance required to obtain a net excess or deficiency, (4) cash borrowing or repayment and interest expenditures are then planned to maintain a minimum cash balance.

h. Prepare a pro forma balance sheet and income statement for Best.

i. Develop a set of recursive equations that can be used to generate each of the budgets developed in parts *a* through *h*.[1]

15–3

Given the following case example and the summary of software systems available in the market (CUFFS, EXPRESS, IFPS, SIMPLAN, XSIM), recommend a software package that would best complement the organization's short-term and long-term needs. Justify your selection by indicating what the systems will provide and how this will enhance the organization's objectives.

Sigma Electronics' planning cycle is a key part of its management philosophy and is at the core of its managerial, strategic, and deci-

---

[1] The original case upon which this case is based is from Horngren, Charles T., *Accounting for Management Control* 3rd Ed.(Englewood Cliffs, N.J.: Prentice-Hall, Inc., 1974), p. 205.

sion-making activities. As such, it is a continuous process that integrates near-term actions, constraints on profitability, and resources with the long-range plans and corporate objectives. The planning cycle begins in August of each year when the operating committee sets the overall priorities that will guide the firm for the upcoming year and the next three years. These priorities define the relative need for growth, profitability, productivity, new-product or process development, and similar issues.

Sigma's planning cycle is implemented through a "four-loop" planning process, as shown in Figure C15–3. The first loop is long-range planning, which focuses on Sigma's direction for the next ten years and the strategies for getting there. The second loop is intermediate-range planning, which concentrates on planning for facilities, manufacturing equipment, and major product cost reductions for the next three years. In this second loop, the current year plus one is most critical because it ties the strategic plan, intermediate plan, and rolling plan together.

The rolling plan, or third loop, is a quarterly update of the current year. It occurs in January, April, July, and October of each year. Rolling plans include a full set of profit and loss and resource objectives, or indices, along with the most current thinking as to volume levels and changing business conditions. The fourth loop is for monthly forecasting. In the first month of each quarter, each product center forecasts for three months into the future. In the second month of a quarter, forecasts are five months; and in the third month, forecasts are four months. This final loop constitutes Sigma's short-cycle profit error signaling and control mechanism.

Throughout the planning process, Sigma managers focus on key indices such as net sales billed (NSB), growth rate, gross profit margin (GPM) percentage, strategic investment (OST) percentage, organization profit percentage, and return on assets (ROA). Once these key indices have been specified for an organization, then all other resources and P & L indices can be developed.

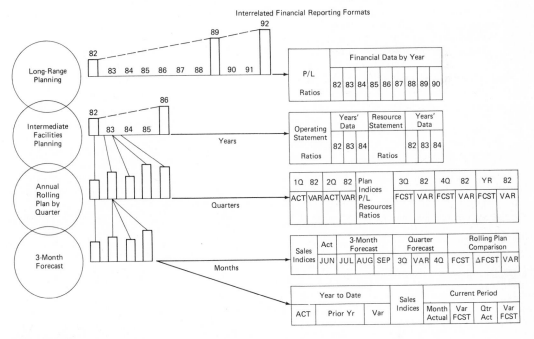

Figure C15–3 Sigma Electronics Planning Cycle

Sales (400,000 regular and 700,000 deluxe)	$ 20,000
Manufacturing costs	12,709
Gross margin	$ 7,291
Marketing costs	4,100
General and administrative	1,000
Advertising costs	200
Profit before taxes	$ 1,991
Taxes (51% of PBT)	1,015
Profit after taxes	$ 976

Figure C15–4(A) L & D Products Inc., Income Statement for Year Ending December 31, 1981 (dollar figures in thousands)

15–4

L & D Products Inc. manufactures small hand-held hair dryers and markets them through manufacturing representatives. The company produces two styles of dryers at its Eaton, Tennessee, plant: (1) a regular model and (2) a super deluxe model.

During the past three years, L & D's sales have increased 15 percent per year. Management expects this growth to continue even though the industry has recently gone through a price decline.

The company's 1981 income statement is shown in Figure C15–4(A), and its cost structure is shown in Figure C15–4(B).

Analysis of the cost structure data shows that the capital investment required in this particular industry is relatively low. Variable man-ufacturing costs are approximately 40 percent labor and 60 percent materials. The variable marketing costs are primarily sales commissions (paid to the manufacturing representatives) and freight expenses.

From past experience, management has noted that when total production volume exceeds 400,000 units, the variable manufacturing costs increase by approximately 25 percent. Therefore, when total production is less than 400,000 units, the manufacturing costs per unit for the two products are $6.00 and $9.50; when total production exceeds 400,000 units, costs increase to $7.50 and $11.87, respectively.

In recent years the company has had an annual advertising budget of $200,000. Previously this expenditure has been allocated equally between the two products; however, manage-

Variable Costs (dollars/units)

	PRODUCT LINE	
	Regular	Deluxe
Selling price	$ 15.00	$20.00
Variable manufacturing costs		
Volume under 400,000	6.00	9.50
Volume over 400,000	7.50	11.87
Variable marketing costs	1.50	1.50

Fixed costs (per year)

Manufacturing costs—$2,000,000
Marketing costs—$3,000,000
General and administrative—$600,000 plus 2% of total dollar sales

Budgeted costs (per year)

Advertising costs—$200,000 (historically, $100,000 for each product)

Figure C15–4(B) L & D Products Inc. Cost Structure Summary—Based on 1980 Results

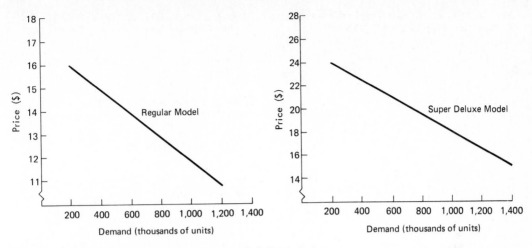

Figure C15–4(C) Product Demand Curves for L & D Products Inc.

ment is now wondering whether this should be divided differently between the two products. Management has also been questioning the effects of advertising on profits and would like to analyze whether the advertising budget, in general, should be increased or decreased.

Based on current advertising, the marketing manager at L & D has estimated that there is an inverse relationship between the prices of the company's products and the demand for its products. These demand relationships are depicted in Figure C15–4(C). The manager has also evaluated some market research data and has come up with the effects of price and advertising on number of units sold for cash production. These data are shown in Figure C15–4(D).

REQUIRED:

a. Develop a model for the company that will allow "what if" analyses for determining the impact of (1) increasing or decreasing an advertising budget and (2) allocating the advertising budget differently between two products. Write the equations for the model.

b. Using the model developed in requirement *a*, evaluate the impact of increasing the advertising budget to $250,000. (Assume that the price of the product remains fixed and that $150,000 is spent on the regular model advertising and $100,000 is spent on the deluxe model.)

c. Modify the model in requirement *a* to take into consideration the impact of price changes.

d. Using the model developed in requirement *c*, evaluate the impact of having a $200,000 advertising budget and allocating it equally between the two products, but assume that the prices of the products have been increased to $16 and $27, respectively.

Figure C15–4(D) Effects of Price and Advertising on Demand for L & D Products Inc.

	PRICE			PRICE	
Advertising	$15	$16	Advertising	$20	$22
$100,000	400	200	$100,000	700	400
$150,000	500	350	$150,000	400	250
	Demand (thousands of units)			Demand (thousands of units)	

e. How would you go about developing an optimal pricing/advertising plan?

f. What advantage would a planning/modeling software package have in terms of performing the analyses in requirements *a* through *c*?

16

LARGE-SCALE SYSTEMS

INTRODUCTION

In Chapter 2 we discussed the advantages and disadvantages of integrated and distributed systems. In Chapter 6 we examined the evolution of these systems. In this chapter we will examine the application of some of these systems.

Note that the title of this chapter refers neither to integrated nor distributed systems, but rather to "large-scale" systems. At one point in time a large system implied an integrated or "total" system; however, as we noted in Chapters 6 and 8, as well as in a number of the application chapters, a system can be large and be distributed in nature. In this chapter we will discuss integrated, distributed, and a combination of integrated-distributed systems; all, however, are large-scale systems.

Four different examples are given in the chapter. Two examples are in the body of the chapter and two case examples are at the end of the chapter. These consist of a manufacturing firm, an electronics firm, a paper manufacturer, and a test equipment and computer manufacturer. In the body of the chapter the examples are fairly detailed, while the end-of-chapter case examples are summary overviews. Each example, however, provides a unique or different systems application.

A MANUFACTURING EXAMPLE[1]

The American Products Corporation specializes in the manufacture of products for the consumer market. The company's sales were $95 million per annum in 1978 and were projected to be about $120 to $125 million by 1983. Its product line consists of fifteen products which can be categorized into three basic product groups. Variations of these basic products are for specific customers whose requirements differ depending on the markets they serve. For large orders, products are shipped directly to the customer from the company's manufacturing plants. All other orders are shipped from the company's warehouses to retailers. Experience has shown that 20 percent of the company's dollar volume represents direct shipments from the plants and 80 percent represents shipments through the company's warehouses.

Corporate headquarters are located in St. Louis; manufacturing plants are located in Minneapolis, Philadelphia, and Los Angeles. Wherever a manufacturing plant is located, a warehouse is attached. The present employment level for the entire firm is approximately two thousand employees.

The organization of American Products is such that the president (the chief executive officer) reports to the board of directors and is assisted by the corporate planning group. The executive vice-president, in turn, reports to the president. In a similar manner, nine vice-presidents (marketing, research and development/engineering, manufacturing, purchasing and inventory, physical distribution, accounting, finance, personnel, and management information system) report to the executive vice-president. Various corporate managers, plant managers, and warehouse managers report to the respective vice-presidents.

American has progressed through a series of data processing systems over the years, limited only by the constraints of available equipment. In the early 1950s, manual systems were augmented by adding machines and calculators. Punched-card equipment and tabulating machines provided expanded system capabilities. As electronic computers became available, the data processing system was adapted to utilize these machines, making the translation of data into information much faster. The company now uses an integrated management information system (batch-processing-oriented), which is being converted to a distributed processing system (interactive-processing-oriented).

The problem encountered with the batch system was that information was not sufficiently timely to effect changes in the operating environment. Too often, information was received too late by corporate headquarters to effect the necessary control over manufacturing and warehousing operations. The batch processing mode of the system did not facilitate day-to-day operational decision making.

Because of the problems with the batch system, it became apparent that a company-wide information system had to be developed. What the company needed was a forward-looking control system that would provide operational control in an interactive processing mode. Because distributed processing systems are capable of accomplishing such a goal, the MIS vice-president

---

[1] Robert J. Thierauf, *Distributed Processing Systems*, © 1978, pp. 136–152. Adapted by permission of Prentice-Hall, Inc., Englewood Cliffs, N. J.

initiated a feasibility study. The study disclosed the feasibility of distributed computing.

The key reasons found in the feasibility study for implementing a management-oriented distributed processing system in an interactive processing mode were

1. Better customer service and improved selling efficiency
2. More timely and improved management information analysis and reporting at the plant and home office levels
3. Improved coordination and control of the overall organization and its individual parts
4. Better opportunity to match demand with production
5. On-line information available from a distributed data base for management analysis of the organization's operations and prospective operations

The Distributed Processing Environment

Based on the feasibility study, the company selected a computer system that integrated satellite minicomputers at each of the three manufacturing plants, including the attached warehouses, with a centralized computer system. Within this hardware configuration, an environment of cooperative software existed thereby allowing the organization to distribute its data base at the appropriate levels and application programs among the remote locations.

Figure 16–1 illustrates the hierarchical or tree network utilized by the American Products Corporation. Essentially, the central or host computer is a Honeywell Level 66 computer that employs a DATANET front-end network processor for controlling all input from the three satellite minicomputers (Four Phase System IV/90, capable of supporting up to thirty-two video displays). Currently, at each of the plants with attached warehouses, four terminals have been installed for use in sales order processing plus four for accounting. In a similar manner, fourteen have been installed for manufacturing and physical distribution.

The executive software for the Honeywell Level 66 Computer System is GCOS (General Comprehensive Operating Software), which controls, schedules, and monitors all activities and adjusts processing activity to changing demands. Processing modes include transaction processing, data base inquiry, time sharing, interactive job entry and execution, and batch processing. These modes are available at the central site and remotely via Level 66 communication facilities, using the corporate data base.

For this particular distributed processing environment, the Data Management–IV (DM–IV) is used because the Level 66 data base management system is designed for high-volume on-line transaction processing and efficient, interactive query and reporting. It uses a common language for defining, managing, and directing data and provides a standard user interface that is simple and logical. Additionally, it allows a common file description to govern the structure of all data but is independent of that structure. In effect, DM–IV gives

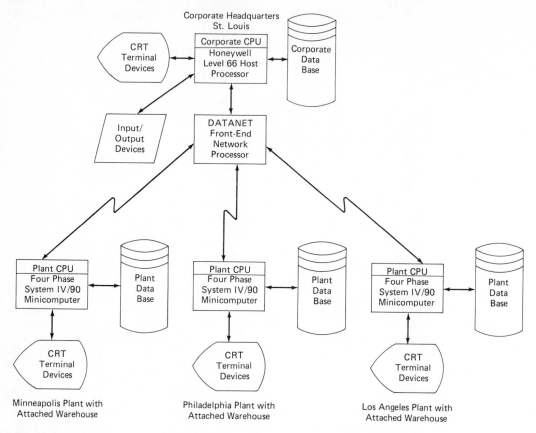

Figure 16-1   Overview of the Distributed Processing System (American Products Corporation)

organizational personnel timely access to vital information and provides data integrity protection, security, and automatic recovery and restart.

The communications network for implementing the distributed operating environment was determined during the equipment selection phase of the systems study. It is a full duplex system that links all of the company's plants, including warehouses, to the corporate headquarters in St. Louis. (A full duplex communication channel, as we noted in Chapter 5, has the ability to transmit information in both directions simultaneously.) In addition, all communication lines from and to corporate headquarters are fully dedicated lines—that is, it is not necessary to telephone in order to reserve a communication line from the plants, including warehouses, to corporate headquarters or vice versa.

Overview of Major Subsystems

From an overview standpoint, the American Products Corporation can be described as a *materials-flow company*. This concept is illustrated in Figure 16–2 as a double-line arrow on the outer rim of the flowchart. Purchased materials, and manufactured materials for stock, flow into the various stages of the production process; here, the materials take on a variety of forms and shapes

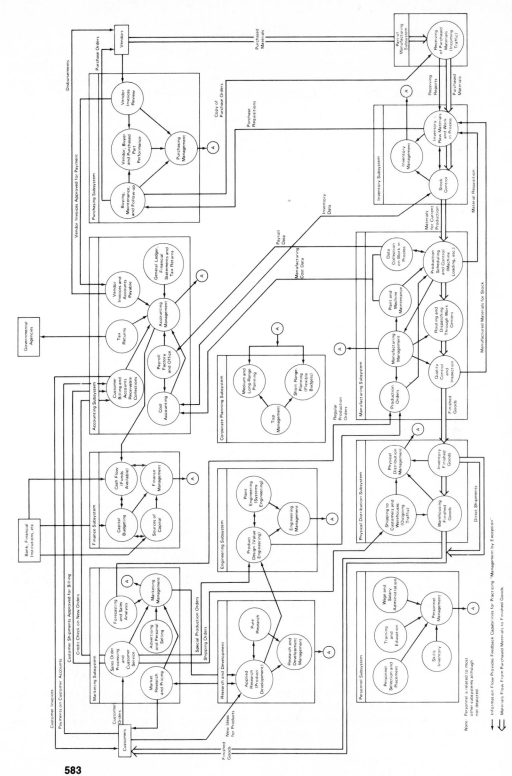

Figure 16-2 Flowchart Depicting the Major Subsystems (American Products Corporation)

583

until they become finished goods. Next, the finished products flow through the distribution system, either directly via direct shipments or indirectly through company-owned warehouses, until they reach the customer. In this materials-flow concept, several of the corporation's subsystems are thus involved, namely, purchasing, inventory, manufacturing, and physical distribution.

Coupled with the materials flow in Figure 16–2 is a corresponding information flow. Materials-flow information is an important factor in coordinating the diversified activities of the three manufacturing plants and attached warehouses with corporate headquarters. The information must be comprehensive, thereby integrating decision making throughout the entire materials-flow process. With an integrated flow of essential information, management and operating personnel can make adjustments swiftly and effectively in response to the ever-changing business environment. The materials-flow approach is therefore an essential part of the distributed processing system.

The information flow for American Products (or any company, for that matter) is not restricted to the materials area only. There may actually be more information being generated for activities that are not directly related to the materials-flow process. For example, many subparts of the corporation's corporate planning, marketing, research and development, engineering, accounting, and finance subsystems are not directly related to the manufacture of the final product. No matter what the source or need of information, the overall distributed processing system must be "open-ended." This approach provides flexibility such that activities can be linked with one another at minimum cost and effort. But more important, the open-ended approach allows for changing the direction and speed of information flow in response to management and operating personnel needs.

Figure 16–3 illustrates the concept of information flow. Here the quarterly sales forecast (marketing subsystem), based on external and internal factors, affects the quantity of finished goods to be produced (physical distribution subsystem), which, in turn, affects materials to be purchased from outside suppliers (purchasing subsystem) and to be manufactured within the company (manufacturing subsystem) by future planning periods. Goods purchased or manufactured are procured on an optimum basis, using the economic order quantity (EOQ) formula, and are eventually handled by the inventory section (inventory subsystem). Both are requisitioned to meet the manufacturing plan in accordance with the schedule of master operations (manufacturing subsystem). The operational or shop status of the final product, material, labor, and similar items is used for operations evaluation control at the manufacturing level. In some cases, operating information is significant enough for review by middle and top management. If this happens, feedback may make it necessary to review future plans (corporate planning subsystem). Also, it may be necessary to revise future sales forecasts. Finally, finished goods are shipped directly to the customers or through plant-attached warehouses.

Due to space limitations, we will not explore all of the major subsystems for American, as set forth in Figure 16–2. Rather, only the basic subsystems (namely, marketing, manufacturing, physical distribution, and accounting) are discussed below. The analysis and design of these selected subsystems serve to highlight the interrelationships of local processing (plants with attached warehouses) to centralized processing (corporate headquarters).

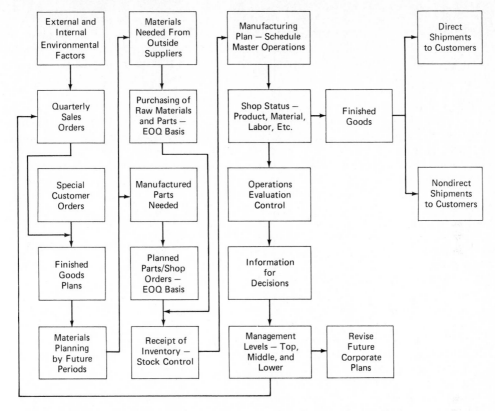

Figure 16-3 The Integrated Flow of Information (American Products Corporation)

MARKETING SUBSYSTEM The firm's marketing subsystem consists of several modules (subparts). The major ones are depicted in Figure 16–2 and are as follows:

1. Forecasting and sales analysis
2. Sales order processing and customer service
3. Advertising and personal selling
4. Market research and pricing

To illustrate how the subparts operate, let us consider sales order processing. The block diagram (an overview of information processing), Figure 16–4, indicates that orders are received and appropriate order forms are prepared and edited before the customer credit is checked. If the order is not accepted because of poor credit, it is returned to the customer and the reason is noted. Generally the order is approved for order entry whereby appropriate files (customer, pricing, and finished goods) are referenced for preparing shipping papers. Shipping papers are then forwarded to the appropriate warehouses for regular shipment or to a particular plant for direct shipment.

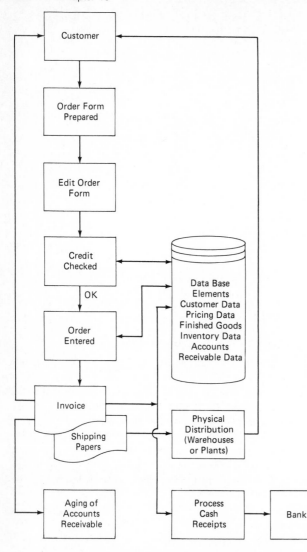

Figure 16–4 Sales Order Processing —A Subelement of the Marketing Subsystem (American Products Corporation)

At this point, other major subsystems interact with sales order processing (marketing subsystem). Shipping papers provide the basis for preparing customer invoices that are eventually used for aging accounts receivable and processing checks received from customers (accounting subsystem). In addition, they are used for assembling goods at the warehouse and plant levels. If items are available for shipment as noted by the perpetual finished goods file during the sales order processing phase, the file is changed from "finished goods on order" to "finished goods shipped" (physical distribution subsystem). Engineering also comes into contact with sales order processing through the receipt of special customer orders (engineering subsystem).

MANUFACTURING SUBSYSTEM The next key subsystem for getting regular or special production orders produced is manufacturing. Its essential subparts are as follows:

1. Receiving
2. Production scheduling and control
3. Manufacturing operations:
   a. Machine shop
   b. Assembly—major and minor
   c. Plant and machine maintenance
4. Quality control and inspection
5. Data collection system

Common questions associated with the manufacturing subsystem are:

1. How much finished goods should be manufactured at one time?
2. What raw materials are required where and when?
3. What is the progress of job orders?
4. How much work-in-process inventory is needed and where?
5. What are the production schedules, and how are they being met?
6. Have the finished goods been completed and/or shipped?
7. What are the manufacturing cost variances?

The manufacturing process is a continuation of the forecasted finished goods marketing subsystem. As illustrated in Figure 16–5, raw materials are ordered on a quarterly basis (purchasing subsystem) and, upon receipt, are placed under the supervision of stock control (inventory subsystem). They provide input for the manufacturing plan of the production scheduling and control section, whose job is to schedule, route, and dispatch orders through the various manufacturing work centers. The quality control section is responsible for making appropriate tests of manufactured and finished products before forwarding them to the warehouse or customer (physical distribution subsystem). As illustrated, there is an interplay between physical activities and data files for operations evaluation, allowing feedback of critical information where necessary.

PHYSICAL DISTRIBUTION SUBSYSTEM The handling of finished goods after manufacturing is the responsibility of the physical distribution subsystem. Subparts of this subsystem include

1. Shipping to customers and warehouses (outgoing traffic)
2. Warehousing—finished goods
3. Inventory—finished goods

The manufacturing process culminates in having the finished goods transported from one of the three manufacturing plants to the customers di-

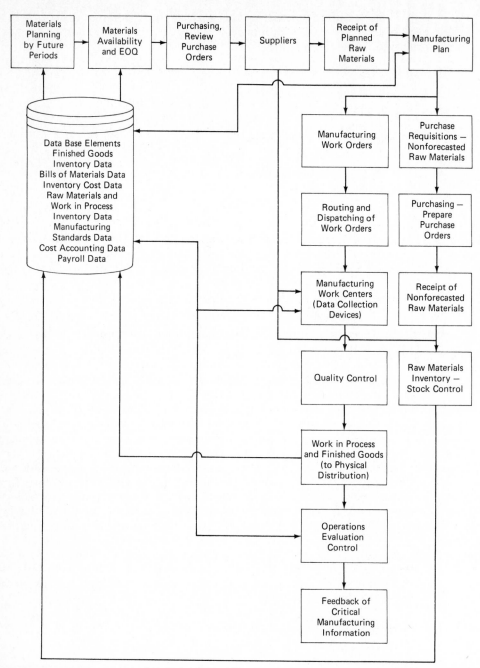

Figure 16-5 Work in Process and Finished Goods—A Subelement of the Manufacturing, Inventory, and Purchasing Subsystems (American Products Corporation)

rectly (direct shipments) or to one or more of the plant-attached warehouses (nondirect shipments). To keep overall shipping costs for the firm at a minimum, the system designed must be capable of responding to these questions:

1. Can finished goods be allocated to warehouses such that customer orders can be filled promptly?
2. Can procedures be devised such that the appropriate quantities desired by customers are in the nearest warehouse to reduce shipping costs?
3. If goods are not available at the closest warehouse, are there procedures for locating goods at the next-closest warehouse almost instantaneously?
4. Does the physical distribution system keep overall costs at a minimum?

The shipment of finished goods, whether it be direct or nondirect, must be reflected in the company's data files. Likewise, certain data on routing finished goods are utilized in effecting the lowest total costs. These files, as shown in Figure 16–6, are referenced when finished goods are shipped to customers via order processing (marketing subsystem). As indicated in Figure 16–

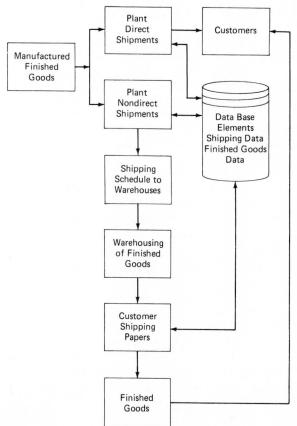

Figure 16–6 Distribution of Finished Goods from Plants to Warehouses and Customers—The Main Subelement of the Physical Distribution Subsystem (American Products Corporation)

4, shipping papers, initiated by the physical distribution subsystem, start the customer billing and collection process (accounting subsystem).

ACCOUNTING SUBSYSTEM The sales and cost factors, generated by the previous subsystems, are accounted for and reported by the accounting subsystem. They provide the required inputs for the following accounting subparts:

1. Receivables and payables
2. Payroll
3. Cost accounting
4. Financial statements and tax returns

The accounting subsystem, which involves keeping records, billing customers, arranging payments, and costing products, among others, is a myriad of details. For accounting information to assist other subsystems, it must focus on answers to such timely questions as the following:

1. Can actual cost data be compared with standard data for the various manufacturing work centers?
2. Can information on the current status of customer accounts be obtained on a "now" basis?
3. Are all accounting data in a machine-processible form for compiling current managerial accounting reports and financial statements?

Generally, accounting activities, as set forth in Figure 16–7, center on those of recording and reporting sales and costs (expenses). Sales revenue and manufacturing cost data—raw materials, labor, and overhead—as well as marketing and general and administrative expenses provide the necessary inputs per the general ledger for producing periodic—overall and detailed—income statements. Cash, receivables, payables, and other accounts are recorded in the general ledger for producing the balance sheet. These financial statements provide inputs for intermediate and long-range analysis (corporate planning subsystem). In a similar manner, detailed income and cost (expense) analyses are helpful in determining future cash flow and capital budgets (finance subsystem).

A MAJOR ELECTRONICS FIRM[2]

Texas Instruments Incorporated is a multinational electronics firm with forty-eight plants in eighteen different countries. The systems problem associated with linking these diverse locations is a major task—the company is in a variety of product markets including the consumer market and is experiencing such a tremendous growth that it has projected a fivefold increase in net sales billed in the next decade. TI employs a large distributed processing network to interlink its plants and activities.

[2] Reprinted with permission of *Datamation* ® magazine, © copyright by Technical Publishing Company, A Dun & Bradstreet Company, (April 1979), all rights reserved.

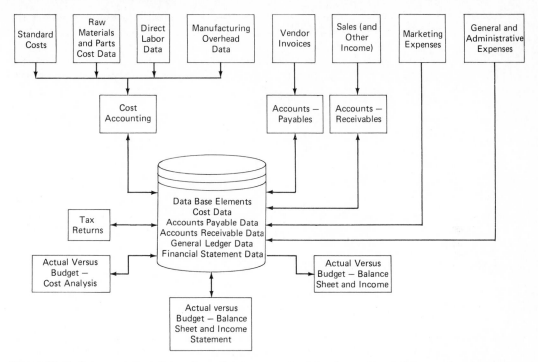

Figure 16–7 Sales and Cost Data—Essential Components of the Accounting Subsystem (American Products Corporation)

Overview

TI's distributed network currently links fifty-one hundred terminals and 190 RJE stations. It is expected that this will grow to twenty-five thousand terminals with ten thousand minicomputers by the mid-1980s. The Information Systems and Services Group has the responsibility for managing this system.

The Corporate Information Center (CIC) is host to many of the distributed minicomputers. It handles the corporate data base and information common to many of the distributed systems. Its capabilities include RJE batch processing, inquiry, time sharing, microfiche and copy service, data preparation, Xerox 1200 printing, and plotting.

The CIC uses two IBM 370/168APs and two IBM 3033s. Each has 8 to 12 megabytes of addressable storage with more than 472 billion bytes of auxiliary storage. Eighty dual-density tape drives are used to access the seventy thousand tapes of corporate information.

The CIC now handles six thousand batch jobs, 320,000 IMS transactions, and 1,250 TSO log-ons per day. Although the use of CIC is large, the use of distributed computers at TI has grown twice as fast as host usage in the past decade.

TI's Communication Grid (TICOG) is the worldwide communication network supporting Information Systems and Services. Figure 16–8 shows the land line and satellite communication channels used by Europe, Asia, and Latin America.

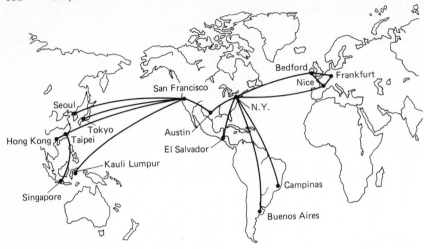

Figure 16–8   TI's Communication Grid (TICOG)

Begun in 1972, TICOG uses packet-switching technology. (*Packet-switching* divides messages into multiple, fixed-size packets. Packet size is chosen to be optimal for reducing system bit error rate.) A TI 98OB minicomputer selects the most effective routing for each individual packet and transmits it. A receiving 98OB minicomputer then reassembles the packets into the original message. The System is also packet-buffered to compensate for error introduction when using satellite channels. In addition to the TI 98OB minicomputer, some special-purpose hardware is used along with ASA data-concentrators with software tailored for satellite communication. The entire communication process is transparent to user data.

TICOG also periodically polls quiescent communication paths. Potential future path failure is detected and repaired before that path is needed. A history of these failures is maintained to aid the identification of faulty equipment.

Most of TI's distributed processing systems use a minicomputer system designed for on-line transaction processing called the DXS (Data Exchange System). Its functions include concurrent batch, interactive communications, and transaction processing; local data base; local and remote data collection; interface to a host (DXS or CIC); multitasking operating system; storing and running the application programs; and hybrid inquiry. A *hybrid inquiry* is a procedure transparent to the operator in which data not available on the local DXS data base are automatically retrieved from the host base and are either displayed or used in the application program (see Figure 16–9).

A DXS can be configured with one or more CPUs. For example, one CPU can be designated to handle applications, one to handle terminal polling, and another to control host communications. The use of multiple CPUs increases throughput and creates communication redundancy in the system. If a local DXS processor goes down, the communication redundancy allows work to continue on another network's DXS or a mainframe host in CIC.

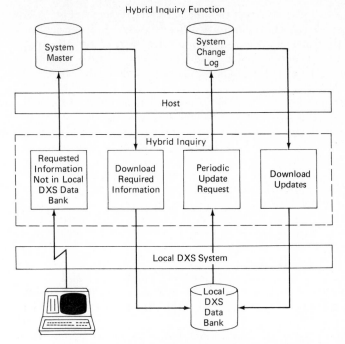

Figure 16-9 TI's Data Exchange System (DXS)

Three models of DXS are used in TI's network. Their disk storage size ranges from 9.2 megabytes to 400 megabytes. One DXS can support up to thirty thousand transactions per day. On the average, the transaction level for DXS is approximately six thousand per day; but with the large growth in distributed use at TI, the number of transactions is increasing 20 to 100 percent per year.

The company uses distributed processing in a wide variety of applications, including automated design of printed circuit boards using interactive graphics. This graphics capability is also used to do design editing on integrated circuits. The data base contains the standard parts library. Another application is a work-in-progress schedule and control system used in production planning that generates statistical engineering data for analysis. Mechanical controls for processing are also controlled by this front-end process system. The company also has a real-time system allowing visibility of job status, dynamic work queue sequencing, and shop load analysis.

Two of TI's more interesting applications are a real-time system for customer service management in the field, and an in-factory use of distributed processing.

The Field Information System

Historically, a major problem for all customer service organizations has been the availability of current customer problem status. In batch systems, when a customer or management makes an inquiry into problem status, it takes research into files and batch printout to answer the questions. The resulting time lag causes management inefficiency and customer frustration.

Texas Instruments' Computer Assisted Repair Effort (TI–CARE) addresses this problem. TI–CARE includes toll-free centralized service dispatch, real-time status on each service request, service history on all equipment, inventory control of service parts and equipment to the customer engineer level, and preventive maintenance planning. Also, the field can change work-order scheduling.

The Field Information System (FIS) is used to implement TI–CARE. FIS is a distributed transaction processing network that allows data collection, scheduling, and resource management of any particular service call in the United States. The FIS network covers the contiguous United States and includes the CIC host.

The need for each dispatcher and manager to know the location of each of his or her customer engineers and the current status of all customer requests led to the development of TI–CARE, for which specifications began in 1975. It took twenty-two months and a great deal of experience learned from the National Centralized Dispatching System before the final specifications were developed.

For ease of use, TI decided to design the system so that the customer with a problem could call any dispatch center in the United States and receive a response to his or her needs. System response had to be quick to reduce both frustration and cost, since either a client or the customer engineer were probably waiting on the phone.

Either very high reliability or automatic redundancy was necessary; a dispatch center disabled for an extended period would leave customers without adequate service response.

Data are collected on all the activity as it occurs and are used to derive indices, which field service managers can use to manage their business. These management reports are generated on a current basis so that operational managers can fine-tune their local businesses and see trends as they develop. This day-to-day information is vital to the proper management of assets and people.

The Field Information System (FIS) was built around the Service Ticket used to generate a customer request. When an equipment serial number is entered, all recent information on that piece of equipment becomes available. To ease the generation of this equipment data base, much of the information is entered when a piece of equipment leaves the loading dock. The Factory Order Control System, which controls factory packaging and shipping, automatically enters equipment data into the FIS when equipment is shipped. This information contains factory ship dates, warranty dates, warranty status, contract status, coverage hours, and the like.

The dispatcher needs to make only a limited input—the serial number for example—to receive a large amount of necessary information. While the customer is still on the phone, pertinent information such as phone number and equipment location is verified.

The FIS then assigns a ticket to the job request and computes the closest service office by using telephone prefixes laid over a geographic grid of the entire United States. This means that a customer can call any of the eleven dispatch centers and the appropriate service office will receive the service request. After selection of the nearest service office, FIS transfers the service ticket into the nearest office's work queue.

When the customer engineer (CE) becomes available, he or she calls into the service office. There the work queue displayed on the CRT shows the work tickets in order of receipt, the equipment model number, the status of the work ticket, and the location of the equipment. From this information the dispatcher can decide which job to assign. The dispatcher then pushes a function key on the 914A terminal, and the entire work ticket is displayed. Information is read off the terminal to the customer engineer for entry onto his or her call report. Errors are reduced by making the screen display and the call report exactly the same format. The dispatcher then keys into the terminal the information that the CE is on his or her way to the customer.

After responding to the request, the CE calls the dispatcher and reads the completed information from the call report. Entering that information into the terminal updates the data bank and work queue. The CE then receives his or her next assignment.

During all of this, FIS has kept track of service inventories down to the customer engineer level. Part of the inventory control system in FIS is an automatic reordering system known as Flowline. When an inventory falls below a predetermined level, it is automatically reordered, in a standard quantity, from the factory warehouse and shipped to the location where it is needed.

The system has also been storing all the transaction data for use in computing indices used to manage the service organization. The performance indices calculated by TI–CARE include the number of incident reports, tickets, trips, and calls; the number of calls requiring parts, the number of calls where parts are not available, and the number of parts red-rushed from each stocking location; the mean time to travel, repair, dispatch, diagnose, and complete; the mean miles traveled and the actual miles traveled; the percentage of recalls and the calls per day; the cost in dollars per hour and in dollars per call; and the number of tickets in each billings status.

The host DXS system contains a centralized data base which is downloaded daily to the eleven dispatch centers that use smaller DXSs. The localized data bases and communication redundancy make a highly reliable combination. For example, the dispatch DXSs in use include two CPUs; one acts as the application processor and the other handles terminal polling and communication routing. Should malfunctions occur, this feature allows terminals to continue functioning by immediately rerouting communication around the malfunctioning CPU to another CPU in the network. Thus, even when a network node goes down, the system remains vital and functioning and terminals can still enter tickets and dispatch CEs. The local daily data base means that each dispatch center can operate autonomously for extended periods even if it loses all communication with the host or other dispatch centers.

As each transaction takes place at the dispatch DXS, the transaction is spooled and transmitted to the host DXS in Houston. The host in turn replies with any new information that will update the district data base. All of this takes place in a few seconds so the DXSs are effectively communicating real time. This provides the advantage that customers can call any service center and find out the status of their request.

Intelligent terminals, in conjunction with DXS, are also used to communicate with the Corporate Information Center's data base. This means that the FIS network both collects field data and gives the field inquiry status to the corporate data base. Information needed by corporate level managers is available on a real-time basis, whereas the access of corporate data is restricted to selected FIS terminals.

The main data base is maintained in 300 megabytes at the host DXS located in Houston. The eleven dispatch sites use DXSs, each with two 9.2 megabyte disks. Remote CRTs and printers are connected to the dispatcher's DXSs, and the entire network is tied together by two high volume data lines.

The Field Information System is continually growing and being enhanced. Some future projects to increase the FIS's power are: operating indices to the CE level, automatic customer billing, automatic service call selection, and CE field communication via portable terminals. Future enhancements to FIS will include failure analysis reports by model number, customer and so forth, to aid in determining and forecasting service problems; distribution of field service charges to other cost centers within TI; cost analysis reports; and daily equipment downtime reports.

In-factory Distributed Processing

Texas Instruments uses an in-factory application of distributed processing known as the Distributed Application Processing System (DAPS). DAPS is based on the belief that proper management of an input rate to an operation is the prime factor in minimizing material buildup in an area and smoothing the work load.

DAPS provides the capability of tracking a part number and quantity through a series of work stations relative to a designated cycle time. The system is linked to the Corporate Information Center. Input to the DAPS DXS computer is through TI 914A intelligent terminals, TI Numeric Entry Terminals (TINETs), and Series 700 terminals.

DAPS manages work in progress by controlling work-station queues and flow rates. It also increases the information available to management concerning individual work-station queues.

Hard-copy scheduling, work status, and problem job reports can be delivered on a daily basis. The increased visibility and real-time status allow flexible rescheduling and priority expediting for hot jobs. Scheduling and managing are also easier because shop load versus shop capacity is now visible. Summary data in the form of schedules, starts, and completions are automatically sent to the Material Control System at CIC.

A team of approximately twenty manufacturing managers and supervisors at all levels developed and reviewed the DAPS specifications. Information for the specifications was gathered at the lowest possible user level. All proposed system functions were approved before the development team started work.

It took six months to install the first DAPS system at Austin, which was put into immediate use. Formal parallel operation of the old system continued for only a short time.

It was important that all definitions and transactions be standardized, with accepted terms and usage. An information inquiry was designed which displays all inquiry types, their definitions, and formats. Any inquiry results in either the presentation of the requested information or an error message precisely describing the problem.

The system replaces manual logging of assemblies as they move through the manufacturing stations, and it eliminates the need for slow verbal and written communication to dispatchers. It also addresses such common production questions as: What is the latest schedule? Where is the part? What do I do next? What are the problems? What is hot? Can we meet the schedule work load?

In addition to on-line information available, customized data listings are distributed to support project and shop management. The Active Record Status report is printed every weekday evening and contains ETAs, commit dates, job statistics, and so forth. A Run History shows the history of work completion and targets for specific work lots. A Shop Load report contains past and future projections of work hours for each work station.

DAPS is made up of distinct units. The largest unit, the shop, is a separate facility or easily identified subset of a fabrication facility or supply organization. A group of stations compose a shop. Stations perform a single operation or series of related operations inside one shop. The station's capacity is expressed in parts/day and hours/day. There are three unique station types:

> *In-basket or queue station* is usually the first station from which orders are released to control the flow.
>
> *Problem stations* are for jobs that cannot continue in the normal flow until certain corrective actions have been taken. The problem job is removed from the queue of workable jobs.
>
> *Close-out stations* follow the last process in a fabrication process and mark job completion.

The specific sequence of stations that a category or family of parts must proceed through is called a *flow type*. The time necessary for completing a certain operation is called *cycle time*. The cycle time for a specific flow type is the sum of the station cycle times for that flow type. This cycle time includes wait, setup, run, and move times for each station.

Flags are used on the station CRT screens to identify problems. Not all problems are shunted to a problem station, since some are temporary and can easily be solved en route to the next designated station. Each shop can define its own set of flags to best fit the operation.

The DAPS system is on-line real-time on DXS; however, changes are only made to the Corporate Information Center's IMS when the Material Control System is updated nightly. The shipping and packaging system, FOCS (Factory Order and Control System), works in conjunction with DAPS. Together they link 170 terminals located at ten sites spread over four cities. Both DAPS and FOCS have access to CIC, as shown in Figure 16–10.

The DAPS runs on a DXS with a 100-megabyte disk. This keeps track of 18,000 to 20,000 lots distributed throughout the 550 stations within twenty shops. (When DAPS was first implemented in 1975, the system operated with only eight terminals.)

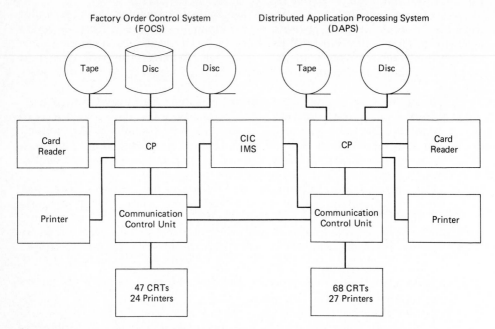

Figure 16–10   Relationship Between CIC and FOCS and DAPS

The DAPS and FOCS operate twenty-four hours a day, seven days a week with time off only for preventive maintenance and backup procedures. Each transaction entered during the day is saved on tape so that complete recovery of data is possible.

While computer-queued scheduling may be the best scheduling plan for overall factory optimization, it may be disrupted occasionally by managers attempting to achieve goals that optimize their individual areas. In such a case, the results may not be best for the factory's goals. This does not mean that blind service to the system is always necessary. For example, a station may not accomplish a job in the same manner as other stations or as the model assumes. In some cases it may not be worth the political and psychological disruption to reorganize that station. But there does come a time when the level of inaccuracies in the model must limit customization—either the differing station must change or the system model must change. TI assumed that one of the problems that might occur was the failure of dispatchers and supervisors to input data quickly. This fear proved unfounded, and the system has been maintained on a continuously updated basis. Part of the reason for successful implementation at that level was the personal commitment of each user.

A problem that was not anticipated was the continuation of previous lines of communication. Even though training programs were carried on at all levels of system use, many of the second- and third-level managers still used an informal system for gathering information. Although they now had the ability to immediately call up operational information on a CRT, they still relied on the managers under them to gather information and bring it to them. Dispatchers were still expected to keep information on paper or in their heads when it was immediately available to them on DAPS. It took time for previous communication channels to atrophy.

TI has learned that the following general considerations must be taken into account when implementing a distributed processing system:

1. Initial success in data processing will encourage new users to bring more and more applications into the system. As a result, new and more-sophisticated functions are continually being added until the machines are overextended and previous system specifications cannot be met. At this point cost-effective expansion must be available.

2. Software and applications must be cost effective before the time new generation equipment is necessary.

3. The total recurring costs need to be determined. In a constantly changing and growing organization, reconfiguration and moving could cause costs to greatly exceed initial estimates.

4. It is important to determine what level of programming/diagnostic expertise is needed in the field. When bugs appear at a remote site, it is often difficult to diagnose the problem, much less solve it. The development of diagnostic software for remote use may be necessary.

5. Many minicomputers have their own sets of languages, different instruction sets, smaller cores and so forth. Thus individuals must be trained to work on a specific type of minicomputer or product family. Furthermore a new class of systems engineers is needed—engineers who understand the architecture, network, and design limitations of these machines.

6. Every effort should be made to ensure an accurate system before it is released to the users. It may take much longer to get over the distrust of a new system if the initial attempts at using it produce error-laden information.

With all of the effort and the many problems involved in implementing a network of this size, Texas Instruments has found that the benefits far outweigh the difficulties. Distributed processing has provided the answer to the company's widely dispersed, multisite, multifaceted data processing needs.

SUMMARY

The development of sophisticated teleprocessing equipment and the advent of mini and micro computer systems has resulted in the development and/or redesign of large-scale computer systems (networks). We have examined two specific cases in this chapter. In each case a distributed processing structure was employed. As we noted in Chapter 8, the movement toward distributed systems will undoubtedly increase in the future. It is therefore not surprising to find that major corporations (such as Texas Instruments Incorporated) have moved in this direction.

Our only objective in this chapter has been to expose the reader to the basic framework of large-scale systems. For the interested reader, the first case is described in detail on a subsystem-by-subsystem basis by Thierauf in *Distributed Processing Systems* (see footnote 1).

SELECTED REFERENCES

BUCKLEY, J. E., "Shared User Networks," *Computer Design*, June 1977.

FOSTER, J. D., "Distributed Processing for Banking," *Datamation*, June 1976.

HADEN, DOUGLAS, *Total Business Systems: Computers in Business*. St. Paul, Minn.: West Publishing, 1978.

JENSEN, F. J., "Centralization or Decentralization in Banking?" *Datamation*, July 1976.

MAYER, JAMES A., "MIS at International Paper: An Integrated Teleprocessing Network," *Management Accounting*, April 1979.

PERSON, RON, "How TI Distributes Its Processing," *Datamation*, April 1979.

RUSSELL, R. M., "Approaches to Network Design," *Computer Decisions*, June 1976.

SAYER, W., "Galion: Blueprint for a Total Management System," *Modern Office Procedures*, February 1970.

THIERAUF, ROBERT J., *Distributed Processing Systems*. Englewood Cliffs, N.J.: Prentice-Hall, 1978.

VANRENSSELAER, CURT, "Centralize? Decentralize? Distribute?" *Datamation*, April 1979.

REVIEW QUESTIONS

1. Identify several alternative ways of organizing the hardware environment of the American Products Corporation in a distributed processing mode.

2. Identify some of the characteristics associated with the distributed processing environment of the American Products Corporation that are not present in the integrated MIS.

3. Assume that the American Products Corporation is much larger than that described in the body of the chapter. What changes, if any, would need to be made in the distributed processing system?

4. Develop a detailed system flowchart for the Field Information System for Texas Instruments Incorporated.

5. What differences, if any, exist in the Manufacturing Subsystem of the American Products Corporation and the In-Factory Distributed Processing System of Texas Instruments Incorporated?

6. Identify some controls and checks that would be required in the Field Information System for Texas Instruments Incorporated.

EXERCISES AND CASES

16-1

International Paper Company is a large multinational forest products corporation, with over \$3.7 billion in sales in 1980.[1] The company is the largest North American producer of paperboard, paper, and pulp products but is also involved in health-care and wood products as well as exploration for oil, gas, and minerals.

In the early 1970s the company's information systems were essentially decentralized with little corporate reporting and control. The only company-wide telecommunications facility was an antiquated paper-tape network for administrative message switching, order entry, and intracompany data flow. From an information systems standpoint, most operating unit locations were on their own; a total of twenty-three separate computer centers and roughly twenty-six mainframes existed. In effect, the limitations of telecommunications prevented any real integration of computer functions.

This environment created problems in the flow of information. Systems at the division level met the requirements of local management with no built-in linkages to corporate level information systems. Passing information from the division level to business unit and corporate management levels was complex, subject to errors and delay. As a result, planning and decision making were being inhibited unnecessarily.

In 1973 IP's senior management directed the financial organization to set an overall direction for MIS activity—with consolidation of the twenty-three data centers and an integrated company-wide information system in mind. To achieve these objectives, IP needed to integrate existing systems or provide a new framework for information company-wide. The result was an "Integrated Information Systems" plan, or IIS. In simple terms, IIS was a plan to feed operating and planning data up through the organization to provide business unit and corporate managers with the information they needed to do their jobs.

Obviously the goal was worthy, the task complex. It meant not only defining information needs at all organization levels and designing application systems to support those needs but establishing an appropriate technical environment to accommodate the data transfer needs of the corporation on a cost-effective basis. In 1976 IP reorganized from a functional structure to one along lines-of-business units— again calling for a better means of distributing information throughout the company.

The first step was consolidation of twenty-three decentralized computer centers into four and, subsequently, two regional computer centers. In effect, the company consolidated the data into a 370/168 in Denville, New Jersey, and two 370/158s in Mobile, Alabama. Corporate Management Information Systems (CMIS) planned and coordinated the move at IP headquarters in Manhattan, providing consolidated computing resources to the corporate staff and seventy-nine IP facilities in the United States.

This, of course, did not solve all of IP's problems. The company had centralized the data but did not have an effective way of moving these data between locations. More than seventeen software technicians were assigned pure maintenance and liaison with locations. Moreover, total voice and data communication costs had increased 122 percent, only partially the result of tariff increases. Data communications costs were almost \$2 million, rising much faster than overhead. In addition, the company was being pressured to add on-line order entry and other applications without disrupting existing operations. It was difficult to meet those demands and get information to existing locations at the same time.

The second step, therefore, was implementation of ITN (Integrated Teleprocessing Network), an under-one-roof approach to data communications. To understand ITN, one has to look at the telecommunications facilities IP had at the time and the objectives of the proposed integrated network.

---

[1] This case has been adapted and reprinted, in part, by permission from, "MIS at International Paper: An Integrated Teleprocessing Network" by James A. Meyer appearing in the April 1979 issue of *Management Accounting*, New York, pp. 24–27.

Historically, commercial teleprocessing environments reflect a lack of overall direction. Software is usually designed and developed for specific user applications without an overall structure in mind. IP was no exception. Each major systems group developed its own application and teleprocessing support. A lot of software development depended strictly on personalities. Nobody really knew exactly what was "out there." To improve an application, or to interface it with similar work at another facility, required costly changes in application code, communication software, and terminal equipment. Moreover, any change in mill applications required a system that accepted paper tape. New applications like on-line order entry had to interface with a number of different manufacturing systems.

In effect, IP was a company of single-application terminal types, with no common standardized teleprocessing software. The company actually had four different networks, each developed and maintained separately, each with its own software, lines, and terminals. The administrative message switch network, the only network serving intracompany communications, serviced 120 low-speed teletype terminals and high-speed computer mainframe links to the regional 370s. The data-entry network serviced forty-seven remote terminals, handling a light volume of data from many locations. Another network supported on-line transactions, mainly file updates. A fourth supported remote job entry for a total of twenty-eight sites.

If viewed separately, none of these networks was deficient; they accommodated the data transfer needs of the users for which they were designed. However, it took three different teleprocessing access methods, five separate teleprocessing control programs, and five data networks to get the job done. It also required some locations to have as many as four different terminals, one for each teleprocessing application. Network integration did not exist.

To solve these technical problems, IP set the following objectives:

Single base telecommunications software to support company needs, including diverse terminal types and networking requirements

Reliable transfer of data from any terminal to any other terminal or data stored in the computer

Cost reduction and cost avoidance

In September 1976 IP set up a group to develop and implement an integrated teleprocessing network to meet these objectives. Two documents resulted. The first was functional specifications for ITN, submitted to five telecommunications vendors. The second evaluated vendor proposals and subsequently recommended the concept of IBM's SNA (System Network Architecture) as the direction for teleprocessing at IP. The SNA approach is basically common teleprocessing software and simplification of all the technical considerations facing a data communications user. With this SNA concept, all data transfer concerns such as line protocol and access methods, and even the choice of the most economical transmission facilities, are "transparent" to the user. For IP this meant that an IBM 3270 display station—or almost any terminal for that matter—could be used to communicate with the company's regional 370 computers. The application did not matter. A person could log onto a 3270 for order entry, switch over to check stock availability, and wind up sending an administrative message—all in one session at one terminal.

In effect, SNA came closest to meeting the ITN objectives. It allowed the company to grow into an integrated network by keeping the application code considerably separate from teleprocessing support.

Corporate systems development manager Jerry Ingersoll sums it up well:

What is key to me is that we can establish input criteria at any location without worrying about which network is involved. In the past we had separate networks for most of our teleprocessing applications. Applications people had to worry about everything from line protocol to access methods and data reliability—in effect all data transfer concerns. Now we provide the format specified to get into ITN and the destination of the data, whether a terminal or an application at one of the computers. In either situation, ITN delivers it. The information is received just as it is sent and everything in between is transparent.

Using SNA, IP implemented ITN in two phases, and the network is now fully in place. Results range from outright savings in hardware and line costs to the three-day business close and a reduced cycle of application development. All levels at IP have been affected, from applications development staff to computer center operations, end users, and general management. IP is truly one company from a data communications standpoint.

A byproduct of ITN and SNA was a reversal of the trend toward centralization of data processing at IP—through distributed processing. SNA makes this possible. The company has shifted some processing to remote sites. Thirty IBM 3790 communications systems have been installed at the Container Division plant locations. Instead of processing all data at regional data centers, plants do remote editing for applications like roll stock inventories, general ledger, and accounts payable. The host 370/168 in Denville provides major data on customers and items as well as network support.

ITN has also helped IP remove most paper-tape facilities. For locations without a terminal operating under SNA and suitable for administrative traffic, the company has installed IBM 3770 keyboard printer terminals and similar devices. Some sixty terminals have been eliminated, including teletype and remote job-entry equipment.

REQUIRED:

a. Prepare a system flowchart showing the initial information system employed by IP.

b. Prepare a system flowchart for the integrated teleprocessing network.

c. In the last section of the IP overview the statement was made that ITN and SNA had led to a distributed processing arrangement. Explain this in light of the fact that in 1974 the company established an Integrated Information Systems (IIS) plan.

16–2

The Hewlett-Packard Company manufactures more than four thousand products for wide-ranging markets that are primarily in manufacturing-related industries.[2] The company has thirty-eight manufacturing facilities and 172 sales and service offices around the world; together these employ about forty-five thousand people. The company has experienced a growth of about 20 percent per year, culminating in sales of $1.7 billion in 1978.

To support the business, HP currently has some fourteen hundred computers. Of these, 85 percent are used to support engineering and production applications, dedicated to specific tasks or arranged in networks. A number of them are also used in computer-aided design applications as front-end processors for large mainframes. The remaining 200 computers are used to support business applications. The largest is an Amdahl 470/V6 located in Palo Alto, California. There are nine medium-sized IBM systems in other large facilities. Seventy HP 3000s are used in HP's factories and larger sales offices, and 125 HP 1000s are scattered about for data entry, data retrieval, and data communications work.

Generally speaking, the HP computers are oriented toward on-line applications, and the large mainframes toward batch processing (although three also support on-line applications). In addition, HP uses about twenty-five hundred CRT terminals in business applications alone.

The network tying all this together consists of 110 data communications facilities located at sales and service offices, at manufacturing plants, and at corporate offices in northern California and Switzerland.

After careful analysis and study, management at HP concluded that systems should be centralized, decentralized, or distributed depending on management needs. The following four examples describe specific HP information systems or facilities and show how they match the organization needs. The first deals with the communication system, which is the heart of a minicomputer network. The second and third examples are of two systems having distributed data bases, one with central master files (at two locations) and the other with both central and dispersed masters. The final example deals with decentralized systems which interface some distributed systems.

110-Node Network

The communications system that supports HP's computing network employs minicomputers at 110 worldwide locations. These minis take care of a number of data communication functions. They handle data entry, format data for transmission, automatically detect and correct errors, and adapt transmission protocols to meet the requirements of various countries. In addition, the minis support on-line access to local data bases.

The company began to build the network in the late 1960s to support a communications network with intelligent terminals. The network was successful right from the start and has continuously been adding to the locations served. In 1974 HP began to install display terminals on the network. More recently distributed data bases and an inquiry capability have been added.

The average worldwide data volume for the network is about 140 million characters per day. This translates into about one hundred thousand messages. But the line cost runs under $50,000 per month, which is very economical compared with the communication costs of other companies using on-line systems at similar data volumes.

The largest communication system applications are for marketing (60 percent of the traffic), accounting (15 percent), employee information (10 percent), and administrative messages (15 percent). About a million orders per year are transmitted over the network, almost 50 percent of which originate outside the United States, and about three million invoices. The network is also used extensively for file transmission.

The system has provided an excellent means for transmitting administrative messages (electronic mail) and has been particularly effective for overseas communication, where the telephone is costly and inconvenient because of time zone differences. Using the system, the cost of transmitting a letter-size message overseas is typically thirty cents. This low cost, coupled with the system's speed and convenience,

has resulted in a large increase in day-to-day communication between people at the operations level in the company's U.S. and overseas offices.

Marketing Administration System

The second application system example is the distributed marketing administration system, which supports the sales and service organization. The primary objective of the marketing system is to provide accurate and consistent information to support customers on a worldwide basis. To do this requires a centrally managed distributed system.

The system is such that centralized, decentralized, and distributed processing all go on simultaneously. Decentralized processing is used for production planning, product configuring, and shipment scheduling at the manufacturing sites, and for order entry and service scheduling at the sales and service offices. Centralized processing comes in for such functions as financial and legal reporting and administration of the employee benefits program at corporate headquarters.

Some forms of distributed processing are employed for maintaining and accessing distributed data bases. All the data for customer records originate at the sales offices, for example, and slices of the customer data base are kept in each sales office, but a complete customer data base is simultaneously maintained at corporate headquarters and slices of the data base also exist at the manufacturing plants.

All the data for product records originate at the sales offices, for another example, and slices of the product data base are kept at each plant, but complete product data bases are simultaneously maintained at corporate headquarters and at each sales office.

Orders and changes are entered at the sales and service offices, transmitted to headquarters where they are entered on central files, and then sent on to the factories for acceptance and delivery acknowledgement. Company order, shipment, and backlog status is maintained centrally to provide information to top management. Delivery information is transmitted from the manufacturing divisions back to the sales offices where orders are acknowledged.

Invoices are centrally processed in Palo Alto and Geneva. The credit and collection functions are decentralized to the sales offices, with central reporting of receivables status to provide financial control.

Files of European open orders are maintained in both Geneva and Palo Alto. An order from a European sales office containing items to be supplied from a European factory and a U.S. factory is processed in Geneva. Complete detail pertaining to the U.S.-supplied items is transmitted to Palo Alto; however, only order statistics are sent to Palo Alto for the European-supplied items. Order status information is transmitted back and forth daily to keep the two files in sync, and a monthly audit procedure ensures that nothing has been overlooked in the daily updates.

Up-to-date order status change information is transmitted daily from the Palo Alto headquarters to the larger U.S. sales offices to provide on-line access for response to customer inquiries. The remote files are syncronized with the master files by computer control. That is, the update program requires each batch update to be performed in the right order. (The January 17 update cannot be performed before the January 16 update.) Local files can be recreated from the central files should recovery be necessary.

Although data communication is handled in a batch mode, the system operates in the same manner as an on-line distributed system in which a significant portion of the data processing is done at more than one location. Data is batch communicated because this is the most economical method to employ with currently available communication facilities.

Personnel/Payroll System

To comply with local laws and customs, an independent personnel/payroll system is maintained by HP in each country in which it has operations. In the United States HP has a distributed system that pays about twenty-five thousand employees. The pay information is entered on display terminals at about thirty remote locations, each with its own daily updated disk file. The data are transmitted to Palo Alto monthly, where the payroll is processed. The paychecks are either transmitted back to the originating locations for printing or directly deposited in the employee's bank account.

The distributed data base that supports the payroll/personnel system operates in a different mode from that which is used for the sales and service system. Each division is responsible for the accuracy of the data relating to its employees. The data are kept on local HP 3000 disk files updated daily. Changes made to these files are transmitted to Palo Alto several times a month, where they are used to update a central file prior to payroll processing.

The audit and control procedure that ensures that the central and remote files are syncronized works in the following manner. After the central file has been updated, the modified records are transmitted back to the local entity for comparison. Any discrepancies are then reported.

Discrepancies can arise from two causes. First, somewhat more stringent edit routines can be applied centrally, so an unedited error is occasionally detected. Second, certain changes to employees' records can be made centrally and these are sometimes not recorded in the local files. A small, but significant, number of errors are detected by this audit and control procedure.

The payroll/personnel system serves a number of departments: finance, accounting, personnel, and tax. An advisory board consisting of members of each of those departments reviews and approves changes to the system's programs, which number several hundred per year.

Eighty-five percent of HP's U.S. employees are paid by this system. The other 15 percent are located in manufacturing divisions that have elected to run their payrolls locally. Personnel data for this 15 percent must still be maintained in the central file to take care of the centrally administered benefit programs. Keeping these independently prepared data accurate and consistent with the data prepared centrally is a significant challenge. This experience has dramatized the advantage of sharing common data used by different functions. The discipline of the payroll system has proved to be invaluable in keeping central personnel records up-to-date and accurate.

The remote personnel files of both kinds permit local entities to produce reports on their employees. In addition, they provide a timely interface to local systems such as cost accounting. The remotely used software is centrally supported, and changes are released periodically.

Factory Management System

The last application system to be described is the factory management system, which is implemented on HP 3000 hardware. This decentralized system supports the functions of order processing, materials management and purchasing, production planning, product assurance, service support, and accounting.

The factory management system consists of a group of functional modules which access a central data base that serves as an information resource for the division. As mentioned earlier, most systems used by the manufacturing divisions are decentralized and locally managed. Although each HP division has unique requirements that must be satisfied by its local support systems, there is a remarkable similarity between the needs of the different divisions. Most HP divisions are oriented largely toward assembly operations, so manufacturing support systems are designed around a bill-of-materials processor. As a general rule, 80 percent of a division's needs can be satisfied with the basic system. HP developed the factory management system to multiply the return on development and support costs by sharing systems between these decentralized locations.

The factory management system was developed over a five-year period, one module at a time. (An example of a system module would be materials management, production planning, or cost accounting.) The development was accomplished by development teams consisting of division personnel responsible for providing the specifications and ensuring that the system meets their functional needs, and of central data processing specialists who make sure that the modules operate efficiently and properly interface other system modules. On completion each module can be shared by other divisions on a voluntary basis.

HP has not attempted to solve all system problems in each module; instead it has followed the 80–20 rule, taking care of major requirements that are common to a number of divisions. In fact, HP has encouraged sharing

divisions to add unique features required to meet their local needs. Quite often these unique features are of value to other divisions and later get incorporated into the "standard" modules.

This approach to shareable system design has been very successful. The company has found that the shared modules save up to 75 percent over the cost of local development and that they can be implemented in a fraction of the time. So far, over half of HP's thirty-eight divisions have elected to participate in this problem, and nearly all have plans eventually to use some parts of the system.

The factory management system has been especially useful to new divisions (which are being added at a rate of about three per year). It has permitted managers in these divisions to have a high level of systems support capability early in their growth cycle. On the other hand, the system has been much less useful to older, established divisions with mature systems. These entities have found it difficult to justify the cost of change (especially retraining people), even though on-line operation and other enhancements would be desirable.

REQUIRED:

a. Compare the communication network of the International Paper Company (Case 16–1) with that of the Hewlett-Packard Company. How do the communication needs of the two companies differ?

b. Describe some of the problems that might exist in the *marketing administration* system in regard to new applications and/or changes in the system. What types of problems probably exist because of the international scope of the systems activities? What, if any, justifications exist for a more distributed system?

c. What reasons would justify HP's decision to process all payrolls at Palo Alto rather than at remote locations?

d. What problems, if any, exist in the factory management system because it uses a central data base that serves as an information resource for the division?

17

SMALL-BUSINESS SYSTEMS

INTRODUCTION

A well-designed and effectively utilized accounting system is essential to the continued success of the small-business organization. Many small businesses fail because of the lack of an effective accounting system that provides management and owners with information for decision-making and reporting requirements. Even small businesses with an efficient, well-designed manual or EDP system may fail because management does not know how to use the information provided by the system.

A small business can best be described by characteristics[1] other than sales or assets in dollars, even though these figures are generally small in comparison with those in a large business. These characteristics lead to specific design, implementation, and control problems not reviewed in earlier chapters. First, a small business is generally a high-risk venture with little capital but much enthusiasm. Thus there often are not enough funds to support expensive systems and the personnel to run these systems. Many small businesses have only a part-time clerk rather than a controller to operate the entire accounting

---

[1] Characteristics are based on William K. Grollman and Robert W. Colby "Internal Control for Small Business," *The Journal of Accountancy* (December 1978), pp. 64–67.

information system. However, the owners are often quite active in the affairs of the business.

Second, managers and owners of small businesses tend to be aggressive risk takers despite the fact that even minor reversals can be catastrophic. This style of management will have an impact on decision needs and the type of system desired to support these needs. This style of management seldom relies on well-structured systems.

Third, the key personnel who run the business tend to have marketing, engineering, mechanical, and artistic talents, for example, rather than financial or accounting expertise. Thus these key personnel often either are not interested in accounting and financial systems or, if they have these systems, do not know how to use them.

Fourth, executives and managers, as well as their families, are likely to own most or a controlling part of the business. Because of family ownership, reports to the owners are often unnecessary.

Fifth, due to their talents and degree of ownership, these small-business executives or owners tend to dominate the affairs of the company. For example, if the owner is an engineer, the basic characteristic of the firm and all of the decisions will reflect the technical side of the business, not the marketing or financial aspects.

Sixth, generally the business is not very complicated. This means that the accounting system required and the reports generated by the system are not as complicated as those for large businesses.

Seventh, generally small businesses are informal in decision and reporting style, making it difficult to implement an accounting system with much structure, especially an EDP system.

Eighth, as with large businesses, many reports such as those listed in Figure 17-1 must be prepared for managers, creditors, owners, and governmental agencies. Moreover, these reporting requirements have increased in complexity but not to the same extent as for large businesses.

In summary, the major differences characterizing large and small businesses result from the dominant role of the owner's and/or manager's influence on the business environment. In a large business, owners and managers are often dominated by the business and its environment. This difference has major implications for accountants as they design and develop information systems for small businesses.

THE SMALL-BUSINESS ENVIRONMENT

Organization and Decision Making

A small business could be organized along functional lines, by projects, or by using a matrix structure. In very small firms the organization will probably be much less formal and will consist of a manager (often the owner) to whom all employees report. Slightly larger businesses may have a few functional, departmental, store, or regional managers. In all cases the organization will be small and often informal, rendering the traditional systems concepts of re-

Sales Analysis (by location, merchandise, and sales person)
Accounts Receivable (including aging and write-offs)
Accounts Payable
Inventory Status (perpetual inventory)
    Inventory on order
    Inventory on hand
    Reorder parts
Cash Receipts
Cash Disbursements
Cash Forecast and Budget
Asset and Depreciation Records
Budgets
    Sales—forecast
    Purchase or production
    Cash
Payroll Register
Financial Statements
Other Special Reports for the Type of Business
    Reports to third parties
        IRS—tax returns
        HEW
        Etc.

Figure 17-1 Typical Reports for Small Businesses

sponsibility and segregation of duties ineffective. This is usually counteracted, in part, by the active participation of the manager and owner in most aspects of the business.

The owners and managers of small businesses will still need to make strategic, managerial, and operational decisions. It is unlikely that these decisions will be made using formal models except in rare cases at the operational level for such activities as scheduling production, ordering inventory, and evaluating investments. Strategic and managerial decisions, however, are based on the same set of information used by larger firms even though it is less formal. The role of the accountant is to see that the small-business owner or manager has sufficient information to make these decisions. The information needed may be a set of operating and financial reports or an organized set of records for inventory, accounts receivable, cash balances, and accounts payable. During the past few years, with the advent of good software for microcomputer systems, internally generated information has been more readily available to small-business users at a reasonable price. An example of this type of system was described in Chapter 14.

Small-business owners and managers must make decisions about where they are headed (strategic planning), how they expect to get there with the resources available to them (managerial planning), and, on a day-to-day basis, how best to use these resources (operational decisions).

Too often, small-business management considers only the processing of transactions. Resource utilization is not planned. Realistic objectives are not formulated with plans to achieve these objectives. Goal setting is a decision-making process. The focal point of this process is the budget. Regardless of the accounting system used, a small business should have a budget or a plan for the future to serve as a framework for operating decisions and to force management and owners to make strategic and managerial decisions about the business. A budget will go a long way toward coordinating the various decision-making activities and will help prevent the typical "seat-of-the-pants" reaction to economic and political events that constantly buffet the small business. An accounting system designed around the budget will give the small business needed direction. The lack of these plans is a major cause of small-business failure.

Information and Reporting Requirements

The information and reporting requirements for small businesses tend to be simple. Often only minimal records are required for management use in decision making. In many cases a *single-entry* accounting system is sufficient for management needs. Moreover, due to the simplicity of operation, a cash basis system will often suffice. Such a system can easily be converted by a trained accountant to an accrual basis at year-end.

This simplicity of information needs arises for two reasons. First, the small-business transactions tend to be straightforward and very repetitive. Simple, easy-to-operate systems can be designed to capture this behavior. Second, because the owner or manager is involved in ongoing operations much of the time, information on unusual events need not be reported in a formal system. Disclosure of unusual or complex events is best handled on a face-to-face basis between the manager, owner, customer, and creditors.

Another important outgrowth of the simplicity and routine nature of information is the increasing use of minicomputers and microcomputers, along with simple accounting software packages for small businesses, such as the one illustrated in Chapter 14. Even when transactions are technical, such as in real estate or tax situations, they are so routine that special software packages have been developed to handle them in small businesses.

Many small-business owners and managers do not really want a complex accounting information system. They prefer the minimum records required to operate the business.[2] The absolute minimum is a record of cash receipts and disbursements (a *check book*), a record of *accounts receivable*, and a record of *accounts payable*. The latter two records may consist of a file of invoices for credit sales and credit purchases. From these minimum records and, if necessary, a physical inventory, a set of financial statements, and tax returns can be prepared at any point in time for any period. Exceptions can be handled at the time of the statement preparation by a CPA if necessary. Most important, the small-business owner or manager can implement and operate this minimal system with little or no training.

Recently there have been several proposals for duality in accounting principles and disclosure requirements. In 1975 the AICPA issued a discussion paper on the application of GAAP to smaller or closely held businesses. The

---

[2] See James B. Bower, Robert E. Schlosser, and Charles T. Zlatkovich, *Financial Information Systems: Theory and Practice* (Boston: Allyn & Bacon, Inc., 1972), pp. 357–76, for a discussion of minimum records.

AICPA Committee on Generally Accepted Accounting Principles for Smaller and/or Closely Held Businesses concluded that there was strong support for consistent application of generally accepted accounting principles, but it recommended that disclosure (the extent of the detail of information) could vary based on the characteristics of the business. The FASB, in issuing *Financial Accounting Standard No. 21,* exempted closely held corporations from previously required disclosures of information about business segments and earnings per share. The basic philosophy underlying these differential disclosure requirements is that the information is not useful to the owners and creditors and does not warrant its preparation cost. More differential disclosure requirements may be issued in the future.

Typical Small-Business Systems

At the present time most small-business systems are manual. Many use a cash register as the only mechanical or electronic device. This is changing, however, and more and more small businesses are beginning to use EDP equipment such as microprocessors and intelligent terminals. We will consider this new development later in the chapter. The accounting system in a small business can be on either a cash or an accrual basis, involving either a single-entry or a double-entry system. The system may also include services provided by individuals outside the small business for a fee.

Cash basis accounting systems recognize revenue when cash is received and expenses when cash is paid, while accrual basis accounting systems recognize revenue in the period earned and expenses in the period in which they are incurred. In some cases the modified cash basis with capitalization of assets (depreciation) may suffice for reporting and tax needs in a small business. In other cases a trained accountant can easily convert cash basis statements to accrual based financial statements by making a series of adjusting entries at the end of the period.

A double-entry accounting system with corresponding debits and credits, detailed records, and control accounts is effective in helping to ensure transaction recording accuracy. The double-entry system is self-checking because debits and credits must balance and the detailed records must add to the control totals in each account. A single-entry system, on the other hand, consists of only one entry for each transaction, either on an original document or on a classified listing of transactions such as daily sales, cash receipts, or purchases. These listings are often transcribed from the cash register tape.

If the file of source documents, such as sales invoices, is used as the accounting record rather than as a basis for posting to a ledger or listing, the system is a *ledgerless bookkeeping system.* The extreme case of a ledgerless system would be a drawer full of unpaid credit sales invoices, purchase invoices, and a checkbook. There are several disadvantages to such a single-entry ledgerless system:

1. There is no double-entry control (no way to balance the books).
2. There are no control accounts to compare with the detailed records or source documents.

3. Great potential exists for lost transactions because of disadvantages one and two above.

4. Partial payments, receipt of part of an order, and other partial transactions play havoc with a ledgerless system because there is no effective way to record partial transactions on a source document.

5. Audit trails are poor. Entire files must be searched to trace transactions.

A single-entry ledgerless system has the following advantages:

1. It is economical.

2. It is simple to use.

3. It can provide sufficient information in a cost-effective way for many small firms.

4. It is relatively simple to use when complete payments on orders are made and received and few exceptions to the transaction are noted on the face of the invoice or other source document.[3]

Some control may be established by using batches for groups of transactions, prelisting the transactions, and, above all, prenumbering the source documents for numerical control and reference.

The accounting profession, service bureaus, and vendors of microcomputers and minicomputers and their associated software packages offer small businesses a wide variety of services that can assist in providing or designing an effective and efficient information system. The periodic audit and review of the system is performed by the certified public accountant. The professional accountant can also assist in designing an effective information system. The professional accountant or a service bureau can provide year-end write-up work and prepare financial statements. Both accountants and attorneys can offer assistance in tax planning. Both the professional accountant and the service bureau can assist in reporting to governmental agencies such as the IRS and FCC. Most public accounting firms, many consulting firms, and the Small Business Administration of the U.S. government offer management advisory services to help the small business with administrative control systems such as budgeting, inventory control, and cash management. Finally, many accounting firms and service bureaus will perform the day-to-day transaction processing activities and routine report preparation needed by the small business.

Internal Control

Due to the environmental characteristics of the typical small business, effective internal control is both more difficult and easier to achieve. Because of the limited resources available for control, the lack of interest in control, and the small number of employees, good internal control systems such as those described in Chapter 9 are rare. The primary problems encountered in small-business internal control were clarified by a field study of more than 120 small

---

[3] Adapted with permission from James B. Bower, Robert E. Schlosser and Charles T. Zlatkovich, *Financial Information Systems.*

businesses.[4] The study used the small-business internal control questionnaire shown in Figure 9-4. The results are shown in Figure 17-2. Many of the small-business systems analyzed did not have common accounting controls involving such transaction processing steps as: the use of a chart of accounts (1b); the listing (2b) and tracing (2c) of cash receipts; the use of imprest petty cash funds (3i); and the use of purchase orders (8a). Moreover, such common administrative controls as the use of budgets (1c), cash projections (1d), financial reports (1e), and perpetual inventory records (6d) were not found in many of these firms. These shortcomings, as well as others, are indicative of the following fundamental problems in internal control for small businesses:

1. Little financial expertise on the part of owners and management,
2. Little segregation of duties (often a part-time bookkeeper does everything),
3. Informal accounting and administrative procedures,
4. Informal styles of analysis, decision making, and reporting,
5. Limited personnel and financial resources, and, most important,
6. The costs of more comprehensive administrative and accounting controls would exceed the potential benefits.[5]

In addition to these problems, there is always the possibility that the owner or manager will influence the managerial and financial affairs of the business because of a closeness to operations and inevitable commingling of personal and business objectives.

On the other hand, because of this closeness to operations, the owner's *supervisory control* (sometimes called *executive control*) over them is much greater than that exerted by the owners and managers of larger businesses. This strength can overcome many of the weaknesses cited earlier. This *control* is especially effective when the owner or manager

1. Uses accounting information or a budget for planning and control and seeks explanations for variations from plans
2. Understands and is alert to unusual events and their potential impact on the business
3. Uses nonaccounting employees for some transaction processing functions
4. Personally observes the operation of the business
5. Plays a key role in each transaction processing cycle
6. Reviews and approves transactions that deviate from the norm and uses standard policies to handle the normal transactions

---

[4] This field study was conducted by graduate students in an accounting systems class over several quarters. See Robert A. Leitch, Gadis J. Dillon, and Sue H. McKinley, "Internal Control Weaknesses in Small Business," *Journal of Accountancy,* December 1981, pp. 97–101.

[5] William K. Grollman and Robert W. Cally, "Internal Control for Small Businesses," pp. 64–67, Reprinted with permission.

1 GENERAL	Weight	Yes	No	N/A or N/R
a Are accounting records kept up to date and balanced monthly?	5	89	33	0
*b Is a chart of accounts used?	3	57	65	0
*c Does the owner use a budget system for watching income and expenses?	1	28	94	0
*d Are cash projections made?	1	23	99	0
*e Are monthly or quarterly financial reports available to the owner?	3	59	60	3
f Does the owner take a direct and active interest in the financial affairs and reports which are available?	5	114	8	0
g Are the personal funds of the owner and his personal income and expenses completely segregated from the business?	4	114	8	0
h Is the owner satisfied that all employees are honest?	2	117	4	1
*i Is the bookkeeper required to take annual vacations?	2	13	16	93
2 CASH RECEIPTS				
a Does the owner open the mail?	5	73	43	6
*b Does the owner list mail receipts before turning them over to the bookkeeper?	5	26	73	23
*c Is the listing subsequently traced to the cash receipts journal?	5	23	76	23
d Are over-the-counter receipts controlled by cash register tapes, counter receipts, etc.?	5	91	23	8
e Are receipts deposited intact daily?	5	88	32	2
*f Are employees who handle funds bonded?	5	9	108	5
g Do two different people reconcile the bank records and make out the deposit slip?	10	71	36	15
3 CASH DISBURSEMENTS				
a Are all disbursements made by check?	5	95	27	0
b Are prenumbered checks used?	5	120	2	0
*c Is a controlled, mechanical check protector used?	5	23	99	0
d Is the owner's signature required on checks?	5	102	19	1
e Does the owner sign checks only after they are properly completed?	5	102	19	1
f Does the owner approve and cancel the documentation in support of all disbursements?	5	78	44	0
g Are all voided checks retained and accounted for?	5	115	7	0
h Does the owner review the bank reconciliation?	5	67	22	33
*i Is an imprest petty cash fund used?	5	35	70	17
j Does the owner *never* sign blank checks?	5	65	24	33
k Do different people reconcile the bank records and write the checks?	10	66	40	16

Figure 17–2 Summary of Results of Internal Control Questionnaire

4 ACCOUNTS RECEIVABLE AND SALES

a Are work order and/or sales invoices prenumbered and controlled?	5	65	36	21
b Are customers' ledgers balanced regularly?	5	74	14	34
c Are monthly statements sent to all customers?	5	61	27	34
*d Does the owner review statements before mailing them himself?	5	29	57	36
e Are account write-offs and discounts approved only by the owner?	5	83	7	32
f Is credit granted only by the owner?	3	62	28	32

5 NOTES RECEIVABLE AND INVESTMENTS

a Does the owner have sole access to notes and investment certificates?	5	26	5	91

6 INVENTORIES

a Is the person responsible for inventory someone other than the bookkeeper?	3	108	7	7
b Are periodic physical inventories taken?	5	83	34	5
c Is there physical control over inventory stock?	5	68	48	6
*d Are perpetual inventory records maintained?	2	33	83	6

7 PROPERTY ASSETS

a Are there detailed records available of property assets and allowances for depreciation?	5	57	8	57
b Is the owner acquainted with property assets owned by the company?	4	69	1	52
c Are retirements approved by the owner?	4	65	2	55

8 ACCOUNTS PAYABLE AND PURCHASES

*a Are purchase orders used?	5	49	72	1
b Does someone other than the bookkeeper always do the purchasing?	5	99	18	5
c Are suppliers' monthly statements compared with recorded liabilities regularly?	4	85	23	14
d Are suppliers' monthly statements checked by the owner periodically if disbursements are made from invoice only?	2	82	30	10

9 PAYROLL

a Are the employees hired by the owner?	3	107	13	2
b Would the owner be aware of the absence of any employee?	3	103	16	3
c Does the owner approve, sign, and distribute payroll checks?	5	94	23	5

*Indicates predominantly negative responses, N/A indicates not applicable, and N/R indicates no response.

Reprinted with permission from Leitch, Dillon, and McKinley, "Internal Control Weaknesses in Small Business."

7. Has an accounting system that generates easy-to-understand, usable, and timely reports (such as those listed in Figure 17–1)[6]

In summary, the small business presents a particular challenge to the systems designer or public accountant because of special administrative and accounting control problems. An effective control system can be built around close supervision of the business's operations on the part of the owner or manager.

Cash Registers and Other Manual Processing Devices

The cash register can serve as an effective focal point for the sales and cash receipt transaction processing cycle. It can be used to record sales at the time of transaction; issue a customer receipt; total various sales statistics by department, type of merchandise, type of sale, and salesperson; generate machine-readable output for further processing; compute taxes; calculate and issue change; and calculate the transaction totals. The cash register can also provide control over assets. Cash is controlled because a protected record is produced on a tape locked inside the machine. The salesperson must be able to reconcile the cash balance in the cash drawer with this transaction record when the register is cleared by management personnel. As we noted in Chapter 13, some cash registers are quite sophisticated. In practice, the effective use of a cash register gives the small-business owner or manager the much-needed assurance that sales transactions are recorded properly and that sales personnel are accountable for the cash assets at their disposal.

Some small businesses may use locked boxes of invoices and cash drawers in lieu of cash registers. One copy of the sales invoice is given to the customer and the other is retained in the locked box. At the end of the day the sales invoices must all reconcile with the beginning and ending balances in the cash drawer. Generally these invoices are prenumbered for numerical control, reference, and an audit trail.

Peg boards also are used to record transactions in many small businesses. Peg boards consist of checks or cash disbursement vouchers overlaying a journal, such as a payroll register. As the bookkeeper prepares the checks, voucher, or invoice, a carbon copy is recorded on the journal. This system has the advantage of being simple and cheap, and of reducing transcription errors. Peg boards are quite useful in summarizing transactions for subsequent posting to the general ledger.

Illustration of Manual System for a Small Business

Many illustrations of manual applications were given in earlier chapters. Figure 17–3 illustrates a very simple system of cash sales designed around a cash register. The register has two drawers, one for each employee. Each employee has the key to that drawer. The register is designed to give the customer a receipt, and to record sales in detail by type of merchandise and by salesperson.

In this simple system each cashier rings up the sale, computes the tax,

[6] Ibid.

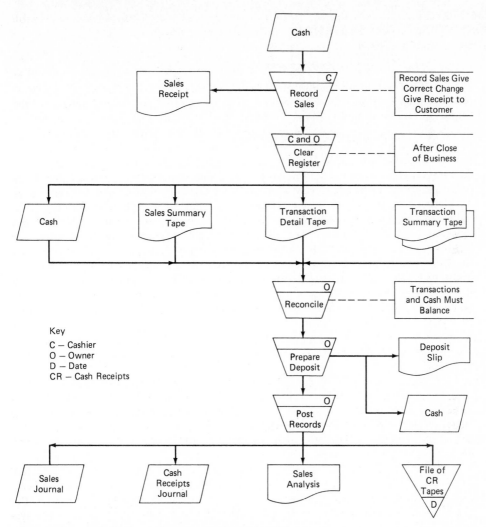

Figure 17-3 Simple Manual System for a Small Business

gives the customer the appropriate change computed by the register, and gives the customer a receipt. While this transaction is taking place, the cash register accumulates summary information on the type of sale, salesperson, merchandise sold, amount of sale, and tax information. At the close of the business day, the owner, in the presence of the cashiers, clears the register. The owner then reconciles the beginning cash balance and ending cash balance with the summary of transactions for each cashier. The owner then prepares the deposit slip and makes the bank deposit. The owner also posts the sales journal, the cash receipts journal, and the sales analysis by cashier and merchandise category for future reference. The cash register detail and summary tapes are filed by date, for reference and to create an audit trail. The key features in this simple system are the focal point of the cash register, the role of the owner, and the recording of data for future planning.

MINICOMPUTER
AND MICROCOMPUTER SYSTEMS
FOR SMALL BUSINESSES

Technological Evolution and Costs

The historical development and current characteristics of minicomputers and microcomputers were reviewed in Chapter 6, and an illustration of a financial accounting system typically offered by software vendors for microcomputers was given in Chapter 14. As we noted in Chapter 6, the microcomputer is quite different from a minicomputer because it is founded on the microprocessor and the micromemory. This difference leads to several characteristics that may be important to a small business. In the mid-1970s, programmable logic was combined with arithmetic circuits on a single chip. This *microprocessor* was then combined with the floppy disk (diskette) in 1977. These developments, along with several advancements in random access memory (RAM), enabled microprocessors to handle the volume and logic necessary for business use. These recent developments have also made it cost-effective for many small businesses to satisfy their decision-making, transaction processing, and reporting needs using a small minicomputer or microcomputer.

An overview of the hardware costs for the major microcomputers is given in Figure 17–4. These are approximate list prices for a minimum config-

VENDOR	MODEL	MEMORY[1] (in 000's of bytes)	OPERATING SYSTEMS[2]	LANGUAGE[3]	WORK-STATIONS[4]	PRICE[5] (in 000's)
Alpha Microsystems	AM–1010	64–384	AMOS	B P	1–14L/R	$15.0
Altos	8000–15	64–208	CP/M	B C F P	1–4L/R	11.9
Apple*†	II/III	16–128	DOS 3.3/SOS	B C F P	1L	7.0
Atari†	800	16–48	Atari	B P	1L	3.9
Commodore†	CMB 8032	16–32	Commodore	B	1L	3.8
Compucolor	II	8–32	FCS	B F	1L	4.0
Cromemco	System Two	64–512	CROMIX	B C F	1–7L/R	10.2
Data General	Enterprise 1000	64	ENTERPRISE/OS	B	1L	9.5
Datapoint	1500	32–60	DOS.H	B	1L, 4R	9.4
Digital Equipment Corporation (DEC)	Datasystem 150	32–64	CTS–300	D	1L	15.7
Hewlett-Packard†	83	16–32	HP	B	1L	8.4
Hewlett-Packard†	125	64	CP/M	B	1L	3.7
IBM*†	Personal Computer	16–256	DOS	B P	1L	4.4
IBM	System/23	64–128	CSF	B	1–2L	9.8
Infotecs	IMP	32	JOEL	H	1L	9.9
Intertec	CompuStar 10	64	CP/M	B C F	1–255L**	7.5
NCR	7520SBS	48	NCR BASIC+6	B	1L	9.9
NEC America, Inc.*	PC–8000	64	CP/M	B F	1–3L	5.3
North Star	Advantage	64	CP/M	B	1L	5.4
Ohio Scientific	CII/C8P	8–48	OS–65D	B	1L	5.0
OSBORNE	1	64	CP/M	B	1L	1.8
Pertec	PCC 2000	64–256	CP/M	B C F	1L, 4R	13.5
Prodigy Systems*	I/II	32–160	O/S	B C F	1–4L/R	12.5

VENDOR	MODEL	MEMORY[1] (in 000's of bytes)	OPERATING SYSTEMS[2]	LANGUAGE[3]	WORK-STATIONS[4]	PRICE[5] (in 000's)
Q1 Corporation	Microlite	48–64	Q1	B C L	1–16L/R	11.4
Qantel	110	48–64	BEST	B	1–2L	13.4
Radio Shack*†	TRS–80 Model II/III	4–64	TRS–DOS	B C F	1L	5.8
SD Systems*	SD–200	32–64	COSMOS	B C	1–5L/R	11.2
Texas Instruments	770	32–64	TPL	B T	1L	8.8
Vector Graphic	System B	64	CP/M	B C F P	1–4L	6.4
Wang	2200–SVP	32	—	B	1L	13.7
Xerox	820	64	CP/M	B C	1L	6.4

Reprinted with permission from Wyune and Frotman, "Microcomputer: Helping Make Practice Perfect," pp. 34–39. Most of the information included in this exhibit is from the *Datapro Directory of Small Computers* (2 vols. [Delran, N.J.: Datapro Research Corporation, a McGraw-Hill Company, 1980]). Because of the rapid changes taking place in the microcomputer marketplace, readers should contact individual computer vendors for the most accurate and up-to-date information. This exhibit covers only a portion of the small-computer industry and is not an endorsement of any product.

*CP/M available.

† VisiCalc available.

[1] Memory—minimum and maximum system memory sizes. The larger the memory size, the more sophisticated applications the computer can support. The least amount of memory for processing business applications should be 48,000 bytes, but 64,000 bytes would be more desirable. An important point to remember is that the operating system of the computer usually takes up a significant portion of the memory. For example, an Apple II Plus computer with 48,000 bytes of random-access memory uses approximately 10,000 bytes of memory for the operating system. The amount of useful memory is therefore less than the system specifications indicate.

[2] Operating systems—"An operating system is a complex group of programs that enables the computer to schedule work in the most efficient manner. Operating systems supervise the overall operations of the computer, control the flow of programs and data through the computer, control input and output devices, and manage the storage facilities of the computer by storing data and programs and retrieving them when needed [*Datapro Directory of Small Computers*]." Application programs designed for a particular operating system (for example, CP/M) generally may be run on any computer that uses that operating system. An operating system is not related to the programming languages, but a good operating system should support all the higher-level languages such as BASIC, FORTRAN and Pascal. Due to its powerful operating features and wide availability, CP/M is the most popular operating system. CP/M is available on many computer systems and the list is growing rapidly. Since CP/M operating systems can be installed on many non-CP/M systems, the user should not, in all cases, decide to "make do" with the operating system supplied by the vendor.

[3] Languages supported by the system—B=BASIC; C=COBOL; F=FORTRAN; P=Pascal; D=DIBOL; H=HIBOL; L=PL/1; T=TPL. It is important to realize that not all similar languages will run on different systems. For example, Apple BASIC will not execute on a TRS–80 machine without modification, albeit minor. Also, if a firm selects a system with a unique language, a problem may occur if at some time the firm plans to change vendors.

[4] Workstations—L=local and R=remote. The number of devices which can input and/or receive data from the microcomputer. In a business environment a workstation usually is a data processing device or terminal. Some single workstation models are aimed at home or small business use.

**Intertec says its model "gears itself to large-volume end users" such as larger businesses and hospitals.

[5] Price—An approximate list price of a minimum system configuration including a printer and floppy-disk system.

Figure 17–4 Major Microcomputer Systems and Their Cost

uration including a printer and a floppy-disk system. Typewriter quality printers and additional storage will increase the price by a few thousand dollars. A sample of software costs for a variety of small systems is shown in Figure 17–5; the software packages illustrated in Chapter 14 cost approximately $500 in 1982.

DIGITAL SYSTEMS HOUSE OF ILLINOIS, INC., Batavia, Il.

General Business—Accounts Payable—Purchase accounting: purchase orders and purchasing, accounts payable cash disbursements and purchase analysis; DEC PDP–8, PDP–11; DIBOL; $1,750 to $3,500 purchase.

General Business—Accounts Receivable—Sales accounting: sales invoices, accounts receivable, billings, and sales analysis; DEC PDP–11; DIBOL; $1,750 to $4,000 purchase.

General Business—General Ledger—General accounting: financial reporting and general ledger; DEC PDP–8, PDP–11; DIBOL; $1,750 to $4,000 purchase.

General Business—Order Entry/Inventory Control—Order fulfillment and inventory control: order processing, inventory control, and warehouse/stockroom control; DEC PDP–8, PDP–11; DIBOL; $2,250 to $4,500 purchase.

General Business—Payroll—Payroll and personnel: payroll; DEC PDP–8, PDP–11; DIBOL; $1,750 to $4,000 purchase.

PROFESSIONAL COMPUTER RESOURCES, INC., Oak Brook, Il.

Accounts Payable—Purchase accounting: accounts payable; IBM S/3, System/34; RPG; 75 users; introduced 1975; $3,000 to $5,000 purchase.

Accounts Receivable—Sales accounting: accounts receivable; IBM System 34; RPG; 75 users; introduced 1975; $3,000 to $5,000 purchase.

DataPlan—Management: financial planning and analysis; RPG, Assembler, 150 users; introduced 1979; $12,000 purchase.

Forecasting—Management: sales/order forecasting and market analysis; IBM System/34; RPG; 75 users; introduced 1975; $3,000 to $5,000 purchase.

General Ledger—General accounting: general ledger, IBM System/34; RPG; 75 users; introduced 1975; $3,000 to $5,000 purchase.

Invoicing—Sales accounting: sales invoices; IBM System/34.

Payroll—Payroll and personnel: payroll; IBM System/34; RPG; 75 users; introduced 1975; $3,000 to $5,000 purchase.

Purchasing—Purchase accounting: purchase orders and purchasing and purchase analysis; IBM System/34; RPG; 75 users; introduced 1975; $3,000 to $5,000 purchase.

Resource Management System—General accounting: general ledger; purchase accounting; purchasing, accounts payable, and order entry; sales accounting; accounts receivable and invoicing; order fulfillment and inventory control; inventory control and warehouse/stockroom control; management; sales/order forecasting and market analysis, manufacturing process/production control, bills of material, and operations planning and control; IBM System/34; RPG; over 100 users; introduced 1975; $50,000 purchase.

DATAMATICS MANAGEMENT SERVICES, INC., Englewood Cliffs, N.J.

Accounts Receivable 225—Sales accounting: accounts receivable; Datapoint 1134; DATABUS; three users; introduced 1978; $525 purchase.

Accounts Receivable 363—Sales accounting: accounts receivable; Datapoint 2200, 6500, 6600; DATABUS; four users; introduced 1978; $475 purchase.

Billing System 362—Sales accounting: billings; Datapoint 2200, 6500, 6600; DATABUS; five users; introduced 1978; $700 purchase.

General Ledger Package 114—General accounting: general ledger; Datapoint 2200, 6500, 6600; DATABUS; five users; introduced 1978; $525 purchase.

General Ledger 329—General accounting: general ledger; Datapoint 1134; DATABUS; four users; introduced 1978; $525 purchase.

Figure 17–5 Sample of Accounting Packages *

*The material in Figure 17–5 is based on a report in *Computer Systems*, a monthly updated looseleaf reference service published by Data Decisions, 20 Brace Road, Cherry Hill, NJ 08034, reprinted with permission. For a complete list see E. S. Walker, "Accounting Packages Selection and Management," *Datamation*, February 1980.

Based on current prices a system that can fill the basic financial accounting and decision-making needs of a small business is within the budget constraints of many small firms. A small-business system generally consists of a computer, a CRT, an input keyboard, dual diskette drives, and a printer. The cost of the printer is generally a major portion of the total cost. To this, the cost of software must be added. The total systems cost may be as low as $5,000–$10,000 for a small business. For slightly larger businesses, modifications, additional storage, and tailor-made software may be added. Note that the IBM personnel computer has 256K, which is equal to that of the large IBM 360 of the late 1960s and early 1970s.

Applications

Minicomputers have software support similar to that available for the large mainframe computer. Good business software packages were not available for microcomputers until very recently. Typical accounting application software packages provided by the manufacturer and general software vendors include payroll, accounts receivable, accounts payable, order entry, inventory, and general ledger. Several examples are shown in Figure 17–5. In addition, many manufacturers and vendors provide word processing capabilities such as mailing list programs, cost accounting programs, tax planning packages, report writing, financial planning, material requirement planning, and statistical analysis packages. Several vendors even specialize in various industries. For example, one vendor may offer an entire array of software as well as hardware to satisfy the more common information processing and accounting needs of a retail pharmacy or a law firm.

One of the more popular software application packages available for several system configurations, similar to those shown in Figure 17–4, is VisiCalc. VisiCalc is especially useful for budgeting and planning. It is a work sheet analysis program where the user defines row and column headings. These rows and columns are labeled and form a matrix work sheet with an x and a y axis. The user can then specify relationships between columns (such as growth in sales) and relationships between rows (such as sales and related expenses via sets of equations). Using these simple functions, the computer will develop the entire budget, forecast, or plan. Any change in values or relationships can also be displayed at the user command so that various alternatives can be analyzed at a glance. The cost of this and similar financial planning models currently ranges from $150 to $1,500.

Microcomputer and minicomputer systems offer many benefits to the small business. The user is put in direct contact with the computer through the CRT and menu processing system which uses random access memory. This interaction is very valuable in achieving better and easier information processing, error correction, report generation, customer relations, inventory management, data input, management control, and accuracy. The primary benefit of small-business systems is not in the periodic processing of payroll checks, the printing of customer statements, and other standard periodic accounting procedures. It may well be that the small-business accountant or service bureau can do this periodic work at a more reasonable cost. The primary advantage of the mini or micro is found in the ability of management to interact with the files in an easy, self-instructed way. For example, this enhanced interaction allows the manager to

1. Query a customer account to answer questions
2. Query the status of a particular inventory item to determine if it is on hand or when it will arrive
3. Determine how much cash will be needed to pay this week's payables
4. Assess the qualifications of a certain employee for a new job
5. Assess the tax effect of a new expenditure
6. Assess various construction plans for feasibility and cost
7. Aggregate and disaggregate financial statements to assess division performance

Many of these and other management questions tend to require immediate answers. The ability to obtain these answers quickly and accurately can have an impact on the profitability of the firm.

Secondary benefits of minicomputer and microcomputer systems are found in the areas of transaction processing and reporting. Transaction processing is simplified. Data are entered once, they are edited, and the files are updated. This streamlined data entry eliminates a considerable amount of paper work, which, in spite of many controls, can create errors that are time consuming to correct. Reporting in many small systems, such as the one illustrated in Chapter 14, can be very flexible. The format of output is not predetermined. Many departmental statements are often available, and comparisons can be made and ratios can be computed. The format of output can be designed by using a generation feature that is common for most good software packages in meeting the business's specific information needs.

Word Processing and Mailing Lists

Many software vendors and hardware manufacturers offer word processing packages. Many packages are priced under $150. Model II SCRIPSIT™ for Tandy's TRS–80™ Model II is typical of the offerings for microcomputers.[7] It has the following features:

1. User-oriented menus and props
2. Table format design
3. Block movement
4. Global word search
5. Page numbering
6. Page ordering and reordering
7. Automatic pagination
8. Spooling so that the printer works independently of typing
9. Interface with Profile II[8] (a filing system) and many special editing features

Other systems are more multifunctional and offer other features such as dictionaries for spelling, record processing, numeric processing for proofing tables, and data-entry procedures for interface with the organization's information system.

In addition to word processing systems, mailing list systems are often offered for the small business that has to write many letters or send information to many potential customers. These packages assist in handling and maintaining large customer and prospect files because of their many update, sort, merge, and print features. In the future, the interoffice communication ability of these systems will become increasingly important.

[7] SCRIPSIT and TRS–80 are trademarks of Radio Shack.
[8] Radio Shack TRS–80 Model II Software, Tandy, Inc.

Selection Criteria

The selection procedure that should be used for a microcomputer or a minicomputer system is no different from that used to select a large mainframe system. Unfortunately many small-business owners and managers purchase a system that does not really satisfy their decision-making, transaction processing, and reporting needs in a cost-beneficial manner.

The system design steps should follow the outline given in Chapters 10 and 11. The selection of software packages must fit the decision-making needs of the business. The difference between the selection process in large businesses and that in small businesses is that in the latter, many of the steps outlined will be less formal. The accountant may be able to render this service. The key to the systems design process is the analysis of the needs of the small business and the subsequent specification of the hardware and software characteristics that will satisfy these requirements. Because the small-business environment is so different from the large-business environment, and because many small newly formed companies are major vendors of minicomputer and microcomputer hardware and software, it is often necessary to seek advice from third parties.

There are several key selection criteria that small-business managers and their accountants must consider. Several of these criteria are based on current limitations in the minicomputer and microcomputer environment. Many of these problem areas should subside with the passage of time.

First, the system must meet management needs. This is a problem with small-business systems because many software packages are so general in design that they do not match the needs of management. This is often due to the limited storage space, which has been a particular problem for microcomputers. Management should avoid modifying these standard packages, for this will lead to many problems later when vendors offer software revisions. Moreover, installation and use are greatly enhanced when standard packages are used. Management should seek the package that meets most of the needs of the business at the beginning of the process.

Second, many systems are weak in internal control due to the historic lack of storage space in many systems and an effort to keep costs to a minimum. The system must have adequate control and data safeguards, or the firm's management and auditors will lose confidence in the information it provides.

Third, a reliable maintenance arrangement must be obtained through a good service network. A backup system at a nearby business may be necessary to allow continuing operations in case of machine failure. This is now the most acute problem because many of the vendors of micro and mini hardware and software do not have good nationwide service networks.

Fourth, adequate documentation is often nonexistent. Many software systems are turnkey systems. Managers and auditors do not know how data are actually processed and what controls and safeguards are available. Moreover, with small systems, user-written programs are often poorly documented. Management and auditors should insist on adequate documentation to give them confidence in the information provided.

Fifth, great care must be taken to obtain audit trails. For example, in the system illustrated in Chapter 14, options are available for transaction listings. These must be required, not optional. Effective numerical document control is necessary because it will enable managers and auditors to trace transactions.

Sixth, input routines should contain menu drives displaying all options and extensive error messages that can easily be understood.

Seventh, although data may be more free of errors due to the input, reasonableness, completeness controls, and editing of input, once data have been entered, it can result in an erroneous update of the master file. Buffers with batch controls would help to increase accuracy at this point by allowing further review of data before the master file has been affected.

Eighth, many systems are not expandable or compatible with larger systems. This may be a severe problem for growing companies. For example, many microcomputer systems are limited as to the number of customers accounts, vendors, and inventory line items that can be handled. In the example cited in Chapter 14, the inventory file is expandable but the others are not.

Ninth, report generation ability must be present so that management can customize its output without writing special programs.

Tenth, applications should be integrated as much as possible so that a single entry will update accounts receivable and inventory systems.

Eleventh, the lack of trained personnel in information processing and accounting will require careful training of users. Training will make the system seem "friendly" and give users more confidence in it.

Finally, obsolescence may be a problem because of rapid changes in technology. Therefore most vendors would rather sell than lease hardware and software. The user might end up with a considerable investment in the system. In some cases had management waited a year or two, a much less expensive system would have provided even better information. From a competitive and economic perspective, it is critical that management and the accountant keep abreast of changes in hardware and software technology.

Special Internal Control Features

Earlier in the chapter we discussed several internal control deficiencies that are found in microcomputer systems and, to a lesser extent, in minicomputer systems. Several practical steps can be taken by the small-business owner or manager to achieve greater control over the system and thereby obtain much greater confidence in the information provided by the system for his utilization.

First, the active participation of management in key transactions and decisions is important.

Second, even though the separation of duties is not economically practical with a small number of employees, better control can be achieved by (a) using a transaction log, (b) specifying a password to restrict use of the designated operator, and (c) prohibiting operators from altering programs. The last measure can be accomplished by employing operators who are not trained in programming.

Third, access can be controlled by simply locking up the computer and diskettes in a closet or safe.

Fourth, passwords should be used for access to key files.

Fifth, control totals should be used for the number of transactions, dollar amounts, and debits and credits in accounting ledger entries. The system illustrated in Chapter 14 is not particularly strong in this respect.

Sixth, exception procedures should be added to flag unauthorized system use, unusual transactions, nonexistent accounts, extraordinary amounts, and other errors. An exception listing procedure would bring any unusual activity to management's attention. In the typical microsystem this is not provided. It should be added for critical activities.

Seventh, data entry errors, transcription errors, and completeness errors are generally reduced due to the interactive menu mode of input which instructs the operator as to exactly what the options are and what to do. This is one of the greatest control strengths of interactive minicomputer or microcomputer systems.

Finally, as far as a small business is concerned, the mere fact that all transactions are processed in a consistent manner is an immeasurable strength because this is seldom the case with informal manual systems. This discipline should give management and the auditor added confidence in the information provided by the system.

Small Systems for the CPA Firm

As in any small business, the smaller CPA firm can make excellent use of minicomputer and microcomputer systems in its decision-making, transaction processing, and reporting needs. Moreover, the access to interactive capability, better turnaround speed, and ease of increasing volume may enable the firm to extend client services and enlarge its practice.

The format flexibility offered by systems such as the one illustrated in Chapter 14 allows the practitioner to better satisfy client requirements for write-up work. The greater speed and lower turnaround time enable the practitioner to increase the volume of this work and give clients much better service on their financial statements and tax returns. Practitioners can add many other write-up and accounting services such as budget preparation, cost analysis, sales analysis, and performance reporting.

Additional types of services that were previously not feasible for smaller CPA firms can also be offered. With the CPA's increased knowledge of accounting systems, the firm can assist some clients in designing their own information systems. A firm can also undertake many more tax and financial planning activities with the aid of an interactive computer system. The practitioner can evaluate the client's financial status by using a system such as VisiCalc and ask many "what if" questions on behalf of the client to help with strategic and managerial planning. For example:

> The microcomputer that one CPA firm uses is a Radio Shack system using a TRS–80 Model I and Model II, both with three disk drives and communication equipment (a modem with an acoustic coupler), valued at approximately $3,000 and $5,000 plus the cost of the software. The firm consists of four partners, four professional staff members, four bookkeepers (one internal), two secretaries and one part-time program-

mer for client work. The professional staff members do not handle the computer. It is used by the internal bookkeeper. The secretaries use the computer for word processing. One partner is totally in charge of computer operations. The other partners and professional staff members are aware of the computer's capabilities but do not otherwise get involved. The firm is constantly seeking new applications to run on the computer. The firm will soon open two new offices and plans to link all three by telecommunications. The following are some of the many applications that are run using the firm's microcomputer:

1. Payroll, W–2 and 941 forms check printing for six clients.
2. General ledger for eight clients.
3. Time and billing using a modified commercially available software package.
4. Accounts receivable using a commercially available DBMS.
5. Worksheet analysis using VisiCalc for tax planning, project control (cash flow), consolidations, summarizing information and survey results.
6. Depreciation schedules and fixed asset reports.
7. Statistical sampling and evaluations.
8. Telecommunications: All TRS–80s located in the clients' offices can communicate with the firm's computer, and information (data files and programs) can be transferred by telephone lines. Clients also may use the firm's computer via time-sharing on evenings when it is not being used internally to access a BVMS package. The time-sharing feature is used to access the Source, MicroNET and AICPA time-sharing libraries for applications (mostly data bases) not available for the microcomputer.
9. Word processing using a letter-quality printer for reports, repetitive letters, confirmations and accounting manuals for clients.[9]

THE FUTURE OF SMALL-BUSINESS SYSTEMS

Because of their simplicity, manual systems will continue to be used in many small businesses. Accounting services will continue to be used for tax planning and financial statement preparation. Whenever feasible and economically possible, however, minicomputer and microcomputer systems will increasingly be used in the future. They are inexpensive and can effectively provide decision-making information, transaction processing speed, precision and consistency, and report flexibility. The small-business manager can command a wealth of information to better plan and manage the business's activities.

This movement toward mini and micro systems will be a major challenge to the accounting profession. When relatively few large organizations had large mainframe computers, the organization could hire experts to run the computer systems. Auditors could call upon experts within their respective firms to assist in the audit of these computer systems. Moreover, the accounting practitioner could also use experts to assist clients in the effective and efficient design of information systems. With the explosion of the number of organizations now purchasing or leasing mini or micro systems, the practitioner

[9] Robert C. Wyune and Alan Frotman, "Microcomputer: Helping Make Practice Perfect," *Journal of Accountancy,* December 1981, p. 39.

will no longer be able to call on the expert for help with system design or audit problems. The accountant must therefore become well trained in information systems design to be able to deal with the problems that will arise. Moreover, accounting professionals employed as controllers and staff accountants by large and small organizations will be expected to function effectively in this new computer environment. This burden of training must be shouldered by the profession. Management will lose confidence in the information provided by these new systems if the accountant is not involved in their design and operation, because these systems will probably lack sufficient controls, be poorly designed, and not meet the information needs of the business. The challenge facing the profession is enormous. Accountants must adapt to this new and rapidly changing technology.

SUMMARY

In this chapter we reviewed the unique characteristics of the small-business environment. We discussed several types of systems designed to meet the decision-making, transaction processing, and reporting needs of the small business. These systems range from simple ledgerless bookkeeping to minicomputer systems. We outlined the internal control strengths and weaknesses involved in each of these systems. The focus and nature of many of these controls differ significantly from those found in large businesses. We also reviewed the costs and benefits of minicomputer and microcomputer systems and discussed the importance of good system design, along with key aspects of the hardware and software selection process. In summary, the transaction processing needs, as well as the operational, managerial, and strategic decision-making needs, must be supported by the information system of the small business in a cost-effective way.

SELECTED REFERENCES

AICPA, "Guidelines for General System Specifications for a Computer System." New York, 1976.

Apple Computer Company, *Apple in Depth*, 1980.

Association of Computer Users Benchmark Report, Vol. 4. Boulder, Colo., 1981.

BLANKENSHIP, RONALD C., and CAROL A. SCHOLLER, "The CPA, the Small Company and the Computer," *Journal of Accountancy*, August 1976, pp. 46–51.

BOER, GERMAIN B., and SAM W. BARCUS III, "How a Small Company Evaluates Acquisition of a Minicomputer," *Management Accounting*, March 1981, pp. 13–23.

BOWER, JAMES B., ROBERT E. SCHLOSSER, and CHARLES T. ZLATKOVICH, *Financial Information Systems: Theory and Practice*. Boston: Allyn & Bacon, 1969.

CERULLO, MICHAEL, "Service Bureaus User Appraisal," *Datamation*, May 1972, pp. 86–89.

"Data pro Directory of Small Computers." Delran, N.J.: Data pro Research Corporation, McGraw-Hill, 1980.

DOWELL, J. RICHARD, "So, You Want to Buy a Minicomputer," *Price Waterhouse Review*, No. 3, 1977, pp. 18–25.

GROLLMAN, WILLIAM K., and ROBERT W. CALLY, "Internal Control for Small Businesses," *Journal of Accountancy*, December 1978, pp. 64–67.

GRUMMAN AND COWEN AND CO., "Annual Minicomputer Survey" (highlights), *Datamation*, November 1980, pp. 145–64.

HIMROD, BRUCE W., "Microcomputers for Small Business," *Journal of Accountancy*, December 1979, pp. 44–50.

KLEIN, PHILLIP J., "When It's Time to Get Your Own Computer," *Journal of Accountancy*, July 1981, pp. 30–34.

LEITCH, ROBERT A., GADIS J. DILLON, and SUE H. McKINLEY, "Internal Control Weaknesses in Small Business," *Journal of Accountancy*, December 1981, pp. 97–101.

McCLELLAN, STEPHEN T., "Distributed and Small Business Computing—A Fast Track," *Datamation*, May 1979 (Special Issue), pp. 124–27.

McDANIEL, LLOYD W., and HENRY WICHMANN, JR., Minicomputers: A Boom to Small Public Accounting Firms and Write-up Work," *National Public Accountants*, February 1979, pp. 22–26.

McGLYNN, DANIEL R., *Personal Computing: Home, Professional and Small Business Applications*. New York: John Wiley, 1979.

Management Science America, *Peachtree/40*™, *Business Software for Apple II*™, 1980.

"Minicomputers Challenge the Big Machines," *Business Week*, April 26, 1976, pp. 58–63.

MITCHELL, JOE, "Expanding the Small Business System," *Datamation*, November 1979, pp. 126–30.

MOSCOV, STEPHEN A., and MARK G. SIMKIN, *Accounting Information Systems*. New York: John Wiley, 1981.

OWEN, JOHN, "The Mini Computer—Threat or Opportunity?" *Accountancy*, July 1979, pp. 76–77.

PAYUE, JOSEPH, "Minicomputers: Big Bucks from Small Systems," *Datamation*, May 1979 (Special Issue), pp. 118–20.

PHILLIPS, J. DONALD, and JAMES L. BOOCKHOLDT, "Mini Systems for Mini Businesses," *Journal of Systems Management*, May 1977, pp. 28–31.

REA, R. C., "A Small Business Internal Control Questionnaire," *Journal of Accountancy*, July 1978, pp. 53–54.

SATRIANO, THOMAS V., "The Practical Aspects of Mini-computer Business Systems for Accounting Practitioners," *National Public Accountant*, April 1978, pp. 8–15.

SCHWARTZ, DONALD A., "Microcomputers Take Aim on Small Business Clients," *Journal of Accountancy*, December 1979, pp. 57–62.

SHAW, ROBERT J., VICTOR GOLDBERG, and JON F. CARMAIN, "Small Companies Can Take Giant Strides with Minicomputers," *Management Focus*, March/April 1978, pp. 28–31.

STELGER, HERBERT J., "Evaluation of Internal Control in Small Audits," *Journal of Accountancy*, November 1964, pp. 55–61.

STENGER, JR., WILLIAM L., "A Sole Practitioner Takes a Hard Look at an Accounting Computer," *Journal of Accountancy*, January 1975, pp. 41–43.

"A Survey: The Small Systems Market," *Datamation*, 1979 (Special Issue), pp. 95–98.

TRS–80™ Computer Catalog No. RSC–5–1981. Fort Worth, Tex.: Tandy Corporation.

WALKER, EWING S., "Accounting Packages Selection and Management," *Datamation*, August 1981, pp. 76–122.

WOHL, AMY, "A Review of Office Automation," *Datamation*, February 1980, pp. 117–19.

WYUNE, ROBERT C., and ALAN FROTMAN, "Microcomputer: Helping Make Practice Perfect," *Journal of Accountancy*, December 1981, pp. 34–39.

"Xerox Bid to Be No. 1 in Offices," *Business Week*, June 22, 1981, pp. 77–78.

ZIMMERMAN, HARRY, "Minicomputers: The Challenge for Controls," *Journal of Accountancy*, June 1980, pp. 28–35.

REVIEW QUESTIONS

1. What should be the focal point of an accounting system for a small business? (Recall where many fell short in the survey of control weaknesses.)

2. What constitutes a set of minimum records for a small business?

3. What is a *ledgerless bookkeeping system*? What are its pros and cons?

4. What is *executive control* and how is it useful for small businesses?

5. What breakthroughs made computer systems cost effective for small businesses?

6. What typical applications are offered by manufacturers and software vendors for small businesses?

7. How can word processing help small businesses?

8. What are some of the limitations of microcomputer systems and how can these limitations be overcome?

9. How can a small microsystem be useful to a CPA firm in expanding its practice?

10. What is the major advantage of small computers, such as the ones discussed in this chapter and in Chapter 14, for the small-business owner?

11. What is the approximate cost of a very small system, and is this cost reasonable for a small-business owner?

12. Should a small-business owner purchase a software package and modify it to suit his or her needs? Or would this person be better off searching for one that is closer to his or her needs rather than modifying the system. If so, why?

13. How do small microcomputer systems and their associated business hardware pose a major challenge to the accounting profession?

14. How can small microsystems improve budgeting and planning activities for small businesses?

EXERCISES AND CASES

17–1

List the major characteristics of the small-business environment and describe how each of these characteristics can influence information systems design.

17–2

Explain what is meant by a single-entry accounting system and how a single-entry accounting system on a cash basis can be converted to an accrual basis system at year-end.

17–3

Clayton County News is a small weekly newspaper. It is the official county organ, and its office is in the county seat. It has a circulation of twenty-seven hundred. The paper is published every Wednesday.

The *News* is an old paper with a colorful history that predates the Civil War. It has had various owners during its existence but is now operated as a sole proprietorship. It was purchased in 1966 from the retiring owner by the present owner and publisher. His wife is the editor and bookkeeper. There are two other employees. One of these employees is an office helper in charge of subscriptions and classified advertisements. The other employee works exclusively in the print shop.

SUBSCRIPTION EXPIRATION NOTIFICATION   Subscription records are maintained on 3-x-5-inch index cards that contain the name of the subscriber, his or her address, and the date of expiration. These cards are filed according to the mailing address. (In some cases the billing address is different.) For example, all the in-county subscribers are maintained in one file, with those of city subscribers in front filed alphabetically according to rural route. Out-of-county subscriptions are filed alphabetically according to zip codes. This same filing system is used to maintain the files of mailing stencils. The *News* uses an Addressograph for printing the address on each subscriber's paper.

NEW SUBSCRIPTIONS   Upon notification of a desired subscription, an index card is made and an address stencil is typed for the Addressograph. The stencil is placed in the active files. If the notification includes payment, the index card is filed as described above. Otherwise it is filed in the rear of the appropriate section.

BLOCK ADVERTISING   Advertising is the lifeblood of a weekly newspaper. Block ads include all those that are enclosed by wide dark lines. For all practical purposes, this is all the commercial advertising except the classified ads.

Orders are received primarily by mail, but occasionally from office visits. Sometimes the editor solicits ads (e.g., for special graduation and Christmas issues). An ad order form is completed by the editor with the name and address of the advertiser, the size of the ad, and the number of times it should be run. She then computes the charge. These orders are maintained chronologically according to the last issue in which the ad is to appear.

CLASSIFIED ADVERTISING   Classified ads are the small ads that are printed together under certain headings. The *News* charges two dollars for the first ten words and ten cents for each additional word.

Most of the classified ads come in over the phone, and the editor or office helper is frequently asked to help in the wording of the ad. The office helper has responsibility for classified ads and performs the following operations unless otherwise indicated.

A classified order form is prepared in duplicate with the name and address of the advertiser, the dates to be run, the charge (if the ad is to run for a definite period), and the body of the advertisement. The original is sent to the shop to be used in setting the ad and proofreading. The carbon copy is kept in the office for further processing.

A copy of the last week's classified page is kept next to the phone, and when an advertiser calls to cancel an ad with unspecified life, that ad is marked out. A notation is also made on the carbon copy of the ad order form of the last date run. When the shop worker is ready to prepare the classified page for the new issue, he comes to the office and requests the canceled classified page with the marked out ads.

The carbon copy of the classified order is used to post a 5-x-7-inch accounts receivable index card with the customer's name and the charges for advertising. These cards are filed alphabetically.

LEGAL ADVERTISING RECEIPTS   Legal advertisements (legals) constitute a large portion of the paper's advertising income. The *News* is the county's "official organ" and thus publishes all the legals for the county. Rates are set by a state regulatory commission.

Legals are received from the various lawyers, the probate judge, and the clerk of the court. They carry instructions as to how many times to run. The editor computes the charge and sends the legal to the shop for setting. The galley (printed copy) and the legal are then returned to the office for proofreading. Necessary changes are made on the galley, and it is returned to the shop. The galley is corrected. The legal remains in the office and is filed by the last issue in which it is to run.

BILLINGS   At the end of the month or shortly after the beginning of the new month, the office helper goes through the subscription files and pulls all those cards that will expire in the coming month. A form is used in which only the name and address of the subscriber and his or her expiration date are handwritten. These form renewal notices, with a printed return envelope, are sent to the subscribers. The pulled index cards are filed alphabetically in back of each division. For new subscriptions, a statement is prepared and mailed with a return envelope.

After each issue, the editor identifies the ad orders that have been run for the last time and records them in the Accounts Receivable account in the general journal. She prepares the statements. Tear sheets (pages with the ad) are provided for those advertisers who require them.

The office helper sends out statements at the end of the month for all classified accounts with remaining balances (from the accounts receivable card file).

After each issue, those legals that have run for the last time are recorded in the Accounts Receivable account in the general ledger, and statements are prepared on general-purpose forms. The statements are mailed each week. The legal is filed by the last date it was run.

CASH RECEIPTS   The editor or the office assistant goes to the post office twice a day—shortly after it opens and then again in the early afternoon. Most of the renewals come in return envelopes which were sent out with the renewal notices. These are turned over to the office helper; however, if the office helper has already gone to the post office, he keeps them and turns the rest of the mail over to the editor.

The office helper notes the receipt in a cash receipts book and, if it is a renewal, discards the renewal notice that has been returned. Then he goes to the subscription file and removes the subscriber's index card from the back of each section, marks a line through the old expiration date, records the new expiration date, and files it alphabetically with the cards of the other subscribers in that section. He puts a check mark on the face of the receipt in the cash receipt book to indicate that the subscription file has been updated. Roughly 30 percent of the incoming renewals are in cash. The cash and checks are placed in the cash drawer. The subscription file is updated in

batches, usually once a day. When a cash receipt book is full, the office helper goes through each page to make sure it has a check mark indicating that the file has been updated. The cash receipt book is then filed with others chronologically.

Address stencils for nonrenewals are pulled once a month. After the last week's issue of that month, all index cards filed in the back of each section are pulled and their address stencil is removed from the mailing file. The index cards and address stencils are filed separately and alphabetically, in case of future payment. When payment is received, the index card is updated with the new renewal date. The issues sent between the expiration date and the end of the month are free. The index card and stencil are returned to the active files and are filed alphabetically.

At the end of the quarter all the cash receipts are copied into the cash receipts journal. Each subscriber's name and amount paid is entered. These are then posted to the general ledger by the editor once a quarter.

Upon payment of an advertising bill, a receipt is prepared by the office helper. It is prepared in duplicate in a prenumbered general receipts book with three receipts to the page. If payment is by mail the original copy is destroyed; otherwise the original is given to the advertiser (payment is rarely made in person). "Classified" is written on the receipt when payment is for a classified ad to indicate that posting is needed to the classified accounts receivable ledger. Upon posting the Accounts Receivable account by the office helper, a check mark is placed on the receipt. The editor posts to the general journal whenever time allows.

Checks are placed in the cash drawer to await subsequent deposits.

REQUIRED:

a. Flowchart the newspaper's current system. Assume that no journal system exists in cases where discussion, which was obtained from the new personnel, was not clear or consistent.

b. Cite the internal control (administrative and accounting) strengths and weaknesses.

c. Suggest ways to resolve the *major* weaknesses.

d. State your opinion as to which parts of the system could benefit from **EDP**, why benefits would accrue, and which characteristics of the EDP systems would help.

e. (optional) Could the Peachtree™ Software Accounts Receivable system be adapted to process subscriptions that are paid in advance? How? See Chapter 14.

f. (optional) Design a microcomputer system for *Clayton County News*. Assume that special programs may be written as needed. Specify a hardware configuration and internal control. How could you use the system to support managerial decision-making needs?

17–4

The Orville Slick Oil Company[1] is a petroleum product distributorship located in Broken Bow, Nebraska. The company distributes the products of the Buffalo Oil Company of Texas as a jobber. All property, plant, and equipment are owned by Mr. Slick. Property used in the business includes two delivery trucks, a service truck, office space, a warehouse for storage of oil and grease, and a plant facility from which gas, fuel, and kerosene are distributed. Gas tanks, gas pumps, and air compressors are kept for use by regular customers. Detailed records are made of customers using this equipment.

The business is run by Mr. Slick. His wife, Gracie, keeps the books. One product delivery man is employed on a full-time basis. Various independent contractors and laborers are hired as needed to help with installation and repair of equipment.

Accounting is done on an accrual basis. A chart of accounts is used. At the end of the year, a local CPA prepares financial statements and tax returns. Mrs. Slick posts the books and reconciles the monthly bank statements. Mr. Slick prepares the monthly sales and excise tax returns.

Revenues are provided by the sale of gas, fuel, kerosene, oil, grease, and related products. Mr. Slick prices all products. The cost of these products from Buffalo Oil fluctuates considerably. Gas, fuel, and kerosene margins are reviewed monthly for this reason, and oil and grease margins are reviewed two or three times a year. Jobbers such as Mr. Slick have had considerable difficulty in evaluating selling prices to keep a reasonable margin and still be competitive.

SALES AND ACCOUNTS RECEIVABLE A delivery man delivers the product and prepares four copies of the sales ticket. Along with the blue original copy, the green copy is the customer receipt, the white copy is for cash or credit-card sales, and the yellow copy is for credit sales. All credit sales are approved by the owner prior to delivery. Since Broken Bow is a small town, this is a simple matter for Mr. Slick because he knows everyone.

Both the white copy along with credit cards and the yellow copy along with the original are forwarded to the bookkeeper, Mrs. Slick. The bookkeeper checks the pricing and accuracy of each type of sale and places the cash in the vault. She then posts cash sales to the daily cash summary report and credit sales to the customer accounts receivable record, which is kept on a 3-x-5-inch card. Both cash and credit sales are posted to a daily sales summary, and the perpetual inventory records are updated. Mrs. Slick then files all original copies by number, all white copies by date, and yellow copies alphabetically by customer name.

Monthly the accounts receivable customer cards are pulled by the bookkeeper along with the alphabetical file of yellow invoices, and statements are prepared and mailed by the bookkeeper. The yellow copies of the invoice are mailed along with the statement. Part of the statement is supposed to be torn off and returned with the remittance.

For accounts that are more than one month past due, service charges are added by the bookkeeper at the same time that the statement is prepared. These charges are posted to the receivables card at the time also.

CASH RECEIPTS Along with cash sales noted above, the owner opens the mail, compares the cash receipts and/or credit cards with the remittance stubs (if the remittance stub is missing, he prepares a new one), and places all cash in the vault. The remittance stubs are forwarded to the bookkeeper, who posts the daily cash summary. Deposit slips are prepared and deposits are made whenever the owner goes to the bank, which is two or three times

---

[1] This case was originally prepared by Professor Sue McKinley. The adapted version is used here with permission.

per week. Credit cards are mailed to Buffalo Oil Company as partial payment for petroleum products. The bookkeeper then posts the accounts receivable cards for the amount of the receipt noted on the remittance stub and files the remittance stub by date.

CASH DISBURSEMENTS   Incoming mail is opened by the owner. Invoices are compared with receiving reports and are attached to purchase orders by the bookkeeper. They are then filed as they are received. A record of employee time is also kept by the bookkeeper. Periodically the owner reviews the unpaid invoice file and writes the necessary checks to pay the vendors. Employees are paid monthly. Buffalo Oil is also paid monthly for the difference between the invoice amount and the credit cards that have been remitted to Orville Slick Oil Company and forwarded to Buffalo Oil (as noted in the cash receipts discussion). All invoices and attached receiving reports are filed by vendor. Cash disbursement information such as name, date, account number, and invoice number is noted on a check stub.

Upon payment of the payroll, payroll records are posted by the bookkeeper. The bank account is reconciled monthly by the bookkeeper.

INVENTORY, PURCHASING, AND RECEIPT OF MERCHANDISE   A perpetual inventory card file is maintained. On each card, the product name, vendor, amount on hand, and amount on order are recorded. This file is arranged according to product name. As noted earlier as part of the sales procedure, the amount on hand is credited as sales are made.

The delivery man makes a casual assessment of items that are in short supply and gives the owner a note. The owner then prepares a purchase order for a reasonable quantity based on his fifteen years of experience as a jobber and sends the original to the vendor. Most products are ordered from the Buffalo Oil Company. A copy is given to the bookkeeper, who pulls the inventory card and updates the on-order amount. She then files the copy by vendor pending delivery of the product.

Upon delivery, the delivery man who works for Orville Slick Oil Company pulls the purchase order copy, compares it with the products received, notes any exception on the purchase order copy, prepares a receiving report, and pulls the inventory cards and updates the on-order and on-hand details for each item received. It is known when delivery will take place because all vendors have scheduled routes and the delivery man who works for Orville Slick Oil Company can be on hand to help the vendor's driver with difficult and often dirty work.

The delivery man then gives the purchase order copy, receiving reports, and inventory cards back to the bookkeeper. The bookkeeper follows up on the exceptions. Receiving reports and purchase orders are filed by vendor, awaiting a copy of the vendor's invoice.

GENERAL COMMENTS   All buildings and inventory items are fenced and locked. Keys are kept in a locked vault (safe), and only the owner and his wife, the bookkeeper, know the combination. All documents are prenumbered. The check stubs, the daily cash summary, the daily sales summary, the accounts receivable file, the inventory file, and all other miscellaneous records are gathered by Mrs. Slick and posted to the general ledger once a month.

REQUIRED: From the notes gathered above on the Orville Slick Oil Company:

a. Prepare a system flowchart for
  (1) Sales and accounts receivable
  (2) Cash receipts
  (3) Cash disbursements
  (4) Inventory, purchasing, and receipt of merchandise
b. Comment on the strengths and weaknesses of both administrative and accounting control.
c. Suggest and flowchart a new system that will relieve the major administrative and accounting control problems by using a microcomputer with (1) accounting applications and reporting packages and (2) capability to generate special reports based on the transactions gathered in a normal course of business as described above.

Assume that there is no formal system where none is noted, and where a conflict occurs, assume that the system is confusing and not effective even for those who use it on a daily basis.

17–5

ABC Leasing[2]   ABC Leasing is a licensee
for a major auto rental company; its location,
in a resort city near the ocean, brings it both
business and vacation customers. Annual sales
volume is approximately $6 million, and the
company has 60 full time employees. Sales are
expected to increase to $9 million over the
next three years. The company has rental offices at the local airport, in several downtown
locations, and in two neighboring towns. A local service bureau has been satisfying all its
data processing needs, but this operation recently increased its charges to ABC to $2,000
per month. At this price the company decided
it might pay to purchase its own computer.

To get some idea of how to approach the
problem, ABC managers attended a seminar
on small business minicomputer systems,
where they talked to some managers from
small businesses who recently had acquired
computers. They learned two important things
from these conversations: (1) approximately
one-half the total costs of the system would
cover the hardware, and the remaining half
would pay for the necessary software, supplies,
consulting help, and assorted start-up costs;
(2) they needed help in gathering the right information, asking the right questions of vendors, presenting the appropriate information
to the vendors, and specifying the exact output
they wanted from the system. ABC management approached its accounting firm for help
in gathering and evaluating information for the
computer purchase decision. The firm's consultant suggested ABC should

1. Study the present data flow within the
   company.
2. Compile and classify information requirements.
3. Get computer system proposals from vendors.
4. Analyze the proposals and then select the
   best proposal from those submitted.

Data Flow within the Company   After several weeks of data gathering by the clerical
staff at ABC, the company was able to compile
the relevant information necessary for specifying the parameters of the system the company
needed (Figure C17–5). The data were important not only to ABC but also to the companies that would write the programs for the
system because company management wanted
all software developed by outside software
vendors. The company president felt strongly
that ABC should not create a data processing
department; therefore, the company would
have to buy all its software from outside suppliers. This decision also meant that programs
and machines acquired by the company would
have to be readily usable by the existing clerical staff.

Finding out what information company
managers need is no easy task, but ABC was
able to identify some obvious needs by looking
at existing problems. For example, monthly accounting reports, useful for controlling operations and for projecting cash flows, arrived
from the service bureau two or three weeks after the close of the month. The clerical staff

General ledger accounts	133
Digits per account number	6
Entries per month to all accounts	900
Contract outstanding on any day	1,600
Payments received each month	1,400
Number of contracts processed monthly	7,900
Number of contracts in rental revenue master file	50,000
Payment vouchers per month	240
Number of entries per voucher	8
Number of vendors serving ABC Leasing	200
Journal entries per month for all disbursements	1
Automobiles bought and sold each month	250
Automobiles on hand	1,200
Number of digits in automobile number	6
Number of digits in automobile serial number	6
Unidentified payments per month	250
Outstanding billable items	900
Unapplied cash items at any time	1,500
Payroll checks per week	100
Full time employees	60

Figure C17–5   ABC Leasing: System Statistics

[2] Reprinted with permission from Boer and Barcus, "How a Small Company Evaluates
Acquisition of a Minicomputer," pp. 13–23.

was gradually getting behind in its preparation of operational analyses, with each sales increase putting them further behind. Given that sales would increase about 50% over the next three years, it was clear the company had to automate existing procedures just to enable the staff to continue performing its present activities.

At the beginning of the output definition process, company managers were convinced that automation of accounting procedures was the most important reason for buying a computer, but as they worked with defining system outputs they began to realize the profit potential of a computerized rental revenue file. Their current system showed a single number of sales revenue; however, the computerized rental revenue application could show rental revenue at a level as detailed as a specific automobile.

Such revenue detail would enable managers to evaluate the profitability of alternative mixes of corporation versus individual renters and small versus large automobiles. It also would allow them to evaluate the relative profitability of their rental locations and to assess the profit impact of various pricing strategies, strategies that involve alternative prices for mileage and day charges. Finally, managers realized that information about the most popular cars would enable them to alter the mix of automobiles they owned by selling less popular cars and replacing them with the more popular ones. In this case, then, output definition activities caused managers to shift their attention from the automation of clerical tasks to consideration of the profit potential of rental revenue information.

After their detailed review of management requirements, the company managers decided to implement the six applications listed below. They decided to start with the general ledger application because doing so would allow company personnel to get acquainted with the system using familiar data before they tried using the new information from the rental revenue system:

1. General ledger and financial reporting
2. Rental revenue
3. Cash payments and bank reconciliation
4. Fleet fixed assets
5. Unapplied cash and items billable
6. Payroll

These applications formed what management considered the basic components of the system the company needed. The information required by each application and the information flows among these applications were illustrated in a visual overview of the system which was most helpful in enhancing communication between managers and technical personnel. It also forced technical personnel to constantly be aware that no system component stands alone. The general ledger application served as the unifying element in the total system.

Not only did ABC managers have to specify the overall information flows, they also had to select those computer systems features compatible with their policy of using the present clerical staff to operate the new system. Working again with its consultant, the company prepared the following list of computer techniques that would satisfy company needs:

1. On-line interactive processing
2. Menu selection and program prompting for data entry, inquiry, file update, and report generation
3. Multi-programming capabilities
4. Printer spooling concurrent with other functions
5. Program prompting for such functions as paper changing and file mounting
6. Preparation of special reports by users through report writing software
7. Multiple security levels to limit file access to authorized individuals

On-line interactive processing with program prompting fits the company requirements well, because input station operators need little experience in computer operations. They simply respond to the questions appearing on the screen, and the system accepts only answers that fit a rigid set of constraints. The third requirement, which allows the machine to perform several activities simultaneously, was included at the suggestion of the consultant who felt the feature would be important for the company. Printer spooling allows operators to continue using terminals while the system prints reports, i.e., running the printer does not tie up the entire system so nobody can enter data during printing operations.

Requirements five and six are important because of the limited data processing knowledge of the personnel operating the machines. Prompting for paper and file changes requires less sophisticated personnel than a nonprompting system. Likewise, report writing software generally can be quickly mastered by nonprograming personnel who can then create nonstandard reports from the data files whenever the company needs them.

The final requirement arose out of management concern about system controls. Large data processing operations employ enough people so that various duties can be segregated to maintain adequate internal control. ABC, however, simply planned to put the machine in a room where present clerical personnel would operate it. This room would be open to all employees, and data entry personnel would also print reports; in short, segregation of duties would be nonexistent. To compensate for this lack of separation, the company wanted to use machine controls to the extent technologically feasible. Purchasing software from an outside vendor helped remove one severe control problem usually present in small companies: program preparation and data entry by the same individuals. Use of a hierarchy of security levels, each higher level giving access to larger portions of the system, allowed the company to carefully control which personnel have access to specific portions of the computer system.

To assure that accurate data entered the system, ABC decided it wanted editing procedures on data input that included both field and multiple field tests. Specifically, the company wanted the system to edit for format, perform range tests on data items, compare values to master file elements, and verify logical relationships between and among fields. Field tests in an interactive system catch data errors while the operator enters data, a feature that increased accuracy and allows inexperienced personnel to correct mistakes before the input data become part of the data files. Both these features were important to ABC because it wanted to use its present clerical staff to operate the system. In addition to these input data editing tests, ABC wanted input data, transaction files, and master files processed under system control with each batch of data processed generating control or audit trail reports for user review.

One other feature the company considered that fits roughly under the heading of information requirements is that of documentation.

System documentation refers to the procedure manuals, program listings, flow charts, listings of test data used to debug programs, and so on. ABC management especially was concerned about this feature because it planned to operate the system with no specialized data processing employees. This meant the instructions for using the programs and hardware would have to be written in clear, precise terms understandable to the present clerical staff; it meant ABC management would have to carefully scrutinize the material provided by the vendors before accepting it, and it meant that ABC would have to specify to the vendors in blunt terms that programs and hardware would be accepted only upon the receipt of documentation suitable for ABC personnel. Documentation is important in companies that have a fully staffed data processing department, but for ABC it wasn't just important—it was absolutely essential. Those factors for which the company decided it needed clear documentation were: systems, programs, equipment and systems operation, user procedures, and data control and error correction procedures.

SOLICITATION OF VENDOR PROPOSALS   After it completed the study of data flow and management information requirements, the company moved to the next step in the computer acquisition process: solicitation of vendor proposals with a request for proposal (RFP). A request for proposal tells hardware vendors, and, in the case of ABC Leasing, software vendors what the company wants from its system. The document describes in detail the specific company requirements for output, performance, and control procedures. In addition, it provides information such as company size, number of employees, and geographic location which helps vendors match their products with the company's needs.

EVALUATING VENDOR PROPOSALS   The final step in the computer acquisition process deals with choosing a system from those proposed by the vendors. ABC management began this final phase by carefully reviewing the proposals for completeness and for responsiveness to the RFP. A list of questions was prepared for vendors submitting proposals with deficiencies such as missing data or incomplete responses to specific points in the RFP. Vendors were asked to answer these questions to clarify the ambiguities in their proposal. Unsatisfactory responses to these questions provided grounds for dropping a vendor because company management felt such unresponsiveness was a good indication of the service it could expect from this vendor in the future. After clarifying these points the company summarized the vendor proposal data in a format that facilitated vendor comparisons. To do this summary, ABC management simply created a large spread sheet that assigned columns to each vendor and rows to the specific elements related to each vendor.

ALL FACTORS ARE RELEVANT   Cost, of course, doesn't give the full picture. For instance, ABC Leasing looked at factors such as current user satisfaction with a vendor, the number of systems sold to date, the total years the software vendors had been in business, and the number of companies using the software produced by the software vendor. Company managers also asked these questions: Is a terminal "locked up" while the printer is running? Are data items protected from erroneous update when two or more programs request that item simultaneously? How much does response time slow down when one additional terminal is added to the system? They looked, too, at the expandability of the system to make sure the system could grow with the business. More importantly, they looked at whether the system could produce reports on time, i.e., regardless of the amount of main memory or the access speed of the disks, management wanted a system that delivered information on time.

Finally, the managers considered how fast the vendors could fix a machine if it broke down; that is, they evaluated the location of maintenance personnel, their hours of availability, the number available, and the comments of present customers on vendor maintenance service. ABC managers visited user installations and attended company demonstrations. They actually used the equipment to see how easily errors could be corrected, screens could be read, and paper could be loaded into a printer.

REQUIRED: Based on the case study above, comment on the following:

a. The degree to which this small business followed the systems design and imple-

mentation procedures outlined in Chapters 10 and 11

b. The internal control considerations

c. The interaction between the accounting firm and management in the preparation of RFP

d. The point at which the vendor bids were solicited

e. The feasibility of using a microcomputer system to provide ABC Leasing with this needed information

f. The need for an interactive system

g. The profitability prospects of a new system

h. The criteria used for selection

17–6

The Kelly Home Building Company is a small building contractor located in the Piedmont area of the Carolinas. The company specializes in custom-built houses and is generally busy enough to retain most of its subcontractors on a regular basis. It has an excellent reputation and is generally asked to bid on many jobs for individuals as well as developers. Its business has grown and it is having a difficult time handling payrolls, billings, bank drawings, accounts payable to vendors and subcontractors, costs distributions, inventories, and scheduling of workers, subcontractors, and material. At the present time it employs a full-time bookkeeper to do the bookkeeping and cost distribution, and Mr. Kelly's son handles all the bid calculations. The company always seems to be two to three months behind and has often lost contracts because of excessive bids and because it has billed some customers for less than it should have due to delays in cost allocations. Quite simply, its financial affairs have been a mess, and Mr. Kelly doesn't even know at the end of the year how profitable the business has really been. He approaches you, as his accountant, for help—he has read and heard and talked to vendor salesmen about the new microcomputers and how they can help managers in his predicament.

REQUIRED:

a. Outline the approach you would advise Mr. Kelly to take to solve his problems.

b. Suggest how microcomputers may be able

to help Mr. Kelly with decision making, transaction processing, and reporting.

c. Suggest some key specifications that Mr. Kelly should spell out when dealing with software and hardware vendors.

d. Design a job cost system including internal control features using a mini or micro interactive computer. This should include data file structure and the flow of documents.

17–7

The Wood Products Lumber Company is a building supply company located in the suburbs of a large metropolitan area, (refer to Chapter 14). The company has been using a service bureau for sales analysis, inventory control, accounts payable, billings, payroll, and financial statement preparation.

The company has been experiencing two problems. First, when a sale is made it really does not know if the item is in stock until it has actually checked the warehouse because the inventory listing is often a week old. The service bureau updates the listing once a week. Using the example given in Chapter 14 on the state of the art in microsoftware for small businesses, suggest an inventory system for Wood Products. Your suggestion should include flowcharts and controls. Why would this be preferable to the current system of accumulating sales invoices and receiving reports and sending them to the service bureau for keypunching and processing?

The second problem, common to many small businesses, is that Wood Products has had considerable difficulty planning future purchases, capital improvements, and new lines of merchandise. As a first step, the company believes that a comparison of monthly and departmental financial statements with "some" plan would be helpful in determining how well it is progressing. For example, is the company making any contribution to profit and general overhead from its lawn care line of products? How could a microsystem such as the one suggested in Chapter 14 help with this problem? Would such a system enable management to engage in "what if" planning? If not, what could be done using the micro-hardware it may have purchased for the inventory problem above?

Finally, would you suggest that Wood Products use a microcomputer system for preparing payroll, processing monthly statements, paying vendors, and preparing financial statements? In your answer to this, indicate the circumstances under which you would make your positive or negative recommendation for these later applications.

17–8

a. Compare the internal control strengths and weaknesses of a small-business microcomputer system with those of a large mainframe system. Be sure to consider the following issues:

   (1) Segregation of duties
   (2) Physical control over assets (files and records)
   (3) Security of records
   (4) Compromise of programs for fraudulent purposes
   (5) Integrity of data input
   (6) Documentation
   (7) Control totals
   (8) Error correction procedures
   (9) Audit trails
   (10) Systems design
   (11) Confidence of management and auditors in information output
   (12) Backup systems
   (13) Supervision and review

b. Compare the internal control strengths and weaknesses of a manual (one bookkeeper) system with those of a microcomputer system by considering the same issues listed above.

17–9

The heart of Duff's Mail Order Seed Company is its mailing list of potential customers and its inventory system. Assume that Duff's specializes in garden seeds and fruit and nut trees for the Southeast. It purchases potential names from such magazines as *Southern Life, Organic Gardeners*, and the better-known seed companies. It pays particular attention to its own repeat customers, whom it believes are keys to its success.

Mr. Duff currently sends promotional material and catalogs free to old customers and to those who respond to letters sent to potential customers whose names are obtained from the list described above. He also solicits names from advertisements in many regional and national gardening and do-it-yourself magazines. Merging all these names, keeping up with address changes, and keeping sales statistics on sources of promotion and purchased mailing lists has been a nightmare for Mr. Duff.

He has heard of some of the new microcomputer systems that have mailing list sales analysis and inventory software. He has asked you, as his accountant, to prepare system specifications for his consideration. Your discussion with him leads you to believe that he is not really sure that such a system would be beneficial, and thus you also want to include in your report a review of the main benefits of such a system as well as its side benefits as they are related to other accounting data processing.

17–10

The firm of Fuller and Drew, CPAs, is located in what was once a small town north of a large fast-growing city in the Sun Belt. Fuller and Drew's practice has expanded considerably. Recently many small businesses have been started in their area in several industrial and office parks located on the beltway that was constructed around the city. Moreover, many apartments and condominiums have been built in the vicinity. Fuller and Drew have expanded

their staff from five to fifteen over the past five years, but they still cannot satisfy the demand for write-up work and tax planning for these businesses, their owners, and the more affluent residents of their growing area.

Their basic problem is that they know they must utilize some of the new computer technology, but neither they nor the rest of their staff are well trained in computer science or data processing. Actually they worry quite a bit about the future with respect to their continued reputation of being one of the best firms in the area and their ability to deal with more and more clients who are now using minicomputers and microcomputers for their accounting needs.

They currently use a service bureau for tax and financial statement write-up work, but they have had many bad experiences lately in the error correction, turnaround, and format of financial statements. Moreover, they would like to expand their tax planning services to more clients and would like to compete with a few aggressive banks in the vicinity that do financial planning for businesses as well as for individuals. They have asked your firm (a large national firm with considerable accounting and information processing and system experience) to assist them. Step by step, how would you proceed to assist Fuller and Drew and what suggestions based on the discussion in this chapter, Chapter 14, and Chapter 15 do you think you might offer? Would you make any staffing or training suggestions and why?

INDEX

A

Accountants, activities and responsibilities, 3–5
Accounting controls, 203, 260, 267–86
Accounting and information systems, 3–5, 29
  traditional, 155–56
  (*see also* Dimensions of accounting systems)
Accounts payable system, 158, 377, 462, 480–90, 610
  aged payables report, 484
  cash requirement report, 484–86
  check register, 487
  open order file, 158
  transaction list, 488
  vendor record, 377, 462, 481
  voucher record and reports, 158, 388, 462, 482–85
  (*see also* Purchasing system)
Accounts receivable system, 461–80, 610
  aging report, 434, 479
  balance forward system, 425
  batch processing order entry illustration, 430–31
  billing cycles, 434–35
  customer accounts list, 477

  customer maintenance, 472
  customer statement, 478
  master files, 422–23, 425–27, 436, 472, 474
  open item system, 425
  real-time on-line, 435, 456, 461–80
  (*see also* Controls; Marketing systems; Point-of-sale system; Sales)
"Active tapping," 248
Adapters, 171
Administrative controls, 15–20, 56, 203, 259
  management and administrative, 265–67
AICPA:
  Committee on Generally Accepted Accounting Principles for Smaller and/or Closely Held Businesses, 611
  management advisory service guidelines, 43
  system for development and implementation of EDP systems, 310–31, 342–60
  (*see also* Statements on Auditing Standards)
American Products Corporation, 580
Analysis and definition, 43–46, 310–31
Application controls, 263, 279–86
Application programs, 241, 349
Arithmetic-logic unit, 109–10
Artificial intelligence, 95